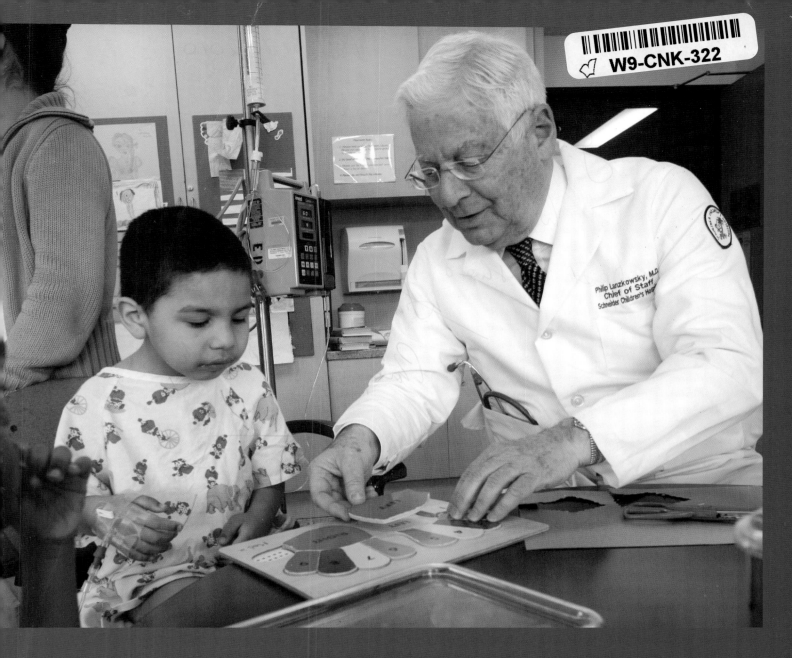

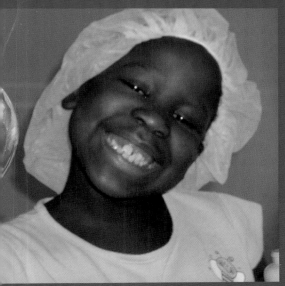

March 17, 2010.

To John,

With compliments and best wishes.

Sincerely,

Philip Langhowsky

How it all began

THE HISTORY OF A CHILDREN'S HOSPITAL

PHILIP LANZKOWSKY, M.B., Ch. B., M.D.,
Sc.D. (honoris causa), F.R.C.P., D.C.H., F.A.A.P.

Executive Director and Chief-of-Staff
Schneider Children's Hospital

Vice President, Children's Health Network
North Shore-Long Island Jewish Health System

Consultant and Chief Emeritus
Pediatric Hematology-Oncology

Chairman Emeritus, Department of Pediatrics
Schneider Children's Hospital

Professor of Pediatrics
Albert Einstein College of Medicine of Yeshiva University
Bronx, New York

How it all began

THE HISTORY OF A CHILDREN'S HOSPITAL

THE
DONNING COMPANY
PUBLISHERS

PHILIP LANZKOWSKY, MD

The Donning Company Publishers
184 Business Park Drive, Suite 206
Virginia Beach, VA 23462

Steve Mull, General Manager
Barbara Buchanan, Office Manager
Pat Swinger, Editor
Amanda D. Guilmain, Graphic Designer
Derek Eley, Imaging Artist
Susan Adams, Project Research Coordinator
Scott Rule, Director of Marketing
Tonya Hannink, Marketing Coordinator

Mary Taylor, Project Director

Library of Congress Cataloging-in-Publication Data

Lanzkowsky, Philip, 1932-
   How it all began : the history of a children's hospital / Philip
Lanzkowsky.
       p. ; cm.
   Includes bibliographical references and index.
   ISBN 978-1-57864-522-0 (hard cover : alk. paper)
1. Long Island Jewish Medical Center--History. 2. Long Island Jewish
Medical Center--History. 3. Long Island Jewish-Hillside Medical
Center--History. 4. Children--Hospitals--New York (State)--Long
Island--History. I. Title.
   [DNLM: 1. Long Island Jewish Hospital. 2. Schneider Children's Hospital.
3. Hospitals, Pediatric--history--New York. 4. History, 20th Century--New
York. 5. History, 21st Century--New York. WS 28 AN6 L297h 2008]
   RJ27.3.N765L36 2008
   362.1109747'21--dc22
                                        2008030763
Printed in the United States of America at Walsworth Publishing Company

Dedicated to all those who made this dream a reality.

"If you will it...it is no legend."
Theodore Herzl
1860–1904

Published on the occasion of the twenty-fifth anniversary of the establishment of
the Schneider Children's Hospital on September 25, 1983.

Table of Contents

Preface

This is the true story of the birth and development of a children's hospital serving Nassau, Suffolk, and Queens Counties in the suburbs of New York City.

The subject could form a best-selling novel, and it could also be an accurate analysis of the medical, financial, and inspirational forces that brought an important medical institution into being in the face of formidable opposition. Dr. Lanzkowsky has thankfully chosen to take the latter route. He presents a case study both for medical professionals and for lay advocates of health-related causes.

His book, "How It All Began: The History of a Children's Hospital," is a mine of important information, presented in straightforward fashion. He has captured not only the medical and corporate politics but also the complex medical and hospital requirements, made even more so by cost exigencies and prevailing notions of public policy. At the same time, he has brought to life the zeal and dedication of the many people who made up the Children's Medical Fund of New York (CMF, originally known as the Children's Medical Center of New York Fund), whose direction, public enthusiasm, and financial resources helped to make it all possible.

Oddly, the hospital is named after a man who was, at the outset, a most vociferous opponent of its creation, although much later he became a significant benefactor. It is such a vitally important facility for children that one wonders how anyone could have opposed it. But as Dr. Lanzkowsky shows, there were second and third helpings of controversy, much of it bitter.

In the very early 1960s, pediatric surgeons Burton Bronsther, MD, and Martin Abrams, MD, introduced the idea of a children's medical center in the Long Island suburbs. They were, in a real sense, missionaries; gathering and indoctrinating friends and parents of patients, indeed, anyone who would listen, and in 1963, they recruited me. They led the way to the CMF, an organization I was privileged to chair for two decades, which in turn spawned a Women's Division, and then a Men's Division. They approached Dr. Lanzkowsky in 1970, not realizing that he was harboring similar notions. Through Dr. Lanzkowsky's professionalism, adroitness, and persuasiveness, a children's hospital materialized at LIJ. It is today an important component of the North Shore-Long Island Jewish Health System, created by mergers.

Doctors Burton Bronsther and Martin Abrams were charismatic men. Campaigning for the children's hospital with them brought new meaning to my life as well as tribulations and joys. Along with the good we all achieved, one of the prime satisfactions for me was a close forty-year friendship with Burt and Marty, both of whom sadly passed away in recent years. That friendship and others of that era were deeply rooted, tempered by adversity, leavened with common ideals.

Philip Lanzkowsky, an internationally acclaimed pediatric hematologist, is one of those whose long-time friendship I value. His bibliography and raft of awards speak to his talent. Born in Cape Town, South Africa, he attended medical school there, and he did postgraduate work in Edinburgh, Scotland, St. Mary's Hospital in London, Duke University in North Carolina, and Utah University in Salt Lake City. In the early 1960s he received a diploma in Child Health from the Royal College of Physicians and Surgeons of London and the Royal College of Surgeons of England. Later he became a member and subsequently a fellow of the Royal College of Physicians of Edinburgh, all the while specializing in children's care. He was, for a short time, in private practice. In 1965, he was appointed director of pediatric hematology at New York Hospital—Cornell University School of Medicine, and four years later became acting pediatrician-in-chief and associate professor of pediatrics at that institution. In 1970, he was named chairman of pediatrics at suburban LIJ. It was a surprising move to a much lesser-known hospital, but one he felt held more promise for the promotion of his ideals of pediatric care.

Dr. Philip Lanzkowsky has served at LIJ and later at the NSLIJ Health System for nearly forty years, eventually becoming executive director and chief of staff of the Schneider Children's Hospital upon its opening in 1983. To my personal knowledge, he was easily the most important person

in its implementation. He brilliantly devised and executed a strategy of affiliation with smaller hospitals in Queens County which reduced the number of their pediatric beds, enabling New York regulators to allocate the number of beds necessary for the successful operation of tertiary care at the children's hospital to be located at LIJ.

With Dr. Lanzkowsky's appearance on the LIJ scene in 1970, there was a previously unknown collegiality among the medical staff. Dr. Abrams said that with Dr. Lanzkowsky's arrival, "Everything began to click." Neonatologist Hedda Acs, MD, recalled, "He never raised his voice; but he was nonetheless very clear. You knew what he wanted, when he wanted it. He was and is very goal oriented." Mark Raifman, MD, one of Dr. Lanzkowsky's early chief residents, said to an interviewer, "There was a marked shift in approach under the new regime. Where his predecessor had dictated, Dr. Lanzkowsky promoted. He initiated a multidisciplinary approach. The concept of doctors getting together to discuss a case became of paramount importance. He ran a taut, productive program with humor, assurance, and deep humanity." It seems clear that Dr. Lanzkowsky was collegial, but no creampuff.

Under his leadership, the establishment of many pediatric subspecialties, the academic atmosphere, the appointment of full-time staff, and the attraction of qualified and promising medical personnel became an important part of the foundation of the children's hospital.

If a measure of parents is their progeny, it is instructive to consider Philip and his wife, Rhona, a practicing psychotherapist, and their five children. Two daughters, Shelley and Leora, are physicians, one a pediatrician, the other a radiologist. Two sons, David and Jonathan, are physicians, one an anesthesiologist and the other an obstetrician-gynecologist. The third son, Marc, became an attorney. Despite his professional and public success, Dr. Lanzkowsky has remained a private man. His family is precious to him and he safeguards its privacy.

Implicit in Dr. Lanzkowsky's narration is justly deserved tribute to the men and women of LIJ who had the institutional courage to back the children's hospital. They had the fortitude to persist in their convictions, and they tolerated the occasional rambunctiousness of CMF.

To me, the pivotal LIJ administrative figure was Robert K. Match, MD, LIJ's executive director during the entire formative period. He was a tower of strength, embracing the ideal and working it through with an occasionally fractious Board of Trustees, despite the opposition of many colleagues in medical regulatory bodies, associations, and groupings. While CMF kept pushing, Bob Match had to reconcile all the financial, institutional, and regulatory forces that could prevent realization. He and I spent much time together, often disagreeing on tactics, planning, and strategy, but he was always patient, never rude, and quick to absorb changes. I'm afraid I tried his soul on more than one occasion, but our bonds of mutual respect and regard for the care of children kept us together. His sudden death in a fiery auto accident deprived the world of a good man.

Former LIJ Chairman, Gus Berne and Aaron Solomon, trustees Mike Stein, Sol Wachtler and Gedale Horowitz, were important in bringing about the CMF-LIJ relationship. William Mack was another fine and unheralded man in the process, who with his keen mind and courteous demeanor was Chairman of the LIJ Building and Planning Committee for The Children's Hospital. He and Gedale Horowitz went on to become Chairmen of the LIJ Board.

Just as New York City's Avenue of the Americas is most commonly referred to as Sixth Avenue though the name was officially changed more than a half century ago, to all of us in CMF, the project that started out being called the Children's Medical Center of New York Fund was always the Children's Medical Center. It was easy to believe, easy to say, and we said it over and over again, to the annoyance of our many naysayers including LIJ people who insisted on the legal change of our corporate name. There were also North Shore Hospital adversaries.

The CMF was a fount of friendship. Really, its heart was its Women's Division. For much of the formative period, the women *were* the CMF; there never would have been one without them. They mixed purpose with socializing; they enjoyed their associations; and they were persistent. They spread the word, participated in policy decisions, raised money, turned out for support, organized multiple chapters, and ran events, many of them complex.

Over the years, people came and left as suburban families do; new divisional chapters were continually coming into existence. In his autobiography, *Always the Young Stranger*, Carl Sandburg identified the strength of America as the constant appearance in each generation of strangers who immerse themselves in public processes and renew society's energy and purpose. At CMF, there were always young strangers to invigorate both the Women's and Men's Divisions, rallying around the CMF banner.

Gladys Cole, as Dr. Lanzkowsky aptly portrays her, was the founding president of the Women's Division. She did an incredible organizational job, and Vivian Kokol succeeded her in fine style. Bernice Mager, Marcia Goodman, Elaine Bisnoff, and Rita Kingsley, all presidents of the Women's Division, come to mind for their leadership roles and devoted attention to the cause in the early periods. So does Marcie Rosenberg, who became president of CMF and from 1993 to 1998 served as chairman of the board of CMF.

Burt Bronsther's widow, Ellyn, is an intelligent woman of charm and determination. Though she never, to my recollection, held office in the Women's Division, she was its original and persistent force. Her determination to cede the stage to Burt should not preclude recognition of her contributing role.

Martin Lifton organized the Men's Division and was its first president. Marty then became chairman and president of CMF, a trustee of LIJ, and a trustee of the North Shore-LIJ Health System. In my tenure at CMF, he was my staunchest colleague; smart, totally reliable, pragmatic, and willing to do anything that had to be done. Marty remains a close friend, a true CMF legacy to me. His son, Steve, eventually became president of the Men's Division, one of a number of men and women who succeeded their parents as leaders of CMF. This intergenerational transfer of interest is heartwarming.

It has been said that success has a thousand parents but failure is an orphan. There are many such CMF "parents" among those thousand, but in truth, there were a number of real parents as well, too many to be named or completely recalled. But I want to take notice of some of the earliest original supporters of the concept of a children's medical center—its pioneers when it was not yet even a blip on any radar screen. A number of such people are described earlier in this text. Add to them Larry Reed, Stuart (Shep) Voisin, Robert Frankel, Elliot Kahn, and Bernard Levy, each a past president of CMF, Bernard and Muriel Martin, Sandy and Carol Gluck, Charlotte Goode, Gene Rothkopf, Wally and Gerry Seid, Harold Kokol, Norman Goodman, Norman Mager, Raphael Weiss, and Roy Blumenthal.

Today, the Schneider Children's Hospital stands tall and proud. Although it is already nationally ranked as a hospital, and indeed internationally known, it is always working on improvement.

So it was! And so it is!

Bertram Harnett
Chairman Emeritus
Children's Medical Fund of New York

Boca Raton, Florida
March 1, 2008

Foreword

For 25 years, the Schneider Children's Hospital (SCH) has provided comprehensive, advanced care for children in this region. Every day, more than 1,200 dedicated physicians, nurses, and other healthcare professionals hold, feed, comfort, and treat patients, and help family members become part of the healing process.

As a resource offering sophisticated medical care for the most fragile of premature infants through adolescents, the Schneider Children's Hospital is a truly unique facility.

Among the fascinating aspects of this book is the startling contrast between the advanced pediatric medical services available today in our region and the practically nonexistent specialty care for children during the not-too-distant past—the 1960s and 1970s. With the exception of Manhattan, there were few pediatric specialists in the New York area. Most children requiring specialty care were treated by the same physicians who provided care to their parents and other adults. If their children were seriously ill, parents had to travel far from home to find specialized pediatric care.

Yet, as this book recounts, there was intense opposition during the 1970s to the creation of a children's hospital on Long Island. After being appointed chairman of pediatrics at Long Island Jewish Medical Center in 1970, Philip Lanzkowsky, MD, faced enormous political obstacles trying to convince others of the need for specialized pediatric care.

There's an old saying: "Pioneers take the arrows; settlers take the land." During those early years, Dr. Lanzkowsky and other visionaries were the targets of many critics in the medical establishment who profited from a local healthcare system that did not differentiate between pediatric and adult medicine. Some of his harshest detractors were members of the medical profession, other hospitals, and even some of the hospital's own medical leadership.

Anybody who knows Philip Lanzkowsky, however, recognizes him as a man of intense conviction and fortitude, unwilling to give up the fight even when outnumbered. Although they struggled mightily at times—and in fact many times they thought the project was dead—he and his supporters overcame countless obstacles to realize the dream of the New York area's first children's hospital. As chief of staff and later as executive director, he has guided the hospital's growth from its opening in 1983 with clinical and administrative expertise, devotion, and boundless energy and enthusiasm.

The Schneider Children's Hospital is not only a one-of-a-kind regional resource but is now among the top children's hospitals in the United States. In fact, patients come there from all over the world. Always eager for the children's hospital to be autonomous and to be recognized in its own right, Dr. Lanzkowsky saw another dream come true in 2003 when I agreed to make the Schneider Children's Hospital a separate entity from LIJ Medical Center, with its own financial, administrative, operational, and clinical oversight. In other words, the children's hospital would sink or swim on its own, and Dr. Lanzkowsky made sure it swam. He quickly established strong administrative and clinical infrastructures and built lasting relationships with hospitals and physicians in local communities. Although many assumed that operating gains from LIJ Medical Center had been sustaining the viability of the Schneider Children's Hospital, the hospital thrived on its own, achieving an impressive track record of financial success and clinical excellence.

In its first "America's Best Children's Hospitals" issue in 2007, *US News & World Report* ranked the Schneider Children's Hospital among the nation's top twenty-five children's hospitals, one of only two hospitals in the entire tri-state area to make the prestigious list. In 2008, *US News & World Report* once again ranked SCH as one of the top children's hospitals in the country.

In 2007, we opened a new chapter in the hospital's history, launching expansion and renovation projects totaling $144 million that will provide badly needed space to meet the ever-growing demands for comprehensive children's

medical care across the region. When the work is completed, the Schneider Children's Hospital will boast the New York region's first and only stand-alone pediatric emergency department and a new pediatric intensive care unit and state-of-the-art imaging center. These new facilities, combined with highly specialized services, advanced technology, and one of the most talented teams of pediatric clinicians in the nation, will further enhance the hospital's reputation as a world leader in pediatric medicine. What is more important for those of us who live and work in the region, these investments will ensure that our children and our children's children can obtain world-class care right in their own back yard.

We are indebted to Dr. Lanzkowsky and other early supporters who led the charge for creating the Schneider Children's Hospital and making it a preeminent hospital for children. The hospital is a monument to their passionate beliefs, their dedication to the care of children, and above all, their perseverance. We thank Dr. Lanzkowsky, too, for recording in painstaking detail the history of its creation, in this beautiful book.

Michael J. Dowling
President and CEO
North Shore-LIJ Health System

Introduction

Parents' instinct to protect and nurture their young is a fundamental element of human behavior.

Society has a collective responsibility to look after its children, and it is ultimately judged by the manner in which it treats them. Their physical and emotional health is our assurance of a better tomorrow.

This is a book about the building of a hospital created exclusively for the care of children—the Schneider Children's Hospital (SCH). This is also a book about change, and the fear it engendered in individuals, institutions, and society. Change is a constant; without it, society makes no progress. Resistance, however, is the knee-jerk response to change of any kind. The fear of change is deep-seated and not easily overcome by logic, reasoning, or data.

SCH stands as a testament to the strength and determination of a group of people who chose to confront that resistance and fear because of their commitment to the health needs of children in the greater Long Island and metropolitan New York region.

It all began with a developing department of pediatrics in a community hospital. In order for this department to morph into a children's hospital, there had to be recognition of the need for change in the healthcare environment on Long Island, an increase in traditional programs, and the introduction of innovative new programs.

The book describes an unswerving commitment to a cause in the face of what appeared to be insurmountable bureaucratic obstacles from government, other hospitals—including NSUH—doctors, and even those who worked at LIJ. Their reasons were different, but they were united in their opposition to the project. Proving to the local and state authorities, and the medical community itself, that there was indeed a need for a hospital exclusively for children was a Herculean accomplishment, especially as during this time there was a moratorium on hospital construction in New York State. But the handful of believers dared to dream big dreams, willed them to happen, and ultimately achieved them—although it took two decades of hard work—because they would not accept defeat. Above all, this is a story of endurance and tenacity.

The people who believed in SCH did not allow themselves to be beaten down by naysayers, and the odds against their project's success did not prevent them from trying.

It is to be hoped that the insights in this book may inspire others who are pursuing a life's dream, encourage them to persevere, and even when those around them scoff, to keep following their principles and their hearts.

"The needs of children should not be made to wait...we can say that although children may be victims of fate, they will not be victims of our neglect..."

John F. Kennedy's Message to Congress
February 14, 1963

Acknowledgements

I started work on this book more than a decade ago in 1996. My first editorial associate was Jan Kahn who interviewed many people on the development of the Department of Pediatrics at LIJ during the past fifty years.

Unfortunately, she did not live to see the project through to completion. Shortly after the work began on June 10, 1999, she died at a young age of fulminating multiple myeloma.

The assistance of Laurie Locastro, my second editorial associate, in the development and production of this book has been invaluable. She has spent more than two years poring over newspaper reports, newsletters, articles, minutes of meetings, and other material and has recorded interviews with fifty individuals who have been involved in one way or another with the department and the hospital.

I am grateful to these "witnesses to history" for the time they spent sharing their memories and the insights they provided, which were incorporated in *How It All Began: The History of a Children's Hospital*. These interviews have allowed us to view the Schneider Children's Hospital story from many perspectives and have helped to ensure the accuracy of the text.

I am indebted to Judge Bertram Harnett, who was involved on a day-to-day basis from the very moment the dream was born, for confirming the accuracy of the record from the early 1960s until the 1980s, and for his editorial suggestions, reminders, and corrections.

I extend my gratitude to my editor, Thea Welch, who was insightful, meticulous, and unflaggingly enthusiastic and who brought me into line every time I strayed into one of my pedagogic habits of repetition for emphasis or was unnecessarily "forthright."

I thank Rose Grosso for her patience in typing and retyping the manuscripts on numerous occasions as new recollections came to mind. Her assistance in other aspects of this book is greatly appreciated.

I thank Lynn Schneider and Mindy Schneider Lesser for reviewing the chapter on their family for its accuracy.

I thank my thirteen-year-old grandson, Jacob Tyler Lanzkowsky, for suggesting the title of the book.

And, finally, I thank my wife, Rhona, for patiently listening to me talk about this project for many years. Because she has traveled the road with me, she has been able to make suggestions and offer criticisms that have enhanced the book.

In a work of this size, with sources of information counted in the hundreds and over two thousand names mentioned, errors inevitably occur. I do not know where they are, because if I did they would have been corrected! I apologize in advance for any omissions or inaccuracies that may have crept in inadvertently.

Chronology of Change

1954–2008

MAY 16, 1954

Long Island Jewish Hospital is officially dedicated.

NOVEMBER 1955

Samuel Karelitz, MD, leaves his post as attending physician at Mount Sinai Hospital in New York City to become the founding director of the Department of Pediatrics at LIJ.

MAY 27, 1956

The premature nursery opens at LIJ.

1956

The pediatric residency program is established at LIJ.

1959

Herbert Goldman, MD, is appointed part-time salaried physician in charge of the premature nursery.

1960

The Cystic Fibrosis Clinic opens under the direction of Jack Gorvoy, MD.

FEBRUARY 1964

The Department of Pediatrics affiliates with the Queens Hospital Center. Frank Desposito, MD, in hematology, and Hedda Acs, MD, in neonatology, are appointed there full time.

JULY 1964

LIJ affiliates with the Queens Hospital Center.

SEPTEMBER 1964

A National Institutes of Health (NIH) adolescent demonstration grant is received, making possible the appointment of I. Ronald Shenker, MD, as the first full-time faculty member in the Department of Pediatrics.

1965

Arturo Aballi, MD, is recruited from Memphis to become director of pediatrics at the Queens Hospital Center.

Norman Gootman, MD, is named full-time pediatric cardiologist at LIJ and founding physician-in-charge of pediatric cardiology.

1968

Dr. Gootman establishes the first pediatric intensive care unit (PICU), a four-bed monitored patient room, at LIJ with a grant from the Rozenberg-Toner Foundation.

The first pediatric cardiac catheterization laboratory is established at LIJ adjacent to the Department of Radiology with assistance from the Saul Littman Save-A-Heart Fund.

NOVEMBER 1968

Construction is completed on a four-story addition to the original LIJ hospital building, a new teaching center, and a research building.

JULY 1, 1968

Dr. Karelitz retires. Benjamin Berliner, MD, is named interim director of pediatrics and a committee begins a national search for a new director.

1969
An eighteen-bed adolescent unit opens at LIJ.

MARCH 1, 1970
Philip Lanzkowsky, MD, leaves his posts as associate professor of pediatrics at Cornell University Medical School and director of pediatric hematology-oncology and acting pediatrician-in-chief at New York Hospital and is appointed director of pediatrics at LIJ.

1970
LIJ affiliates with the new medical school of the State University of New York at Stony Brook.

The division of pediatric hematology-oncology is established with Dr. Lanzkowsky as the founding physician-in-charge.

Leonard Sussman, MD, pediatric endocrinologist, is appointed founding physician-in-charge of endocrinology at LIJ and the Queens Hospital Center.

The Learning Diagnostic Center opens under the direction of Eugene Schwalb, MD, in the basement of the Speech and Hearing Center with a grant of $40,000 from the Rosenstock Foundation.

A Division of Adolescent Medicine program for adolescent drug abusers opens at Christ Episcopal Church in Manhasset.

1971
Marvin Klein, MD, pediatric neurologist, is appointed founding physician-in-charge of pediatric neurology.

Bruce Bogard, MD, is appointed founding physician-in-charge of general pediatrics.

JANUARY 1, 1971
A station wagon modified to hold an incubator is the first neonatal transport van, dubbed the "Flying Squad."

APRIL 1, 1971
A meeting is held at the Caucus Restaurant in Mineola with Dr. Lanzkowsky, Judge Bertram Harnett, president of the Children's Medical Center Fund of New York (CMFNY) and Martin Abrams, MD, to discuss the building of a children's hospital at Nassau County's Meadowbrook Hospital in East Meadow, Long Island. Lanzkowsky suggests LIJ as the appropriate location for a children's hospital.

APRIL 17, 1971
Judge Harnett and Drs. Lanzkowsky and Abrams meet with Robert K. Match, MD, executive director of LIJ, to elicit his support for a children's hospital at LIJ.

NOTE

Over the passage of time, Long Island Jewish Hospital (LIJ), in Queens County, changed its name several times (see page 40). North Shore Hospital, located in Nassau County, changed its name to North Shore University Hospital (NSUH) in the early 1970s. From 1989 to 1995, NSUH affiliated with Glen Cove Hospital (formerly Community Hospital of Glen Cove), Forest Hills Hospital (formerly LaGuardia Hospital), Syosset Hospital (formerly Syosset Community Hospital), Huntington Hospital, Southside Hospital in Bay Shore (Suffolk County), Franklin Hospital (formerly Franklin General Hospital) in Franklin Square, Plainview Hospital (formerly Central General Hospital) and Staten Island University Hospital to form the North Shore Health System. The North Shore Health System merged with LIJ in 1997 to form the North Shore-Long Island Jewish Health System (NS-LIJ Health System). Throughout this book, the acronyms "LIJ," "NSUH," and "NS-LIJ Health System" will be utilized to refer to these entities. The Schneider Children's Hospital is referred to as such or as "SCH."

Judge Harnett meets with Dr. Lanzkowsky in the new Nassau County Court House in Mineola to strategize the next moves.

JULY 19, 1971

Judge Harnett and Dr. Lanzkowsky meet with Jack Platon Collip, MD, chairman of Meadowbrook's Department of Pediatrics, to elicit his support.

JULY 1971

First comprehensive sickle cell clinic is established at the Queens Hospital Center by Gungor Karayalcin, MD.

NOVEMBER 8, 1971

Judge Bertram Harnett and Aaron Solomon, chairman of the Board of Trustees, sign an agreement between the CMF and Long Island Jewish Medical Center to build a hospital to be known as the Children's Medical Center of New York at a proposed cost of $10 million.

1972

The first specially equipped ambulance to transport newborns and older children goes into operation thanks to a donation of $25,000 from Abraham Meltzer, a grateful grandfather.

The Committee of Interns and Residents, a housestaff union, calls for a strike of interns and residents. They do not report to work for forty-eight hours, during which time Dr. Lanzkowsky acts as "resident" in the emergency room and Dr. Gootman is the "resident" on the inpatient unit.

APRIL 1972

Eugene Pergament, MD, is appointed the founding physician-in-charge of human genetics in the Department of Pediatrics, and the laboratory in genetics is established with a grant of $200,000 from the CMF. Dr. Pergament is joined by Audrey Heimler, MS, genetics counselor.

The Division of Human Genetics at LIJ is designated a Regional Diagnostic Center by the Birth Defects Institute of the New York State Department of Health.

JULY 8, 1972

Bruce Ackerman, MD, is appointed first full-time physician-in-charge of neonatology.

NOVEMBER 22, 1972

Mayor Lindsay designates Children's Medical Center Week in New York, issuing a proclamation at City Hall to this effect.

FEBRUARY 1, 1973

LIJ acquires St. Joseph's Hospital, Rockaway, and renames it LIJ-South Shore Division. Philip Lipsitz, MD, is appointed its first director of pediatrics.

FEBRUARY 11, 1974

Affiliation is established with Booth Memorial Hospital in Queens (presently called New York Hospital of Queens) for rotation of pediatric residents to Booth and transfer of complicated pediatric patients to LIJ.

MARCH 8, 1974

Dr. Lipsitz is appointed physician-in-charge of neonatology in the Department of Pediatrics at LIJ.

MAY 1974

A clinic for children with mental retardation is established at LIJ in collaboration with the Association for the Help of Retarded Children (AHRC) with Jack Storm, MD, as director of the clinic.

JUNE 7, 1974

LIJ submits a formal application to New York State to construct a $24 million, 150-bed children's medical center.

DECEMBER 20, 1974

The Health and Hospital Planning Council of Southern New York and the New York State Department of Health approve Part I of the application.

JULY 1, 1975

Bernard Gauthier, MD, is appointed founding physician-in-charge of the Division of Nephrology in the Department of Pediatrics.

1975

Perkins and Will, a hospital consulting firm represented by David Ginsberg, is hired by LIJ to develop a program for the children's hospital for submission to the state.

JANUARY 1976

"Call-a-Consult" system is established, making staff specialists available without charge to the entire medical community on a round-the-clock basis.

1976

Louis A. Rossetti of Detroit is appointed architect for the children's hospital project.

LIJ sells the South Shore Division to the Church Charity Foundation, which renames it St. John's Episcopal Hospital.

JUNE 1976

Cyril A. Abrams, MD, is appointed physician-in-charge of endocrinology to succeed Dr. Leonard Sussman, who died of a brain tumor.

JULY 1976

Lazar Fruchter, MD, who trained at Children's Medical Center Boston, is appointed as founding physician-in-charge of pediatric immunology.

DECEMBER 1976

Chronic hemodialysis is performed on a child at LIJ for the first time.

1976–1977

Eighty pediatric beds in Queens County, at Hillcrest General Hospital, LaGuardia Hospital, and Queens Hospital Center, are closed because of low occupancy. Services are taken over by Department of Pediatrics at LIJ.

1977

The Department of Pediatrics affiliates with the Association for the Help of Retarded Children (AHRC), Brookville.

The New York State Hospital Review and Planning Council approves the children's hospital project without additional beds because of the "present fiscal crisis" in New York State, and the commissioner of health declares a moratorium on new hospital bed construction.

JANUARY 1977

Peninsula Hospital Center in Far Rockaway affiliates with the Department of Pediatrics at LIJ.

FEBRUARY 3, 1977

Over a hundred CMF members crowd the meeting room of the Health and Hospital Planning Council of New York in Albany wearing diapers pinned to their chests bearing the slogan, "Save the Children's Medical Center." That night the protest is on national television.

FEBRUARY 1977

Hillcrest General Hospital affiliates with the Department of Pediatrics at LIJ and closes its fifteen pediatric beds.

APRIL 1977

The first hemoprofusion column is used successfully by Dr. Gauthier for reversing coma due to overdose of dilantin.

JUNE 1978

The project to build a children's hospital is approved at a public hearing in Kew Gardens before the Queens Project Review Subcommittee of the City's Health System Agency (approved 9-4 in closed door vote) and at the New York City Health System Agency. The Project Review Committee of the HSA votes 11-2 for building the hospital and the executive committee votes 19-0 in favor. The State Hospital Review and Planning Council and finally the State of New York approve the project to create a children's hospital and convert ninety-seven pediatric beds at LIJ into a 150-bed children's hospital.

JANUARY 1979
Dr. Aballi retires as director of pediatrics at the Queens Hospital Center to be replaced by Murray Davidson, MD. Dr. Davidson will also serve as the founding physician-in-charge of gastroenterology at the Queens Hospital Center and LIJ.

JULY 7, 1979
Transposition of great vessels during open-heart surgery is performed on a six-month-old baby from Bolivia.

JULY 20, 1979
Department of Pediatrics of Franklin General Hospital, Valley Stream affiliates with LIJ's Department of Pediatrics.

MAY 18, 1980
Ground is broken for the construction of a children's hospital at LIJ.

1980
Multidisciplinary rounds are teleconferenced for the first time via Bell Telephone's Gemini-100 System. St. Charles Hospital, Port Jefferson, Huntington Hospital, and Queens Hospital Center receive the transmissions.

SEPTEMBER 1980
For the first time, a patient receives continuous ambulatory peritoneal dialysis (CAPD) at LIJ.

JUNE 1981
An $85.58 million Federal Housing Administration (FHA) mortgage is awarded to LIJ to build the children's hospital, a multilevel parking garage, a food services building, and to expand operating room and outpatient facilities.

1981
The Architects Collaborative, Inc. of Cambridge, Massachusetts, is appointed architect for the children's hospital, replacing the Detroit firm of Louis Rossetti. Morse Diesel, Inc., of New York City, is the construction firm.

JULY 1982
Dr. Lanzkowsky is named chief-of-staff of the new children's hospital.

JULY 1983
Lorry G. Rubin, MD, is appointed founding physician-in-charge of pediatric infectious diseases.

1983
The working name of the children's hospital, the Children's Medical Center of New York, is officially changed to Schneider Children's Hospital to honor Irving and Helen Schneider.

The first Child Life Program on Long Island is established at SCH with Joan Chan as its director.

SEPTEMBER 1983
Paul Kessler is appointed first divisional administrator of SCH, Arnold I. Tannen is appointed associate administrator, and Mary Lou Martin first associate director of nursing. Ruth Blustein, CSW, is appointed associate director of social work services.

SEPTEMBER 25, 1983
New York Governor Mario Cuomo opens the Schneider Children's Hospital, in a formal ceremony attended by 1,500 guests.

JUNE 1984
Emile Scarpelli, MD, PhD, is appointed director of the pediatric research center and establishes a separate research center for Schneider Children's Hospital. Robert Bienkowski, PhD, is appointed associate director of the pediatric research center.

SEPTEMBER 1984
Michael Frogel, MD, is appointed chief of general pediatrics.

Norman Ilowite, MD, is appointed first pediatric rheumatologist at SCH.

MARCH 1985
The first Ronald McDonald House on Long Island, with eighteen rooms (the 100th house worldwide), is built on the grounds of SCH.

JUNE 15, 1985
Dr. Marvin Klein resigns his position as chief of pediatric neurology.

JULY 1985
Vincent Bonagura, MD, is appointed founding chief of the division of allergy-immunology.

Dr. Scarpelli is appointed founding chief of pulmonary medicine and director of the pulmonary function diagnostic laboratory. He also establishes the first home ventilator care service.

APRIL 1986
Joy Nagelberg, MD, becomes the founding chief of emergency medicine. For the first time, pediatric emergency medicine is covered by full-time pediatric attendings.

JUNE 1986
The Schneider Children's Hospital is designated an AIDS clinical trial center by NICHD (National Institute of Child Health and Development) with Dr. Bonagura as principal investigator.

JULY 1986
Lydia Eviatar, MD, who was acting chief since Dr. Klein's resignation, is appointed chief of pediatric neurology.

1987
Stanley Levin, formerly director of pediatrics at Kaplan Hospital in Israel and professor of pediatrics at Tel-Aviv University, is appointed assistant chief of staff at SCH.

SCH is designated a Regional Perinatal Center (RPC) by New York State.

MARCH 1987
An asthma center is established at SCH.

OCTOBER 1987
Surfactant replacement is used for the first time in premature quintuplets on Long Island.

1988
Cynthia Sparer is appointed administrator of SCH.

The teleconferencing system is updated. Optel Communications system offers an electronic writing tablet that replaces the Gemini system's blackboard.

MAY 1988
Raj Pahwa, MD, establishes the bone marrow transplantation program using a converted single-patient room fitted with a HEPA filter.

1989
The *Children's Hospital Quarterly Journal* is initiated under the editorial leadership of Dr. Stanley Levin.

JUNE 1989
Robert Cassidy, PhD is appointed first director of bioethics and social policy for the Schneider Children's Hospital with a grant from the Rudin Foundation.

JULY 1989
LIJ affiliates with Albert Einstein College of Medicine and is officially designated the medical school's Long Island campus.

1990
LIJ and SCH are selected as one of four sites in New York State for a designated epilepsy center with Gerald Novak, MD, as physician-in-charge.

Lydia Eviatar, MD, establishes a sophisticated neurovestibular laboratory evaluating dizziness and balance difficulties with the help of a special computerized rotational chair decorated as a space capsule.

DECEMBER 1990
The American Council for Graduate Medical Education (ACGME) certifies training program in allergy-immunology.

1991

Fredrick Z. Bierman, MD, is appointed chief of cardiology to succeed Dr. Gootman.

OCTOBER 1991

The four-bed bone marrow transplantation unit opens on the fourth floor of SCH. It has a laminar air flow system and is the only such unit approved by New York State specifically for pediatrics.

JUNE 1993

Dr. Pahwa performs one of the first allogeneic bone marrow transplants utilizing cord blood stem cells in a patient with acute leukemia.

1994

Pediatric Urgicenter opens at SCH under the direction of Dr. Frogel.

Nonsurgical closure of ductus arteriosus is successfully performed in cardiac catheterization laboratory.

Surgical ligation of ductus arteriosus in premature infant is performed at bedside in the neonatal intensive care unit (NICU).

1995

High-frequency oscillator is used in respiratory failure in newborns and infants for the first time at SCH.

SCH affiliates with the Lexington School for the Deaf in Queens County. Eric Weiselberg, MD, is appointed medical director.

Nitric oxide is used in newborn respiratory failure at SCH.

NOVEMBER 10, 1995

First subspecialty satellite center is established in Hauppauge, Long Island.

MAY 1, 1996

Food allergy center is established at SCH.

JULY 1996

Pediatric house staff rotate at St. John's Episcopal Hospital in Far Rockaway and St. John's Episcopal Hospital in Smithtown.

SEPTEMBER 1996

Second subspecialty satellite is established in Hewlett.

OCTOBER 1996

Picturetel, the third incarnation of teleconferencing, commences.

1996

Hauppauge satellite center relocated to Commack.

JUNE 1997

The Schneider Children's Hospital is designated a Level I Trauma Center by New York State.

SEPTEMBER 1997

Extracorporeal membrane oxygenation (ECMO) program started at SCH.

OCTOBER 29, 1997

The merger between LIJ and the North Shore Health System creates the North Shore-Long Island Jewish Health System.

MARCH 8, 2002

NSUH's pediatric department is renamed Schneider Children's Hospital at North Shore.

DECEMBER 2002

Center for HOPE (Healing, Opportunity, Perseverance and Enlightenment) is established at SCH for bereavement care in partnership with Baptist Memorial Health Care System of Tennessee.

"Play doctor" and "play patient" program is developed with the Science Museum of Long Island to alleviate anxiety of children going to the doctor or hospital.

JANUARY 2003

Dr. Lanzkowsky is appointed executive director of SCH; Eric Chaikin, associate executive director for operations; John Brandecker, associate executive director for finance; Carolyn Quinn, RN, associate executive director for patient care services.

JUNE 2003
New endoscopy suite opens in the Division of Gastroenterology and Nutrition.

JULY 2003
Anastassios Koumbourlis, MD, is appointed chief of pulmonary medicine.

2004
The Schneider Children's Hospital subspecialty center opens in Bensonhurst, Brooklyn.

APRIL 30, 2004
Bus service to transport patients and families to SCH from Bensonhurst, Brooklyn, is initiated with a donation from Kohl's Care for Kids Fund.

JUNE 2004
New York State Department of Health sponsors Women, Infants and Children (WIC) program at Schneider Children's Hospital.

JUNE 23, 2004
Division of Cardiology moves to new suite on first floor of SCH with eight examination/testing rooms and state-of-the-art imaging.

JULY 2004
Vincent Parnell, chief of pediatric cardiothoracic surgery, is appointed surgeon-in-chief of Schneider Children's Hospital.

OCTOBER 2004
Queens Child Advocacy Center is established to provide comprehensive healthcare to abused children in partnership with the New York City Police Department, the Queens County District Attorney's Office, the mayor's office and Safe Horizons.

2005
Ronald McDonald House expands from eighteen to forty-two rooms.

FEBRUARY 2005
Child Magazine ranks SCH among the nation's top children's hospitals.

AUGUST 2005
The Schneider Children's Hospital initiates bloodless surgical program under the direction of Michael LaCorte, MD.

SEPTEMBER 2005
U.S. Postal Service selects SCH as the site for the official New York launching of the 2005 postage stamp celebrating the year of the healthy child.

JULY 1, 2006
Dr. Bierman succeeds Dr. Lanzkowsky as chairman of the Department of Pediatrics, the third since LIJ was established in 1954.

AUGUST 2006
SCH opens New York City surgical office.

AUGUST 2007
Construction starts for new neonatal intensive care unit, ambulatory chemotherapy unit and atrium.

SCH signs an affiliation agreement with South Nassau Communities Hospital to provide pediatric residents and surgical coverage.

SEPTEMBER 2007
Bikur Cholim Room opens, providing a hospitality room for families of Orthodox Jewish patients.

U.S. News & World Report ranks SCH among the nation's top twenty-five children's hospitals, one of only two hospitals in the tri-state area to make the prestigious list.

OCTOBER 9, 2007
The Schneider Children's Hospital subspecialty center opens in Williamsburg, Brooklyn.

The Schneider Children's Hospital gets honorable mention on the floor of the House of Representatives for providing the first Diamond Blackfan Anemia (DBA) Comprehensive Clinical Care Center for patients across the country and developing a national DBA Patient Registry.

JUNE 2008
U.S. News & World Report once again ranks SCH among the nation's top children's hospitals.

AUGUST 2008
Groundbreaking for new inpatient tower consisting of state-of-the-art emergency department, pediatric imaging center, twenty-five-bed medical/surgical unit and a twenty-five-bed pediatric intensive care unit. Construction to be completed in 2011.

NOVEMBER 2008
Opening of new neonatal intensive care unit, ambulatory chemotherapy and atrium at SCH.

OUR ETHOS

Society is judged by the way it looks after its children—
its greatest asset.

We seek to build a world where the best interests, health, and security of every
child have a place at its center and not on the margins.

The health and welfare of our children are our raison d'etre.

CHAPTER 1

LAYING THE FOUNDATION

THE HISTORY OF LONG ISLAND JEWISH HOSPITAL

It is appropriate to look first at the institution whose Department of Pediatrics was nurtured and developed to become a pediatric hospital in its own right: the Schneider Children's Hospital (SCH).

Like their counterparts at North Shore University Hospital (NSUH), the founders of Long Island Jewish Medical Center (LIJ) were driven by the desperate need for hospital facilities to serve the developing communities straddling the Nassau-Queens border. The post-World War II boom drew thousands of young families to suburban Long Island. The local healthcare facilities were quickly overwhelmed; in the late 1940s, Nassau County had only 1.8 hospital beds per 1,000 people. A group of local businessmen, including Saul Epstein, Louis Gertz, and Gustave Berne, who was known as Gus, developed a plan to build not just a hospital but an outstanding teaching and research facility. They were also motivated, during this era of marked discrimination, to build a facility that would offer equal access for physicians, surgeons, and patients of all races and religions.

Eugene Rosenfeld, MD, executive director LIJ, and founders Morris Brecher and Philip Weisberg set out to visit major hospitals in the U.S., 1951.

Before LIJ came into being, there was North Shore Hospital, which was first proposed in 1945 after the injury of a local boy made very clear the need for a community hospital on the North Shore of Long Island. The original plan was to build the proposed 150-bed North Shore Memorial Hospital in Saddle Rock, Great Neck, on twelve acres--seven acres purchased from Mrs. Roswell Eldridge, who donated the remaining five acres. The hospital was to serve the North Shore, as its name indicated, including the Douglaston, Great Neck, Little Neck, Port Washington, Manhasset, and Roslyn areas.

A ten-man pro-tem committee was established consisting of five Christians and five Jews. It was agreed that Jews would share equally in the hospital's governance, and a Jew and a Christian would alternate in the position of president of the hospital. This condition was met for many decades. It was also agreed that Jewish doctors, who were not accepted on the staffs of the Mineola, Glen Cove, and Flushing hospitals, would be welcome on the proposed hospital staff. (Judith S. Goldstein: Inventing Great Neck, Rutgers University Press, 2006)

The main drivers for the creation of the North Shore Hospital were Willie Cohen, Jack Hausman, Sol Atlas, and William Levitt. They teamed up with John May (Jock) Whitney, a millionaire newspaper publisher and former ambassador to Britain, who drew upon the support of his wife, Betsy, his sister, Joan (Mrs. Charles S.) Payson, and his sister-in-law, Babe Paley--all financial and social heavyweights. This led in 1949 to the donation of ten acres of land adjacent to Greentree on Valley Road (later renamed Community Drive) by Jock Whitney and his sister. Joan Payson became president of a board whose thirty-two members were a balance of Christians and Jews.

The groundbreaking ceremony was held on May 6, 1951, with all the pageantry and patriotism of the time. Elizabeth Taylor and her director husband, Mike Todd, joined hospital trustees and CBS chairman William Paley at the North Shore fundraiser ball in 1952. After eight years and at a cost of $4 million, North Shore Hospital opened its doors on July 27, 1953.

The LIJ building fundraising campaign got a boost from former first lady Eleanor Roosevelt. Mrs. Roosevelt addresses a group of supporters at the home of Mr. and Mrs. Saul Epstein, 1949. Mr. Epstein was the first chairman of the LIJ Board of Trustees.

According to an internal LIJ memo from the early 1950s, "It [was] recognized that a teaching hospital [was] not only essential to the practice of good medicine, but such a hospital [would] provide sorely needed training opportunities for young Jewish doctors who found doors difficult to open elsewhere."* Simultaneously, a group of visionaries were working on the establishment of North Shore Hospital.

Judith S. Goldstein: Inventing Great Neck, *Rutgers University Press, 2006*

Mr. Epstein and Mr. Berne obtained a $500,000 grant for the building of LIJ from the Federation of Jewish Philanthropies, which was established in the mid-nineteenth century to provide financial support for the large numbers of Jewish immigrants to America from Eastern Europe. The founders of LIJ, most of whom were businessmen, took their task seriously, and with tremendous energy and intensity educated themselves in the complexities of the new hospital's requirements. They traveled to other hospitals around the country and met with medical, architectural, and administrative experts for nearly a year. They came to know what they wanted to build: a medical center with specialized services, research laboratories, educational programs and facilities, and residents for staff.

By 1949, a 120-member board of founders and a thirty-nine-member board of trustees were in place. The first critical decision was hiring Eugene Rosenfeld, MD, as the hospital's initial executive director. Dr. Rosenfeld was followed by

Schumacher potato farm on which LIJ was built, 1952. The church presently called St. Philip and St. James, founded in 1950, still stands on Lakeville Road, New Hyde Park.

The house on Schumacher farm was moved to clear space for LIJ, 1952.

Peter Rogatz, MD, with Donald Meyers as the associate director. In 1969, Robert K. Match, MD, was named executive director and served in this position until he resigned in 1993. (Sadly, he was killed the following year in a car accident on the Long Island Expressway.) The Board of Trustees of LIJ then appointed an interim committee to run the hospital, consisting of Alan Abramson,

MD, David Dantzker, MD, John Kane, MD, and myself. A national search for the CEO of LIJ was conducted, and Dr. Dantzker was appointed CEO and president of LIJ in November 1994.

It took five years of planning and fundraising to bring LIJ into existence. A fundraising goal of $7.5 million was set and reached, with contributions from the trustees, the local communities,

bed facility had the most modern equipment of the time, including heating and air conditioning, operating facilities, and a pneumatic tube system to send information, supplies, and even prescriptions to any point in the hospital.

The structure was designed for expansion, as the board envisioned a 500-bed facility. According to the June 1953 edition of *LIJ Reporter*, the $8 million cost of construction was made up of $1.5 million of government funding through the Hospital Survey & Construction Act (also known as the Hill-Burton Act), $4.9 million in contributions from 26,000 families, and $1.6 million in contributions from board members.

Dignitaries including New York State Governor Thomas E. Dewey and Senator Lister Hill, an author of the Hill-Burton Act, attended the official dedication on May 16, 1954. The hospital design garnered national recognition when LIJ won

Construction of LIJ began in 1952.

the Modern Hospital of the Year award in 1955 from *Modern Hospital Magazine*, "for excellence of architectural design, functional planning, economy of construction and operation and proper provision for hospital needs of the community."

It was the first start-to-finish Federation-sponsored hospital, and the first voluntary hospital on Long Island with research and education programs. As was stated in a 1953 article in the *LIJ Reporter*: "It is the first contribution of the entire Jewish community to the health and welfare of the Island. The hospital marks the coming of age of the Long Island Jewish community. The hospital has already shown evidence

and the federal government. A forty-eight-acre plot of land, known as the Schumacher farm, was acquired in Queens, on the border with Nassau County, adjacent to Hillside Hospital.

Construction of LIJ began in 1952. The architect was Louis Allen Abramson. It was completed in May 1954, a year after nearby North Shore Hospital opened its doors. The five-story, 215-

The new hospital, complete with sign, 1954.

The official dedication of LIJ attended by Governor Thomas Dewey accompanied by Saul Epstein, chairman of LIJ Board of Trustees, May 16, 1954.

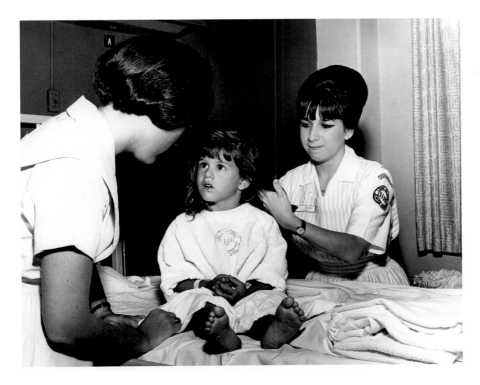

Junior volunteers engage a patient, circa 1960.

The first eight chiefs, who also constituted the Medical Board,1954. Left to right: Drs. Alexander Rosenthal (ob-gyn), James Berkman (laboratory), Leon Eisenbud (dentistry), Samuel Karelitz (pediatrics), Eugene Rosenfeld (executive director), Philip Lear (surgery), Bernard Epstein (radiology), Sylvan Surks (anesthesiology), Edward Meilman (medicine).

Medical Board
First Year 1954-55

Meeting of the Medical Board at LIJ, 1954.
Left to right: Drs. Alexander Rosenthal (obstet-
rics-gynecology), Eugene Rosenfield (executive
director), Philip Lear (surgery), Samuel Karelitz
(pediatrics), Edward Meilman (medicine),
Ms. Henny Reinhardt (secretary), Sylvan Surks
(anesthesiology), Bernard Epstein (radiology),
and James Berkman (laboratories).

that it will continue in the great traditions set by Jewish hospitals in the United States."

A critical decision made early on by the trustees was to staff the hospital departments with full-time chiefs, making it one of the first community hospitals to do so. The trustees decided to pay all chiefs the same salary, irrespective of specialty, and so the chief of surgery was paid the same as the chief of pediatrics and was accorded equal status and authority. As the board of trustees argued, all chiefs were equally important to the management of the hospital. This decision, unusual for the times, had a profound effect on the hospital and the quality of its medical care for decades to follow. In contrast, North Shore Hospital's early medical leadership was made up of nonsalaried community-based practitioners.

The Women's Service Guild, an entity that was created before LIJ ever opened, assembled a group of 100 trained volunteers to deliver additional services. The hospital's thirty outpatient clinics opened less than three months after the

hospital itself and provided even more services to Long Island's residents.

The hospital grew quickly, and by the late 1950s it was clear that more space would be needed. The board created the Committee for a Master Plan, which was responsible for developing a workable plan to expand the hospital. Their recommendation was to add four floors to the existing five-story structure, wings for outpatient care, a research institute, and a teaching center.

By 1964, ten years after the hospital opened, the occupancy rate had risen from 70 percent of capacity to 92 percent. The number of laboratory tests performed had grown from 130,000 in 1954 to close to 600,000 a decade later. The initial $8 million expenditure grew into a ten-year $15 million project that nearly doubled LIJ's capacity. Ground was broken for the expansion in April 1965, and the construction was completed in November 1968.

In 1964, LIJ contracted to administer the medical services of the Queens Hospital Center, which was then operated by the New York

City Health & Hospitals Corporation (HHC). The LIJ administrators at the Queens Hospital Center, who served from the affiliation agreement's inception to its termination in the late 1980s when Mount Sinai Hospital assumed responsibility for the facility, included Robert Bruner, Gerald Katz, Murray Rimmer, William Kozma, and Stephen Grabel.

In 1966 LIJ's Hearing and Speech Center was created through the efforts

Volunteer play therapists in playroom on Four South of LIJ, circa 1960.

Expansion to LIJ built in 1965. Peter Rogatz, M.D., Director of LIJ showing Congressman Lester L. Wolff the construction site.

The LONG ISLAND JEWISH HOSPITAL BUILDS FOR TOMORROW A $15,000,000 EXPANSION PROJECT

AFFILIATED WITH THE FEDERATION OF JEWISH PHILANTHROPIES

LOUIS ALLEN ABRAMSON ARCHITECT
F.S. DUBIN ASSOC MECHANICAL CONSULTANTS
WENBERGER, FRIEMAN LEIGHTMAN + CO
L. NOVICK LANDSCAPE CONSULTANT
P.J. CARLIN CONSTRUCTION CO. GENERAL CONTRACTOR

ONE HOUR PARKING 8 AM TO 6 PM

Children in pediatric clinic on Four South LIJ, 1966.

of Joe and Jean Leigh, the founders and prime movers of the Long Island Hearing and Speech Society. About the same time, additional clinics were opened for adolescents, hemophiliacs, and children with cystic fibrosis, as well as one of the first kidney dialysis centers in the area.

LIJ's informal alliance with Hillside Hospital was formalized in 1972 when the two agreed to a merger. Hillside was founded in 1927 and the institution's physical proximity made the relationship a natural one. Interestingly, the merger was recommended in the report that resulted from a study conducted in 1959-1960 for the

Federation of Jewish Philanthropies by Professor Eli Ginzberg and Peter Rogatz, MD. (Ginzberg, E., and Rogatz, P: *Planning for Better Health Care.* King's Crown Press, 1961). All mental health services were provided by Hillside, and LIJ's commanding presence in the community allowed Hillside to expand its services to a wider population.

In 1973, LIJ acquired the old St. Joseph's Hospital on Beach 51st Street in Far Rockaway, Queens (LIJ-South), with the aim of building a hospital similar to LIJ on the South Shore in the Five Towns area of Nassau County, east of the Rockaways. This project was thwarted, however, by objections from community and regulatory bodies, and in 1976 LIJ sold the hospital to the Church Charity Foundation. It was renamed St. John's Episcopal Hospital.

LIJ underwent a major expansion with the addition of the Schneider Children's Hospital in 1983. The Joel Finkelstein Cancer Foundation, a new oncology building, was added in 1985, enhancing LIJ's ability to treat cancer patients.

LIJ expanded and improved upon several areas in the early 1990s. Additional women's services were added, including a labor/delivery/recovery unit to smooth the birth process for mothers. The merger with the North Shore Health System in October 1997 allowed the LIJ hospitals to continue their long tradition of service to the community, expanding their sphere of influence and increasing services to the public. It also led to the further development of the Schneider Children's Hospital.

MEDICAL SCHOOL AFFILIATIONS

Soon after opening, LIJ became affiliated with the State University of New York Health Sciences Center at Brooklyn, known as SUNY Downstate. Philip Lear, MD, LIJ's chief of surgery, acted as the local dean for the medical school. This affiliation lasted until 1970 when LIJ

Aerial view of LIJ campus showing LIJ Hospital and Schneider Children's Hospital, 1983.

became affiliated with the newly created Health Sciences Center of the State University of New York at Stony Brook.

Interest in an affiliation with Albert Einstein College of Medicine of Yeshiva University (AECOM) had been gestating at LIJ since 1952, even before either institution had formally opened. Dr. Eugene Rosenfeld, the first executive director of LIJ, had proposed the idea of turning LIJ into a Long Island campus for Yeshiva University's developing medical school. The negotiations took a long time. A formal academic agreement between LIJ and AECOM was finalized at last in 1988 and students made their way

to LIJ the following summer.

In the 1970s and 1980s, under the leadership of the dean of the clinical campus, James Mulvihill, DMD, LIJ considered developing its own medical school with Adelphi University, Touro College, and finally the Sophie Davis School of the City University of New York. Despite prolonged and labor-intensive negotiations, none of these alliances came to fruition.

On March 26, 2008, the North Shore-Long Island Jewish Health System signed an agreement with Hofstra University to form a new medical school, the first one in Nassau County, Long Island. This new medical school promises to raise the reputation of the NS-LIJ Health System and Hofstra University to national prominence. The founding dean of the medical school is Lawrence Smith, MD, Chief Medical Officer of North Shore-LIJ Health System. The first medical students are scheduled to be admitted in the fall of 2011.

The following table contains further historical information, including the evolution of LIJ's name, its bed counts, its medical school affiliations and a list of chairmen of the Board of Trustees.

EVOLUTION OF THE NAME

1954   Long Island Jewish Hospital (LIJ)

1970   Long Island Jewish Medical Center (LIJMC)

1972   Long Island Jewish—Hillside Medical Center (LIJ-HMC)

1983   Long Island Jewish Medical Center (LIJMC) which consisted of the following divisions:
- Long Island Jewish Hospital (LIJ)
- Schneider Children's Hospital (SCH)
- Hillside Hospital

    Note: Schneider Children's Hospital was referred to as the Children's Medical Center of New York prior to start of construction and in 2002, Hillside Hospital was renamed Zucker-Hillside Hospital

2003   LIJMC was separated into:
- Long Island Jewish Hospital
- Schneider Children's Hospital
- Zucker-Hillside Hospital

NUMBER OF HOSPITAL BEDS (BY 1983)

Long Island Jewish Hospital	370
Hillside Hospital	223
Schneider Children's Hospital	150
Total	**743**

HISTORY OF MEDICAL SCHOOL AFFILIATIONS

State University of New York Health Sciences Center at Brooklyn—1955–1970

Health Sciences Center of the State University of New York at Stony Brook—1970–1988

Albert Einstein College of Medicine of Yeshiva University —1988–present

Hofstra University School of Medicine in partnership with NS-LIJ Health System—2008

CHAIRMEN OF THE BOARD OF TRUSTEES OF LIJ FROM ITS INCEPTION UNTIL 1997:

Saul Epstein*	1950–1956
Jack Liebowitz*	1956–1968
Gustave Berne*	1968–1971
Aaron Solomon*	1971–1976
Irving Wharton*	1976–1981
Martin Barell*	1981–1986
William Mack	1987–1991
Irving Schneider	1991–1995
Gedale Horowitz	1995–1997
Roy Zuckerberg	1997–present

    Deceased

CHAIRMEN OF THE BOARD OF TRUSTEES OF NORTH SHORE-LIJ HEALTH SYSTEM

Saul Katz/Roy Zuckerberg (co-chairmen)	
	Oct 29, 1997–Feb 9, 1998
Saul Katz	Feb 9, 1998–2000
Roy Zuckerberg	2000–2004
Dan C. deRoulet	2004–2006
Saul Katz	2006–Present

LIJ president Robert K. Match, MD, board chairman William Mack, Albert Einstein's Burton Resnick and Dominick Pupura, MD, celebrate the affiliation between LIJ and Albert Einstein College of Medicine in 1988.

Signing the affiliation agreement between North Shore-Long Island Jewish Health System and Hofstra University for the development of a new medical school, 2008. Seated, left to right: Saul Katz, chairman of the Board of Trustees, North Shore-LIJ Health System, and John Miller, chairman of the Board of Trustees of Hofstra University. Standing, left to right: Michael J. Dowling, president and CEO of North Shore-LIJ Health System, Lawrence Smith, MD, the founding dean of the medical school, and Stuart Rabinowitz, president of Hofstra University.

CHAPTER 2

HE CARED ABOUT CHILDREN

THE KARELITZ YEARS
1955-1969

A hospital can only be as good as the women and men who practice there. It will be illuminating, therefore, to look closely at the people who shaped the early Department of Pediatrics at LIJ.

When Long Island Jewish Hospital opened its doors in 1954, the founding director of the fledgling Department of Pediatrics was Samuel Karelitz, MD. Already a legendary figure, both locally and nationally, he was an outstanding academician and a dreamer who understood pediatric medicine as well as the needs of children.

Dr. Karelitz was born in Russia in 1900 and came to the United States as a child. He worked all his life, including waiting tables to put himself through Yale Medical School. Not surprisingly, he demanded the same work ethic from the house staff, and he was fiercely loyal to those who matched his commitment.

Recruited from Mount Sinai Hospital in Manhattan, Dr. Karelitz had done distinguished research under Bela Schick, MD, developer of the famous Schick test for the diagnosis of diphtheria. Schick called Karelitz "the best resident I ever had." Karelitz was a gifted clinician,

Marilyn Antokoletz, M.D., Beatrice Holland, R.N., and Samuel Karelitz, M.D. on rounds in the Premature Center at LIJ circa 1960.

whose studies included babies' cries, diabetes (after Banting and Best discovered insulin), and measles. In particular, his work with the placenta to find ways to immunize against measles led others to the discovery of gamma globulin. He was among the first to employ continuous intravenous therapy to counteract dehydration.

In keeping with the era in which he practiced, his experiments were clinical in nature. While he did write many papers, all his research was based on clinical findings and observation. In this regard, he is generally looked on as one of the most outstanding physicians of his era. As Henry Isenberg, PhD, the chief of microbiology at LIJ, recalled, "Karelitz encouraged research. He diminished the distance between science and medicine, still aware of the art that goes into medicine, but respecting the enormous part science plays." According to those who worked under him, to describe him as a colorful personality would be an understatement. A short, rotund, dynamic man, Karelitz was famous for his ability to relate to children on their own level and put them at ease. He was actually seen entering a patient's room doing a cartwheel.

Samuel Karelitz, MD, director, Department of Pediatrics, LIJ, 1954–1969.

As I have heard repeatedly, however, he did not exude this teddy bear warmth with his staff. He was a strict, demanding, exacting taskmaster who was the captain of his ship. Indeed, you might call him a dictator. Funny stories were circulated about the World War II unit he commanded in North Africa as a lieutenant colonel in the Medical Corps and the chief of medicine of Mount Sinai's Third General Hospital. Apparently, the troops serving under him actually debated whether to go after the Nazis or after Dr. Karelitz!

Dr. Isenberg also recalled that Dr. Karelitz used to send a shaking resident into a patient's room to observe him or her for five minutes with strict orders not to ask a single question. Then, based on the silent observation, the resident had to come up with a diagnosis on the spot. If you were wrong, or if he disagreed with you on any issue, it was a long time before he let you forget it.

Still, members of his house staff also remember wonderful parties at his home, being invited to his summer place in Connecticut on weekends, and his willingness to take residents with him to conferences, once driving three of them all the way to Montreal. S. David Sternberg, MD, staff pediatrician under Dr. Karelitz, recalled, "He was hard, demanding, and he would chew you out. But if anyone else chewed you out, he was a mother hen."

This toughness can be attributed not simply to the man's personality but also to the era in which Dr. Karelitz trained. In the first half of the century, the chief physician was considered just that—the chief. There were no specialists in any discipline, and there were very few scientific tests to confirm whether the chief was right or wrong in his diagnosis—only the course of the disease, or, on a grimmer note, the autopsy. In medicine today, everybody is a Monday morning quarterback and everything is on instant replay. But back then, the chief doctor's opinion was not opinion, but akin to law.

While sooner or later everyone felt his wrath, everyone agrees on one thing: Dr. Karelitz was never motivated by anything other than providing excellent pediatric medicine. As surgeon Martin Abrams, MD, noted, "He really gave a damn about kids."

Hedda Acs, MD, recalled being berated more or less incessantly for a few days because

Dr. Karelitz disagreed with her on the treatment of a child. Then she passed the open door to his office and was called in. She groaned inwardly, thinking that she couldn't bear to listen to his litany one more time. But when she entered the office, he merely handed her a piece of hard candy. "That was all, no apology or reference to the subject of our disagreement whatsoever," she said. "But I knew it was over." She also remembered a time when her own young child was very ill with a fever. Worried, she mentioned it at work. That night, Dr. Karelitz arrived to care for the child himself.

The reminiscences of Benjamin Berliner, MD, who served as one of four attending physicians under Dr. Karelitz and as acting director of the Department of Pediatrics upon Dr. Karelitz's retirement in 1968, are particularly vivid. A great admirer of Dr. Karelitz, he was nevertheless unafraid to confront him when, in Dr. Berliner's judgment, he had been behaving "like a little Napoleon." Dr. Berliner noted with wry appreciation, "Sam took it." He also recalled one particularly sad and difficult case: "The child, about a year old, was hopelessly ill. He had spina bifida and meningitis, he was paralyzed, and his head was one-fourth the size of the bed. Well, Karelitz ordered all sorts of heroic measures to prolong his life. He genuinely felt that every child's death was a personal defeat. I said nothing while he gave his orders, but later that day I marched into his office to tell him how I felt about it. The office was empty so I took a piece of paper and wrote on it a quote from Shakespeare's King Lear. It comes at the end of the play, after Lear dies and Edgar attempts to revive him. The Earl of Kent stops him with these words:

Vex not his ghost. 0 let him pass! He hates him
That would upon the rack of this tough world
Stretch him out longer.

"I didn't sign it, but he knew whom it was from although he never acknowledged that he read it. But he rescinded his orders and quietly let the boy die. And at his retirement he mentioned the quote in his speech. He said in front of all those people that he was grateful. It had taught him something."

The story is interesting not only for what it says about both Dr. Karelitz and Dr. Berliner, but also as an indication of how far the concept of bioethics has come. Back then the chief was judge and jury. Ethical issues were decided based on the judgment and conscience of the individual physician. Today we have a full-time bioethicist and an entire educational program devoted to such matters.

Dr. Karelitz may not have been attuned to the concept of bioethics as a specialty, but he was fully attuned to the need for specialists in the practice of pediatric medicine.

In the 1950s, pediatrics was mostly devoted to the care of well children. The feeding of babies was a prime concern, as was helping essentially well kids through the common diseases of childhood. Dr. Karelitz saw the distinct need for the pediatric specialist, well versed in childhood diseases, to treat the sick child—perfectly obvious to us now, but revolutionary for his day. He was pioneering in his insistence that the baby is different from the child, who is in turn different from the adolescent. He set about staffing his department with the best physicians he could find, and then pointed a finger at them, named a specialty, and basically said, "You're it."

Since nobody was specialty-trained, everyone self-trained. Dr. Sternberg, who became a specialist in pediatric neurology, had had a mere three months at the Neurological Institute at Columbia Presbyterian Hospital before coming to work for Dr. Karelitz. Other self-trained specialists were Jack Gorvoy, MD, and later, Hedda Acs, MD, for cystic fibrosis; I. Ronald Shenker, MD, who had

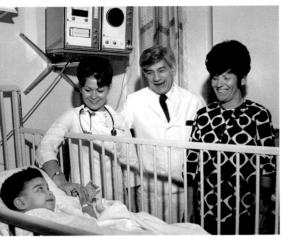

Benjamin Berliner, MD, one of the first four attending physicians in the Department of Pediatrics, late 1960s.

previously worked in school health, for adolescent medicine; and Richard Reuben, MD, for neurology. And thus an incredibly distinguished team was created.

Herbert Goldman, MD, who became LIJ's first specialist in neonatology, recalled his entry into the field. "I just liked to hang around the nursery and observe the newborns. Back then, the newborns were the province of the nurses. The head nurse at that time was a wonderful and formidable woman named Beatrice Holland. Dr. Karelitz noted my interest and designated neonatology as a specialty for me. I worked with him on formula studies." Those studies led to the fortification of infant formulas with Vitamin K, and the discontinuation of high-protein formulas in premature infants.

Norman Gootman, MD, was the first trained specialist appointed by Dr. Karelitz in 1965. He had done formal fellowship training in pediatric cardiology with Abraham Rudolph, MD, at Jacobi Hospital, Albert Einstein College of Medicine. In 1968 he established the first four-bed monitored intensive care unit with funds from a grateful patient and a pediatric cardiac catheterization laboratory with equipment discarded from adult cardiology.

In 1966 Dr. Karelitz contracted with New York City to provide ambulatory and preventive pediatric care to the Rockaways in a project known as PRYME, and in 1977 the administration of this project was transferred to the Church Charity Foundation.

By the time Dr. Karelitz's tenure came to an end in 1969, he had established an impressive Department of Pediatrics. When he retired, Dr. Berliner was appointed interim director of the department while the search committee sought a new chairman. The search committee consisted of Edward Meilman, MD, chairman of medicine, James Berkman, MD, chairman of laboratory medicine, Philip Lear, MD, chairman of surgery, and Alexander Rosenthal, MD, chairman of obstetrics and gynecology.

One of the candidates for the chairmanship, Dr. Berliner, served the department well as interim chief. Well-liked and an outstanding and dynamic teacher, he helped the staff decompress after the autocratic tenure of his predecessor. By this time, the practice of pediatrics had changed dramatically, and the staff was ready to change with it. Dr. Berliner, who later became a professor at the University of Connecticut Farmington Medical School and the director of the Waterbury Regional Department of Pediatrics, recalled that interim year with pleasure. He was reluctant

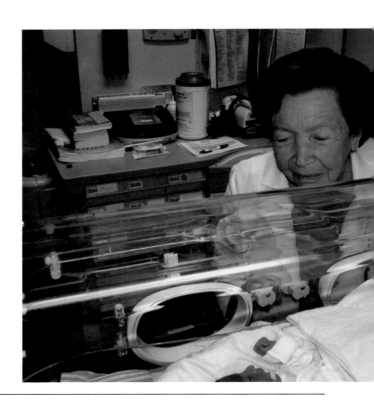

for it to come to an end, "But," he added, "Philip Lanzkowsky's arrival freed me to teach, which is what I love best. When I saw how incredibly active, organized, ambitious, and dedicated Dr. Lanzkowsky was, and saw his goals for a children's hospital unfold, I realized he was the man for the job, and that the department was in wonderful hands." Or, as Dr. Martin Abrams put it, "When Phil came, everything started to click."

Plaque dedicated to Samuel Karelitz, MD, in the lobby of SCH.

SAMUEL KARELITZ, M.D.
1900 - 1980

FOUNDING CHAIRMAN OF PEDIATRICS, LIJ-HMC
1954 - 1969
DISTINGUISHED CLINICIAN, TEACHER AND RESEARCHER, SAMUEL KARELITZ WAS A MAN WHOSE STRONGEST MOTIVATION WAS HIS LOVE FOR CHILDREN.
PRESENTED BY THE BOARD OF TRUSTEES, LIJ-HMC '80

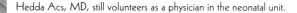

Hedda Acs, MD, still volunteers as a physician in the neonatal unit.

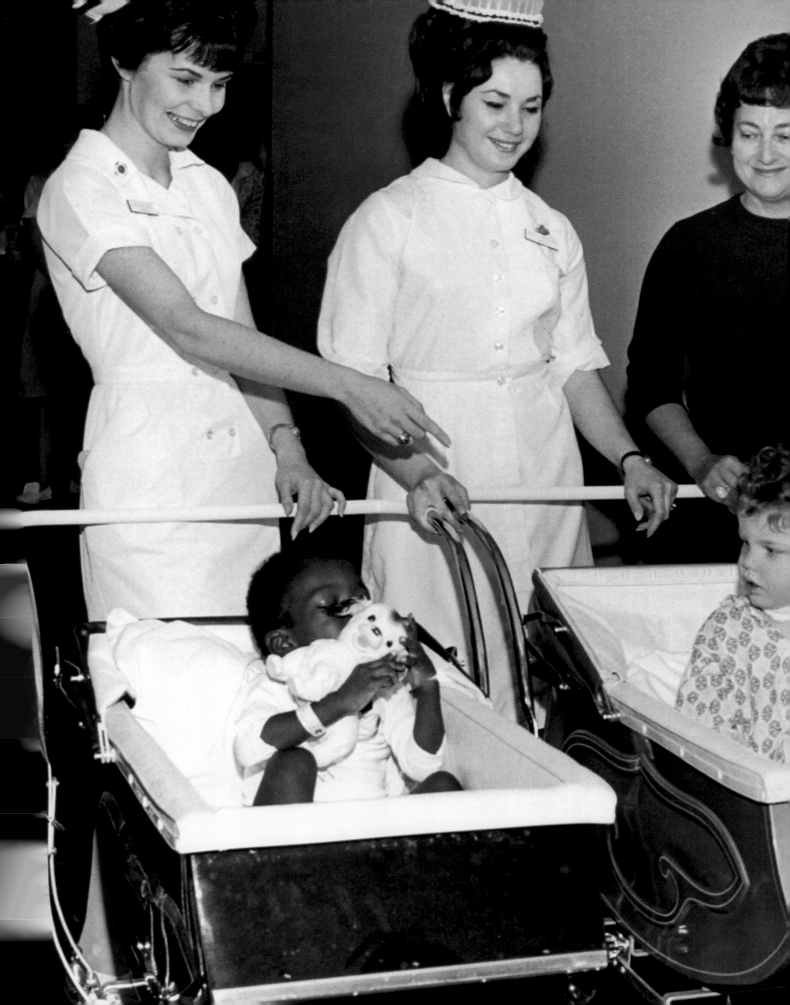

CHAPTER 3

SHAKING UP THE STATUS QUO

THE LANZKOWSKY YEARS, 1970-1983

Following a national selection process involving a search committee of the senior LIJ directors of departments with the participation of key members of the Board of Trustees, I assumed the post of director of pediatrics at Long Island Jewish Medical Center (LIJ) on March 1, 1970, leaving my positions at the New York Hospital-Cornell University Medical School. (see Appendix I)

My contract gave me immediate tenure to age sixty-five. I was grateful to the board of trustees for the confidence that they had in me and for the twenty-seven years of job security that allowed me to proceed at the appropriate pace to carry out the plans and policies I felt were in the best medical interests of children.

But let's go back a bit. In 1965 I was recruited from South Africa to become the director of pediatric hematology at New York Hospital and associate professor of pediatrics at Cornell University Medical School. Later I became the acting chairman of pediatrics at Cornell Medical School and acting pediatrician-in-chief at New York Hospital. When Robert K. Match, MD, president of LIJ, approached me to ask whether I was interested in the directorship being vacated by Dr. Karelitz, I immediately replied that I was, indeed. New York Hospital was a well-established

A mother and a grandmother visit their child in the hospital during Sunday afternoon visiting hours, circa 1970s.

LONG ISLAND JEWISH MEDICAL CENTER NEWS RELEASE

New Hyde Park, NY— Dr. Philip Lanzkowsky, Associate Professor of Pediatrics at Cornell University Medical School, has been named Director of Pediatrics at Long Island Jewish Medical Center.

Recently named Professor of Pediatrics at Downstate Medical Center, Dr. Lanzkowsky has served as Director of Hematology at New York Hospital since 1965. Dr. Robert K. Match, Director of LIJMC, said Dr. Lanzkowsky will join the staff on March 1.

In announcing the appointment, Dr. Match spoke for both the Center's Board of Trustees and its administration when he said, "We welcome Dr. Lanzkowsky to our growing Medical Center, confident that he will further enrich its program. Our pediatric service has earned an outstanding reputation over the years and, we look forward to extending and broadening this service under Dr. Lanzkowsky's leadership."

Dr. Lanzkowsky, who is 37 years old, was born in Cape Town, South Africa, and has had a distinguished medical career. He graduated from the University of Cape Town Medical School in 1954 and was awarded a Doctorate of Medicine in 1959 for his research on iron deficiency anemia in infants and pre-school children. In the same year he received from the University of Cape Town the Joseph Arenow Prize for original postgraduate research in the field of science, medicine and applied science. In 1960 Dr. Lanzkowsky, during the tenure of a Cecil John Adams Memorial Traveling Fellowship, did postgraduate studies at the Hospital for Sick Children in Great Ormond, London and the University of Edinburgh, Scotland. He received a diploma in Child Health from the Royal College of Physicians and Surgeons of London.

Dr. Lanzkowsky first came to the United States in 1961 as a clinical and research fellow in Pediatric Hematology at Duke University. He then attended the University of Utah College of Medicine in Salt Lake City as a research fellow in Pediatric Hematology.

He returned to South Africa in 1963 as Consultant Pediatrician and Pediatric Hematologist at the Red Cross War Memorial Children's Hospital in Cape Town.

A member of the Royal College of Physicians and Surgeons, Dr. Lanzkowsky has served as acting Pediatrician-in-Chief at New York Hospital and acting Chairman of the Department of Pediatrics at Cornell University Medical School. He was director of the Pediatric Hematology Training Program at New York Hospital for the National Institutes of Health and presently serves as scientific advisor to the division of Pediatric Hematology of the Department of Pediatrics of the University of Chile.

He has written more than 60 articles which have appeared in various medical and scientific publications and has contributed to standard textbooks in pediatrics and pediatric hematology.

Dr. Lanzkowsky is married and lives in Great Neck with his wife and five children.

2/11/70

institution, but I sensed there was little opportunity for change on the pediatric horizon. While I had not heard much professionally of LIJ, I felt that as a new institution it had the potential to embrace change.

When I visited LIJ and met its department directors, many of whom hailed from prominent academic institutions, I became even more interested. This, I thought, might be the institution at which I could implement my ideas from my training in children's hospitals in South Africa, Edinburgh, Scotland, and London, and my philosophy of medical care for children and the training of pediatricians. I was in sync with the threefold mission of the Department of Pediatrics that dated back to its founding: to provide state-of-the-art clinical care for children and their families, to advance the scientific understanding of pediatric medicine, and to educate house staff to become knowledgeable, skillful, and dedicated pediatricians. It seemed the ideal place to develop an outstanding department of pediatrics, and it was my hope and goal that a hospital just for children might even grow out of this new hospital in the burgeoning suburbs of New York.

At that time, the department was small, relatively unstructured, and not geared for an academic department of pediatrics. My wife, Rhona, and my

Cornell colleagues did not share my enthusiasm. In fact, when I brought my wife to the pediatric unit, she was horrified. She actually asked why I had taken the position. She and my colleagues wondered why I was leaving an institution with an international reputation for a community hospital "out in the sticks." One colleague described it as moving from a cathedral to a shtiebel, a Yiddish word for a small room, humbly set in a home or place of work, devoted to prayer. They characterized the move as academic and professional suicide. Frankly, I was not unaffected by their doubts.

Despite my doubts, I immediately felt welcome at LIJ. Michael Stein, who at the time of my appointment was chairman of the Joint Conference Committee of the LIJ Board of Trustees, a committee consisting of trustees and chiefs of the departments, recalled in an interview with Laurie Locastro, my editorial associate, "We liked his accent. Phil was a charmer, he came with great credentials, he was very convincing and persuasive in the search process, was highly recommended, and we were thrilled to get him. If we hadn't had him, the chances are that we never would have had a children's hospital."

Dr. Philip Lanzkowsky, MD, ScD, FRCP, DCH.

Up to the 1940s, pediatric wards worldwide consisted of ten to twenty beds in drab surroundings with minimal activities for children and minimal parental visiting hours.

In the early 1950s, the entire pediatric department at LIJ consisted of thirty beds in four-bedded rooms in a more child-friendly environment. The "premature center" was built as an afterthought in 1956, an appendage to the emergency department consisting of eighteen beds. With the expansion of LIJ in 1968, the department grew to forty-five beds on Four

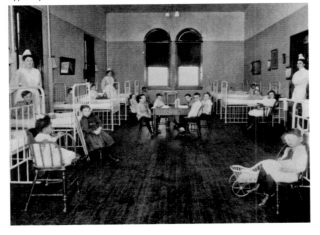

Typical pediatric ward of the 1930s.

Pediatric playroom at LIJ in the 1950s before the days of computers and interactive art.

A nurse playing with a patient in a patient room at LIJ in the 1950s.

South (including a four-bed monitored critical care unit), with a small playroom and a conference room, and the premature unit was expanded to twenty-four beds. In 1969, an eighteen-bed adolescent unit was established on Four North. Just before my arrival, the neonatal physician offices were relocated and ten more neonatal beds were added. When I was appointed in 1970, the department of pediatrics at LIJ had a total of ninety-seven beds, including thirty-four neonatal beds, and was responsible for the 109-bed Department of Pediatrics at the Queens Hospital Center under an affiliation agreement with the New York City Health & Hospitals Corporation (HHC). In 1973 LIJ purchased St. Joseph's Hospital in the Rockaway's (LIJ-South Division), which added twenty-four pediatric beds. I recruited Philip Lipsitz, MD, chief of neonatology at Beth Israel Medical Center in New York City, to become director of pediatrics at LIJ-South. When Dr. Lipsitz became physician-in-charge of neonatology at LIJ-North Division, Maurice Teitel, MD, took his position. The total bed complement of the department of pediatrics was 230 beds distributed as follows:

LIJ-North Division

Medical-surgical beds, Four South	41
Intensive care beds, Four South	4
Adolescent beds, Four North	18
Neonatal beds	34
TOTAL	97

Queens Hospital Center (QHC)

Surgical beds, Seven West	40
Medical beds, Seven East	41
Infectious disease beds, Five Center	8
Neonatal beds, Seven Center	20
TOTAL	109

LIJ-South Division   24

NEW LEADERSHIP

While I greatly respected Dr. Karelitz, I felt that changes in the times and in medical care for children required a different style of leadership and a different approach to the practice of pediatrics. It was clear, however, that one of my biggest challenges would be breaking down perceived barriers to change. Without change there would be no progress and, without progress there would be no future.

To the staff, the differences in style between us were immediately apparent. Henry Isenberg, PhD, the chief of microbiology and a close colleague of Dr. Karelitz, recalled, "Lanzkowsky came on quietly, firmly, and won the confidence of the Old Guard." Hedda Acs, MD, a neonatologist and a trainee and protégé of Dr. Karelitz, recalled, "Dr. Lanzkowsky never raised his voice. But he was nonetheless very clear. You knew what he wanted, when he wanted it. He was and is very goal oriented but much more academic. Dr. Karelitz's emphasis was more of the clinical nature."

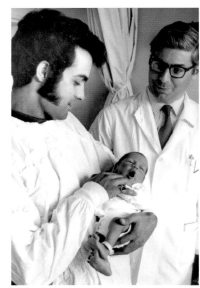

Dr. Lanzkowsky chatting with a new father, Joseph Gallinam, on obstetrical rounds, April 1970.

In contrast to the era of fear and trembling, Mark Raifman, MD, one of my early chief residents, recalled that rounds with the new chief "were actually fun." I paid particular attention to encouraging collegiality in the medical staff and initiated a Thursday morning 11:00 a.m. gripe session for interns and residents in my office. (In those days, they could actually all fit into my office!). In earlier times, such an airing of griev-

LIJ department chairs, circa 1975. Standing: Drs. Murray Baron (radiology), Charles "Buddy" Rabiner (psychiatry), Arthur Sawitsky (hematology), Mary McLaughlin (community medicine), Joseph Rovinsky (obstetrics and gynecology), David Rosen (ophthalmology), Leslie Wise (surgery). Seated: Drs. James Berkman (laboratory medicine), Sylvan "Sy" Surks (anesthesiology), Philip Lanzkowsky (pediatrics), Edward Meilman (medicine), Leon Eisenbud (dentistry).

ances could not have been imagined. Although, I must confess I did sometimes use the time to delineate proper conduct.

Shortly after my arrival, I inevitably began to clash with my fellow chairmen. I was only thirty-seven years old, and there was a thirty-year age gap between me and the more senior and influential chairmen. I was trained in a different era than they as an internist, pediatrician, and pediatric hematologist-oncologist. I was committed to the development of a department along full-time academic lines, consistent with my previous training and experience. I was trained at the dawn of the development of pediatric subspecialties, which required specific clinical training including a core curriculum and research. These differences set the stage for divergence between

many of my colleagues and myself, and I found that diplomacy was frequently required.

As is the way in the British system of medicine in which I had trained, I started making rounds in obstetrics to speak to the mothers (and occasionally the fathers) about their newborns, the importance of breastfeeding, and other aspects of newborn care. Again, there was conflict: The obstetricians claimed that the mother was their patient, and the pediatricians were worried about my contact with their future patients.

As increasing numbers of community-based pediatricians applied for staff privileges in the burgeoning department of pediatrics, the battle over appointments began to rage. Having staff privileges gave the physician the right to admit patients to the hospital as well as the right to attend departmental meetings and educational activities. This required a review of the practitioner's credentials by a number of hospital committees. Appointing a staff physician was like climbing Mount Everest. "Why do you need another pediatrician on the staff?" cried other departmental directors and the voluntary staff itself, who had seats on the hospital Credentials Committee. "We have enough! What special expertise does he bring to the department?" they asked. I had to prepare extensive support for each new appointment. There was no doubt that being a member of the LIJ staff enhanced the reputations of the community-based pediatricians and their practices. But they saw it as a privilege, like belonging to a private club, while I saw it as a right, belonging equally to all qualified community pediatricians. In my view, the more pediatricians who had staff privileges, the higher the standard of care for children. The objective was to provide a wide array of services dedicated to children and their families exclusively. As the numbers of community-based pediatricians on the LIJ staff increased and the divisions expanded within the hospital, the sphere of influence of the department and the hospital would widen, and an increasing number of diverse and interesting patients would be available for teaching and research. For the first time, patients could be referred to pediatric specialists on Long Island for diagnosis and treatment instead of being referred to specialists in Manhattan or beyond, usually to Children's Hospital Boston or the Children's Hospital of Philadelphia.

When it came to facilities and supportive services such as radiology, laboratory, emergency, and the operating room, the same objections arose. There was a failure to appreciate that children need different facilities and supportive services. Over the years, new objections were added to the old, well-worn arguments such as "It is more expensive to create separate and distinct facilities catering to the special needs of children." Never mind that those facilities would provide better and more appropriate care for children.

The first summer of my tenure, I was startled to note that the total census in the pediatric department was six patients exclusive of the neonatal unit. The nursing staff, which determined the admission policy, was discouraging admissions because of the limited nursing staff assigned to pediatrics. At my insistence, the policy for admission of sick children was liberalized so that no infant or child requiring hospital admission was turned away. Until the administration relented and assigned more nurses to pediatrics, there was what I called "organized chaos."

I was concerned not just with the number of nurses, but also with the quality of nursing in pediatrics, and that led me into another confrontation. One day I noticed that a nurse attending to a baby had long, polished nails. This was long before a "nail policy" existed for nurses. The director of nursing was Rachel Rotkovich, RN, an icon of nursing in her day, who was single-handedly responsible for raising the status of nursing in hospitals nationally. I asked her to fire this nurse.

The next morning, Rachel marched into my office. She was a large woman, and she wrapped her arm around my neck in a smothering embrace. "Who hires the nurses here?" she demanded. "You do, Rachel," I gasped, turning somewhat cyanotic. "Who fires the nurses here?" she again demanded to know. "You do, Rachel," I said meekly. With that she released me. The following day the nurse was transferred to the Department of Medicine. Rachel and I have remained close friends. I knew that I had overstepped my authority, and she knew that my request was warranted.

Raising standards caused a good deal of discomfort all around. After my first ward rounds, the chief resident came down to tell me the house staff was distressed because they could not take my demands. Norman Gootman, MD, a cardiologist, a full-time faculty member, and a cheerful, kind-hearted friend of everybody, came to warn me that the house staff was threatening to go on strike—an unprecedented event. I said, "That's

Rachel Rotkovich, RN (left), director of nursing at LIJ, speaking to members of the nursing staff in the late 1960s. Variations in the nurse's caps indicate rank.

fine, Norm...then you and I will do the work." The house staff did not strike, and the program began to turn around almost immediately, becoming a desirable place for residency training. In July 1970, we matched,* for the first time in a long time, with four American residents.

In 1972, however, when house staff unionized and joined the Committee for Interns and Residents (CIR) in New York State, a strike of the interns and residents did occur. When they did not show up for work, we were put to the test. Dr. Gootman manned the inpatient ward and I ran the pediatric emergency department.

Fortunately, the strike only lasted for forty-eight hours.

HIRING FACULTY

The 1970s was a decade of major programmatic expansion. Regardless of the constant controversy, we continued pushing on the agenda for the development of pediatrics. Expansion of the department and enhancement of physician education were primary goals. In 1970 the entire faculty consisted of Dr. Gootman, who spent half his time at the Queens Hospital Center, and I. Ronald Shenker, who was the only full-time pediatrician on staff and was supported by a National Institutes of Health (NIH) adolescent medicine demonstration grant that he had received in 1964. There were only twelve foreign residents

*The National Residency Matching Program (NIRMP) was established in 1952 to ensure that students receive their highest choices of the residency programs that are interested in them. Each year, senior medical students apply directly to residency programs. The students and residency programs then interview and evaluate each other. Once the students have determined which programs they prefer and the programs have decided on the students they want, both the students and the programs submit their preferences to the NIRMP in the form of rank order lists. The NIRMP processes these lists using a computer algorithm that is designed to optimize the rank-ordered choices of students and programs. The results are announced by the NIRMP on Match Day in the third week in March every year.

in pediatrics; four residents in each of three years of training. Research was another important area to be developed. We wanted to attract the best people by creating a scholarly atmosphere where inquiring minds could flourish.

Serious planning for a children's hospital at LIJ had begun in 1972, only two years after I arrived, and we were traveling the rocky road toward receiving necessary approvals from many governmental bodies. We were also garnering public support for the project, staging a huge fundraising campaign, and forging affiliations with surrounding hospitals to provide specialty medical care in one form or another. But just as important were the development of all the pediatric specialties and the recruitment of faculty from all over the country to lead these new divisions.

At that time, internists who maintained their own practices in the community were running the pediatric subspecialty services at LIJ. Although many of them were outstanding clinicians, they were generally not interested in the development of an academic department of pediatrics. They tended to view pediatrics as a stepchild of medicine. Still, these internists, who had meager to nonexistent knowledge of pediatrics, were providing specialty care to children. The new paradigm, with pediatricians and pediatric subspecialists taking their rightful place in the management of childhood illnesses, signaled a threat to the status quo—not only clinically but also financially. I presented the concept of interdisciplinary consultation, and encouraged the view—not new—that the patient was not the "captive" of a single practitioner who would provide the approach to diagnosis and management. That the complexities of medicine mandate a multidisciplinary approach seems obvious today, but to the medical staff at LIJ it was a new and threatening way of doing business. This led to strong opposition to the appointment of full-time pediatric subspecialists to the medical staff.

Drs. Norman Gootman, Philip Lanzkowsky, and I. Ronald Shenker—the entire full-time pediatric staff in 1970.

When I was about to appoint Marvin Klein, MD as the first chief of pediatric neurology, the chief of neurology, who was in private practice at the time, asked me, "Why do we need them when the patients' needs are being covered by us—the internists?" His view was that an adult neurologist could take care of a neurological condition in a premature infant just as competently as he could in an octogenarian. I then challenged him as to why there was a need for a pediatric department. On reflection he said, "Well, I believe that internists can look after all sick children."

The need for pediatric specialization had been recognized for over a century and pediatric specialists had been practicing in most first world countries for decades. Long Island internists were far behind the times. For historic perspective, it should be noted that the Pediatric Section of the AMA was founded in 1881, the American Pediatric Society in 1888, and the Section of Pediatrics of the New York Academy of Medicine in 1889. In 1887 in the Section of Children's Diseases of the IX International Congress of Medicine, the officers and council members emphasized the importance of pediatrics itself and its neglect by the main body of medical practitioners in the

United States.* In 1889 Abraham Jacobi's presidential address to the first scientific session of the American Pediatric Society in Washington, D.C., entitled "The Relations of Pediatrics to General Medicine," a 12-page masterly and prophetic document, claimed that pediatrics should be considered a separate specialty emphasizing the differences between child and adult. In his article, Dr. Jacobi professed that, "...there is scarcely a tissue or an organ which behaves exactly alike at different periods of life" in respect to physiology and pathology. He discussed growth and development and gave a long list of diseases and disorders that are peculiar to childhood or predominate during that period.

As I began to recruit, I discovered that there were inherent difficulties in attracting talented faculty from top medical schools in the country such as Johns Hopkins, Harvard, Columbia, Cornell, and the Albert Einstein College of Medicine, from the well-known children's hospitals such as Seattle Children's Hospital, Children's Hospital Boston, and the Children's Hospital of Philadelphia, and from other well-established institutions. However, many pediatricians were interested because of the possibility I held out to them of a children's hospital in the not-too-distant future. I spent hundreds, probably thousands, of hours talking, influencing and convincing academicians to leave the hallowed halls of the ivory towers. Breaking the umbilical cord with established medical schools was very difficult. I interviewed ten, fifteen, and often more candidates for every single individual appointed. The medical staff had to be carefully selected, specially trained and above all, sensitive to the needs of children.

Senior and even junior faculty recruited from well-known medical schools and hospitals had demands for salary, security, staff, space, and

often support for their research endeavors. I was attempting to figure out how to meet those demands while dealing with plenty of resistance from the powers that be at LIJ. There were few full-time faculty in any of the departments at LIJ at the time and my fellow chairmen could not understand the need to build a full-time faculty of specialists in Pediatrics.

Controversy arose over each and every specialty appointment in pediatrics during the 1970s. Appointive actions had to be defended first to the executive director of the hospital, then to the chairman's group, then to the Credentials Committee and the Medical Board, and finally to the Joint Conference Committee of the Board of Trustees.

It all required resources, ingenuity, and innovation. Developing a faculty is like building an orchestra; not only the candidates' skills and academic achievements but also their personalities and adaptability had to be considered, so they could function as a team and work harmoniously together in the "children's hospital orchestra."

We needed shared goals and objectives and a shared philosophy. As subspecialties proliferated, there would be more and more emphasis on teamwork so that the care of every child could become the concern of many professionals.

CREATING DIVISIONS

Before a subspecialty division such as nephrology or endocrinology could be staffed, it had to be created. This was in itself a tortuous process, meeting with the same resistance and requiring changes to the medical staff bylaws and approval after approval including that of the full Medical Board. You could say that the creation of the subspecialty divisions created a lot of division at LIJ!

*Faber, HK and McIntosh, R., History of the American Pediatric Society; McGraw Hill, 1966.

Once each division was approved, it was built in a very deliberate manner, brick by brick, as a foundation for the planned children's hospital so that it could fulfill its clinical and academic mission. Clinically, it would bring the expertise needed to provide sophisticated tertiary and quaternary medical care and programs to the Long Island community. Academically, it would form the basis for the development of a teaching and research program. I needed to make my selections very carefully and deliberately, always bearing in mind that this was an evolutionary process; quantum leaps would meet obstacles that might prove insurmountable.

The first step was to appoint a chief in each subspecialty division. These chiefs had to be excellent clinicians, well known in their respective fields, who generally had the qualifications to become full professors at the medical school, which meant they had achieved national recognition. Each appointment required a national search—a difficult and tedious process. But it was vitally important to get the right people in the right jobs. After the chief, each division grew exponentially in faculty, ancillary staff, sophisticated equipment, and the insatiable need for space. The table at right shows the year each division was created (before the children's hospital was built), the founding physician-in-charge (in the late 1970s this title was changed to chief), the divisional chief in 2008, and the number of present staff by categories.

With the growth of the divisions and the appointment of more and more specialists the house staff grew in number from twelve residents in 1970 to twenty-four by 1983 and there was considerable growth in the number of fellows being trained in the subspecialty areas. The additional staff was the result of merging the LIJ and the Queens Hospital Center pediatric programs in 1972.

DEVELOPING REGIONAL NETWORKS

In the early 1970s, I was an early proponent of the need for regional networks. This would entail implementing the regionalization of pediatric care by developing a tapestry of pediatric services in the surrounding communities consisting of primary and secondary care provided by the community-based pediatricians and the local community hospitals, while concentrating all tertiary-care pediatrics in the relatively safe environment of a pediatric department with many qualified and well-trained subspecialists.

I worked out written agreements with the Queens Hospital Center, Catholic Medical Center, LaGuardia, Flushing, Peninsula, Hillcrest, and Jamaica Hospitals in Queens County. These arrangements included rotating LIJ pediatric residents, providing faculty coverage, and transferring serious cases to the Department of Pediatrics at LIJ. An arrangement had been concluded with the Association for the Help of

Faculty and pediatric house staff, 1971. Front row, left to right (in suits): Drs. I. Ronald Shenker, Hedda Acs [Queens Hospital Center (QHC)], Philip Lanzkowsky, Arturo Aballi (QHC), Norman Gootman and Herbert Goldman (part-time).

DIVISON	YEAR OF INCEPTION	PHYSICIAN-IN-CHARGE AT INCEPTION	CHIEF IN 2008	FACULTY NUMBER	FELLOW NUMBER	ANCILLARY STAFF	TOTAL STAFF
Neonatology+	1956	Herbert Goldman	Dennis Davidson	11	11	9	31
Adolescent Medicine	1964	I. Ronald Shenker	Martin Fisher	7	3	11	28
Cardiology	1965	Norman Gootman*	Fredrick Z. Bierman	11	6	19	35
Endocrinology	1970	Leonard Sussman*	Phyllis Speiser	5	2	9	15
Hematology—Oncology++	1970	Philip Lanzkowsky	Jeffrey Lipton	10	6	23	36
General Pediatrics	1971	Bruce Bogard*	Michael Frogel	14	0	2.5	39
Neurology	1971	Marvin Klein*	Joseph Maytal	7	5	13	25
Human Genetics+++	1972	Eugene Pergament	Joyce Fox	3	0	13	16
Nephrology	1975	Bernard Gauthier	Howard Trachtman	3	0	4	7
Immunology++++	1976	Lazar Fruchter	Vincent Bonagura	1	0	1	2
Gastroenterology+++++	1979	Murray Davidson*	Gastroenterology: Jeremiah Levine Nutrition: Michael Pettei	9	2	14	25

*deceased; +Name changed to Neonatal-Perinatal Medicine; ++Name changed to Hematology-Oncology and Stem Cell Transplantation;

+++Name changed to Medical Genetics; ++++Name changed to Allergy-Immunology; +++++Name changed to Gastroenterology and Nutrition

Retarded Children (AHRC) in Brookville, New York, for clinical programs and research at LIJ. Informal agreements were made with most of the private and voluntary hospitals in Queens and many of the hospitals in Nassau and Suffolk for consultation and referral of patients. The agreements gave these institutions priority for admission and immediate access for specialty consultations. The aims of these affiliations were to assist the pediatricians in the community, benefit patients, raise the standard of pediatric care in the entire Queens, Nassau, and Suffolk region, and establish LIJ as the hub for complicated cases. Many of these arrangements dating back to the early seventies have endured to this day, and over time affiliations have been added and dropped.

This strategy greatly widened the sphere of influence of the department of pediatrics, filled beds, provided a realistic "live" demonstration of regionalization of sophisticated medical care, and strengthened the case for the imperative need to build a children's hospital. The facts were being created on the ground. As Jack Welch said, "When it comes to strategy, ponder less and do more."*

Because of its concentration of subspecialties, the pediatric department at LIJ admitted children not just from Queens, Nassau, and Suffolk, but

*Jack Welch and Suzy Welch; Winning, 1st Ed, Harper Collins Publishers, Inc, New York

Faculty and some pediatric house staff, 1982. Second row, left to right: Drs. Lazar Fruchter, Cyril Abrams, Barbara Stewart, Marvin Klein, Leonard Fogel (administration), Mary Lou Martin (nursing), Philip Lanzkowsky, Murray Davidson, I. Ronald Shenker, Philip Lipsitz, Marie Casalino, Bernard Gauthier, Bruce Bogard. Third row, standing, left to right (in suits): Drs. Robert McGovern (QHC), Florence Marshall (QHC), Robert Festa, Ashok Shende, Krishna K. Gupta (QHC), Alan Shanske (QHC), two department secretaries, Avelina Maralit (QHC), Hedda Acs (QHC), Dov Nudel, Michael Nussbaum, Ernest Lieber, Daniel Silbert, Audrey Heimler (genetics counselor). Missing from the photo was Dr. Norman Gootman.

department had no interest in participating with LIJ on that project. The idea died right there. At the time I lacked the audacity to pursue it.

INFANT TRANSPORT SYSTEM

Prior to 1971, the City of New York Department of Health, operating out of Bellevue Hospital, provided neonatal transport. Infants were transported in metal boxes with oxygen piped in. The boxes had no temperature control, and when the infants arrived at their destinations, they were frequently hypothermic. Occasionally during transport the oxygen source became disconnected and the babies became cyanotic and hypoxic.

Because of the increasingly apparent need for safe neonatal transport from community hospitals in Queens, Nassau, and Suffolk, LIJ initiated an infant transport program in the spring of 1971. The *Daily News, Long Island Press*, and *Queens Ledger* all announced in April 1971:

Special Auto Is Set Up for Sick Babies

A new service for critically ill newborn babies was started last week by Long Island Jewish Medical Center in New Hyde Park. Everything a small baby needs for survival is included in the new specially equipped ambulance put into service by Long Island Jewish Medical Center. Instead

also from the five boroughs of New York City, New Jersey, Connecticut, and beyond. As the dream of a children's hospital began to seem more and more real, it attracted additional highly qualified pediatricians, both to be trained and to join the faculty, from major academic institutions both in this country and abroad.

Not all my efforts were successful. A plan to develop a mobile van to provide care to the indigent in conjunction with Nassau County Department of Health did not win approval. At a meeting with John J. Dowling, MD, commissioner of health of Nassau County in 1971, Dr. Gootman and I were told in no uncertain terms that it was not a good idea and that the health *of waiting for a sick baby to be brought to the hospital, the hospital goes out and gets him with a sick-baby transport. The newborn infant may be premature or full term. Sometimes he is just two or three pounds of very sick baby. He is carried in an envelope of protection from the minute he is picked up, sometimes as much as an hour's distance from the hospital. Specially trained personnel and equipment within the vehicle give the tiny patient the protection he needs. The mobile transport incubator is heated to a steady 90 degrees F., although it might be 10 degrees outside. "This is critically important," said Dr. Philip Lanzkowsky, the hospital's director of pediatrics, "because a tiny baby exposed to cold may experience a severe drop in temperature which could be dangerous." The sick baby transport also carries a pediatric resuscitator to revive or maintain a baby's respiration, suction equipment to ensure a clear respiratory airway, a tank of oxygen and an analyzer to measure the concentration of oxygen in the transparent plastic "isolette." In addition to the ambulance driver, the transport carries a specially trained pediatric nurse from the hospital's premature nursery center and, if necessary, a pediatrician. The small patients come to the medical center on referral from other hospitals. The transport goes to Queens, Brooklyn, and the Bronx to bring ill newborn infants to the intensive care unit of the hospital's premature nursery center. The child's medical history and the mother's obstetric record, including her blood type, go along with the infant. The transport answers emergency calls any hour of the day or night. Before this, the center was dependent on other ambulance services. "Sometimes," Lanzkowsky said, "babies in crisis could not be transported during late night hours. Often they were exposed to cold*

enroute and, sometime they did not receive the protection of full emergency equipment and staffing."

Initially, the hospital station wagon was used for neonatal transport. The rear compartment was slightly modified to allow for the safe carriage of a premature baby incubator and a transport team consisting of a neonatal nurse and house physician.

The incubator was secured to the floor of the station wagon, and the power for the incubator came from an electrical outlet connected to the station wagon's battery. Eric Gould, MD, a pediatric intern at the time, recently vividly recalled his experience riding in the improvised ambulance. "I hated when I had to ride in the wagon," he said. "We were in a jump seat right behind the driver, and if we had to stop short, I thought I would fly through the windshield." This program was described in a medical journal article entitled "Regionalized neonatal intensive: Development of transport service using improvised vehicle," by Drs. H. Goldman, P. Lanzkowsky and S. Sun in the *New York State Journal of Medicine* 74:1835-1840, 1974. It read:

A modified nine-passenger Ford Country Esquire station wagon was used as the transport vehicle. Metal tracks were securely fastened to the rear floor of the station wagon immediately in front of the rear seat. These tracks were designed so that an Air Shields transport incubator could be firmly fixed into position by means of removable pins. An electrical outlet was installed in the rear of the station wagon and connected to the automotive battery. A DC cord of the transport incubator was modified to fit into this outlet. The transport incubator could then be operated in three different ways in the vehicle and four ways altogether: (1) into the special outlet by means of the modified DC cord, (2) into the station wagon cigarette lighter by a standard

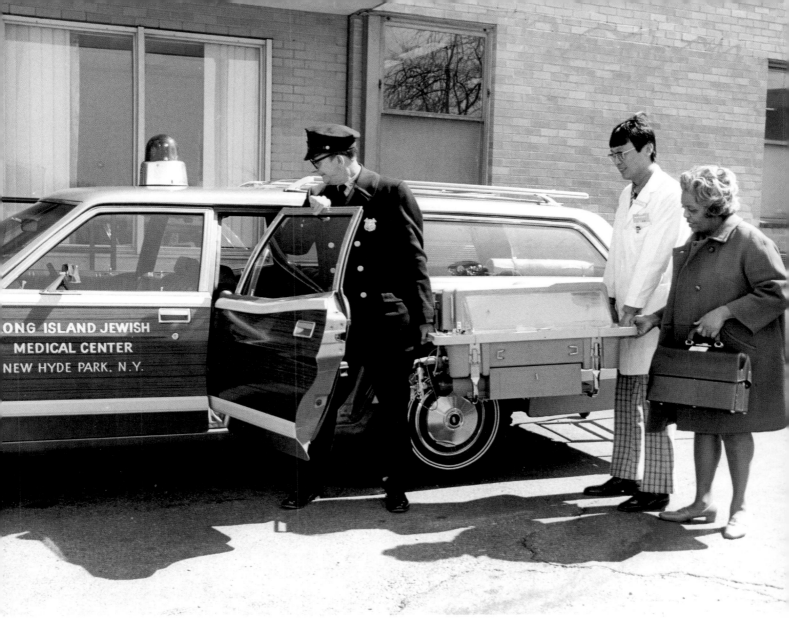

Beatrice Holland, RN, Shyan-Chu Sun, MD, and Mr. Hoffman, the security guard who drove the station wagon, 1971.

Beatrice Holland, RN, and Eric Gould, MD, pediatric resident, in the back of the station wagon modified to serve as an infant transport vehicle, 1971.

The Meltzer family with three-year-old Ross Meltzer and Dr. Lanzkowsky in the new mobile intensive care unit donated by the Meltzer family, 1972.

Ross Meltzer at 36 years old.

DC cord, (3) into its own battery by the standard DC cord and (4) into the AC outlet by the AC cord. Considerable attention was devoted to keeping the infants warm during transport. Efforts were made to keep the interior temperature within the vehicle at 75 to 80 degrees.

Fortuitously, an occasion arose to make a marked improvement in the transport of sick infants and children. A 10-day-old infant named Ross Meltzer was admitted to the Community Hospital of Glen Cove with severe anemia associated with Rh disease and the doctor told the parents that the child was not going to survive.* The child's grandfather, Abraham Meltzer, who

lived in Kings Point, Long Island, called me and I went to see the baby at Glen Cove Hospital. I resuscitated him and gave him a blood transfusion, but he needed to be transferred to LIJ immediately for further, more advanced treatment than Glen Cove could provide. I had brought along an incubator, and I accompanied the baby on the ambulance ride to LIJ. Happily, he survived. Without the incubator, I believe the baby would have died in the ambulance.

Mr. Meltzer called to thank me for saving his grandson's life and expressed his willingness to make a monetary contribution of a few thousand

Lanzkowsky, P., Gootman, N., Salemi, M.: "Photo-therapy: A Note of Caution," Pediatrics 48:969, 1971

dollars to show his gratitude. "That would buy a wheel," I told him. "A wheel for what?" he asked. "A wheel for the ambulance," I replied. I explained that a custom-built, specialized ambulance would permit the safe transport of neonates to a tertiary-care center such as LIJ and would save the lives of many babies like his grandson. The cost, however, would be $25,000. That was on a Wednesday. I had a check from him for the full $25,000 by Friday.

The neonatal transport van donated by Abraham Meltzer was delivered in January of 1972. I called it the Flying Squad. It took many months to develop, requiring engineers, physicians, and nurses to pool their experience to determine what equipment should be included. The ambulance was twenty-one feet long and eight feet high and contained everything necessary to keep a sick or injured infant alive. It had fourteen electrical outlets, a high-power emergency generator, a sink with hot and cold running water, and monitoring equipment to chart an infant's vital signs.

This mobile intensive care unit, one of very few in the country, permitted us to extend our services through and beyond the tri-county area. This unit and subsequent models were used to transport not only neonates but also infants and children, from hospitals as far away as upstate New York. Approximately 300 infants were transported annually during the seventies. Today, ten times that number are transported to SCH yearly, and the mode of transport makes the above description sound very primitive indeed, although it undoubtedly saved lives. *(For a description of the method of transport of neonates and non-neonates to SCH today, see Chapter 14.)*

In the 1970s, police helicopters were employed to transfer critically ill infants and children to LIJ, especially during peak traffic hours. The helicopters landed either on the

Helicopter coming in for a landing on the parking lot in front of LIJ on a snowy day, with the station wagon waiting to receive the patient, circa 1973.

Hillside property or, at night, in the parking lot in front of LIJ. Car headlights formed a circle in the darkness so the pilots could see where to land. By the end of the 1970s this mode of transportation was abandoned. The vibration and noise in the helicopter prevented stethoscopes from being used, interfered with the monitoring equipment making therapeutic interventions en route impossible, and it was too dangerous for patients and staff.

MULTIDISCIPLINARY TELECONFERENCING

In 1973 I started holding multidisciplinary conferences weekly with the full-time faculty and house staff in order to discuss difficult diagnostic

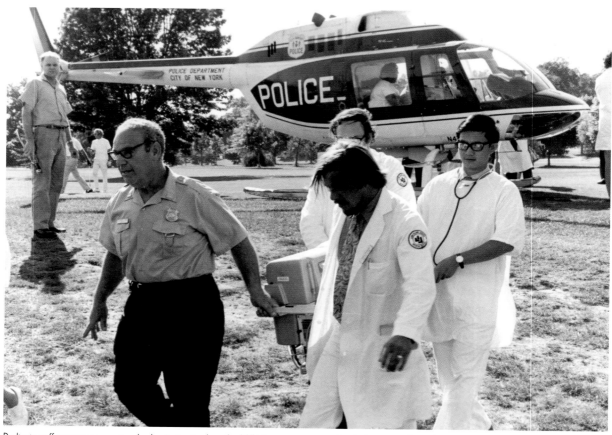

Pediatric staff receive a neonate who has just arrived on the Hillside property in a police helicopter in the early 1970s

problems. These sessions became extremely popular. The material presented, including radiology and pathology, was so elegant and instructive that I decided to look into a mechanism whereby this information could be transmitted to other hospitals in the area.

By the end of the decade, the New York Telephone Company had developed a system that met my needs: an electronic "blackboard" that had the capacity to transmit images via the telephone wires to TV screens in distant locations. A portable conference telephone and speakerphone gave it audio capability. This system, developed by Bell System was called *Gemini*. This system was a model for and the forerunner of interactive teleconferencing. However, it had significant limitations since it could not transmit x-rays, blood slides, or pathology. This program was the first of its kind in the country in which physicians

affiliated with a community hospital participated in seminars of a teaching hospital miles away (*New York Times*, May 4, 1980). *Gemini*, though very helpful, was rendered obsolete by technological advances. The current state-of-the-art teleconferencing system is still called *Gemini*, after the original system.

CALL-A-CONSULT PROGRAM

"Call-a-Consult" was another innovative program that was instituted in 1976. This was recognized in the local press (*South Shore Reporter, Nassau Herald, Far Rockaway Record, Great Neck Record* in January 1976) and nationally in *Pediatric News*, (April 1976).

The service assisted the practitioner in the investigation and treatment of children with uncommon conditions and was the precursor of the successful Schneider Children's Hospital

On-Call Program. Its aim was to provide immediate and up-to-date information to practicing pediatricians, as well as serving as a new form of postgraduate education to the physician. The article in the January 1, 1976, edition of the *Great Neck Record* read:

Hospital Establishes MD's 'Call-A-Consult'

If a doctor comes across a difficult problem when treating a child, instant feedback from a wide variety of pediatric subspecialists is now only a telephone call away. The department of pediatrics at Long Island Jewish-Hillside Medical Center has instituted a service called 'Call-a-Consult' which makes its staff specialists available, without charge, to the entire medical community on a round-the-clock basis.

Practicing pediatricians, family physicians and general practitioners are invited to telephone a private extension at the hospital when they encounter an uncommon condition in a young patient. The 'Call-a-Consult' service then puts the doctor in touch with a senior physician who specializes in the problem area. In this way, the doctor has immediate access to pediatric cardiologists, hematologists-oncologists, neurologists, neonatologists, and geneticists among others. The subspecialists, for the most part, are also professors at Stony Brook State University.

Dr. Philip Lanzkowsky, chairman of the department of pediatrics at Long Island Jewish, points out that the instant consultations are designed "as a community health service utilizing our growing staff of full-time subspecialists. With the rapid technological strides now being made in pediatrics, we believe it essential that we make our resources available to all physicians in the vicinity."

Programs similar to 'Call-a-Consult'

Multidisciplinary teleconferencing using the electronic blackboard that was part of the Gemini System, circa 1981.

are currently utilized in Nova Scotia and Southern California. Statistics gathered in California have shown that in 36 per cent of the telephone calls made by physicians, information obtained results in significant change in the management of the child being treated.

Initially this program was viewed as an innovative way for pediatricians in practice to get free telephone advice about the diagnosis and management of their patients from specialists at the hospital. With the passage of time and the increased number of specialists in the department of pediatrics who became well known on Long Island and who developed personal relationships with practicing pediatricians, this service became informal, frequently utilized, and very helpful to the practicing pediatricians and their patients.

PSYCHOSOCIAL PROGRAMS

No doubt owing to my previous training at St. Mary's Hospital School of Medicine of the University of London with Professor Donald Winnicott, the father of child psychiatry, I have always been deeply concerned about the psycho-social management of hospitalized children and the impact of a child's illness not only on the child but on the whole family. When I arrived at LIJ, parents were permitted to visit on Wednesday and Sunday afternoons only, and nurses wore starched white uniforms. I quickly reversed these archaic practices. Parents were permitted to visit every day, despite complaints from the nursing staff that the presence of parents 24/7 interfered with their ability to effectively carry out their nursing duties. The regulations on nurses' attire were also liberalized.

The Schneider Children's Hospital represents the fulfillment of so many of my highest ideals for the care of the hospitalized child, but none was more important and was carried out more successfully than the care of his or her psychological state and, indeed, that same concern for the child's family—expressed by the compassionate staff and also by the warm, child-friendly environment.

Playroom in the department of pediatrics at LIJ in the early 1970s.

CHAPTER 4

THE DREAM

HOW IT ALL BEGAN

A hospital dedicated to the care of children was an exciting dream. Its materialization would require the combined dedication and efforts of many people and institutions.

    The dream was born with Martin W. Abrams, MD, and Burton Bronsther, MD, who passed it to Judge Bertram Harnett, who subsequently handed it to me. Judge Harnett's focus would be on marshaling community support in the political, board, planning, and "lay" arenas; mine would be on the academic and programmatic considerations necessary to bring this dream to reality. Judge Harnett provided decades of leadership experience and the intellectual vigor required to gain approval for the building of a children's hospital and to attract funding and community support. The grassroots support of the Children's Medical Center Fund of New York (later the Children's Medical Fund of New York, or CMF, as we will refer to it hereinafter) and the foresight of several members of the LIJ Board of Trustees and its executive director would also be instrumental in achieving the objective.

    But let's start at the beginning.

Signing the agreement of affiliation between the CMF and LIJ-HMC, November 8, 1971. Seated left to right: Irving Wharton, vice-chairman, LIJ Board of Trustees; Aaron Solomon, chairman, LIJ Board of Trustees; Hon. Bertram Harnett, chairman CMF Board of Trustees. Standing, left to right: Hon Sol Wachtler, trustee, LIJ, and Robert K. Match, MD, executive vice-president, LIJ.

DRS. BURTON BRONSTHER AND MARTIN W. ABRAMS

Burton Bronsther, MD and Martin W. Abrams, MD were partners in a pediatric surgical practice located in Rockville Centre, Long Island. Both understood the need for a children's hospital to provide optimal care for children. Dr.

Bronsther trained under Willis J. Potts, MD, at the Children's Memorial Hospital in Chicago. Dr. Abrams trained under C. Everett Koop, MD, at the Children's Hospital of Philadelphia. In 1965, Drs. Bronsther and Abrams had become frustrated with their dealings with small hospitals all over Queens and Nassau County. With the encouragement of Drs. Potts and Koop, they assembled an advisory board to study the possibility of developing a children's medical center for New York.

Top: Burton Bronsther, MD
Bottom: Martin W. Abrams, MD

Burton Bronsther was a big bear of a man, but kindly and gentle. Martin Abrams was energy personified; an athletic man, a wonderful conversationalist and story teller. Both had outgoing personalities, were articulate and persuasive, and shared a great sensitivity to the needs of children. The parents of many of their patients fell under their spell, drawn in by memories of their children's medical treatment. Some of their stories had tragic endings. These men were natural magnets for anyone who felt deeply about the quality of medical care of their children. Decades later, Sylvia Bakst, director of LIJ archives, interviewed Dr. Bronsther for the Fall, 1991 edition of Memories & Milestones. In it, he commented with pride on the hospital: "These days when I drive past Schneider Children's Hospital I feel so good because our dream became a reality. Today the hospital has certainly achieved national acclaim. Dr. Philip

Lanzkowsky deserves tremendous credit for its accomplishments and for its outstanding staff."

Judge Harnett had unusual advocacy and organizational skills, and Bronsther and Abrams turned to him in 1963 for assistance in formulating the project and moving it forward.

BERTRAM HARNETT

It must be understood just how unpopular the notion of a children's hospital was back then in the regulatory and medical communities. There was no public constituency supporting this project in any of the three Long Island counties. Oddly enough, there was a prevailing concern that a children's hospital would negatively affect fundraising for other medical needs in the New York City metropolitan area. Private practitioners were afraid that centrality of high-level childcare would take away patients and cut their incomes. A children's hospital was seen as a cost-intensive specialty hospital—not a necessity. The bean counters were hard at work!

From the late sixties to the early eighties, Bertram Harnett was the engine that drove the effort to establish a children's hospital on Long Island. During a versatile career that has spanned over six decades, Harnett served as a trial justice of the New York State Supreme Court and, in earlier days, county attorney of Nassau County, New York. He was since 1948 a practicing lawyer, a partner in several well-known law firms in New York City and Nassau County specializing in insurance, corporate, tax, and estate planning law. He taught law at Columbia, Rutgers, Kansas, and Hofstra Universities' schools of law, as well as the New York Practicing Law Institute. A frequently published legal author and a nationally recognized insurance law authority, he often testified in court as an expert witness. Harnett was a founding public member of the Nassau/Suffolk Regional Planning Board, founding chairman of both the Nassau/Suffolk Comprehensive

Health Council and the Mitchell Field Development Corp., and chairman of the Nassau Legal Aid Society, all underlining his savvy in public affairs and causes.

One frightening experience and one important person in Judge Harnett's boyhood in Sea Gate, Brooklyn, led to his commitment. He had been sickly as a child and had been in and out of hospitals. When he was nine years old, he was run over by an automobile while at play with his brother, Joel. His parents were not at home, and he was taken to the emergency room at Coney Island Hospital by the shaken driver of the car, where he was left for hours in a crowded room.

Decades later, he still remembers the experience clearly: "A nurse came over to me and said, 'Shut up, stop your crying, you're going to be dead in a few hours anyway.'" He was eventually patched up, but when he woke in a ward the next day, a doctor similarly lacking in compassion said, "What! You still here?" By then, Harnett's parents had found him, but the next night, the boy in the adjacent bed died after receiving last rites from a priest. It was a terrifying hospital stay.

The second great influence in Harnett's early days was his mother's mother, Rae Barnett. "She fought unremittingly for what she believed in," said Harnett. "One of her causes was indigent pregnant women, many of whom were recent immigrants. She, who was poor herself, begged for money for them from wealthy

Judge Bertram Harnett, chairman of CMF 1966-1984

women in her community." Harnett recalled, "I stood in the doorways and watched her with these poor women. She was encouraging and warm. She was big, forceful, maybe gruff, but she had a heart of gold. My heart still fills with love when I remember this tough-looking lady holding the face of some poor soul, gently, offering comforting words, with tears from both of them. She was for those who could not help themselves." Children, like the needy, are not an "articulate constituency," in Harnett's words.

On September 9, 1963, Judge Harnett received a fateful call from Dr. Abrams, whom he had met once before. Harnett was just finishing a stint as the Nassau County attorney, and was going back into private practice. "Marty called me and said, 'Hey, Bert, how would you like to have your first client—no fee? Burt Bronsther and I have an idea for the creation of a children's hospital. Will you be our lawyer?'" Harnett asked him, "What's a children's hospital?" Halfway through his explanation, Harnett interrupted him and said, "Stop, Marty. You have me for life." Harnett thought it would be easy—after all, who could be against children? He had no idea that this cause would indeed bind him and Marty together for the rest of their lives.

Harnett's law office founded the CMF, which was incorporated in 1966 to create a legal foundation for the efforts. He became its first chairman, and maintained the position for two decades. He devoted endless hours to the organization and was the inspirational leader of the tireless group of dedicated individuals who waded through the stormy bureaucratic waters of the regulatory bodies, built community and political support, and eventually helped win over the government and medical authorities whose acquiescence was necessary for the building of the children's hospital. From these early days until the hospital was built on the grounds of LIJ, there were many different people involved as the project evolved through many different phases of development.

THE INITIAL PHASE

In the mid-sixties Drs. Bronther and Abrams spoke incessantly about their plans to build a children's hospital with parents of patients and their personal friends, of whom they had many. For a brief period, they brought in a public relations firm to help spread the word.

Gladys Cole helped form the Women's Division of the CMF, and under her leadership it rapidly become a cohesive force, multiplying into numerous chapters, with attendant activities such as social luncheons, speaking programs, and annual dinner dances. The Men's Division, under the leadership of Martin Lifton, developed later.

In 1965, Drs. Abrams and Bronsther assembled a distinguished advisory board with the objective of further developing the CMF. A private dinner symposium for the board was held in 1965 at the old Garden City Hotel. Several CMF members and most of the board attended to discuss and develop the concept in order to clarify what they should seek, and what should be avoided. This group met only on two occasions; it produced a document but nothing else.

THE MITCHELL FIELD PHASE

By 1966, the need to have a tangible product became a significant objective with the group, and the architectural firm of Morris Lapidus was asked to create an architectural rendering of the proposed hospital. The firm came up with a circular building containing 550 beds with a parking garage surrounding it. When, on February 1, 1996, an article and photo of the rendering of this space-age building that would house a new children's hospital on Long Island appeared in the *New York Times*, written by Raymond H. Anderson, the glimmer of reality, however dim, began to shine through the rhetoric. The article read:

New Children's Medical Center Is Proposed for Nassau County

Plans for the construction in the New York area of a children's medical center that ultimately would be the largest in the United States were announced here yesterday. The $34.5 million center is to be built in Nassau County, possibly on a 16-acre site of the former Mitchell Air Force Base in Garden City. Negotiations have been initiated with Nassau County for a possible donation of the land.

A fund drive for the first stage of the project was announced at a news conference in the Plaza Hotel by the governing committee of the Children's Medical Center Fund of New York.

Dr. Edward L. Pratt, a Cincinnati pediatrician said that the plan was to raise about $3 million in private donations and then turn to the Federal and State governments for grants. Such grants, he added, probably would cover 50 to 60 per cent of the total cost. The nonprofit, independent children's center would open with 329 beds and be expanded later to 550 beds. But its emphasis will be on outpatient care, reflecting a trend in pediatrics toward prevention, early diagnosis and rehabilitation.

The circular main building, designed by Morris Lapidus, the architect, would have a multi-level garage with ramps to permit outpatients to be driven to the level of the clinics. One of two auxiliary buildings will have 50 rooms to allow children to live with one of their parents while receiving treatment.

Mr. Lapidus, who has designed several medical centers including Mt. Sinai Hospital here, said his design for the project was aimed at creating a "non-hospital atmosphere." "It will be no more traumatic to a child than a kindergarten or a school," he added. "The concept is that we are really creating a community – a community for children."

The design incorporates suggestions by pediatricians working in children's hospitals throughout the United States. Dr. Pratt said that the planners had decided upon Nassau County as the best site for the children's center because of a rapid increase in the area of young people under the age of 15.

Citing Census Bureau figures, he noted that from 1950 to 1960 the number of residents under 15 in Nassau increased 143 per cent, compared with an increase of 37 percent throughout the country.

Other members of the governing committee of the Children's Medical Center Fund include Dr. C. Everett Koop, chief surgeon at the Children's Hospital of Philadelphia, Dr. Martin W. Abrams of the Morrisania Division of the Montefiore Medical Center and Joel W. Harnett, vice president of Cowles Communications, Inc.

Several members of the Long Island Federation of Labor, A.F.L.-C.I.O., attended the conference to express their support of the children's medical center.

But, in the end, this was a fantasy. It was a pipe dream. There was no real program development, no support from any hospitals in the region or regulatory agencies, no medical leadership, no capital funding, no operational business plan for the hospital.

In 1966, Judge Harnett contacted the Mitchell Field Development Corporation, which he had earlier founded and chaired, and CMF was given a public hearing, at which a grant of land was requested on the condition that enough construction capital was raised. According to the November 12, 1971 issue of *Newsday*, The Mitchell Field Planning Commission rejected

this plan because the hospital would operate in isolation from other medical centers. Local hospital and community leaders affiliated with such hospitals communicated their opposition directly to the county and town administrators. There were some later negotiations, but they led nowhere.

THE MEADOWBROOK HOSPITAL PHASE

The Meadowbrook Hospital, known today as Nassau University Medical Center, was at that time a brand-new nineteen-story county hospital in East Meadow, Long Island. When the hospital was built in 1974, the local fire department did not have a ladder tall enough to fight a fire on the top floor—should one break out there—and so a certificate of occupancy was never issued; nor was the floor ever used. It is vacant to the present day.

In the late 1960s, the CMF board had the idea to sponsor a separate facility for children on these top two floors. It would be a stepping-stone toward further construction on county grounds. There were no detailed discussions about the difficult features of the hospital, including the separation between the emergency room and the surgical operating suite. James Ericson, who was the director of the Meadowbrook Hospital, and Jack Platon Collip, MD, its chairman of pediatrics, were interested in having a children's hospital located in their facility, and there were many meetings and discussions with the Nassau County commissioner of health on the subject.

Because of the public nature of the proposal, it was necessary to gain the support of the local Republican and Democratic parties. Democratic representatives were favorably inclined, but the Republican side was not. A lot of opposition was generated, again, from local hospitals and their well-positioned patrons. The potential for a political explosion necessitated that the negotiations maintain a low public profile. But before the proposal was presented to the Nassau County Board of Supervisors, a fateful lunch would put an end to the Meadowbrook phase.

THE LIJ PHASE

Only a week or two after my arrival at LIJ in the spring of 1970, Drs. Bronsther and Abrams marched into my office to share their long-held dream of building a hospital where the needs of sick children were the only concern. Whether they suspected it or not, Drs. Bronsther and Abrams had come to the right man. My training had taken place in children's hospitals in Cape Town, South Africa, Edinburgh, Scotland, and London, England. I understood that by assembling pediatric experts trained in medical, surgical, psychiatric, and dental disciplines, a children's hospital would encourage research directed solely to the improvement of the health and welfare of children and would act as a focal point for educating the community in matters of child care and child health. It would do all this in a physical environment that would cater exclusively to the needs and comfort of children.

About a year after I met with Drs. Bronsther and Abrams, I received a phone call from Judge Bertram Harnett, who was at that time with the New York Supreme Court in Mineola. Judge Harnett introduced himself, told me he was calling at the urging of Dr. Abrams, and invited me to lunch. I said to him, "Well, what's the subject? I just don't meet with judges without knowing what it's all about." Judge Harnett replied, "I think we have some common interests." He was right.

On the first day of April, 1971, Dr. Abrams and Bertram Harnett met me for lunch in a Mineola restaurant prophetically named the Caucus. Dr. Bronsther wasn't available. At that meeting, the concept of building the children's hospital went into dramatic forward gear. While it might stall, it was never to be reversed.

Ostensibly, the purpose of our lunch meeting was to solicit my support, as the newly appointed director of pediatrics at Long Island Jewish Medical Center, for the Meadowbrook Hospital proposal. I listened patiently for two hours to the presentation. In my mind, the idea was a spectacular one—consistent with my own dreams and aspirations for children in the region—but I thought their plan lacked sufficient foundation ever to materialize. A county hospital was the wrong place to base a children's hospital. It would never gain national standing there, it would never gain public support, and it would not attract top academicians from around the country. It would also lack academic independence, and if it ever got off the ground, it was unlikely to be successful. Ultimately the CMF came to the same realization.

When it was nearly 2 o'clock and I had to return to work, I commented, "It is a great idea, but the location and sponsorship are wrong. It should be at LIJ, where we have a nucleus of pediatrics and a resident training program." To this, Harnett responded, "Would LIJ be interested?" I committed to pushing the idea and told him the first approval would have to come from Robert K. Match, MD, the executive director of Long Island Jewish Medical Center. In retrospect, I realized that we were selling to each other the idea of a children's hospital at LIJ. Apparently, we both had the same hidden agenda!

Dr. Match listened to me and was willing to consider the possibility with an open mind. On April 17, 1971, at 9:30 a.m., a breakfast meeting was scheduled at the home of Dr. Abrams in Kings Point. Drs. Match, Lanzkowsky, Abrams, and Bronsther, and Judge Harnett were in attendance. Harnett clearly expressed his views and philosophy about a children's hospital, which were very sound, because Harnett had spent several years learning all he could about the subject.

The meeting was a success; Dr. Match liked the prospect of building a children's hospital affiliated with Long Island Jewish Medical Center.

On June 16 and 17, 1971, I met with Judge Harnett in Room 319 of the new Nassau County Court House in Mineola to decide how to proceed. Next, since the plan was to move the project away from Meadowbrook Hospital to LIJ, on July 19, Judge Harnett and I met with Dr. Jack Collip, chairman of pediatrics at Meadowbrook, in the John Peel Room of the Island Inn in Westbury, New York. We hoped to elicit his support, and we were gratified that he understood why we had come to our decision and was cooperative. So, on to the next hurdle....

The next step was for Dr. Match and me to present a proposal for a children's hospital to the Board of Trustees of LIJ. Some thought well of the idea, but others were opposed to it. The knee-jerk reaction to the proposal from some board members was: "There is only one LIJ, and, we are not going to split LIJ up."

We realized that seeing our plan become a reality would be no cakewalk—especially with this outspoken and opinionated board. But we went about our work, often one on one, educating and convincing individual board members about the need for a children's hospital and what it would do for LIJ. The LIJ professional staffs, especially the directors of departments, were at best indifferent but mostly opposed. They were uninformed about what a children's hospital really was, they were satisfied with the status quo, they feared competition for attention of the board and allocation of resources, and they were concerned about the demands a children's hospital would make on their services and departments. After considerable discussion, the board reluctantly agreed to affiliate with the CMF in pursuit of building a children's hospital.

Because of the prevailing indifference and lack of information about our idea, I felt it was necessary to develop and circulate a document entitled, "Rationale for a Children's Medical Center," for purposes of discussion (Appendix II). Because of its provocative and "threatening" nature, this document was passed around with great discretion. Some thirteen years later, its basic principles became the foundation of the philosophy, organization, and program for the Schneider Children's Hospital.

The November 5, 1971 issue of *The Long Island Press* reported that the organization had originally considered affiliation with the Nassau County Hospital in East Meadow because a site near the county hospital had already been selected, but that the group had had "second thoughts" because of fears of getting bogged down in government bureaucracy and red tape.

The general public first learned about the proposed 100-bed children's hospital at LIJ on November 4, 1971, when the venture was disclosed in Walter Kaner's column in *The Long Island Press*. The article was entitled "Hospital for Children—First of Kind in Metropolitan Area" and was followed by articles in *Newsday* (November 12, 1971); *Glen Oaks News* (November 18, 1971), and the *Long Island Herald* (November 18, 1971). The *Queens Ledger* (November 18, 1971) revealed that the CMF had signed a contract with Long Island Jewish Medical Center to build a hospital on the grounds in New Hyde Park at a proposed cost of $10 million. The hospital, to be known as the Children's Medical Center of New York, was expected to be completed in 1975. Initially there would be 100 beds, with provision made for later expansion. Also planned, according to the article, were ambulatory care, research, and educational facilities, as well as residential accommodation for parents and pediatric patients not requiring in-hospital care.

The *Queens Ledger* article read:

Announcement of the contract signing was made by State Supreme Court Justice

Bertram Harnett, chairman of the Children's Medical Center Fund of New York, and Aaron Solomon, president of Long Island Jewish Medical Center.

The agreement, as explained by Solomon, stipulates that the Children's Medical Center will assume responsibility for building and equipping the new hospital while Long Island Jewish Medical Center will provide the site and be responsible for staffing and running the hospital. Planning and development will be carried on jointly. Provisions have been made for cross representation on the respective boards.

The stated purpose of the projected Children's Medical Center will be to treat "the whole child" including diseases and disorders from the prenatal period through adolescence. Presently the closest children's hospitals are in Philadelphia and Boston.

"The Long Island Jewish Medical Center," said Judge Harnett, "is a particularly appropriate institution for this affiliation for a number of reasons. This voluntary hospital already has the nucleus for the formation of a children's hospital—the staff, facilities and equipment. It has a premature nursery center, intensive care units for the child and the newborn baby, an adolescent unit, an infant transport service and a full range of specialized pediatric clinics. The institution has also distinguished itself in the sub-specialty areas of pediatrics such as pediatric hematology, cardiology, adolescent medicine and pediatric surgery. The recent affiliation of Long Island Jewish Medical Center with the Health Sciences Center of the State University at Stony Brook is also of great significance."

In addition, Judge Harnett pointed out that the highly accessible location of Long Island Jewish Medical Center figured in the decision. The Children's Medical Center will be under the administrative supervision of Dr. Robert K. Match, executive vice president and director of Long Island Jewish Medical Center. Dr. Philip Lanzkowsky, director of pediatrics of LIJMC, will be in charge of the professional services.

While this statement appeared significant and substantial in its own right, in reality, it formed the basis for a battle that raged for more than a decade with surrounding physicians, institutions, and regulatory agencies, all of which were bent on thwarting the development of a children's hospital in this region of the country. The motivation for these objections was, regrettably, self-interest and a desire to maintain the comfortable status quo of the delivery of medical services for children.

The Future Home
OF THE
CHILDREN'S
MEDICAL CENTER
OF NEW YORK
the total health care of Children

CHAPTER 5

HELP FROM THE GRASS ROOTS

THE ROLE OF THE CMF

"There are a lot of charities. Every charity is worth something, but some are worth more than others."
—Bernice Mager, President of Women's Division, 1975

The Children's Medical Center Fund of New York (CMCFNY), a not-for-profit corporation, was established in 1966. Although in the 1970s the corporate name was changed to the Children's Medical Fund of New York, the same organization, which generally in this text will be known as the CMF, has devoted over forty years to the development of a children's hospital and then to its support when it became a reality.

Judge Bertram Harnett, who was chairman of CMF's Board of Trustees until 1984, founded the organization and was the driving force behind it and its role in the building of the children's hospital. Harnett was followed in this role by a succession of equally dedicated chairpersons, all of whom made major contributions to the advancement of the organization's goals and objectives. These included:

Martin Lifton	1984-1991
Bernard Levy	1991-1993
Marcie Rosenberg	1993-1998
Jeffrey S. Jurick	1998-2002
Richard J. Goldberg, MD	2002-2004
Stephen Lifton	2004-2006
David Blumenfeld	2006-present

One of the potential sites on the LIJ campus considered for the future home of the children's medical center. Members of the women's division of CMF headed by Gladys Cole stand proudly on either side of the sign, 1972.

A volunteer-driven organization, CMF is structured with a board of directors, an office and staff, and both a Women's and a Men's Division, which at their height had a combined membership of over 10,000 drawn from all over Long Island as well as Manhattan and Westchester. The CMF's membership consists of parents, physicians, civic leaders, and other dedicated people, and it was represented on the LIJ Board of Trustees.

The CMF played a key role in the establishment of the Schneider Children's Hospital. Its members participated in the planning and were unrelenting advocates of its separation from LIJ. They worked for legislative approval, raised building funds, and helped in surmounting vigorous opposition to the proposed hospital from state and private medical authorities. Today, the CMF's main focus is fundraising (it continues to be the largest contributor to the hospital), but in the beginning it was predominantly an activist organization.

Together, its members created the largest public interest group in Queens and Long Island, which eventually played a role in altering the political equation that had stymied the early efforts for a separate children's hospital.

This level of commitment is epitomized by this description of a CMF volunteer in *Newsday*, in September 1972:

> "The children's hospital could not have been possible without the help of the countless volunteers who have worked tirelessly on behalf of this venture. Their commitment is without equal. In addition to bringing in dollars, they are out in the community telling our story and enlisting support."
>
> Martin Lifton
> CMFNY President
> *North Shore Community Papers*
> September 18, 1982

Carole Zorfas was sitting in somebody's living room when her gaze caught the flutter of an upraised hand. Her eyes traced the hand down along the arm to its owner, whereupon she made an interesting discovery: it was hers. She looked twice to makes sure, but yet it was hers, and she was doing something she had never done before. She was volunteering, and not only that, she was thinking "I'd do anything, scrub floors, and sweep hallways, anything."

Thus is the mentality of a dedicated volunteer. Mrs. Zorfas plunged into fundraising for a proposed children's medical center, but the syndrome is universal and a bit spooky, and for that reason volunteering has never been taken lightly. When you are a volunteer in what you consider to be a good cause, a strange new attitude seizes you. Whole vatfuls of new adrenaline course through your blood. Unknown energies stir to life. A wild recklessness possesses you, and you find yourself giving your 9-year-old the keys to the house and letting her grub out her own survival because you are too busy at the campaign office answering telephones and opening up letters with $1 checks in them, usually accompanied by a hand-written note saying somewhere in it "God bless you." What had driven Mrs. Zorfas, and of course, the other members into the ecstasies of the sacrificial life, was a campaign to raise money for the Children's Medical Center.

THE WOMEN'S DIVISION

In the beginning, promoting the CMF rested almost entirely on the Women's Division. As the years unfolded, a Men's Division followed, as did broad community support. But its original dynamic force sprang from women who agonized over their own children's medical misfortunes, and indeed, even some deaths. The women who led the division had extraordinary abilities, particularly in building and maintaining such a large force for so long without anything tangible in front of them. It is the essential truth that these women were the mothers of the children's hospital and kept it alive until it walked on its own Long Island Jewish feet.

The drive of women for a children's hospital is embodied in the experiences of Marcia Goodman, one of the early project supporters. Marcia was a mother of two children who died when they were very young, one from cancer and one from pneumonia. She vividly remembered the problems they encountered in a pediatric ward of a major hospital in Manhattan and described her experience in the September 21, 1983 issue of Newsday. "I'll never forget the day my son [who had cancer] was sitting in my lap," she said, "and the doctor came over and told me he had three weeks to live. It was as if I were with a child who was deaf and dumb. We transferred him to Children's Hospital Boston. The entire attitude, the entire feeling of the place was different. They geared the hospital toward children, and they treated them with greater compassion and more efficiently."

Remembering this terrible time, Mrs. Goodman said, "I know the anguish of being miles away from family and friends, of having no one to turn to when you need support. The opening of a children's hospital here on Long Island will be a blessing for so many."

This was not an isolated experience. Many of the early supporters were mothers of sick children who learned that they had to travel to

A CHILD

Bitter are the tears of a child

Sweeten them

Deep are the thoughts of a child

Quiet them

Sharp is the grief of a child

Take it from him

Soft is the heart of a child

Do not harden it.

Lady Pamela Wyndham Glenconner

Boston or Philadelphia for optimal care for their children. Some professionals and members of boards of trustees of hospitals on Long Island and in Manhattan grew angry when they heard these comments. They were displeased with the fact that these women found resonance with other mothers of sick children, and most particularly that their concept of a separate and distinct hospital for children was gaining traction.

There was a subtle correlation between the changing role of women in society and that of the Women's Division of the CMF. They were a group of vibrant, intelligent people who worked tirelessly and stood unwaveringly behind what they believed. They strove for two decades to shape the concept into concrete reality. The hospital is really a monument to them.

Just over a year after its formation, the Women's Division had over 1,300 members in chapters scattered throughout Long Island and Queens, and in the 1980s this number increased to 6,500. Many of these women were mothers and grandmothers of children with medical problems who had to go elsewhere for comprehensive care. Others were simply aware that they might have to travel to another city for assistance some day if a children's medical center was not built in the New York metropolitan area. Most of the members realized that the road ahead would be long, and though they hoped to open the center in 1975, many millions of dollars were required before construction could begin.

The women envisioned a time when new frontiers in medicine would be reached by the new hospital. But until it was built, they and their associates would pour hundreds of cups of coffee and tea as they proselytized all over Long Island and the five boroughs of New York for members, money, and womanpower. They hosted dinner dances, luncheon after luncheon, coffee after coffee, to fundraise, boost their membership, and create awareness and support in all of the communities in the area.

The Women's Division's very first luncheon was hosted in 1972 at the Waldorf Astoria in New York City, and included important guests such as Mayor and Mrs. John Lindsay and guest speaker Barbara Walters. Events continued, one after the other, sending out the message that the New York Metropolitan area needed a freestanding children's hospital.

In an interview, Mrs. Gladys Cole said, "Other hospitals created a lot of political flak, like Columbia Presbyterian. They said they were a children's hospital, but they were not like the children's hospitals in Boston, Philadelphia, or Chicago, which were the models that CMF had aspired to emulate."

In order to grow most effectively and provide the best possible support throughout Long Island and the boroughs of New York City, the Women's Division was organized by strategically located chapters, each with a president. There were eight initial chapters located in Queens, Suffolk, Mid-Island, Merrick, Garden City, the Five

Towns, Roslyn, and Great Neck. The number of chapters grew as the membership expanded, and soon there were chapters in Westchester, Glen Cove, Jamaica Estates, South Shore East, and South Shore West. The ranks grew into the thousands and represented all the boroughs and counties surrounding New York City.

In the beginning, Ellyn Bronsther and Gladys Cole were the two major drivers of the project. Ellyn Bronsther was the very embodiment of the Women's Division. As Burt Bronsther's wife, she

CHILDREN'S MEDICAL CENTER of NEW YORK

at LONG ISLAND JEWISH HILLSIDE MEDICAL CENTER

New Hyde Park

DAIS GUESTS

Mayor & Mrs. John V. Lindsay   Hon. & Mrs. Ralph G. Caso   Miss Barbara Walters

Hon. Bertram Harnett   Dr. Philip Lanzkowsky   Mr. Aaron Solomon

Dr. Robert Match   Mrs. John Alliger   Mrs. Malcolm Steiner

Dr. Martin Abrams   Dr. Burton Bronsther   Hon. Shirley Amerasinghe

Mrs. Mary Egginton   Mr. Lawrence M Reed   Mr. Stuart Voisin

Mr. Robert Frankel   Mr. Martin Dwyer

CMF Women's Division inaugural luncheon program cover,
April 12, 1972.

chose to appear in a secondary role, helping to shepherd the dream. Charismatic and articulate, she encouraged many women and was tireless in her commitment. Many recruits joined up as a direct result of Ellyn Bronsther's efforts and attention.

Laurie Locastro, my editorial associate, recalls her visit to interview Gladys Cole for this book:

"I stepped into the elevator and pushed the button for the Penthouse, then checked myself in the mirror to make sure everything was in place. I rang the bell and was greeted by Gladys Cole, a stately and attractive woman. She invited me into her home, which was just as I expected, beautiful

and meticulous. My first question, of course was, 'How did you get involved with the Children's Medical Fund?"

Mrs. Cole told Laurie her story. "I spent many years bringing up my kids, and when my son was seven, he was diagnosed with a bone disease. I went from one hospital to another all over the country, looking for a pediatrician who could help my son, and I finally found a doctor at Children's Hospital Boston. I used to take my son back and forth to Boston on crutches because he wasn't able to walk any more, although he had been an outstanding young athlete. During this time, Dr. Marty Abrams, a very dear friend who was helping me with my son, approached

and asked for their support. I thought it would be a good idea to start a women's group. Before we knew it, we had several in the metropolitan area."

I was invited to speak at many of these gatherings at various locations from the North Shore to the South Shore of Long Island and beyond.

As the organization grew, it was decided within the organization that the president of the Women's Division would hold a two-year term. In 1973, Vivian Kokol became the second to serve. Armed with a velvet voice, iron hands, and an indomitable will, Vivian took the helm from Gladys and guided the women calmly through the long and trying wait for state approval.

Judge Harnett once told me that he believed that Gladys and Vivian both could have run General Motors. The judge said with a chuckle, "Gladys's son, Kenneth, eventually rose to the top in retailing. A lot of people thought he inherited his father's business ability, but I think his acumen came from Gladys."

Vivian Kokol hosted the second annual luncheon, which was an elegant, large-scale affair held in the Grand Ballroom of the Americana Hotel in May 1973. It was attended by over 1,000 women and raised over $20,000. The large ballroom danced with the reflections of crystal chandeliers and beautiful flowers adorned every table and corner. The guests were dressed as if they had just stepped out of Vogue. The guest speaker was Jonas Salk, MD, the eminent scientist who developed the first effective vaccine

me with the idea of building a children's hospital and asked if I would get involved. I said I am involved, without even a 'yes'. It was something New York was in very much need of. It was a lot of hard work. We started with three or four of us, and after realizing we had good ideas and good things to do, I had a big meeting in my home in Kings Point, and invited everyone I knew, men and women. We explained our goal to raise money to build a children's hospital in New York. When we started, we called it seed money, and we went to different areas to raise seed money. I was getting everyone involved. I traveled around and spoke to hospital administrators, and absorbed anyone who could help us into our organization. I met a lot of well-known people, but none of them wanted to help us with seed money. They all wanted to be big shots and get involved once the hospital was open. We started to go to different communities in the metropolitan area—Springfield Gardens, Whitestone, Syosset, and Huntington. We would find someone we knew in the community and ask her to invite all the women she knew to come to her home, and we informed these women about the children's hospital we were trying to build

pay a formal public tribute to Dr. Jonas Salk for his contribution to the health and the prevention of suffering of children worldwide. Children from the tip of South America to Greenland and from San Francisco to Calcutta all owe you a debt of gratitude, Sir, for saving them from the ravages of paralysis and death due to poliomyelitis.

I can recall with nightmarish clarity the polio epidemics of the early 1950s as they swept through the community in which I lived in South Africa leaving behind the deaths of so many innocent children and paralysis, deformity and crippling in others. In 1954 one of the major breakthroughs in the history of modern medicine occurred—you discovered the polio vaccine. In 1955 the vaccine was employed throughout the world virtually ending a scourge on the world's children caused by the polio virus.

Dr. Salk is a native of New York City where he was born in 1914. He received his MD degree in 1939 from New York University College of Medicine where he was Christian Herter Fellow in chemistry and experimental surgery.

In 1942 he attended the University of Michigan, sponsored by the National Foundation March of Dimes, to work with Dr. Thomas Francis, Jr. and in 1947 he went to the University of Pittsburgh as associate research professor of bacteriology and

against paralytic polio. He was the director of the noted Salk Institute for Biological Studies located in San Diego, California, and world renowned for his research in immunology. Other guests included Geraldo Rivera, Alexander Dobkin, Susan Perl, and Loretta Long, star of "Sesame Street." I made a presentation to Dr. Salk on behalf of CMF and made the following remarks:

Dr. Salk, honored guests on the dais, ladies and gentlemen:

It is my singular honor and privilege to

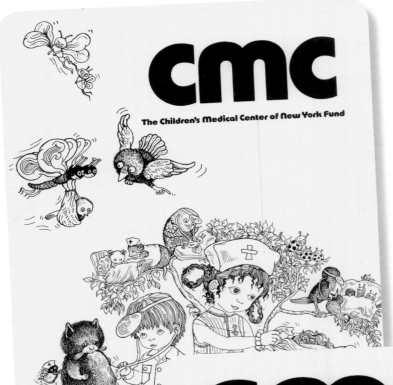

cmc

The Children's Medical Center of New York Fund

Program for second annual luncheon featuring Dr. Jonas Salk, Geraldo Rivera, Alexander Dobkin, Susan Perl and Loretta Long.

cmc

The Children's Medical Center of New York Fund

proudly invites you to

THE SECOND WOMEN'S AUXILIARY LUNCHEON

Mistress of Ceremonies Loretta Long

honorary title in the field of *Medicine*—DR. JONAS SALK

Eminent scientist, who developed the first effective vaccine against paralytic polio. He is director of the noted Salk Institute for Biological Studies in San Diego, Calif. and is world-renowned for his research in immunology. A native of New York City, Dr. Salk received his M.D. from N.Y. University College of Medicine, where he was a Christian A. Herter Fellow in Chemistry and Experimental Surgery.

honorary title in the field of *TV Communications*—GERALDO RIVERA

Contemporary TV newscaster of the current scene, Mr. Rivera is the best there is. He has won numerous awards for his probing reportorial work on WABC-TV's "EYEWITNESS NEWS" program. A graduate of Brooklyn Law School, Mr. Rivera won the coveted Emmy Award for his report on conditions at the Willowbrook State School for Retarded Children and two major broadcast journalism awards.

He believes his function is to change the world in some measurable way...and he will!

honorary title in the field of *Art*—ALEXANDER DOBKIN

The creator of the beautiful color lithograph designed exclusively for this event was born in Genoa, Italy. Mr. Dobkin's work has been critically acclaimed around the globe for more than forty years. In addition to his lithographs, Mr. Dobkin has also published several books and is a distinguished teacher. His paintings, drawings and lithographs are in the permanent collections of the Metropolitan Museum of Art, the Museum of Modern Art and the Whitney Museum. He has won the Childe Hassam Purchase Award of the American Academy of Arts & Letters. He was graduated from City College & received his Masters Degree in Art from Columbia University.

honorary title in the field of *Illustrating*—SUSAN PERL

You may not recognize the name, but the work of Susan Perl is instantly recognizable to anyone who comes in contact with The New York Times, just about any magazine you can name, any one of her shelves of books or the TV set. She is the illustrator for all seasons. And although she is most famous for her drawings of children and animals, Ms. Perl can capture anything in pen and ink. When she's drawing, Ms. Perl devotes a major portion of her time to getting children and animals together in real life the way she does in her drawings. Ms. Perl was born in Austria and now lives in New York City.

honorary title in the field of *educational entertainment*—LORETTA LONG

She is not the Pied Piper, but her magical appeal has millions of children following her. She is Loretta Long, star of "Sesame Street," Children's Medical Center Mistress of Ceremonies. She delights in children and they know it. There is no mistaking the special twinkle in her eyes when she is "Susan of Sesame Street." Loretta was born on a farm in Kansas and is presently enrolled in a doctoral program in humanistic studies. She is sparkling, sincere, sensitive and enthusiastic and it is easy to see why she has captured the hearts of youngsters in this country.

Philip Lanzkowsky, MD presents Jonas Salk, MD, with an award on behalf of CMF, May 1973.

director of its virus research laboratory. In 1948 he became full professor and in 1954 chairman of the department of preventive medicine.

While at Pittsburgh, Dr. Salk developed the vaccine for paralytic poliomyelitis and in 1954 the safety and effectiveness of the vaccine were demonstrated by vast nationwide field trials.

In recognition of this and other contributions, the State of Pennsylvania in 1955 created a newly endowed chair at the University of Pittsburgh, appointing Dr. Salk as the first Commonwealth Professor of Preventive Medicine. Dr. Salk received many honors, including a citation from President Eisenhower and in 1956 a Congressional Gold Medal for "great achievement in the field of medicine."

In 1960 the people of San Diego voted to donate a tract of land to build an institute of biological studies and today this institute—the Salk Institute—leads the world in biological research.

The people assembled here today are dedicated to the building of a children's hospital and your research achievements will act as inspiration and a standard to be emulated by this emerging institution.

On behalf of those present, we salute you, Sir, and it is my honor on their behalf to present you with this award.

The affair was a financial and motivational success that helped propel the efforts of the committee. Year after year, these affairs continued, each more successful than its predecessor. They were held in the grand ballrooms of elegant hotels in places like Port Chester, Flushing, Meadow Park, New York City, and Garden City. Fashion shows were very popular features at these affairs and were supported by top retailers such as Saks Fifth Avenue and

CMF Women's Division Lollipop Campaign poster, November 1972.

Bloomingdale's, and fashion designers like Aldolfo, Christian Dior, Geoffrey Beene, Anne Klein, and Ralph Lauren. I was invited to attend these events frequently to give motivational talks on care available in a children's hospital compared to that received in a general hospital, and the need for a hospital exclusively for children on the North Shore of Long Island, and also to assist CMF in maintaining the interest and momentum for this project.

The Women's Division torch, which was so brilliantly held aloft by Gladys Cole and Vivian Kokol, was passed the summer of 1975 to the capable hands of Bernice Mager. Bernice had been actively involved in the CMF since its beginning, serving first as president of the South Shore West Chapter. As with many of the volunteers, it was a personal circumstance that prompted her participation in CMF. Following her youngest son's surgery in 1972, Dr. Burton Bronsther, who had been one of the surgeons, asked Bernice if she would consider joining him and others in a philanthropic organization whose goal was to build a children's hospital. She was more than happy to be among the pioneers. Mrs. Mager is still involved, as a member of the Board of Trustees.

When asked to sum up her thoughts on all the hours she'd spent fundraising, getting approval, and building the children's hospital, she responded, "To laugh often and much; to win the respect of intelligent people and the affection of children; to earn the appreciation of honest critics and endure the betrayal of false friends; to appreciate beauty; to find the best in others; to leave the world a bit better, whether through a healthy child, a garden patch, or a redeemed social condition; to know even one life has breathed easier because you lived—this is to have succeeded."

In September 1972, the Women's Division announced its first public campaign to solicit funds throughout the greater New York area. It was to run from November 22 to November 25, 1972, and was called the Lollipop Campaign keyed to the symbol of kindness to children.

During these four days, 5,000 volunteers gave two hours of their time to be "lollipop people." They fanned out all over the metropolitan area, from Manhattan to Montauk, northern New Jersey to southern Connecticut, offering lollipop pens or buttons for donations

Carol Zorfas, member of the CMF Women's Division leaves lollipops in a local business, November 1972.

Carol Zorfas and Robert Frankel (extreme left) receive the "Children's Medical Center Week in New York" proclamation from the Office of the Mayor of New York City kicking off the Lollipop Campaign, November 25, 1972.

of one dollar or more toward construction of the children's hospital. They were everywhere—in banks, stores, and malls, at Madison Square Garden, the Coliseum, Yankee Stadium, bridges, tunnels, and anywhere else a crowd was likely to be. Donation cans were everywhere, too, and so were posters. In buses, trains, grocery stores, gas stations, dry cleaners, butcher shops, beauty shops, delicatessens, and restaurants, they urged: "Look for the Lollipop People."

The committee, which was co-chaired by good friends Carol Zorfas of Jericho and Elaine Wolbrom of Hollis Hills, had an enormous undertaking on their hands. They put in fifteen-hour days in preparation for the campaign. During the four days, the women met thousands of people face-to-face, explaining the need for the children's medical center and gaining recognition and support from the communities on Long Island, the boroughs of New York City, northern

New Jersey, and southern Connecticut.

All the newspapers covered the campaign and New York City's Mayor Lindsay even designated the week of the campaign Children's Medical Center Week in New York, with a proclamation to that effect at City Hall.

The lollipop fundraising effort turned out to be a branding campaign that was probably more successful than any they could have paid an advertising agency to create for them. It exceeded its goal of $100,000.

For the women who had made it all happen, this great success was simply another step toward their goal of opening a children's hospital in the metropolitan New York City area. They were still a long way from having enough money to build the hospital.

Many different fundraising events followed this campaign. There were tennis galas, dinner dances, quilt auctions, walkathons, children's art shows, bazaars, house and garden tours in the spring, and golf tournaments. They sold calendars and cookbooks, and through ongoing networking, received many donations from events held by other organizations to support the children's medical center.

Many of the women with long-term involvement in the CMF shared similar stories. These women include Marcia Goodman, Marcie Rosenberg, Muriel Martin (Springfield), and Elaine Bisnoff. All served as officers, some more than once, and some are still involved.

One typical story is that of Rita Kay, a vivacious member of the Women's Division who has much love and compassion for children. After having two healthy boys, Rita and her husband wondered whether there was a children's hospital in the metropolitan area, just in case they needed it. The children's hospital had just opened, and Rita came to visit. She says that as she walked through the hospital, she could feel the love and compassion for the children there, and she loved what the institution stood for, which was the total care of children. Thrilled to hear about the existence of CMF and its role in fundraising for the children's hospital, Rita joined a chapter on Long Island, and has remained enthusiastically involved ever since.

THE MEN'S DIVISION

"Wonderful people created a wonderful hospital, and they can be proud of what they did. The key was the people. We were the catalyst and everyone worked very hard—each in his or her own way. The result is that we have a children's hospital serving lots and lots of people today."

—Martin Lifton

As the organizational structure of the CMF changed and Men's and Women's Divisions were created, Martin Lifton became the founding president of the Men's Division.

When asked how he got involved, Mr. Lifton replied, "My son Steve had been in an accident and broke his femur. No children's hospital existed to take care of him. My wife, Ellie, heard that people were planning to build a children's hospital. She went to one of the meetings and got involved, and she said to me, 'You have to come to the next meeting.' So I went to the meeting. Judge Harnett was organizing a group for the Men's Division. My wife volunteered me, and the rest is history. I became the founding president of the Men's Division. We started by supporting the events that were already planned. Then we organized our own fundraising event, the first annual golf outing, named for the late Bernard Martin, and held at the Plandome Country Club. We asked friends and family members to participate in the golf tournament for a fee. After the event, we solicited all participants to become members and supporters of CMF. The event raised between $18,000 and $25,000 and we thought it was the most fantastic thing that could ever happen. Now it has grown into a million-dollar

event every year. So that was my involvement in the beginning."

The Men's Division was not structured into chapters; instead, it remained an integral division. With the help of Howard Katz, director of development at LIJ, it started to build its membership. The first goal was to find 1,000 people to give $1,000 within a set period of time. The Women's Division joined this effort. They called it the Angel Campaign, and when the hospital was built, blocks with the donors' name were put up in the Wall of Angels. Once the $1,000 donation was given, donors were asked to repeat the donation. Many did, and their blocks on the Wall of Angels contained a star. In 2006, these blocks were removed and replaced by glass "bricks," recognizing the original contributing angels.

The men soon became very involved in planning the children's hospital. They traveled to other children's hospitals to speak to their administrators and observe the programs. They provided support throughout the long process

of gaining approvals. They attended the community hearings while continually building their membership with new supporters. But the reality was that the CMF needed an advocate from the hospital who shared their dream and could help the CMF and the hospital work together in a more collaborative way.

As Mr. Lifton said, "Dr. Lanzkowsky and Bertram Harnett stepped into the picture and became the advocates to solicit the hospital's support, and the two of them together became a powerful force to move the project forward. Lanzkowsky spent a huge amount of time with the CMF, attending and speaking at some of their functions and reporting at their board meetings. Lanzkowsky is a wonderful man," he continued, "and very dedicated. He understood the realities of the world, and there weren't many people who could have gotten as much done as he did."

The battle the CMF waged on behalf of the children's hospital could be described as Churchillian. You may remember these words: "We shall fight on the beaches, we shall fight in the streets, we shall never surrender." The rallying cry of Judge Harnett as quoted in the March, 1977 issue of *In Touch* signaled a renewed determination on the part of the CMF to accomplish its goal: "We will go to every government official, to every health planning body in the state hierarchy, every newspaper editor, every child-health group in the metropolitan area to press for more beds. We've worked too hard and come too far. The needs of our children are too great...we will not be turned back now."

The organization launched a campaign that awakened both the general public and the medical community to its grit and determination. Because it was striving for a higher level of pediatric care, the CMF was already seen to be casting aspersions on the existing level of care, and on the institutions and physicians providing it. This campaign both embarrassed and angered some at LIJ.

On February 3, 1977, over 100 CMF members, almost all women, braved the bitter cold weather to travel to Albany. They crowded uninvited into the meeting room of the Hospital Review and Planning Council of New York, where a hearing on the children's hospital application was being conducted, wearing cloth diapers pinned to their chests that bore the slogan, "Save the Children's Medical Center."

In the days preceding the trip, members of the Women's Division and the Men's Division coordinated a huge mail campaign. They sent out 50,000 postcards and 5,000 letters to people in the community, elected officials, thirty-one members of the Hospital Review and Planning Council, and Governor Hugh Carey, explaining their cause and eliciting support. Additional letters were sent to corporate executives. Health service agencies in the community were urged to send their own letters in support of the children's hospital.

The diaper may have been a rather inelegant choice as a means for conveying the CMF's message, but it got attention—too much attention, according to some at LIJ. When the topic of the children's hospital came up for discussion, the group rose en masse, and Judge Harnett attempted to present their case. At first, the chairman of the council would not allow the judge to speak; in fact, he said no one from the audience would be granted the floor, and he threatened the judge with a charge of contempt. However, TV cameras were present, thanks to Ray Weiss, an early CMF board member who worked for NBC. The judge pointed this out, and he also pointed out that it would be a disgrace if such a substantial delegation, representing thousands of residents of the State of New York who were fighting for children, could not have their say.

Members of the CMF Women's Division attending the New York State Hospital Review and Planning Council Meeting.

The council president had no choice but to accede. The cameras rolled. The judge spoke. The women cheered. And hundreds of thousands more watched NBC's news program that evening, on which Judge Harnett and Bernice Mager spoke eloquently of the need for a children's hospital.

In retrospect, while actions such as this one were somewhat clumsy and certainly inflammatory, the medical community needed a wake-up call, and Judge Harnett and the CMF furnished it. Like most wake-up calls, it was not well received. They had my support but because of my position, I could not be too vocal against the medical establishment.

Despite the efforts to encourage the CMF to work in partnership with LIJ, it was hard for some members of the organization to realize that the children's hospital now had a home and that it was appropriate for LIJ to take over the project. When LIJ did take over, the CMF was enveloped politically. And that didn't sit well with many.

It isn't hard to understand. When they put so much time into something they believed in, most of them found it very hard to let their feelings of ownership go. The members of the CMF were the ones who had been traveling to children's hospitals all over the country to see their programs and facilities. They were the ones who had gained support from the surrounding communities. They were the ones who had been fundraising for years to see this dream. And they were the ones who now had to take the back seat of LIJ's bus. That was the feeling shared by many of CMF's staunchest members. Nonetheless, the group managed to move past personal feelings to rally behind the cause. The children's hospital would happen at LIJ.

The contract was signed on November 8, 1971, and LIJ and the CMF were now partners. Judge Bertram Harnett's and Gladys Cole's names were submitted for appointment to the Long Island Jewish Hospital Board of Trustees. Gladys continued to travel around to gain support and fundraise for the new children's hospital. But after all the years of volunteering for the cause, Gladys Cole ran into political problems with some LIJ board members. After consulting with others, Bertram Harnett had to contact Gladys Cole and tell her that some were fighting her appointment to the board. They felt that in her missionary zeal, Gladys Cole was criticizing LIJ.

When the CMF met with the LIJ board (as they'd done with the boards of all of the other hospitals in the area), the trustees told them that they felt their Department of Pediatrics was as good as any children's hospital. Gladys' reply to Long Island Jewish was the same one she'd given to all of the hospitals: "New York needs a free-standing children's hospital," she said. "Your Department of Pediatrics is nothing like the Children's Hospital Boston, the Children's Hospital of Philadelphia, or Memorial Children's Hospital in Chicago. They all have free-standing hospitals, and they all have support services for children as well as parents." Gladys knew her stuff, because she had seen these hospitals first-

hand. But some trustees did not like her message: "You don't know what a children's hospital is. You have a wonderful hospital, you have very good care, you have ninety beds in your Department of Pediatrics, but you do not have what other children's hospitals have."

"I'll never forget the day one of the trustees took me aside and told me that if I stopped criticizing LIJ, the board would consider appointing me as a member," Mrs. Cole said. "I replied, 'I never spoke against LIJ, and I never will—I am just telling you what we need.'" That discussion marked the end of Gladys Cole as a LIJ board member. Gladys walked away, never to return.

"I probably never should have—it was so much of my life," she said. "But I was hurt, and that was it."

I spoke recently with Judge Harnett, and he told me that Gladys was the biggest personnel loss that the Children's Medical Fund ever encountered. She was a dynamic, well-spoken, and determined woman who gave her all to the cause. The CMF did not stand behind her because it did not want to damage its fragile new relationship with LIJ. But twenty-five years later, Bertram Harnett met with her in Palm Beach, Florida, to offer her a formal apology for what had transpired.

From the early seventies through 1980, Judge Harnett and later Martin Lifton reported to the LIJ Board of Trustees on their fundraising events and accomplishments, and at most board meetings they handed over the money they had raised.

In 1981, the CMF raised $1.84 million. In the first quarter of 1982, it raised $620,000, as Martin Lifton stated at an LIJ Board of Trustees meeting in April 1982. In June 1982, it raised over $500,000 at a one-day golf outing. As of December 1982, CMF had raised approximately $8 million since its inception, as Judge Harnett announced at a board meeting that month. To date, the total amount raised for the Schneider Children's Hospital by the CMF is in the range of

$40 million.

Still today, this volunteer-driven, nonprofit organization provides important support to the Schneider Children's Hospital. At the CMF's insistence, the first child life program on Long Island was established in 1983, with Joan Chan appointed as its director. Initially it was fully funded by the CMF, which continues to help finance this wonderful program designed to minimize stress on children, both inpatients and outpatients, and their families who are coping with the hospital experience. Highly trained child life specialists help children learn about the hospital and their illnesses while providing therapeutic play through the Heather Fessler Music Therapy Program, art therapy, pet therapy, and the Clown Care programs.

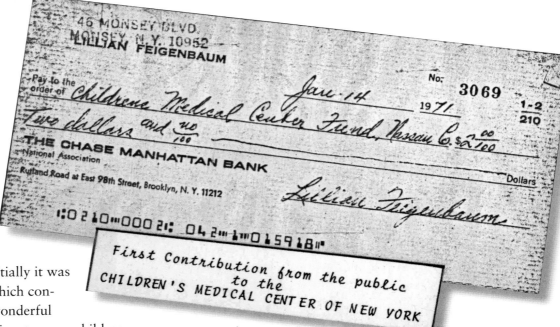

First donation (two dollars) given to the Children's Medical Fund on June 14, 1971.

Marcie Rosenberg and Jeffrey Jurick presenting a check for $1,200,000 to SCH, circa 2000.

Among the programs and services the CMF has supported over the years are the following:

Cancer Center
Center for H.O.P.E.
Child Advocacy Center
Childhood Diabetes Center
Child Life Program
Child Protection Center
Clown Care Unit
Cystic Fibrosis Center
Cardiopulmonary Rescue Center
Heart and Lung Center
Heather Fessler Music Therapy Program
Hematology/Oncology Program
Institute for Childhood Asthma
Institute for Pediatric Neuro-Oncology
Neurology EEG Laboratory
Pediatric Ambulatory Program
Pediatric Cardiology Program
Pediatric Emergency Department
Pediatric Urology Program
Pediatric Research
Pet Therapy Program
Quality of Life Service
SCH On-Call Program
Sleep Disorders Program

CMF has utilized a number of interesting logos from the 1960s to the present day.

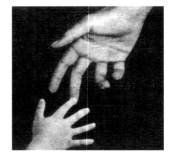

On October 22, 1988, the CMF paid tribute to Philip Lanzkowsky, MD, at its twenty-fifth anniversary celebration held at the Glen Oaks Club in Old Westbury, New York. As he accepted a crystal figurine from Martin Lifton, Chairman of the CMF board, Dr. Lanzkowsky thanked the CMF for its contribution to SCH over the past twenty-five years as well as its yeoman service in making the hospital a reality. He said, "We have a gigantic task ahead of us—to continue to build so that the hospital can stand as a beacon of hope and as a magnet to all those who seek medical, surgical, psychiatric, dental, and other care."

In July of 1997, a plaque was placed in the SCH lobby honoring Judge Bertram Harnett for his contribution to the establishment of the Schneider Children's Hospital. Pictured here at the occasion are (left to right) Burton Bronsther, MD, Ruth Harnett, Judge Harnett, Ellyn Bronsther, Martin W. Abrams, MD, Marie Abrams, and Philip Lanzkowsky, MD.

On May 1, 2007, the CMF, in conjunction with the North Shore-LIJ Foundation, organized a major benefit at Cipriani Wall Street, New York—a grand and luxurious setting for special events. Occupying an entire city block, this New York landmark served as the home of the New York Merchants' Exchange, the New York Stock Exchange, and the U.S. Customs House, as well as the headquarters of the National City Bank. The 16,000-square-foot venue is framed by four sets of monolithic Corinthian columns, and a seventy-foot ceiling has a Wedgewood dome.

I was the guest of honor as well as twenty-five members of the CMF Men's Division who had received the Bernard L. Martin Award from 1981 to 2006. This award was given to members who best exemplified commitment to children's healthcare.

CMF also recognized my contribution to SCH by presenting me with a lifetime achievement award. In accepting the award, I commented on my deep and longstanding belief in the importance of high-quality pediatric health care. I said that "society is measured by the manner in which it cares for its children and our children are our greatest and most vulnerable asset." The event drew a record attendance of 940 people, and Ray Romano, star of one of the most popular sitcoms in television history and winner of numerous awards. Elvis Costello and

Philip Lanzkowsky, MD, demonstrating a model to the Blumenfeld family, showing the future development of SCH, May 7, 2008. Left to right: David, Anna, Susan, Edward Blumenfeld, Philip Lanzkowsky, MD, Francie and Brad Blumenfeld.

the Impostors entertained the guests. The evening raised $40 million for the rebuilding of SCH. The evening also paid tribute to the Edward Blumenfeld family—a family with a long history of passionate commitment to pediatric health care on Long Island—for one of the largest single contributions to SCH. Edward and Susan Blumenfeld became members of CMF in the early seventies.

Roy Zuckerberg, chairman emeritus of the NS-LIJ Health System Board of Trustees, presents Philip Lanzkowsky, MD, with a lifetime achievement award.

BUILDING ON A DREAM

A BENEFIT FOR SCHNEIDER CHILDREN'S HOSPITAL

May 1, 2007
Cipriani Wall Street

CHAPTER 6

SKEPTICS ABOUND

WINNING THE TRUSTEES' APPROVAL

Attaining the approval of the LIJ Board of Trustees for the building of a children's hospital at LIJ was a long and difficult process that was complicated by some surprising turns of events.

The LIJ board consisted of a number of judges (Sol Wachtler, Samuel Rabin, Charles Margett, and Leonard Hanower), lawyers (Gustave Berne, known as Gus, Martin Barell, and Aaron Solomon), and prominent businessmen (Saul Epstein, Jack Liebowitz, Irving Schneider, Irving Wharton, Michael Stein, called Mike, William Mack, called Bill, and Joseph Wohl). While there were many other trustees, it was this group who were most active and essentially determined the hospital's course from inception to the end of the 1970s.

Gus Berne was the dominant trustee. He was chairman of the board of LIJ, and a charismatic man who had made his fortune in real estate and the law. Aaron Solomon, an urbane, highly effective labor lawyer, succeeded Berne as chairman. Both provided initial impetus for the children's hospital. Lawyer Martin Barell was a member of the New York State Board of Regents, and Irving Schneider was well known in the New York City real estate arena.

Aaron Solomon, Chairman of the LIJ Board of Trustees 1971–1976, Philip Lanzkowsky, MD, and Judge Bertram Harnett at the signing of the affiliation agreement between LIJ and CMF, November 8, 1971.

Gustave Berne, chairman of the LIJ Board of Trustees from 1968 to 1971.

Irving Wharton, chairman of the LIJ Board of Trustees from 1976 to 1981.

They were also major players. Interestingly, many of these trustees were sons of first-generation immigrants.

Most active board members were very successful and philanthropic and shared a consuming interest in building an outstanding hospital in the tradition of other Jewish hospitals, such as Mount Sinai in Manhattan and Montefiore Medical Center, the teaching hospital of Albert Einstein College of Medicine in the Bronx. Many worked very hard day and night at reaching this objective. They were articulate, highly intelligent, and analytical. A couple were argumentative, provocative, and opinionated, which often made meetings of the Joint Conference Committee of the LIJ Board of Trustees sound like the House of Commons of the English Parliament. The Board was deeply committed to LIJ and intimately involved in the affairs of the hospital in a very constructive way. However, high-flown rhetoric, on occasion, complicated decision-making.

The proponents of the children's hospital were occupied with warding off attacks not only from outside regulatory bodies, institutions, and professionals who were vehemently opposed to it, but also, and surprisingly, from some elements of the LIJ Board of Trustees who had strong negative feelings about it.

For some time, even before I arrived, informal discussions had been held inside and outside the hospital walls about the need for a children's hospital. But these discussions were only talk, had no substance, and never produced a plan. In 1968, Judge Sol Wachtler was appointed New York State Supreme Court Justice in Nassau County, along with Bertram Harnett. "He [Harnett] was constantly telling me that there was a need for a children's hospital, and that they [CMF] were looking for a home to build it," recalled Judge Wachtler. At that time they were working with Meadowbrook Hospital (presently known as Nassau University Medical Center). A meeting that Judge Harnett had with me in 1971 opened new doors and opportunities. Encouraged by the mutuality of our goals and objectives Harnett grew interested in putting a proposition before the Long Island Jewish Board of Trustees.

Prior to broaching this idea at a formal Board of Trustees meeting, Wachtler arranged

Martin Barell, chairman of the LIJ Board of Trustees from 1981 to 1986.

Honorable Sol Wachtler, member of LIJ Board of Trustees.

a meeting in his Kings Point home with board members Irving Schneider, Irving Wharton, Michael Stein, Robert K. Match, MD, and Judge Harnett. In an interview with Laurie Locastro, my editorial associate, Judge Wachtler recalled that Judge Harnett presented the goals and vision of the CMF in his usual cohesive and persuasive manner. Harnett told them about the fundraising that had been going on for years on behalf of a children's hospital, and the support of the local communities on Long Island and in all the boroughs of New York City and Westchester County. There were certain conditions that had to be met before the CMF would bring the money it had raised and its support and prestige to LIJ, according to Judge Harnett.

"I remember it so clearly," Judge Wachtler said. "They wanted, number one, a separate hospital—even if it was separated by two inches. It could not be part of the same building. They did not want a floor, or a wing—they wanted a separate hospital. The second condition was that two members of the CMF become members of the LIJ Board of Trustees, and three members become associate trustees." (Giving

away the associate trusteeships was not a terribly meaningful thing; associate trustees were not then actual members of the board.)

Judge Harnett left the members of the board alone to discuss his proposition. One of the most powerful and influential members was very resistant to the whole idea and was particularly outraged by Harnett's request for representation on the board. He thought that such a position should require making large contributions to the hospital, becoming active in its support, and then waiting your turn. "It's a great honor to be a member of our board," he proclaimed. Years later, once the LIJ board was solidly behind the building of a children's hospital, this board member accepted its reality and became its major supporter.

At the time that the proposition to build the children's hospital was presented, LIJ had another major preoccupation: building a new hospital on the South Shore of Long Island, which was to be the South Shore Division of LIJ. Negotiations were under way, and finally, in 1973, LIJ purchased St. John's Hospital for this purpose. A financially failing hospital located on

Beach 51st Street in Far Rockaway, Queens, it would have to be torn down and the new hospital rebuilt on the site. The LIJ board had really wanted to build the new hospital in Lawrence, just across the line from Rockaway in Nassau County. But the people in the Rockaways did not want to lose their hospital, and the people in Lawrence did not want to have one. A considerable amount of acrimony ensued, and eventually LIJ abandoned the idea and the hospital was sold. The diversion of the LIJ Board of Trustees' attention to this project helped delay the children's hospital project from going forward as rapidly as it might have.

The failure of the LIJ South Shore project offered many key lessons in what not to do when building a children's hospital. A handful of LIJ trustees desirous of improving healthcare facilities on the South Shore had aroused community animosity because they had failed to take into account the need for community and public support. Medical and public health needs had never been articulated, and the planning process had not been sufficiently transparent. Tearing down an old hospital and replacing it with a state-of-the-art institution, while a noble objective, required the groundwork and involvement of more professional, medical, administrative, and lay personnel than LIJ was then willing to commit. Though the eventual building of the children's hospital proved that such dreams could be realized, in the end, public support, fervent dedication to the realization of ideals, and medical professionalism carried the day. The South Shore experience proved that good intentions alone were not enough.

From the beginning, a very influential and vocal member of the board and Judge Harnett did not hit it off. Both had forceful and determined personalities, both were tough, and neither shied from confrontation. Judge Harnett was correctly critical of medical care for children on Long Island, and some members of the board took these views personally as criticism of LIJ. Since Judge Harnett personified the ideals and objectives of CMF, these board members were antagonistic to the organization and all of its supporters both before and after the children's hospital was built. Because it aspired to higher standards for pediatric care, CMF was perceived as casting aspersions on existing standards of care, on the institutions providing this care, and on the physicians and surgeons delivering the care. This was not well received in many quarters.

Another point of contention between the CMF and the LIJ Board of Trustees (who carried fiduciary responsibility for the hospital) was one of idealism (seeing the dream become reality) versus practicality (managing costs effectively). The CMF wanted a separate operating suite, emergency department, radiology department, and ancillary services such as pathology. LIJ was basically unwilling to acquiesce to these requests based on capital expense, operating expense, and a lack of volume to justify such a separation. Because it carried ultimate responsibility for managing the children's hospital, LIJ had to be pragmatic, whereas the CMF had the luxury of being uncompromising. They'd set their sights on creating an institution such as those in Boston or Philadelphia. This basic conflict caused long-lasting tension between the two entities.

It must be said that, in the ultimate analysis, the CMF was correct in wanting what it wanted for the new hospital—but it was ahead of its time. Rome was not built in a day. After all, the distinguished children's hospitals key members had visited in Boston and Philadelphia had acquired the reputation, capital, endowment, and operational and academic experience over a period of more than 100 years.

The critically important LIJ players who favored the children's hospital were Aaron Solomon, Gus Berne, Mike Stein, and Sol Wachtler.

Mike Stein said, "As chairman of the LIJ Board of Trustees' Development Committee, I saw the CMF bringing to LIJ a new group of potential donors." Irving Wharton was initially critical but in time came on board. Eli Cohen discarded neutrality to favor the children's hospital. Most board members seemed neutral, taking no public positions but instead watching the forensic action as if at a tennis match. Irving Schneider, who had several allies, maintained continuous skepticism of the concept and of the impact a separate children's hospital would have on LIJ.

Gus Berne was chairman when the children's hospital was formally proposed. One prominent member of the board, vehemently opposed to the idea, declared, "Absolutely not, forget it—it's not going to happen! LIJ is one hospital, it always will be, and we are not splitting it into two." However, this blatant opposition did not stop other members of the board. Negotiations went on and on, there were meetings and more meetings, and the board went back and forth. Aaron Solomon, Mike Stein, and Sol Wachtler exercised initiatives. Gus Berne had become very sympathetic; he and Aaron Solomon were pivotal. Irving Wharton vacillated between supporting the program and supporting some of the vocal opposition voices. Every board meeting was very anxiety provoking for me, because I never knew where the next opposition to the children's hospital would come from. I had no official voice, although I used every opportunity to educate board members about the need for a children's hospital and I actively campaigned for their support. The battle raged on and on but eventually, on November 8, 1971, the board agreed to put the matter to a vote. The children's hospital won.

This was only the beginning. The board and CMF still had many battles ahead. There were difficulties encountered in the appointment of "acceptable" CMF trustees and in the development of a contract between both parties, and

there was unexpected opposition from the Federation of Jewish Philanthropies to CMF's raising money for hospital operations. More years of acrimony, negotiations, and compromises! The climate of the arduous and lengthy negotiations that took place is best understood by sampling the minutes from several meetings of the Board of Trustees of LIJ from this period:

Special Meeting of Board of Trustees
August 24, 1971

JUDGE HANOWER, CHAIRMAN OF THE NOMINATING COMMITTEE, said that the nominating committee had considered certain names submitted as prospective Trustees and Associate Trustees to represent the Children's Medical Center (CMC). He said that the meeting was quite lengthy because of the extended discussion of the entire subject. The Committee decided to recommend that the Board elect Trustees and Associate Trustees only at such time as a contract with the Children's Medical Center had been consummated and signed. After a very lengthy discussion, and upon motion duly made and carried, it was RESOLVED that a Committee be appointed by the President to proceed with the negotiations and preparation of a suitable agreement with the Children's Medical Center; and further RESOLVED that this Board of Trustees undertakes to elect two Trustees and three Associate Trustees to represent the Children's Medical Center upon the execution of the contract.

The president, Gus Berne, then appointed for this purpose an Ad Hoc Committee consisting of Eli B. Cohen, Martin C. Barell, Saul J. Beldock, Irving Schneider, Hon. Sol Wachtler, Irving L. Wharton and Joseph S. Whol with Eli B. Cohen as Chairman of the Ad Hoc Committee.

September 20, 1971

ELI B. COHEN, CHAIRMAN OF THE AD HOC COMMITTEE on the Children's Medical Center, reported on the meetings and discussion that took place with representatives of the Children's Medical Center. He said that his Committee had suggested two or three programs that could be funded by the Children's Medical Center, and that CMC were studying the details of these proposals.

October 1971

IRVING WHARTON reported that he and Judge Sol Wachtler had met with Judge Bertram Harnett to complete the negotiations for an agreement for an affiliation with the Children's Medical Center. He stated that agreement had been reached on all of the details; that a written agreement had been prepared and approved by the Ad Hoc Committee previously appointed.

MR. WHARTON stated that CMC had agreed to contribute to LIJMC during the short term no less than $200,000.00 by April 1, 1972, and $200,000.00 in each year thereafter for programs selected by LIJMC which relate to children and the provision of a comprehensive Children's Medical Service over which LIJMC would have control. He also stated that the long term objective was the erection of a children's facility of at least 100 pediatric beds, and that CMC would pay the cost of planning, equipment and construction of such facility; that they expected to raise five million dollars in pledges payable annually over a five year period, and that if they did not secure such pledges within three years from the date of this agreement, the agreement should be deemed renewed for each subsequent year unless either party cancelled within thirty days after such anniversary date. The short term program was to continue for a period not longer than two years after CMC obtained five million dollars in pledges or upon the opening of the new facility, whichever comes first.

MR. WHARTON also said the LIJMC had the right to construct such a facility as part of the Institute of Community Health, and that the delivery of medical care would be the sole responsibility of LIJMC; that administration of the facility would be under the direction of the Executive Vice President of LIJMC; that appointments to the pediatric staff would be in accordance with the Medical By-Laws, and that the LIJMC Director of Pediatrics would be the Medical Director of the new facility.

MR. WHARTON stated that in addition to other details, the agreement provided for election to the Board of two Trustees and three Associate Trustees sponsored by CMC, and that LIJMC would have similar representation on the CMC Board. After a discussion during which many questions were asked and the answers discussed fully, and upon motion duly made and carried, it was RESOLVED that the proposed agreement with Children's Medical Center, presented to this meeting, be approved and the President is authorized to execute the same on behalf of LIJMC.

Judge Sol Wachtler was then the chairman of the legal committee of the Board of Trustees of LIJ, and the head of the CMF was Judge Bertram Harnett. Both were brilliant jurists and had been outstanding lawyers before they ascended to the bench. They were very friendly and collegial. With Judge Wachtler acting for the hospital and Judge Harnett acting for the CMF, they had collectively drafted an agreement between the two entities that would become the basis of the cooperative effort to build a children's hospital at Long Island Jewish Medical Center. This document had a long preamble and many provisions.

Melvin Ruskin, who is now a seasoned member of the law profession but was then a young attorney and outside counsel for LIJ, was contacted by LIJ president Dr. Robert K. Match and asked to review the contract and meet with him to provide his comments. Mr. Ruskin reviewed the contract and declared that it was an ineffective document from a legal perspective. In particular, he felt that it was an agreement to agree, which, under the law of the State of New York, was nonenforceable. In addition to that, it contained inconsistent

Aaron Solomon, chairman of the LIJ Board of Trustees from 1971 to 1976 and Judge Bertram Harnett, chairman of the CMF Board of Trustees, signing the affiliation contract between the institutions, November 8, 1971.

provisions about who might control certain elements of the children's hospital, and who would determine certain issues that would affect it. Mr. Ruskin reported all of his findings to Dr. Match, who asked Mr. Ruskin to come to the executive board meeting and report his conclusions.

Mr. Ruskin said, "It will put me in a very awkward position to be critical of a contract drawn by the two judges." But Dr. Match insisted. Mr. Ruskin attended the meeting of the executive committee of the Board of Trustees, which was then composed of businessmen as well as attorneys, and presented his report as diplomatically as he could, indicating the unenforceability of the agreement, its inconsistencies, and the fallacies he had found from a legal perspective in the document itself. When he finished

his report, Mr. Ruskin recalled, "Gus Berne stood up, walked over behind me, and put his hands on my shoulders. Then he addressed the meeting. As I remember his words, he said, 'This young lawyer just gave us a brilliant legal analysis of this contract, and he is absolutely correct. But it doesn't mean a thing. We are going to sign this contract, put it in the drawer, and build a hospital.' In effect, he was saying that if the Board of Trustees continued to negotiate to get perfection in the document, the deal would evaporate."

The executive committee of the Board of Trustees adopted the contract between LIJ and the CMF and subsequently signed it. Both parties agreed upon the contract, and it was signed on November 8, 1971.

Then LIJ and CMF, acting in good faith for a common objective, executed the plan to build the children's hospital. Ruskin said he learned something very important from this experience: that sometimes business realities trump the legal documents involved. "The wisdom of the members of the board was evident, because the facility was built, and it is one of the premier facilities in the area today," he said.

Supreme Court of the State of New York
Justices' Chambers
Mineola, N. Y. 11501

Bertram Harnett
Justice

February 25, 1972

Philip Lanzkowsky, M.D.
Long Island Jewish/Hillside
    Medical Center
New Hyde Park, New York

Dear Phil:

        I thought you might like
to have for your souvenirs copies
of some photographs taken at the
Long Island Jewish/Children-s
Medical Center signing on November
8th.

        Hold on to these. Fifty
years from now they will be col-
lector's items of old timers in
old timers' dress at a historic
occasion.

                    Sincerely,

                    Bert

Letter sent from Judge Harnett to Philip Lanzkowsky, MD, on February 25, 1972 with the photos of the LIJ-CMF affiliation contract signing.

The contract called for the CMF to elect two trustees and three associate trustees to the LIJ board. Judge Harnett and Robert Frankel represented the CMF in the early seventies. Members of the CMF who are currently serving on the board of the North Shore-Long Island Jewish Health System include Martin Lifton, Barry Rubenstein, Gedale Horowitz, Marcie Rosenberg, Edward Blumenfeld, Richard Horowitz, Jeff Jurick, Jay Raubvogel, and Howard Weingrow. The current associate trustees of the NS-LIJ Health System board who were originally members of CMF include Harvey Bernstein, Anthony Fromer, Agnes Funk, Alan Goldberg, Arthur Goldberg, Herbert Krauss, Alexander Levy, Michael Mann, and Warren Sabloff. Barry Rubenstein and Gedale Horowitz, ex-chairmen of the LIJ board, who became interested in LIJ through the CMF, ultimately played important roles on the LIJ board and subsequently on the NS-LIJ Health System board.

The contract was amended in April in 1972 to include the following:

"If this agreement is terminated, all funds remaining shall be applied for child care purposes at Long Island Jewish-Hillside Medical Center in such manner as Long Island Jewish-Hillside Medical Center and Children's Medical Center of New York Fund shall mutually agree. In such event, all contributors to the Children's Medical Center of New York Fund will be accorded the same credits and acknowledgements given to contributors of equivalent sums directly to Long Island Jewish-Hillside Medical Center."

In the 1970s, LIJ was receiving annual support from the Federation of Jewish Philanthropies with an understanding that LIJ would not raise money for operations from the community because that was the federation's function. Because of this, it was felt that a further amendment of the agreement was necessary. The board adopted another resolution, on June 27, 1972,

as follows:

"WHEREAS the Federation of Jewish Philanthropies has raised questions regarding the activities of the CMC Fund (CMF) affecting the relationship between Federation and LIJ-HMC; and WHEREAS representatives of the CMC Fund (CMF) and LIJ-HMC have tentatively agreed on arrangements which will satisfy the requirements of Federation and the CMC Fund (CMF);

NOW, THEREFORE, be it RESOLVED that the Officers of LIJ-HMC be authorized to work out arrangements with CMC Fund (CMF) and Federation of Jewish Philanthropies to accomplish the following results:

1. CMC (CMF) will discontinue raising money for operational purposes for LIJ-HMC.

2. The project of the CMC (CMF) will be submitted for inclusion in the Federation Building Fund Campaign.

3. The publicity of Federation, the CMC Fund (CMF) and LIJ-HMC will be coordinated giving reasonable weight to the needs of each organization.

4. That all monies and pledges raised by CMC Fund (CMF) shall be turned over annually to LIJ-HMC and such monies shall be deposited in a special account earmarked for the CMC (CMF) project as approved for inclusion in the Federation Building Fund Campaign. In such special account, there shall also be deposited all other monies hereafter raised for said purposes from Federation or the public, and all such funds including any interest earned thereon shall be earmarked for the said project."

In January 1973, the Communal Planning Committee of the Federation of Jewish Philanthropies agreed in principle to the affiliation with the CMF, contingent on approval of the project by the Hospital Review and Planning Council of New York and appropriate state approving bodies, and the inclusion in the Building

Fund Campaign of the Federation of Jewish Philanthropies of a sum of $20 million, with a philanthropic component of approximately $6,667,000. Additionally, there was a stipulation that all aspects of the CMC project, including fundraising, conform to the federation's bylaws as well as to the guidelines and regulations of its Building Fund Campaign.

There were several meetings attended by Judge Harnett, Howard Schneider, then a CMF activist, and various federation committee members in an effort to resolve matters. The fundamental problem was that the federation was a long- and well-established philanthropy with many constituent parts, and CMF was an amorphous grassroots organization with thousands of diverse participants. The federation insisted that all CMF funding should be cleared through them. Unfortunately, many of its members were skeptical of a need for a children's hospital.

The Federation of Jewish Philanthropies' issue of limiting CMF fundraising or advocacy methods was never resolved. CMF is an independent organization and could not by its very nature function within the rules of another organization. Its fundraising became seriously impaired, and ultimately, CMF elected to go its own way. Judge Harnett told me that he knew of no further discussions between LIJ and federation people. In retrospect, all of the amendments and approvals surrounding the federation negotiations were a waste of time. When the hospital was built in 1982-1983, that organization did not contribute any financial assistance to LIJ.

In a September 1973 meeting of the LIJ board, Irving Wharton reported yet again on the status of negotiations. As evidence of the unease felt by both parties, Mr. Wharton reported that the establishment of a suitable time for either party to withdraw from the agreement was still under consideration. Irving Schneider recommended that the contract be resubmitted to the Executive Committee for further deliberation and

then presented to the board for final approval. Upon a motion duly made and carried, this recommendation was passed.

The uneasiness between CMF and some LIJ trustees persisted, fanned by personality clashes, lack of trust, and the relatively insular LIJ board's recurring fear of giving up some of its domain to a "group of outsiders" who didn't deserve to be members of the board because they had not earned it "the old-fashioned way." This situation was evidently complicated by the Federation of Jewish Philanthropies' controversy over CMF. An attempt to resolve matters was embodied in the amendment of the agreement with LIJ on June 27, 1972.

Wrangling over the contract between CMF and the hospital continued until March 1976 when a new contract was signed, changing some of the commitments and previously agreed-upon arrangements.

In September 1980, in a last desperate, eleventh-hour move to prevent the hospital from going forward, a prominent LIJ trustee appealed to the Board of Trustees to re-review the project "with reference to the necessity and importance of the CMF to the community." His written presentation to the board read:

"Mr. Irving Wharton, Dr. Robert Match and fellow Board members: I have spent a great deal of time carefully considering the recent events that have taken place regarding the hospital's expansion program. After much deliberation, I have reached the conclusion that the Board should now consider re-evaluating its initial decision to proceed with the program, as it is currently constituted. I fully understand the importance of rehabilitating operating rooms, heating, electrical, plumbing and air conditioning systems, as well as the necessity of constructing a new food-processing center and loading dock. I am, however, extremely apprehensive about the

20% increase in overall costs now facing us and think it would be far more prudent on the part of the Medical Center to only float a bond issue of $40 million which would be spent to upgrade the facility, rather than the $80 million plus now currently contemplated to upgrade the facility and to build a Children's Medical Center which will only yield 60+ new beds. Although I was part of the approval process which recommended the construction of the Children's Medical Center, and though I am acutely aware of the vast amount of time, energy and commitment on the part of many that resulted in this decision, I believe the circumstances have now changed sufficiently enough to warrant a comprehensive re-review of the necessity and importance of the Children's Medical Center to our community. I am aware of the fact that the State and Federal government is now taking the position that they will not approve the construction of the Children's Medical Center until after January 1981. This raises an obvious question concerning the importance of such a facility to the community if in fact governmental agencies take this position. As a hopefully responsible trustee, I must raise the question of why we are now building something that may significantly affect the financial viability of the Medical Center. Would it not be more responsible for us as trustees to seek other alternatives, which could accomplish the same end? For example, the State takes the position that there are too many hospital beds in New York. Might we not exercise more prudent leadership in trying to deal with upgrading other facilities, such as Queens, that are not fully occupied, by lending our expertise both administratively and medically to increase occupancy and promote the attractiveness of such an institution without the expenditure of huge sums of capital investment thereby eliminating the need to spend $40 million to build additional beds. I recognize that such questions have broad implications. However, I feel the time is now right to raise

these questions at the Board meeting in order to make certain that we are prudently exercising our responsibility as trustees."

This letter to the board, coming from within the very core of LIJ, dealt a potentially fatal blow to the realization of a children's hospital. It came out of left field, from one of the few board members with whom I had had little previous contact and who had, as he stated, previously voted in favor of the project. The day was saved, however, by Irving Wharton and Gus Berne. Mr. Wharton responded to this communication in the following way:

"Reevaluating the Board's decision to go forward with the program by the Board would not be as productive as obtaining an objective view of the feasibility of the program in spite of the increase in costs. The view of the many members of the Board would be influenced by their emotional feelings about the need for a Children's Hospital and would be subjective both in favor of and in opposition to the program. An objective view from disinterested organizations would be of greater value at this time. Therefore, it is better that we should look to the judgments of the government agencies whose approval is necessary for a commitment rather than to have another debate at the Board level. Although we know that the governmental trend towards limiting construction is becoming stronger all the time, we must assume that after all of these agencies approve our project, they will do it on the basis of demonstrated need and economic feasibility. We have, so far, been approved by all of the agencies up to the United States Department of Health and Human Services (HHS). It is the obligation of HHS to review not only the economic feasibility of the project, but also the cost of the project. When they are through with their processing and they have approved the project both regionally and in Washington, it goes to

FHA for further approval. All of these approvals, when granted, will demonstrate the propriety of the cost factors and economic viability of the project. These approvals will have greater meaning than any other evaluation that would be attempted. It is interesting, too, that our financial staff, our outside auditors, Loeb and Trope, and the firm of Ernst and Whinney, which specializes in hospital feasibility studies throughout the country, have all established economic feasibility

As a result of the increased cost, it will be necessary, too, that our equity requirements be increased from $5 million to approximately $8 million, which our financial advisors have said is feasible."

Mr. Barell, chairman of the board at that time, commended the trustee on his detailed written exposition of an extremely complex problem and thanked him for his sincere efforts and interest in the continuing fiscal stability of LIJ. He also thanked Irving Wharton, who, together with several other trustees, had contributed an inordinate amount of time and energy over a period of several years, for his forceful and vital role in moving the process forward through the various agencies, consulting organizations, mortgage bankers, planning staff, architects, and others who reviewed and eventually passed on the viability of the project.

The call for reconsideration was denied.

This was the last action of the Board of Trustees. After years of wrangling, the building of the children's medical center was approved.

Since I was not present at board meetings, I did not until recently grasp the degree of dissension among the board members concerning the children's hospital and the degree of vehemence against CMF by certain members. I was busy building hospital relationships, assisting in the closure of pediatric beds at small community hospitals, developing pediatric programs at LIJ, preparing statistics and documents for regulators,

and assisting CMF in maintaining momentum for the children's hospital within the community. Interviewing board members and reviewing minutes of board meetings in preparation for this book made me more cognizant of the heat of these behind-closed-door discussions. In retrospect, the LIJ board took a bold step in approving the building of the children's hospital, increasing its bed capacity, enlarging the physical plant by 200,000 square feet, assuming debt for the first time in LIJ's history, and tolerating its concomitant financial risk. It was a leap of faith for the board, and it is to their credit that they went through with it. It was a triumph for the visionaries on the board.

Finally, forward progress—fast-forward! The groundbreaking ceremony for the children's hospital took place on May 18, 1980. On February 11, 1981, the U.S. Department of Health, Education and Welfare (HEW) approved mortgage financing. On December 13, 1982, Dr. Match reported to the Medical Board: "Dr. Philip Lanzkowsky has been given the administrative title Chief-of-Staff of the Children's Hospital to allow him to deal effectively with many of the professional responsibilities, the overall environmental issues of quality assurance in all disciplines of the facility." The following article in the *Great Neck Record* on July 14, 1983, announced this appointment.

LANZKOWSKY NAMED CHIEF OF CHILDREN'S HOSPITAL

Dr. Philip Lanzkowsky, of Great Neck, chairman of the Department of Pediatrics at Long Island Jewish-Hillside Medical Center since 1970, has been named Chief of Staff of the new Schneider Children's Hospital of LIJ by Dr. Robert K. Match, president of the Medical Center. The 150-bed hospital will open in late fall.

In announcing the appointment Dr. Match said, "Dr. Lanzkowsky has been one of the major forces in creating this hospital which we believe will be a model of excellence. Under his direction, the department of pediatrics has grown into one of the region's outstanding facilities for clinical care, teaching and research."

Dr. Lanzkowsky is a pediatric hematology/oncologist, internationally recognized for his work in children's blood diseases. He is a professor of Pediatrics at the Health Sciences Center of the State University of New York at Stony Brook.

Under Dr. Lanzkowsky's leadership, the Department of Pediatrics at the Medical Center has broadened its services, pioneering in such areas as neonatal and adolescent medicine. He has developed one of the most active teaching and residency programs in pediatrics in Greater New York with 60 residents on staff.

Before joining the staff of LIJ, Dr. Lanzkowsky was acting chairman of the Department of Pediatrics, acting pediatrician-in-chief of New York Hospital and Associate Professor of Pediatrics at Cornell University Medical College. He is the author and co-author of more than 200 publications, and his most recent book is "Pediatric Oncology, A Treatise for the Clinician," published this year by McGraw Hill.

Dr. Lanzkowsky received his training at the University of Cape Town, South Africa and served his residency at St. Mary's Hospital, London, England. He earned a diploma in Child Health from the Royal College of Physicians and Surgeons in London, was appointed a fellow of the Royal College of Physicians of Edinburgh and came to the United States in 1961 as a fellow in Pediatric Hematology and Oncology at Duke University in North Carolina and University of Utah in Salt Lake City, Utah.

With the opening of the Schneider Children's Hospital just a few months away, Dr. Lanzkowsky has already recruited a cadre of full-time pediatric specialists. Available at the new facility will be a full range of specialties including hematology/oncology, nephrology, neurology, endocrinology, gastroenterology, genetics, adolescent medicine, neonatology, cardiology, dentistry, psychiatry and child development as well as the surgical sub-specialties of urology, orthopedics, cardiothoracic surgery and oral surgery.

Dr. Lanzkowsky lives in Great Neck with his wife, Rhona, and their five children.

Letters of congratulations on this appointment poured in from many sources including New York State Senator Frank Padavan and New York State Assemblywoman May W. Newberger.

In March 1983 Arnold Tannen was appointed facilitator in the programmatic planning and staffing of Schneider Children's Hospital. In August 1983 Paul Kessler was named divisional administrator, Arnold Tannen, associate administrator, Mary Lou Martin, RN, associate director of nursing and Ruth Bluestein, MSW, associate director of social work services. In August 1983, the board formally changed the name of the children's hospital from Children's Medical Center of New York to Schneider Children's Hospital.

Paul Kessler, first divisional administrator for SCH, and Philip Lanzkowsky, MD chief of staff, 1984.

Sometimes all we need is someone who will take us by the hand and lead us in the right direction.

CHAPTER 7

LET THE PLANNING BEGIN

In March 1972, a planning committee (named, appropriately, the Planning Committee) was established under the auspices of the Children's Medical Center Fund of New York (CMF).

At the meeting of the Board of Trustees of Long Island Jewish Medical Center (LIJ) on May 23, 1972, Judge Bertram Harnett, the CMF Planning Committee chairman, reported that a series of planning meetings was being held to study all of the factors involved in the construction of a children's hospital, and that the committee would continue to seek out as much information as was available so that it could, sometime in the near future, submit a proposal or a plan to LIJ. The LIJ board was not enamored with this idea; it maintained that planning was the responsibility of the board and not of a fundraising group. The CMF saw it differently. Its members thought of themselves not only as fundraisers but as enablers, campaigners, and planners. They did not want just any facility—they wanted the children's hospital of their dreams. The board gave in, thanks to the dogged determination of Judge Harnett.

LIJ-CMF Planning Committee meeting in the LIJ boardroom, 1976. Left to right are Philip Lanzkowsky, MD, Michael Stein (chairman of the Joint Planning Committee), Robert K. Match, MD, and Judge Bertram Harnett with the Rossetti plan in the foreground.

The Planning Committee of CMF scheduled eight public hearings, which were held in the LIJ boardroom. Judge Harnett arranged for a court stenographer to record the meetings. They were held to create the community interest needed to support the building of the children's hospital and to establish the desired requirements.

Many guests were invited to attend, including people who held executive positions at LIJ and doctors from various specialty areas in pediatrics and surgery. Dentists, nurses, educators, social workers, program planners, consultants, architects, lawyers, parents, health organizations, community planning and action groups, civic associations, directors of outside hospitals and children's hospitals, and mothers of sick children—all participated in these hearings.

Announcements of the dates, times, and purpose of the public hearings were disseminated in a number of ways. Letters were sent to the Nassau, Suffolk, and Queens medical societies inviting participation, press releases were printed in local papers, and public service announcements were carried by radio stations WNBC and WHLI. Letters and telegrams were sent and phone calls were made to invite professionals on a comprehensive list provided by LIJ medical leadership, and an advertisement was placed in Newsday soliciting participation. A genuine effort was made to contact all organizations and individuals who might have an interest in the children's hospital.

The dynamics of these meetings were interesting. There was the evangelistic fervor of a group of mothers of sick children who had traveled to Children's Hospital Boston to get them medical help. This experience had opened their eyes to a different, higher level of care for sick children. These mothers knew the difference between the care provided in a children's hospital and that given in an institution that did not specialize in children's care far better than trustees of hospitals and many Long Island medical professionals, because they'd experienced both first hand. The mothers were vocal and passionate; they embarrassed the trustees and medical professionals present, who were made to feel they had failed in their mission to provide excellent care for children. Representation of the LIJ Board of Trustees at those meetings was sparse.

Harold Light, deputy administrator of LIJ, represented Robert K. Match, MD, executive vice president and director of LIJ, who was unable to attend. Mr. Light indicated that Dr. Match would prefer to participate in the actual planning process and was more concerned about the proposed hospital's integration into the existing operation and site and program planning. Aaron Solomon, chairman of the LIJ Board of Trustees, could not attend, but Mr. Light read a statement he had written:

"It gives me great pleasure to participate in these hearings which have been called by the Children's Medical Center and to convey to you, as the President of the Board of Trustees of the Long Island Jewish-Hillside Medical Center, my own sentiments and those of the rest of the Board as it relates to our present and on-going relationship with the Children's Medical Center.

We at Long Island Jewish take great pride in

Burton Bronsther, MD, Philip Lanzkowsky, MD, Judge Bertram Harnett, and Martin W. Abrams, MD following a Planning Committee hearing, 1972.

the fact that the Children's Medical Center came to us with their proposal to create a special facility for the treatment of children and children's diseases. We think you made the right choice in coming to Long Island Jewish, because there is no other health facility in the Long Island area, and for a very good distance beyond the Long Island area, which has consistently demonstrated the dynamism, the medical know-how and the administrative-managerial-fiscal ability to launch the kind of quality programs we feel are necessary in this geographic region. We have come a long way in eighteen years because of the drive and the determination of LIJ's founders, and we see in yourselves a group of individuals with the same kind of vision, drive and determination that brought the goal of the creation of the Long Island Jewish Medical Center to fruition. We have every confidence that the Children's Medical Center will produce that which it has contractu-

ally committed itself to produce in our affiliation agreement, and we have every conviction that the creation of such a center on the grounds of Long Island Jewish-Hillside Medical Center will enhance this institution's position as the regional facility for medical and health care.

A number of people have asked the Trustees at Long Island Jewish whether the need for a children's medical center really exists. They have pointed out to us that we already have one of the largest, if not the largest, pediatric service in the entire metropolitan region. Our 97 pediatric beds, exclusive of 42 newborn bassinets, would seem to be a sufficiently large number of pediatric beds to meet the needs of sick children, especially in light of medicine's continuing success in eliminating most of the childhood illnesses with which pediatric beds were formerly filled. We think the case for a children's medical center has been made.

"In order for the professional planners to proceed, they must be given a set of guiding principles; what the project is about, what we want to accomplish, and what the objectives are. We are trying to derive maximum information and advice, and set it down so that not only those who are present but all of those involved in the process will have the benefit of the comments and recommendations made here.

The process we are undertaking is relatively unusual and innovative in that we are planning a medical center right out in the open, inviting full public participation. It is the position of the committee that it is important that the view of all persons connected with the health delivery process, the consumer groups as well as healthcare providers, are being sought. We are trying to get all of the value factors and value inputs that we can for forging our own planning proposal.

The net result of these hearings, hopefully, will be a printed record which will contain the maximum input factors going into the formulation of the Children Medical Center."

Judge Bertram R. Harnett
Chairman, CMFNY
Proceedings of the Planning Committee
Of the CMF. May 21, 1972

We think that the fact that we are running over 90 percent occupancy on our pediatric unit and over 104 percent occupancy in our premature nursery is an indication that practicing physicians will refer their patients to such a medical center when they recognize that the quality of care given at that center and the level of medical knowledge and practice are such as to make it illogical not to do so.

Dr. Philip Lanzkowsky has been instrumental in bringing to LIJ the kinds of special know-how required to run modern pediatric services, and we have every confidence that he will continue to recruit the necessary expertise to make for a truly great children's medical center.

Long Island Jewish-Hillside Medical Center is already well on its way to becoming the regional center for the treatment of children's illnesses. Our premature nursery, with the help of the transport service developed by Dr. Lanz-

kowsky, already serves this purpose for a broad geographic area. Our affiliation relationship with LaGuardia Hospital in Queens, which has now closed its pediatric services because of our affiliation, is another such indication. The pediatric service at the Queens Hospital Center and the Children and Youth Project at Operation Pryme in the Rockaway area are further indication of our outreach activities in the pediatric sphere. Our Board of Trustees has just approved an affiliation relationship with the Catholic Medical Center which, in return, will refer its more complicated and complex pediatric cases to us out of their own recognition that the knowledge and wherewithal necessary to provide such treatment exist, at Long Island Jewish Medical Center.

One final word on the question of regionalization and the specific location of the Children's Medical Center at Long Island Jewish-Hillside Medical Center. What I have to say on this specific subject is colored in large measure by my long-standing relationship with the division of communal planning of the Federation of Jewish Philanthropies. In the early stages of the population movement, eastward from the city, most of the individuals who had made the move towards suburbia did not give up their ties to the core city and continued to be active in philanthropic and cultural endeavors in the inner city area. Despite great inconvenience, it was not uncommon for people to continue to travel back to the city to satisfy many of their cultural and philanthropic activities of the past. The major health needs of these individuals also were taken care of, generally, by return visits to the inner city where it was felt the 'real' medical know-how existed and where 'real' serious medical problems could be taken care of.

We at Federation have noticed, in the relatively recent past, a very different kind of attitude emerging as it relates to these kinds of needs. Increasingly, people are looking to the satisfaction of such needs and to a variety of services in a geographical area more proximate and more convenient to them than New York City proper. Health care is no less different in this regard than anything else. If anything, quite the reverse is true.

We see, increasingly, a demand for and an expectation of the provision of services of a high level in the geographic area in which people reside. More and more people are refusing to cross the river to get the care they need. More and more people are turning to regional medical centers like Long Island Jewish to provide them with the quality medical care they have every right to receive.

The Board of Long Island Jewish-Hillside Medical Center, when it created Long Island Jewish, determined that it was going to create an island of medical excellence in the Long Island region because no facility existed which could satisfactorily take care of such needs. We think we have been successful in creating that island of excellence, and we think that the addition of the Children's Medical Center to our family will strengthen and enhance our position as the island of medical excellence in this area. Long Island Jewish is already the only facility between Montauk Point and New York Presbyterian Hospital which can deliver a number of children's medical programs. More and more, the people in this area have reason and a right to expect that such kinds of services should be available here without having to make the long and unreasonable journey into Manhattan. Programs for the treatment of cystic fibrosis, hemophilia, cerebral palsy, cleft palate, and learning disabilities are but a few of the programs people can receive in the Long Island area. With the financial assistance provided by the Children's Medical Center we will be adding programs in genetics, genetic counseling, and virology as well.

As I have already indicated, we expect the Children's Medical Center to quickly achieve its fundraising goal and to tell us they are ready to move ahead with the development of plans for construction. These hearings are an important first step in the process. I have appointed a small subcommittee which I hope will be meeting with members of your Planning Committee to begin to take a real hard look at where the Children's Medical Center would most logically belong on our grounds and how it can be smoothly and effectively integrated into our existing operation. Your own drive and dynamism have lent further impetus to our own drive and determination to meet the community's needs. We have every belief that our joint resources and energies will effectively meet those needs for the years to come."

—*From the Proceedings of the Planning Committee of the CMF, May 21, 1972*

Gus Berne, the intellectually agile chairman emeritus of the LIJ board and an early supporter of the children's hospital, did attend the hearings. In typical humorous, insightful Berne style, he spoke about the goals and objectives of the hospital and the role and responsibilities of trustees. Harnett, who chaired these meetings, was grateful that Mr. Berne attended and participated in the process.

I submitted to the planning committee statements concerning my vision for the hospital:

"Mr. Chairman, Members of the Planning Committee,

This document, which I have entered into the record, is my own remarks and personal views without approval of the Board of Trustees of the Long Island Medical Center, and without prior discussion with the Directors of Service of this institution. The children's medical center should be a referral center for medical, surgical, dental, and psychiatric care for the newborn, the child, and the adolescent. It should provide primary care when called upon to do so for a defined area surrounding the hospital. In addition, it should become a center for undergraduate and postgraduate training for pediatricians, surgeons, psychiatrists, and dentists, as well as other professionals such as nurses, physiotherapists, and para-professionals. It should play a leading role in the development of basic and applied research with reference to children.

To this end it should attract men and women of high academic caliber with a full-time commitment dedicated to these aims, to establish an institution of excellence in all three areas. I am proposing that the bed allocation should be in the region of 200 beds, and the reasons for this are the following: 1) It is a reasonable projection of the need and it is important that we don't build an institution that is larger than our needs; 2) this realistic number of beds is more likely to receive approval from the NY State Department of Health; 3) the ability to staff the hospital with competent nursing and ancillary staff; and 4) the comparative size of other children's hospitals indicates that about 200 beds would be a reasonable size for the hospital. A significant outpatient department will be required to take into account all the various disciplines in pediatrics and pediatric surgery.

Some of the highlights of the physical plant should include the formation of modules of four-bed units with flexibility to be able to reduce these four-bed units down to one-bed units when this is required; e.g., for isolation of children with infectious diseases. Every unit should have a playroom for reasons that have already been entered into the record. Conference rooms for purposes of training of doctors, and also computer terminals should be available to print out various laboratory and x-ray results.

The general facilities should include central and outpatient pharmacies, x-ray facilities, and regional x-ray facilities. A regional x-ray facility and regional laboratories are very important; they should be available in certain parts of the hospital such as in the neonatal unit, intensive

care unit and emergency department. The outpatient facility should have its own x-ray department as well as its own laboratory.

There should be an auditorium for lectures and for some of the educational activities and a library. There should be research facilities including animal facilities. There should be a surgical suite, which should include a pre-anesthesia room, an induction room where anesthesia induction occurs, operating rooms and recovery rooms. The intensive care unit should be within the same area so that the child can go to a pre-anesthesia room, through surgery, to a post-anesthesia room, and if he is critically ill to an intensive care unit all within the same geographic area of the hospital.

There should be a school facility. This usually is for children who have been in the hospital for some time so that they continue with their educational program.

We should also look to a heliport for purposes of transportation in keeping with the concept of a regional center—transportation of patients from all over the region.

These, in general, are some of the major high points of the physical plant with reference to the medical aspects.

Thank you, ladies and gentlemen."
—*From the Proceedings of the Planning Committee of CMF, May 21, 1972*

Many of the organizations the CMF contacted for support and cooperation were joined together to form the Council of Affiliated Organizations, whose purpose was to receive information and recommendations. Many thought it would be impossible to unite these healthcare organizations in our community, but this was proved not to be so. They were able to work together because of many shared problems and one common objective: healthy children. The council consisted of forty-two organizations ranging from the Nassau Heart Association to the Parent Teacher Association (PTA) from each county. Below is a partial listing of its members:

Nassau-Suffolk Comprehensive Health Planning Council

Parent Teacher Association, Nassau Chapter

Association for Children with Learning Disorders, Nassau County

New York Association for Brain Injured Children, Queens Chapter

National Foundation for Ileitis and Ulcerative Colitis

Cooley's Anemia Blood & Research Foundation

Association to Aid Emotionally Disturbed Children, Nassau County Chapter

National Cystic Fibrosis Research Foundation, Nassau County Chapter

Human Growth Foundation, Nassau County Chapter

Cleft Palate Parents' Council

Dysautonomia Foundation

The Riley-Day Syndrome Foundation

Nassau Heart Association

Economic Opportunity Council of Nassau County

National Tay-Sachs and Allied Disease Association

Epilepsy Foundation, Nassau County Chapter

Association for Children with Down's Syndrome

Nassau-Suffolk Hemophilia Guild

United Cerebral Palsy of Queens

Lost Community Civic Association

The Lost Community Civic Association was a community organization created by the individuals living in an area bounded by 76th Avenue, Union Turnpike, Lakeville Road, and 163rd Street, on the border of Nassau and Queens. Because they were on the border, they felt neglected by NYC, receiving inadequate city services such as snow removal, street repairs, and lighting. The people of this area called themselves the Lost Community and created a civic association to represent them.

All of these organizations participated in the planning meetings, presented their membership statistics, and discussed the specific requirements of the programs needed by the children they represented. They expressed the importance of regionalized care as well as interdisciplinary care in one location. They expressed their frustration at getting less than optimal care from existing medical facilities. They were appreciative of the opportunity to be heard, as their previous pleas had largely fallen on deaf ears. The future children's hospital promised to be a fulfillment of their dreams.

A large number of healthcare professionals nationwide participated in the planning hearings for the children's hospital. These included the chairmen of departments at LIJ, local pediatricians, pediatric subspecialists from existing children's hospitals, physicians from medical schools, and physicians from local hospitals and the State University of New York at Stony Brook. Representatives of NSUH's board and administration chose not to attend these hearings. A partial list of the participants and some of their comments follow:

Marc Rowe, MD
Professor of Surgery and
Chief of Pediatric Surgery
University of Miami

David R. Murphy, MD
Director of Surgery
Montreal Children's Hospital
Montreal, Quebec, Canada

"We appeal to you to help us establish a clinic where the children's needs could be met and where the staff specialized in this type of conditions. At this moment we go from one place to another. We should have our own place."

Mrs. Hartman, Director
Association for Children with Down's Syndrome
Proceedings of the Planning Committee of CMF, 1972

David Steward, MD
Chief of Anesthesiology
Hospital for Sick Children
Toronto, Ontario, Canada

Edward Pratt, MD
Chairman, Department of Pediatrics
University of Cincinnati Medical School
Chief of Staff, Cincinnati Children's Hospital
Medical Center
Director, Children Hospital Research
Foundation
Chief of Pediatrics, Cincinnati General Hospital
Cincinnati, Ohio

Dale G. Johnson, MD
Pediatric Surgeon
Primary Children's Hospital
Salt Lake City, Utah

Tague C. Chisholm, MD
Chief of Pediatric Surgery
Children's—Minneapolis
Minneapolis, Minnesota

Harry Bishop, MD
Chief of Medical Staff
Children's Hospital of Philadelphia
Philadelphia, Pennsylvania

Robert Filler, MD
Associate Professor & Pediatric Surgeon
Children's Hospital Boston
Boston, Massachusetts

Anthony Shaw, MD
Professor & Pediatric Surgeon
University Medical Center
Charlottesville, West Virginia

William B. Kieswetter, MD
Professor & Chief of Surgery
Children's Hospital of Pittsburgh
Pittsburgh, Pennsylvania

Earle L. Wrenn, MD
Pediatric Surgeon
Le Bonheur Children's Medical Center and
St. Jude's Children's Medical Center
Memphis, Tennessee

Judah Folkman, MD
Chief of Pediatric Surgery
Children's Hospital Boston
Boston, Massachusetts

S. Sakaguchi, MD
Pediatric Surgeon
Children's Hospital of Wisconsin
Milwaukee, Wisconsin

The following are extracts from local physicians attending the hearings and were taken from the Proceedings of the Planning Committee of the CMF, 1972:

"First I am delighted to see that the Children's Medical Center has really moved along to this stage of planning; really coming close to actuality....

A Children's Medical Center associated with Long Island Jewish and contiguously then associated with us would be an addition to our resources, because there is none anywhere on Long Island as you well know.

We do need one (a children's medical center) on Long island when you consider the population of Queens, Nassau, Suffolk and probably Brooklyn. I do not want to create a Kings territory, but certainly, if you look to the east we are not going to have one."

Edmund Pellegrino, MD
Vice President for Health Sciences Center
State University of New York at Stony Brook

"I have been in practice in pediatrics in Nassau County for twenty years and we have been waiting for this event for a long, long time. I think the main benefit to the pediatricians of Nassau County will be the presence of an autonomous unit which is not a wing of another institution in which the naturally vying competition for priorities in funds within such an institution might push pediatrics into the background—and I think we need the presence of a Children's Hospital in which we feel our priorities were top, and that cooperation in the care of our referrals would be available.

Once the hospital comes, we sincerely hope it will be of the caliber so that I can, in good conscience, say to Mrs. Jones, "No, we are not going to go to Texas, we are going to come to New Hyde Park."

John Pisacano, MD
Chief of Pediatrics
Long Beach Memorial Hospital

"Speaking both as Chief of Franklin and as President of the Nassau County Pediatric Society, we heartily endorse the concept of a children's medical center in the area. We have been disappointed that such has not been more available directly in Nassau County to service the children in that area more thoroughly.

The development of a Children's Medical Center at Long Island Jewish in no way precludes the future prospect for the center to serve the 1.6 million population of Nassau and the 1.2 or 3 million of Suffolk; we are admiring both the prospects of development of the Center and the present pediatrics personnel that probably will form its nucleus under the leadership of Dr. Lanzkowsky."

Albert Beckman, MD
Chief of Pediatrics
Franklin General Hospital

At these hearings, all aspects of the children's hospital, including fundraising, medical specialties needed, the physical plant, and the opening

"And if you are building a children's medical center, what you are doing is building a regional center, really, in the true sense which would take care of all complex cases."

Marc Rowe, MD
University of Miami

"I am full of admiration for you people for what you are doing and what you aspire to do, and I hope that you do it right."

David R. Murphy, MD
Montreal Children's Hospital

"Well you see, my view is that a children's hospital is an implement, a tool to improve the care of children, and I don't think many people appreciate that. Children are discriminated against in that they do not vote, they are not very vocal, and they are outnumbered and so I think it is up to us who deal with them to promote what makes for their best care, and I'm sure a children's hospital will do that."

Edward Pratt, MD
Cincinnati Children's Hospital Medical Center

"The children, from the standpoint of nursing, diets and overall care, are just so different than the requirements of adults. Children get the short end of things.

There are many intangible things that go into a children's hospital, which I think are very, very important; just the whole attitude of the place, toward the needs of the child and the relationship of the parent to the child. They can be built up in a children's hospital and they can go down the drain in an adult hospital."

Dale G. Johnson, MD
Primary Children's Hospital

"I think that probably most of us have no question that it is a great advantage to have a children's center where everyone devotes their ideas, expertise, and care purely to children. So many different problems arise with children. There is no doubt that a children's hospital is a better way to do it."

Robert M. Filler
Children's Hospital Boston

Proceedings of the Planning Committee of the CMF, May 1972

of satellite clinics in the communities surrounding the hospital, were discussed. They served as a forum to express needs and ideas and to gain support from the community. One of the suggestions from these meetings was to broaden our knowledge using the best resource available: other children's medical centers.

From May to September 1972 I led a group consisting of Silas Edman, CMF's vice president for planning and development, I. Ronald Shenker, MD, Martin W. Abrams, MD, and Jerrold Becker, MD, to Boston, Cleveland, Toronto, Philadelphia, Cincinnati, New Haven, and Montreal. Each of these children's medical centers was quite different in terms of its physical plant and organizational and governance structure. The doctors spent a good deal of their time visiting with the medical staff in their respective departments while Silas Edman spent time with the administrative and planning staff to get a feeling for the way their facility projects were conceived, completed, and maintained. We gathered a voluminous amount of information and brought it back to the committee.

I took a mini-sabbatical from my hospital responsibilities and went to Europe to study state-of-the-art construction and administration of children's hospitals there, visiting facilities in London, Paris, Berne, Zurich, Amsterdam, Copenhagen, Malmo, Stockholm, Upsalla, and Gothenberg. Their clinical programs, their organizational structure, and the special features of their physical plants were of great interest. Numerous photographs were taken for the architects and planners.

The last of the public planning hearings organized by the CMF concluded at 10:25 p.m. on October 25, 1972. In total, the Planning Committee had collected an overwhelming amount of information. A report was rendered to Peat, Marwick, Mitchell & Co. containing a feasibility study, which included an analysis of the economics, statistics, and other factors pertinent to the proposed children's medical center. The committee concluded that the children's hospital should be built on the site of the current parking garage, which was across the street from LIJ and would be a very visible location upon entering the campus; a site favored by the Women's Division of CMF.

The idea was that the CMF Planning Committee and the medical leadership of LIJ and the boards of both organizations would formulate the final program recommendation, which would then be contained in the application for approval submitted to the State of New York.

It did not quite work out that way. The consensus arrived at by the various experts who presented at the hearings called for a self-contained, more extensive hospital, but LIJ was restrained by philosophical and financial considerations and the burden of getting state approval. LIJ had to compromise on a building with its own entrance and public spaces but shared laboratories, operating rooms, and emergency department.

While at the time these compromises seemed necessary if one wanted the building to be built, they had a profound effect on the future of the children's hospital. The passage of time proved that failure to build the services CMF, Judge Harnett, and I fought LIJ for and were denied, prevented the children's hospital from reaching its full potential. In the 2008 expansion of the hospital, thirty-five years later, many of the deficits will be corrected.

THE SITE

LIJ was not overly influenced by the CMF Planning Committee and in fact snubbed the whole process. LIJ appointed its own planning committee, on which I served. It was chaired by Mike Stein who was simultaneously chairman of the Board of Trustees' Joint Conference Committee and its Development Committee. LIJ board members on this new committee included

William Mack (known as Bill), Sol Wachtler, Gus Berne, Dr. Robert K. Match, Robert Boyer, director of LIJ's planning department, and representation of CMF led by Judge Harnett. The LIJ planning committee and the CMF planning committee met jointly for several years. LIJ had the preconceived notion of maximizing LIJ services for the children's hospital and appointed consultants with this concept in mind. The first order of business for this new committee was to determine the site for what CMF wanted, a "free-standing" children's hospital on the LIJ campus.

At this point, the architectural firm Perkins and Will Partnership was hired to complete the master plan for program development. David Ginsberg was appointed as the project's master planner. Having worked with LIJ on many other projects, Ginsberg was well known and liked within the hospital. He proved to be enthusiastic, extremely intelligent, very knowledgeable, and a valuable member of the planning team. Working with the LIJ committee, David Ginsberg collected the information for a layered feasibility analysis of potential sites. The committee was considering a total of nine sites on the property. All of them were evaluated to determine which would best suit the project. For each site, the feasibility study considered the following factors:

- Identity: The children's hospital should be located so that it retains its own identity.
- Public visual impact: The site should allow the children's hospital to be visible for public access.
- Appropriate scale: The site must be most in scale with existing facilities (e.g., Hillside Division).
- Appropriate character: The site should be located away from the Geriatric Institute (presently known as Parker Jewish Institute for Chronic Care and Rehabilitation) to maintain the architectural character related to the children's hospital that does not clash with the architectural design of the Geriatric Institute.

Philip Lanzkowsky, MD, and Judge Bertram Harnett at a LIJ-CMF Planning Committee meeting with the Rossetti plan, 1976.

- Site sufficiency: The site must be large enough.
- Expansion potential: The site must provide room for future growth.
- Expansion interface: The site must be suitable for long-range plans of LIJ.
- Legal Restrictions: The site should have minimal legal restrictions related to easements, highways, and development of local streets.
- Demolition interface: The site should offer the least amount of demolition.
- Utility interface: The site should accommodate utility interfacing.
- Traffic rerouting: The site should require the least traffic rerouting.
- Patient/public access: The site should be accessible to present and future parking.
- Parking location lost: The site should provide the least loss of existing parking space.
- Ambulance access: The site should be accessible to incoming ambulance traffic.
- Service access: The site should be accessible to the shared service areas of LIJ.

In addition to environmental and physical considerations, relationships among the children's hospital's potential future departments had to be examined. A functional framework for the various types of services and facilities that already existed and those that were contained

Philip Lanzkowsky, MD promoting the children's medical center during a radio interview for WNBC in the 1970s.

in the long-range plan had to be evaluated. The feasibility study identified space needs for the following services:

- Inpatient care
- Ambulatory care
- Education and research
- Diagnosis and treatment
- Administration

After what seemed like an unending series of meetings, and after review of the feasibility studies, it was determined that the children's medical center should not be built as a completely freestanding facility on the site the CMF planning committee had originally chosen, but instead should be built as an integrated part of LIJ, so they could share services such as food, radiology, and operating rooms, and most important, so there would be easy access to the neonatal intensive care unit from LIJ's labor and delivery suites. One fundamental dictum was: "Never when the child is awake should he or she experience the adult environment." With this in mind, it was determined that the best location was contiguous to the rear of LIJ, so that the two entities would be connected at the back, but the front of the children's hospital would be free from the so-called adult environment, as would all of the rooms, clinics, and children's wards. The back of

the neonatal unit would connect like an umbilical cord to the labor and delivery unit for immediate and easy access for sick newborns. From the front, the children's hospital would appear as a freestanding children's facility.

It was, to be sure, another compromise, but one that all sides could acquiesce to. Again, the governing motive was to keep up the momentum.

After what seemed like endless months of planning, LIJ was now prepared to approach New York State with the recommendation of building a children's hospital and the rationale of need.

MAINTAINING MOMENTUM

It was a challenging task to maintain interest, enthusiasm, and commitment on the part of all of the constituents and stakeholders when nothing tangible had happened for over a decade—and when, in fact, there were stretches when the project appeared dead. There were pediatricians on staff and in the community who were convinced it would never materialize. There were chairmen of various LIJ departments who had not been enthusiastic about a children's hospital in the first place and saw no reason to change their minds. There were members of the Board of Trustees who needed an infusion of enthusiasm from time to time to keep them on course. There were the men and women of the CMF who required "updates" at dinner parties, fundraising events, and golf outings from the South to North Shore of Long Island and in Westchester. There was the opposition (hospitals, physicians, and some politicians), who were using this time to undermine the project. There were the regulatory bodies (often spurred on by political motivation) requesting repeated and increasingly detailed data to justify the need for a children's hospital, in frequent verbal presentations, in written form, as well as at formal hearings. In addition, there was the public, whose interest and support had to be maintained through frequent radio and television interviews.

In March 1973, a seminar entitled "Today's Child" was held in the Teaching Center auditorium for trustees, patrons, and friends of LIJ, to fan interest in the children's hospital project, which at that point was so tied up in a bureaucratic web that it needed resuscitation. In addition, a "seminar series" to examine the children's medical center was organized in June of 1973, cosponsored by the Council of Affiliated Organizations and LIJ's Department of Pediatrics, to help maintain momentum.

The first seminar in the series was presented to a group of 150 interested community leaders on Sunday, June 10, 1973, at a buffet supper in the Teaching Center. Vivian Kokol and Sanford Gluck, members of the CMF, co-chaired the program, which was coordinated by Silas Edman, director and vice president for planning and development.

Robert Frankel, president of the CMF, in his brief keynote address, praised the pediatric department for its progress in achieving excellence in pediatric care. "I am sure that, while you will be deeply impressed by the marvels our distinguished panel will discuss, implicit in every statement will be the need for larger physical facilities, more equipment, especially designed for pediatric practice, increased research facilities, and most importantly, a special and separate environment for children," Mr. Frankel said.

The panel members strongly supported this assertion in their presentations. I introduced the specialists in various divisions of the pediatric department: Norman Gootman, MD, cardiology; I. Ronald Shenker, MD, adolescent medicine; Marvin Klein, MD, neurology; and Eugene Pergament, MD, and Audrey Heimler, MS, genetics. In addition, Jerrold Becker, MD, pediatric surgery, and Leon Eisenbud, DMD, dentistry, discussed cooperation between their departments and the pediatric specialists in the care of sick and handicapped children.

In my comments, I traced the development of pediatrics at LIJ and outlined the program then available, which utilized the services of fourteen full-time specialists and a total of 241 pediatricians, including interns, residents, fellows, and attending physicians, making it the largest and most comprehensive pediatric program in the area. "Why then a children's medical center in this area?" I posed rhetorically. "Because our 1.6 million children under age 19 do not yet have the kind of facilities for care available in a children's medical center, care that they need and are entitled to, and that is provided in cities throughout the country with populations far smaller than the Long Island tri-county area." (*In Touch*, Vol 1 No 3, 1973)

Judge Harnett and I worked together very closely during this period. Scarcely a week passed that we did not spend an evening or a Sunday morning writing copy and planning ways to propagate the idea of a children's hospital. Even during the darkest period, Judge Harnett and I continued to dream, remained committed to the concept, and were determined to see it come to fruition. Judge Harnett was a true believer, and he did whatever he thought had to be done in service to the ideal. He didn't seem to mind stepping on toes, nor was he deterred by personal attacks. As chairman of pediatrics at LIJ, I had to be slightly more restrained, but I was cautiously vocal, nevertheless.

And so we waited. We hoped for the best. We endured further vicissitudes in pursuit of our goal. And the years passed...

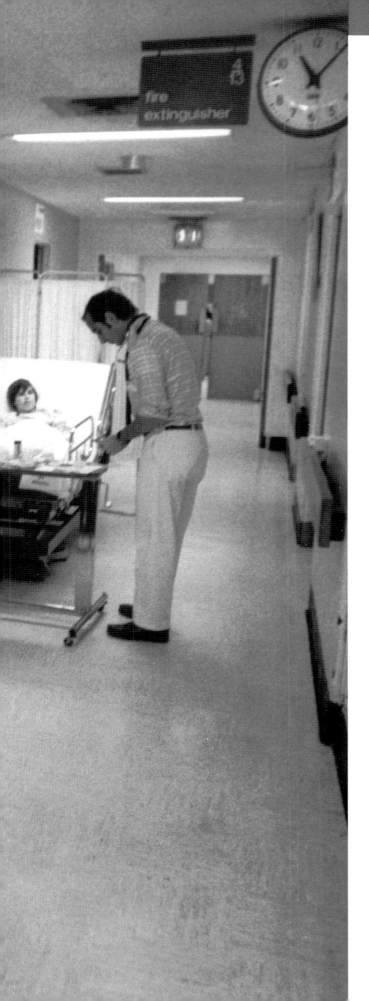

CHAPTER 8

WHY A HOSPITAL FOR CHILDREN?
THE RATIONALE

"A child is not a small adult" was our mantra, and it said it all. Children do not need smaller facilities. They need entirely different ones. A child's physical and emotional needs differ from those of adults; only at a hospital designed specifically for children can a child receive the kind of comprehensive care he or she requires. This was the unified message we presented to the state regulatory bodies, and to anybody else who would listen to our story.

We knew that this premise had emotional and intuitive appeal. But we realized that of itself, our mantra would not speak strongly enough to the New York State Department of Health to win the necessary approvals. We knew only too well that the road to approval would be rocky and we would have to come up with reasons that could withstand objective medical, economic, and planning scrutiny; facts that were compelling and irrefutable. It certainly seemed to us that there was a glaring deficiency in the provision of health services to the New York metropolitan area (defined as the five boroughs of New York City, Nassau, Suffolk, and Westchester Counties, southern Connecticut, and northern New Jersey): the lack of a children's medical center with staff and facilities to provide an adequate range and

Overcrowded corridors in the Department of Pediatrics at LIJ in the late 1970s.

quality of care in sufficient volume to meet the needs of its vast pediatric population.

How could there be such a lack in a geographic area bursting with children? The population explosion between 1950 and 1960 swelled the number of children under the age of 15 in America by almost 80 percent. In the five boroughs, this population group grew by 51 percent, in Nassau County, 143 percent, and in Suffolk County a whopping 259 percent!

Yet ours was the only major metropolitan area in the United States without a medical center exclusively and independently serving children.

Because of its high volume of complicated cases and its specialized medical staff, the Department of Pediatrics at Long Island Jewish Medical Center (LIJ) had become one of the largest, finest, and most advanced pediatric services in the region. Our success, however, had become a problem. LIJ's Department of Pediatrics, opened in 1954, was finding its allotted space hopelessly inadequate. It no longer met the needs of all members of the community, for the following reasons:

- The high occupancy rate, resulting from the transfer of very ill children from other hospitals, often required that patients be cared for in the corridors.
- Isolation areas were inadequate to handle a constantly increasing number of immunocompromised patients, for example, leukemics, children on cytotoxic agents, and the critically ill.

> "It was many years ago, but the memory still brings a rush of tears...the memory of walking out of the hospital room in a distant city as her little daughter cried, her face pressed against the bars of the crib. But the mother had been away from her other two children for a week. She had to catch a plane back to Long Island. It was the price the family was paying to have the kind of care found only in a children's hospital. There was nothing like it near home. This story is true. It is one reason why a children's hospital had to be built."
>
> —Parent of a Sick Child

- Outpatient facilities for expanding pediatric programs were hopelessly inadequate.
- Intensive care unit facilities were too small.
- There were no dedicated operating rooms or recovery areas for children.
- There were no school facilities.
- Playroom facilities were inadequate.
- There were no parent facilities for lounging or sleeping.
- Laboratory research space was hopelessly inadequate.
- Lecture rooms for pediatric students (para-professional, medical, and nursing) were scarce.
- Office and secretarial space had fallen behind needs.
- A separate pediatric radiology facility did not exist.
- Many outpatient programs, such as adolescent medicine, were housed in trailers or in office space in adjacent buildings.

We were convinced that LIJ's pediatric program, with its specialized services, would be a strong foundation for the first children's hospital in the region. But regionalization of pediatric care was essential and was going to be a tough sell to New York State at a time when its regulators were in no mood to hear of escalating costs for medical care, especially in the face of unused pediatric capacity in every hospital in the region. We would have to be eloquent in stating the advantages of regionalization in meeting all the special needs, both medical and emotional, of the hospitalized child, as opposed to those of the adult.

THE ARGUMENT FOR REGIONALIZATION

In Queens, Nassau, and Suffolk Counties, there were too many small hospitals providing pediatric care that had low occupancy (often below 60 percent), inadequate physical facilities, and incomplete medical coverage. By their very nature, small units tend to lack the necessary expertise for the optimal care of children because of the expense required to provide it, and the related inability to attract well-trained pediatric

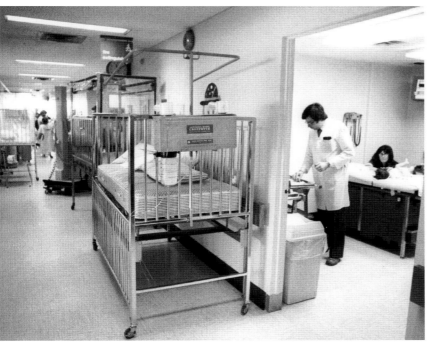

Overcrowded corridors in the Department of Pediatrics at LIJ in the late 1970s.

subspecialists in sufficient numbers. Regrettably, inefficient small units are expensive to operate as well as being mediocre or even inadequate in their delivery of pediatric care.

Of the forty-nine hospitals in Queens, Nassau, and Suffolk Counties in 1972, other than LIJ, only two had intensive care units for children or neonates, and none had special adolescent facilities. At every forum or meeting, public or professional, as well as those held before commissions and regulators, we argued that a proper environment, in which everyone was totally devoted to children, was essential to providing children optimal care. But many hospitals and medical professionals were offended by the implication that they were not providing optimal care, and our arguments were met with vehement

contradiction, strong rhetoric, and powerful opposition. Often it seemed that nobody was listening to the real message: *what the children needed.*

Every phase of a child's care, from collecting a urine specimen to taking x-rays, should differ from the routine care in an adult institution, we insisted. More caregivers are needed to serve the infant and young child, and therefore, more nurses for bedside care. In the general hospital, the child is in competition with a larger and more demanding group of adult patients and is frequently the loser! The child is generally regarded as a second-class citizen, and as a result, gets second-class care. Worldwide experience supported the belief that total care of the child can best be provided by an independent children's hospital. Although it is desirable that such a children's hospital be associated with a medical center with its academic atmosphere, the children's hospital should be a separate entity, and should be administered separately.

The list below summarizes our arguments concerning the advantages of regionalization of medical care for children:

- Reduction of costs of medical care by increased bed utilization and decreased length of stay per disease process.
- Provision of essential programs that small units cannot provide because of cost restrictions, lack of medical expertise, and insufficient volume, for example, a cardiac surgery program, bone marrow transplantation program, sophisticated critical care for neonates and children, pediatric surgical specialties such as neurosurgery and orthopaedic surgery.

- Improved quality of care and patient safety in large units where specialized medical staff is available on a twenty-four-hour basis, as is specially trained staff in the emergency department.
- Specialized units with appropriate equipment and facilities, for example, neonatology, intensive care, and adolescent medicine.
- Specialized operating rooms and laboratory, radiological, and emergency facilities.
- Attraction of top academicians in various pediatric specialty areas, for example, hematologists, endocrinologists, cardiologists, geneticists, neonatologists, radiologists, surgeons, urologists, and orthopaedic surgeons.
- Attraction and retention of nurses and other healthcare professionals, for example, respiratory therapists and technologists specially trained in the care of children.
- Facilities and opportunities to train physicians, nursing staff and technologists in the care of children so that these professionals could become specialists in pediatric medicine and surgery.
- Opportunities to promote clinical and basic research in pediatric medicine and surgery.
- Better public dissemination of health education concerning children.
- Recreational and educational facilities, art therapy, pet therapy, music therapy, parents' sleeping accommodations, all designed to reduce children's emotional trauma.

On the topic of children's emotional trauma, we know today that not just the physiological but also the emotional makeup of a child is wholly different from that of an adult. Children should be managed in a hospital environment designed to appeal to them and make them feel comfortable and at home.

Numerous studies have shown that children under five years of age are emotionally disturbed by hospitalization; that improved hospital

conditions can lessen trauma for them, and that arrangements for the mother or father to stay with the child in the hospital are effective measures for trauma prevention. An improper approach to a hospitalized child can produce an adverse psychological impact, the effects of which are felt for many years.

At this time, some local pediatric departments had already closed and it appeared to me that others would soon follow. A number of smaller institutions already had informal arrangements with LIJ's Department of Pediatrics to transfer their more complicated cases, and our special programs were drawing patients from all over Long Island and beyond. (This trend continues, supporting our belief in the advantages of regionalization.) We argued that it would be far better to plan regionalization of care than to have it imposed by government and regulatory agencies.

It was abundantly clear to us that the time was right to establish a physical plant specifically designed for the needs of children. It was also abundantly clear that we were going nowhere unless and until we solved the problem of too many underutilized pediatric beds in the region.

CLOSING BEDS

We understood that the state was short on the political will needed to mandate the necessary closing of beds. This could only come about voluntarily, and since we were the largest provider of medical care for children in the region, we would need to play a role in accomplishing it. I had my work cut out for me!

In 1973, there were twenty hospitals in the Borough of Queens providing pediatric care services, for a total of 660 pediatric beds, as follows:

Astoria General Hospital*	21
Booth Memorial Hospital+	20
Boulevard Hospital*	17
Elmhurst Hospital	94

Flushing Hospital	53
Hillcrest General Hospital*	15
Jamaica Hospital	38
Kew Gardens General Hospital*	8
LaGuardia Hospital++*	12
LIJ (now SCH)	95
LIJ-South Shore+++	24
Mary Immaculate Hospital	40
Parkway Hospital*	10
Parsons Hospital*	4
Peninsula General Hospital	30
Physicians Hospital*	12
Queens Hospital Center	109
St. John's Hospital, Queens*	24
Terrace Heights Hospital*	18
Whitestone General Hospital*	6
TOTAL	660

*These hospitals no longer have pediatric beds or have closed
+Now called NY Hospital of Queens
++Now called Forest Hills Hospital
+++Now called St. John's Episcopal, Far Rockaway

On the face of things, there were already too many pediatric beds in the Borough of Queens—and we wanted to add fifty-three new ones.

To justify building a children's hospital, the net number of regional pediatric beds could not increase. We had to convince a number of hospitals to close them because they were underutilized and too expensive. I met with the CEOs, executive directors, and pediatric department chairmen of twenty hospitals to negotiate affiliation agreements. Some were prepared to transfer their pediatric patients, close their pediatric beds, and utilize them for other services. In return, LIJ's Department of Pediatrics agreed to provide medical services for their pediatric patients. The medical services offered varied with each institution, from resident, fellow, and attending staff coverage to coverage for neonatology, emergency services, and specialty clinics. In addition, LIJ was prepared to grant staff privileges to qualified pediatricians at these hospitals. Not all hospitals were happy with our negotiating stance. Some had a long-standing antipathy to LIJ. After all, we were relatively new and highly successful. But while some hospitals were not willing to collaborate, happily, a few wanted to close their pediatric departments for their own reasons, and we provided them with a mechanism to achieve this objective.

From 1970 to 1980 LIJ facilitated the closure of 251 pediatric beds in Queens County. In keeping with our concept of regionalization, the Department of Pediatrics created affiliations with almost all hospitals that had pediatric units, and made a commitment to receive their tertiary-care patients as well. Many of these relationships have survived the passage of time and the vicissitudes of the medical marketplace and are still in place to this day.

Some hospitals closed some of their pediatric beds, as shown in the list below, and some hospitals, namely, Hillcrest, Kew Gardens, LaGuardia, Parkway, Parsons, Physicians Hospital, Terrace Heights, and Whitestone General, closed their pediatric service completely.

The following table lists the distribution of the 251 beds closed in Queens' borough hospitals.

Astoria General Hospital	17	Parkway Hospital	10
Boulevard Hospital	5	Parsons Hospital	4
Elmhurst Hospital	17	Peninsula General Hospital	14
Flushing Hospital	22	Physicians Hospital	12
Hillcrest General Hospital	15	Queens Hospital Center	65
Jamaica Hospital	6	St. John's Hospital, Queens	4
Kew Gardens General Hospital	8	Terrace Heights Hospital	18
LaGuardia Hospital	12	Whitestone General Hospital	6
Mary Immaculate Hospital	16		

From 1970 to 1980 the closure of pediatric beds required the development of the following affiliation arrangements:

INSTITUTION	TYPE	WRITTEN AGREEMENT	FINANCIAL AGREEMENT
Booth Memorial Hospital	* †	Yes	No
Brookhaven Memorial Hospital	Neonatology †	Yes	No
Brunswick Hospital Center	Neonatology †	Yes	No
Catholic Medical Center of Brooklyn and Queens	* †	Yes	Indirect
Franklin General Hospital	* †	Yes	No
Hillcrest General Hospital	Neonatology* †	Yes	No
Jamaica Hospital	Resident Rotation	Yes	Yes
	Neonatology†	Yes	Yes
La Guardia Hospital	* †	Yes	Yes
Mid-Island Hospital	Neonatology †	Yes	No
Peninsula Hospital Far Rockaway, NY	* †	Yes	Yes
Queens Hospital Center	* †	Yes	Yes
St. John's Episcopal Hospital – South Shore Division	Cardiology * †	Yes Yes	Yes No
St. Mary's Hospital	Pediatics †	Yes	No

For Children-Bayside, NY South Nassau Community Hospital	Neonatology †	Yes	No
OTHER INSTITUTIONS: Association for the Help of Retarded Children, Brookville, NY	Attending Staff	Yes	Yes
City Health Dept. Jamaica Clinic	Cardiology	Yes	No
New Directions	Attending Staff	No	No
Project Outreach	Attending Staff	No	No
Queensboro Society For the Prevention of Cruelty to Children	Attending Staff	Yes	Yes
State University of New York of Stony Brook Student Health Services	Adolescent Fellow	Yes	No

*Residents and attending staff (these arrangements varied from year to year and did not all exist at the same time)
†Patient transfer agreement

Closure of these beds in Queens County resulted in:

- Improvement in care and cost saving by eliminating duplication of services.
- Soaring occupancy rate for LIJ's Department of Pediatrics (close to 100 percent).
- Pressure to receive tertiary-care cases in numbers that exceeded LIJ's capacity to deal with them effectively in the existing facility. This enhanced our case with the regulatory authorities.
- Long waiting lists for elective admissions to many of the components of LIJ's pediatric services. This also enhanced our case with regulatory authorities.

Our affiliation strategy worked very well, is ongoing to this day, and strengthens the Children's Health Network while improving care in the region.

Following are letters from Terrace Heights Hospital, the New York City Health and Hospitals Corporation, Hillcrest General Hospital, and St. John's Episcopal Hospital of the Church Charity Foundation (all Queens hospitals) describing the relationships that were developed with these hospitals.

TERRACE HEIGHTS HOSPITAL
87-37 Palermo Street Hollis, NY 11423
776-1000
—

I. IRVING COOPER
Executive Director

December 2, 1977

Dr. Philip Lanzkowsky
Chairman of Pediatrics
L.I. Jewish-Hillside Medical Center
New Hyde Park, N. Y.

Dear Doctor Lanzkowsky:

First I would like to thank you for the excellent cooperation which you have extended to our Pediatric and Neonatal services in the past. Whenever a problem arose on either of these services, we always knew that you were there ready and willing to help us out.

The purpose of this letter is to inform you that Terrace Heights Hospital has discontinued its formal Pediatric service. Because of this, we would like to ask you to continue our association and accept Pediatric patients from Terrace Heights Hospital, with emphasis on those requiring tertiary care.

The Board of Directors at its last meeting on November 28, 1977, approved sending this letter to you.

Sincerely yours,

IIC;fi

I. Irving Cooper
Executive Director

NEW YORK CITY
HEALTH AND HOSPITALS CORPORATION
125 Worth Street, New York, N.Y. 10013

December 6, 1977

Robert K. Match, M.D.
President
Long Island Jewish Hillside
  Medical Center
270-05 76th Avenue
New Hyde Park, New York

Dear Dr. Match:

As per our recent conversations, I am writing to you to indicate the Corporation's thinking with regard to pediatric beds in our two hospitals in Queens. On the basis of our analysis of recent years' utilization, it would appear that we could reasonably consider reducing our total pediatric complement of 99 beds (Queens 44, Elmhurst 55) by about 25 beds and still be able to maintain an adequate bed supply to meet current utilization. We have not yet completed our analysis and, of course, these figures are subject to change, particularly if we see a significant change in demand as facilities in the Borough undergo changes and as our own hospitals develop different modes of pediatric services.

I hope that this information, tentative as it is, will be of use to you. Please do not hesitate to contact me if you have any questions.

With kind personal regards.

Sincerely,

LeRoy Carmichael
Executive Vice President,
Operations

LETTER OF UNDERSTANDING BETWEEN
HILLCREST GENERAL HOSPITAL – GHI AND
THE DEPARTMENT OF PEDIATRICS OF
LONG ISLAND JEWISH-HILLSIDE MEDICAL CENTER

Hillcrest General Hospital – GHI is planning to close its fifteen (15) pediatric beds while maintaining and developing pediatric services that are necessary for the community. This has become possible because of the back-up potential offered by the Pediatric Department of the Long Island Jewish-Hillside Medical Center which is a tertiary pediatric unit. The type of back-up which Long Island Jewish is prepared to provide is supervision of neonatology by a Board Certified Neonatologist, Pediatric Consultation and transfer of emergency patients in a timely and prudent manner, and a transfer agreement which will effectuate timely transfer of patients for evaluation and required admission. In addition the Center is prepared to grant pediatric privileges to qualified pediatricians subject to the credentials process of Long Island Jewish-Hillside Medical Center.

We feel because of this regional resource the closure of Hillcrest General Hospital-GHI pediatric unit will enhance rather than jeopardize the medical service to children in the immediate area served by Hillcrest General Hospital-GHI.

The acceptance of this joint endeavor is dependent on and subject to the development of a mutually acceptable program designed for the comfort and protection of the patient and in the best interests of the participating institutions and the communities they serve.

Dated: January 25, 1977

Irwin W. Schenker
Executive Director for
Hillcrest General Hospital-GHI

Philip Lanzkowsky, M.D.
Chairman, Department of Pediatrics
for Long Island Jewish-Hillside
Medical Center

✝ THE CHURCH CHARITY FOUNDATION
of Long Island
480 HERKIMER STEET | BROOKLYN, NY 11213

March 9, 1977

Dr. Philip Lanzkowsky
Chairman of Pediatrics
Long Island Jewish-Hillside Medical Center
Lakeville Road
New Hyde Park, New York 11040

Dear Dr. Lanzkowsky:

The staff of St. John's Episcopal Hospital, South Shore Division welcomed the opportunity to discuss our mutual areas of concern for the provision of pediatric care for the residents of the Far Rockaway, Southwest Nassau community served by our hospital. We look forward to the development and further enrichment of working relationships between the Department of Pediatrics of your institution and our facility located in Far Rockaway.

We are extremely supportive of your plan to establish the Children's Medical Center as the tertiary care regional center for Pediatrics located on the present Long Island Jewish/Hillside Medical Center campus at New Hyde Park. We appreciate the support that your Department has offered South Shore during the several months of transition of operating auspices from Long Island Jewish to the Church Charity Foundation. I believe that because of this spirit of cooperation, not only has the provision and quality of care been unabated, but in fact it has been improved. As you know, we have established an approved residency training program in Pediatrics under the Chairmanship of Dr. Shulman and the Directorship of Dr. Teitel. It is our institutional goal to continue to upgrade this service. In keeping with this goal, we believe that there are many specialized services available at your facility which are not desirable to duplicate at every community hospital. We hope that through joint planning, these areas can be further outlined and that unnecessary and costly duplication of expensive services will be avoided. Out primary goal is to provide access to the full range of services for the patients served. It will be our intention to transfer those patients to your Center where it is medically desirable and when the highly specialized facilities are available.

We look forward to continuing and enlarging the relationships which have been established over the last year.

Sincerely,
Gil Bernstein
Director of Development

cc:
Paul J. Connor, Jr.
Marguerite Tighe
Dr. Bernard Shulman
Dr. Maurice Teitel
Matthew Kurs

CHAPTER 9

A PIPE DREAM?
WINNING OVER
THE REGULATORS

It was time to stop preaching to the converted; we now had to convince skeptics outside our immediate circle of the need for a children's hospital through objective criteria. It was time to begin the arduous process of obtaining approvals from the governmental regulatory authorities that would permit us actually to build the children's medical center.

One would think getting approval to build a children's hospital would be an easy job. Who could possibly be opposed to a facility devoted to the total care of children? But it proved to be a long, grueling process, and at times the opposition seemed insurmountable. The resistance of the medical profession and the hospitals in Queens, Nassau, Suffolk, and Manhattan was fierce.

It took two years to construct the Eiffel Tower, three to complete the Sears Tower, but *thirteen years* to build the children's hospital! Seeing it through required the patience of a Job, the strength of a Samson, and the commitment of a saint. So...let's walk along that twisting, winding, and occasionally torturous road!

Even though Long Island Jewish Medical Center (LIJ) had become committed to the concept of build-

Members of the CMF Women's division attending the New York State Hospital Review and Planning Council Meeting (uninvited).

ing a children's hospital on its campus, much work had to be done to prepare the application for submission. Initially, the application was submitted to the Health and Hospital Planning Council of Southern New York (HHPC), but during the years of submitting and resubmitting applications, delays, disapprovals, and reevaluations, a new agency came into being called the Health System Agency (HSA). (Actually, we had to deal with the Queens HSA, the Nassau-Suffolk HSA, and the HSA of New York City because of the geographic location of the hospital on the Queens-Nassau border). That approval was required in order to proceed. In total, the following agencies had to approve the construction of the children's hospital—none of which *a priori* was enthusiastic about building an institution that would add more pediatric beds in an era of cost containment:

- Comprehensive Health Planning Agency (CHPA)*
- Facilities Review Committee of the Health and Hospital Planning Council (HHPC) of Southern New York
- Health and Hospital Planning Council of Southern New York (HHPC)**
- Queens Health System Agency (HSA)
- Nassau-Suffolk Health System Agency (HSA)
- New York City Health System Agency (HSA)
- New York State Department of Health (NYSDH)

*This agency was the predecessor of the Health System Agency (HSA).

**This agency was the predecessor of the present NY State Hospital Review and Planning Council.

I authored a document entitled "Rationale for a Children's Medical Center," (Appendix II) which contained the philosophy and reasoning behind building a children's medical center. Written in January 1971 and marked "confidential," this document became the roadmap for application to the state as well as the basis for discussions concerning the children's medical center with professional and "lay" audiences.

The year 1971 was a significant transition period for healthcare in the United States, especially in the State of New York. Healthcare costs were escalating at alarming rates. Policymakers were trying to get their arms around the rising costs and, somehow, rein them in. The issue was especially acute in the State of New York, and a section of the NYSDH was delegated to focus on this very problem. Its "solution" was to eliminate acute-care beds wherever it could and close as many hospitals as possible, with particular focus on the small proprietary (for-profit) hospitals that dotted the landscape in many parts of the state. (There is nothing new under the sun. The present-day Berger Commission was set up by the NYSDH in 2006 to recommend consolidation, closure, conversion, or restructuring of healthcare facilities in order to reduce the total number of beds as a cost containment strategy. Its recommendations, approved by the governor and the legislature, became law to be implemented by the commissioner of health.)

I realized that the children's hospital would only be approved if pediatric units were closed or reduced at many Queens County hospitals. The state did not have the desire or the political will to close beds so it (cleverly) expected LIJ to do the legwork. Each time a target was reached, a higher target was set, requiring more and more time and effort. In short, this was a period of subtraction of healthcare in New York State, and the building of a children's hospital was an addition, and so a contradiction. The state would very much have preferred that those advocating a children's hospital would grow tired and give up. Of course, this did not happen!

In the early 1970s the first regulatory hurdle was the CHPA, which, again, was a forerunner of the HSA. The CHPA established a three-person panel to hear the case for the building of a children's hospital. Dr. Frank Cicero, deputy commissioner of the NYSDH, was responsible for appointing the panel with a view to broadening the base of participation to include CHPA, the New York City Department of Hospitals, and representatives of the voluntary hospitals in New York City. Dr. Cicero appointed Joseph Terrenzio, the commissioner of hospitals for New York City, Irving Wilmont, executive director of NYU Medical Center, and Robert Popper, chairman of the CHPA. They unanimously approved the concept—but their nod was only the first that was required before we could go forward.

At that time, in order to build a hospital in the State of New York, it was necessary to submit a two-part application for a certificate of need (CON) to the NYSDH.

PART I OF THE CON APPLICATION

Part I of the CON application provided information in support of the need for the hospital. It included a community needs assessment, examination of existing healthcare resources, and the basic program criteria for the project, including number of beds, patient visits, admissions, procedures, and other related operating statistics. It required a room-by-room description including the number and type of spaces needed, functional relationships, and the amount of floor area needed for each function. Part I also asked which functions would be located in the existing Long Island Jewish Medical Center. The plans were on a relatively small scale (1/16 inch = 1 foot). A project construction budget, equipment list, and budget, financing plan, staffing plan, and reimbursement plan were also submitted.

PART II OF THE CON APPLICATION

Part II required more detail and concentrated more on the design of the building. The plans were on a larger scale (1/8 inch = 1 foot) and furniture and equipment placement was indicated. Plans on an even larger scale were required for important rooms like bedrooms, operating rooms, and the like. The site plan was enhanced to show roads, walks, retaining walls, landscaping, site lighting, and grading. Mechanical, electrical, and plumbing plans were provided. Life safety information related to sprinklers, smoke detectors, and alarms was included. An outline specification was prepared to show the materials, systems, and services to be provided. The budget was updated, and a construction schedule was prepared. The financing approval, zoning approval, and community approval were also provided.

The drawings for Part I and Part II that related to the building design were done by the Perkins and Will architectural firm. They did Part I because LIJ had not yet selected an architect, and later, they did Part II because LIJ was in the process of changing architects from the Rossetti Group of Detroit to the TAC Group of Cambridge, Massachusetts, and did not want to lose time. David Ginsberg, of Perkins and Will, prepared the plans, which were followed closely for the actual building, except for the fact that the auditorium on the ground floor next to the cafeteria was eliminated. When TAC was appointed architect for the project, it modified Ginsberg's design and prepared the exterior elevations and interior details.

On February 26, 1973, LIJ submitted Part I and Part II to the NYSDH to build a 150-bed children's medical center. The plan constituted a fifty-three-bed addition to the present ninety-seven-bed pediatric complement within the Department of Pediatrics at LIJ. The original letter from Robert K. Match, MD, to Richard Nauen, MD, associate commissioner for New York City Affairs, NYSDH, which accompanied the application, read as follows:

LIJ HMC

LONG ISLAND JEWISH-HILLSIDE MEDICAL CENTER ° NEW HYDE PARK, NEW YORK 11040 (212)343-6700, (516)437-6700

ROBERT K. MATCH, M.D.

Executive Vice President and Director

February 26, 1973

Dr. Richard Nauen
Associate Commissioner for New York City Affairs
New York State Department of Health
270 Madison Avenue
New York, New York 10016

Dear Dr. Nauen:

I am enclosing for your review Parts I and II of an application for approval of construction of hospital and related facilities in accordance with Article 28 of the Public Health Law of New York State.

Long Island Jewish-Hillside Medical Center is presently a 661-bed institution consisting of 438 general care beds and 223 psychiatric beds. Following the completion of construction of an additional 32 beds, approval for which has already been received by the New York State Department of Health, we will be a 693-bed institution at our present location. In addition, effective February 1, 1973, a merger with the South Shore Hospital (formerly the St. Joseph's Hospital of the Catholic Medical Center in Far Rockaway) has added 223 beds to our overall complement, thus giving us a grand total of 916 beds; to this would be added 78 bassinets and 4 temporary post-cardiac beds for a total of 998.

Our present application is requesting approval for the construction of a 150-bed unit in which we will consolidate the existing inpatient and outpatient programs of the Department of Pediatrics at LIJ-HMC. Presently, the pediatric service consists of 45 pediatric beds at the LIJ Division (including 4 intensive care beds), an 18-bed adolescent unit at the LIJ Division, 34 neonatal beds (including 8 neonatal intensive care bassinets) at the LIJ Division and 24 general pediatric beds at the South Shore Division. In addition, LIJ-HMC is responsible for the professional services provided at the Queens Hospital Center of New York and in this location we provide pediatric services in 109 pediatric beds which includes 20 neonatal beds.

It is also important to note that LIJ-HMC provides all the inpatient pediatric care for patients of the LaGuardia Hospital which closed its pediatric unit in 1971, that LIJ-HMC has transfer arrangements with a number of hospitals in Queens County, all of whom transfer their more complicated cases to LIJ-HMC, and that LIJ-HMC is presently in negotiations with several other hospitals who are interested in closing down their pediatric units because of their own low occupancy rates.

This new facility, upon completion of construction, would house all of the existing pediatric beds at LIJ-HMC, would allow for a very moderate increase in the overall number of general pediatric beds, would allow for the creation of a 15-bed psychiatric unit for children under 13 years of age, would allow for the creation of a 15-bed chronic care unit and, finally, would allow for a modest expansion of our neonatal unit to 40 beds. We welcome the opportunity of discussing with you the utilization of the space to be vacated by the existing pediatric beds.

We are aware of New York State's present attitude as it relates to the construction of new beds in the New York City area. Nevertheless, we feel justified in submitting this application on the following grounds:

1.   The creation of a facility expressly geared toward providing for the health care needs of children is sorely needed in the Tri-County area of Long Island.

2.   The number of beds we anticipate in this new facility represents a figure which constitutes no real net increase in the total number of pediatric beds presently under the medical supervision of LIJ-HMC and, indeed, actually represents a modest decrease when one takes into account the projected reduction of the pediatric bed complement at the Queens Hospital Center.

3.   A facility in which the consolidation of primary, secondary and tertiary care pediatric services can be housed is necessary in the face of declining occupancy rates on pediatric units throughout the area and, most particularly, the uneconomic, inefficient and questionable quality of care provided in a variety of marginal units throughout this area.

4.   All of the new beds which would be constructed will be in conformance with all existing codes and regulations of the New York State Department of Health.

5.   The addition of these beds would not create a substantial change in the Medical Center's present program though it would clearly hasten and solidify the Medical Center's move toward the regionalization of pediatric services in one location.

6.   The LIJ-HMC is located on the border of Queens and Nassau Counties in the area which continues to experience population growth and is likely to do so for some time to come.

7.   The Medical Center's bed occupancy for pediatric services in 1972 was 85.6 for the general pediatric beds, 97.3 for the neonatal unit and 89.4 for the adolescent unit. Our percentage-of-occupancy projections for calendar year 1973 exceed those figures in every area.

The total number of admissions to LIJ-HMC over the last three years on the pediatric service is as follows:
1970 <u>2,301</u>
1971 <u>2,845</u>
1972 <u>3,024</u>

In giving consideration to this request, we think it important that the New York State Department of Health take into account the following factors:

1. There are probably too many pediatric facilities in the Tri-County area attempting to provide child care with extremely low occupancy, in inadequate physical facilities and providing, as a consequence, incomplete medical coverage

2. Small pediatric units do not have available the necessary expertise for the optimal care of children because of the expense involved in the development of these types of services and the inability of such units to attract well-trained specialists on a full-time basis.

3. The spiraling costs of medical care dictate the need for high bed utilization and centralization of services in order to accomplish a meaningful program of child health care.

4. A reasonably large size regional center can help reduce the costs of medical care by increased utilization and by decreasing the stay per disease process. To some extent, we have already demonstrated this in the Department of Pediatrics at LIJ-HMC.

5. Such a center can provide optimum care for children by providing programs that smaller units cannot provide because of cost restrictions and the lack of medical expertise, for example, cardiac surgery, a hemophiliac program, a program for the treatment of cystic fibrosis, leukemics, etc.

6. Reasonable safety for pediatric patients can only be provided in large units where medical staff is available on a 24-hour basis.

7. The availability of special units with special equipment and facilities can only be maintained in a reasonably large size center.

8. The availability of high-class academicians in the various specialty areas for consultation, for example, pediatric hematologists, neurologists, endocrinologists, cardiologists, geneticists, neonatologists, radiologists, surgeons, urologists, orthopedic surgeons, etc., can only be sustained by a unit such as we are describing.

9. The advancement of basic knowledge in pediatric medicine and surgery through research can only be developed in units of this kind.

10. The dissemination of health education materials concerning children can most effectively be rendered through a facility of this kind.

11. Special facilities for children, and for the parents of children requiring such care, can only be provided in units of this size so as to help reduce the emotional trauma of separation to such children.

As already indicated, LIJ-HMC has already begun to function as a regional center for pediatric care by providing the necessary specialty services to lesser staffed and equipped hospitals. Increasing recognition on the part of other health facilities as to their own inability to provide adequate pediatric care has led to a situation at LIJ-HMC where our own ability to continue to provide the quality of care necessary is hampered by inadequate isolation areas for the constantly increasing number of patients who are immuno-compromised, for example, leukemics and children on cytotoxic agents, a recognition of the fact that we are in need of additional intensive care unit facilities, a recognition that we lack a separate pediatric pre-anesthetic and recovery room, a recognition that we lack adequate school facilities, adequate playroom facilities and adequate facilities for parents in which they might sleep.

Additionally, we are in need of additional laboratory research space, additional lecture rooms for pediatric students (medical, nursing and paraprofessional), additional office and secretarial space for the cadre of full-time physicians presently on board and those that we anticipate bringing on board and because the existing facilities, at the time they were built, were not designed with an eye toward taking care of the specific needs of children.

This letter would not be complete without our calling to your attention the fact that our recognition of the need to expand ambulatory facilities for pediatric care has led us to project a fairly large amount of floor space for such services. At present, LIJ-HMC provides 8,980 visits for pediatric patients in our outpatient department and, in addition, provides 9,239 visits to pediatric patients in our emergency room. The trend toward the provision of specialized pediatric care in regionalized centers such as the one we are projecting is likely to continue and accelerate in the years to come. The ability of a Medical Center to provide such services is largely dependent upon their ability to attract subspecialists of pediatric medicine and pediatric surgery under one roof for the provision of optimum care for such children. We anticipate a facility which will make provision for an expansion of services in these areas, for space in which to provide health education programs for parents and children and for adequate space in which to provide teaching to those healthcare specialists who will be dealing with children through their professional careers.

I look forward to an early response from you. I will be most happy to meet with you and members of your staff to substantiate, in greater detail, our need for this new facility.

Sincerely,

Robert K. Match, M.D.
Executive Vice President
and Director

/yf
Enclosure
cc: Jack C. Haldeman

This letter was the opening conversation in what turned out to be a five-year dialogue with various regulatory bodies leading to final approval to build the children's hospital, which came in June 1978. During this period, there were significant delays in the NYSDH review and approval process. The lack of timely processing of Part I and Part II of the CON application delayed the project at least one year. Although it should have been under construction long ago, it was in the position of being "reevaluated" and subject to still further delays. The unfavorable impact of these delays on the project's costs and fundraising efforts is incalculable. The number of people and committees involved in approving a not-for-profit endeavor, which delays progress and escalates cost, stands in high contrast to the number involved in the approval process for a for-profit endeavor. The following is a chronology of the steps in the process after the submission of Part I and Part II:

June 4, 1973—New York State requests financial information to be submitted within thirty days.

June 27, 1973—LIJ requests an extension of 120 days to respond to this request.

The slow response to this request on the part of LIJ, despite prodding by Judge Harnett and me, reflected the institution's ambivalence concerning this project and its fear of the economic impact of a children's hospital on the medical center itself. There were also delays on the part of the state, which took ten months to respond.

In the interim, in order to gain support of the proposed concept, location, and development of the program for services of the proposed children's hospital, meetings were held with individuals and representatives of regulatory and planning agencies and others interested in children and their healthcare needs. During this time the following meetings occurred, which included discussions of program, site location, regional planning, and off-site services.

March 19, 1974	Queens Board No. 13	Dr. M. McFarland, Mrs. S. Noreika,
	NYC Planning Board (Queens)	Mrs. W. French, Mr. R. Jacobson, J. Wills
	Queens Borough President's Office	Ms. L. Avery, Mrs. A. Hayes, Mrs. C. Schulman
	NYC Planning Board (Central)	Mr. J. Merrill
	Nassau & Suffolk CHP	Mr. W. Warner
March 24, 1974	NYC District Health Office	Dr. N. Kuo
March 25,1974	Queens Children's Hospital	Dr. Faretra, Dr. Hartman, Mrs. Wolf, Mr. Kulik
March 26, 1974	NYC Dept. of Health	Dr. I. Leveson, Ms. J. Cooke, Ms. L. Lanz,
March 26, 1974	NYC Health & Hospitals Corp.	Mr. R. Boyar
March 26, 1974	NYC Dept. of Mental Health & Retardation Services	Miss S. Schrenze1
March 27, 1974	L.I. Health & Hospitals Planning Council	Mr. H. Bang, Mr. D. B. Herd

March 28, 1974	NYC Youth Services Agency	Mr. R. Lucas
March 28, 1974	Nassau County Medical Ctr.	Dr. P. J. Collipp
April 3, 1974	NYC School Task Force	Mr. D. Koren
April 4, 1974	CHPA (Queens)	Mr. R. Larsen, Mr. Thompson,
	CHPA (NYC Office)	Mr. R. Popper,
		Mr. N. Schwartz

April 23, 1974—New York State takes no action on the original Part I application.

The letter from Donald Dickson, MD, Deputy Commissioner of the Department of Health, stated that on June 4th, 1973, New York State had requested additional financial information to be submitted in thirty days. Although an extension of 120 days had been granted, LIJ had not supplied the necessary financial information within the extended time frame. Since NYS did not act on the application it was tantamount to a rejection.

The rejection was disappointing; however, it did not slow down LIJ or the LIJ Planning Committee, which pushed forward to complete the master plan analysis and compile all of the financial information. We continued to meet with hospitals to combine services for regionalized medical care for children in their communities, and LIJ leadership and Planning Committee members continued their meetings with the regulatory and planning agencies.

May 7, 1974—LIJMC submits the amended Part I and the financial information to the NYSDH that had been requested the previous year.

May 22, 1974—New York State acknowledges receipt of the amended Part I.

September 1974—The application (Part I) is approved by the CHPA, a predecessor of the Health System Agency (HSA), and the Facilities Review Committee of the HHPC of Southern New York.

December 16, 1974—NYSDH approves Part I of the application for a CON to construct a $24 million comprehensive children's medical center to serve an area from Queens to Suffolk County. (Newsday, *December 21, 1974*).

In celebration of that approval, Judge Harnett and Dr. Match made the following statement in the hospital publication *New Horizons* in the spring of 1975:

Having cleared the hurdle of State approval, it is important to share some considerations which affect the thinking behind the new children's facility.

The paramount consideration is, of course, the continuation of excellence in medical care at all levels by a staff specially trained and dedicated to the ill and injured child. While every attempt will be made to maintain the essential character of a true children's hospital, interconnection to the main hospital will occur in those instances when duplication of services would be clearly uneconomical or contrary to the environmental and psychological needs of the ill child.

The planning process will take into account the experience of the various children's medical centers across the country. Not the least of the considerations which will enter into the conceptualization of our children's facility will be the philosophical premise by which CMCFNY was founded many years ago—that children are not small adults and therefore need and deserve special care in their own separate facility designed specifically for the medical and emotional needs of children.

We look forward to a children's health facility which will become a major referral center in this area, a place in which highly specialized professional people work to elevate the quality of pediatric care in the region and in which the entire body of personnel is sensitized to the needs of children. To this end, it is our intention to give every planning consideration to the creation of the best, most efficient, distinct facility where the LIJ-HMC tradition of excellence of medical care can be carried out in an environment totally committed to children.

April 25, 1975—LIJ requests and is granted an extension from February 16, 1975, to July 15, 1975, to submit Part II. The original Part II submitted on February 26, 1973, was not formally considered because the procedure called for Part I to be approved before Part II could be submitted.

April 25, 1975—NYSDH informs LIJ that the 28B Housing Finance Agency (HFA) funding proposed and approved in the Part 1 application is no longer available.

June 1975—A total moratorium on approval of hospital beds anywhere in New York State is declared by the New York State Department of Health.

Dr. Match reported to the Board of Trustees that final approval from the state had not been granted because of the state's withdrawal of funds for hospital construction and the moratorium. This was a major setback (actually, two tough blows) for the project. As a result of all these delays, and the concomitant increases in cost estimates, raising enough money had become a problem. LIJ had been relying on the HFA

for funding. Incidentally, this was the first time in the institution's history that the board had agreed to borrow money to finance construction. It had been LIJ's policy not to borrow money, but to spend only what could be raised in charitable contributions. In an age when hospitals' reimbursement was based on the previous year's expenses (retrospective reimbursement), this was a bad business decision, since all debt service could have been rolled into the bed reimbursement and paid for the following year by an increase in hospital rates to cover this expense of the debt service.

Although the LIJ board consisted of entrepreneurs used to taking risks in their own businesses, they were unusually cautious and conservative when it came to taking risks for the hospital. Overall, their feeling was that hospitals should not have mortgages.

In 1975 Perkins and Will, which had prepared the drawings for Part I and Part II, was asked by LIJ to collate, refine, and further develop all of the programmatic data we had accumulated over the years for the children's hospital for submission to the state.

July 15, 1975—LIJ submits Part II with drawings.

May 4, 1976—New York State rejects Part II.

The letter, marked "disapproved," stated, "We shall withhold Part II application from the formal determination by the Commissioner of Health contingent upon satisfactory resolution of a number of items, including satisfactory resolution of the suspension of 28B funds through the Housing Finance Agency no later than August 2, 1976."

The estimated cost for the children's hospital in 1974 was approximately $24 million. Housing Finance Agency (HFA) financing and $3 million raised by the Children's Medical Fund would cover this. After the HFA funds dried up, new loan arrangements were made and approved through the Federal Housing Authority (FHA) to begin construction as soon as we received approval, by which time the estimated cost had risen from the original $24 million to approximately $35 million! This would mean that the FHA loan would be approximately $32 million. Rising construction and operating costs were of great concern to the Board of Trustees of LIJ.

July 30, 1976—LIJ submits Part II containing the required revisions prior to the August 2 deadline.

August 26, 1976—New York State requests an amendment to the financial section of the Part I application within thirty days, because of the change in financing from HFA to FHA.

September 24, 1976—LIJ submits the amendment to the Part I application.

At this point, New York State HHPC, without serving LIJ notice, unilaterally decided to reevaluate the project.

December 16, 1976—The HHPC conducts meeting #1 re: CMC "reevaluation."

Without notification to the affected institutions, NYSDH placed on the HHPC agenda the "reevaluation" of several Part I "pipeline" projects, including the children's hospital project. The HHPC, taking issue with the lack of notification, established a special subcommittee, the New York State Special Subcommittee for the Reevaluation of Previously Approved Projects, to meet with the affected institutions and review the "reevaluated" projects.

Early January 1977—The New York State Special Subcommittee for the Reevaluation of Previously Approved Projects recommends that LIJ be permitted to build a children's medical center, but without an increase in the pediatric bed complement.

This was totally unacceptable. It defeated the whole purpose of building a children's hospital. LIJ appealed the decision, submitting additional information in support of the need for the expansion of pediatric beds.

January 7, 1977—LIJ submits a written

report and verbal presentation to the New York State Special Subcommittee for the Reconsideration of Previously Approved Projects.

This was in response to a New York State staffing report questioning the experienced high percentage of occupancy, the appropriateness of the experienced lengths of stay, the tertiary nature of the care provided, LIJ's efforts in regard to the regionalization of pediatric services, and the closure of pediatric beds in the community. They had already been presented with reams of data, but it was not enough, they stated. LIJ had no choice but to supply further documentation.

In addition to the political and philosophical objections to getting the project approved in the seventies and early eighties, the certificate of need (CON) process was difficult because it was tied not only to establishment of need but also to hospital reimbursement rates. When a capital project was approved by the HSA followed by approval of the New York State Health and Hospital Planning Council (presently called the New York State Hospital Review and Planning Council, or HRPC), the capital budget for the project would also be approved and the cost of the project (debt service and depreciation) would be amortized into a "pass-through" amount added to the rate established for a particular hospital. This amount was paid by Medicaid and Blue Cross, the major insurance companies. Commercial payors paid 13 percent more than Blue Cross and Medicaid. Because capital expense for hospital construction determined the reimbursement rate, the NYSDH was very concerned about new construction and put rigorous regulatory controls in place. With the development in the eighties and nineties of multiple commercial payors, market forces determined hospital reimbursement and dominated decision-making. Control of the CON process by the state became less rigorous because there was no longer a fixed guaranteed reimbursement to hospitals by the state and hospital reimbursement rates fluctuated with payors. Accordingly the CON process was drastically simplified and centralized within the NYSDH, which appointed one body—the New York State Hospital Review and Planning Council—to review all CON applications. Parts I and II of the old process were eliminated.

February 3, 1977—Both the special subcommittee and the HHPC, after re-review of the data, recommend approval of the children's medical center project without additional beds, but with the ability to convert existing LIJ acute-care beds to children's hospital specialty-care beds during the Part II submission.

Additionally, the subcommittee recommended approval without prejudice of additional beds at a later date should circumstances change.

February 11, 1977—The New York State HHPC approves the "reevaluated" children's medical center project.

The project could proceed, with no beds added to the total capacity of LIJ. The reason given for this decision was the "present fiscal crisis in New York State, and the moratorium on construction of new hospital beds."

On February 14, 1977, I pointed out to the Medical Board that since over fifty pediatric beds had been closed in Queens, and LIJ pediatric occupancy was 100 percent, building the children's medical center without additional beds would impose an insurmountable burden on the institution.

The March 1977 issue of *In Touch* reported,

We know we have a strong case in the light of the large number of pediatric beds that have been closed in hospitals that cannot maintain the staff, the facilities or the overall level of care required. For tertiary care—that is, the highest level of care on a comprehensive scale—a regional medical center is needed. The CMC will be that regional center.

We are, in fact, a regional center for childhood diseases and disabilities right now. But much of the time we've got to care for children under the most crowded conditions because we're filled to over capacity.

"We're documenting all of this," Dr. Lanzkowsky said, "and we're going back to the Hospital Review and Planning Council. I'm sure that ultimately its membership will understand our need for 150 beds if we are to satisfy the needs of children in Queens and Long Island, as well as other areas of the city."

March 28, 1977—Dr. Match and staff meet with Glen Haughie, MD, deputy commissioner of the NYSDH, and the department's staff to discuss the need for the additional fifty-three beds that were originally proposed.

The NYSDH agreed to review the issue pending the submission of data documenting the pediatric case mix and the appropriateness of the pediatric lengths of stay. Back to the drawing board…to prove, once again, the obvious. We prepared for the state an estimate of the number of pediatric, adolescent, neonatal, and psychiatric beds that were needed at the children's medical center. We calculated the number of beds using the following formula:

$$\frac{\text{Length of stay x annual number of admissions}}{365 \text{ days}} \div \text{desired occupancy rate} = \text{bed need}$$

The length of stay (LOS) figures were different for pediatric, adolescent, and neonatal beds. The statewide average LOS for pediatric patients was 5.8 (pediatric patients defined as patients under 14 years of age); for adolescents 10.8 (adolescent patients defined as children 14 years of age and older); and for neonates between 20 and 25 days (neonatal patients defined as under 31 days of age).

The justifying data was furnished, using LIJ's 1975 experience:

PEDIATRIC BED NEEDS:

5.8 days (LOS) x 3,088 annual admissions = 17,910 patient days

$\frac{17,910}{365}$ = 49.1 ÷ 0.8* occupancy = 61 beds needed at CMC

ADOLESCENT BED NEEDS:

10.8 days (LOS) x 859 annual admissions = 9,277 patient days

$\frac{9,277}{365}$ = 25.4 ÷ 0.9** occupancy = 28 beds needed at CMC

NEONATAL BED NEEDS:

22.5 days (LOS) x 579 annual admissions = 13,028 patient days

$\frac{13,028}{365}$ = 35.7 ÷ 0.9*** occupancy = 40 beds needed at CMC

*State-required minimum occupancy rate was 75 percent for maximum efficiency.

**Adolescent beds were included under medical/surgical methodology. The state-required minimum occupancy was 90 percent.

***State-required minimum occupancy rate for neonatal beds was 90 percent.

Using the state methodology, the total beds required at CMC was:

Pediatric	= 61
Adolescent	= 28
Neonatal	= 40
Total	**129**

After battling with the NYSDH and the New York State HHPC from February 1973 until early 1977, and having made considerable progress, LIJ was informed that the project had to be reviewed from scratch by a new agency that had come into being in the interim—the Health System Agency.* This was ominous, because the Nassau-Suffolk HSA, the organization created to review federal grant applications and certify need for hospital expansion, had concluded that by 1982 there would be a surplus of 216 pediatric beds in the Nassau-Suffolk area. It had found that in 1976 only seven of the thirteen hospitals with pediatric services in Nassau County reached the recommended occupancy rate of seventy-five percent. In Suffolk, only four of the twelve hospitals had reached the recommended level. Ironically, LIJ's proposal for a children's hospital in Queens was not even within the jurisdiction of the Nassau-Suffolk HSA but because of LIJ's location on the Queens-Nassau border they felt their review was justified. That organization had also found a significant decline in the 0–19-year-old population in the region—all bad news for the children's hospital project. (*Long Island Daily News*, June 4, 1978). The Nassau-Suffolk HSA concluded that "these factors indicate that an expansion of pediatric services at LIJ cannot and should not be substantiated on any projected pediatric needs for the Nassau-Suffolk region." But it did not rule out Queens.

The Queens HSA, now in charge, immediately questioned the length of stay (LOS) figures, and because they were higher than the statewide average we had to justify them.

The state's claim at that juncture was that we were admitting children who were not severely ill (low case mix intensity) who could be treated in a community hospital. It was my task to convince them otherwise. David Ginsberg of Perkins and Will and I analyzed several hundred admissions to demonstrate that a high percentage of them were tertiary in nature. Together we crunched the numbers, often into the wee hours of the

---

* In 1975 the National Health Planning and Development Act signed into law the establishment of federally funded health system agencies (HSAs), which required community participation in the decision-making process. These HSAs were established and became operative in 1977.

morning, to justify the data we had presented. We argued that because we were a tertiary-care center for pediatrics, our LOS should not be compared to the statewide average. Data were submitted supporting our longer than average length of stay because of our higher case mix intensity. Because of the specialized care we provided at LIJ, a substantial number of patients were difficult to diagnose and treat and required a longer length of stay. We were ahead of our time, as the current diagnostic related group (DRG) system recognizes these concepts.

The HSA reviewed the rate of Medicaid denials from November 1976 to March 1977. It determined that LIJ's Medicaid reimbursement denial rate was significantly lower (2.9 per 100) than the average (5.2 per 100)—in fact, it was the lowest rate of all hospitals reviewed. The HSA uncovered only four days of unnecessary care in two cases—again fewer unnecessary patient days than the other hospitals, and better utilization of patient care services.

The HSA finally accepted 5.8 as the appropriate length of stay for our pediatric patients, and by applying the 1975 occupancy rates and using a 1981 needs methodology, their estimated need for pediatric beds at LIJ was 121, still less then our goal of 150 beds. In order to reach the required 150 beds, we submitted the program to the state that described, in addition the need for rehabilitation and psychiatric beds in a comprehensive children's hospital. No methodology was offered to substantiate the need for pediatric rehabilitation and psychiatric beds. A survey of the HSA staff indicated that there were no pediatric rehabilitation (chronic) beds in Queens and that the long-term psychiatric beds maintained at the Queens Children's Psychiatric Hospital had an occupancy rate of 90.5 percent—but they still planned to close one ward.

The HSA determined that since the children's medical center project program offered a combined multimodel treatment program for pediatric patients, it would be consistent to include a rehabilitation and psychiatric component. Bed need figures for this type of tertiary-level integrated care were not available.

The concept of including psychiatric and rehabilitation beds at the Center was viewed favorably by the regulatory bodies.

By accepting the actual length of stay for pediatric patients at LIJ, a need for 121 pediatric beds at the hospital was projected. The HSA determined that an excess of twenty-eight pediatric beds would exist in the county by 1981. They recommended that the total pediatric beds at LIJ be increased from the existing 97 to 121 beds on the basis that LIJ would continue to provide tertiary-level pediatric care. Furthermore, they encouraged LIJ to work with the other hospitals in Queens to decertify additional pediatric beds. Then the HSA staff would be willing to approve the additional pediatric beds LIJ had requested in its application. The staff recommended approval of the construction of the children's medical center to house all pediatric beds if Part II on the CON application indicated that it would make more sense architecturally and financially than adding twenty-four beds to LIJ.

*June 20, 1977—LIJ submits the Supplementary Data Report as requested by the NYSDH to review the need for the additional fifty-three CMC beds and documents this request with the submission of the actual professional activity study (PAS) data.**

LIJ also submitted an analysis, by diagnosis, of its pediatric service activities for the first quarter of 1977.

To indicate how badly needed the beds were, at the Joint Conference Committee** of the Board of Trustees at LIJ on June 13, 1977, I had reported that in the past month approximately seventy-seven children requiring tertiary care had to be cared for in the halls of the hospital or sent to another hospital.

July 15, 1977—The NYSDH requests additional data consisting of the diagnosis of pediatric admission to LIJ for the year 1976.

August 20, 1977—LIJ submits the data for 1976 as requested by the NYSDH.

September 1977—New York State informally advises LIJ that the submitted PAS data support the tertiary nature of the pediatric case mix at LIJ, the appropriateness of the resultant lengths of stay, and the unusually high percentage of occupancy, and thereby support the need for the additional fifty-three pediatric beds. Additionally, LIJ is advised that the project will be placed on the November agenda of the HHPC.

Success at last!...but no, not quite. The hospital didn't make the November agenda. We were assured, however, that the project would be placed on the December agenda.

November 30, 1977—Dr. Match and I travel to Albany to meet Kevin Cahill, MD, an expert on tropical medicine, special assistant for health affairs, and one of the most powerful members of then-Governor Hugh Carey's political inner circle, to ask him to present our case to Governor Carey.

November 30, 1977—While Dr. Match and I are in Albany, LIJ staff meets with representatives of the NYSDH to review the status of the project. They are informed that, to date, the children's medical center project is not on the December HHPC agenda.

They were also told that although the need for the fifty-three additional pediatric beds had been documented, it had to be viewed in relation to the available pediatric beds in Queens County. This was accomplished, and they were assured

that every attempt would be made to put the project on the December agenda.

December 2, 1977—LIJ is advised that the project has made the December HHPC agenda.

LIJ was also given the date of the meeting of the Special Subcommittee for the Reconsideration of Previously Approved Projects of the HHPC as required, prior to the December HHPC meeting. It learned that the staff of the HHPC recommended that the projected bed complement go back to 121 beds, instead of the 150 requested, and should include pediatric, adolescent, psychiatric, and chronic care beds. It also learned that approval to construct the children's facility would be granted if it were determined, based on the Part II submission, that this were more feasible than adding beds in the already existing facility, meaning LIJ, and that the HHPC would be receptive to further increased capacity at LIJ if more than the fifty-six beds were subsequently decertified in Queens County (data based on existing capacity of 473 pediatric beds in Queens County). This put the onus on the Department of Pediatrics to effectuate the closure of pediatric beds in Queens.

December 12, 1977—LIJ Medical Board is made aware by Dr. Match of the fact that approval of an additional fifty-three beds is critical to the financial viability of the children's hospital project.

Since the construction was to be supported by mortgage financing, the ability to pay the mortgage debt and depreciation and maintain a balanced operating budget would be dependent upon the number of beds. In general, the various healthcare agencies had been supportive of the request for additional beds; however, LIJ was informed that there had been continuous opposition encountered from "various local organizations."

Early in December, the Queens Health System Agency became aware that the children's medical center was on the HHPC agenda for December 15. The chairpersons of the nine district boards in Queens sent mailgrams and letters to the HHPC requesting that the application be pulled from the

---

*This is a hospital discharge abstract called the PAS case abstract prepared in the medical records department from medical records of every hospital discharge including newborns, mandated by the federal government. The data was used to create and maintain a computer-accessible file of the PAS data for use by the scientific community, healthcare and governmental agencies. This antedated the diagnostic related group (DRG) system.

**A standing subcommittee of the board of trustees composed of an equal number of trustees and chairmen of the clinical departments.

agenda to allow the Queens HSA to review it for the first time, especially in light of demographic changes over the past three years.

December 14, 1977—Citing the need for additional information (and responding to the mailgrams and letters from the HSA chairpersons), the Special Subcommittee for the Reconsideration of Previously Approved Projects of the HHPC advises LIJ to remove the CMC project from the December HHPC agenda.

Under duress, LIJ acquiesced to the request of the subcommittee.

December 30, 1977—The HSA of New York City informs LIJ that it needs to review the project.

Citing the withdrawal of the project from the December HHPC agenda as the precipitating action, the HSA informed LIJ of its intent to review the CMC project for determination of need. LIJ's investigation of this action indicated there was no legal basis for such a review. Despite this, approval from the NYSDH and its subsidiary agencies was required, irrespective of their legal status, in order for the project to move forward.

March 1978—The HSA of New York City informs LIJ of a meeting on April 6, 1978, to review and make comments on the application.

Once again, this required that I present the project to a new group of people, who knew nothing about the project's history, in order to convince them of the need to build a children's hospital.

April 1978—At an LIJ Medical Board meeting, Dr. Match reports as follows: "The project has finally moved to the brink of approval by the New York State Department of Health."

But at this late stage, still another review at the state level was required—the HSA's.

May 4, 1978—The Children's Medical Center project is approved by the HHPC.

May 24, 1978—At the Medical Executive Committee meeting, Dr. Match reports: "The children's medical center was approved by the Health and Hospital Planning Council on May 4th after a blatant political attack from Nassau County elements."

"Over the course of the last few months," Dr. Match stated, "there has been a naked attack on this program led by North Shore Hospital not only to oppose the program but [to meet] in other political arenas in the state to accuse LIJ of falsifying data and of dishonesty." A lengthy discussion ensued regarding the motivations of the opposing institution's attempt to block the building of this sorely needed facility at this late date, especially when 250 pediatric beds in Queens had been already closed over the last few years, and at a time when the need for this facility had been clearly demonstrated. Dr. Match further proclaimed his "total abhorrence on the part of hospital staff participating in opposition to a project of another hospital based upon self-interest" and stated that he would never condone similar behavior on the part of LIJ staff.

For five long years, the staff at LIJ had basically jumped through hoops to provide all of the state agencies involved in this approval process with information, reports, patient data, and whatever else they asked for. But, it finally paid off. In May 1978, LIJ had at last gotten the state's go-ahead to build the children's medical center...but not so fast. The project needed the approval of still more agencies.

June 1978—The Queens HSA Project Review Subcommittee approves the project at a public hearing in Kew Gardens before the Queens Project Review Subcommittee of the New York City Health System Agency. The closed-door vote was 9 to 4.

In all, twenty-three speakers appeared at the Queens public hearing, most of them from Queens and most favoring the project. One of the most effective speakers on behalf of the children's hospital was a young mother who had her infant in her arms as she sat patiently until it was her time to speak. She recounted her experience of arriving at another major hospital while in labor with the baby's birth imminent and being turned away for financial reasons. She concluded that she was welcomed at LIJ and showed her healthy baby as proof of the care given to her and her child. Her story brought tears to the eyes of some members of the audience and even made one of the later speakers, who represented the hospital that turned her away, ask only for a name change but not to deny the building of the children's hospital. LIJ won a strategically important first-round victory.

Because of the potential impact of this project on Manhattan hospitals, the New York City HSA demanded an opportunity to review this project.

July 1978—After a tense meeting and a lively debate, the Project Review Subcommittee of the New York City Health System Agency voted 11-2, and its executive committee voted 19-0 to approve the project.

The HHPC approved the project by a 12-9 vote, and, finally, the NYSDH approved the creation of the children's hospital partly on the recommendation of the local federal planning agency. The Department of Pediatrics' ninety-seven beds were to be converted into a 150-bed children's hospital with the following configuration:

Bed type	LIJ	Children's Hospital
General pediatric	41	50
Adolescent	18	18
Intensive care	4	12
Neonatal intensive care	34	40
Psychiatric	0	15
Chronic care	0	15
TOTAL	97	150

A federal health planner admitted that many of the existing general-care pediatric beds in Queens were outmoded, and that the state was in the process of closing a large percentage of them. As a result, the planner said, there was a need for highly specialized pediatric beds, and LIJ was the only medical center in Queens with the sophisticated medical resources to accommodate them.

Both federal and state planners agreed that a major reason they had approved the expansion was their belief that many Queens residents didn't have automobiles and would have a tough time traveling to a hospital in Nassau. Even though Nassau pediatric beds are only a few miles farther away, they contended that there was no direct public transportation to them from Queens. (*New York Times*, June 13, 1978)

Richard A. Berman, who made the state's decision in his role as director of the NYSDH's Office of Health Systems Management, said that it had been a "tough call." The plan for the facility had drawn vigorous opposition from Nassau hospital administrators and other health officials in Nassau and Suffolk. North Shore Hospital, which led the battle, had argued that the project was too costly, and would duplicate specialized pediatric facilities that already existed in Nassau, and were underused.

Mr. Berman said, however, that he was impressed by the facts that: (1) state and city health-planning staffs both had recommended approval, (2) public transportation was virtually nonexistent between Nassau and Queens, making travel to Nassau facilities difficult for the poor who live in Queens, and (3) the new facility would be one of quality. "Each new bed costs more money," Berman said. "But I felt the weight of the evidence said if there were a children's facility more available with a wide range of special services, the people would be better served.

"Costs are still under review," Mr. Berman said. "But the state's cost-containment strategy is not aimed at stopping development of all needed programs. Its purpose is to make sure that we selectively and responsibly identify those additional programs that are desirable and affordable." The new facility, whose first three floors would be connected by walkways to LIJ's main building, would be designed for children needing the highest level of care. It would include rooms with sleeping arrangements for mothers, an accredited school for long-term patients, play and recreation areas, pediatric operating rooms, and a spectrum of children's clinics.

Dr. Match's response was, "We are all very elated about it. LIJ first filed an application for the facility in 1972. It has been a lengthy process. But we are pleased that the end results reflect that the system can work…and political and emotional factors were not able to impede the forward movement of the project." North Shore officials declined to comment. (*Newsday*, June 13, 1978)

Even after the approval, an official of an adjacent hospital continued his objections to the project, saying it was "ludicrous" to view the project strictly from a Queens perspective. "Long Island Jewish is clearly designed to serve the Queens-Nassau area, as viewed by its location," he pointed out. "If it was designed to serve the Queens metropolitan area it wouldn't be put in the easternmost tip of Queens in a relatively affluent area. That has got to be a distortion of reality of the highest order. In a day and age when everyone is trying to hold down escalating costs, it is absurd to hide behind that technicality." (*Long Island Daily News*, June 4, 1978)

But, it was too late!

June 19, 1978—Dr. Match reports to the Medical Board that LIJ had received Part I approval from the state for the children's medical center, and that construction would start within a year.

He stated that limitations had been placed on the cost but every attempt would be made to preserve the important components of the original plan. The name of the center (the working name was the Children's Medical Center) would be selected at a later date.

The next issue that had to be faced was the financing of the project. In order to pay for the children's hospital, upon request of the U.S. Public Health Service, Region 2 office, the following LIJ Board of Trustees resolution was duly made, seconded, and adopted:

RESOLVED, that the Board of Trustees of Long Island Jewish-Hillside Medical Center does hereby authorize and approve the filing of an FHA242 mortgage insurance application by this corporation for the purpose of financing and construction with respect to the proposed modernization, construction and alteration projects for Long Island Jewish-Hillside Medical Center. RESOLVED, that the Board of Trustees of Long Island Jewish-Hillside Medical Center does hereby authorize any of the following:

Irving Wharton, Chairman of the Board
Stanley Grey, Treasurer
Robert K. Match, MD, President

To act as its agent in all matters pertaining to approval and construction of the facilities described herein.

The original FHA loan application was for $76 million, $35 million of which was allocated for construction of the children's medical center.

The federal funding program, through which the bulk of the funds would flow, required that we select a reliable construction manager (CM) and secure a guaranteed maximum price (GMP) from the CM. The industry was well aware of this project and, of course, it was considered a desirable one. Carl Morse, of Morse-Diesel (MD), a prominent contractor in New York at the time, had set his sights on the job. He knew several of the most important board members and lobbied them to be the one selected, and he succeeded.

Although he was well aware of the federal requirements (all of which were on paper in a circulated publication), we had significant difficulty in securing the required GMP. It took us over nine months to acquire it, which, of course, added to the overall length of the project. Part of the problem, and this is endemic to the issue of a GMP, was that "the project," in addition to the building of the children's hospital, involved the phased implementation of several subcomponents, for example, a 684-space, multilevel parking garage, a food service plant for the entire LIJ complex, a new emergency generator building, renovations to the boiler plant, and extensive renovations to the LIJ ambulatory care facilities as well as a totally new design and expansion of the surgical operating suite. All this was to take place while LIJ itself remained in full operation. Also, at this time LIJ was running an occupancy of over 100 percent, with patients in beds in corridors, something quite unheard of at the time, especially with low occupancies in many of the other area hospitals.

December 11, 1978—It is reported to the Medical Board that the children's medical center is in the final stages of detailed programming for an FHA application for long-term financing.

The FHA application required LIJ to provide collateral to support the borrowing, with a lien on an income stream. The hospital was not prepared to give the land it owned as collateral because it wanted to reserve it for future collateral. Melvin Ruskin represented the hospital to the FHA, and he was able to negotiate a lien on the footprint of the children's hospital only, and not on any of the other real property. This enabled the hospital to have the full future use of its other real property for collateral, which could be used to fund future expansion. LIJ was pleased at the high level of cooperation shown by the FHA, and by the final outcome.

June 1979—The FHA mortgage awarded to LIJ is $85.58 million to build the children's hospital as well as the other structures previously referred to.

January 1, 1979—Dr. Match reports to the Board of Trustees that a contract for architectural work on the "children's facility" is being negotiated with the Architects Collaborative (TAC), and a discussion is held about Morse-Diesel acting as the construction manager.

April 19, 1979—A report to the Medical Board indicates approval for the Part II Application—all systems are go!

The architects were on board and designs were scheduled for completion by July 1979. Construction was to begin about April 1, 1980, with some preliminary work starting in November 1979.

May 18, 1980—Groundbreaking ceremony is held for the children's hospital.

But...even after the groundbreaking, the project faced yet one more stormy Board of Trustees meeting in September 1980. When William Mack reported that the expected GMP was $2.3 million above the amount processed for the mortgage, the last shot at preventing the children's hospital from being built was fired unsuccessfully by a vocal board member. (See Chapter 6.) After a heated debate, the day was saved by Irving Wharton and Gus Berne, who made a motion that the board indicate its full accord to go ahead with the plans for the construction of the children's hospital. The motion was seconded and carried, with all trustees present, and only one voting nay.

In the end, the LIJ board proved to be united. The hard work of the LIJ staff with the regulatory authorities, led by Dr. Match, and the rationale and program development by the professional staff, led by me, formed the basis of the state's approval. The Children's Medical Fund of New York (CMF) aroused the community and caught the allegiance of the local legislators, and the state gave in. It was a victory that had earlier seemed impossible. All of the hours of courting community support, the endless cups of coffee poured and cakes made, the enormous amount of time spent coordinating fundraisers, selling lollipops, and speaking with anybody and everybody, had all paid off. The children's hospital was going to be built. The dream of providing children with medical care in physical surroundings that would help them feel safe, comfortable, and secure, provided by specialized physicians who understood their own particular needs, was no longer a dream. It was now to be a reality!

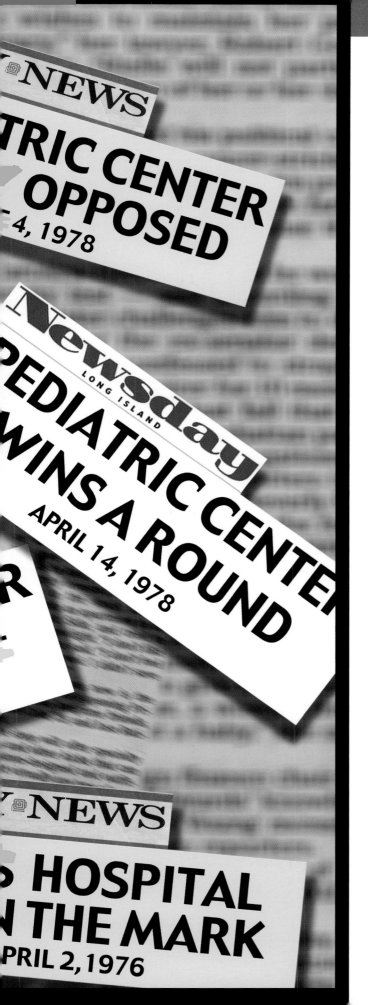

NEWS

TRIC CENTER
OPPOSED
— 4, 1978

Newsday
LONG ISLAND

PEDIATRIC CENTE
WINS A ROUND
APRIL 14, 1978

NEWS

HOSPITAL
N THE MARK
PRIL 2, 1976

"WE DON'T NEED IT AND WE DON'T WANT IT!"

THE PUBLIC CONTROVERSY

The children's hospital created a storm of controversy. People who were afraid of change—medical and "lay" people—objected loudly, in the political arena and in the press.

While we struggled to win the necessary approvals, the debate raged. But it didn't stop us. We established facts and collected data to prove the need for the children's hospital. We addressed consumer groups throughout Long Island for over a decade and we testified before agency after agency created by bureaucratic organizations. Many were newly created during the long period that we were seeking approval. We even took our fight to the office of the governor of New York.

The opposition was angry, fierce, and persistent. The story was followed closely by the press in the local papers, Newsday, even the New York Times. It was on local and national television. The debate went on from 1971 to 1983, when the hospital opened its doors, and even into the first few years following its opening.

There were many professionals, who should have known better, who testified against its establishment before the Queens and New York City Health System Agency (HSA). These included the chairmen of pediat-

Newspaper headlines in the late 1970s and early 1980s.

rics of medical schools in New York City and hospital representatives and pediatricians who were scared that an institution of this nature would threaten their very livelihood. Objections also came from within—certain board members, departmental chairmen, and other professionals who feared competition from a children's hospital for LIJ's limited resources. They didn't understand (although they were told over and over) that children's hospitals raise the standard of pediatric practice in the community and provide important aid to children in the region. Like ostriches with their heads in the sand, they remained willfully ignorant of the fact that almost every large city in the western world boasted at least one if not two children's hospitals, and many had been in existence for over a century.

> "The children's medical center is a product of our caring...and of a tremendous indication of the need in Queens for a center to take care of children who can't be taken care of in any other facility in the county."
>
> Irving Wharton
> Chairman of the Board
> Long Island Jewish-Hillside Medical Center
> *Newsday*, May 1, 1978

The controversy over the new 150-bed children's hospital had split health officials on both sides of the Queens-Nassau County line, and state officials conceded that the issue was an exceedingly difficult one to resolve because of the strong political pressure both sides exerted. There were many who were opposed to the project who publicly predicted failure for the children's hospital.

On November 12, 1971, an article entitled "Medical Center to Serve Children to be built on LI [Long Island]," was published in the *New York Times*. In the early to mid-seventies, many more articles were printed, mostly containing general information about the children's hospital, the plans, and the supporting organizations and their fundraising activities. This generally placid period proved, however, to be the calm before the storm.

The announcement of the New York State Health Department's approval of Part I of the CON application for the creation of Long Island's first children's hospital in the *New York Times* on December 21, 1974, summed up the opposition to the project:

"Children's Hospital Planned on Island" by David A. Andelman, *NY Times*, December 21, 1974

> *NEW HYDE PARK—The State Health Department has approved the creation of Long Island's first children's medical center. It is to be built and operated by Long Island Jewish-Hillside Medical Center on its grounds here.*
>
> *The center, estimated to cost $25 million, is expected to be completed within five years, according to Dr. Robert K. Match, executive vice president and director of Long Island Jewish, and will be the first comprehensive center for the treatment of children in Queens and Long Island.*
>
> *Its creation, however, has not been without controversy, even some hesitant opposition although it is not related to the hospital's disputed proposal for its South Shore Division in Lawrence.*
>
> *With the falling birth rate, hospitals throughout the region, and the nation, have also found sharply dropping occupancy rates in their pediatric units. Many are contemplating closing pediatric wards and the prospect for the future is a continuation of such trends.*
>
> *"There was some unofficial opposition from some hospitals in the region who were concerned about their own pediatric occupancy," said Dr. Jack C. Haldeman, president of the Health and Hospital Planning Council of Southern New York, which nevertheless approved the facility.*

Several Changes Made

The approval did not come, however, before the hospital submitted several substantive changes in plans for the new facility at the request of the council.

Now, the children's medical center, while maintaining a separate entrance that one state official conceded "will help them raise money," will be connected with Long Island Jewish on every floor—sharing such services as x-ray and laboratory facilities, operating rooms and other functions with the main hospital.

"We insisted that they integrate the children's facility with Long Island Jewish in such a way that if at some future date, that many beds were not needed, they could be converted to medical-surgical beds for adults," Dr. Haldeman said.

"Children's hospitals all over the country are in trouble—those that are standing on their own," Dr. Haldeman added. "Unless they are integrated with a general hospital, they are in very bad shape."

In Queens, a state official said, occupancy rates for many hospitals' pediatrics units are hovering between 50 to 60 percent—substantially below the 70 percent that the state requires be maintained for efficiency of operation. As a result, some hospitals are reportedly considering closing pediatric beds.

Nevertheless, Dr. Haldeman said that the state council decided to approve the Long Island Jewish facility because "first rate centers such as this are needed. We expect it to become a referral center for all of Long Island and Queens."

And, he added, the increase in total beds at the hospital will be minimal since 15 of the 150 beds will be used for psychiatric care of adolescents and 15 for long-term medical care. In addition, 97 existing pediatric beds in the main hospital will be closed when the new facility opens.

Long Island Jewish officials are also concerned about raising $25 million given the present state of the economy. Already some $3 million in pledges and cash have been collected and Dr. Match said that 1975 would be devoted to fundraising with ground broken possibly in 1976.

But Dr. Philip Lanzkowsky, chairman of pediatrics at Long Island Jewish, who is expected to head the new center, said that the need for such a children's hospital is, in fact, immediate.

"For children requiring complex surgery or suffering from severe medical diseases, this center is essential," Dr. Lanzkowsky said. "There are many conditions that the primary doctor and an ordinary community hospital simply cannot handle."

Fast-forward ten years

"The Schneider Children's Hospital has an occupancy rate ranging from 95 percent to a little over 100 percent. It is consistently being utilized to its maximum and beyond as shown on a flowchart in the conference room of the hospital."

Philip Lanzkowsky, MD
Chairman of Pediatrics LIJMC

Great Neck News, February 25, 1988

The ruckus over the building of a children's hospital reverberated throughout the community, as reported in the Rockaway Journal on December 31, 1974. People in the Rockaways (Queens County) thought they would be deprived of pediatric services as a result of the new children's hospital. At the time, LIJ was planning to purchase the St. John's Hospital in Far Rockaway and to move it to a new facility to be constructed in the Lawrence area of Nassau County.

South Shore To Lose All Pediatric Beds

Dr. Lanzkowsky reassured the community that Pediatrics at the South Shore would take on a "new direction," that "although the pediatric hospital bed section in the Far Rockaway facility will be terminated when the Children's Medical Center is built, there will still be full out-patient care, emergency pediatric care and specialty clinics at the South Shore Division in Far Rockaway," stressed Dr. Lanzkowsky.

The State Health Commissioner's office requires the closure of the present 97 pediatric beds in New Hyde Park. The South Shore Division, if still under LIJ, which now has 24 pediatric hospital beds, would be required by the City and State to close that division, and the 24 beds would then be transferred and included into the 150 bed Children's Medical Center complex.

"The new building is 4 or 5 years down the pike," explained Dr. Lanzkowsky, who hails from South Africa. At the time that the CMC (Children's Medical Center) is completed, then, the Far Rockaway pediatrics hospital beds will close down. Until then, they will function as long as LIJ operates the hospital in Far Rockaway.

The CMC will not be competing with local hospitals. It will ensure a "major team approach" to esoteric problems in the field of pediatric medicine.

Various malignancies in children would necessitate calling in specialists in pediatric radiology, pediatric surgery, pediatric neurology, explained a hospital spokesman. This type of medical specialist is available in a team situation in a pediatric hospital. Children who have leukemia, hemolytic anemia, would need a radioisotope laboratory. Cleft palate defects would be treated by ten different pediatric specialists at a Children's Hospital Center.

Local hospital pediatric departments will be consulting with the regional CMC for treatment of unusual diseases when the new facility is constructed. The CMC began and has gained impetus through active community support in the South Shore of Long Island. The many active women's auxiliaries have attracted large groups of idealistic young women, who have raised funds through various activities. It was affiliated with the Long Island Jewish Medical Center in 1971.

Rockaway Journal, *December 31, 1974*

In 1978, with state approval imminent, the controversy really heated up.

A prominent chairman of pediatrics on Long Island said the children's hospital was a hoax. (*Newsday*, May 1, 1978). A spokesperson for Flushing Hospital said that his institution was opposed to the plan because it would "lead to an excess of beds in Queens." Flushing Hospital was completing a $28 million construction and rehabilitation project that included thirty pediatric beds and twenty premature-baby beds. Administrators were worried that patients who would have gone to their hospital would now go to the children's medical center. Major Karl Nelson, associate director of Booth Memorial Hospital in Central Queens (presently called New York Hospital of Queens), said, "Although the beds were designed to handle children who need specialized care, the children's hospital may attract children who can be cared for at existing facilities." But then he added, "The Borough of Queens needs this technical improvement in pediatric care. The level of pediatric care in this borough is poor as a rule, and this kind of care is needed. Long Island Jewish has the medical and scientific experts to do it." (*Daily News*, June 4, 1978)

The opposition came almost entirely from the general medical community, predominantly from the doctors and hospitals on Long Island, although the Manhattan hospitals and medical schools were not silent. Everyone had an opinion, and many were not very positive. The fundraising and publicity campaign waged by the Children's Medical Center Fund of New York (CMF) contributed to the controversy. Its underlying message was that existing specialized facilities and specialized medical and surgical services for children in the area were inadequate and not specific to the needs of children. The Nassau County Medical Society labeled the CMF campaign an "insult to the integrity and dedication of hundreds of local pediatricians." The Nassau-Suffolk Hospital Council (NSHC) strongly protested.

Carol M. McCarthy, executive vice president of NSHC, sent a letter to Martin Lifton, president of the Men's Division of CMF, dated June 27, 1977, that stated, "Inflammatory and misleading statements have been made to support the establishment of 150 beds at the center," and, further, "Needless apprehension and fear are created in our area's parents and children." She firmly requested that they alter their approach in future public relations campaigns (See page 166).

CMF founder Judge Bertram Harnett responded strongly to this letter. He said that it paid no attention to the facts, and emphasized

Pediatric fund seen as affront to other hospitals

Long Island Daily News
June 4, 1978

that LIJ was located in Queens County and therefore not a member of NSHC. He went on to say that 250 pediatric beds had been closed in Queens, and the resultant pediatric burden on LIJ was particularly heavy since it was the only hospital in the area providing any level of tertiary care for children. Representatives of the NSHC had declined to attend the planning hearings for the proposed children's medical center, even after a formal invitation had been issued. "You overlook the central fact entirely—that of the public interest," Judge Harnett stated in his response. "While there are some fine pediatric facilities in this region, there remains a need for more and better tertiary care. There are better ways to treat children. Parents know that. Do you seriously believe that they have worked...by the thousands for many years because of 'public relations'?" He concluded, "This is no place for self-compliment, or complacency, or the acting out of antagonisms, or petty jealousies. You are a hospital council, not a business association. You should not be on the sidelines, or worse, hindering those trying to do something constructive. Join with us in our effort for enhanced regional tertiary pediatric care. The bruised egos will heal easier than desperately ill children."

Surrounding hospitals blasted the CMF, asserting that it had "unfortunately gone so far as to plant significant doubts in the minds of parents in the Long Island region, with respect to the availability of comprehensive pediatric services." (*Daily News*, June 4, 1978) In response, LIJ cited the local and state planning and health agencies that had already approved the project as objective evidence of the need for a children's hospital. Frankly, the trustees and I were sometimes uncomfortable with the CMF's aggressive approach. It was often provocative and inflammatory, straying from what a member of the medical profession or a hospital could say in public.

NASSAU – SUFFOLK HOSPITAL COUNCIL, INC.

560 BROADHOLLOW ROAD
MELVILLE, NEW YORK 11746
(516) 752-1355

June 27, 1977

Mr. Martin Lifton
Sterling Company
41 East 42nd Street
New York, New York 10017

Dear Mr. Lifton:

The Board of Trustees of the Nassau-Suffolk Hospital Council, representing the twenty not-for-profit hospitals in the bi-county area strongly protest the recent publicity on behalf of the Children's Medical Center. Inflammatory and misleading statements have been made to support the establishment of 150 beds at the center. Such statements as "if we cannot get those beds...there will be children...who will die" ignore the many fine medical institutions on Long Island with excellent and available pediatric facilities, including neonatal and pediatric intensive care units. Needless apprehension and fear are created in our area's parents and children.

We are cognizant of the sensitivity to the problems related to obtaining State approval for projects deemed necessary and appropriate by a facility and its community. We are also aware of the value of general public support in attempting to have the State Hospital Review and Planning Council and Commissioner Whalen alter an earlier decision. However, neither fact is sufficient justification for the present public relations campaign. We firmly request that you alter your approach and base future media efforts on supportable fact and responsible statements.

We will be discussing this matter once again at the next meeting of the Hospital Council Board. Please let me know by July 31 of changes in approach you plan to implement.

Sincerely,

Carol M. McCarthy
Executive Vice President

CMM/gpw

An organization to promote and coordinate cooperative activities of its membership.

A particularly bitter battle was waged by hospitals in Nassau County in close proximity to LIJ. One of the hospitals hired a bus to take people, including their employees, to Albany to oppose the building of the children's hospital. Many of their employees collected signatures in petition against the hospital being built at railroad stations and at bus stops. While Long Island Jewish, which was a major medical center affiliated with the Federation of Jewish Philanthropies of New York, sought to bring strong political pressure on all levels of government to defend its pediatric expansion, Nassau hospitals repeatedly attacked the project as unneeded. One hospital official called the new facility a "medical absurdity" and contended that there were empty pediatric beds at several Nassau County hospitals within several miles of LIJ. (*New York Times*, June 13, 1978) At that time, North Shore Hospital was maintaining an occupancy rate of only about 82 percent, while LIJ generally had a census over 100 percent. Nassau County hospital officials were concerned about additional beds for pediatrics being built in close proximity to the Queens-Nassau border, and one official viewed the proposed children's hospital as providing services that would be duplicative. (*Newsday*, May 1, 1978) Doctors and hospital officials in Nassau and Suffolk Counties and the five boroughs were adamant in their determination to stop the project. (*Long Island Daily News*, June 4, 1978) We had come to an impasse.

In order to resolve this dispute, move forward with the building of a children's hospital, and achieve true regionalization, I recommended to some members of the LIJ Board of Trustees that we offer the top floor of the children's hospital to North Shore University Hospital for its department of pediatrics. If looks could kill, I would have been dead! On this occasion, and at many other times during the struggle to get the hospital approved, I nearly was. This was not the first or the last time an idea of mine was met with ridicule and even hostility. It wasn't easy to swallow, but I remained firmly convinced of the advantages a children's hospital would provide for children and determined to fight to the end. My only consistently reliable allies were Judge Harnett and Robert K. Match, MD, president of LIJ.

The arguments were becoming even more vocal and passionate. Smear campaigns moved away from the basic issue and became personal attacks on the individuals promoting the building of a children's hospital.

An executive vice president of one of the Nassau hospitals publicly called Dr. Match a "bum," and said that I (Lanzkowsky) was "another guy I'd like to punch through the walls." Questions were raised about LIJ's integrity; it was accused of falsifying occupancy figures and deceiving the public. The facts were that data produced by LIJ were official verified PAS data submitted by all hospitals in a uniform manner to the State. "The crux of the problem," a certain hospital official said, "is that LIJ has expansionist designs." (*Newsday*, May 1, 1978) Suspicion of the motives on both sides made any cooperation between LIJ and its neighboring institutions impossible.

The LIJ treatment center for drug users in a church on Northern Boulevard in Manhasset, enlargement of the cardiac program at LIJ, the

> "Problems occur where one institution does something that is in direct conflict with the other institution's plans and goals."
>
> Lawrence Sherr, MD
> Chief of Medicine
> North Shore University Hospital
>
> *Newsday*, June 14, 1978

> "Waste and inefficiency are the unavoidable by-products of a failure to work cooperatively. I tell you there must be waste by not having joint comprehensive planning."
>
> Judge Sol Wachtler
> State Court of Appeals
> LIJ Trustee
> NSUH Associate Trustee
>
> *Newsday*, June 14, 1978

development of a South Shore division in the Five Towns area, LIJ's purchase of the Manhasset Medical Center on Northern Boulevard—these LIJ projects were also subject to heated opposition from surrounding hospitals. But the most publicized dispute of all (and the one at the apex of the controversy) was the development of the children's hospital.

The location of LIJ, on the Queens-Nassau border in New Hyde Park, was a complicating factor. It is officially regarded as a New York City health resource and falls within the planning jurisdiction of the federally funded Health System Agency (HSA) of New York City. The opposition's point was that LIJ was emerging as the regional center for Queens County and should continue to do that, and that Nassau hospitals should play a similar role for Nassau County.

There should be parallel development of the hospitals in the two counties, and programs could not merge. (*Newsday,* May 1, 1978) In the absence of rational regionalization of medical services by government agencies, there was no one single government agency to provide leadership or authority in this area.

Dr. Match and the LIJ Board of Trustees, however, viewed the geographic location of LIJ on the Queens-Nassau border as an accident of history and not as the product of careful planning of the location of the

> "They view Nassau as their turf, but sick people are sick people. They come to us not only from Nassau and Suffolk.. North Shore [hospital] must accept the fact that there is lebensraum (living space) for both of us."
>
> Irving L. Wharton
> Chairman
> Board of Trustees LIJ
>
> *Newsday,* June 14, 1978

> "Geographic proximity of the two hospitals is an example of what happens without integrated regional planning. Because these major hospitals are not logically spaced apart, travel for specialized care has been made more difficult for patients from Western Queens, Southern Nassau and Suffolk Counties."
>
> Thomas Cranshaw
> Nassau-Suffolk HSA
>
> *Newsday,* June 14, 1978

hospital in relationship to other hospitals in Queens and Nassau Counties. They maintained that county lines drawn to delineate separate political jurisdictions presented no barrier to access. In 1976 approximately 40 percent of pediatric admissions, 20 percent of neonatal admissions, and 50 percent of adolescent admissions to LIJ had come from Nassau and Suffolk Counties. The argument of geographic restriction did not hold water.

From the *Long Island Daily News,* June 4, 1978:

"There will be a tremendous amount of money spent on something people say is ridiculous," said Dr. Mervin Silverberg, director of pediatrics at North Shore. "A number of institutions are making major investments in this area. For instance, the Nassau County Medical Center is planning to open a 33-bed psychiatric adolescent center."

He pointed out that last fall his hospital spent money to reconstruct the prenatal area and that Nassau Hospital in Mineola is now establishing itself as a specialist in child care along with Long Island Jewish, North Shore and the Nassau County Medical Center—all of which are within a 10-mile radius.

"The local communities can go on ego trips and have nice health temples but somebody has to say that with limited health resources we have to be careful in our planning because everybody is asking for money," Silverberg said.

Asked why all of the local and state organizations have thus far approved this project, Silverberg said it must have been as a result of "politicizing because there is no way they could have sold it on need."

FINANCIAL ISSUES

Finances became the next front in this battle. Certain hospital officials called the proposed children's hospital a "travesty on cost containment." (*Newsday*, May 1, 1978) The Nassau-Suffolk Hospital Council, a group of twenty nonprofit hospitals on Long Island, pointed out that the estimated construction cost was $35 million. "That is $880,377 per bed. Such large expenditures can only be justified if there is a clear determination that access to and quality of care would be adversely affected if a project is not approved." It continued, "Press releases...have insinuated that such is the case, that present facilities are inadequate. The Nassau-Suffolk not-for-profit hospitals bring the fallacy of these statements to your attention..."

In an attempt to respond to these comments, Dr. Match indicated that the project would add only $16 a day to the bill of every patient admitted to LIJ, which would be paid by Blue Cross, Medicaid, and Medicare. He said he had been assured that Blue Cross rates would not be affected by the added cost because the $16 would be spread out among all nine million subscribers.

And then the Nassau-Suffolk Hospital Council gave this scary warning: "Approval of the project will place an additional strain on existing expensive facilities." Further, if the project got the go-ahead, Queens health officials who approved it "...may well find that you have placed too many eggs in one basket, that too few dollars remain to meet the urgent modernization, renovation and equipment needs of the remaining health care institution in their Health System Agency region." (*Long Island Daily News*, June 4, 1978)

All the rhetoric failed to take into account that not all beds are the same. A children's hospital requires specialized pediatric beds, including state-of-the-art critical-care beds, neonatal critical-care beds, psychiatric beds, and beds for rehabilitation. The critics also failed to appreciate that we weren't just talking about beds: there would be much-needed ambulatory space—space, in fact, occupying almost 40 percent of the hospital. This would include clinics to accommodate 40,000 outpatient visits per year, a cardiac catheterization laboratory, an ambulatory chemotherapy unit, and laboratories for endoscopy and pulmonary function testing. This was innovative and counter to the financial interests of LIJ (hospital reimbursement is driven by its bed occupancy) and not even on the radar screen of the regulators. I strongly believed that all patients should be treated in the same dignified facilities by the same physicians and nursing staff irrespective of their insurance coverage—privately insured, Medicaid, and uninsured. This would do away with the traditional clinic and two-tier system of medical care. This was a bold and provocative stance in the 70s. The naysayers simply failed to understand what a children's hospital was all about. As medical science progressed, I argued, more and more children would be treated in the ambulatory arena rather than being admitted. The prediction was correct because the hospital, built for 40,000 ambulatory visits, twenty-five years later has close on 160,000 ambulatory visits annually. This improved care, in the long run, reduced the trauma of admission, reduced expenses and meant that children were treated in a more suitable environment. For most, my logic fell on deaf ears.

On June 4, 1978, Stuart Ain reported as follows in the *Long Island Daily News*:

It (the children's hospital) could very well signal the beginning of the end for pediatric units at 25 Long Island hospitals and that is why officials at most of these hospitals are holding their breath as they *await the decision from Albany on the fate of the $35 million pediatric center at the Long Island Jewish-Hillside Medical Center in New Hyde Park.*

Long Island doctors and hospitals view the planned 150-bed facility as one that will act as a magnet for all pediatric cases in the entire metropolitan area.

With such a dynamic facility straddling the Nassau-Queens border, Nassau and Suffolk county hospital officials believe their own facilities will be forced to eliminate beds.

In fact, the process of patient migration to LIJ had already begun. LIJ had already negotiated agreements with the majority of hospitals in Queens to utilize LIJ as their regional resource for their pediatric patients, resulting in the closure of over 250 pediatric beds in Queens. A federal health planner contended that there was a justified need for highly specialized pediatric beds in Queens, and LIJ was the only area medical center with the sophisticated medical resources to accommodate them.

In an act of desperation, a hospital official made the following public appeal:

"You are giving this plum to an institution that has not proven itself. This thing is inappropriate, not right, and not fair. Somebody has to blow the whistle." (*Newsday,* May 1, 1978)

While no ground was broken, the talk continued:

The first solid plans for a children's medical center for the metropolitan New York City area were disclosed recently at Long Island Jewish-Hillside Medical enter, New Hyde Park, New York. The new health facility, exclusively for children, will contain 150 beds and will be built at a cost of $25 to $30 million. Planning and fund raising will

be a joint effort of the Children's Medical Center of New York Fund, Inc. and Long Island Jewish-Hillside Medical Center. The new facility will be built adjacent to the present Center in New Hyde Park. Within an 8 mile radius of the new facility live 800,000 children under 19 years of age. In addition, children of the broader, tri-state region (New York, New Jersey and Connecticut) will rely on the new center for sophisticated medical services that local community hospitals cannot provide. The new facility will contain beds for intensive care, general pediatric use, neonatal care, psychiatric crises and chronic care. Included among special features of the Center will be sleepover accommodations for parents, day care center for siblings and an accredited school for children hospitalized for extended periods. More than 40 full-time physicians will be on the Center's staff. Philip Lanzkowsky is Chairman, Department of Pediatrics, and Robert K. Match is President, Long Island Jewish.

Pediatric World News, Vol 14, No 12, 1976

To my knowledge, no other hospital issue had ever prompted such heated debate. "It has opened up a hornet's nest among physicians," said Carl Pochedly, MD, of Nassau County Medical Center. "One could only guess the remarks passed in private conversations, by some of the statements made in public hearings." (*Newsday,* May 1, 1978)

Newsday took a strong opposing stand throughout the controversy. In an article published on May 3, 1978 (before the final approval to build the children's medical center), once again it questioned the wisdom of building a new hospital for children.

"Why a New Hospital When Beds Are Empty?"
Newsday, Garden City, NY, May 3, 1978

Q. You have two hospitals within three miles of each other. Both offer first-rate medical care for children. Hospital A's pediatric section is badly overcrowded. Hospital B's has plenty of unused space. What do you do?

A. Expand Hospital A's pediatric services more than 50 per cent by building a new children's medical center, which will cost $35 million and increase per-day rates for all Hospital patients by $16. Illogical?

Not to the sponsors of the proposed children's facility at Long Island Jewish-Hillside Medical, Center. They've been working on the project for 16 years. They've raised $6 million in private contributions for it. They've won official approval from several key health-planning agencies. And they're hoping that the state's Hospital Review and Planning Council, which ordered the plan scaled down early last year, will endorse it in full tomorrow.

Newsday hopes the council will make a different decision. Neither the high professional reputation of LIJ-Hillside nor the sponsors' admirable concern for quality care is in question. The prime issue, in a period of intense public anxiety about the cost of health services, is simply this: Is the new Queens center really needed?

We don't think so. Less than three miles from LIJ-Hillside is North Shore University Hospital in Manhasset, with a general pediatric bed occupancy rate of 82 percent. The rate at Nassau County Medical Center in East Meadow, nine miles or so from LIJ-Hillside, is still lower at 69 per cent. By 1982, the Island is expected to have a surplus of 216 pediatric beds. To the west are outstanding Manhattan hospitals,

some more easily accessible from Queens than LIJ-Hillside. Newsday science editor David Zimmerman has reported these facts in detail lately. They do not justify a new, 150-bed, three-story children's hospital at LIJ-Hillside or the $29 million federal loan required to construct it. Indeed, there are persuasive arguments against the project.

Actually, the conflict obscured many instances of inter-county sharing. There was already a significant exchange of young patients between Queens and Nassau. In 1976, of the children admitted to LIJ, 31 percent came from Nassau, while North Shore evidently got about 25 percent of its admissions from Queens. The idea of battling for admissions or erecting barricades at the border was ludicrous. Even the location of LIJ right on the Queens-Nassau line suggested many opportunities for regional health service balancing, a kind of official osmosis in which county lines would be easily penetrated, and concentrations of young patients could reach comparable levels in pediatric facilities.

After the project was approved in June 1978, it continued to be bitterly criticized by the Nassau County hospital officials, who described it as a "waste of resources" and a threat to their own pediatric services. One of the most outspoken critics of the new children's hospital from a neighboring hospital said: "Despite the fact that the State approved it, nobody will ever convince me that the new addition makes any sense at all. When push comes to shove, the bottom line of this entire affair is that 27 beds will cost a total of $35 million." He also said, "How can anyone justify that kind of expense when everyone else is trying to contain health costs?"

But LIJ could and did justify the cost of building a children's hospital. Small hospitals in the area could not afford pediatric specialists because they did not have the patient base to support specialty care. If LIJ were going to provide the children of Queens, Nassau, and Suffolk with the pediatric medical care they needed, it needed a facility large enough to justify the expenses and provide the room to offer multidisciplinary care. LIJ didn't spend $35 million on an addition; it spent $35 million on a state-of-the-art medical facility just for children, one they and their families desperately needed; a facility that housed the best pediatric specialists in the area; a facility that would offer the kind of medical expertise and care that once was available only to adults.

THE NAME GAME

Controversy also raged over the mere name of the facility. From early on, many professionals, most hospitals on Long Island and in Manhattan and the Nassau-Suffolk Hospital Council, were opposed to naming the hospital the Children's Medical Center of New York.

Children's Medical Center of New York had been the "official" name for the children's hospital starting way back in the sixties, when it was no more than a dream shared by a few visionary individuals. Other area facilities thought that the name suggested that we held a preeminent position among the other pediatric centers nearby. Babies Hospital of Columbia Presbyterian even threatened to sue LIJ if the new hospital was named the Children's Medical Center of New York, and argued that use of that name impugned Babies Hospital, which they viewed as a children's hospital in New York.

Similar reactions came from Queens and Nassau hospital officials. One official said it suggested that it was the ultimate facility for specialized care. "It tends to put comparable institutions at a lower status," he said, "and it might seriously affect our occupancy and recruitment of professional staff." (*Newsday*, May 1 1978)

In the same article, I was quoted as saying, "Patients should have the freedom to go to the hospital they think gives them the best care." The logic for the objection to the name escaped me, I reportedly said. "People go for quality. They are not swayed by names." In an effort to placate the opposition, having heard some unofficial rumblings by the state, LIJ agreed not to use the name Children's Medical Center of New York but instead to refer to the putative hospital as the Children's Medical Center.

Back in 1974, at a June meeting of the Joint Conference Committee of the Board of Trustees of LIJ, Dr. Match had stated that from its inception the children's hospital concept had threatened many hospitals and pediatricians in the area, but that the concept had gained greater acceptance from the reviewing bodies because it did not call for any significant increase in general pediatric beds, but called instead for the creation of specialized-care beds lacking in the area. Dr. Match suggested that other hospitals' opposition was in large measure to the use of the proposed name.

Fast-forward to 1983. At its annual dinner dance, LIJ announced that the children's hospital was to be named Schneider Children's Hospital in honor of Helen and Irving Schneider. Mr. Schneider, who was vice chairman of the LIJ Board of Trustees, was the evening's guest of honor. Martin C. Barell, then chairman of the LIJ board, described Mr. Schneider as a "forceful influence in bringing the idea of a pediatric hospital to fruition." Now, that was interesting because when the idea of building a children's hospital was first proposed, Irving Schneider was totally against it. Subsequently, he had made the most substantial contribution of any single individual during the long and complex fundraising process.

WILL IT EVER END?

It's hard to believe, but even during the construction, the controversy continued.

New Hospital Nears Finish Amid Debate

By Merle English

As workers put the finishing touches on a $50-million, 150-bed Children's Hospital that Long Island Jewish-Hillside Medical Center is building near the Nassau-Queens border, experts are debating whether the new facility will result in an oversupply of pediatric beds in the area. Daniel McGowan, executive director of the Nassau-Suffolk Health System Agency, said last week that Nassau already has more pediatric beds than it needs. Although Children's Hospital is considered to be a New York City facility, its proximity to Nassau is expected to draw patients from that county. "We are calling for fewer pediatric beds," McGowan said. "We're not pushing to close beds, but we would not mind if some of the pediatric beds closed or were converted." He said Nassau has 368 pediatric beds but need only 315. Western Suffolk, with 252 pediatric beds, also has an adequate supply, according to McGowan, because only 245 are needed. He said the East End, with 30 pediatric beds, needs three more. But Dr.

John Partin, chairman of the pediatrics department at the State University at Stony Brook, said there is "a major deficit" in the quality of care that children in the Queens-Nassau-Suffolk area are receiving. He called for a 150-bed children's hospital at Stony Brook. He said LIJ's Children's Hospital "perched on the border between Queens and Nassau," would need 200 more beds to adequately serve a population of 4 million. The debate over the need for pediatric beds comes at a time when a shortage of general-care beds is being reported at many hospitals on Long Island. Officials at Long Island Jewish defend the need for their Children's Hospital, which is scheduled to open in October. They said that although it primarily would serve Nassau and Queens, it also would serve Suffolk and other sections of the metropolitan area. Philip Lanzkowsky, chairman of the pediatrics department who will be chief of staff of the Children's Hospital, said LIJ's existing 97-bed pediatrics division was "running at close to 100 per cent occupancy." Dr. Partin, the Stony Brook official, questioned whether LIJ's Children's Hospital actually will serve Suffolk. "How far do we expect people to travel when, increasingly, both parents are working?" he asked. University Hospital at Stony Brook has 30 pediatric beds and has been approved for 20 more, McGowan said. Officials at LIJ said the new Children's Hospital would handle pediatric treatment, training and research. The five-story cement and glass structure will serve newborns and children up to 18 years old. Among its features will be:

• More than 60 pediatric residents, making it the second largest training program in the state, and more than 100 attending pediatricians. In addition, 400 new employees, including doctors and nurses are being hired to staff it.

• A public school for kindergarten through 12th grade staffed by two full-time teachers and closed circuit TV presenting educational programs.

Newsday, August 7, 1983

In response to this article, Dr. Match sent the following letter to *Newsday*:

With the dedication of the new Schneider Children's Hospital of the Long Island Jewish Medical Center scheduled for September 25, it is difficult to understand why Newsday would headline an issue that has been resolved for several years. In the Aug. 7 Newsday, you highlight negative attitudes about the new pediatric beds the Children's Hospital is bringing to Long Island rather than examining the facility and how it will serve our population ("New Hospital Nears Finish Amid Debate").

You surely know that there was a complex system of approvals and proof of need before the first shovelful of earth could be turned. The Nassau-Suffolk Health System Agency, along with its New York City counterpart and the New York State Department of Health, all gave official approval for this 150-bed children's hospital. No hospital can be constructed today without thorough investigations proving need for the facility via careful documentation.

Building a hospital that is exclusively for children is very different from simply adding pediatric beds. It will serve a special population in need of tertiary care. With a full-time staff of pediatric specialists in every major discipline, a children's hospital stands as a resource for the entire community: its doctors, its families and its local hospitals.

The Schneider Children's Hospital is a place that will care for the most seriously sick children—those with cancer, with heart and other congenital problems, with chronic disease and with acute psychiatric problems.

Surely you must be aware of the fact that nowhere in the entire metropolitan region is there a hospital offering in-depth, total pediatric care in an environment designed specifically for children. There are parents on Long Island who travel to Boston and Philadelphia for this kind of specialized service.

Another vital component of the Schneider Children's Hospital will be its extensive teaching and research. It is essential that pediatricians in the area have ongoing educational programs conveniently available to keep them in touch with all that is new in their field.

The new Schneider Children's Hospital answers a proven need and is a real contribution to progress on Long Island.

Dr. Match's response was an eloquent one. But even more eloquent was that of Maria Polsone of Holbrook, dated August 26, 1983:

I was prompted to write this letter after reading the article on the new children's hospital to be opened at the Long Island Jewish-Hillside.Medical Center. Daniel McGowan, executive director of Nassau-Suffolk Health System Agency, stated: "Nassau already has more pediatric beds than it needs." I was astonished by this statement, having just had my infant daughter recently hospitalized for six days at Long Island Jewish. Even though she was just five months old, there was no crib available for her in the nursery. She was admitted and we spent our first night at LIJ in the hall along with seven other pediatric patients, their mothers or fathers sleeping alongside their children in chairs. Our daughter finally did receive a room at 5 PM the next day.

For six days I saw this picture repeated night after night. Although our daughter received excellent care from the dedicated nurses, there was overcrowding—far above 100 per percent occupancy, which I am told is a normal occurrence.

The trauma of having a child hospitalized, whether it be for a long stay or a short stay, can certainly be eased by having beds available and a facility geared entirely to the needs of the small patient and his or her family.

I do hope McGowan never has to experience having one of his children hospitalized and discovering, contrary to his opinion, that there is, indeed, "no room at the inn."

In 1991, the very same Daniel McGowan, now head of planning at LIJ, came to me with Jerrold Hirsch, PhD, a member of his staff, to inform me that the region had a shortage of neonatal intensive care beds as determined by the New York State Health Department. Would I increase the neonatal beds at the children's hospital from the original forty to forty-four beds? Mr. McGowan had changed his opinion about the need for beds since 1983, when he was executive director of the Nassau-Suffolk Health System Agency.

Newsday wasn't giving up. As late as September 21, 1983, David Zimmerman, the Newsday science writer, posed the question again: "Why is there a need for a hospital exclusively for children?"

I responded as follows:

"Children generally get short shrift in a general hospital. It is difficult to deal with geriatric patients one minute and pediatric patients the next. Most radiologists don't have the time or patience to wait for a child to stop screaming. If adults have emergencies they are often pushed in to the OR (operating room) ahead of children. So children are often kept late in the day, which is psychologically traumatic and medically undesirable. The difference between the new children's hospital and our old pediatric ward is the difference between providing optimum care and just getting by." In order to assuage the fears of pediatricians and surrounding community hospitals I said: "It is not designed to take care of cases presently being taken care of by pediatricians in their offices. It is designed to take care of highly specialized pathology in medicine, surgery, psychiatry and dentistry."

But while they were tearing us down, the hospital was going up. *Newsday* wrote in September 1983:

Once built many directors of smaller hospitals on Long Island felt that the center will eliminate trips to major pediatric centers in Manhattan, Boston, Philadelphia and Washington. "It will answer a need that has not been met for a long time," said Martin F. Nester Jr., administrator of Long Beach Memorial Hospital. "The care of children is changing, and a tertiary (specialty) center is really in the best interests of the community of Long Island."

The changes Nester referred to include the specialized care now available to premature babies only in major centers, plus the growing tendency to hospitalize only the sickest children, a practice that increases the need for community hospitals to have back up help.

Most hospital administrators agree. "We were initially opposed to the idea of a large children's hospital," said Charles J. Hackett, executive director of Hempstead Hospital. "But since they have built it, we certainly expect to take advantage of it. Anytime we have a child needing services they provide and we don't have, we're going to be right on their doorstep."

Not everyone was prepared to comment on the question of the need for the hospital. Silverberg declined to be interviewed about his current view.

Newsday, September 1983

After the hospital was completed—in fact, on the very day it opened—the *New York Times* (September 25, 1983) continued the crusade with the headline: "Children's Hospital Being Dedicated but Doubts Remain." Instead of hailing the hospital as a major advance in medical care, the article dug up the tired old objections to its construction, quoting various healthcare administrators who were concerned about the impact of the children's hospital on their services, duplication of services, a flat birthrate on the Island, the surplus of pediatric beds, and on and on and on. Once again, I was called upon to defend the hospital.

"The delivery of pediatric services in a physical plant built specifically for children will be very different from those of general hospitals, and they have to be," said Dr. Philip Lanzkowsky, chief of staff of the hospital and chairman of the department of pediatrics. "To my knowledge we are the only facility in the New York State area providing this totality of multidisciplinary care under one roof."

Dr. Lanzkowsky, a professor of pediatrics at the Health Sciences Center of the State University of New York at Stony Brook, said: "We must have a concentration of children and pediatric beds in order to bring together this large number of pediatric specialists in medical, surgical, psychiatric and dental disciplines. If you have 20 beds, you cannot attract the staff. You cannot afford to keep them because the bed base is not large enough to support the staff economically."

About 225 health professionals will be hired, including pediatric specialists, nurses, social workers, respiratory therapists and child life specialists.

Work is continuing at the hospital, which plans to admit its first patients in November. On the main floor of the facility is a flower-lined courtyard enclosed by glass-walled corridors and a skylight. The courtyard opens on all five floors—each floor covers one acre—to the outdoors.

There is a parents' suite for overnight stays. Seven sleeping rooms, a living room, kitchenette and bathrooms are provided for parents of patients in the neonatal and intensive care units. Single and double rooms also have sleeping accommodations for parents.

A public school with full-time teachers, playrooms and day care for visiting brothers and sisters will also be available. Rooms are painted in cheerful colors.

New York Times, Sept 25, 1983

The controversy was loud, bitter, and expensive—cost increases over the years of postponement of construction totaled millions of dollars. But the hospital was built, and its almost instant success was validation of the concept.

Summing it all up, the *New York Times*, more than thirty years later on May 20, 2007, ran the following article:

Did a Children's Hospital Make Sense? Yes, to Put It Mildly

By Marcelle S. Fischler

NEW HYDE PARK—Opening the Schneider Children's Hospital in 1983 was an uphill battle for Dr. Philip Lanzkowsky, the executive director and chief of staff, but a plan to expand it is proving a lot easier.

Critics initially wondered whether a hospital devoted solely to children's care was viable, Dr. Lanzkowsky said; they worried that it would duplicate the services that other hospitals provided with only a few dozen pediatric beds and that it would have a detrimental effect on surrounding medical institutions.

Dr. Lanzkowsky, a South African-born hematologist oncologist, was determined to prove his detractors wrong. He advocated for the children's hospital from the time he arrived at Long Island Jewish Medical Center as chairman of pediatrics in 1970. "This was a place that was ripe for a children's hospital," recalled Dr. Lanzkowsky, 75, referring to the burgeoning suburban landscape. The hospital provided "one-stop shopping," he said, and was designed to fill "the unique medical, surgical and psychological needs of children" and their families. Still, it took him thirteen years to get approvals from the state and other regulatory bodies before the hospital's doors could open.

Within a few months the hospital's 154 beds were fully occupied. Built for 40,000 ambulatory patients a year, it now has 160,000, attracting patients from "Nassau, Suffolk and Queens as well as from across the country and overseas," Dr. Lanzkowsky said. "We are bursting at the seams," he added. "We are unable to accommodate all the children who need our care."

The hospital's expansion will take place in two phases. Next month, a $22 million, two-story addition over part of the existing building will add 24 modern neonatal intensive-care beds to the existing 45, as well as physicians' and faculty offices. The open courtyard off the lobby will be enclosed with glass, creating an indoor winter garden and atrium that will be used for activities like concerts and performances by clowns from the Big Apple Circus.

By the end of the year, ground is expected to be broken for Phase 2, a $110 million, five-story patient tower that will include the region's first stand-alone children's emergency room, a children's imaging center and 50 additional surgical beds, all in single rooms. "Some people may be here for a long time," Dr. Lanzkowsky said, "so they have to be comfortable."

To kick off the expansion, $40 million was raised at a recent gala for the Children's Medical Fund, the hospital's philanthropic arm, which raises funds for special programming, research and new technologies as well as buildings. A substantial portion came from the family of Edward Blumenfeld, a local real estate developer who is the fund's chairman.

The children's hospital has a budget of just over $200 million annually and is part of the North Shore-Long Island Jewish Health System. "You never make money, but you don't lose money," Dr. Lanzkowsky said. "We pay our way."

Michael J. Dowling, chief executive of the health system, said the goal was to elevate Schneider from "the top echelon" to "one of the premier [children's hospitals] in the country. To do that we have to expand," Mr. Dowling said. The children's hospital also *has satellite centers in Commack, Hewlett, Flushing, Bensonhurst and Williamsburg.*

From the start, Dr. Lanzkowsky tried to make the hospital as inviting as possible. Visitors are greeted outside by fanciful Keith Haring and Niki de Saint Phalle sculptures. A player piano in the lobby is often used for performances. Large candy murals made from jelly beans, candy corn and marshmallow twists decorate the walls, along with several pieces by Andy Warhol and whimsical William Wegman dog portraits. Outside the admitting office, children create kaleidoscope images on computers.

"When they come here they have an educational experience in addition to repairing the hole in the heart or curing their cancer," Dr. Lanzkowsky said. Pet therapy, art therapy and music therapy are offered. Playrooms are outfitted with toy kitchens, puzzles, paints, riding toys and books.

When a child comes to Schneider Children's Hospital, Dr. Lanzkowsky said, "He is so preoccupied with the diversion of the activities that he forgets why he came here in the first place, and that is a wonderful thing."

After this article was published, some changes were made in the construction plans which replaced the physicians' and faculty offices with a new state-of-the-art ambulatory chemotherapy unit and the size of the patient tower was reduced to four stories.

Michael Pettie, MD, PhD, demonstrating an endoscopy procedure to members of the house staff.

Howard Seiden, MD, reviewing the anatomy of the heart with cardiology fellows.

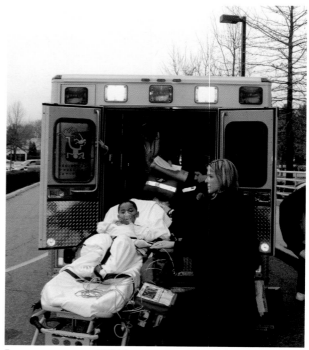

Emergency transport to SCH from a community hospital, winter 2001.

Clowns entertaining a young fearful patient.

Learning the ropes at a pre-surgical orientation.

Mark Atlas, MD, reading blood smears with his colleagues.

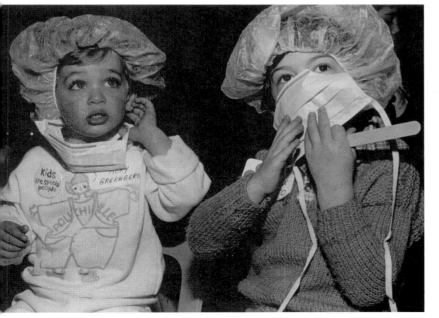

Future physicians learning the ropes.

CHAPTER 11

BUILDING AT LAST!

CONSTRUCTION IS APPROVED

During the development phase of the children's hospital, a number of architects were engaged as the location, scope, and programs changed.

In 1966, when the children's hospital was only a dream, the firm of Morris Lapidus was asked to present a design.

Lapidus, who died in 2000 at the age of 98, was the son of a Russian immigrant who was raised on Manhattan's Lower East Side. He studied architecture at Columbia University and started his career designing innovative shopping outlets that changed the way people shopped. He had also designed several hospitals, including Mount Sinai in Manhattan. The flamboyance of his designs, including their use of brilliant lights, compelling forms, and opulent materials, attracted wide interest. His work was curvy, dramatic, showy, ornamental, accessible, and whimsical, and these characteristics brought him both critical backlash and commercial success. At that time, circular buildings were in vogue; the University of Connecticut hospital and the State University of New York at Stony Brook hospital both had circular structures, impressive from the exterior, but with many functional disadvantages.

Groundbreaking for the children's hospital on May 18, 1980. Left to right are Irving Wharton, chairman of LIJ Board of Trustees, Judge Bertram Harnett, chairman of CMF Board of Trustees, Robert Frankel, Congressman Lester L. Wolff, and Robert K. Match, MD, president of LIJ.

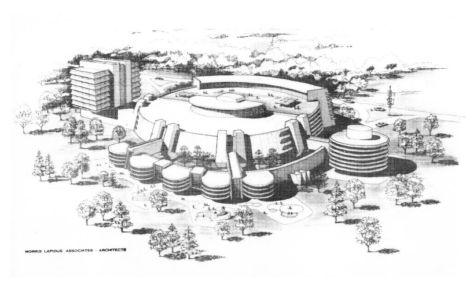

Rendering by Morris Lapidus of the Children's Medical Center of New York. *New York Times*, February 1, 1966.

Here are excerpts from his "architectural concept" for a 550-bed children's hospital:

"This design has evolved from the principle of separating and differentiating the environment and traffic of children and their parents from the technical core facilities of the hospital. These core facilities are incorporated into a semicircular building. By employing the semicircle, all peripheral points are equidistant from the central facilities; there are no remote areas or long tortuous corridors.

The ward facilities are in a curved building connected by enclosed ramps to the semicircle. The space between these two facilities is used as a garden court, portions of which will be glassed over to create a winter garden. The wards are single-loaded, the rooms located on one side of the corridor, all facing the park and the most beneficial exposure.

Located adjacent to the wards and adjacent to the central building is the Auxiliary Treatment Building (Parent-Child Residence), a new concept in hospital care. This facility fulfills a threefold function: it serves as a motel for parents whose children are hospitalized; an outpatient residence where children undergoing special outpatient care may stay with their parents; and a place where patients requiring only cursory medical care may stay with their parents.

The central road runs past the flat side of the semi-circular central facilities building and the flat side of the semi-circular parking garage, which is directly opposite. Within this garage are located a pair of ramps serving a double purpose. They enable swift parking of vehicles on various levels and they permit direct vehicular access to any level of the central facilities building, with corresponding immediate parking. Thus, the standard concept of a single hospital entrance is nullified. Separate entrances are now possible for all departments that so require them."

Mr. Lapidus' "concept" also included staff apartments "looking out over landscaped grounds" with access to the hospital "under cover" and a recreation area for staff on the roof of the parking facility. It was designed for a site in Nassau County at Mitchell Field, however, when the Mitchell Field deal died, so did the Lapidus design. It had many valid and novel features, but the grandeur and scope of the plan were not consonant with the fiscal and regulatory realities of the day—nor would they pass muster even today.

When the building of the children's hospital at LIJ became a reality, the need for architectural service became immediate, and a number of architectural firms were interviewed in September 1975.

In January 1976, Rossetti Associates of Detroit, which had designed the Charles Mott

Children's Hospital of Detroit Medical Center, was engaged to draw up the architectural plans. Rossetti Associates was founded in 1969, and the fact that it had won multiple awards set it apart from other architectural firms. Its success was based on its tenacity and passion.

The following article describing the hospital's special features that were part of the Rossetti design appeared in the *Long Island Press* on April 10, 1976.

Hospital On The Way
LIJ to Start Children's Unit in a Year

After five years of fund-raising and planning, construction of a new children's hospital at Long Island Jewish-Hillside Medical Center is expected to begin in about a year, officials said yesterday.

The roughly $30 million structure, connected to the New Hyde Park hospital's main building with an entrance planned for 76th Avenue, will take about two-and-one-half years to complete, said Sam Popkin of Rossetti Associates, the Detroit architects recently hired to design the 150-bed facility.

For the first time in its expansion career, LIJ will be borrowing money to finance construction, said Michael Stein, chairman of its development committee, who noted that LIJ has built a $50 million, 46-acre plant solely through contributions.

LIJ will apply, within the next four months, for Federal Housing Administration loans to cover two-thirds of the cost of the new Children's Medical Center, said president Dr. Robert K. Match.

The rest of the money will be raised by the Children's Medical Center of New York Fund, whose 4,000-member women's auxiliary has gathered $3 million over the last five years, said the chairman, Nassau Supreme Court Judge Bertram Harnett.

Stein noted that as the "finest pediatric facility from the East River to Montauk," the center was the "logical next step in the master plan of the Medical Center."

Match said the hospital was looking into future uses—perhaps a physical rehabilitation unit—for the space now occupied by LIJ's 97 pediatric beds.

The Children's Medical Center, tentatively planned as five stories with room for expansion, will serve children under 19 from as far away as New Jersey and Connecticut,

Renderings of proposed hospital and atrium of the Children's Medical Center, by Gino (Louis A.) Rossetti 1976.

will handle 25,000–45,000 outpatient visits annually, have 40 pediatric specialists and will create an estimated 300 jobs, officials said.

Among its special features, said LIJ pediatrics chairman Dr. Philip Lanzkowsky, will be:

- Facilities for parents to stay overnight with their children
- A school for patients
- A day center for other children in the family
- One-day stays for hernia operations, tonsillectomies and other surgery
- A kidney dialysis unit, new cardiac diagnostic unit and a center for cancer, "the second commonest cause of death in children," with a large blood bank operation
- 15 psychiatric beds and 15 beds for the chronically ill
- Separate operating rooms and emergency unit for children
- Child-scale rooms designed to let nurses observe patients at all times

Louis A. Rossetti, president and principal of Rossetti Associates, who was called Gino, described the design in an interview for *In Touch*, Summer 1976.

"We have designed a strong separate statement for the Children's Medical Center, allowing for an economically and operationally feasible relationship to existing LIJ structures and programs and for logical future growth and development." With this introductory statement, Gino (Louis A.) Rossetti, President and Principal of Rossetti Associates, architects of choice for the Children's Medical Center to be constructed at Long Island Jewish-Hillside Medical Center, presented preliminary plans for the projected CMC to the Joint Planning Committee.

In addition to the preliminary CMC model were site plans, traffic pattern studies and recommended solutions for parking for the total complex. In developing the basic scheme for the CMC the architects had considered, in addition to the hospital relation to existing structures, such natural phenomena as the solar path for all seasons, prevailing wind directions and natural ground levels.

The basic elements proposed included a "bed tower," five and one-half stories above ground, outpatient department and emergency room space, pediatric operating rooms, lobby, amphitheatre-teaching center, and mechanical and service support. The open "atrium" space was upheld by the architect on aesthetic and environmental grounds. The three patient floors, with two patient stations to a floor, are designed as a right angle providing patient room with a view and corridors, backup space and play areas overlooking the atrium. The patient stations would be located so that nurses can have visual contact with patient rooms and can control traffic to and from.

Rossetti's design was ahead of his time. While his architectural plan was outstanding, appropriate in scope and size for a children's hospital, it was not viewed with favor by the LIJ Board of Trustees. They were concerned with the cost and that the state would not approve a hospital of that size. It is interesting that more than thirty years later a similar plan is materializing in the new construction of SCH (see Chapter 20). The state was interested in controlling costs, and the LIJ trustees were concerned about raising enough money through philanthropic contributions to construct a hospital of such a large size, as well as its operating budget. The square footage of the building had to be reduced. Robert Boyer, director of the LIJ Planning Department, and I were saddled with the task of shrinking the building size in half, from approximately 400,000 square feet to 200,000 square feet, in order to gain board approval.

A series of meetings was scheduled over three weeks with each of the various disciplines of the pediatric department to review space requirements. They were comprehensive, attended by physicians and nurses in each of the disciplines. It was a democratic approach to planning; everyone had his or her say and became part of the solution. The meetings taught us that such efforts are an activity in compromise.

We were careful to separate desires from the necessities. We were prepared to fight for the necessities if we had to, but we would not necessarily be able to provide all the staff's desires. At the end of this difficult process, we did arrive at a reduced square footage that corresponded to the state's mandate, and the architects were readily able to modify the schematic plans. Once the plans were accepted by the LIJ Planning Department they were reviewed with representatives of each of the relevant disciplines. The architects were then free to move forward to the next phase of design development. Unfortunately, however, differences of opinion developed between the LIJ Planning Department and the Board of Trustees and Gino Rossetti, which led to the termination of his firm as the architects.

The Architects' Collaborative (TAC) was engaged in 1979. An American architectural firm founded in 1945 by Walter Gropius in Cambridge, Massachusetts, TAC had created many successful projects and had gained wide respect for its broad range of designs. One of its specialties was designing public school buildings; they were located all over New England, as were a large number of TAC-designed hospitals. TAC's philosophy reflected Gropius's central preoccupation with the social responsibilities of architecture. Collaboration was its mantra. Accordingly, not just one architect, but instead, an entire group of architects contributed to a project, with a partner-in-charge who would meet with the clients and have the final say. This method had been practiced by Gropius himself when he was an instructor at the renowned Bauhaus school, in Dessau, Germany, which he had founded. The closest meaning for its name in English is "architecture house." Bauhaus style became one of the most influential currents in modernist architecture.

The Architects' Collaborative (TAC) model of the children's hospital, 1979.

The partner-in-charge on the children's medical center project was Richard Brooker, who was assisted by Edmund K. Summersby as the lead architect. Both of them worked very collaboratively with the staff to develop the design. After over a year of design development, TAC submitted a model and architectural drawings to the LIJ Planning Department.

Moving the project from architectural drawings to reality required two further steps: securing financing and appointing a construction manager. Financing had to go through the fairly lengthy process of mortgage approval by the U.S. Department of Housing and Urban Development (HUD) and the Federal Housing Administration (FHA). The construction manager selected was Morse-Diesel, which had to provide the board with a guaranteed maximum price (GMP) after having received bids from various subcontractors,

Robert K. Match, MD, and child
at groundbreaking ceremony,
May 18, 1980.

especially the early and largest trade contracts for excavation and foundation, concrete, steel, plumbing, electrical, and heating, ventilation, and air conditioning (HVAC). Both the financing and the GMP required and received LIJ board approval before any construction could begin.

The TAC plan called for a large central courtyard in the building. The New York State Department of Health (NYSDOH), whose approval was necessary to proceed, were very concerned about the cost of the courtyard and the energy costs to maintain appropriate heating in the building. After several meetings with the NYS-DOH we convinced them that it was necessary for the esthetics of the building and for creating a suitable environment for children.

When the plans were submitted to the New York City Building Department, there was one more snag. There was a street on the city maps that had never been built, which ran through the site. This paper street, unknown to anybody at LIJ, connected the old Motor Parkway on the north of the property to 76th Avenue at the south end. Before any building could occur, we had to go through a "demapping" process, which, among other things, required consent from the community. After several meetings and much discussion, we were successful in getting the community to agree that the phantom street, which even the residents did not know existed, could be demapped to clear the way for the building of the children's hospital.

The cost of the hospital had escalated from original quotes of approximately $18 million in the early 70s to $35 million by 1982. It was financed through an $86 million bond issue of the State Dormitory Authority, which included new parking facilities, a central food-processing center and other improvements to LIJ.

Groundbreaking took place under a tent in the pouring rain on Sunday, May 18, 1980. I participated in the ceremony as chairman of the Department of Pediatrics, along with Irving Wharton, chairman of the Board of Trustees, LIJ; Robert K. Match, MD, LIJ's president; Michael Stein, vice-president and chairman of development; Judge Bertram Harnett, chairman of the CMF Board of Trustees; Rita Kingsley, president of CMF's Women's Division; and Harvey Bernstein, president of its Men's Division. In attendance despite the deluge were hundreds of CMF members.

Dr. Match's remarks were as follows:

"This is a very special day for all of us. We have certainly waited a long time for today's groundbreaking ceremonies. This groundbreaking is the culmination of years of dedicated work on the part of many people—board members, professional staff, community leaders, and our good partners in this effort—the Children's Medical Fund of New York.

It is a particular pleasure for me to see so many of you here and to welcome everyone on this important occasion.

From the day LIJ opened its doors 26 years ago, the pediatric department, under the leadership of a full-time chairman, has been one of our most important, heavily utilized services. And, over the years, it has continued to grow, adding expert full-time staff in all the major specialties and gaining national renown for its accomplishments.

This is why we are now beginning to build our new 150-bed hospital for children. Twenty-six years of expanding and intensifying pediatric programs has led to our current position as a regional resource for physicians and community hospitals

Philip Lanzkowsky, MD, determined to see the job done, moves a tractor on the site.

During the flu season, a seven-year-old girl in coma was rushed to LIJ from Huntington Hospital. She had a rare brain inflammation called Reye's syndrome that sometimes follows the flu. Extremely delicate procedures and constant monitoring saved her. Her case was diagnosed correctly only because of the educational pediatric program televised from LIJ to Suffolk hospitals every week. It enabled her doctor to recognize a problem he hadn't seen in his seventeen years of practice and to send her here.

Then, last week, TV and newspapers ran the story of a little boy who spent a year and a half in our neonatal unit. He came to LIJ from Mary Immaculate Hospital and survived six dangerous and complex operations to correct a gangrenous intestinal tract. He is alive and thriving—not only because of surgical and pediatric treatment but also because of the team that watched over him—doctors, nurses, a psychologist, physical therapist, and social worker. Last week, a young boy was brought to us from Brookhaven Hospital with symptoms that could have been meningitis or Rocky Mountain spotted fever. His condition was deteriorating rapidly when he arrived. Careful testing proved that it was the first case of Rocky Mountain spotted fever on Long Island this year and a regimen of antibiotics halted the progress of the possibly fatal illness. Just a few days ago, he left our pediatric intensive care unit and went home as good as new.

The experiences of these children explain why we are here today. They demonstrate the close relationship we have with community hospitals throughout the island. By building this new hospital for children, we are broadening and strengthening the care and services we can give. In about three years, I hope you will all be with us again when we dedicate our new hospital for children—one that we feel sure will be a model for the nation. You can all be proud to have had a hand in creating such a special place for all our children."

in the entire Long Island area and beyond. In this role, as a regional resource, LIJ has been called upon more and more to answer a growing demand for highly specialized pediatric care for the most acutely ill children.

Perhaps these brief case histories will give some insight into the part we play as a highly skilled tertiary care center, which means we are a facility with the most advanced technology and medical talent to go with it. These seriously ill children are often rushed here by helicopter or by our 'flying squad,' a specially equipped ambulance for newborn babies in jeopardy. Let me tell you about a few of the children who have recently been brought to the pediatric unit from hospitals throughout long island.

Children's hospital under construction, 1982.

Mr. Barell added:

"As I watch the Children's Hospital rising, I see beyond the structure, all the years of concerted effort. The process of gaining official approval meant complex demographic studies, hearings at many governmental levels to prove the rationale for this essential resource, and creative planning to build on a sound financial foundation. We are proud to have had the devotion of so many wise and talented men and women who made it possible."

Here is an excerpt from Judge Harnett's speech:

"The idea of the Children's Hospital began 20 years ago. Its fruition is a tribute to the unswerving spirit and determination of the people in the Children's Medical Fund of New York. Keeping this flame burning for so long a time has involved two generations of supporters. Today sons and daughters of our founders are also carrying the message about this important pediatric resource into their communities. The Children's Hospital has been an intrinsic part of our lives and now that it is a reality, it will stand as guardian for the health of our children."

I made these comments:

"The past decade has produced a new era in the evolution in the field of medicine. Because of the tremendous acceleration in scientific and technical knowledge many treatment decisions are now being made by teams of specialists. Such a combined approach has meant dramatic changes in the practice of pediatrics. Our Children's Hospital is the logical arena for the entire spectrum of advanced medical practice and this team approach assures the highest quality of care for all children."

In the summer of 1980, construction began. At last, it was achieving steel-and-concrete reality, with the steel superstructure of the five-story

building from South Africa and the outer "skin" of precast concrete slabs from Canada. As construction moved forward, regular meetings were held with the construction manager, the Planning Committee of the Board of Trustees led by William Mack, the architects, the engineers, and the LIJ Planning Department. The purpose was to bring any issues that had arisen to a forum where decisions could be made immediately so that there would be no delay. At these meetings requests for change orders were reviewed. Careful attention was paid to both the validity and the cost of change orders. Because they involved additional expenses for LIJ and potential additional income to the subcontractors, they were addressed fairly, firmly, and on a timely basis rather than being left to the end of construction. Only the ones that passed a strict and comprehensive review were approved. These meetings proved very helpful in moving the project along.

Members of the LIJ Planning Department were on the site every day to ensure that the quality of the work and the progress were satisfactory.

The children's hospital opened on September 25, 1983, one week later than originally projected. Its working name through the long process of planning, approvals, and actual building had been the Children's Medical Center of New York and then the Children's Medical Center. It was announced only a couple of months before it opened that its official name would be the Schneider Children's Hospital, in honor of generous benefactors Helen and Irving Schneider.

At completion, the sleek, five-story glass and cement building sat gracefully on the Long Island Jewish-Hillside Medical Center campus in New Hyde Park. Having outlasted more than a decade of stormy controversy, the hospital consisted of 150 beds, including sixty-eight medical-surgical beds, fifteen psychiatric beds, and fifteen long-term care and rehabilitation

Children celebrate nearing the completion of the construction of the children's hospital, 1983.

beds. The pediatric intensive care unit had twelve beds and the neonatal unit forty beds equipped with advanced, computerized bedside monitors. (Because of a need for more acute medical beds, the long-term rehabilitation unit was converted into a hematology-oncology unit shortly after the opening of the hospital.) The hospital was originally built with a parents' suite on the third floor for overnight stays. Seven rooms, a living room, kitchenette and bathrooms were provided. By 1989, this area was converted into additional office space for faculty. In addition to comprehensive services in medicine, surgery, dentistry, and psychiatry, the Schneider Children's Hospital was built with the capacity for broadened pediatric research and teaching programs.

The sensitivity to children's needs was clear as soon as you walked through the doors into the bright, airy lobby.

Disney tunes flowed from the player piano, and light streamed from the courtyard garden and from a skylight that looked like a giant building toy. There were comfortable couches to sit on, wonderful pictures to look at, games to play, even juice for children while they waited. The playrooms had glass roof bay windows to let in natural light. The walls were painted with bold splashes of color—a palette of sixty-four colors was used. A turn in the chartreuse-and-yellow corridor led to a purple-and-bright red stretch, then on to a blazing blue-and-green passage and then to cobalt-and-pink. The core of the building was a flower-lined courtyard with walls of glass letting in the brightness of the outside world. This was designed to be the focal point for patients, personnel, and visitors.

Great expanses of double-thick, heat-absorbent, energy-efficient glass were used throughout the building, to let in sunlight for its therapeutic effect. A series of direct-access passageways connected the hospital to LIJ: on the first floor to the LIJ lobby, on the second floor to LIJ radiology, and on the third floor from neonatology to LIJ's obstetric unit. The building also incorporated special environmental features aimed at reducing stress for children. These included sleeping

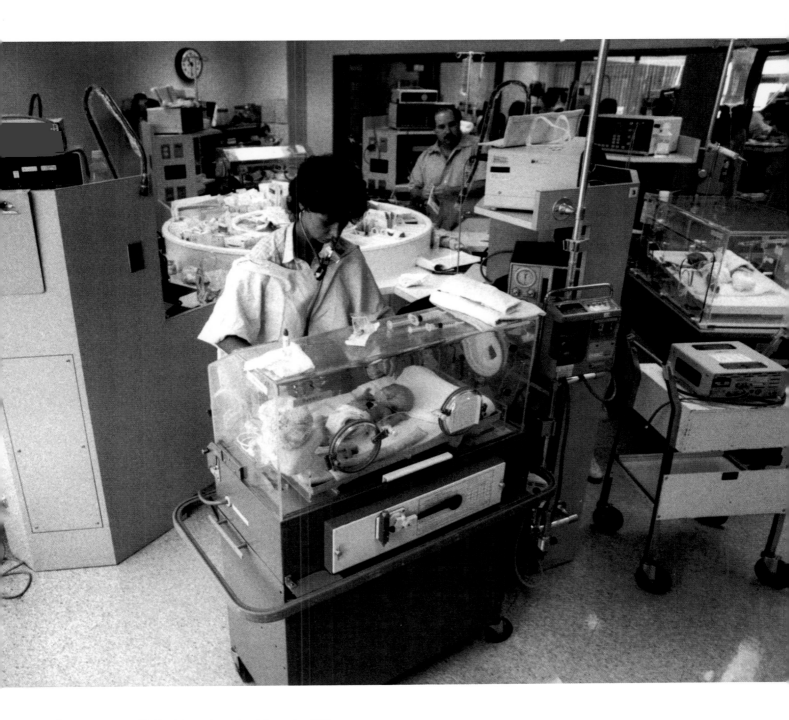

Opposite page top: Children's hospital completed, September 1983.

Opposite page bottom: Children's hospital lobby, as depicted in *The New York Times* and *Newsday*, 1983.

This page: The neonatal unit of the children's hospital.

Every level overlooks colorful landscaped atrium—the core of the Hospital

accommodations for parents in their children's rooms, brightly decorated waiting rooms, play areas, and a schoolroom for inpatients.

"We've tried to create spaces with a sense of openness and lightness," said Edmund K. Summersby of TAC.

To further enhance the quality of life for patients being treated at SCH, especially those who lived far away, and abroad, in 1986 an eighteen-room Ronald McDonald house, a "home away from home," was built on the grounds of SCH. Through the efforts of Lynn Jurick, the founding chairperson of the Ronald McDonald House Board, and myself, the LIJ Board of Trustees agreed to permit the building of the House on land owned by LIJ.

The house provided (and continues to provide) a place for parents to stay near their children while they are treated for life-threatening diseases. It was the 100th Ronald McDonald House built worldwide, and its board of trustees consisted (and continues to consist) of represen-

tatives from the LIJ board and the community and Ronald McDonald owner/operators. I have been its medical director since it was built (its bylaws require that the medical director is the chief of staff at the Schneider Children's Hospital). In 2005 the house was expanded to forty-two rooms.

In 1991 the hospital was expanded to include a four-bed bone marrow transplantation unit equipped with a laminar airflow system on the fourth floor of the hospital. The unit was donated by the Gambino Medical and Science Foundation and is the only one approved by New York State exclusively for children. This unit required a certificate of need (CON) application and state approval. To justify it and establish the necessary statistics, I had to make a presentation before the New York City Health System Agency.

In 2007 the first phase of a master plan to rebuild SCH commenced.

Opposite page top: Children's hospital courtyard, 1983.

Left: 100th Ronald McDonald House built on the grounds of SCH, 1986.

Below: Ronald McDonald House showing the 2005 expansion.

Bottom left: Children's hospital courtyard, 1983.
Bottom right: Family area in the Ronald McDonald House, 2007.

CHAPTER 12

STAUNCH ADVOCATES

THE SCHNEIDER FAMILY

Irving Schneider was a member of the Long Island Jewish Medical Center (LIJ) Board of Trustees during the long, drawn-out development and building phases of the children's hospital.

He was at first a strong and vocal opponent. Gradually he became neutral, then willing to be persuaded, and finally convinced of the need for the hospital. In fact, when the hospital opened in 1983 its official name was the Schneider Children's Hospital, in acknowledgment of the generosity of Irving Schneider and his wife, Helen. At that time, their gift was the largest single contribution received.

But it was a personal experience that had a profound effect, as so often happens; he became a passionate supporter of the hospital that bears his name and of the entire children's hospital concept after the life-threatening illness of his first grandchild, Jeremiah, in June 1989.

As an infant, Jeremiah developed profound, life-threatening stridor, a condition marked by difficult and noisy breathing due to obstruction of the windpipe and brought about by a hemangioma of the larynx. He was treated by Allan Abramson, MD, chairman of otorhinolaryngology (ENT), and Philip Lipsitz, MD, chief of neonatal-perinatal medicine. A discussion, initiated by Robert K. Match, MD, president of LIJ, was held as to whether the baby

Bottom photo: Schneider Children's Medical Center of Israel. Kaplan Street, Petach Tikvah, Israel.

Helen and Irving Schneider.

should be sent to Children's Hospital Boston or Children's Hospital of Philadelphia. Jeremiah's parents, however, were staunch in their belief in the excellence of the hospital and their trust in its physicians; they insisted that Jeremiah be treated there, and not moved to another hospital, even one of the most famous children's hospitals in the world.

Dr. Abramson went forward with the treatment, performing delicate laser surgery, which was successful. Throughout the ordeal, and during Jeremiah's recovery, Irving Schneider lived in the neonatal unit at his grandson's side. Witnessing the level of the care his grandson received and having the baby restored to health were transforming, as Irving Schneider told me himself.

For years afterward, Mr. Schneider would remind people of his early opposition to the idea and comment that he really had not understood what a children's hospital was about. He'd become a star convert, consumed with passion, idealism, and energy. His wife, Helen, and his daughters, Lynn and Mindy, shared his commitment.

For twenty years, from 1983 until he became ill in 2003, I spoke to Mr. Schneider almost every day, usually at 6:30 in the morning, after he had already been at work for an hour or two. The conversation always had the same pattern. "How is business?" he would ask. That was his code for asking, "What is going on?" He wanted to know the news of the previous day—what the census was, who visited, any anecdotes about the

Irving Schneider "advising" Philip Lanzkowsky, MD, on hospital matters, June 2000.

staff (he knew most of them by name and was friendly with many on a personal basis), and any interesting patients. He had an excellent working knowledge of the inner operations of a hospital from having been active on various hospital boards for close to fifty years, and he would pepper his comments with advice or recommendations. He was, in fact, as knowledgeable about the operations and finances of a hospital as the most astute and competent CEO.

He visited the hospital several times a month, always looking closely at the condition of the building and the cleanliness of the place. I have no doubt that in a subtle or not so subtle way he protected the interests and the separateness of the children's hospital at meetings of the LIJ Board of Trustees. Mr. Schneider was a powerful personality whose motto was that any objective could be accomplished by "devastating logic and brute force." His other motto, taken from the scriptures (Psalms 121:4), was "...The Guardian of Israel neither slumbers nor sleeps."

Irving Schneider enjoyed bringing visitors to see the hospital, and he liked to relate to them how it all began. He would always ask me to start giving the history, and then he would fill in parts that he especially loved to tell. These largely concerned the unexpected impact of the hospital and its sphere of influence. His favorite comment during my historical discourse to visitors was, "Nobody could have imagined, Philip,

the difference between a department of pediatrics and a children's hospital." This was my cue to detail the unique contributions that a children's hospital makes to the totality of medical care for children.

Mr. Schneider spread his generosity beyond the children's hospital at LIJ. He was also responsible for the building of the children's hospital in Petach Tikvah, Israel, which is named the Schneider Children's Medical Center of Israel (SCMCI) and became one of the most outstanding children's hospitals in the world and a jewel in the crown of the largest Israeli health care system, Kupat Cholim Klalit. The hospital is a beacon of hope for children in the Middle East and the Mediterranean basin amidst the turmoil and terror that has engulfed that region in recent years. It was his fervent desire that the Schneider Children's Medical Center of Israel would be a bridge to peace between Israel and its neighbors. His contribution to the State of Israel was acknowl-

IRVING SCHNEIDER: A LIFE OF SERVICE

Mr. Schneider was an active member of the LIJ Board of Trustees from 1965 until 2003. He was also director of the Jewish Community Relations Council of Greater New York, vice chairman of the Association for a Better New York, and a member of the Brandeis University Board of Trustees. Long active in Jewish service organizations, he was honorary chairman of the Board of Governors of the Greater New York UJA-Federation of Jewish Philanthropies, trustee emeritus of the Jewish Communal Fund, and a member of the Board of Directors of the Hebrew Immigrant Aid Society (HIAS) and the American Jewish Joint Distribution Committee.

His service in the field of healthcare also included appointment as trustee of the Health Insurance Plan of New York (HIP) and membership on the Board of Trustees of Maimonides Hospital.

In his professional life, he served as executive vice president of HelmsleySpear, director of Reliance Group Holdings, Inc., and vice president of the Realty Foundation of New York. He also served as governor of the Real Estate Board of New York.

edged by the President of Israel's presentation of the Child Protection Shield Award to Helen and Irving Schneider.

Irving Schneider brought his trademark energy, enthusiasm, and determination to the building of the first children's hospital in Israel. First came a detailed analysis of the situation, and then he asked Robert Derzon, principal of Lewin Associates of San Francisco, Marvin Bostin, president of Bostin Associates, and me to study factors such as the following: A) Does Israel need a children's hospital? B) If so, where should it be located? C) Under whose auspices should it operate?

After months of study, we decided that Israel did indeed need a children's hospital, that it should be located in the densely populated area near Tel Aviv, and it should be operated under auspices of the Kupat Cholim Klalit organization. Once the decision was made, Mr. Schneider fully committed his resources and personal time to the effort. He appointed Jerry Switzer, AIA, founding partner of MorrisSwitzer Environments for Health, LLC, an American architectural firm with children's hospital experience, to work with the Israeli architects. He visited Israel every month and sometimes even more often during the planning and construction of the hospital. On a number of occasions during and after the construction of the hospital, I accompanied Irving and Helen Schneider to Israel to review the progress of the hospital and its medical programs. Irving Schneider was determined to see to it that construction proceeded in a manner that met his exacting standards, and indeed it did. From 1997 through 2002 the Schneider Children's Medical Center of Israel has won the annual five-star title from the Council for a Beautiful Israel as "the most aesthetic hospital" in the country. In 2003, the Council for a Beautiful Israel awarded the medical center the "Flag of Beauty," which is

Atrium of Schneider Children's Medical Center of Israel.

Irving and Helen Schneider on the dais at SCH house staff graduation ceremony. Left to right: Irving Wharton, Helen Schneider, Irving Schneider, Mark Sperling, MD (keynote speaker), Robert K. Match, MD, and Philip Lanzkowsky, MD (at podium), 1993.

bestowed once every five years. With unsurpassed generosity, Mr. Schneider paid for most of the 225-bed children's hospital. I know of no other philanthropic commitment of this magnitude to any children's hospital.

The Stephen Auster Fellowship in Pediatric Cardiology, supported by the Schneider family, is awarded annually at graduation to the most academically accomplished fellow in pediatric cardiology. Stephen Auster, a nephew of Irving Schneider, died suddenly of a cardiac condition (idiopathic cardiomyopathy) on the ball field at a young age, and the fellowship was established in his honor.

Irving and Helen Schneider loved graduation day at SCH, when they sat proudly on the dais and enjoyed listening to the keynote speakers who had come from all over the country to attend the event. Irving Schneider would hand out the diplomas to the graduating house officers, and Jeremiah, his eldest grandson, assisted in later years by Max, Katie, and Jake, his other grandchildren, would hand out the gift books and awards to the residents.

In June 1996, Irving and Helen Schneider and I were honored by the LIJ Board of Trustees at its annual dinner dance at Glen Oaks Country Club in Old Westbury, New York. The theme of the evening was "For the Children."

In December 1999, at the annual SCH gala at Tam O'Shanter Club in Brookville, New York, Irving and Helen Schneider were honored by the faculty and staff of the Schneider Children's Hospital for their contributions to the hospital.

In April 2002, the Schneider name was joined to the Department of Pediatrics at North Shore University Hospital and other pediatric components of the North Shore-Long Island Jewish Health System, a further honor for the family. Irving remarked on that occasion that the children's hospitals, both here and in Israel, had given his life meaning.

Helen Schneider, who had once aspired to become a nurse, was a volunteer in the pediatric playrooms at LIJ for many years before SCH was built. She was also committed to the Women's Service Guild at LIJ. Helen Schneider understood that medicine and technology alone do not cure patients; comfort, solace, kindness, and a friendly environment contribute to the healing process. She didn't want any child entering the hospital to be traumatized by the experience.

A person with a highly developed aesthetic sense, Helen left her mark on the Schneider

Irving Schneider and grandson Jeremiah at 1994 graduation ceremony.

Philip Lanzkowsky, MD, on behalf of the LIJ Board of Trustees, presents Helen and Irving Schneider with a token of the board's appreciation for the Schneiders' contributions to the children's hospital, June 1996.

Children's Hospital as a place where children can appreciate art and sculpture and the beauty of nature. From the inaugural day until the present day, there is always a beautiful bouquet of real flowers at the information desk, which was initiated and funded by her.

The art that decorates the grounds and the halls—the Keith Haring, Niki de Saint Phalle, and Clyde Lynn sculptures and the Andy Warhol lithographs—was selected and funded by Helen Schneider and her daughter Lynn, who believed that "real" art was not wasted on children, particularly sick children.

Helen Schneider was also an active member of the Board of Trustees of the Ronald McDonald House for sixteen years. She died on December 8, 2001, after a courageous battle with cancer.

The elder Schneider daughter, Lynn Schneider, a graduate of the Harvard University School of Architecture, became a member of the Planning Committee of LIJ in 1984, an associate trustee in 1985, and a full trustee in 1996. She is presently on the North Shore-LIJ Health System Board of Trustees. When Irving Schneider became ill in September 2003, Lynn continued the Schneider tradition of involvement and interest in the children's hospital.

Mindy Schneider Lesser holds a master's degree in public administration with a major in health administration from New York University. She became involved at LIJ as a "candy striper" during her senior year in high school and volunteered in that role for several years after college.

Top: Helen Schneider thanks the staff and faculty for honoring the Schneider family. From left to right are Helen Schneider, Philip Lanzkowsky, MD, and Irving Schneider, December 1999.

When Helen Schneider died, Mindy became a member of the Board of Trustees at the Ronald McDonald House; she serves today with enthusiasm and dedication that match her mother's.

Irving Schneider, his wife, and daughters had a major and lasting impact on the hospital that bears their name.

Mr. Irving Schneider and his grandchildren distributing books and diplomas at house staff graduation 2004.

Ribbon-cutting ceremony naming Schneider Children's Hospital at North Shore University Hospital. Left to right: Philip Lanzkowsky, MD, Mindy Schneider Lesser, Irving Schneider, Lynn Schneider, Jon Cohen, MD, and Michael Dowling with patients, April 2002.

Playroom at Ronald McDonald house reflecting Helen Schneider's interest in creating a child-friendly environment.

COME CELEBRATE WITH US

Dedication of the
Schneider Children's Hospital of
Long Island Jewish-Hillside Medical Center

CHAPTER 13

Sunday, September 25, 1983

[3]0 p.m. Dedication Ceremonies
[F]ollowed by Champagne Party

Under the Tent
[o]n the Grounds of the Hospital
[7]6th Avenue and 270th Street
New Hyde Park, New York

[S]peaker: Governor Mario M. Cuomo

RSVP

SOMETHING TO CELEBRATE

THE DEDICATION

The hospital's dedication ceremony was held on September 25, 1983, three years after the groundbreaking ceremony had taken place.

Actually, celebration of the project's completion had started earlier, in the summer of 1983, with a dinner dance in the Grand Ballroom of the Waldorf Astoria. Irving Schneider was the guest of honor. New York City Mayor Koch attended and gave a speech in which he commented, "New York's medical facilities are its greatest glory. But it has not been blessed with a special hospital for children. For Irving Schneider to help make this possible will assure his place in heaven."

Among the other guests at the Waldorf Astoria Grand Ballroom were Mayor of Jerusalem Teddy Kollek, former New York City Mayor Abe Beame, Congressmen Tom Downey and Charles Schumer, New York State Senator Frank Padavan, Assemblyman Arthur Kremer, and Manhattan Borough President Andrew Stein. Speakers included the Most Reverend Bishop Joseph M. Sullivan, Auxiliary Bishop of Brooklyn;

Invitation to the dedication of the Schneider Children's Hospital, September 25, 1983.

Dedication
Schneider Children's Hospital of
Long Island Jewish-Hillside Medical Center

Reverend Carl E. Flemster, Executive Minister of the American Baptist Churches of Metropolitan New York; and Jack Bigel, president of the Community Council of Greater New York and head of the Program Planners, Inc.

After twenty years of hard work, endless meetings to gain support, fundraising, planning, justifying the need over and over to every bureaucratic agency in New York City and on Long Island, Saturday morning meetings at kitchen tables discussing

Sol Chaiken, Martin Barell and Robert K. Match, MD, attending the dedication ceremony.

plans and tactics—what amounted to thousands upon thousands of hours spent by a dedicated team of individuals—the day had come. Invitations had been sent out far and wide and a large crowd was in attendance.

Robert K. Match, MD, Mindy Schneider, Irving Schneider, Governor Mario Cuomo, Helen Schneider, Lynn Schneider, Philip Lanzkowsky, MD, and Martin C. Barell at the dedication ceremony for the Schneider Children's Hospital.

Philip Lanzkowsky, MD, Rhona Lanzkowsky, and Richard Brooker (partner in charge of the The Architects' Collaborative) in the cafeteria of the children's hospital on dedication day.

Under a sparkling September sun, more than 1,500 guests gathered in celebration. It was a gratifying, joyous, emotional day that felt perfect in every way: blue skies, bright sunshine, and an atmosphere charged with the electricity generated by the excited guests. Kites bounced gaily in the sky above, children held tight to helium balloons, and clowns wandered through the crowds. Music from the U.S. Merchant Marine Academy Band sent spirits soaring. I made a welcome speech, as did Martin C. Barell, chairman of the Board of Trustees of Long Island Jewish-Hillside Medical Center (LIJ), Honorable Donald R. Manes, Borough President of Queens, Robert K. Match, MD, LIJ's president, Helen Schneider, Honorable Justice Sol Wachtler, Judge Bertram Harnett, chairman of the Children's Medical Center Fund of New York (CMF), and New York State Governor Mario Cuomo.

Among the attendees was Sol Chaikin, known as Chick, president of the International Ladies Garment Workers Union, who was helpful in winning governmental approval for the project. Also present were the leaders of the Women's Division: Gladys Cole, Vivian Kokol, Bernice Mager, Marcia Goodman, Barbara Kleinberg, Marcie Rosenberg, and Muriel Martin, and from the Men's Division were Norman Goodman, Jesse Gottlieb, Alan Hoffman, Gedale Horowitz,

PROGRAM
Martin C. Barell, Program Chairman
Chairman, Board of Trustees, LIJ-HMC

STAR SPANGLED BANNER
Elaine Malbin

INVOCATION
Rabbi Israel Mowshowitz

WELCOME
Martin C. Barell

SPEAKERS
Philip Lanzkowsky, MD
Chief-of-Staff, Schneider Children's Hospital

Honorable Donald R. Manes
Borough President, Queens

Honorable Bertram Harnett
Chairman, Children's Medical Fund of NY

Robert K. Match, MD
President, LIJ-HMC

Helen Schneider

Honorable Sol Wachtler
Justice, Supreme Court of the State of NY

Honorable Mario M. Cuomo
Governor of the State of New York

BENEDICTION
Rev. Frank. N. Johnston
Associate Trustee, LIJ-HMC

Yale University "Alley Cats" Chorus

RECEPTION
Music by the U.S. Merchant Marine Academy Marching Band

Band Master, Capt. Kenneth R. Force

We appreciate the cooperation of Rear Admiral Thomas A. King, Supt. of the Merchant Marine Academy, Ms. Elaine Malbin, the L.I. Klown Enthusiasts, Adelphi University Mimes, the Yale University "Alley Cats" and members of the Children's Medical Fund of NY who served as hosts and hostesses.

U.S. Merchant Marine band at the dedication ceremony.

Richard Horowitz, Ron Kisner, Frederic A. Kleinberg, Jack Lyons, William Mack, Harold Schwartz Jr., and Walter Seid. Richard Brooker, a partner of TAC, and Edmund Summersby, the lead architect, were also in attendance.

The afternoon's festivities began with the national anthem sung by well-known opera star Elaine Malbin. Entertainment included the U.S. Merchant Marine Academy Marching Band, the seventeen-voice Yale University "Alley Cats," and the Long Island Klown Enthusiasts.

Helen and Irving Schneider and their family, for whom the hospital was named, stood beside Governor Mario Cuomo at the ribbon-cutting ceremonies, along with two children who were winning their fight against leukemia. Nine-year old Donna Edlinger and her seven-year old brother, David, were patients who were being

treated for leukemia in the pediatric cancer program at Long Island Jewish-Hillside Medical Center. Judge Sol Wachtler introduced Governor Cuomo, who delivered the keynote address, which follows:

"Today is a time for prayer and for a simple thanksgiving that the dreams and hopes represented by this hospital have come true—that there is now such a special place for children who are sick or in pain, a place dedicated to healing and comforting them, giving them the most technically advanced care possible and doing so with gentleness and understanding.

A commitment is required by New York State to the work at this children's hospital, a commitment to achieve decent healthcare for all our children, a commitment to seeing to it that no child in this state goes hungry or is condemned to

David and Donna Edlinger, July 2008.

Governor Mario Cuomo, Helen and Irving Schneider and their daughters, Mindy (on left) and Lynn (on extreme right) and Donna and David Edlinger at the ribbon-cutting ceremony, September 28, 1983.

Governor Mario Cuomo and Robert K. Match, MD, sharpening the scissor blade for the ribbon-cutting ceremony.

a life of sickness and disability because his or her parent couldn't afford even the most basic level of medical attention or nutrition.

In New York State we will continue to act according to the principle that was the inspiration for this hospital that rests at the very heart of both the Jewish and Christian faiths...the principle of need.

The principle that human affairs can be left neither to the laws of evolution nor to a lifeless and abstract logic that says that fairness requires that we treat everyone equally and the handicapped child will receive only as much care as the healthy one, and if we cut ten percent of the budget then it must be across the boards, the sick and homeless and destitute bearing the same sacrifices as the wealthy and the able bodied.

You rejected that logic when you set out to build this hospital, you insisted that the so-called fairness is not enough, that the measure of our humanity is how we respond to those who can't help themselves, who depend on us to help them...the chance to live and stand on their own two feet, to be free from pain, to grow and take some small part of the happiness we all seek.

Long after the social Darwinists and apostles of despair and the proponents of abandonment to the commitment that makes us human have left the stage and taken their place in historical footnotes, the work you have done will still continue.

Children will be treated here, cured and made whole and given some reason to believe that there is real goodness and real compassion in the world around them. The coming generations will build on your achievement, expand it and improve it, treasuring the sacrifices you made, remembering your faith and your struggle. Schneider Children's Hospital represents the composite of the best available in medical technology today."

He was given a standing ovation by an audience consisting of civic leaders, people from all sectors of the health and service professions, legislators, government officials, nurses, doctors, and the friends and family of Helen and Irving Schneider.

Delivered softly and emotionally, Helen Schneider's speech was extremely moving:

"Governor Cuomo, Borough President Manes, distinguished legislators, eminent clergy, trustees, and children of all ages.

Our family agreed that I should write and deliver this speech. The program committee set three conditions which were to be followed—namely to be brief, to the point and not to be repetitive. In the first version that I wrote, I didn't do too well. I wrote very little because I cried a great deal.

But, I continued on, and after the third version I was doing well when I received the outline of two other speeches that were delivered earlier today, and discovered that mine would be repetitive. I wrote another draft in which I wanted to thank everyone—from the founders of this great medical center who set the high standards, to all of the people who were involved in the creation and building of the children's hospital. And I realized that it was too long. Therefore, I decided that we should continue to thank each individual personally instead.

Now let me briefly give you some of my thoughts.

This is a glorious day in our lives. What brings us to this day is a culmination of ideas and feelings that we have:

Our interest in helping others,

Our long-term association with the delivery of healthcare,

Gratifying but difficult days as volunteers in the pediatric playroom,

The reputation of this medical center and its continuing determination to be not only better, but the best.

And what we believe private philanthropy should be.

We thank you for the honor which you bestow upon us today in naming this children's hospital for us.

Irving, Lynn, Mindy and I look upon this day as a new beginning, and pledge our continued support of the Long Island Jewish-Hillside Medical Center.

Thank you."

Chairman of LIJ's Board of Trustees, Martin Barell said:

"This children's hospital is a product of a joint effort. Its initial moving force was the Children's Medical Fund of NY, whose members devoted countless hours to fulfill the dream. The trustees of LIJ worked together consistently with the fund. Dr. Robert K. Match, together with his staff, put forth tremendous effort year after year. Generous donors such as the Schneider family, along with countless others, contributed significantly. Government officials and private citizens all lent their support. And today the dream is realized."

In my own remarks, I stressed the need for regionalization and the attraction of medical professionals, stating:

"Mr. Chairman, Governor Cuomo, Borough President Manes, members of the clergy, distinguished members of the dais, ladies and gentlemen:

The opening of the Schneider Children's Hospital is a unique and historic event. It relegates the dream of the need for, and the planning of a children's hospital to the pages of history. It dedicates the realization of this dream—the product of the coordinated efforts of many. We recognize today:

The perspicacity of the LIJ Board of Trustees for embracing the concept and bringing it to fruition;

Dr. Robert K. Match, president of the hospital, for his sterling leadership during its inception and passage through the stormy waters of the approval process, and, with the help of Mr. Irving Wharton, successfully navigating the complexities of the financing of a project of this magnitude;

Judge Bertram Harnett and the Children's Medical Fund of New York for their unswerving commitment to the pristine concept of a children's hospital;

Drs. Burton Bronsther and Martin Abrams for the seed they planted of the idea of a children's hospital in the hearts and in the minds of man;

The Schneider family for their benevolence and generosity;

The untiring efforts of Mr. Robert Boyer, director of planning of this institution, the architects, engineers, builders, and numerous artisans who gave of their special skills and expertise;

Central to a project of this type, the hard work, talent, and dedication of the medical staff, both full time and voluntary, for their critical role in program development and planning;

The nursing staff for their assiduous care of children entrusted to them;

And, ultimately, the public at large, who have held this institution in high esteem.

The spiraling costs of medical care dictate the need for the concentration and regionalization of specialized equipment and services, as well as the need for high and effective bed utilization. The

Schneider Children's Hospital is a beautiful five-story building, each floor being an acre in size. The architects were The Architects Collaborative from Cambridge, Massachusetts, descendants from the famous Bauhaus school of architecture.

The inpatient area consists of medical, surgical, psychiatric, neonatal, and intensive care units, for a total of 150 beds. The ambulatory care area comprises twenty-four examination and treatment rooms and specific diagnostic modules for the various specialty areas. All of these treatment areas wrap around a landscaped courtyard to be utilized for children's recreation and entertainment. The building is replete with numerous consultation rooms, conference rooms, and laboratories for both clinical and research purposes. The entire building will be fully computerized, using the most advanced of technology. There are playrooms, a school, sleeping facilities for parents, patient and parent libraries, all built specifically for children and decorated in a cheerful array of colors. This hospital represents a composite of the best available in medical facilities in the western world.

This children's hospital represents a societal and political challenge of the greatest magnitude; the poor, the sick, the handicapped, and the neglected children need our intervention. They need us to exercise both our muscle and our ingenuity on their behalf so that they and their families do not continue to bear a disproportionate burden of cutbacks and retreats in our social responsibility. Our children's good health, competence, and vigor are central to our national interest. We must not turn our backs on the most vulnerable of America's assets.

Truth to tell, there were some who were opposed to the construction of the children's hospital but, fortunately, there were many men and women of good will who were resolved to make this a reality and a great institution. Now that it stands as a magnificent resource for the community at large and for this entire region, it merits the support of the public, of the community of health professionals, and of all those interested in the welfare and future of our children.

The essence of a children's hospital is the gathering under one roof of a galaxy of scholarly professionals who are dedicated to the combined attack on the manifold problems of health and disease of the newborn, the child, and the adolescent with the aid of the techniques and the specialized knowledge available in the medical world today.

The children's hospital has an obligation to join with other institutions of similar dedication to teach, to share, to learn, to work in concert—all in the interests of children. This professional interaction should weave a tapestry of comprehensive and coordinated services enhancing the welfare of children in the tri-county area.

All who care about children must care deeply about the education of those who provide their health services. The children's hospital will play a major role in medical education and act as a lodestar for the training and teaching of all health professionals concerned with children. It should be the trendsetter in modern technology and techniques for the humane care of children. It should become a spearhead for research in all the disciplines of pediatrics so that the fruits of biological research and clinical investigation can benefit future generations of children.

At this time the children's hospital is a mere building; a promise to the children of this region. We have a gigantic task ahead of us—to build medical programs for children in this region on a sound fiscal basis so that this hospital stands as a beacon of hope and as a magnet to all those who seek medical, surgical, psychiatric, and dental and other care.

The driving force and rationale for this children's hospital is the fact that children are not miniature adults; their entire medical and emotional make-up is wholly different from that of the adult and hence, they should be managed in a separate environment—an environment designed to appeal to children and make them feel comfortable and secure. When we open our doors: we shall be judged by the immediate community we serve for the medical care that we render; we shall be judged by students from all over for the truths they glean in

Standing ovation for Dr. Philip Lanzkowsky following his address at the dedication ceremony.

our classrooms and the clinical skills they perfect in our wards; we shall be judged by the national and international scientific community for the quality of research that emanates from our laboratories; and, ultimately we shall be judged by the most critical of all—the individual ill child who is comforted by our staff and restored to health. We will succeed in all these areas.

In conclusion, permit me to share with you one of the many thoughts that enter my mind on this occasion. The most poignant of all is the traditional Judaic blessing, which has been uttered on special occasions for centuries, and I quote it to you in the original Hebraic tongue: She'Hecheyano, V'Keyamanoo, V'Higyahnoo Lazman Hazeh.

'We regard ourselves privileged to have been granted life and sustenance and permitted to reach this day.'

We have come a long way and we recognize the monumental task ahead of us.

I thank you, ladies and gentlemen."

Dr. Robert K. Match was warmly received. His speech was as follows:

"Well, they said it couldn't be done—and here we are. It's taken twenty years—an uphill fight all the way. But what we have here will have a profound impact on the health of children and the well being of families for generations to come.

This dedication marks the beginning of an exciting era in the delivery of the most advanced health services for children of this region. It is a tribute to the many thousands of people who persevered for two decades in the efforts to build this special pediatric hospital. Today is a day of sharing in the success of a dream.

That dream began in the early 1960s with a core of women and men led by Judge Bertram Harnett, Dr. Burton Bronsther, and Dr. Martin Abrams. They formed the Children's Medical Fund of New York, and in 1971 we combined forces, via an official contract, to work together to build a children's hospital.

There were many rocky years ahead. There were obstacles that would have stopped any less determined group. There were voices raised against us from many quarters. But we had many friends, too. Friends who had the vision to see the necessity for a hospital built exclusively for pediatric medicine. Some of our most stalwart allies were people in the official health agencies who recognized the validity of our cause. They studied the volumes of demographic reports, analyses of medical records, and statistics about our patient population. And, most important, they recognized the quality of our pediatric care and became our allies.

Even so, it took six tough years before official approval was granted. As we dedicate this very special hospital for children, we want to thank the farsighted experts in the health and hospital field who added their voices to ours in the government agencies and legislative chambers where the decisions were made.

And here in our own family were those invaluable members of our board of trustees who worked long and hard for our goal. It would have been a 'mission impossible' without their total support. These are men and women whose business and professional backgrounds were a priceless resource. They are people like Irving Wharton. During his five years as chairman of the board, his secretary found him in our offices more than his own. You already know about Helen and Irving Schneider. Their names over the door of the new hospital signify a profound commitment and involvement. They have done more than help raise an edifice—they will have helped enrich the lives and assure the health of literally millions of children.

As you came to this tent, you saw the Schneider Children's Hospital. I'm sure you agree that it is a beautiful structure. What we have to offer all of you, your families and friends is a hospital that is five stories tall, with five acres of floor space, 150 beds for inpatients, twenty-four examination/treatment rooms for outpatients, expanses of windows overlooking a landscaped courtyard, halls and rooms in remarkably cheering colors, laboratories built into a diagnostic

and treatment area, intensive care units with the most advanced computerized monitoring beside every bed and crib. At last, we have beds designated specifically for psychologically sick and chronically ill children. We even have a waterbed for pediatric inpatients because it was learned that it has special therapeutic value.

Let me tell you what was involved in some of the basic design. Of course we recognize the role of the architects, the planners, and the builders. But there is another, less obvious factor. To make this hospital really function, our nurses and doctors were intimately involved in helping to work out the use of space, the choice of equipment, the arrangement of special units. For example, we had a section of the neonatal intensive care module section set up in the LIJ basement. They tested it for every possible situation that could arise. They visited other teaching hospitals with neonatal units. As a result, what we have now is a unit for premature and very sick newborns that will set the pace for all others.

And making all these beautiful components work is an army of dedicated, enthusiastic health professionals. Under the guidance of Dr. Philip Lanzkowsky, chief of staff, and for many years the chairman of LIJ 's Department of Pediatrics, we have attracted a staff of outstanding pediatric specialists. They have come here from some of the most prestigious medical institutions in the country. There is one point more I would like to make and I think it is a tremendously important one. There is a philosophy of care and compassion welded into the very structure of this building. At every stage of its planning and development, we asked: 'How will this affect the child? Will it lessen apprehension? Will it lessen stress on parents?' And with the Schneider Children's Hospital we feel the answer is 'YES.'

Thank you for coming here so that we can celebrate together."

Judge Harnett addressing the audience at the dedication ceremony.

Judge Harnett spoke with great feeling. He stated:

"There was, in the beginning, the Children's Medical Center Fund of New York, to become Children's Medical Fund of New York (CMFNY). The Schneider Children's Hospital of LIJ-HMC will always stand as a testament to the courage and determination of the thousands of women and men of the fund who devoted two decades to its creation. They believed that a child is not a small adult and that a child has special emotional needs and physical tolerances to be taken into account in a hospital environment. They proved that idealism can be the ultimate practicality, that the dedication of tough-minded parents could move bureaucratic mountains. We are grateful to the trustees and staff of LIJ-HMC for their own Herculean efforts in bringing into being this special place for children.

It has to be said that the Women's Division of CMCFNY, to become CMFNY, has been the most positive force in lifting the children's hospital from a mere idea to a concrete and medical reality. They were on the mark all the way. Many of these women are here today. To them and to those not here, I say, 'Thanks very much for our children's hospital.'"

Honorable Donald Manes, Borough President of Queens, said:

"There would be no children's hospital here right now if not for the tremendous effort of a lot of dedicated, caring people.

I know about the countless meetings, hearings, and appeals; about the mountain of documents you had to prepare; about the reams of red tape you had to cut through.

In Queens alone, there are more than 463,000 children between infancy and eighteen years of age. Add Nassau and Suffolk Counties, and that figure skyrockets to one-and-a-quarter million children.

What we're dedicating today is a major healthcare resource for millions of children in

Invitation to the dinner dance sponsored by the Children's Medical Fund of New York celebrating the dedication of SCH.

The Children's Medical Fund of New York

Dinner Dance

Martin Lifton
Guest of Honor

Saturday, October 1, 1983
Glen Oaks Club

celebrating the dedication of the Schneider Children's Hospital of Long Island Jewish-Hillside Medical Center

PROGRAM

Robert E. Morrow, Dinner Chairman

WELCOME
Martin C. Barell, Chairman
Board of Trustees, LIJ-HMC

Robert K. Match, M.D., President
LIJ-HMC

Philip Lanzkowsky, M.D.,
Chief of Staff,
Schneider Children's Hospital,
LIJ-HMC

DINNER AND DANCING

PRESENTATION
Hon. Bertram Harnett, Chairman
Board of Trustees, CMFNY

RESPONSE
Martin Lifton

ROLL OF HONOR

Arrangements and Decor — Ellie Lifton

the region—a healthcare resource that's strong in treatment, teaching, and research, all in the fine tradition of Long Island Jewish-Hillside Medical Center. When it comes to health care, we can't ask for more than that."

And there was more celebrating to come. On Saturday, October 1, 1983, the CMF held a dinner dance at Glen Oaks Club celebrating the dedication of the Schneider Children's Hospital. The Honorable Bertram Harnett made a presentation to the guest of honor, Martin Lifton. I spoke, as did Martin C. Barell and Dr. Match.

MOVING DAY—NOVEMBER 1, 1983

It was a happy time. It was a sad time. A week earlier the pediatric nursing and house staff had held a farewell party on LIJ's Four South. They called it a "lost our lease" party, and there

were many memories shared of crises faced, children who made them laugh or cry, as well as the excitement and anticipation of packing up the pediatrics department for the move to the new children's hospital.

C-Day was Children's Day—the day when patients were moved from LIJ into their new beds in the Schneider Children's Hospital next door. The advance strategy would have awed a five-star general. In an inch-thick procedural manual, maps showed the route from the old locations to the new. Every staff member was listed, with specific assignments for the day. They ranged from dispatcher in the children's hospital lobby to members of one of two emergency code teams ready to go at a moment's notice.

Twenty-three departments and divisions were involved in the planning coordinated by the nursing department. Security officers and key personnel had walky-talkies. Children were tagged according to medical priorities, destinations in the new units, and modes of transportation: bed, stretcher, and wheelchair. Box lunches were ordered. Equipment was color-coded for time and date of relocation.

The checklist seemed endless. The day before the move, every detail was reviewed for what seemed the thousandth time. Was the oxygen in place? Were medication supplies fully stocked? Were all the beds made? Were soap and toilet paper in every bathroom?

Pediatric staff from other shifts or with the day off came in to help with the move. "After all," one nurse said, "we've been waiting a long time for this day."

Transport teams composed of pediatric staff, as well as volunteers from other departments,

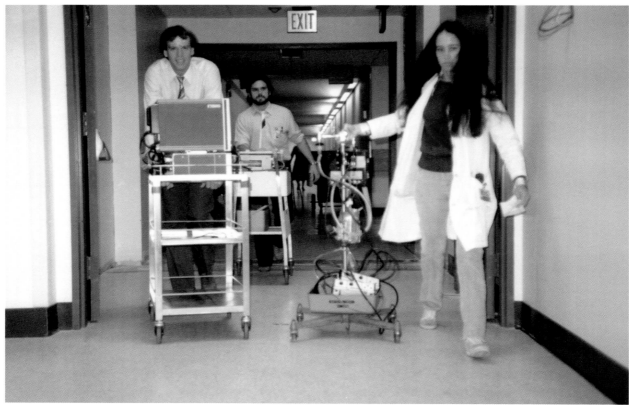

Moving day—hospital staff moving equipment...

accompanied each child from the old bed to the new. First came the patients from the intensive care unit. Each had been tagged "A" priority and was shepherded by a team consisting of a physician, a nurse, and a respiratory therapist. Some were on complex life-support systems; some in traction, some with cardiac monitors. Their passage from LIJ to the new second-floor ICU was followed by a relay of security officers continually in touch with central dispatching.

Through the morning and into the afternoon, new inpatient units steadily filled with young patients. Last to make the move was the adolescent group. All but the sickest teenagers considered the experience an adventure.

New patients were not being admitted yet, but a steady stream of parents and children were soon arriving at the first two outpatient modules to open in the Consultation and Diagnostic Services.

The sigh of relief might have been heard all the way to Lakeville Road!

During the day, the media came to see and film the activities and interview the participants. TV crews vied with newspaper reporters, photographers, and radio broadcasters, all eager to get first-hand reactions from young patients, their parents, and staff. ABC-TV and NBC-TV featured the move on their news programs. The *New*

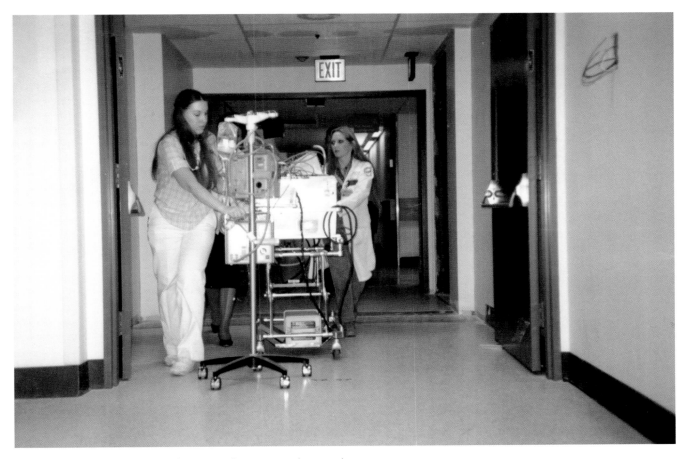

...and finally the moment everyone has been waiting for—moving in the patients!

York Times, Newsday, the *Daily News*, and the *New York Post* all carried stories that highlighted the hospital's warm and supportive environment. Agreeing with them were the scores of visitors who entered the cheerful lobby with its red walls, blue carpeting, and broad expanse of glass. And topping the scene was the unusual seasonal floral arrangements on the information desk in the lobby, a gift of Helen Schneider.

The Schneider Children's Hospital was open for business!

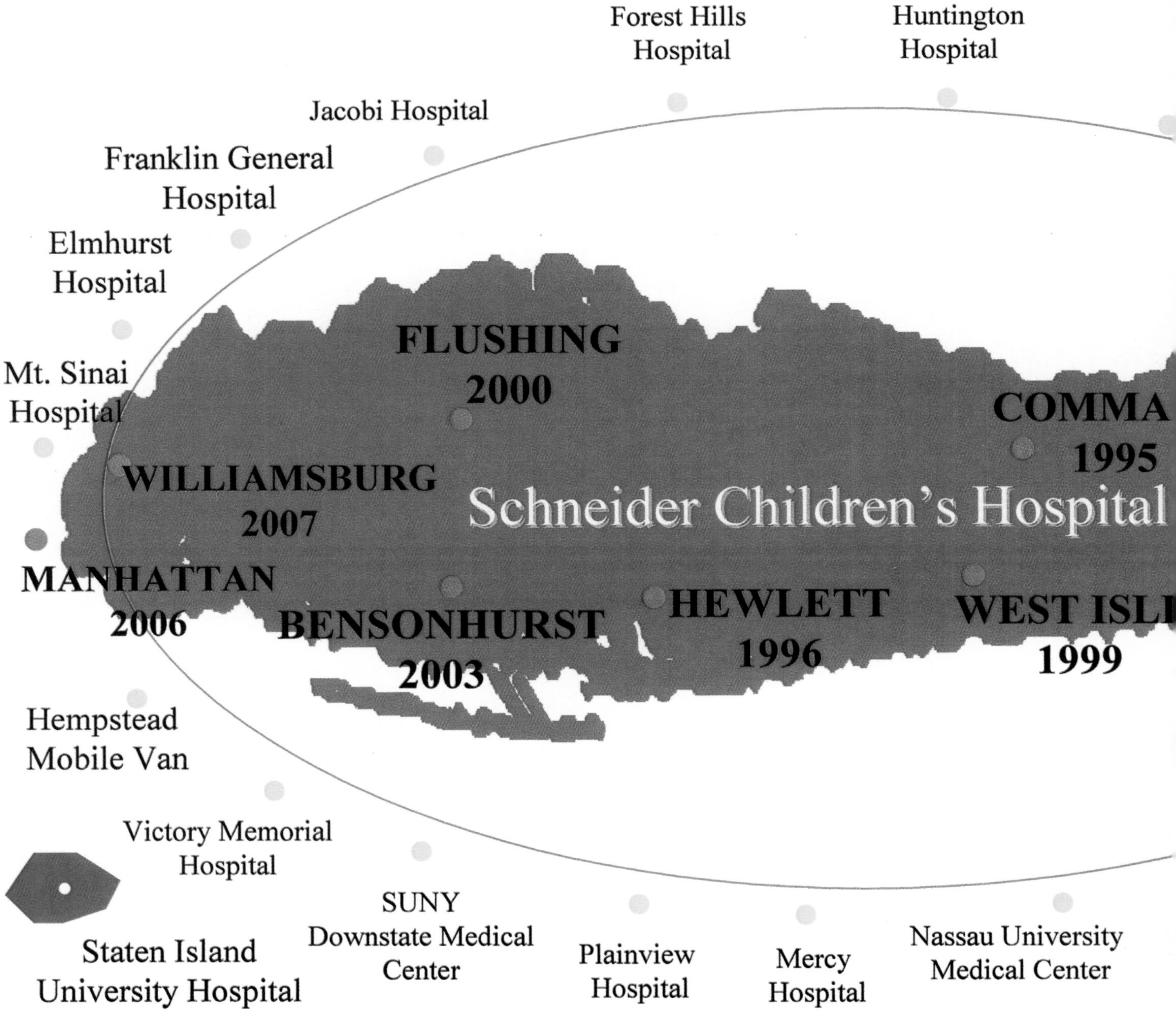

Forest Hills
Hospital

Huntington
Hospital

Jacobi Hospital

Franklin General
Hospital

Elmhurst
Hospital

**FLUSHING
2000**

**COMMA
1995**

Mt. Sinai
Hospital

Schneider Children's Hospital

**WILLIAMSBURG
2007**

**MANHATTAN
2006**

**BENSONHURST
2003**

**HEWLETT
1996**

**WEST ISLI
1999**

Hempstead
Mobile Van

Victory Memorial
Hospital

SUNY
Downstate Medical
Center

Plainview
Hospital

Mercy
Hospital

Nassau University
Medical Center

Staten Island
University Hospital

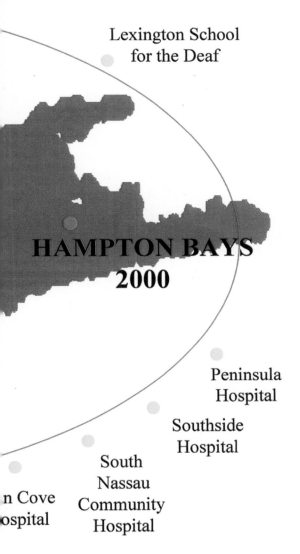

CHAPTER 14

St. John's
Rockaway Hospital

Lexington School
for the Deaf

**HAMPTON BAYS
2000**

Peninsula
Hospital

Southside
Hospital

South
Nassau
Community
Hospital

n Cove
ospital

BUILDING ON THE DREAM

THE LANZKOWSKY YEARS 1983–2008

With medical crises day and night, and physicians and staff under nearly constant pressure and stress, a hospital is never a peaceful place.

Compared to the cramped quarters of the Department of Pediatrics at Long Island Jewish Medical Center (LIJ), however, the newly opened Schneider Children's Hospital (SCH) was an oasis of peace and tranquility. No longer were children bedded in the corridors. No longer were children receiving chemotherapy in an adult waiting room. Pediatric care could and would now be taken to another level.

In my professional life, I, too, had found (relative!) peace and tranquility. For thirteen years, I had been battling for the creation of a children's hospital. Many times I believed that the dream was about to die. And now here it stood, an architectural wonder, warm and bright, with room under its one roof for our wide array of services for children, with proper play and school facilities and accommodations for parents. Everyone felt the excitement—patients, parents, visitors, nurses, doctors, and prospective faculty and house staff from all over the country to whom we could now offer a very inviting workplace.

Schneider Children's Hospital showing recent hospital affiliations and multidisciplinary satellite centers on Long Island.

Endurance and tenacity are the words that best characterized my efforts during that thirteen-year period. With only a few staunch allies at my side, I had attended meeting after meeting, filed application after application, while being bombarded from every direction with skepticism and doubt. And at the same time I was running the Department of Pediatrics. It's somewhat surprising, looking back, that we were able to build the foundations for so many important programs during those LIJ years. But build we did, and at SCH we were able to see these programs evolve and flourish.

PSYCHOSOCIAL PROGRAMS

Once the hospital was built, the first child life program on Long Island was created, with its diversionary and educational art, music, pet, and clown programs.

Helen Schneider and her daughter, Lynn, who shared an interest in art, generously purchased

significant works of art for SCH that were unique for a hospital and had a transforming effect on the institution. The art includes works by Keith Haring (the outdoor sculpture became the logo for the hospital), the colorful enameled Magic Tree by Niki de Saint Phalle, and the Astronomy Lesson by Clyde Lynn, all outdoor sculptures. Also included are the Cowboys and Indians and Endangered Species suites by Andy Warhol, and William Wegman's charming photographic studies of his Weimaraners. Interactive exhibits were installed to help minimize the fear of hospitalization and make the hospital a child-friendly place. Programs were established for parents to help them cope with children's chronic and terminal illnesses. In addition to being cured of their disease, the goal was that the children should be discharged without having acquired any emotional scars in return, and indeed hospitalization at SCH was a positive life experience. A children's art gallery and a children's museum would temper the hospital experience.

Child playing with computerized interactive exhibit.

SCHNEIDER CHILDREN'S HOSPITAL PEDIATRIC FACULTY
Prior to Merge, 1998 (Partial Listing) Names listed left to right
1st Row (sitting): Jeremiah Levine, MD, Michael Pettei, MD, Lorry Rubin, MD, I. Ronald Shenker, MD, Philip J. Lipsitz, MD, Philip Lanzkowsky, MD, Fredrick Bierman, MD, Howard Trachtman, MD, Dennis Carey, MD, Andrew Adesman, MD, Norman Ilowite, MD,
2nd Row: Rose Grosso (Executive Assistant), Bradley Kessler, MD, Susan Schuval, MD, Gungor Karayalcin, MD, Jack Gorvoy, MD, Joyce Fox, MD, Lydia Eviatar, MD, Vincent Bonagura, MD, Mayer Sagy, MD, Michael Frogel, MD, Robert Bienkowski, PhD, Robert Cassidy, PhD, Raj Pahwa, MD, Andrew Steele, MD, Hedda Acs, MD, Cheryl Kurer, MD, Angela Romano, MD, John Brandecker (Departmental Administrator)
3rd Row: Shari Fallet, MD, Toba Weinstein, MD, David Gold, MD, Doug Yoon, PhD, Martha Arden, MD, Eric Weiselberg, MD, Neville Golden, MD, Marc Jacobson, MD, Arlene Redner, MD, Joseph Maytal, MD, Bernard Gauthier, MD, Peter Silver, MD, Laura Nimkoff, MD, Robert Koppel, MD, Kalpana Patel, MD, Barry Goldberg, MD, Karen Powers, MD, Ann Zaslov, PhD, Yehuda Shapir, MD
4th Row: Steven Weiss, MD, Nancy Rosenblum, MD, Robert Gochman, MD, Philomena Thomas, MD, Roy Vega, MD, Robert Katz, MD, Clifford Nerwen, MD, Lynda Gerberg, MD, Scott Svitek, MD, Dorie Hankin, MD, Sunil Sood, MD, Katherine King, MD, Dennis Davidson, MD

EXPANSION OF HOUSE STAFF, FACULTY, AND DIVISIONS

Once the hospital was built and space became available, we were able to grow the house staff and the faculty. The pediatric house staff increased from twenty-four to fifty-four when SCH opened, and by 2008, with the merger with North Shore University Hospital (NSUH), to 131 residents and 58 fellows. The full-time faculty, both medical and surgical, increased from the time of the opening of SCH when there were twenty-four, to 142 due to an increase in the number of faculty in existing divisions and the formation of new divisions. As shown in the table on the following page, new chiefs were appointed and new divisions cre-

ated; our ability to attract outstanding staff from around the country was enhanced by the available space and the atmosphere, both academically and for patients, of the new children's hospital. Expansion occurred not only within the Department of Pediatrics but also in the surgical disciplines with the appointment of full-time surgical specialists in general surgery, orthopaedics, urology, and rehabilitation medicine.

The merger of LIJ and NSUH considerably enhanced the regional network that SCH had developed over the years with the addition to the network of a number of Nassau and Suffolk County hospitals that had previously belonged to the North Shore Health System.

SCHNEIDER CHILDREN'S HOSPITAL PEDIATRIC HOUSE STAFF Prior to Merger, 1998 (Partial Listing) Names listed left to right

1st Row (sitting): Chitra Ravishankar, MD, Joan Dowdell (House Staff Coordinator), Frank Fanella, MD, Robert Katz, MD, Philip Lanzkowsky, MD, Robert Cassidy, PhD, Rajesh Savargaonkar, MD, Rose Grosso (Executive Assistant), Sheryl Cohen, MD

2nd Row: Navyn Naran, MD, Ronit Herzog, MD, Francisco Campos, MD, Johanna Mallare, MD, Jennifer Balasny, MD, Dorothy Telega, MD, Minu George, MD, Mary Baldauf, MD, Halina Borowska, MD, Marla Sheflin, DO, Monica Relvas, MD, Laurie Massey, MD, Margaret Wren, DO, Marina Milman, MD, Deepti Mehrotra, MD

3rd Row: Nancy Chiang, MD, Lai Ping Lew, MD, Yamo Deniz, MD, Maria Galoso, MD, Malathi Sreedhara, MD, Brenda Marcano, MD, Natasha Tellechea, MD, Liliana Palacio, MD, Sangita Modi, MD, Linda Moerck, MD, Suzanne Hartley, MD, Tara Fusco, MD, Saumitra Biswas, MD, Louis Dizon, MD

4th Row: Gregory Telega, MD, Gregory Kraus, MD, Gorge Lujan-Zilbermann, MD, Miro Ukraincik, MD, Renat Sukov, MD, William Krief, MD, Yakov Yagudayev, MD, Kenneth Nalaboff, MD, Jayati Singh, MD, Albert Bassoul, MD

5th Row: Paul Sirna, MD, Gadi Avshalomov, MD, Ioannis Moissidis, MD, Isaac Braverman, MD, Betty Luna, MD, Bruce Gerberg, MD, Ian Marshall, MD, David Teng, MD, Joseph Cohen, MD, Maqbool Qadir, MD

6th Row: Brian Rabinowitz, MD, Manuel Pedroso, MD, Stephen Sondike, MD, Richard Rosencrantz, MD, David Berman, MD

SCHNEIDER CHILDREN'S HOSPITAL PEDIATRIC FELLOWS
Prior to Merger, 1998 (Partial Listing) Names listed left to right.
1st Row (sitting): Stefano Amodio, MD, Mahmut Celiker, MD, Yaser Mohamed, MD, Rafael Barilari, MD, Philip Lanzkowsky, MD, Aruna Ramanan, MD, Elizabeth Ong, MD, Beth Gottlieb, MD, Cynthia Stevens, MD

2nd Row: Gina Murza, MD, Marion Rose, MD, Naomi Zilka, MD, Ramon Lacanilao, MD, Atul Shah, MD, Itzak Levy, MD, Maqbool Quadir, MD, Narinder Bhatia, MD, Mikhail Mirer, MD, Amyn Jiwani, MD, Eleni Lantzouni, MD, Aliya Khan, MD

3rd Row: Deepa Limaye, MD, Elizabeth Suarez, MD, Rosa Gamundi, MD, Luz Galand, MD, Christine Hom, MD, Jose Serruya, MD, Li Kan, MD, Tabassum Shamim, MD, Anna Alshansky, MD, Stella Ocampo, MD, Johanna Mallare, MD

4th Row: Fernando Ginebra, MD, Santosh Eapen, MD, Zoltan Zentay, MD, Rohit Talwar, MD, Fred Schwartz, MD, Jon Igartua, MD, Louisdon Pierre, MD

DIVISION	YEAR OF INCEPTION	CHIEF AT INCEPTION	CHIEF IN 2008	FACULTY NUMBER	FELLOW NUMBER	ANCILLARY STAFF	TOTAL STAFF
Infectious Diseases	1983	Lorry Rubin	Lorry Rubin	3	2	5	10
Pulmonary Medicine	1984	Emile Scarpelli	Anastassios Koumbourlis	3	0	5	8
Allergy-Immunology*	1985	Vincent Bonagura	Vincent Bonagura	6	3	11	19
Developmental & Behavioral Pediatrics	1985	Yeou-Cheng Ma	Andrew Adesman	6	1	8	15
Critical Care Medicine	1985	Janis Schaeffer	Mayer Sagy	10	6	3	17
Emergency Medicine	1986	Joy Nagelberg	Joy Nagelberg	10	6	0	16
Bone Marrow Transplantation**	1988	Raj Pahwa	Indira Sahdev	2	0	4	6
Bioethics & Social Policy	1989	Robert Cassidy	Robert Cassidy	1	0	1	2
Rheumatology	1991	Norman Ilowite	Beth Gottlieb	3	2	3	7

*This was a combined division of Allergy-Immunology and Rheumatology until 1991.
**Incorporated in the Division of Hematology-Oncology and Stem Cell Transplantation.

CLINICAL PROGRAMS

The twenty-five years between 1983 and 2008 saw major advances in medical care nationwide, and SCH was in the forefront of adopting, and in some instances initiating, new treatments and procedures.

In the field of neonatology, SCH became a lung rescue center for the advanced treatment of lung disease in premature infants, providing not only conventional ventilation but also high-frequency oscillatory ventilation (HFOV) and high-frequency jet ventilation which ventilates lungs at hundreds of little breaths per minute, reducing the likelihood of barotrauma. In addition, SCH has pioneered the use of inhaled nitric oxide for persistent pulmonary hypertension. Dennis Davidson, MD, was in the forefront of research in this area, and the hospital became a site for a national multicenter clinical trial. Extracorporeal membrane oxygenation (ECMO) is utilized in cardiopulmonary failure when other methods are not effective. SCH is one of only two sites in the New York region where ECMO is available. All of these measures have considerably improved the prognosis of neonates with lung disease. SCH has also participated in studying another major clinical advance in

neonatology: selective brain cooling for hypoxic ischemic encephalopathy, a major breakthrough in the management of hypoxic infants resulting in a 50 percent reduction in severe neurologic disabilities.

In my early years, Christiaan Neethling Barnard, MD, and I were in training at the same time at Groote Schuur Hospital in Cape Town, South Africa—he in surgery and surgical research and I in pediatrics. When he performed the first heart transplant in 1967 my competitive spirit was kindled and I began to contemplate performing bone marrow transplantation on patients with bone marrow failure. In 1970, while I was at the New York Hospital, the opportunity arose to perform one of the first bone marrow transplantations in the United States on a twelve-year-old girl with aplastic anemia. My colleagues and I demonstrated that it can be done, but unfortunately the patient died from overwhelming graft-versus-host disease. (Hilgartner, MW, Lanzkowsky P, Nachman, RL, and Weksler, MD: "Bone Marrow Transplantation for Aplastic Anemia following Hepatitis." American Pediatric Society and the Society for Pediatric Research, 1970)

These experiences made me determined to start a bone marrow transplantation unit at SCH. I recruited Raj Pahwa, MD, from Memorial Sloan-Kettering Cancer Center in New York to head the transplantation program. It began in isolation rooms on the fourth floor of LIJ, but in 1991, following a rigorous certificate of need (CON) application to the state and presentations before the New York City Health System Agency, a four-bed laminar flow transplantation unit was approved—the only one exclusively for children in the state. Since the inception of this program, hundreds of patients have received allogeneic (including cord blood) and autologous stem cell transplantations, saving the lives of many children with bone marrow failure, hematologic diseases, solid tumors, and metabolic diseases.

Cardiology is another area in which medical care has been transformed at SCH under the guidance of Fredrick Z. Bierman, MD. Cardiac catheterization is no longer used for diagnosis only but is now used therapeutically. With interventional cardiac catheterization, percutaneous coils and devices close patent ductus arteriosus and other shunts and stents are able to open strictures in the cardiovascular anatomy such as aortic coarctation and stenosis of branch pulmonary arteries. Various devices attached to the ends of catheters (like umbrellas) close atrial septal defects and in some cases ventricular septal defects. In addition, percutaneous ablation of life-threatening arrhythmias by radio-frequency and cryo-ablation have cured children with these disorders. These procedures are done in an ambulatory setting and do not require thoracotomy and cardiopulmonary bypass, dramatically reducing pain and morbid-

Multidisciplinary teleconferencing using state-of-the-art technology, 2007.

ity. At SCH in the past five years (2002–2007) 1,246 cardiac catheterizations have been performed, of which 549 were interventional cardiac catheterizations (117 valvuloplasties, 62 angioplasties, 72 stent deployments, 108 atrial septal defect device closures, and 190 electrophysiology ablations for arrythmias).

Dramatic advances have occurred in laparoscopic surgery in children. At SCH most surgery today is done laparoscopically through pinhole incisions. More and more, abdominal scars and post-operative pain and discomfort are being relegated to the pages of medical history.

Neurosurgery at SCH has seen major advances in craniofacial surgery, microscopic techniques, endoscopic skull base and intraventricular surgery, epilepsy surgery, and surgery for movement disorders.

Major advances have also occurred in the management of cystic fibrosis: comprehensive specialized care, new pharmaceutical agents, improved antibiotics, development of enteric-coated pancreatic enzyme supplements, availability of lung and heart transplantation, better understanding of the pathophysiology of cystic fibrosis, and ongoing clinical research at SCH and other institutions. These have all contributed to a significant increase in life expectancy.

Advances in drug therapy (antimicrobial, antifungal, and antiviral agents) for infections, antiretroviral agents for the treatment of AIDS, and immunotherapeutic agents in the treatment of hematologic, immunologic, rheumatologic, and gastroenterologic disorders have had a profound effect on the outcome of these conditions. Advances in psychopharmacology have dramatically enhanced the management of psychiatric and behavioral disorders in children. New drugs, dosage schedules, and protocols to treat childhood cancers have resulted in remarkable cure rates in most childhood malignancies. Newer and safer anesthetic agents and techniques have improved surgical results and made new surgical procedures possible.

SCH has kept ahead of the curve in advances in medical genetics, adopting new procedures and techniques for genetic diagnosis as they became available.

SCH has been in the forefront of adopting cutting-edge technology, including physiologic monitoring equipment in the intensive care units; state-of-the-art ventilation equipment; wireless telemetry monitoring cardiac rhythm in patients; wireless capsule endoscopy, in some cases replacing flexible endoscopy in the examination of the gastrointestinal tract in children; continuous veno-venous hemodiafiltration for removal of drugs or toxic metabolites from plasma; videoelectroencephalography (video EEG) for identifying seizures, pseudoseizures, and movement disorders; and flexible bronchoscopy with children.

The most impressive advance has been in pediatric imaging. With the use of CAT scan, MRI, ultrasonography, PET scanning, PET-CT, and neuroimaging, the anatomy and pathology are revealed in a most exquisite and precise manner, allowing accurate diagnosis and guiding surgical intervention. Fetal ultrasound, another major advance, permits the diagnosis of fetal anomalies, including intracardiac defects, very early in fetal gestation making fetal surgery and medical intervention possible.

All of these sophisticated programs have required physical space, financial support, and talented and well-trained faculty working with a dedicated team of nurses, technicians, and other medical specialists. SCH has made it all possible.

RESEARCH PROGRAMS

The Research Programs have flourished since the opening of SCH in 1983. Thousands of abstracts and scientific papers have been published in peer-reviewed national and international journals as well as numerous chapters and text books. Members of the faculty present their research at national and international scientific meetings on a regular basis. Details of research conducted at SCH are described in Part II of this book entitled Development of Divisions of Schneider Children's Hospital.

THE GEMINI CONFERENCE

Back in 1973, I started holding weekly multidisciplinary conferences with the full-time faculty and house staff to discuss difficult diagnostic problems. I wished I could transmit the material to other hospitals, and that became possible by the end of the decade with the development of the New York Telephone Company's Gemini teleconferencing system, an electronic "blackboard" that could transmit images via the phone lines to TV screens in remote locations.

In 1988 Optel Communications came out

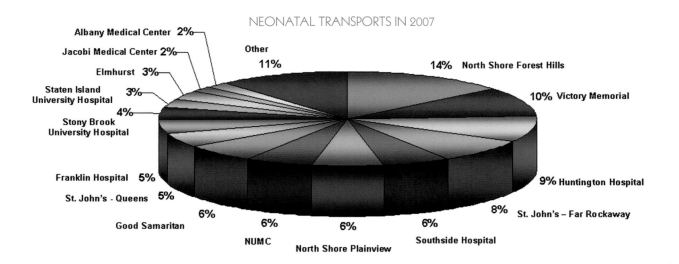

NEONATAL TRANSPORTS IN 2007

Albany Medical Center 2%
Jacobi Medical Center 2%
Elmhurst 3%
Staten Island University Hospital 3%
Stony Brook University Hospital 4%
Franklin Hospital 5%
St. John's - Queens 5%
Good Samaritan 6%
NUMC 6%
North Shore Plainview 6%
Southside Hospital 6%
St. John's – Far Rockaway 8%
Huntington Hospital 9%
Victory Memorial 10%
North Shore Forest Hills 14%
Other 11%

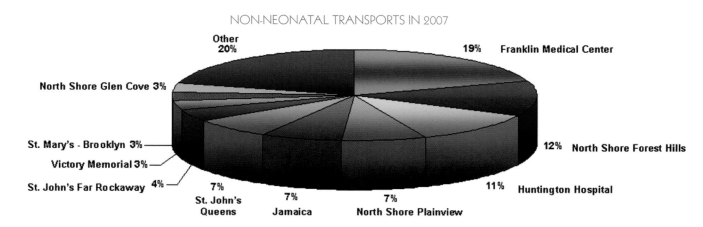

NON-NEONATAL TRANSPORTS IN 2007

Other 20%
North Shore Glen Cove 3%
St. Mary's - Brooklyn 3%
Victory Memorial 3%
St. John's Far Rockaway 4%
St. John's Queens 7%
Jamaica 7%
North Shore Plainview 7%
Huntington Hospital 11%
North Shore Forest Hills 12%
Franklin Medical Center 19%

with a more sophisticated system in which an electronic writing tablet replaced the original electronic blackboard. The electronic tablet was linked to a computer that was loaded for every session with the patients' history as well as graphs, pathology slides, and radiographs, including ultrasonographs, CT scans, and MRI. In addition, there was two-way audio contact with all the sites to permit interactive discussion between the Schneider Children's Hospital (the presenting hospital) and the receiving hospitals in the area. While continuing to use standard telephone lines, the system allowed for more computerized functions to be incorporated into the weekly presentation. Using this tablet, the moderator could annotate images on the screen in different colors and zoom down on images for

greater detail. This system was more fully described in *Academic Medicine*. (Rosner, F., Gandhi, M.R. and Lanzkowsky, P.: "Teleconferencing for Graduate and Continuing Medical Education," *Academic Medicine* 67:384, 1992)

In 1995, we upgraded again, to the current Picturetel System. The new state-of-the-art technology allows for two-way transmission of both audio and video images using dedicated ISDN telephone lines and integrated computer and medical equipment. Each location receives a real-time broadcast of the program. The system permits two-way transmission of audio and sophisticated images between all locations independently. This technology has resulted in the transmission of diagnostic-quality imagery throughout the network.

Initially, transmissions went to the Queens

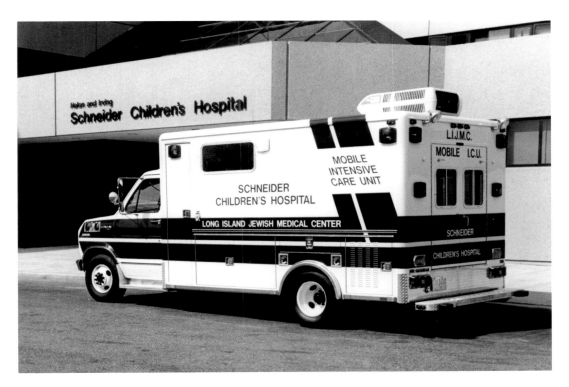

The third mobile intensive care unit employed by SCH, 1984.

FIG. 14.1: Growth of the SCH transport system for neonates and total transports, 2003–2007.

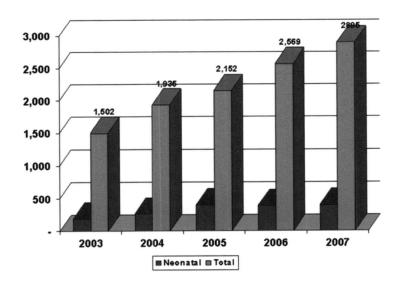

Ribbon-cutting ceremony for first multidisciplinary satellite center in Hauppauge, 1995.

the reign of King Charles II), which never closed throughout the blitzkrieg except for the twelve compulsory days between September 4 and 16, 1939, the Gemini conference has virtually never been canceled because of inclement weather or for any other reason. My signature tune at the beginning of each session is: "It's eight-zero-zero Eastern Standard Time, broadcasting from the Schneider Children's Hospital." The music would play even if the audience was small.

In keeping pace with today's technology, grand rounds and interactive teleconferencing (Gemini conferences) are available for viewing on the Schneider Children's Hospital Website. A complete library of conferences held from the fall of 2006 to the present is available for viewing over the Internet. Continuing medical education credits are also available upon complete viewing of these conferences.

Hospital Center and Elmhurst Hospital in New York City, and to Huntington and St. Charles Hospitals on Long Island. Currently the program is transmitted to twenty-five sites including private pediatric offices, SCH satellite centers, and eleven hospitals in the North Shore-Long Island Jewish Health System. As an indication of the system's scope and versatility, it is also transmitted to Semmelweis University in Hungary.

This system permits institutions at long distances from large university centers to receive information in a very cost- and time-efficient manner. Physicians no longer need to travel long distances to get their continuing medical education. Although the official name of this system should be Interactive Teleconferencing, it continues to be dubbed the Gemini conference after the original equipment utilized in the later 1970s.

The session is held every Friday at 8:00 a.m. at the Schneider Children's Hospital and is an extremely popular educational exercise both for SCH staff and the medical and nursing staffs of the hospitals receiving these educational programs. Like the Windmill Theatre (located in London, near Piccadilly Circus where a windmill stood in

SCH ON-CALL PROGRAM

The SCH On-Call Program was developed in 1997 to provide relief and support for community-based pediatricians at night and on weekends and holidays. After-hours calls from patients of the

Consultation Center at Brooklyn service brochure.

participating pediatricians are transferred to this service and their calls are responded to in less than half an hour. Run by a nurse practitioner and senior residents and supervised by a member of the faculty, this program fields all incoming patient calls. In accordance with agreed-upon protocols, patients receive medical advice and treatment over the phone. If necessary, patients are advised to go to the emergency room. The pediatricians receive faxed updates on their patients.

Today more than 200 pediatricians are enrolled in this system and over 30,000 calls are answered every year.

INFANT TRANSPORT SYSTEM

Back in the seventies, seriously ill infants were transported to LIJ in a converted station wagon equipped with an incubator or by helicopter. Today state-of-the-art ambulances, manned 24/7 by dedicated teams of critical care nurses, physicians, emergency medical technicians, and respiratory therapists, are transporting many more neonates, infants, and children from a much wider geographical area.

The ambulances are linked by phone to the pediatric intensive care unit and their locations are tracked at all times by a global navigating system. After LIJ's department of pediatrics' first

Mobile health van.

specially equipped infant transport ambulance (a gift from a grateful grandfather) went on the road, 300 babies were transported (nearly a baby a day). Today, that number is close to 3,000—nearly ten babies a day! (Fig. 14.1) The pie diagrams on page 230 show the various institutions from which neonates and non-neonates are transported.

MULTIDISCIPLINARY SATELLITE CENTERS

The development of a large subspecialty faculty and the need for consultations in communities distant from the hospital led to the concept of satellite consultation centers. The first center was developed on Long Island in Hauppauge in 1995. This center had to be relocated to Commack in 1996 because it had outgrown the original space in Hauppauge.

This was followed by the development of centers in Hewlett, Nassau County (1996), West Islip, Suffolk County (1999), Hampton Bays, Suffolk County (2000), Flushing, Queens County (2000), Bensonhurst, Kings County (2004), and Williamsburg, Kings County (2007). These satellites are very convenient for patients for initial diagnoses and continuing care by specialists. They expand the network of services provided to the community, reduce the need for patients to travel long

FIG. 14.2: Schneider Children's Hospital Consultation Center Patient Visits.

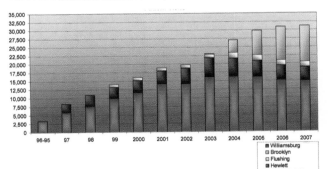

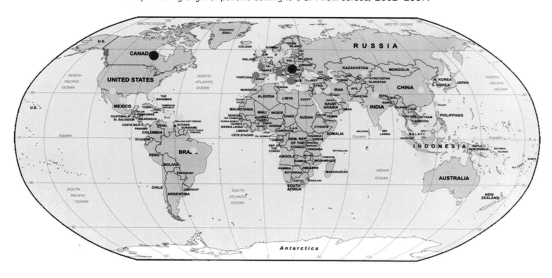

Map showing origin of patients coming to SCH from abroad, 2002–2007.

● 1 – 5 patients   ● 5-10 Patients   ● 10 or more Patients

other staff, the program delivers primary health services to children in underserved and high-risk communities throughout Long Island.

The program has three goals: (1) to improve access to high-quality healthcare for vulnerable populations; (2) to offer direct medical services and education programs to at-risk families; and (3) to target statistically important chronic and acute illnesses and deliver meaningful assistance.

The Mobile Health Program was expanded in 2008 with the purchase of a mobile dental unit. The thirty-eight-foot vehicle unit is equipped with two dental chairs and staffed by a dentist and support personnel. The dental van provides a full range of dental services to needy residents in Hempstead, Central Islip, Bay Shore, Brentwood, and Riverhead, both children and adults.

THE INTERNATIONAL PROGRAM

As the Schneider Children's Hospital's reputation grew and its faculty became more well known on a local, national, and even an

distances for specialty care, enlarge the sphere of influence of the Schneider Children's Hospital, and serve as a major referral source of tertiary-care patients to the hospital. In 2007 over 30,000 patients were seen in these centers. (Fig. 14.2)

Before these centers are established, SCH senior faculty meet one on one with local doctors to ascertain which medical services are needed in that particular area. The consultation centers provide uniform, high-quality, comprehensive services conducted by senior faculty. They do not compete with the local pediatricians for primary care, but instead support community-based pediatricians by providing tertiary care.

MOBILE HEALTH PROGRAM

In order to provide medical care to about 75,000 uninsured children on Long Island, a mobile health program was instituted in 1999. This was made possible by a generous donation from the Sanjay and Sylvia Kumar Foundation and New York State grants. An attempt to accomplish this in the early 1970s was unsuccessful.

Using a Winnebago-sized vehicle equipped with two examination rooms, a registration/waiting area, and a team of doctors, nurses, and

FIG. 14.3: Emergency department visits, 2002–2007.

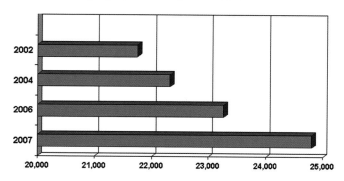

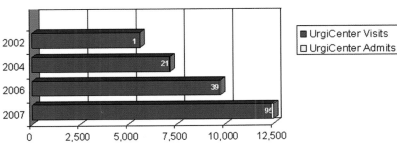

FIG. 14.4: Urgicenter visits and number of patients admitted to the hospital from the urgicenter, 2002–2007.

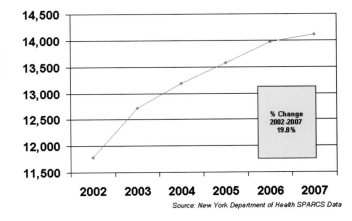

FIG. 14.5: SCH discharges (inclusive of neonates and normal newborns), 2002–2007

Source: New York Department of Health SPARCS Data

international level, patients were referred to it from various parts of the world. (See the map at left showing the countries of origin of patients coming to SCH.) Frequently, relationships of SCH faculty with physicians in many countries abroad have facilitated and promoted these referrals. These patients and their families live at the Ronald McDonald House on the grounds of the hospital.

Patient referrals occur in many disciplines, particularly bone marrow transplantation, oncology, cardiovascular surgery, and neurosurgery, although other disciplines are also on the list. They come from countries all over the world, as shown on the map on the opposite page.

EMERGENCY DEPARTMENT AND URGICENTER

The volume of patients in the emergency department has increased considerably over the years. (Fig. 14.3) The acuity of illness has also increased. In 1984, only 12.4 percent of all patients presenting in the emergency department were admitted to the hospital; in 2007 that number had risen to 20 percent. The increased volume and acuity led to the establishment of an urgicenter in October 1992. (Fig. 14.4)

The purpose of an urgicenter is to treat patients with relatively mild acute illnesses who come to the emergency room for medical care. This "fast-track" system decants patients from the emergency department, easing the emergency department's load. It has been met with consider-

able patient satisfaction. Initially the center was open from 6:00 to 10:00 p.m. when private pediatricians were not usually available. Over time the hours were extended from noon to midnight Monday through Friday and on public holidays and weekends 9:00 a.m. to midnight. The urgicenter provides coverage for walk-in patients, voluntary and full-time faculty referrals, and most importantly, for the triaged pediatric emergency department patients with non-emergent but acute care needs. This has resulted in a decrease in the number of walkouts from the emergency department due to excessive waiting time. The urgicenter has also permitted expertly trained pediatric emergency medicine physicians to be able to focus on the truly acutely ill patients. The volume of the urgicenter has grown as the availability of this service has become known in the communities we serve. In 2007, approximately 12,500 patients were seen.

HOSPITAL DISCHARGES

As a consequence of all these innovative programs and services, the number of discharges at SCH has increased every year.

There has been a 19.8 percent increase in discharges in the last five years. (Fig. 14.5) (In 1970, the first year that I was director of pediatrics at LIJ, the total pediatric discharges at LIJ were 2,301.) SCH has become the major provider of tertiary-care services to children in Queens,

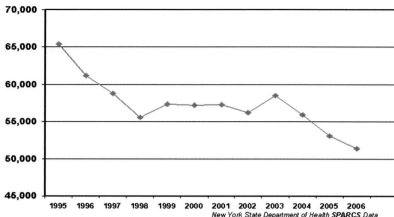
FIG. 14.6: Trend in pediatric discharges in the region, 1996–2006.

New York State Department of Health SPARCS Data

Nassau, and Suffolk Counties, part of the borough of Brooklyn and beyond, a population totaling more than seven million people. This increase in pediatric discharges occurred at a time when there was a 21 percent reduction in pediatric discharges at other hospitals in the region. (Fig. 14.6) In 2007 the Schneider Children's Hospital had the largest number of discharges of any one of the 215 hospitals providing pediatric care in New York State. (Table 14.1)

FINANCIAL SUCCESS

In 2007, the operating revenue (almost exclusively from patient services) was $165 million, with an operating gain of revenue over expenses of approximately $16 million and an operating margin of 9.6 percent. Since the children's hospital has no endowment, the margin was entirely from hospital operation. The faculty practice plan of SCH comprising physician billing, contracts, contributions, and hospital-

supported services was approximately $51 million. The SCH grant activity from the federal government, New York State, and foundations was approximately $3,500,000, with over $4,700,000 in philanthropy. The total revenue received from all services was approximately $224 million. Compared to other hospitals, SCH is highly successful from a financial perspective. The factors creating the favorable operating margin include:

High occupancy: Since the hospital was built, it has typically seen an occupancy rate in excess of 95 percent. At peak times, the occupancy exceeds 100 percent, with a large number of patients being treated in the hallways because of the inadequate number of beds. The total inpatient discharge in 2007 was 14,115 (including neonates and normal newborns).

Percentage of surgical discharges: With the appointment of a cadre of full-time pediatric general surgeons and pediatric surgical subspecialists, the percentage of surgery to pediatric medicine has reached 22 percent. Since the margin on surgical cases is greater than that on medical patients, this is financially advantageous to the hospital.

Number of critical-care beds: The number of critical-care beds at SCH is sixty-eight (44 percent), which is very high, even for a tertiary-care hospital. This includes neonatal intensive care, pediatric intensive care, and the bone marrow transplantation unit. The trend during the past

TABLE 14.1: Top five New York State Hospitals Inpatient Pediatric Providers

Hospital	County	Discharges[*]
Schneider Children's Hospital	Queens	7,266
New York Presbyterian – Columbia Presbyterian Center	New York	6,306
Womens and Children's Hospital Buffalo	Erie	6,198
Montifiore Medical Center – Henry & Lucy Moses Division	Bronx	6,036
Westchester Medical Center	Westchester	4,499

*Excludes neonates and normal newborns.

New York State Department of Health SPARCS Data

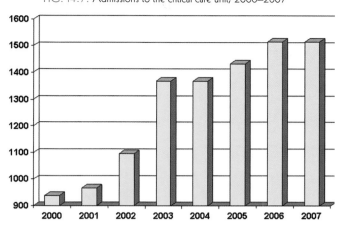

FIG. 14.7: Admissions to the critical care unit, 2000–2007

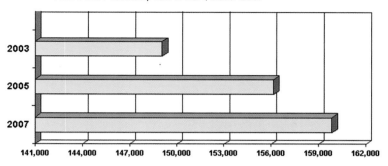

FIG. 14.8: Ambulatory visits at SCH, 2003–2007

few years has been toward greater demand for pediatric critical-care beds. (Fig. 14.7)

The planned construction will bring the number of critical-care beds to 55 percent. This is reflective of the very high acuity level of the patients referred to SCH.

Ambulatory patient visits: The number of ambulatory patient visits has increased considerably over the years. (Fig. 14.8)

Pediatric trauma center: Since SCH was approved in 1996 as a Level I Trauma Center for pediatrics, trauma cases from all over the region are referred to SCH, contributing to the high occupancy rate. (Fig. 14.9)

Case intensity: Because of quaternary-care programs such as bone marrow transplantation, ECMO (extracorporeal membrane oxygenation), and high-risk neonatology, the hospital has a very high case intensity index.

Length-of-stay reductions: A very aggressive case management system and the use of hospitalists and firm directors (full-time physicians who have total responsibility and authority for the effective management of a hospital unit—part of the organizational structure in hospitals in Great Britain but uncommon in this country) have driven down the length of stay, increased the throughput of the hospital, and improved patient satisfaction and the margin. The average length of stay in 2007 was 4.2 days for medical patients, 3.3 days for surgical patients, and 15.7 for neonatal patients.

Hospital and physician relationships and contracts: The development of a network of over 1,000 pediatricians on Long Island and beyond who are connected to SCH at various levels, and our relationships with surrounding hospitals, have resulted in the transfer of a large number of cases to SCH.

The infant transport, international, and satellite center programs described earlier, have also contributed to the hospital's financial success.

Proving all of its critics wrong, SCH is thriving, a children's hospital whose name is synonymous with excellence in pediatric care. The systematic development of SCH over the past twenty-five years has catapulted the institution into national and international prominence.

When it opened its doors, we enjoyed the luxury of all that pristine new space; twenty-five years later it is bursting at the seams. The hospital has to be expanded in size to accommodate the increased number of patients seeking care.

FIG. 14.9: Number of Admissions from pediatric trauma center, 2000–2007

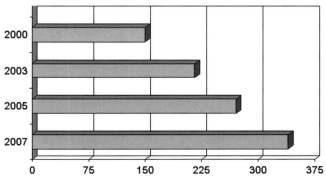

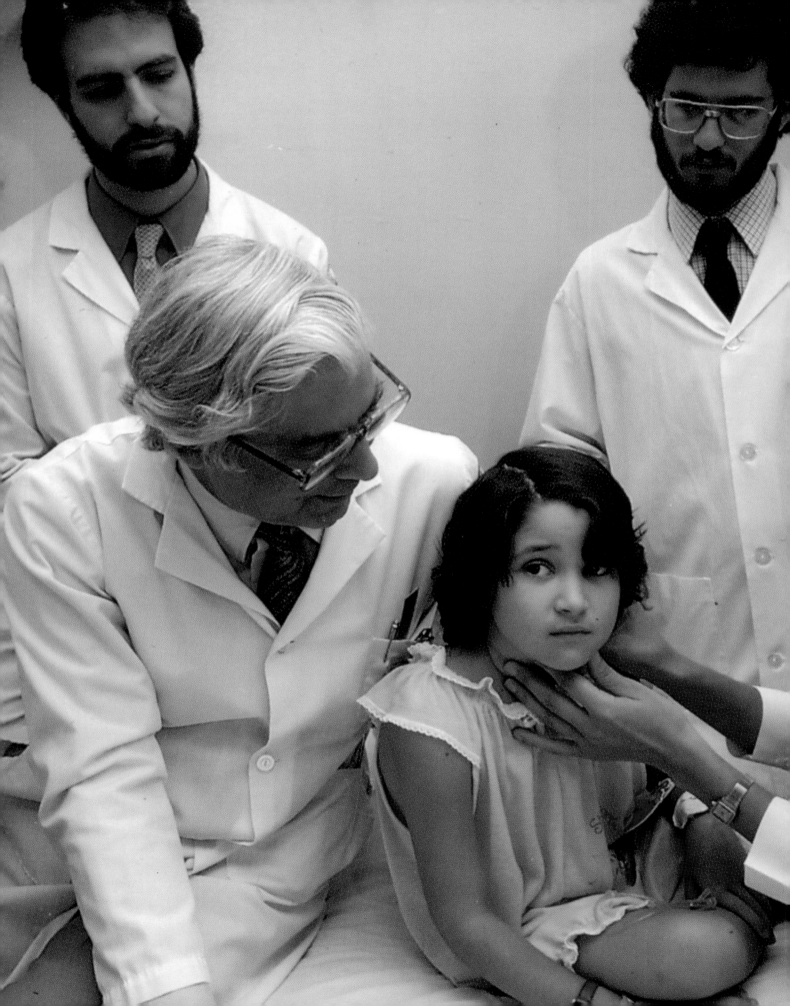

CHAPTER 15

THE EDUCATION PROGRAM

TRAINING THE NEXT GENERATION

"All who care about children must care deeply about the education of those who provide their health services. The children's hospital will play a major role in medical education and act as a lodestar for the training and teaching of all health professionals concerned with children. It should become a spearhead for research in all the disciplines of pediatrics so that the fruits of biological research and clinical investigation can benefit future generations of children."

From the remarks of Philip Lanzkowsky, MD, at the Schneider Children's Hospital dedication ceremony, Sept. 25, 1983.

UNDERGRADUATE MEDICAL EDUCATION

Educating the pediatricians of the future has always been an important part of the mission of the Department of Pediatrics of Long Island Jewish Medical Center (LIJ) and the Schneider Children's Hospital (SCH). In 1955, LIJ affiliated with the State of New York Health Science Center at Brooklyn, better known as SUNY Downstate, and its third-year students did clerkships in pediatrics at LIJ for sixteen years. In 1970, when LIJ switched its affiliation to the newly opened Stony Brook University School of Medicine, also part of the SUNY system, between four and six pediatric clerks rotated for seven-

Bedside rounds in the hematology-oncology unit with Philip Lanzkowsky, MD, and house staff in 1984.

week blocks throughout the year, and many chose to come back as pediatric residents. In 1989, when LIJ became the Long Island campus for the Albert Einstein College of Medicine of Yeshiva University, SCH received its clerks in pediatrics in six-week rotations. Following the merger of LIJ and NSUH, medical students from New York University School of Medicine, in addition, rotated in pediatrics at SCH.

Over the years, fourth-year medical students from many medical schools around the country and abroad took elective rotations at SCH, which provided them with a combination of extensive clinical experience and systematic teaching.

GRADUATE MEDICAL EDUCATION

The Pediatric Residency Training Program at LIJ was established in 1956 and has been approved by the RRC (Residency Review Committee of the American Council for Graduate Medical Education, or ACGME) every year since then—usually receiving commendation. At first, a two-year pediatric residency was preceded by a one-year rotating internship consisting of four months of medicine, four months of surgery, two months of obstetrics and gynecology, and two months of pediatrics. In the mid-1960s, the rotating internship was abolished and a three-year training in pediatrics became a requirement for eligibility for board certification in pediatrics. LIJ established a three-year pediatric residency accepting twelve pediatric residents, four in each year. In 1972, the LIJ program grew to twenty-four residents when it merged with the Queens Hospital Center (QHC) pediatric residency training program and incorporated its residents into the LIJ residency complement. With the opening of SCH in 1983, the residency program was further increased to fifty-four, and it grew in 1989 to seventy-two residents because of the Bell Commission requirements.

In 1995, eight more residents were added when the primary-care track was established. This was a program designed by the New York State Department of Health specifically to increase the number of primary care physicians state-wide and it provided financial incentives to hospitals toward that end. With the merger of the North Shore pediatric program with SCH in 2003, the residency training program finally grew to a total of 131 pediatric residents, becoming one of the largest programs of its kind in the country. The table below details the growth of the residency program over the past fifty years.

NUMBER OF RESIDENTS

1956	LIJ-2-year residency (plus rotating internship)	3
1957	LIJ-2-year residency (plus rotating internship)	4
1958	LIJ-2-year residency (plus rotating internship)	5
1960	LIJ-2-year residency (plus rotating internship)	7
Mid 1960s	LIJ-3-year pediatric residency	12
1972–1992	Pediatric residency merged with QHC (12)	24
1983	SCH (30)	54
1989	Bell Commission (18)	72
1995	Primary-care track (8)	80
2003	Combined SCH-NSUH program (NSUH- 51)	131

The first fellowship training programs at LIJ started in the late 1960s, in neonatology and cardiology. The hematology training program started in 1970, followed over the years by the other sub-specialty areas as full-time faculty were appointed. In 2002, a year before the merger of the NSUH pediatrics program with the Schneider Children's Hospital, SCH had forty-six fellows in twelve subspecialty areas as follows:

Division	Number
Adolescent medicine	3
Allergy-immunology	3
Cardiology	5
Critical care medicine	5
Developmental-behavioral pediatrics	3
Emergency medicine	5
Endocrinology	3
Hematology-oncology	6
Infectious diseases	1
Neonatal-perinatal medicine	6
Neurology	4
Rheumatology	2

At that time, NSUH had seventeen fellows in seven subspecialty divisions as follows:

Division	Number
Adolescent medicine	2
Allergy-immunology	3
Cardiology	3
Endocrinology	1
Gastroenterology	2
Infectious diseases	1
Neonatal-perinatal medicine	5

When the fellowship training program was combined, the number of fellows was reduced to fifty-eight, distributed in the following subspecialty divisions:

Division	Numbers
Adolescent medicine	3
Allergy-immunology	5
Cardiology	6
Critical care medicine	6
Developmental-behavioral pediatrics	1
Emergency medicine	6
Endocrinology	2
Gastroenterology	2
Hematology-oncology	6
Infectious diseases	2
Neonatal-perinatal medicine	12
Neurology	5
Rheumatology	2

THE EARLY YEARS

The man who led the pediatric training program in pediatrics at LIJ upon its establishment in 1956 was Samuel Karelitz, MD, who embodied the standards and spirit necessary to fulfill an educational mission. Even though the program was small in those days, Dr. Karelitz insisted on a full academic slate. Bedside rounds were held every day from 10:00 to 11:00 a.m, with private practitioners in the community who served as teaching faculty for three months at a time. From 11:00 to 12:00, Dr. Karelitz held teaching rounds, taking up the most "interesting" cases across the whole spectrum of pediatric problems. He made his afternoon rounds every day precisely at 4:00 p.m. The residents, attending physicians, and nurses were lined up in front of the nurses' station on Four South, starched and standing at attention as their chief descended on them from his first-floor office. Rounds would continue until all the patients had been seen, the problems understood, and the management decided upon.

In 1964, six months before the Queens Hospital Center affiliated with LIJ, the Department of Pediatrics at LIJ affiliated with the Queens Hospital Center, which was operated by the Health and Hospitals Corporation of New York. At that time, the Queens Hospital Center had 109 pediatric beds, including twenty neonatal beds, and its own independent residency program with twelve residents. Franklin Desposito, MD (hematology), and Hedda Acs, MD (neonatology), were appointed full-time to the Queens Hospital Center and were the main teachers in the early days before the Queens Hospital Center residency program was combined with LIJ's. Dr. Acs was chief of the neonatal unit and residency program director and in 1989 became the director of the Department of Pediatrics. She worked assiduously to provide first-rate care for children in an understaffed, underfunded inner-city hospital for over thirty years (1964 to 1997) and was an inspiration in her devotion and commitment to sick children.

In 1972 the Queens Hospital Center residency program merged with LIJ's residency program, and this combined residency lasted until 1992, when LIJ discontinued its affiliation with the Queens Hospital Center. The Queens Hospital Center was "the worst of times, it was the best of times." Supplies were inadequate. Ancillary staff was "difficult." Parents were unavailable. But despite the conditions, the residents found out what it really meant to be a doctor—to be responsible, to make decisions, and to make a difference. They found out how good they could be—and how good that felt.

Arturo Aballi, MD, director of pediatrics at the Queens Hospital Center, 1965–1979.

No one made a more indelible mark in pediatrics at the Queens Hospital Center than Arturo Aballi, MD, the director of pediatrics under the affiliation agreement with the Health and Hospitals Corporation of the City of New York. In 1965, he was recruited from Memphis to become the first director of pediatrics. Born and educated in Cuba, Dr. Aballi was the son of the famous Arellano Angelo Aballi (1880–1952), professor of pediatrics at the University of Havana, Cuba. He was board certified in both neonatology and hematology, and a perpetual student, with extraordinary expertise in infectious diseases. Thirty years after the Queens Hospital Center experience, an SCH faculty member was still proclaiming that his goal in life was to be Dr. Aballi. What was his distinguishing mark? He knew everything! He knew medicine. He knew diagnostics. He knew his patients. He knew your patients—all there was to know about them. And he expected you to demonstrate your commitment by always working to know more and care more.

Dr. Aballi was always available, always there. But he was more than just physically present;

he was always interested, excited (and exciting), and deeply invested in whatever was going on. Thriving on three hours of sleep a night, he read prodigiously, his energy was boundless, and his spirit infectious.

And, finally, he was such a great teacher, able to channel all his knowledge, enthusiasm, and concern into the teaching of others. He was a model and a mentor for all he taught.

THE LANZKOWSKY ERA

I served as program director from 1970 until the pediatric program merged with the NSUH pediatric program in 2003 when Harvey Aiges, MD, became the program director. When I became chairman of pediatrics, I did most of the teaching, assisted by Norman Gootman, MD, I. Ronald Shenker, MD, and a cadre of voluntary staff. As the full-time staff grew, the teaching faculty grew as well, and greater specialization developed, providing a broader scope of expertise to be imparted to students and residents.

In 1984 I appointed the first full-time coordinator of pediatric training. After studying medicine at Albert Einstein College of Medicine, completing an LIJ pediatric residency, serving as chief resident at the Queens Hospital Center and as an attending for four years at that hospital, Michael Frogel, MD, came back to SCH to run the residency program and become chief of the Division of General Pediatrics with the responsibility for quality assurance. For ten years Dr. Frogel handled the enormous demands of managing the second largest pediatric residency in New York State, including recruiting about twenty-five new house staff each year. In 1987 I appointed Stanley Levine, MD, formerly director of pediatrics at Kaplan Hospital and professor of pediatrics at Tel Aviv University in Israel, as my assistant chief of staff. Professor Levine, born and trained in South Africa, was a well-known immunologist and had interest and expertise in medical education. He was the first editor of the Children's Hospital Quarterly Journal, which was published from 1989 until 1999 and contained original papers written by members of the faculty. Dr. Levine assisted Dr. Frogel and me in house staff training and ran a course on the logic and art of medical diagnosis. After Dr. Frogel decided to devote all his time to general pediatrics, Robert Katz, MD, joined by Robert Cassidy, PhD took on the task of residency training.

Michael Frogel, MD, Robert Cassidy, PhD, and Robert Katz, MD, circa 1989.

Over time the teaching program remained remarkably constant. Work rounds, professorial rounds, noon lectures, consultants' order-focused teaching, senior residents' learning and teaching one step ahead of juniors and rich and varied pathology in the patient population formed the backbone of the training program.

Dr. Cassidy, the director of bioethics, shadowed me on most of my rounds and teaching assignments, ostensibly to complement my teaching but actually to check that the correct and "ethical" message was being conveyed to these young, impressionable trainees.

Reflecting on the teaching program, Dr. Cassidy stated: "1970 was the dividing line between B.L.E. and L.E.: Before the Lanzkowsky Era and the Lanzkowsky Era. Seldom have the principles and spirit of one individual so defined such a large and complex institution. For nearly half a century he has cared for the sickest children, published nearly 300 academic papers, written six textbooks on pediatric hematology-oncology, developed and led a department of over 125 full-time pediatric faculty, trained almost 1,000 house officers and thirty-eight hematology-oncology fellows, and, most noticeably, planned, produced, and nurtured what was initially the only children's hospital in the greater New York area."

Although many faculty members were recruited in the 1970s, there were still many areas left uncovered, meaning that the existing faculty had to be more expansible and truly collegial in managing care and teaching. I made professorial rounds every day in a different area of pediatrics. If it's Monday, it must be the adolescent unit; Tuesday the intensive care unit; Wednesday the hematology-oncology unit; Thursday the neonatal unit; and Friday, to bring all the spheres into harmony, the multidisciplinary teleconference (a.k.a. Gemini) and grand rounds. Grand rounds, usually conducted by a member of the full-time faculty or a visiting professor from one of various medical schools around the country, were (and still are) held every Friday at 11:00 a.m.

Neonatal rounds with Fredrick Battaglia, visiting professor from University of Colorado. Left to right: Drs. Herbert Goldman, Joel Sussman, Philip Lanzkowsky, neonatal fellow, Fredrick Battaglia and Shyan-Chu Sun, a neonatal fellow, 1971.

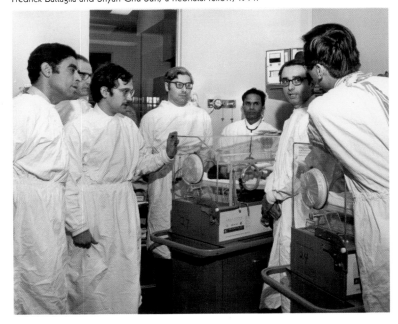

Dr. Cassidy and Laurie Locastro, my editorial associate, interviewed members of the house staff of the seventies, eighties, and nineties to gather their recollections of the training program:

Many faculty who were members of the house staff in those "good old days" remember cramming all night on the twenty different ways that neuroblastoma could present and all the conceivable causes for an obstructed airway. "Who was Fanconi?" Good enough was never good enough. As their survival skills became finely honed, they learned to feed "the chief" alluring (and craftily selected) topics. ("Looks like the baby has hyperbilirubinemia, Dr. Lanzkowsky.") Occasionally he bit, but often, to their great disappointment, he did not.

Former residents remembered that knowing all the "stuff" was only the beginning. Above all, they had to know their patients. Quoting Osler, Dr. Lanzkowsky was prone to reminding them "Listen; listen to the patient. He tells you the diagnosis." The complete history! The immediate condition! The laboratory data! The diagnostic thinking! The management plan! The expected consequences of each intervention! And no notes to help your memory or calm your nerves. The resident was the patient's pediatrician and the only acceptable standard for the pediatrician, as they recalled, was Dr. Lanzkowsky. "Tell me everything you know about hypertension," he would demand. "We have an hour. You appreciated a mass? Take me in and show me how you examined that abdomen. Did you look at the smear?" They were expected to demonstrate how to be a pediatrician.

"They remembered that Dr. Lanzkowsky wanted to teach them three things," Laurie Locastro reported. "First, to think systematically...to take a handful of branches and turn them into a tree. Structure the questioning; discipline the probing. Sort all that garbage into defined categories. (Remember those mnemonics, such as CTMIND—congenital, traumatic, metabolic, infectious, neoplastic, degenerative.) And, systematically build the connections between the categories until their vision had encompassed everything and given them command over all. 'Don't think like a technician,' he exhorted them. 'Think like a creator...create a consistent, coherent, and comprehensive order to ground your practice.'

"Second, he sought to inspire the house staff (no matter how busy or tired or frustrated or fearful) with the wondrous intellectual excitement of their profession. The complexity of the human organism, the sensitivity and ingenuity of a good clinical work-up, the aesthetic elegance of disciplined scientific thinking—it was at one and the same time the most morally serious work and the most stimulating fun.

"And third, he taught them professional honor. Duty, responsibility, honesty, integrity...these professional virtues are the bedrock of practice. They will never forget that Dr. Lanzkowsky demanded an unqualified commitment to serving their patients, to respecting their colleagues, and to being true to their work. With this, as with systematic thinking and intellectual excitement, he served as an example of how the physician put these principles into practice. Anything less, as many remembered hearing him say many times, was 'unacceptable...totally unacceptable.'"

Rounds almost always had everyone going in to the patient's bedside. All of the faculty knew and worked with all the residents. There was no formal morning report until 1984, as every new patient was shared and discussed informally. The house staff recalled that every Thursday morning, they all squeezed into my office (for a while, along with the department's cages of iron-deficient rats, which I kept there to be sure they were properly cared for during my research work on iron deficiency). Sitting on the floor, they might raise their gripes, which I would return to them, miraculously transformed into deficiencies they needed to work on. In those early days, the program was much smaller, and more intimate. I used to hold regular parties at my home for house staff and I was able to get to know them and their significant others quite intimately.

Teaching was shared by all in the residency family. The chiefs really ran the daily work of the hospital, including the intensive care unit, which had no regular attending until 1983. And they taught as they worked, especially at night, when the senior residents would administer teaching boluses to the interns. Every case was a teaching case. Why? Because, as Dr. Cassidy eloquently phrased it: "Inspiration flowed down from the top like a mighty stream—the need for knowledge was a pressing reality for those who had front-line responsibility for patients." It was indeed a different era.

The proof of the educational efficacy of this intense communal residency is the remarkable number of our outstanding full-time faculty who

Bedside rounds in critical care unit with Philip Lanzkowsky, MD, and house staff, 1987.

Rounds with Philip Lanzkowsky, MD, Kevin Bock, MD, and Kevin Roy, MD in the critical care unit, 2005.

Bedside rounds in the adolescent unit with Philip Lanzkowsky, MD, and house staff, 2006.

SCHNEIDER CHILDREN'S HOSPITAL

Grand Rounds Program

Sponsored by:
Schneider Children's Hospital
New Hyde Park, NY

Long Island Jewish Medical Center,
The Long Island Campus for the
Albert Einstein College of Medicine

 Schneider
Children's Hospital

trained in our residency program. (See alumni appointed to full-time SCH faculty in Part III, page 468.) They are a tribute to how well the program put its principles into practice.

CHANGES...NOT ALL OF THEM GOOD

My intimate involvement with every phase of the education program over nearly four decades gives me a unique vantage point from which to view its evolution. There have been many advances, and many steps back.

Site visits by the RRC of the ACGME (the Residency Review Committee of the American Council for Graduate Medical Education) occurred every three years, and later every five years. The early site visitors were pediatricians well known to me, such as Edward Joyner, MD, formerly chairman of pediatrics at Lenox-Hill Hospital, and Gertrude (Trudy) Stern, MD, retired from New York Hospital-Cornell faculty. The visitations were informal and social and after lunch, some reminiscences, and an exchange of pleasantries, there would be a comment such as, "We know you run a good program," and they would leave and we would receive full accreditation. In the last decade or two, things have changed. The PIF (program information form) has become more detailed and searching, and evaluations of residents and faculty have grown more exacting. Greater detail about curriculum and lectures is required, and rigorous adherence to rotations and requirements is demanded. The site visits have become more formal and less pleasant.

Required outpatient continuity clinics were added in 1977 and in 1989 the resident complement expanded to meet the demands of the Bell Commission. This was a heavy blow to traditional training. Resident fatigue was believed to have been a contributing factor in the death of a young patient, Libby Zion, at New York Hospital in 1984. This case resulted in the formation of the Bell Commission, an ad

hoc advisory committee established by the New York State Commissioner of Health in 1984. The committee, led by Bertrand Bell, MD, a professor at Albert Einstein College of Medicine, recommended limiting resident working hours to eighty hours a week and no longer than twenty-four hours at a stretch. This recommendation was passed into law by the New York State Legislature and went into effect on July 1, 1989 (section 405 of the New York State health code, referred to as the Bell Commission Regulations). This rule has been carefully policed by state regulatory bodies and very forcefully imposed and regulated by the New York State Department of Health.

Many of the old-time "giants" are still grieving for those "no Bell" days, when the patients, not the schedule, decided when the work was done. Regulation 405 has had a major impact on the residents' attitude. A "shift mentality" has developed, with residents becoming less committed to completing care of the patient. Because they could work a specific number of hours and then hand the patient off to someone else, their sense of personal and professional responsibility diminished significantly. This was a sea change in the way house staff perceived and carried out their responsibilities.

The curtailment of the work hours for residents increases the number of times patients are "handed off" to fellow residents and further fragments the care the patient receives at the bedside. New technology will be necessary to enhance the transfer of information and to ensure patient safety.

Many would agree, however, that there is a danger to residents who have worked long hours at a stretch: the danger of getting to a

> "The clinician who keeps one eye on his watch while in the wards is rarely successful."
>
> —Sir William Osler, Albany Med Ann 1901:22:1-11

car accident when driving home overtired. This has happened to residents in this program and elsewhere.

How else has the residency changed in the "modern era"? The commitment to academic seriousness in a state-of-the-art children's hospital endures, but educationally, two shifts in emphasis are notable. Increasingly, primary care has become a major focus of our academic programs. Originally, LIJ and SCH concentrated on training house staff to care for the sickest children in the optimal tertiary-care setting. Those who went on to fellowships were well prepared to handle the pressures and complexities of sub-specialty care. But over half of the graduating residents headed for a primary-care career. Our responsibility to prepare them fully melded with the change in the RRC requirements and the socioeconomic pressures in the early 1990s for more primary-care specialists. In response, the department initiated the Private Pediatrics Residents Education Program (PPREP) in 1992, which places residents in private pediatricians' offices for their continuity clinic. Now almost half the residents spend half a day per week for three years acquiring the knowledge, skills, and sensitivity necessary for the specialty of "real world" office pediatrics. This primary care commitment also led us in 1995 to create a primary track concentration for up to eight residents each year who spend double the time in a primary-care setting, and receive extra primary-care specialty training. In recognition of this investment of resources, SCH was officially recognized by the New York State Department of Health as one of the selected group of primary-care training programs.

Complementing this humanistic focus has been the addition of a full-time director of bioethics and social policy Robert Cassidy, PhD, in 1989 to help the residents sharpen their decision-making skills when dealing with ethical dilemmas. Further, recognizing the inescapable psychosocial dimensions of all pediatric care, two special educational programs have been created by Dr. Cassidy to help the residents understand and manage the personal and familial problems associated with both primary care and critical care.

As the house staff grew in numbers, an educational committee was developed to take responsibility for their recruitment, retention, evaluation, teaching, and curriculum development. Prior to the merger, Dr. Katz and Dr. Cassidy assumed this role. With the merger of LIJ and NSUH, they were joined by Harvey Aiges, MD (program director at NSUH), and later by Stephen Barone, MD, who became program director in 2006.

In the beginning, training programs were more like apprenticeships. There were relatively few trainees under a small number of pediatri-

Robert Cassidy, PhD, Stephen Barone, MD (program director) and Robert Katz, MD, discussing resident selection, 2008.

cians who were not specialists but who trained the residents in all aspects of pediatrics, including the subspecialty areas. The content and quality of the programs varied considerably, based upon the effectiveness and focus of the chairman of the Department of Pediatrics. There was no fixed curriculum nor were there absolute requirements for board certification other than spending three years in a "pediatric residency." There were no

The most essential part of a student's instruction is obtained not in the lecture room, but at the bedside.

Oliver Wendell Holmes
(1898-1894)

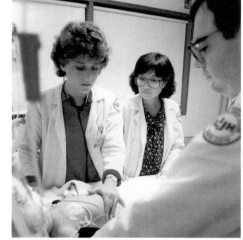

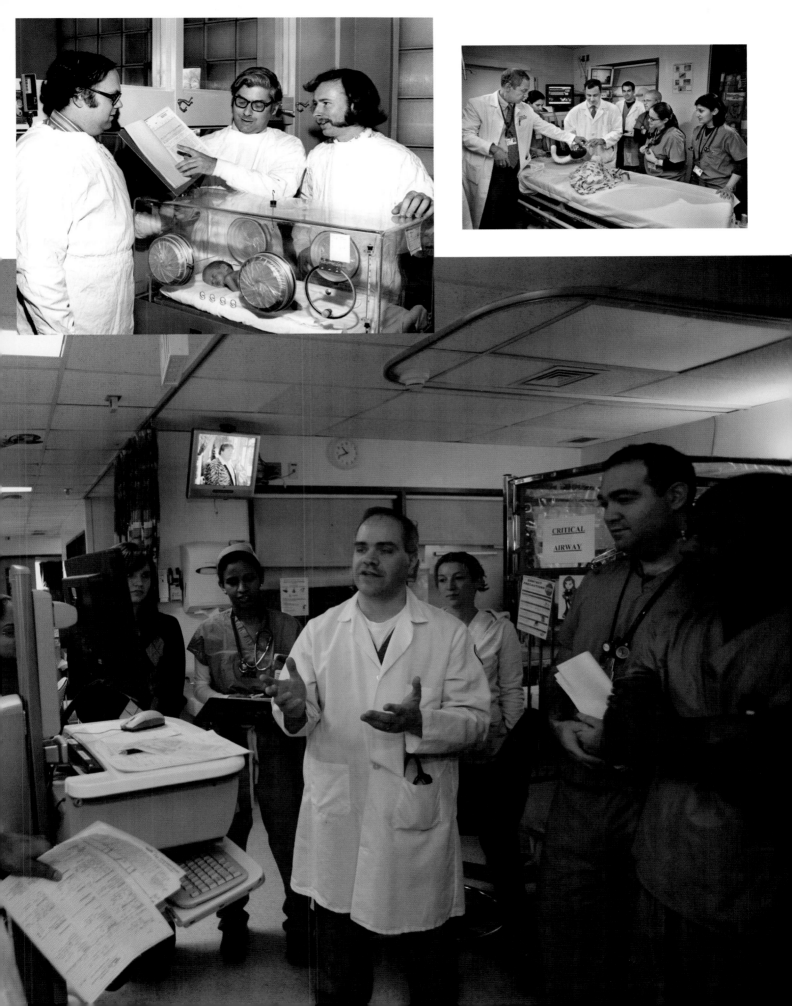

formal evaluations of the program, the residents, or the faculty, and the RRC approval was relatively informal.

At LIJ in the early 1970s, there was considerable emphasis on detailed history taking and careful, meticulous physical examination of all patients. There were no limits on work hours and house staff were expected to take personal responsibility for their patients, irrespective of the number of hours they'd been on the job, only leaving the hospital after their work was complete. With the increased use of ultrasound, CT scan, and MRI for extensive investigation of children, careful history taking and physical examination tended to take a back seat to medical technology. A more accurate and precise diagnosis of a neurological condition was possible with a CT and an MRI, compared to the relatively crude physical examination of the central nervous system. Accordingly, the house staff and subsequently the faculty became less skilled in physical examination and were more prone, as specialization grew, to go to special investigations in every discipline very early on in the management of a patient. I regret that as a result pediatricians in training became less likely to accept the intellectual challenge of developing a logical, comprehensive differential diagnosis based on history, physical examination, and appropriate laboratory testing. Instead, frequently they would simply "call for consultants."

There was a major shift when the DRG (diagnostic related group) reimbursement system was put into place and hospitals were paid by diagnosis and not on a per-diem basis. The pressure was on to reduce patients' hospital length of stay, often shortening weeks to days. The turnover rate within the wards increased, and therefore the time available to spend on any particular patient decreased. The shortened length of stay also prevented them from observing the psychosocial aspects of the patient and family. This was another blow to the traditional training of residents.

Another change was brought about by the RRC's strict regulation of the rotations for residency training. They prescribed the number of months in critical-care medicine, neonatal intensive care, ambulatory pediatrics, and emergency medicine, as well as rotations in certain specialty areas. This large number of obligatory rotations resulted in a very fragmented experience. The resident was prevented from being in a general medical and surgical unit for several months so that he or she could become familiar with its workings, the patients admitted, and the natural history of certain diseases.

Managed care, which was a sea change in the economics of practice, has led more pediatricians in training to become pediatric specialists rather than primary-care pediatricians. A specialist is more able to control his or her work hours and increase remuneration (procedure-oriented specialists earn more than primary-care physicians). A greater number of pediatricians are looking for salaried positions or joining group practices rather than becoming solo practitioners. Today, more house officers are married and have families and other responsibilities. The medical profession has become viewed less as a calling and more as just a highly skilled job. In short, it's no longer a way of life, but merely a way of making a living.

In the early 1970s, the vast majority of residents were men. This is another area where we have seen enormous change with the passage of time. The present house staff resident program has close to 80 percent women. This complicates the program because many of these women may either become pregnant during their training period or have child care responsibilities which may prevent them from completing their residency within the established time frame creating logistical problems for the program. To alleviate the added burden this places on the residents several solutions have been proposed. One is the extension of the residency training beyond the traditional three years and another is the creation of split residencies. Both of these suggestions have problems not the least being continuity of care for the patient.

The challenge for medical educators is to respond to these problems with innovations in the educational program that will recapture the intellectual excitement about the medical profession as well as the sense of personal responsibility and "ownership" of patient care. Training programs in which residents are expected to provide a disproportionate amount of service may need to be reevaluated and eliminated. Technology will need to assist in meeting some of the training goals. Computers, hand-held devices, and simulation laboratories are the tools to enable residents to quickly acquire both the medical information they need and critical technical skills. Training programs have moved too slowly to adapt to the new realities for training residents.

As mentioned at the beginning of the chapter, today the Schneider Children's Hospital has one of the largest training programs in the nation. It is committed to providing the highest standard of pediatric education through the delivery of state-of-the-art comprehensive care in an academic and research-oriented environment supervised by more than 125 full-time faculty members who specialize in all subspecialty areas of pediatric medicine and surgery. Its well-deserved reputation is based on the success of generations of graduates who are now clinicians, researchers, and academicians. From its inception until June 30, 2008, 1,294 pediatricians and pediatric subspecialists graduated from the program and are now practicing in almost every state in the country and in many countries around the world.

In the early 1970s, graduation ceremonies (an extremely important event for the faculty, graduates and their families) took place in the relatively drab surroundings of the LIJ Teaching Center. With the opening of SCH, graduation exercises became an important academic and social event attended by graduates and their families, the faculty, members of the LIJ Board of Trustees, and senior administrative staff. It is a festive event held in a tent on the front lawn of the hospital that features a dais for the chiefs of divisions and the distinguished guests. There are photographers and videographers present, the podium is decorated with flowers and balloons, and the atmosphere is one of joy and excitement. Each graduate receives a certificate of completion of residency from the Schneider Children's Hospital and a calligraphic copy of the oath and prayer of Maimonides.

The keynote speakers are always nationally known figures. A list of keynote speakers and their topics follow:

LIST OF KEYNOTE SPEAKERS AND THEIR TOPICS AT GRADUATION

1976　Robert McGovern, MD
　　　Practicing Staff Pediatrician
　　　"Styles in Pediatrics"

1977　Leonard Ehrlich, MD
　　　Practicing Staff Pediatrician
　　　"The Graduate: 40 Years Later"

1978　Arturo Aballi, MD
　　　Director of Pediatrics, Queens General
　　　Hospital, Queens, New York
　　　"Four Decades of Pediatrics"

1979　Louis Fraad, MD
　　　Professor of Pediatrics, Albert Einstein
　　　College of Medicine
　　　"Ethical Perspectives on Pediatric
　　　Practice"

1980　Harry Shwachman, MD
　　　Professor of Pediatrics and Chief of Clinical Nutrition, Children's Hospital Boston,
　　　Harvard Medical School
　　　"Reflections"

1980　Henry Barnett, MD
　　　Professor and Chairman of Pediatrics,
　　　Albert Einstein College of Medicine
　　　"Role of Specialists in Pediatric Practice"

Robert Haggerty, MD, second right, accompanied by (left to right), Philip Lanzkowsky, MD, Irving Schneider, Mrs. Shoshana Arbeli-Almozlino, Minister of Health of the State of Israel, Robert K. Match, MD, and Irving Wharton, 1986.

Graduation ceremony, 1988. Left to right: Cynthia Sparer, (associate executive director of SCH), Helen Schneider, Drs. Edmund Pellegrino (at podium), I. Ronald Shenker, Philip Lanzkowsky, and Seymour Cohen (dean of the clinical campus at LIJ).

1981   Harry Gordon, MD
        Professor of Pediatrics, founding director
        of the Rose F. Kennedy Center
        for Research in Mental Retardation and
        Human Development, Albert
        Einstein College of Medicine
        "On Talking with Patients"

1982   Kenneth Tardiff, MD, MPH
        Professor of Psychiatry and Public
        Health, The New York Hospital-
        Cornell Medical Center
        "The Caring Physician in the Medicine of
        the Future"

1983   Carola Eisenberg, MD,
        Dean of Student Affairs, Harvard Medi-
        cal School
        Leon Eisenberg, MD
        Professor of Psychiatry and Professor and
        Chairman, Department of Social
        Medicine and Health Policy, Harvard
        Medical School
        "Eisenberg's Uncertainty Principle or
        What to do Until the Biochemist Comes"

1984   Rabbi Irving Greenberg, PhD
        Founding president of CLAL—The

        National Jewish Center for Learning
        and Leadership
        "The Covenental Ethic of Medicine"

1985   Professor Stanley Levin, MD
        Associate Chief-of-Staff, Schneider
        Children's Hospital
        "Back to the Future"

1986   Robert Haggerty, MD
        Professor and Chairman of Pediatrics,
        University of Rochester School of
        Medicine
        "The Future of Pediatrics"

1987   Edmund Pellegrino, MD
        Vice President and Director of the Health
        Sciences Center, State University of New
        York at Stony Brook
        "Are We Still a Profession?"

1988   Ruth Westheimer, PhD
        Psychosexual Therapist and Author
        "The Challenge of Being in the Helping
        Profession"

1989   Samuel L. Katz, MD
        Professor and Chairman of Pediatrics,
        Duke University School of Medicine
        "The News Never Changes, It's Just the

Samuel L. Katz, MD, 1989.

Thomas K. Oliver, Jr., MD, 1990.

People"
1990 Thomas K. Oliver, Jr., MD
    Professor of Pediatrics, University of
    Pittsburgh School of Medicine
    "Pediatric Manpower: Past, Present and
    Future"
1991 Frank A. Oski, MD
    Professor and Chairman of Pediatrics,
    Johns Hopkins School of Medicine
    "Plant a Radish, Get a Radish"
1992 Mark Sperling, MD
    Professor and Chairman of Pediatrics,
    Children's Hospital of Pittsburgh
    "Child Health: Society Ills"
1993 James Stockman, III, MD
    President, American Board of Pediatrics
    "Needed: A Way to Train Doctors"
1994 Joe M. Sanders, Jr., MD
    Executive Director, American Academy
    of Pediatrics
    "Your Future in Pediatrics"
1995 Elias Schwartz, MD
    Professor and Chairman of Pediatrics,
    Children's Hospital of Philadelphia
    "Hippocrates at the Millennium"

1996 R. Alan B. Ezekowitz, MD
    Professor and Chairman of Pediatrics,
    Massachusetts General Hospital
    "How to Aim at Moving Targets, a
    Professional Guideline"
1997 Joel J. Alpert, MD
    Professor and Chairman of Pediatrics,
    Boston University School of Medicine
    "Is It Good for the Children?"
1998 Alan R. Fleischman, MD
    Senior Vice President for Medical and
    Academic Affairs, New York Academy of
    Medicine
    "Pediatrics in the 21st Century"
1999 Robert Cassidy, PhD
    Director of Bioethics and Social Policy,
    Schneider Children's Hospital
    "Make a Joyful Choice: of Robin and
    Lambs, Butterflies and Donuts"
2000 Chester Edelmann, Jr., MD
    Professor of Pediatrics and Associate
    Dean, Albert Einstein College of
    Medicine
    "Pediatrics and the New Millennium"
2001 Jack P. Shonkoff, MD

James Stockman, III, MD, 1993.

Jack P. Shonkoff, MD, 2001.

Dean of the Heller School and Professor of Human Development, Brandeis University
"Becoming a Pediatrician in Interesting Times"

2002   Joel J. Alpert, MD
Professor and Chairman of Pediatrics, Boston University School of Medicine
"Mommy—Daddy...Who is My Doctor?"

2003   Victor Dubowitz, MD
Professor of Pediatrics, Hammersmith Hospital, University of London
"Ramblings of a Peripatetic Pediatrician"

2004   Michael J. Dowling
President and Chief Executive Officer, North Shore-LIJ Health System
"Healthcare Concerns—2005"

2005   Lawrence G. Smith, MD
Chief Medical Officer, North Shore-LIJ Health System
"The Changing Role of Physicians"

2006   Ms. Leah Olverd
Pediatric cardiology patient
"Personal Reflections of a Pediatric Cardiology Patient"

The Samuel Karelitz Intern-of-the-Year Award given for clinical diligence and humanity is presented each year at the graduation ceremony to the outstanding intern. Mrs. Ethel Karelitz, widow of Dr. Samuel Karelitz, presented the award to the outstanding intern-of-the-year from 1971 until her death in the late 1990s. The recipients of the Samuel Karelitz Award are listed below:

1971   Lynn Burkes, MD
1972   *
1973   David Brown, MD
1974   Irwin Hametz, MD
1975   Marcia Bergtraum, MD
1976   Gilbert Dick, MD
1977   Abbott Laptook, MD
1978   Richard Sosulski, MD
1979   Bruce Morgenstern, MD
        Janis Schaeffer, MD
1980   Marvin Resmovits, MD
1981   Thomas Klein, MD
        Morris Charytan, MD
1982   Sidney Randel, MD
1983   Aimee Telsey, MD
1984   Joseph Werther, MD
1985   Lin Lan Tang, MD
1986   Mark Hausdorff, MD
1987   Joanne Greising, MD
1988   Andrea Yaris-Newman, MD
1989   Ana Dellorusso, MD
1990   Howard Apfel, MD

*In 1972 the residents supported a strike organized by a new resident and intern union. Due to the walkout, I did not present the Samuel Karelitz award in that year.

THE OATH AND PRAYER of MAIMONIDES

A 12th Century Physician

THY eternal Providence has appointed me to watch over the life and health of Thy creatures. May the love for my art actuate me at all times; may neither avarice nor miserliness, nor the thirst for glory nor for a great reputation engage my mind for the enemies of truth and philanthropy could easily deceive me and make me forgetful of my lofty aim of doing good to Thy children. May I never see in a patient anything but a fellow creature in pain. Grant me strength, time and opportunity always to correct what I have acquired, always to extend its domain, for knowledge is immense and the spirit of man can extend indefinitely to enrich itself daily with new requirements.

Today he can discover his errors of yesterday and tomorrow he may obtain new light on what he thinks himself sure of today.

O God, Thou hast appointed me to watch over the life and death of Thy creatures. Here I am, ready for my vocation.

Congratulations to _____

upon graduation from the Department of Pediatrics, Schneider Children's Hospital, North Shore-Long Island Jewish Health System.

_____
Date

Calligraphies~(631) 321-0079

_____
Chairman and Professor of Pediatrics

The oath and prayer of Maimonides certificate given to graduating house staff. Maimonides was a 12th century rabbi, philosopher, and physician. He was appointed court physician to Vizier el-Fadil, Regent of Egypt.

1991   Ron Newfield, MD
1992   Steven Weiss, MD
1993   Beth Gottlieb, MD
1994   Lorraine Catalano, MD
1995   Robert Goldman, MD
1996   Deepti Mehrotra, MD
1997   Margaret Wren, DO
1998   Barbara Brown-McDaniel, MD
1999   Jeffrey Bocchicchio, MD
2000   Chie-Youn Shih, MD
2001   Hildred Machuca, MD
2002   Robert Marchlewski, MD
2003   Kevin Roy, MD
2004   Kena Richardson, MD
2005   Lisa Williams, MD
2006   John Ciannella, MD
2007   Maureen Banfe, DO
2008   Eliyahu Rosman, MD

Mrs. Ethel Karelitz presents Joseph Werther, MD, with the Samuel Karelitz Intern-of-the-Year Award, 1984.

Applications for residency annually exceed 1,000 from almost every state of the union and from many countries abroad.

The education program as it has evolved during the past fifty years has established a remarkably sound foundation for our educational future. Present-day healthcare economics require a reshaping and sharpening of the pediatrician's clinical decision-making without excessive utilization of resources such as laboratory and radiological studies. The new paradigm of managed care, as well as reduced governmental investment in healthcare, demands a more selective use of resources and a more disciplined defense of those choices. The program is committed to providing the pediatricians of the future with the training to master these challenges.

The goals of our training program remain the same: disciplined judgment, clinical competency, therapeutic commitment, and professional honor. The principles, the spirit, and the resources are available to provide a solid academic and clinical bridge to our next fifty years of residency training.

POSTGRADUATE MEDICAL EDUCATION

The first postgraduate course was established in 1970 with a "grant" of $1,000 provided by Robert K. Match, MD, who was at that time the executive director of the hospital. The money was designated not only to provide education to practicing pediatricians, but also to invite pediatric luminaries from this country and Europe to visit LIJ and meet with the pediatric faculty. This was another way to get broad national recognition for the pediatric program. The first annual pediatric postgraduate course was held in the hospital Teaching Center in November 1970 and was entitled "Learn More About Drugs." Guest faculty included Edmund D. Pellegrino, MD, vice president and director of the Health Sciences Center, dean of the Medical School, State University of New York at Stony Brook; Robert Haggerty, MD, professor and chairman of pediatrics,

University of Rochester School of Medicine; Jerrold F. Lucey, MD, professor and chairman of the Department of Pediatrics, University of Vermont Medical School; and Felix Heald, MD, professor and chairman of pediatrics, George Washington University School of Medicine.

These courses were held at first in close proximity to the hospital, and later at resort locations in Mexico, the Caribbean, and Europe. At the peak of the program, hundreds of pediatricians attended. The courses, conducted over a three-day period, were carried out annually for more than thirty years and provided remarkable national and international exposure for the program and its faculty.

Another postgraduate education activity was the annual pediatric board review course designed to prepare candidates for the pediatric board examination. It was run by the pediatric faculty and attended by board candidates from the New York metropolitan area.

Dr. I. Ronald Shenker was responsible for organizing postgraduate medical education programs.

Pediatric Postgraduate Course, 1988.

1979 postgraduate course held in Puerto Rico. Speakers from the left: Drs. Thomas K. Oliver Jr., Vincent Fulginetti, C. Everett Koop (who later became surgeon general to the United States), and Philip Lanzkowsky.

CHAPTER 16

SMILES, LAUGHTER AND CHEER

THE ART OF THE CHILDREN'S HOSPITAL

For a sick child confined to a hospital, the hospital is his or her universe. As far back as 1970, we began to design this universe with insight and compassion—as a place where children are made well, which is most important, of course, and also as a place where smiles, laughter, and cheer drive out sadness and fear.

We are proud of the fact that the Children's Hospital has taken on another dimension for children—it has also become a children's art gallery and a children's museum.

Practicing the art of healing, our specially trained physicians, nurses, and health professionals provide skilled medical treatment to their patients. They are united in their love for children and their passionate desire to make a difference in their young lives.

Known worldwide for the excellence of its clinical care, the Schneider Children's Hospital is also associated with another kind of art—the kind that decorates the grounds and adorns the halls and walls, providing enormous visual impact.

Patients come in many sizes and shapes: a "preemie" so small she almost fits in the nurse's hand; a high school athlete who looms over his physician; a toddler deftly steering an IV pole through the hall. The art in the hospital has been carefully chosen to attract the interest

Patients having fun with "Roller Ball" game.

Celebration at the placement of the Keith Haring sculpture. Standing: Lynn Schneider, Mindy Schneider (in red), and Helen Schneider. Sitting: Keith Haring with a group of children, November 1987.

of these disparate age groups. It helps them cope with stress, stirs their imaginations, and gives them an opportunity to express their feelings. The art also speaks to the parents, who are here day and night, providing untiring love and support for their children.

This chapter is a tribute to the latter type of art, much of it provided over the years by the Schneider family. Helen Schneider, a volunteer at LIJ for many years and a warm and compassionate person, was always particularly concerned about the emotional well being of the hospitalized child. She and daughter Lynn shared a love for and knowledge of art, and much thought went into their selections. Through the years, they provided a variety of wonderful works.

THE KEITH HARING SCULPTURE

When you pull into the drive at SCH you know right away that it is a unique hospital. You can't miss the twenty-foot sculpture designed by noted artist Keith Haring. Exuberant and playful, the sculpture depicts a parent figure—whether it is mother or father is in the eyes of its beholder—that's dancing on its head while balancing a child on each foot. "Children will see something happy the minute they reach the hospital," Mr. Haring said at the installation ceremony.

Commissioned by Irving and Helen Schneider in 1987, the 2,500-pound statue was fabricated at the Lippincott Foundry of North Haven, Connecticut, and shipped to Long Island in huge crates. With its bright, cheery primary colors, it the place that he came back on his own time with cans of paint. While the children watched, he decorated a 200-foot hallway on the second floor with his characteristic bold, black, graffiti-style people and animals.

THE "MAGIC TREE"

While those seeing it for the first time may gaze at it in awe and even, perhaps, bewilderment, the brilliantly colored cloisonné statue is a familiar part of the landscape of the children's hospital for those who work here and for frequent visitors.

Noted Franco-American artist Niki de Saint Phalle, who was born near Paris and raised in New York, created the statue. Her passionately lived life provided the raw material for her work, which allowed her to triumph over her pain. Her sculptures of oversized creatures and fantasy figures are in major museums all over the world. In 1989, Helen Schneider, who loved Ms. de

Celebration at the placement of the Keith Haring sculpture. Left to right: Irving Wharton, Keith Haring, Helen, Lynn, Irving, and Mindy Schneider, and Philip Lanzkowsky, MD, November 1987.

Keith Haring painting with a group of hospitalized children, November 1987.

has become the logo of the hospital.

The celebration held when the sculpture was formally installed in November 1987 was filled with laughter and applause. Its highlight was a drawing session with Keith Haring, who helped the children sketch their own versions of his sprightly enameled steel design. After masses of balloons were released, he set out to visit patients who had not been able to leave their beds for the occasion. All young party-goers were given T-shirts emblazoned with the yellow, blue, and red design of the Haring sculpture.

Keith Haring visited the site many times, walking around to explore the hospital and speaking to the children. He was so taken with

Second-floor hallway painted by Keith Haring.

Saint Phalle's work (particularly the "Nanas," the round maternal figures in riotous colors for which she is best known), contacted the artist and began the long collaborative process of commissioning a work for the hospital. Ms. de Saint Phalle had spent some time in hospitals recuperating from various illnesses, so she knew what it was like to be a patient, and she was very enthusiastic about the commission. The tree was Niki's idea, and as she worked she had the inspiration that it should be a fountain, with water squirting out in all directions. She well understood the healing aspects of seeing, hearing, and touching water.

The colors of the "Magic Tree" are so arresting that one doesn't notice at first that the branches are actually snakes with open mouths but snakes they are. There was some concern by the hospital that the finished work would frighten the children, but they are really very benign in appearance. The caduceus, an ancient symbol depicting two snakes twined around a herald's wand, is traditionally associated with healing.

The whimsical and witty "Magic Tree" looks as if it grew right out of the lawn next to the hospital cafeteria, and it is reflected in its surrounding landscaped pool. The vibrancy of its colors lends it an air of playfulness, and the sculpture captures the attention of all visitors and patients at the hospital.

THE "ASTRONOMY LESSON"

At night, the Schneider Children's Hospital is a peaceful place, with the hallways softly lit and the staff quietly providing care and comfort.

Though most of us don't think of it in this way, the hospital is home for many children—often parents, too—for a night, a week, or even longer. Also providing comfort is the work of art in the center of the atrium, called "The Astronomy Lesson," which was created by artist

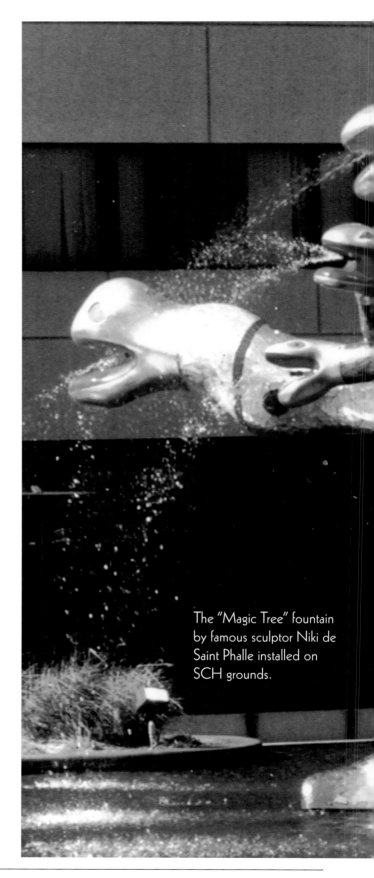

The "Magic Tree" fountain by famous sculptor Niki de Saint Phalle installed on SCH grounds.

Clyde Lynn, a native of New Jersey. His work is in numerous public and private collections, including the National Gallery of American Art, the Smithsonian Institution in Washington, D.C., and the Wadsworth Atheneum in Hartford, Connecticut. Clyde Lynn combines the talents of a sculptor, a painter, an engineer, and a magician. His cast stone sculptures use fiber optics to create lights that flicker across the concrete surfaces like slow, silent fireworks. The moon and stars are familiar to all children. A favorite bedtime book for many is "Goodnight Moon," in which the moon is a friendly figure, like a member of the family. The sculpture provides a sense of reassurance and constancy for children during what is often a stressful time.

ANDY WARHOL'S "ENDANGERED SPECIES" AND "COWBOYS AND INDIANS" SUITES

The "Endangered Species" Suite was actually the first art hung along a main hallway on the first floor of SCH. Ten silkscreens in the artist's "Cowboys and Indians" Suite were hung in the main hallway of the second floor of SCH. Cowboys and Indians, monkeys and frogs—these child-friendly images are bright, colorful, and playful.

Andy Warhol, born in Pittsburgh in 1938, was one of New York's most successful commercial illustrators. He became a legend in the art world, known as the Prince of Pop.

In the 1960s Warhol used as his subjects common, mass-produced articles like Campbell's

A group of children admiring the "Magic Tree" fountain.

Night photo of two children looking at the "Astronomy Lesson."

Andy Warhol's "Cowboys and Indians" Suite.

Andy Warhol's "Endangered Species" Suite.

Dogs at the Hospital!

Soup cans and Coke bottles. From 1962 on he made silkscreen prints of famous personalities like Marilyn Monroe and Elizabeth Taylor. Andy Warhol died on February 22, 1987, from complications of gall bladder surgery.

DOGS AT THE HOSPITAL!

The whimsical photographic dog studies are the work of well-known photographer William Wegman, which have been exhibited in museums and galleries around the world. As soon as the Weimaraners were hung on the wall, children, adults, doctors, and nurses were looking at them and laughing.

The Cat in the Hat

"THE CAT IN THE HAT"

In celebration of the fiftieth birthday of "The Cat in the Hat," the Animazing Gallery in Soho presented Schneider Children's Hospital with a 1,000-pound, seven-foot tall monumental bronze representation of the beloved Dr. Seuss figure, which will grace the entrance of the hospital for years to come. Universal Studios commissioned Leo Rijn to develop and oversee the creation of numerous Marquette scale models of Dr. Seuss sculptures. Rijn has been identified as one of today's brightest sculptors because of his ability to transform two-dimensional ideas into three-dimensional works of art.

"BICYCLING IN THE SUN"

This statue brings to life a young boy pedaling his bicycle. A girl hangs on behind, feet lifted in the air and pigtails blowing in the wind. The artwork welcomes visitors to a place where children—and their dreams—are the greatest priority. This life-size bronze statue, which stands almost five feet high, is a limited-edition work by Prince Monyo Mihailescu-Nasturel Herescu. Prince Monyo was born and raised in Bucharest. After escaping political unrest and years of imprisonment, he moved to the United States. For the past forty-five years Prince Monyo has worked as a prolific and prestigious sculptor and painter. His work is collected all over the world and displayed in many museums and public places. "Perhaps one of the children who see it will someday create sculptures as I do," says Prince Monyo. "But if I could put a smile on just one of their faces, this is the greatest contribution of my life."

"Bicycling in the Sun"

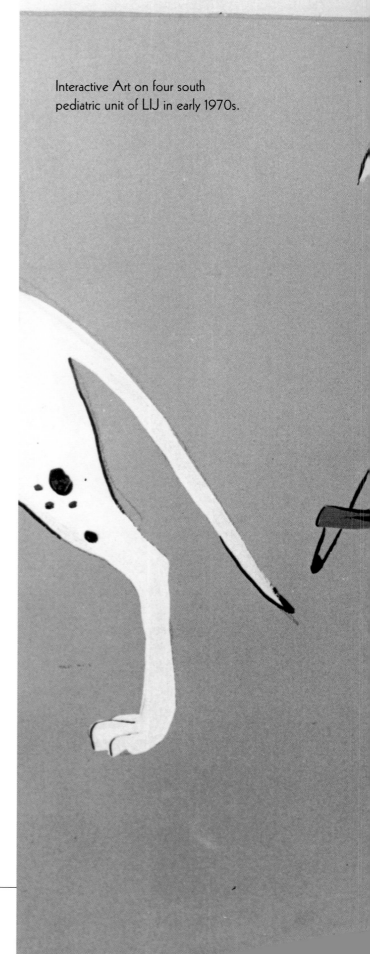

Interactive Art on four south pediatric unit of LIJ in early 1970s.

INTERACTIVE ART

Back in the seventies, it was felt that art played a vital role in creating a bright and cheerful atmosphere for children and their families.

A four-year old boy who was a patient on the pediatric floor at LIJ was seen talking to the playroom wall for the entire week that he was in the hospital. This was quite understandable, because the wall was alive with cartoon and nursery rhyme characters. Every day he would say "Hi" to Dennis the Menace and then exchange a few pleasantries with Donald Duck or Yogi Bear. He and his fellow patients loved the menagerie.

Philip Lanzkowsky, MD, entertains a young patient on a kaliedodraw kiosk.

"KALEIDODRAW KIOSKS"

This interactive display brings out the artists in kids, while lessening the anxiety of a hospital visit. These computer-operated kiosks feature the Kaleidodraw, Sandy Art, and Doll House software programs that entertain children of all ages. This software allows budding artists the opportunity to create images using their selection of pictures and icons. Images from the center computer are broadcast to a large plasma screen mounted about the unit. This exhibit helps children get lost in their creativity and eases their minds as they wait for medical care.

"ROLLER BALL"

A dynamic rolling marble ball interactive game greets children in the lobby of the Schneider Children's Hospital. This interactive device continually lifts colored glass marbles to the top of a seven-foot tower where they are released into a maze of downhill ramps. On their way down, the marbles activate fiber optic tracks and various lights and sounds. On the side of the tower are controls for children to interact with the sculpture.

THE "SPACE WALK"

These enormous murals (forty-six feet by eight feet) placed on either side of the hallway joining LIJ to SCH are designed to ease the stress of young SCH patients. The rubberized flooring puts a spring in your step that helps you imagine you are walking on the moon. There's also motion-triggered music that plays, and astronaut chatter recorded from the actual space explorations. You can see faces brighten when families walk through this exhibit.

The "Space Walk"

"Sweet Distraction"

"SWEET DISTRACTIONS"

This art collection is made of bright, whimsical murals that depict images designed to capture the imagination of children, including an astronaut, a caterpillar, a butterfly, a circus train full of animals, and an under-water world of fish. The pictures are literally "eye-candy" for kids. The murals are "painted" with hundreds of candy morsels, pieced together to create scenes.

These murals were assembled by two preschool teachers who volunteered their talent and time, spending hours patiently piecing together the candy that brought the drawings to life. There are many of these artistic renderings in the passages and hallways of SCH.

THE "AQUA CIRCUS"

These are no ordinary aquariums. With buttons, levers, and cranks at their disposal, children can control the movements of fish, sea creatures, and other objects inside the virtual aquariums. They are not filled with water, and the fish and other sea creatures inside are not real. In fact, these "fish tanks" are unlike any you will find anywhere else. That's why the children and their families love them so much. When a patient giggles as she causes the seaweed to swirl, there is no doubt the art is doing its job!

A mother amuses her daughter with the "Aqua Circus" while they wait for their doctor.

A hospital patient entertains himself with the projected animated tiger.

Self-portrait tile hallway

WATCH OUT FOR THE WILD ANIMALS!

Wild animals can be seen climbing the walls, soaring near the ceiling, and scurrying across the floor. Created by Polish artist Dominik Lehman, twelve daylight projections of different animals were filmed at various zoos (the Bronx and Central Park Zoos and the New York Aquarium). After the animals were filmed, the background and foreground were removed. When these animals are projected on the wall throughout the hospital they truly inhabit the space.

THE SELF-PORTRAIT TILE HALLWAY

This is an extraordinary display of more than 400 self-portraits painted on square-foot ceramic tiles by the children of Daly Elementary School in Port Washington, New York.

Each tile has been framed and permanently mounted along the corridor most patients pass through when they are admitted to the hospital. The combined tiles create a mural that resembles a cheering crowd of happy children, who seem to say to the apprehensive young patients: "Don't be afraid—you are not alone. Look at our smiling faces—we are thinking of you and we want you to feel better soon."

SANDCASTLE MURAL

A forty-five-foot long panoramic photo-mural of sandcastles on a beach wraps around the walls of the Children's Heart Center.

This mural, which was built by Al Jarnow during the summer of 2004 at Green Hill, Fire Island, is a composite of dozens of elements. Using only sticks and shells found on the beach, Mr. Jarnow worked, or as he describes it, played, for three weeks building different sand castles. Each day he would photograph the sandcastles from all angles. After completing the castles, he used computer software to create the beautiful kingdom of castles that now adorns the walls of the waiting room in the Division of Pediatric Cardiology. The castles are fantasies drawn from a wide variety of architectural styles; they help to transform the waiting room into the beautiful and serene world of a warm summer day.

Libby Pataki, New York State's First Lady, entertains the children in the playroom celebrating the opening of the Clown Care Unit, March 1995.

OUR SPECIAL VISITORS

Over the years, in addition to visiting professors and academicians from this country and abroad, many other prominent visitors have come to the children's hospital. They include:

Pediatrician Benjamin Spock, MD
Sir Raymond Hoffenberg, President, Royal
    College of Physicians of London
Árpád Göncz, President of the Republic of
    Hungary
Libby Pataki, New York State's First Lady
Mayor Rudy Guiliani

From the art and entertainment world, they came to bring joy and cheer to the children:

Sunil Dutt, one of India's foremost film
    producers and actors
Violinist Midori
Entertainer Marie Osmond
Sesame Street's Bob McGrath

Benjamin Spock, MD (on left) honored by SCH at a party for the hospital's tenth anniversary, October 1984.

Acclaimed violinist Midori, gives a concert for the children at SCH, 1983.

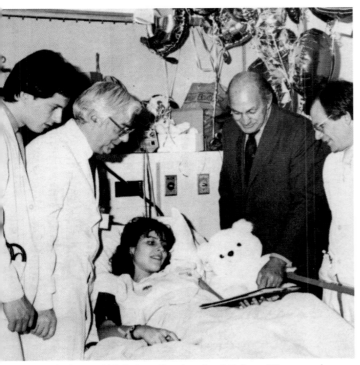

Sir Raymond Hoffenberg, President, Royal College of Physicians of London, making rounds in the pediatric intensive care unit. Left to right: George DeNoto, medical student, Philip Lanzkowsky, MD, Sir Raymond Hoffenberg, and Andrew Steele, MD, April 1987.

Árpád Göncz, President of the Republic of Hungary, touring the bone marrow transplantation unit with Philip Lanzkowsky, MD, 1992.

Mayor Rudy Guliani holding an abandoned baby, with Philip Lipsitz, MD, chief, neonatal-perinatal medicine, February 22, 1998.

Olympic figure skater Sarah Hughes
Anchorman Dan Rather
Miniature horse Thumbelina
Meteorologist Dr. Frank Fields

Prominent sports celebrities visited the hospital too:
The Long Island Ducks
The New York Mets' "Mr. Met"
Mets outfielder Ben Johnson and infielder Rubin Gotay

The art, the interactive games, the music in the lobby, and the clowns all join together to transform the hospital into a place not only of healing but also of smiles, laughter, and cheer.

ACKNOWLEDGEMENTS

Irving and Helen Schneider and their family donated:
The Keith Haring sculpture
TheNiki de Saint Phalle sculpture, the "Magic Tree"
The Clyde Lynn sculpture, the "Astronomy Lesson"
Andy Warhol's lithographs, the "Endangered Species" Suite
Andy Warhol's lithographs, the "Cowboys and Indians" Suite
The William Wegman prints, the Weimaraners
Dominik Lehman's projections of zoo animals

The Animazing Gallery of Soho, New York donated:
Leo Rijn's sculpture of Dr. Seuss's "Cat in the Hat"

Sandy and Joel Busel donated:
Prince Manyo Mihailescu-Nasturel Herescu statue, "Bicycling in the Sun"

Discover the Smile Foundation, started by Lisa Epstein, donated:
Protozone Interactives
    "Kaleidodraw Kiosks"
    "Roller Ball" interactive game
    The "Space Walk"
    The "Aqua Circus"

Celebration following production of movie with Sunil Dutt.

Sunil Dutt, one of India's foremost film producers and actors, makes a film at LIJ entitled "Dard Ka Rishta" featuring Philip Lanzkowsky, MD as a pediatric hematologist-oncologist, June 1982.

Lisa Cusano and Amy Rubenstein's "Sweet Distractions" art collection
Al Jarnow's sandcastle murals
Daly Elementary School students' self-portrait tile hallway

Bob McGrath, the most popular and longest-lasting "human" character of the hit show Sesame Street, visits SCH to entertain children, October 1996.

Marie Osmond visits patients at SCH as part of the Children's Miracle Network telethon produced by the Osmond Foundation featured on WOR-TV (Channel 9), May 3, 1985.

Sarah Hughes, Olympic gold medal figure skater, visits SCH, January 2003.

Dan Rather, anchorman for the CBS evening news, flanked by Philip Lanzkowsky and Michael Dowling on a visit to SCH, January 25, 2003.

Dr. Frank Field, a television personality and meteorologist on New York TV for decades, visits SCH to create a documentary about the children's hospital, December 2007.

Members of the Long Island Ducks, a triple-A baseball team, visit the hospital, August 2005.

"Mr. Met" visits children and their families in the hospital, January 2005.

Mets outfielder Ben Johnson, far left, infielder Rubin Gotay, far right, and "Mr. Met" visit SCH, 2007.

Thumbelina, the smallest horse in the world at only 17.5 inches tall, visits SCH, August 2007. Inserts: Thumbelina with visitors Carly Beatrice Lanzkowsky and Aliza Herz.

CHAPTER 17

BUILDING A SYSTEM

THE CREATION OF THE NS-LIJ HEALTH SYSTEM

Two tertiary hospitals, North Shore University Hospital (NSUH) and Long Island Jewish Medical Center (LIJ), are located only one and a half miles apart; NSUH very close to Queens in Nassau County and LIJ actually straddling the Queens-Nassau border on the North Shore of Long Island.

While many community-based physicians are on the staffs of both hospitals, the hospitals themselves have been in conflict almost from their founding within a year of each other, about fifty years ago. The tension between the two was heightened when LIJ declared its intent to build a children's hospital.

There have always been huge differences in the hospitals' management and governance. LIJ trustees believed in the need for salaried full-time chairmen, whereas NSUH's first chairmen were culled from the voluntary physicians in the community. LIJ always had a physician as its chief executive officer, and physician leadership was its hallmark, while at NSUH, the chief executive officer was a non-physician. NSUH trustees were more diverse, from a cultural and religious

Signing the agreement of the merger of the North Shore Health System (NSHS) with Long Island Jewish (LIJ) Medical Center, 1977. From left: Saul Katz, NSHS chairman; David Dantzker, MD, president of LIJ; Roy Zuckerberg, chairman of the LIJ Board of Trustees; and Jack Gallagher, CEO, NSHS.

point of view, while LIJ, a Federation of Jewish Philanthropies hospital, always had predominantly Jewish medical and lay leadership.

Roy Zuckerberg, chairman of the LIJ Board of Trustees.

As to management, at NSUH the administration ran everything, whereas at LIJ, the Board of Trustees was more intimately involved in the operations of the hospital. NSUH trustees believed in borrowing money for hospital construction, while the LIJ trustees' philosophy was to carry no debt. Over the years, this difference led to considerable disparity between the physical plants of the two institutions. This was clearly a great advantage to NSUH, which over the years was expanded, renovated, and updated in a variety of ways. But despite the differences, the two hospitals had plenty in common, such as the desire to provide top-notch medical care, train future physicians, and invest in research.

Many attempts over the years to bring the administrations and trustees from both sides together were unsuccessful, generally because of conflicting personalities and agendas.

From 1989 to 1995 NSUH affiliated with Glen Cove Hospital (formerly Community Hospital of Glen Cove), Forest Hills Hospital (formerly LaGuardia Hospital*), and Syosset Hospital (formerly Syosset Community Hospital*), Huntington Hospital, Southside Hospital in Bay Shore (Suffolk County), Franklin Hospital (formerly Franklin General Hospital) in Franklin Square, Plainview Hospital (formerly Central General Hospital), and Staten Island University Hospital to form the North Shore Health System (NSHS). Peter Stamos, a Rhodes scholar and founder and chief executive officer of Stamos Associates, Inc., a healthcare-consulting firm, worked with Saul Katz, chairman of the NSUH board, and Jack Gallagher, the hospital's CEO, during the development of this network and the

Both of these hospitals were acquired from the Health Insurance Plan of New York.

eventual merger of NSHS with LIJ as well.

Toward the end of the twentieth century, factors such as fear of managed-care companies and their dominance in determining hospital revenue, the expense of duplication of major medical equipment, the need to rebuild the infrastructure of both institutions in a computer-based age, and the need for more modern hospital facilities compelled the two hospitals to consider joining forces. By this time, there was a new generation of trustees more amenable to discussion.

Saul Katz, chairman of the NSUH Board of Trustees.

Roy Zuckerberg was chairman of the LIJ board, and Saul Katz was chairman of the NSUH board. Sol Wachtler, a member of the LIJ board, had a close relationship with both men and played an important role in the initiation of discussions between them. He told Laurie Locastro, my editorial associate, that a dinner meeting was held at Saul Katz's home attended by a committee made up of representatives from both hospitals: Roy Zuckerberg, Sol Wachtler, Gedale Horowitz, Irving Schneider, and David Dantzker, MD, from LIJ, and Saul Katz, Abraham Krasnoff, Alan Greene, Robert Kaufman, and Jack Gallagher from NSHS. A decision was made at that meeting to attempt to draft an agreement between LIJ and NSHS. Peter Stamos played an important role in the creation of the merger documents and the development of the governance structure of the new entity.

When the merger was proposed in 1997, the federal government filed an antitrust action in an attempt to block it. Its position was that the health system that would be created would be so large it would be considered in restraint of trade and therefore a virtual monopoly. However, the government lost a legal contest in the Eastern District, and the merger went forward. It was finalized on October 29, 1997, and the North

Shore-Long Island Jewish (NS-LIJ) Health System came into being.

The decision, which was a significant defeat for the government, was endorsed by State Attorney General Dennis C. Vacco after the two entities signed an agreement guaranteeing a two-year price freeze for managed-care contracts and the return of a minimum of $50 million of its savings to the public in the form of new prevention and other community programs.

Merging two institutions that were so close geographically and yet so far apart culturally was not easy, but overall, the merger proceeded remarkably well. A single board of 120 members was established, a central administration was put into place, new medical staff bylaws were written, and the merging of certain administrative departments such as legal, planning, and human resources went rapidly forward.

For a short period, Jack Gallagher representing NSHS and Dr. David Dantzker representing LIJ shared the position of chief executive officer. Jeffrey Menkes and Michael J. Dowling shared the chief operating officer position. In May 2000 Dr. Dantzker and later that year Mr. Menkes resigned their positions. When Mr. Gallagher resigned his position in January of 2002, Mr. Michael Dowling was appointed president and CEO of the NS-LIJ Health System. At the end of the day the LIJ culture did not survive, nor did the LIJ administration.

The merging of clinical departments went at a slower pace, but the Department of Pediatrics led the pack. I expressed my thoughts on the future growth and development of pediatrics for the system in a document I named "A Proposed Master Plan for the Development of Children's Health Network of North Shore-LIJ Health System," written on November 15, 1997, and revised January 15, 1998, excerpts of which make up Appendix III. Written with Larry Levine, administrator of SCH at the time, it

represented the end-game strategy, but because of the "sensitivities" and the fear of change that the merger had engendered, senior members of the NS-LIJ Health System administration who agreed with its contents advised me to lock the document in a drawer for the time being.

Shortly after the merger in 1997, I was appointed vice president of the Children's Health Network (CHN), a newly formed organization of the NS-LIJ Health System.

On June 30, 1999, I presented my ideas of the master plan for the CHN to the newly combined Department of Pediatrics at a faculty retreat and to a combined chairmen's meeting of the NS-LIJ Health System on March 28, 2000. This master plan set out the following goals:

Establish an integrated continuum of care for children.

Provide improved and consistently high quality of care, irrespective of point of access.

Increase accessibility of care geographically and for all segments of the population.

Seek opportunities to serve unmet needs in the community.

Develop new and innovative programs.

Provide value to payers.

Carry out the educational and research mission.

Increase public visibility and market presence.

Ensure that all children receive the best possible care from the most qualified people and in the most appropriate setting at the best value (quality/cost).

Treat children in facilities designed for children and staffed by personnel specifically trained in pediatrics.

Mervin Silverberg, MD, chairman of the Department of Pediatrics at NSUH, attempted to keep the Department of Pediatrics at NSUH intact, while I sought to consolidate and regionalize pediatrics at SCH, consistent with the master plan for the combined Department of Pediatrics and the Children's Health Network. Several uneasy years followed. Although there was no overt conflict, we had obvious differences in goals, objectives, style, and vision. The forces at play were two inwardly focused cultures, paralyzing indecision, parochial politics, a low level of trust between the parties, lack of teamwork between the NSUH and SCH pediatricians, and the general human fear of change and things unknown.

Philip Lanzkowsky, MD, and Jack Gallagher, at the SCH 1999 winter gala.

Because of his commitment to NSUH, Jack Gallagher could not readily entertain a different model. He spoke of two great and equal departments, "like the Twin Towers," but I saw it "like the Empire State Building," with SCH being the edifice of pediatric care dominating the landscape for the system.

Gallagher encouraged the NSUH doctors to stay the course with the belief that, at the end of the day, there would be a separate and distinct Department of Pediatrics from SCH serving the North Shore. To me this spelled duplication of sophisticated services in two locations in close proximity to each other and a denial of the basic objectives of the merger.

Actually, I underestimated how hard it would be to drive people out of their comfort zones.

With the passage of time, it became clear that many of the leaders of the Department of Pediatrics at NSUH were unable to accept change, and this fact resulted in many voluntary resignations.

Shortly after my appointment as vice president of the Children's Health Network, I had to confront two major obstacles. First, the faculty practice plan for the two departments had to be merged into one. This was necessary to eliminate the economic incentive for the faculty members to remain competitive, and to open the way for closer clinical cooperation and interchange of patients. Second, each of the pediatric divisions had to have a single chief and a common, unified goal and objective. This was not easy, since each department had its own chiefs of all the divisions, for example, cardiology, neonatology, neurology, and hematology-oncology. One of the two existing chiefs had to be chosen for each combined division.

This was done as fairly and objectively as possible, through the use of criteria such as academic rank, leadership ability, and previous accomplishments. Everybody in the department was given assurances regarding salary and tenure. This selection process created anxiety, fear, and tension in what was already a war zone, but it had to be carried out in order to move the plan forward.

At a number of "town meetings," which were well attended by all faculty, I explained my vision for the future of the combined Department of Pediatrics. I tried to assuage the faculty's concerns and reassure everybody of his or her tenure. Mr. Gallagher asked me not to announce the new chiefs of the combined divisions, since he continued to have questions about these decisions. Many of the leaders of the new health system attempted to dissuade me from the course I had embarked upon. After many discussions with people in the health system, however, I remained convinced that creating a strong, nationally recognized children's hospital that concentrated all tertiary-care pediatrics in one place would benefit not only the children of the region but also the health system.

Because of the fundamental differences between Jack Gallagher and me regarding how pediatric services should be delivered by the health system in the future, he appointed the Katz Consulting Group, Inc. (presently Kurt Salmon Associates) in 2001 to recommend future direction for the Department of Pediatrics and SCH. After extensively interviewing faculty, reviewing data, and studying other children's hospitals nationwide, they developed the following guiding principles:

- All pediatric specialty programs will be focused at SCH on the LIJ campus, with faculty assigned to NSUH to support pediatric inpatient, ambulatory surgical, and emergency room services and provide limited outpatient visits there.
- All faculty will have offices in divisional office suites at SCH.
- Faculty in cardiology, hematology-oncology, and infectious diseases will have assigned offices at NSUH. Neonatology and critical care will have dedicated offices and examining rooms at NSUH. All other faculty will utilize shared office and examining space when at that hospital.
- Neonatal-perinatal medicine, necessary to support the large obstetrical service at NSUH, would remain at NSUH.

While this attempt at merging the departments had some rational basis, it had a big political component in order to satisfy some of the needs of both parties. I viewed the report as an expedient interim plan. Its importance lay in its recognition that ultimately, SCH would house all of pediatrics for the system.

In my June 1999 address to the graduates, faculty, administration, and trustees, I commented on the merger of LIJ and NSUH with particular reference to the discipline of pediatrics:

"The NS-LIJ Health System has established the Children's Health Network as an entity, which is unparalleled in its scope and objectives anywhere in this country. It has approximately 1,000 pediatricians and subspecialists, 13,000 inpatient admissions, 300,000 outpatient visits and serves a population of several million people. This new network will be one of the largest providers of pediatric care in the United States and should be a model to be emulated.

It will combine two great departments of pediatrics, each with its own national and international reputation, to work in unison in a single integrated, unified entity, for the common good of children, to further pediatric education and all professionals concerned with the health and welfare of children, and to further the objectives of biomedical research in the developing child.

The merger will allow us to develop an innovative integrated healthcare delivery system for children, the purpose of which is to provide quality-driven, cost-effective care that meets the needs of children whether they are healthy or require specialized medical care. It will be based on the fundamental concept of a principle-based meritocracy.

This mission will be accomplished through the development of a comprehensive continuum of children's health services which will ensure that children are treated in the most appropriate setting, at the right time, by the best qualified and most suitable physicians under an umbrella of a uniform standard of excellence throughout the region.

The new pediatric network will be academically based and provide broad geographic access to high-quality care to children from Staten Island to Montauk through the vast array of primary care pediatricians, pediatric subspecialists, satellite centers, and hospitals.

A network of this type will ensure value, cost-effectiveness, and satisfaction to all the

stakeholders—patients, payers, and physicians.

If the building of the children's hospital was a major step forward for pediatrics, then the effective and successful development of the Children's Health Network under unified management is a quantum leap in the delivery of medical care for the children in this region.

This is a unique opportunity and a massive challenge for us. This merger on paper is being translated into a living entity benefiting all children so that the services it provides can act as a 'Pied Piper' for sick children throughout the island in a uniform system with a common mission which will ensure optimum care for children.

It must also fulfill its mission to provide care to the underinsured and uninsured children within our region. The latter is going to require resources, which have to be built into our overall mission.

We have to recognize and appreciate and be sensitive to the insecurities that change entails for all the stakeholders involved, but change is essential for progress and to attain our wider mission. The opposite, lack of change, leads to stagnation and lack of progress. If we do not ride the wave of change we will find ourselves beneath it. We have to have the resolve and courage to change that which requires change.

Without change there can be no breakthroughs. Without breakthroughs there can be no future. We should remember that the bend in the road is not the end of the road, unless we fail to make the turn.

According to a recent front-page article in *Crain's New York Business* regarding children's hospitals, I quote: 'Children's health services will serve as the centerpieces of new health care networks and will be compelling marketing showcases that networks will use to attract patients, insurers and employees.' But more important than that, it is good for the health and welfare of children, and that is why we want this dream for children to become a reality."

When Michael J. Dowling became president and CEO, he realized that in order for there to be proper clinical integration, there should be one chairman of pediatrics, and I was the one he appointed for the position. That cleared the way for a complete and ultimately successfully combined North Shore-Long Island Jewish Health System Department of Pediatrics. In April 2002 the department at NSUH was renamed Schneider Children's Hospital at North Shore.

As the pressure for space for other departments at NSUH developed, the subspecialty clinics in endocrinology, hematology-oncology, immunology, gastroenterology, nephrology, and eventually cardiology were transferred to SCH. This had two effects:

1). It reduced the number of pediatric admissions and occupancy at NSUH. This led to the closure of pediatric beds, the number of which was reduced stepwise from an original complement of forty-two medical/surgical beds and fifteen critical-care beds to twelve medical/surgical beds, and twelve critical-care beds by 2005.

2). It created pressure on the space at SCH, which led to the development of clinics at 410 Lakeville Road in New Hyde Park, Nassau County, and 865 Northern Boulevard in Great Neck, Nassau County, and to the consolidation of general pediatrics (NSUH general pediatrics had been at 865 Northern Boulevard) at 410 Lakeville Road. Allergy-immunology, pulmonology, and cystic fibrosis clinics moved to 865 Northern Boulevard. The academic offices of endocrinology moved to 400 Lakeville Road. Finally, in 2007, the division of neurology and its clinics moved out of SCH to 410 Lakeville Road. These clinical specialties, which had shown enormous growth but whose practice did not require

being in the hospital, were moved to provide more space for the ambulatory chemotherapy unit within SCH. This was not ideal, and the aim is that ultimately these programs will return to the hospital when expansion makes this possible.

It soon became apparent that running a department consisting of twelve medical/surgical beds and twelve ICU beds at NSUH was very difficult and inefficient. As further construction occurs at SCH and space becomes available, SCH at North Shore will close with the exception of neonatology, which will remain at NSUH to support its Department of Obstetrics. This will complete the consolidation of all pediatric beds at one location at SCH.

As a result of the merger and the growth of all the programs, expansion of the hospital became inevitable. In 2007, the process began.

The two pediatric training programs (NSUH had fifty-one residents and SCH eighty residents) were combined into one, effective July 2003, which made it one of the largest pediatric training programs in the nation. The first director of the combined 131-resident program was Harvey Aiges, MD. The fellowship programs were also merged.

On the whole, the merger was a great success, programmatically and financially, fulfilling the aspirations of the trustees who set the process in motion. The fusion of the separate boards of trustees into a single leadership unit worked well. The first few years of the merger were tense, however, both for the administration and for the medical staff, because of the necessary consolidation of leadership roles that inevitably had to occur.

After about five years, the dust had settled. It took about the same amount of time to settle on a logo for the system. It was difficult to find one that everybody was comfortable with that represented both NSUH and LIJ in the most equitable way.

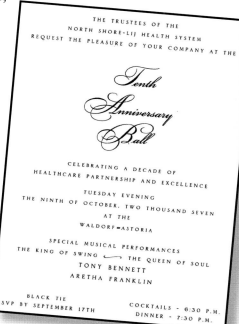

To celebrate this successful healthcare partnership, a tenth anniversary ball attended by about 1,500 people was held at the Waldorf Astoria in New York on October 9, 2007, with entertainment provided by Tony Bennett and Aretha Franklin. It was a celebration of the vision, determination, and extraordinary leadership demonstrated by the NS-LIJ Health System and its board in creating one of the finest and most successful health systems in the nation.

CHAPTER 18

FULFILLING THE DREAM

CUTTING THE TIES

When the Schneider Children's Hospital (SCH) opened, it was not an independent facility but instead, for ease of operation, was grafted onto the fiscal and organizational structure of Long Island Jewish-Hillside Medical Center (LIJ).

The two institutions had a single budget and financial statement and single governance, and the executive director of LIJ was responsible for SCH even though he had no special knowledge of or expertise in running a children's hospital. He did appoint an associate executive director for SCH, the first of whom was Paul Kessler,* who reported to him.

Unfortunately, this organizational structure caused problems because it did not recognize the unique needs of the children's hospital. For example, nobody knew how each hospital was performing financially on its own, which was essential for effective management. In the absence of any data to the contrary, SCH was always viewed as a

Mr. Kessler was followed by Cynthia Sparer in 1988, Martin Fink in 1990, and Larry Levine from 1992 until 1999.

Dr. Philip Lanzkowsky confers on a hospital matter with Dr. Fredrick Z. Bierman, Chairman of the Department of Pediatrics, (on his right), Dr. Vincent Parnell, Surgeon-in-Chief, (on his left) and Dr. Andrew Steele, Medical Director (standing).

significant financial burden on LIJ. (It was not until the children's hospital's finances were separated from LIJ's that it became apparent that the operations of the children's hospital in fact had always shown a significant positive balance.) Despite constant urging, the LIJ administration would not grant any degree of independence to the children's hospital. In fact, they sought to link the two as closely as possible, frequently referring to the Schneider Children's Hospital as a division of LIJ.

This policy was in sharp contrast to and at times in conflict with my goals and vision for the hospital. I had always wanted the children's hospital to be separate from LIJ, with its own mission, its own constituency, and the right to self-determination. These philosophical differences created a conflict that simmered for almost two decades, during which time the Schneider Children's Hospital was held back from assuming its rightful place among independent children's hospitals in the country, and during which time I was perceived in certain quarters as a truculent adolescent creating unnecessary disharmony in the institution. I was extremely frustrated, but the odds appeared insurmountable.

Then, in January 2002, Michael J. Dowling became the president and CEO of the newly merged North Shore-Long Island Jewish (NS-LIJ) Health System. Mr. Dowling had a

Philip Lanzkowsky, MD, and Michael J. Dowling in SCH lobby.

broader vision; he had the authority, and he took the bold step previous leaders had feared to take for almost a quarter century. He removed the shackles that bound the children's hospital and became one of its most powerful and staunch supporters. This was a turning point in the history of SCH.

Mr. Dowling rapidly appreciated that the children's hospital was sui generis, and not only that; he saw it as a "jewel in the crown" that would help to catapult the system into national and international prominence. To fulfill that mission, SCH needed to develop its own governance structure and independent budget. On January 1, 2003, Mr. Dowling separated SCH from LIJ, both organizationally and operationally, to the maximum extent possible given the close proximity of both institutions to each other and the fact that there is at present a single Article 28 license from the New York State Department of Health for both institutions. After having been chief-of-staff of the hospital since it opened, I was now appointed, in addition, its first executive director. In turn, I appointed Eric Chaikin as associate

First executive management team, from left: John Brandecker, Eric Chaikin, Philip Lanzkowsky, MD, and Carolyn Quinn, RN.

executive director for operations, John Brandecker as associate executive director for finance, and Carolyn Quinn, RN, as associate executive director for patient care services.

I later added to the management team an associate executive director for human resources and an associate executive director for quality management and patient safety. A separate administrative structure and table of organization were developed, formal medical bylaws for the hospital were established, and its own governance structure, the Medical Leadership Council, was put into place.

The Medical Leadership Council (MLC) had the following composition:

Executive director of SCH
Medical director of SCH
Chairman of the Department of Pediatrics
Vice-chairman of the Department of Pediatrics
Chairman of the SCH Performance Improvement Coordinating Group (PICG)
Chief of neonatal-perinatal medicine
Chief of pediatric critical care medicine
Chief of general pediatrics
Chief of pediatric general surgery
Chief of pediatric otorhinolaryngology
Chief of pediatric cardiothoracic surgery
Chief of pediatric neurosurgery
Chief of pediatric radiology
Chief of pediatric anesthesiology
Chief of pediatric emergency medicine
Chief of child psychiatry
Chief of pediatric dental medicine
Chief of pediatric ophthalmology
Chief of pediatric orthopedics
Director of bioethics
Associate executive director for patient care services
Graduate medical education pediatric program director
Four community-based pediatricians
Executive director of LIJ
Chief medical officer of NS-LIJ Health System

Table of Organization of Schneider Children's Hospital

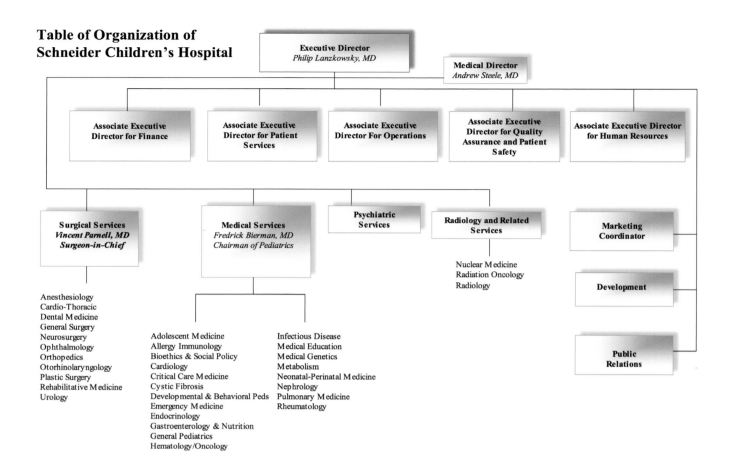

The Medical Leadership Council formed subcommittees in these areas:
- Credentials
- Critical care
- Emergency preparedness
- Graduate medical education
- Medical ethics
- Medical records
- Nutrition
- Performance improvement coordinating group
- Perioperative
- Pharmacy and therapeutics

The formation of the Medical Leadership Council was a milestone in the history, evolution, and governance of the Schneider Children's Hospital. It facilitated major administrative appointments that laid the foundation for the next phase of its development. Fredrick Z. Bierman, MD, was appointed president of the Medical Leadership Council. In addition,

I appointed Vincent Parnell, MD, as the first surgeon-in-chief and Andrew Steele, MD, as the first medical director of SCH.

The Medical Leadership Council itself, its subcommittees, and these appointments drew in representatives of all clinical disciplines. We now had a governance structure similar to those in place at other children's hospitals in this country; one that was designed to respect the needs of a complex tertiary-care children's hospital and ensure the continuity of excellence that would uphold the hospital's reputation.

LIJ's Article 28 license from the Department of Health incorporated both SCH and Zucker-Hillside Hospital. For legal and regulatory reasons, SCH's Medical Leadership Council to this day reports to the LIJ Medical Board. On April 28, 2008, a Board of Visitors was created for SCH with Mr. Sean Simon as its first chairman. Although this board carries no operational or fiduciary responsibility (this resides with the NS-LIJ Health System board) the function of the Board of Visitors is fundraising and the important role of ambassadors to enhance and promote the SCH "brand" in the community. It is anticipated that in the future, SCH will have its own discrete Article 28 license and board of trustees—the final separation.

SCH has 1,214 employees who can be broken down in the following categories:

Full-time faculty	142
Residents	131
Fellows	58
Nursing	645
Social workers	47
Child life specialists	18
Housekeeping	45
Secretaries	66
Medical assistants	34
Security	9
Dietary	6
Respiratory therapy	6
Engineering/maintenance	7

The staffs of the laboratory medicine and radiology departments, surgical operating suite, security, dietary, respiratory therapy, engineering, and maintenance are all shared between LIJ and SCH. It is anticipated that some of these areas and departments will be the exclusive domain of the children's hospital as it continues to grow.

A ranking of children's hospitals in the United States published in the February 2005 issue of Child Magazine made it clear that the Schneider Children's Hospital had arrived; we were seventeenth on that list. That September, the U.S. Postal Service selected the hospital as the site for the official New York launch of the new 2005 postage stamp celebrating the Year of the Healthy Child. The stamp, created by postal service art director Carl Herrman and stamp artist Craig Frazier, showed a silhouette of a healthcare

provider placing a stethoscope on a child's chest. The stamp had the phrases "Regular medical checkups," "Car seats each time," "Balanced diet and exercise," and "Caring for our future," printed around its border.

Catherine Cassidy, U.S. Postal Service district manager and Joseph Capone, New Hyde Park postmaster with new stamp released in conjunction with the U.S. Surgeon General's declaration of 2005 as the Year of the Healthy Child.

In September 2007, *U.S. News & World Report* ranked SCH twenty-fourth on an even more prestigious list of best children's hospitals in the nation. Ranked below us were well-known, well-established institutions such as Children's Memorial Hospital in Chicago; Children's Hospital and Clinics of Minnesota in Minneapolis; Mayo Clinic Children's Hospital in Rochester, Minnesota; and Children's Hospital of Wisconsin in Milwaukee.

The hospitals were ranked based on national

reputation, mortality rates (brain surgery, bone marrow transplantation and congenital heart disease), number of annual discharges, nurse staffing ratio, Magnet status (for nursing excellence), and advanced care (technology, palliative care program, and FACT [Foundation for the Accreditation of Cellular Therapy] approval).

It's interesting to note that SCH was the youngest children's hospital on the *U.S. News & World Report* list; the twenty-four ahead of SCH had been established at least fifty years earlier. SCH is only a quarter of a century old and already known and respected around the world. In June 2008, *U.S. News & World Report* again ranked SCH as one of the top children's hospitals in the nation.

All this is a testament to the fact that the geographic location was right, the time in the development of pediatrics was right, the connection to LIJ was right, and so was the "dream team"—Judge Harnett, the men and women of the Children's Medical Fund, and I. Despite the struggles and the skepticism and the animosity of the seventies, these elements came together and the children's hospital became a reality. The Schneider Children's Hospital was simply meant to be, to the benefit of the thousands of children it has served and will continue to serve.

US News & World Report rank Schneider Children's Hospital as the top twenty-fourth children's hospital in the country.

Top Ranked

Two Years in a Row

2007

2008

U.S.News & World Report ranks Schneider Children's Hospital among the best children's hospitals in the nation.

We are proud to be recognized for our outstanding pediatric care for the second consecutive year. But we know that our work doesn't end here. To continue meeting the growing need for world-class pediatric care, we've embarked on a significant expansion project which includes the construction of a new four-story pavilion to house metropolitan New York's first stand-alone children's emergency department, new pediatric radiology center, new pediatric intensive care unit, expanded neonatal intensive care unit and a state-of-the-art medical and surgical unit.

SCHNEIDER CHILDREN'S HOSPITAL

Schneider Children's Hospital is continuously ranked one of the best! To help support the expansion project, please call 516-465-2551.

Schneider Children's Hospital New Hyde Park, NY

North Shore LIJ Schneider Children's Hospital

North Shore-Long Island Jewish Health System

Setting New Standards In Healthcare℠

SCHNEIDER CHILDREN'S
HOSPITAL
SCHNEIDER CHILDREN'S
HOSPITAL

CHAPTER 19

PASSING THE TORCH

GRADUATING WITH THE GRADUATES

After thirty-five years as chairman of pediatrics at LIJ and the Schneider Children's Hospital (SCH), in 2005 I decided that the time had come for me to retire from that position.

In my June 2005 graduation address, I announced that I had informed Michael J. Dowling, the President and CEO of the North Shore-Long Island Jewish (NS-LIJ) Health System, of my intent to step down, effective July 1, 2006, although I would continue to serve as executive director and chief-of-staff of SCH. This would allow adequate time for recruitment of a new chairman and an orderly transfer of responsibilities.

My tenure as chairman, while filled with challenges, obstacles, and setbacks, accom-plishments and triumphs, was above all a wonderful experience. I enjoyed clinical medicine as a practicing pediatric hematologist-oncologist and as a general tertiary-care specialist and the intellectual challenge of a difficult diagnosis or a complicated patient. I was excited about teaching medical students and residents the fundamentals of clinical medicine—its scientific basis, its clinical application, its intellectual opportunities—and instilling in them the need to adopt a systematic

Philip Lanzkowsky, MD passes the "baton" to the new Chairman of the Department of Pediatrics, Fredrick Z. Bierman, MD, July 2006.

approach to diagnosis based on fundamental principles. I enjoyed my years in the laboratories doing basic research and in the wards with patients garnering information and making observations.

Unlike many in my position, I did not mind its administrative aspects. It helped that I have always found it easy to make decisions—even major ones. When I think I have enough information to make a tough call, I resist perseverating. I was never out to win a popularity contest but instead wished to lead a community of physicians toward a shared goal. Above all, I was inspired in my work by a deep, all-consuming excitement about all aspects of medicine and an overriding drive to improve the healthcare of children. I thought about the hospital day and night. I cared about my patients, my colleagues, the faculty, and the hospital employees. I cared about the welfare of the hospital—that it would stay the course and remain true to its mission.

During the many years as chairman and during the long period it took to build the children's hospital, I learned to deal with disappointment (from regulatory authorities and others) and even rejection at times; the vision of building a great hospital exclusively for children helped me to endure.

To the faculty and the thousands of students and house officers whom I was privileged to teach, I attempted to impart core values, consistent with the finest traditions of Hippocrates and Maimonides. I stressed that industry, hard work, service to others, competency, dependability, and loyalty are the hallmarks of their chosen profession. I exhorted them not to be swayed by expediency, appeasement, or opportunism but always to think for themselves, to be goal directed, and to use their time efficiently. I encouraged them to approach problems realistically, recognizing that one's zone of concern should not overwhelm one's zone of action. I insisted that they learn to make incremental improvements on the path

to their goals rather than attempting quantum leaps that could lead to failure. I believe, as a matter of dogma, in the sanctity and incalculable value of human life, and I attempted to instill in my students the primacy of compassionate and competent patient care. I did my best to convey, in words and actions, that a physician should possess all the attributes of a mensch and have his or her moral compass in operation at all times. I would like to think that this is the legacy I have left behind.

THE GRADUATION ADDRESS

In my 2006 address to the graduates, faculty, and trustees, I formally announced my retirement as chairman of pediatrics in these words:

"The time has come for me to graduate with the graduates. It is appropriate for me to reflect on the thirty-six years that I have been chairman of this wonderful and great department of pediatrics that has received national and international recognition. The number 36, twice Chai, has a special connotation and has great significance in ancient mythology.

It has been a very exciting experience to have been chairman of the Department of Pediatrics

Dr. Philip Lanzkowsky delivering his graduation address in 2006 announcing his retirement as Chairman of Pediatrics.

Standing ovation following Dr. Lanzkowsky's address.

for this period of time—a period in which there have been astronomical advances in the practice of medicine and a quantum change in the healthcare delivery system in this country. A true healthquake.

I came to LIJ in March 1970 with a dream and with a vision:

- To establish a children's hospital,
- To develop a tapestry of services for children on Long Island,
- To establish the foremost training program for pediatrics in this country, and
- To establish a department of pediatrics that had academic credibility and was recognized in academic circles nationally and internationally for its excellence in clinical care, teaching, and research.

The challenges were immense, the obstacles were vast and often unpredictable, the achievements were considerable, and the satisfaction was immeasurable, for which I thank all of you. But this was only possible with the help of a loyal and dedicated faculty who shared these ideals and this wonderful dream. I salute them and pay tribute to them today. I also pay tribute to members of the Board of Trustees, particularly Mr. Irving and the late Mrs. Helen Schneider, and former and present members of the hospital administration.

Speaking from this very same podium on September 25, 1983 at the opening ceremonies for the children's hospital attended by Governor Mario Cuomo, I said at that time, and I quote: 'The essence of a children's hospital is the gathering under one roof of a community of scholarly professionals who are dedicated to the combined attack on the many problems of health and disease of the newborn, the child, and the adolescent.' This has been achieved over the years by bringing together, 'under one roof' so to speak, a community of scholars as loyal and dedicated faculty who shared these ideals and whom I have carefully culled over the past three to four decades from premier medical schools around the country. At the present time, of the more than 100 faculty, we have twenty-three full professors and twenty-two associate professors in the department, and fifty-five faculty who are assistant professors, as evidence of our commitment to developing a scholarly environment. At the recent national academic meetings in May in San Francisco, the faculty of Schneider Children's Hospital had numerous presentations and posters reflecting the outstanding research done here. To be precise, there were fifteen presentations and posters by our faculty, which boosted our academic credibility nationally.

This week's *New York Magazine* features seventeen of our faculty in the list of the Best Doctors in New York.

I continued to say on that occasion in 1983 and I quote again: 'Schneider Children's Hospital has an obligation to join with other institutions of similar dedication to teach, to share, to learn, to work in concert, all in the interests of children.' I predicted that this professional interaction would weave a tapestry of comprehensive and coordinated services enhancing the welfare of children in the tri-county area. Over twenty years later we met this commitment through our multiple relationships with many hospitals, our satellite system, and our weekly teleconferencing to hospitals and community-based pediatricians.

At that time in 1983 I turned to the empty building that had just been completed and said that the hospital was a mere building; a promise to the children of this region. We have a gigantic task ahead of us to build medical programs for children in this region on a sound fiscal basis so that this hospital stands as a beacon of hope and as a magnet to all those who seek medical, surgical, psychiatric, dental, and other care.

It was designed for 40,000 outpatient visits a year, and we now see almost four times that amount. I commented that when the doors of the children's hospital opened to serve the public, we would be judged by:

- The immediate community we serve for the medical care that we render;
- Students from all over for the truths they glean in our classrooms and the clinical skills they perfect in our wards;
- The national and international scientific community for the quality of research that emanates from our laboratories; and Ultimately, the most critical of all, the ill child who is comforted by our staff and restored to health.

Although the accomplishments have been great over the years and have catapulted us into the position of one of the top children's hospitals in this country, we have to be ever mindful of the facts:

- That complacency and smugness are the enemies of progress and innovation;
- That failure to take prudent risks leads to missed opportunities; and
- That expediency and avoidance of conflict are not always the right paths to follow and, while those paths may be comfortable and may lead to short-term gains, they may compromise certain core values and may not be in the best interests of our basic

objective—to provide excellence in medical research and care for children.

A sense of the history of the children's hospital, where we have come from and where we are going, is crucial; it is the lodestar and compass for our future direction so that we continue to fulfill the dream.

The time has come to hand over the responsibility of the chairmanship to the next chairman, like the torch relay in the Olympics.

During the past year, a committee formed by Mr. Michael Dowling conducted a national search for the next chairman. There were numerous highly qualified applicants from all over the nation. After many interviews, the unanimous decision of the committee has been to recommend Fredrick Zachary Bierman, MD, as the new chairman of pediatrics, the third chairman in fifty-two years. He will carry this program to new heights in the years ahead. As when the Olympic torch is passed, there is a sense of continuity.

Dr. Bierman is an individual of sterling character, an outstanding clinician and teacher, who has received national acclaim. It is my pleasure now to salute Dr. Bierman, hand my stethoscope over to him, and give him his new seat on the dais.

I would also like to recognize my wife, Rhona, and all my children, who have put up with my chairmanship for thirty-six years with patience and understanding.

Thank you, ladies and gentlemen."

On July 1, 2006, I passed the torch into the capable hands of Dr. Fredrick Z. Bierman who became the third chairman of pediatrics since the creation of the department in 1954. Dr. Bierman is a graduate of SUNY Downstate. He did his pediatric residency at Mount Sinai Hospital and his cardiology training at Children's Hospital Boston and Harvard Medical School and was on the faculty in cardiology at Columbia until his appointment to SCH in 1991 as chief of cardiology and associate chairman of pediatrics.

A TRIBUTE TO ROSE

This book would not be complete without recognizing my loyal, hardworking, and talented executive assistant, Rose Grosso.

While I was developing and running one of the largest departments of pediatrics in the country, she assisted me on a day-to-day basis. She is well known to generations of house staff, pediatricians, administrators, trustees, and others who had business with the department. Rose worked in that capacity for over thirty years, playing an important behind-the-scenes role, even though she sat at the front desk.

Rose is intuitive and perceptive and possesses the ability to communicate with professors, chairmen of the board, trustees, and all members of the staff with the same level of concern and interest. She remains calm and unruffled even under the pressure that inevitably occurs in the "hot seat," the office of the chief-of-staff. She shares my enthusiasm for the hospital and my concern that it be built and operated with excellence. I must confess that I was not happy when in October 1994 she decided to change her name from Rose Yannaco to Rose Grosso. My concern was that her marriage would dilute her loyalty and commitment. I was absolutely wrong. She was and is able to cope beautifully with the demands of married life and the job.

Rose Grosso at her desk, 2008

CHAPTER 20

BUILDING ON EXCELLENCE

INTO THE FUTURE

Every year thousands of children come to the Schneider Children's Hospital (SCH). As the reputation of SCH increases there is an exponential increase in the number of patients coming to the hospital.

Built in 1983, it is bursting at the seams and is no longer able to meet present-day needs. This is due not only to an increase in the number of patients but also to the fact that state-of-the-art treatment at the bedside demands more space.

The need for ambulatory clinic and critical-care space has increased tremendously, because advances in pediatric medicine have made it possible for children to undergo procedures and receive therapies for more complex diseases in an ambulatory-care setting, and because those who require admission are generally very sick and require critical-care beds.

When the Schneider Children's Hospital opened its doors in 1983, it was designed for 40,000 ambulatory patient visits per year. Building an ambulatory facility that would meet that demand was a major achievement because, in those days, many thought the projected patient number was excessive, and the cost of operating so large an ambulatory program would be astronomical. (Reimbursement in hospitals is dependent almost

View of proposed new inpatient tower with adjacent existing SCH building. Construction started 2008 and scheduled for completion 2011. Architectural rendering by MorrisSwitzer — Environments for Health.

exclusively on in-patient revenue.) There was considerable resistance from the Long Island Jewish Medical Center (LIJ) administration and regulatory bodies to build ambulatory facilities. Seeing the trend of pediatric care toward ambulatory services, I was insistent that SCH have a significant ambulatory component. In the year 2000, the number of ambulatory patients treated was 115,000. In 2008, we provided ambulatory services to over 160,000 children—four times the number the hospital was built to serve!

The current number of critical-care beds is inadequate. When the hospital was built, it had twelve critical-care beds. The demand for critical-care beds has risen and continues to do so, far outstripping the increase since the hospital was built—only eight more critical-care beds, for a total of twenty. In the last five years alone the number of patients admitted to the critical-care unit has risen from 1,095 to 1,511, an increase of 38 percent.

Specialty programs and numbers of personnel have outgrown their space within the hospital, and in order to make more room, in the early 1990s, "decanting" of academic offices and clinics to locations outside the hospital had begun. The merger that created the North Shore-Long Island Jewish (NS-LIJ) Health System in 1997 only compounded the problem. A large number of divisions that didn't require an in-hospital location were relocated in other buildings in close proximity to the hospital. In response to the need to expand the capacity of the hospital, enhance the experience for the patients and families, and allow SCH to stay ahead of the curve, a master plan for future development was required.

In 2001, the Katz Consulting Group, Inc., developed a master program plan that would support a redefined, expanded mission for the current and future needs of SCH. The goal was to create a child- and family-friendly environment that incorporates the latest in technological advancements, some of which may not have been invented. Rather than entering a place of stress or sickness, the child and his or her family would enter a place of health and healing.

The master plan includes a five-floor ambulatory services building adjacent and connected to the Schneider Children's Hospital, each floor containing 30,000 square feet of space to house all the ambulatory programs currently "exiled" to locations outside the hospital.

Model of SCH master plan consisting of (A) existing SCH building; (B) proposed five-floor ambulatory services building and (C) proposed nine-floor inpatient tower. The architect is Morris Switzer Environments for Health.

The plan also calls for a new nine-floor inpatient tower that would house 175 beds. In keeping with modern hospital construction and expectations of patients and their parents, the hospital will have only single-patient rooms. Patient rooms will consist of a section for medical and nursing personnel, a section for the patient, and a discrete sleeping facility for parents that would have Internet access. This "universal room" concept will be used to allow for varying levels of intensity while maintaining a family-centered focus for each child. The building will also have its own separate pediatric emergency department and a state-of-the-art imaging suite.

The space that connects the two new buildings to the existing children's hospital will be a large, four-story, glassed-in atrium, which will serve as the heart of the new complex. The atrium will function as a focal point for the total complex and will provide a sense of wonder and excitement for the children entering the hospital. The Niki de Saint Phalle sculpture

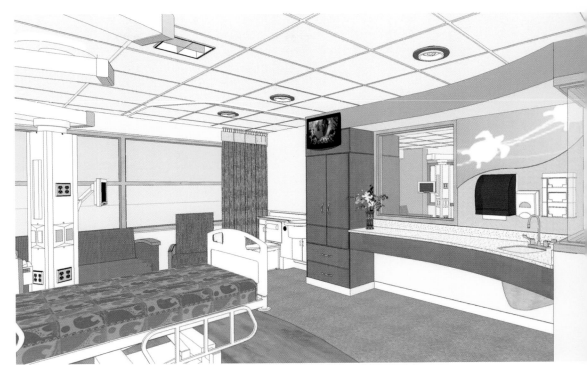

Conceptual renderings of interior design in SCH master plan showing pediatric intensive care patient room and ambulatory waiting area.

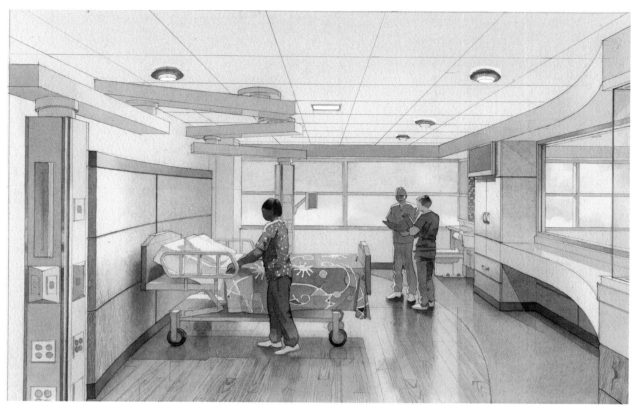

Architectual rendering of new pediatric intensive care patient room.

will be relocated to the atrium, offering year-round enjoyment. A remodeled main lobby will be both inviting and informative, and new design elements and signage will welcome all who enter the hospital. The hospital will also have a large auditorium for clinical and public meetings.

This master plan also called for the existing Schneider Children's Hospital to be retrofitted to contain a distinct pediatric surgical suite with pre- and post-operative recovery areas, faculty offices, and support space. The surgical suite will be designed and equipped especially for children so that they no longer have to utilize the operating rooms designed for adults at LIJ. The child-specific surgical facility will have the very latest technology and robotic surgery equipment, built-in cameras, remote robotic surgical capabilities, and voice-activated hardware. It will provide ample space for recovery and a comfortable lounge near the operating room where families

can wait for their children to return from surgery.

The design for the new complex was developed by MorrisSwitzer-Environments for Health, LLC, of Vermont. Jerry Switzer, AIA is its founding partner.

The total space designed to accommodate the programs, including the existing Schneider Children's Hospital, will be 560,000 square feet. The cost to realize the master plan will be approximately $250 million. After several years of planning, and the escalation of building costs during that time, we came to the realization that because of the enormous capital requirements, this master plan will have to be carried out in phases over a period of several years—a long-term dream, hopefully to be realized in the next decade.

Phase I of the master plan consisted of expansion of the existing neonatal intensive care unit (NICU), a new ambulatory chemotherapy area, and the enclosure of the existing SCH

Official groundbreaking ceremony for the first phase of rebuilding SCH showing construction in progress. Left to right: Saul Katz, (Chairman of the board of NS-LIJ Health System), Philip Lanzkowsky, MD, Fredrick Z. Bierman, MD, Karen and Joe Zangri with children Felicia and Ben (a NICU graduate) and Dennis Davidson, MD, September 19, 2007.

courtyard to create an atrium, commenced in July 2007. The official groundbreaking ceremony took place on September 19, 2007. My remarks at the groundbreaking ceremony are included below:

"This is a great day for Schneider Children's Hospital, our patients, the communities we serve, and our staff. SCH opened in 1983 amidst considerable controversy. Opposition came from all sources—regulators, doctors, and hospitals.

On September 25, 1983, on the eve of the dedication of the hospital, the *New York Times* ran an article with the headline, 'Children's Hospital Being Dedicated but Doubts Remain.' Opposition to building the children's hospital was repeatedly aired on television, and it was described by some in the local newspapers as 'a hoax.' The arguments advanced against the building of the children's hospital were that it would cause a duplication of services, there was a flat birthrate on Long Island, there was already a surplus of pediatric beds, and it was far too expensive. Never before has such a good idea met with such vociferous and widespread acrimony.

The predictors of doom and gloom were wrong! SCH has become:
• The Pied Piper and lodestar for sick children,
• A beacon of hope for many children and a place of last resort for some, not only from this community, but from around the country and around the world,
• One of two top children's hospitals in this region ranked among the top twenty-five children's hospitals in this country, according to a survey in *U.S. News & World Report*. Those institutions ahead of us in the list are prestigious institutions established fifty to 150 years before SCH and those below us on the list are such great institutions as the Mayo Clinic, Children's Memorial Hospital in Chicago, and children's hospitals of Minnesota, the University of Wisconsin, and the University of Michigan.

It was built for 40,000 ambulatory patient visits per year. We now have close to 160,000 visits annually.

Physicians from all around the world come to train at Schneider Children's Hospital.

In 1971 we made a promise to develop a specialized children's hospital on Long Island so we could provide outstanding pediatric care, right here in the New York area. We fulfilled our promise by establishing a hospital responding to the unique medical, surgical, and emotional needs of children. Our success has been built on the reputation and talent of our nursing staff and our physicians and surgeons culled from the finest medical institutions in this country and abroad. Superb medical care can only arise from a community of highly trained physicians working together as a team, in concert, to heal sick children in an environment specifically designed for children and their families.

We recognize that our children's good health is central to our individual and national interest and that society is measured by the manner in which it treats its children. Our children are our greatest and most vulnerable asset.

The construction happening around us today, the first phase of a grand master plan for the next decade, will propel us to even greater heights. We are building twenty-four state-of-the-art NICU beds for a total of sixty-eight NICU beds, one of the largest units in the nation, a state-of-the-art ambulatory chemotherapy unit, and a 20,000-square-foot, four-story-high atrium that will contain a winter garden, a performance stage for children, an art gallery and interactive games, and a virtual children's art gallery and museum. And this is only the beginning.

An institution of this caliber does not arise de novo—it is the product of a clear-cut vision perceived over thirty years ago and executed with deliberate determination by many people over the decades.

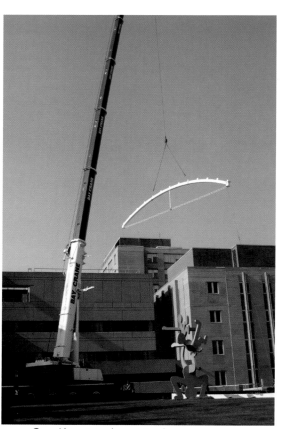

Crane lifting struts of new atrium frame.

We thank our physicians and nursing staff—the backbone of this children's hospital; our many benefactors and donors, without whom this would not be possible; Michael Dowling, CEO and president of the North Shore-LIJ Health System; and Saul Katz, chairman of the Board of Trustees, for their leadership."

As mentioned in my remarks, the first phase consisted of expanding the NICU by 5,900 square feet and constructing twenty-four state-of-

Top: Struts being placed in position to support roof of new atruim, 2007.
Bottom: Rendering of main passage of new neonatal intensive care unit
completed November 2008.
Left: Completed atrium, 2008

the-art neonatal intensive care beds. This brought
the neonatal bed complement to sixty-eight,
making it one of the largest units in the country.
An ambulatory chemotherapy unit, with 16
treatment bays, was built above the new NICU
to accommodate the increasing number of cancer
patients.

Since this construction took place in the very
middle of a busy hospital, considerable planning
and ingenuity were required so as not to interfere
with the facility's day-to-day operations.

The new construction also converted the
existing Schneider Children's Hospital courtyard
into a 20,000-square-foot, four-story glass-
enclosed atrium consisting of a playground for
hospitalized children, including a performance

Conceptual renderings of the new four-story glass-enclosed atrium.

Conceptual rendering of the new SCH lobby.

Conceptual rendering of the new SCH lobby looking into the atrium.

Lobby, another view.

Close-up view of proposed SCH entrance.

real boon for sick children and their parents throughout the region. The total bed complement at the completion of this second phase of the construction will be 228 beds, of which 117 (51 percent) will be dedicated to intensive care. This construction project is scheduled to be finished in 2011, and the building has been designed to accommodate a five-floor expansion to house an additional 125 beds.

stage, winter garden, and areas dedicated to pet therapy, music, and art therapy. This phase was completed in November 2008 at the cost of $22 million dollars.

Phase II of the master plan started in August 2008 consisting of the first four stories of the nine-story inpatient tower. There will be a bright and airy new lobby to welcome children and their families joining the glass-enclosed atrium of SCH to the new inpatient tower.

This phase of construction will provide 100,000 square feet of new space that will include a twenty-five-bed medical/surgical unit, a twenty-five-bed pediatric intensive care unit (PICU), a state-of-the-art imaging center, and Long Island's first stand-alone pediatric emergency department. This emergency facility will be outfitted with equipment designed just for pediatric patients and staffed with physicians and nurses who specialize in caring for children. The new children's-only emergency department, with its own radiology suite and CAT scan, will be a

Phase III of the master plan will consist of adding five further floors to complete the nine-story inpatient tower. Decanting some beds from the existing SCH into the bed tower will permit the development of a surgical operating suite exclusively for children to be built in the vacated space in the existing SCH building.

Phase IV of the master plan calls for the creation of an ambulatory services building to accommodate all ambulatory pediatric services presently located in facilities outside the children's hospital.

In addition to realization of the master plan that will guide expansion of the children's hospital in the decade ahead, we anticipate that there will be major advances in medicine and healthcare that will affect the hospital and the way we deliver care to the children we serve. The ways that patients physically experience the hospital, including everything from registration to food service to filing complaints, are primitive by today's information technology standards. In the future, electronic check-in will allow patients to register at home online and print out a bar code. When patients go to the hospital to be admitted, they will hand their bar codes to the receptionist. This will give the hospital the ability to recognize patients immediately, address them by name, know why they came to the hospital, and direct them accordingly. Bedside computers and interactive televisions will enable patients to order food, communicate with doctors, nurses, and housekeeping staff, file complaints, learn about their health conditions and medications, and have more control over their environment. All of these innovations will make the hospital stay a less dehumanizing experience.

SCH already has computers-on-wheels (known as COWs) in the intensive care units. This equipment permits the ordering of laboratory tests, radiological studies, and medications and tracks their status at the bedside. It allows for the display of serial laboratory results,

Computer on Wheels.

radiological images, operative notes, and pathology reports, as well as the recording and display of nursing and medical records. It also minimizes errors of transcription and helps to ensure a safer environment for patients.

Robots, omnipresent in industry, are already present in the world of healthcare in the form of robotic telerounding and robotic rounding. Robotic rounding includes real-time audio and visual communication with the patient, electronic chart review, and discussion with nursing staff regarding treatment. The six-foot-tall robot used in the telerounds is equipped with a fifteen-inch flat screen, two high-resolution cameras, and a microphone, and uses a videoconferencing system to conduct two-way communication with a remote console. During each session, the physician at the control station computer is able to drive the robot to the patient's room, emulating an on-site experience. Adult patient satisfaction with robotic rounding has been good, and children will especially enjoy this technological advance. Robotic rounding has been demonstrated to reduce the length of hospital stay and permits doctors to check on their patients while they are away from the hospital.

Another use of robotics in the hospital is to perform surgery. Remote minimally invasive surgery and unmanned surgery are major medical advances aided by surgical robots. Potential advantages of robotic surgery lie in precision and miniaturization. Since January 17, 2002, when surgeons at Children's Hospital of Michigan in Detroit performed the nation's first advanced, computer-assisted, robot-enhanced surgical procedure at a children's hospital, surgical robotics have been used in many types of pediatric surgical procedures including tracheoesophageal fistula repair, cholecystectomy, Nissen fundoplication, Morgagni hernia repair, Kasai portoenterostomy, congenital diaphragmatic hernia repair, and others. Additionally, the future will bring us biobots and bio-nanites (robots small enough to enter and travel through the body with the capability of reinsulating cells on nerves), as well as robots utilized for synthetic tissue replacement and repair systems. Nanotechnology holds the promise of the use of tiny machines with the tools and intelligence to perform specific tasks, (e.g., administering drugs), kill certain viruses, repair certain cells, and manufacture certain needed proteins or enzymes.

One of the most highly publicized and exciting areas in medical technology is human gene therapy, which seeks to replace missing or malfunctioning genes that are associated with a specific disease, thereby eliminating the illness or reducing its symptoms. The mapping of the human genome will determine the entire sequence of the human chromosome and will revolutionize biology and medicine. It will open the door to a vast repertoire of potential new treatments that will lead to cures for many diseases. Gene therapy for single-gene diseases will be routinely and successfully administered in the decades ahead.

There are two essential components for successful gene therapy. First, a therapeutic gene must be identified, and second, the gene must be safely delivered and transduced (incorporated) in the appropriate cells and DNA segment of the patient. The vehicles used to transport and deliver genes to targeted cells are referred to as vectors. For years scientists and physicians have faced the hurdle of finding a way to deliver therapeutic genes into the targeted cells efficiently and safely. Researchers are currently evaluating numerous gene delivery systems, including viral vectors (viruses rendered incapable of reproducing themselves) and nonviral vectors ("naked" DNA or lipid-coated DNA).

Patients' medical records may include the complete genome as well as a catalog of single base-pair variations that can be used accurately to predict responses to certain drugs and environmental substances. Patients will be treated as biochemical and genetic individuals, making medical interventions more specific, precise, and successful. This will reduce or eliminate

Architectural renderings of Emergency Department Waiting Areas

treatment side effects, save patients from taking unneeded drugs, and apply optimum therapy—the one that fits the patients' genetic profiles. In the genomic era, hospitals may be transformed in ways we cannot today envision.

There are other changes in healthcare that may have a profound effect on the children's hospital. Advances in health-oriented telecommunications, medical imaging, databasing, memory miniaturization, satellite technology, and other information systems are laying the groundwork

View of proposed new inpatient tower showing the new emergency department to be completed in 2011.

for fundamental changes in the organization of healthcare. Scanning massive databases containing millions of cases will determine what therapies actually work best in particular circumstances. The use of information technology as a management tool tends to make the practice of medicine more of a science and less of a craft, driving costs down and quality up. Broadly applied, it will also open the gates to a number of highly effective and inexpensive nonmedical methods that are considered "alternative" or "complementary" in western countries. The ability to measure all interventions by outcome and cost (outcome management) will push all therapies toward greater uniformity, bring a wider range of therapies into official payment systems, and allow true comparison of intervention and prevention strategies. Medical knowledge is expanding faster than any human can learn it. Computer programs called "expert systems"

help physicians and other health practitioners move much more rapidly and effectively through the decisions of diagnosis and therapy, isolating rare diseases, differentiating between similar syndromes, and discovering the latest research on the most effective therapies. Their widespread use is likely to change the doctor role significantly, bringing him or her away from knowing facts and toward the more human elements of the craft, such as making difficult judgments and helping patients change their behavior.

The Schneider Children's Hospital of the future will have to incorporate scientific discoveries as they become available. Future construction and allocation of beds and resources will be influenced by the direction and the impact of these changes in medicine as they become incorporated into daily practice.

All architectural renderings in this chapter were by MorrisSwitzer – Environments for Health.

The beginning of education lies in imitation—therefore pick someone worth imitating.

Martin H. Fisher
(1899 – 1962)

Some members of the SCH faculty

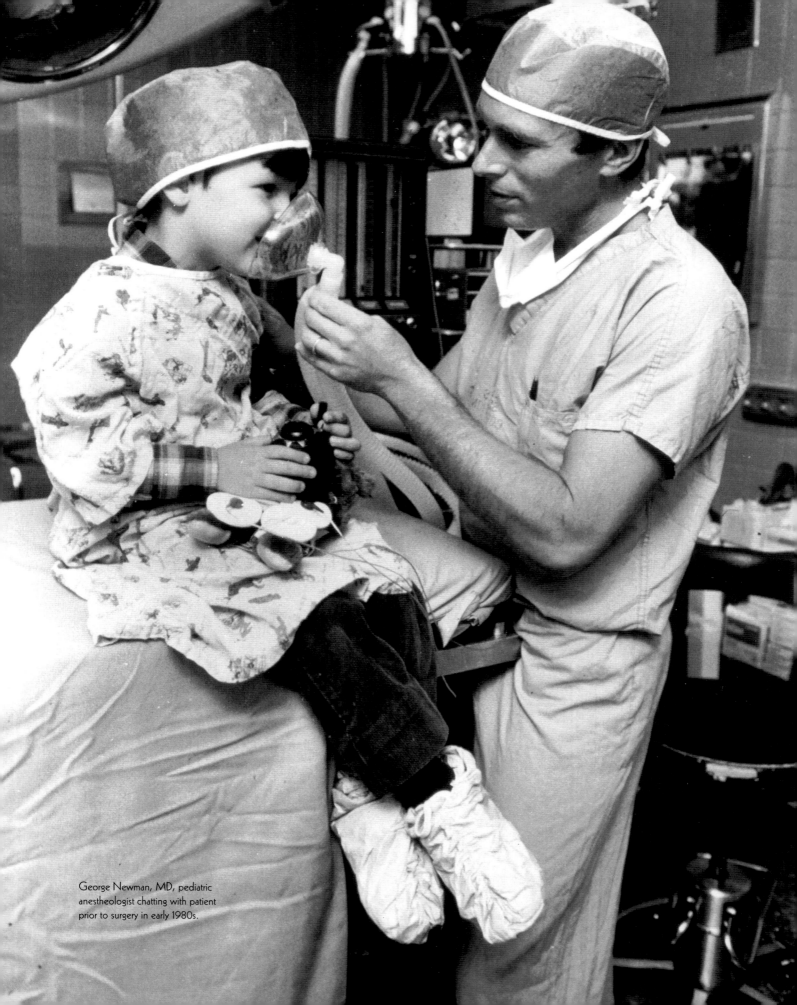

George Newman, MD, pediatric anestheologist chatting with patient prior to surgery in early 1980s.

Dr. I. Ronald Shenker, founding physician-in-charge of the Division of Adolescent Medicine, 1965–2000, speaking with patient.

chairmen of departments and physicians-in-charge of divisions became chiefs. Also, during the early years of the merger when North Shore University Hospital (NSUH) and SCH had their own divisional chiefs, some pro-tem titles were in use until chiefs of combined divisions were appointed.

It is hoped that the above explanation will account for some of the inconsistencies the reader may encounter in this section of the book. Some differences in style and emphasis may also be spotted because the individual chiefs wrote the histories of their divisions.

The faculty listed in the boxes are or were all full time, unless otherwise indicated.

INTRODUCTION

Apart from the Department of Pediatric Medicine (Pediatrics), the other services are, for academic reasons (residency approval), officially pediatric divisions of their respective departments at Long Island Jewish Medical Center (LIJ), even though they operate exclusively within SCH. From an administrative, organizational, and financial perspective, the responsibility for these services rests jointly with SCH and LIJ. Nursing, child life, and social work services are autonomous within SCH and have no reporting relationships to their corresponding LIJ departments.

With medical advances over time, the names of some divisions changed, for example, child development to developmental and behavioral pediatrics; human genetics to medical genetics; gastroenterology to gastroenterology and nutrition; neonatology to neonatal-perinatal medicine; and immunology to allergy-immunology-rheumatology and later separate divisions of allergy-immunology and rheumatology. Titles of faculty also changed over time. In the late seventies directors of departments became

PEDIATRIC MEDICINE

ADOLESCENT MEDICINE

The recognition that adolescents were underserved in the pediatric community dates back to the early 1960s when Children's Hospital Boston opened its first adolescent clinic. Samuel Karelitz, MD, chairman of pediatrics at LIJ at that time, with the support of the hospital and a promise of funding from the New York State Department of Health, sought to establish adolescent medicine as an integral part of the department. In September 1964, I. Ronald Shenker, MD, returned to LIJ after a three-year hiatus following his internship and pediatric residency here, with experience in public health and student (college) health, to establish a section of adolescent medicine in the pediatric department. In 1965, the Division of Adolescent Medicine of the Department of Pediatrics at Long Island Jewish Hospital came into being, with Dr. Shenker serving as the founding physician-in-charge.

A section in the department of pediatrics on the fourth floor of LIJ (Four South) was cordoned off to create a small office in which the adolescent program had its modest start. Initially patients were seen in the general outpatient clinic on two afternoons weekly. Obesity, acne, somatopsychic complaints, and problems of adolescent growth and development were typical cases seen. With state and Federal Children's Bureau funding, a clinical nurse specialist, a part-time secretary, a part-time nutritionist, and a social worker were added. This multidisciplinary team received federal support for almost two decades and demonstrated that appropriate adolescent care can be delivered to an underserved population within a department of pediatrics. They established a close liaison with the child psychiatry department at LIJ, and increased clinical services by utilizing a core of voluntary pediatricians who spent one afternoon per week with the program. This core group included Ruth Miller, MD, Stanley Blatt, MD, Marie Louise Rie, MD (deceased), and Esther Friedenthal,

ADOLESCENT MEDICINE FACULTY	
Chiefs	
1965–2000	I. Ronald Shenker, MD
2001–present	Martin Fisher, MD
Staff	
1978–1986	Michael Nussbaum, MD
1985–2008	Marc Jacobson, MD
1990–2008	Martha Arden, MD
1991–2006	Neville Golden, MD
1995–present	Eric Weiselberg, MD
2000–2006	Elba Iglesias, MD
2000–present	I. Ronald Shenker, MD
2002–2008	Rollyn Ornstein, MD
2008–present	Ronald Feinstein, MD
2008–present	Linda Levin Carmine, MD
Ambulatory Visits	
2007	8,472

MD. Weekly meetings were held in the home of Mollie Schildkraut, MD, from the psychiatry department, who provided an educational forum to enhance the team's skills in diagnosis and management of psychosocial conditions and the developmental assessment of the adolescent.

With the construction of the research building at LIJ in 1969, the adolescent team left its Four South office space. Its members were scattered in other areas of the hospital, while the chief settled into space close to the newly constructed office of Benjamin Berliner, MD, the interim chairman of pediatrics. At the same time, with additional bed capacity in the newly expanded LIJ, the eighteen-bed adolescent unit was opened on Four North, supported by a generous gift from the Abraham and Frieda Bernstein family.

In 1970, the Division of Adolescent Medicine opened a clinic in Christ Episcopal Church in Manhasset for drug-abusing adolescents.

Upon the arrival in 1970 of Philip Lanzkowsky, MD, to head the Department of Pediatrics, the Division of Adolescent Medicine moved to temporary quarters in the trailers behind the main hospital. With 1,600 square feet of offices and examining rooms available, the division expanded to its current format. The staff began to see an increasing number of teenage patients with eating disorders, and the division embarked upon studies (which continue) to elucidate the medical complications of these conditions.

In its own dedicated space and with community recognition, the division established an identity as the provider of confidential care to the adolescent. A comprehensive adolescent gynecology program was established, which allowed the adolescent access to a self-contained area for medical services. Subspecialty consultations such as dermatology, endocrinology, and orthopaedics were regularly available within the self-contained area. The advantages of a site separated from the

ABRAHAM AND FRIEDA BERNSTEIN ADOLESCENT UNIT

Opening of new Abraham and Fieda Bernstein Adolescent Unit on Four North LIJ, 1969. From left: Robert K. Match, MD, Richard Casden, grandson of the Bernsteins, Frieda and Abraham Bernstein.

main hospital outweighed the disadvantage of isolation of the program.

The adolescent medicine fellowship training program began in 1974, with Jonathan Horwitz, MD, the first fellow. The early fellows recruited from the house staff included Susan Trecaratin, MD, Eric Kaplan, MD, Michael Nussbaum, MD, and Martin Fisher, MD. The Student Health Service at Stony Brook University was also utilized

as a training site. One-year fellowship positions soon evolved into a two-year program. Some of the early graduates of the program included Dr. Nussbaum, who then joined the full-time faculty as a second attending in the Division of Adolescent Medicine, and Dr. Fisher, who joined the faculty at North Shore University Hospital (NSUH).

Fellows were soon being recruited from institutions outside the pediatric training program as the division began to be recognized as one of the pioneering programs in the country. Trainees came from programs such as the University of Miami, the University of South Carolina, Brown, and New York area institutions, including New York University, Columbia, and Cornell. Graduates of the program currently hold leadership positions locally, as well as in the national Society for Adolescent Medicine and the Section on Adolescent Health of the American Academy of Pediatrics.

With the opening of the Schneider Children's Hospital (SCH) in 1983, the Division of Adolescent Medicine moved back into the new hospital. With the luxury of having its own dedicated examining rooms, clinical and investigative activities were reorganized so that we could see patients three afternoons weekly. Services were expanded to include school-based health programs to care for adolescents who are at high risk for problems such as teenage pregnancy, drug and alcohol abuse, violence at home and on the streets, and chronic illnesses such as asthma, obesity and diabetes. These services are provided in ten high

Dr. Martha Arden, director of school-based programs, 1990–2008.

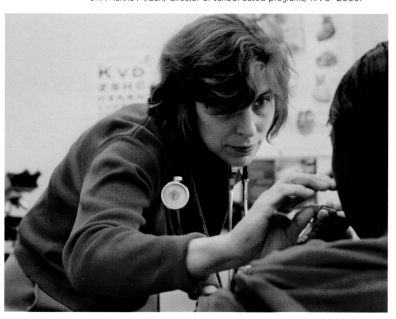

schools on Long Island, and a school-based health program with New York City Department of Health funding at Franklin K. Lane High School, the largest high school in Queens.

Over the following decade, the division's full-time faculty expanded with the recruitment of Marc Jacobson, MD, from the University of Maryland to establish the Center for Atherosclerosis Prevention within the Division of Adolescent Medicine; Neville Golden, MD, to replace Dr. Nussbaum in the position of director of the Eating Disorders Center; Martha Arden, MD, a former fellow, as director of school-based health programs; and Eric Weiselberg, MD, also a former fellow, as medical director of the Lexington School for the Deaf in Queens.

In the late 1990s, as SCH grew and space was at a premium, the division moved into dedicated space at 410 Lakeville Road where it continued to focus on nutritional disorders in adolescents (anorexia nervosa, bulimia, hyperlipidemia, obesity) along with providing adolescent-specific medical and gynecological healthcare in the office-based and school-based locations.

In 2000-2001, as part of the merger that created the North Shore-Long Island Jewish (NS-LIJ) Health System, the division merged with the Division of Adolescent Medicine of North Shore University Hospital (NSUH). The merged division moved into larger space at 410 Lakeville Road, Lake Success and added outpatient programs at two schools (a junior and a senior high school in Far Rockaway) and three large group homes in Brooklyn, Queens, and Nassau Counties. The division also participated in satellite programs of the Department of Pediatrics in Commack, Hewlett, and Brooklyn.

In January 2002 Dr. Martin Fisher became chief of the division and Dr. I. Ronald Shenker became chief emeritus. Additional attendings (Elba Iglesias, MD, 2000; Rollyn Ornstein, MD, 2002) joined Drs. Fisher, Shenker, Jacobson,

Dr. Martin Fisher, chief of Division of Adolescent Medicine, 2001–present.

Golden, Arden, and Weiselberg, to bring the total to eight full-time faculty. This current faculty represents a broad spectrum of academic interests, has garnered national recognition for contributions to the literature and program development, and provides a sound base for teaching and monitoring of the pediatric house staff and the three fellows in the division. By 2008, the division also included a full complement of nurses, nurse practitioners, nutritionists, and social workers to help meet the medical, gynecologic, nutritional, and psychological needs of adolescents from multiple communities and in diverse settings throughout the local and regional area. In 2008 Ronald Feinstein, MD, a former pediatric resident, and Linda Levin Carmine, MD, joined the full-time faculty.

ALLERGY-IMMUNOLOGY
(Formerly Allergy-Immunology and Rheumatology)

In the 1950s, clinical allergy was handled by a group of voluntary staff pediatricians. Eli Perlman, MD, was chief, assisted by Howard Scalettar, MD, Howard Kantor, MD, Philip Schneider, MD, and Seymour Kaplan, MD. They ran the allergy clinics for children at Long Island Jewish Medical Center (LIJ) and were responsible for teaching allergy to the house staff. They continued in this role for several decades, until the formal Division of Allergy-Immunology was established in 1985.

In July 1976 a clinical program in pediatric immunology was established at LIJ by Lazar

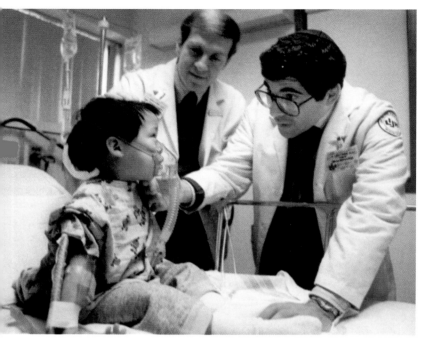

Dr. Vincent Bonagura, chief of Allergy-Immunology, 1985–present, and Dr. Hylton Lightman.

Fruchter, MD, who completed his training at Children's Hospital Boston and became the first physician-in-charge of immunology of the Department of Pediatrics at LIJ. In 1983 Dr. Fruchter immigrated to Israel, and the care of patients with allergic and immunologic diseases was turned over to Naynesh Kamani, MD, who in 1984 became responsible for running the pediatric allergy clinic and separately, a pediatric immunology clinic. Dr. Kamani, who resigned in 1985, established the clinical laboratory in immunology and rheumatology with Norman Ilowite, MD, who was a pediatric rheumatologist recruited from Seattle Children's Hospital, and who became the first chief of the Division of Rheumatology in 1991.

In 1985 Vincent Bonagura, MD, was appointed the first chief of the Division of Allergy-Immunology and Rheumatology. Dr. Bonagura was previously at Columbia Medical School and the New York Presbyterian Hospital. Hylton Lightman, MD, the first fellow in the Division of Allergy-Immunology and Rheumatology, was appointed in 1985, and Dr. Bonagura

also recruited David Valacer, MD, to head the Section of Pediatric Allergy. Eileen Pagano, RN was the first nurse clinician in the Division of Allergy-Immunology and Rheumatology.

In June 1986, SCH was designated an AIDS clinical trial center by the National Institute of Child Health and Human Development (NICHD) with Dr. Bonagura as principal investigator.

In order to satisfy the Residency Review Committee (RRC) of the American Council for Graduate Medical Education (ACGME) requirements for a conjoined pediatric and adult training program in the discipline of allergy and immunology, William Nicholas, MD, was appointed to head the Section of Adult Allergy in 1986. Frederick Siegal, MD, was recruited from LIJ's internal medicine faculty to be the adult immunologist and coordinator of the residency training program in internal medicine in 1989. The Division of Allergy-Immunology was formally recognized as a certified training

program in the discipline of allergy and immunology by the ACGME in 1990. At that time, three fellows were enrolled in the training program.

Dr. Peter LoGalbo

In 1991, the Division of Allergy-Immunology and Rheumatology was separated into two distinct divisions. Dr. Ilowite, who was head of the Section of Pediatric Rheumatology in the Division of Allergy-Immunology and Rheumatology, became the founding chief of the Division of Rheumatology at SCH. During the same year, Dr. Valacer left SCH to become the training director of pediatric allergy and immunology at

New York Hospital-Cornell Medical School. Dr. Bonagura recruited Peter LoGalbo, MD, board certified in allergy and immunology, pediatric rheumatology, and clinical and diagnostic laboratory immunology, to head the Section of Pediatric Allergy, the position vacated by Dr. Valacer, and to assist Dr. Ilowite in developing a training program in pediatric rheumatology.

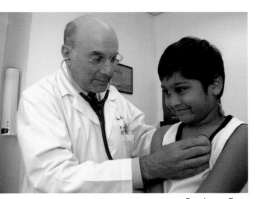

Dr. James Fagin

Also in 1991, Susan Schuval, MD, a previous fellow-in-training in allergy and immunology at LIJ, was appointed head of the Section of Clinical Immunology for HIV Infection. In 1993, Eric Applebaum, MD, also a previous allergy-immunology fellow, was recruited to assist Dr. Nicholas in further developing the Section of Adult Allergy for the training program. Dr. Applebaum served as instructor in internal medicine for two years, and was replaced by John Rooney, MD, in 1994 when Dr. Applebaum entered private practice. Dr. Rooney left the division as a full-time member to enter private practice in 1995. He remains as a voluntary member of the Section of Adult Allergy along with Drs. Mitchell Boxer, MD, and Ellen Epstein, MD. Dr. Boxer was appointed co-head of the Section of Adult Allergy, along with Dr. Nicholas, in 1996.

In July 1996, Steven Weiss, MD, PhD, a former pediatric resident at the Schneider Children's Hospital and fellow in the allergy-immunology training program at LIJ, became the newest member of the faculty. Dr. Weiss added his extensive research expertise to that already present in the division. Dr. LoGalbo became the first director of the Pediatric Asthma Center at SCH in 1999,

the first of its kind on Long Island. Blanka Kaplan, MD, joined the division in 2000 and became head of the Section of Adult Allergy, replacing Dr. Nicholas, who retired in 1998. Maria Santiago, MD, was recruited from the Division of Pulmonary Medicine to join Dr. LoGalbo as co-director of the Pediatric Asthma Center at SCH in 2001. In 2005, Dr. LoGalbo left the division to enter private practice, and that year James Fagin, MD, previously the chief of general pediatrics at North Shore University Hospital, joined the division and assumed Dr. LoGalbo's role as co-director of the Pediatric Asthma Center. Also in 2005, Marie Cavuoto, MD, previously a fellow in allergy and immunology at LIJ, joined the division. The Division of Allergy-Immunology currently trains three to five pediatric or internal medicine residents in allergy and immunology over a two-year period.

ALLERGY-IMMUNOLOGY FACULTY

Chiefs

1976–1983	Lazar Fruchter, MD
1984–1985	Naynesh Kamani, MD (pro-tem)
1985–Present	Vincent Bonagura, MD

Staff

1985–1991	Norman Ilowite, MD
1985–1991	David Valacer, MD
1991–Present	Susan Schuval, MD
1991–2005	Peter LoGalbo, MD
1994–1995	John Rooney, MD
1996–1999	Steven Weiss, MD, PhD
2000–2002	Savita Pahwa, MD
2000–Present	Blanka Kaplan, MD
2001–2003	Gadi Avshalomov, MD
2005–Present	Marie Cavuoto, MD
2005–Present	James Fagin, MD
2008–Present	Punita Ponda, MD

Ambulatory Visits

2000	4,125

Since the Division of Allergy-Immunology's inception, it has developed a national and international reputation. The research laboratory headed by Dr. Bonagura has presented 130 abstracts at various national and international meetings including the Society of Pediatric Research, the American Academy of Allergy, Asthma, and Immunology, Federation of American Societies for Experimental Biology (FASEB), the American College of Allergy, Asthma, and Immunology, the American College of Rheumatology, and the American Association of Immunologists. Several abstracts are presented yearly by the faculty and fellows at each of these meetings. In addition, more than 120 manuscripts have appeared in prestigious peer review journals, including *Nature, Structural Biology, Immunology Today*, the *Journal of Clinical Investigation*, the *Journal of Immunology*, the *Journal of Experimental Medicine*, the *Proceedings of the National Academy of Science USA, Arthritis and Rheumatism*, the *Journal of Pediatrics*, the *Journal of Infectious Diseases, Clinical Immunology*, and *Clinical and Vaccine Immunology*. Dr. Bonagura is a director of the American Board of Allergy and Immunology, a member of the American Board of Pediatrics, and vice chair of the Allergy and Immunology RRC of the ACGME.

Over the past seven years, members of the faculty have been invited to give many presentations at international symposia dealing with molecular immunology, autoimmunity, primary immunodeficiency, HIV infection in children, immunodeficiency associated with long-term survivors of pediatric acute lymphocytic leukemia, asthma, and other atopic diseases.

The Division of Allergy-Immunology Research Laboratory has been very successful in obtaining support for clinical and basic research covering several projects involving primary immune deficiency, HIV-related immune deficiency, autoimmunity, and most recently,

defective host responsiveness to human papillomaviruses (HPVs). Funding institutions that support the research efforts of the Division of Allergy-Immunology include the National Institutes of Health, the Arthritis Foundation, the Lupus Foundation, Inc., the Campbell Foundation, and the Easter Seals Foundation. To date, the total number of research dollars obtained by the Division of Allergy-Immunology at SCH is in excess of $15 million.

The division has also formed national and international collaborations with several institutions through its research efforts. An ongoing research relationship with the University of Oslo, the National Hospital of Norway, was established in 1995. Dr. Bonagura gave a lecture at the University of Oslo in December 1995 and implemented an important collaborative effort between SCH and the University of Oslo. A long-standing relationship with the University of California at Los Angeles with Sheri Morrison, MD, and Elaine Reed, MD, continues to produce research support and many publications in the areas of autoantibody characterization at the molecular level and immunogenetic control of the response to HPV infection. A research collaboration with the University of Naples was also established by Dr. Bonagura and Fulvio Invernizzi, MD. In this collaboration, both SCH and the University of Naples examined the expression of disease-specific rheumatoid factors in patients with type-2 mixed cryoglobulinemia. A strong collaboration also exists between the Division of Allergy-Immunology and Bettie Steinberg, PhD, from the Department of Otorhinolaryngology at LIJ. This collaboration includes studying host defense in human papillomavirus infection in patients with recurrent respiratory papillomatosis (RRP). Since 1992 the collaboration has been productive, yielding many publications and a National Institutes of Health (NIH) program project that combined three independent NIH Research Project (R01) grants over a fifteen-year period, and a separate independent R01 grant from NIH.

The faculty of the Division of Allergy-Immunology has also been innovative in the establishment of new programs. In addition to the Pediatric Asthma Center established by Drs. Bonagura and LoGalbo which coordinates care of children with mild, moderate, and severe asthma by the staff clinicians at SCH, a food allergy center, presently directed by Dr. Cavuoto, was formed by Dr. LoGalbo in 1995. This center addresses the complex area of food-related allergy in a scientific manner, and provides more accurate diagnoses, "cutting-edge" clinical care, and an opportunity for clinical and basic scientific research.

Drs. Bonagura and Schuval have established a Pediatric AIDS Center that is funded by the National Institute of Child Health and Development. Funding for a Center of Excellence in Pediatric and Adolescent HIV Care was also obtained from the New York State Department of Health AIDS Institute. The center conducts clinical trials of antiretroviral and immune-therapeutic reagents with the goal of providing the most advanced care for children with HIV infection and monitors highly active antiretroviral therapy (HAART) compliance in providing comprehensive care for HIV+ infants, children, and adolescents. A joint program with the Division of Pediatric Hematology-Oncology was established to provide stem cell transplantation for children with primary immune deficiency. As a result, children with Omen's syndrome, severe combined immune deficiency, bare lymphocyte syndrome, and Wiskott-Aldrich syndrome have received transplants at SCH's bone marrow transplantation unit.

With the North Shore-LIJ Health System merger, Savita Pahwa, MD, a highly respected national authority on AIDS and chief of immunology at NSUH, joined the Division of Allergy-Immunology, and the pediatric AIDS programs of NSUH merged with those of SCH. Dr. Pahwa left the division to join the research faculty at the University of Miami in 2002.

BIOETHICS AND SOCIAL POLICY

From decisions to forgo life-extending treatment through questions of truth-telling and confidentiality, and challenges to professional principles in a managed-care world, ethical issues

Robert Cassidy, PhD, founding director, Division of Bioethics and Social Policy, with a group of medical students.

permeate pediatric care. Recognizing the need for disciplined understanding and management of these issues in hospital practice, and also for systematic training of pediatric house staff in ethical decision-making, the Bioethics and Social Policy Division was formed in 1989. Robert C. Cassidy PhD, who trained at Princeton and Oxford, was chosen as full-time director. This program has received significant support from the Rudin Foundation.

The program has developed two vehicles to reach its two major goals. First, bioethical issues in current clinical cases are reviewed and adjudicated by the Schneider Children's Hospital Ethics Committee (CHEC). With twenty-five members from pediatrics, nursing, social work, and child life, CHEC is responsible for reviewing all cases that raise critical bioethical challenges. Its mission also includes formulating policies to enlighten and guide clinical decisions about ethical issues.

In addition, Dr. Cassidy has developed a series of "ethics rounds" for house staff on the critical-care services, noontime lectures for all house staff, and intensive seminars for the Albert Einstein College of Medicine medical students, which build the foundations for systematic bioethical judgment and sharpen the decision-making tools needed to put ethical principles into practice.

In sum, the educational program in bioethics has made a significant contribution to the development of young pediatricians at SCH, and CHEC has served as a reflective complement to the faculty's and staff's responsive and responsible care of children and their families.

CARDIOLOGY

For over forty years, the Division of Cardiology within the Department of Pediatrics at Long

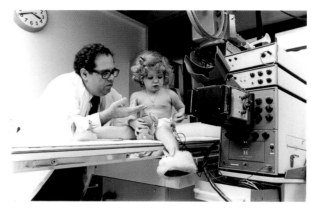

Dr. Norman Gootman, founding divisional chief of cardiology, 1965–1991, comforting a child prior to cardiac catheterization, circa 1970.

Island Jewish Medical Center (LIJ) and then at the Schneider Children's Hospital (SCH) has been a creative, progressive service caring for the fetus, the newborn baby, and the child, as well as the adolescent with congenital and acquired heart disease. In 1965 Norman Gootman, MD, who trained with Abraham Rudolph at Albert Einstein College of Medicine, was appointed the founding physician-in-charge of cardiology. His associate was George D. Rook, MD, a board-certified pediatric cardiologist on the voluntary staff. The division has evolved from a satellite program of LIJ at the Queens Hospital Center to a multidisciplinary cardiology division at the Schneider Children's Hospital, with faculty recruited from leading pediatric cardiology centers in this country.

The Division of Cardiology designed by Dr. Gootman was based on scholastic and clinical excellence. Clinical pediatric cardiology at LIJ began in 1965 with the first cardiac catheterization (initially performed in the adult cardiac catheterization laboratory) and open heart surgical procedure performed on a pediatric patient. In 1968, the scholastic commitment of the pediatric cardiology faculty led to the establishment of one of the earliest New York fellowship training programs in this discipline, which to date has produced twenty-five fellows and more than seventy research papers. Dr. Gootman,

Dr. Norman Gootman's animal laboratory, circa 1970.

accompanied by his wife, Phyllis Gootman, PhD, professor of physiology at SUNY Downstate College of Medicine, conducted seminal research on the central nervous system's control of cardiovascular function in newborn piglets.

In 1980 a dedicated pediatric cardiac catheterization laboratory was opened, setting a new standard of subspecialty care for the community served by LIJ.

Following Dr. Gootman's retirement due to serious illness in 1991, Fredrick Z. Bierman, MD, was appointed chief of the Division of Cardiology.

In concert with his colleagues, Angela Romano, MD, Cheryl Kurer, MD, Yehuda Shapir, MD, and Barry Goldberg, MD, Dr. Bierman coordinated the clinical and academic activities of the division. In collaboration with other subspecialty disciplines at SCH, the Division of Cardiology has made many innovations in diagnosis, nonsurgical treatments, and screening for pediatric cardiovascular diseases. Fetal cardiovascular imaging services introduced by Dr. Bierman and his colleagues established fetal cardiac medicine as a nationally recognized diagnostic and therapeutic subspecialty of pediatric cardiology. In addition to advances in classical management of congenital heart disease, the division has focused attention on the care of complex cardiovascular anomalies in the fetus

CARDIOLOGY FACULTY

Chiefs

1965–1991	Norman Gootman, MD*
1991–present	Fredrick Z. Bierman, MD

Staff

1976–1986	Dov Nudel, MD
1979–1991	Sandra Brunson, MD
1979–1989	Daniel Silbert, MD
1986–1989	Donald Leichner, MD
1987–present	Angela Romano, MD
1990–1998	Cheryl Kurer, MD
1991–present	Yehuda Shapir, MD
1992–1993	Robert Voght-Lowell, MD
1993–1995	Frank Ing, MD
1996–1998	Barry Goldberg, MD
1998–1999	Rohit Talwar, MD
1999–2006	Devyani Chowdhury, MD
1999–2006	Amyn Jiwani, MD
1999–2001	Steven Ritz, MD
1999–present	Dipak Kholwadwala, MD
2000–2005	Robert Boxer, MD*
2000–2005	Steven Fishberger, MD
2000–present	Therese Giglia, MD
2000–2005	Jared LaCorte, MD
2000–2002	Irene Sadr, MD
2000–2004	Russell Schiff, MD
2003–present	Michael LaCorte, MD
2004–present	Howard Seiden, MD
2005–present	Andrew Blaufox, MD
2006–2008	Sanah Merchant, MD
2007–present	Shilpi Epstein, MD
2008–present	Deborah Mensch, MD
2008–present	Preeta Dhanantwari, MD

*deceased

Ambulatory Visits

2000	6,348
2007	7,610

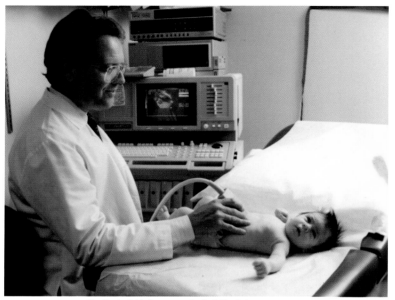

Dr. Fredrick Z. Bierman, chief of Cardiology, 1991–present, examining an infant with cardiac ultrasound.

and neonate. Advances in ultrasound imaging of the fetal heart permits medical therapy of rhythm abnormalities to be initiated before such problems adversely affect the fetus and newborn. In addition, state-of-the-art cardiac ultrasound permits prenatal diagnosis of complex abnormalities of heart structures. Families now have the opportunity to meet with specialists at SCH from maternal-fetal medicine, neonatal-perinatal medicine, and human genetics, who assist the pediatric cardiologists and cardiothoracic surgeons in the care of their child after birth.

In January 1994, with the addition of Frank Ing, MD, to the faculty, the Division of Cardiology transformed the cardiac catheterization laboratory from a diagnostic to a therapeutic laboratory for the management of congenital heart disease. It had been almost sixty years since routine closure of the ductus arteriosus was performed as the first successful cardiovascular procedure. In 1994, the same treatment was accomplished at SCH, not in the operating room but rather in the cardiac catheterization laboratory. Today, hundreds of infants, children, adolescents, adults, and senior citizens have undergone catheter-guided closure

of the ductus arteriosus. A therapy that previously required thoracic surgery, general anesthesia, and inpatient postoperative supervision was transformed by the faculty and staff of the Division of Cardiology into a same-day outpatient procedure. That milestone was quickly followed by percutaneous stent therapies for stenosis of branch pulmonary arteries and aortic coarctation. In 2001, Dipak Kholwadwala, MD, head of the Section of Pediatric Cardiac Catheterization advanced the nonsurgical treatment of congenital heart disease with the closure of interatrial septal defects by catheter.

Andrew Blaufox, MD, head of the Section of Electrophysiology, treats life-threatening pediatric rhythm abnormalities by catheter intervention. Dr. Blaufox's collaboration with the Division of Maternal-Fetal Medicine at LIJ has resulted in state-of-the-art therapies for fetal rhythm anomalies. Care of critically ill pediatric patients with acquired cardiovascular disease and management of patients who have undergone cardiothoracic surgery is provided by Therese Giglia, MD, and Howard Seiden, MD, who share this responsibility with the Division of Critical Care Medicine. The faculty of the noninvasive imaging laboratory, Drs. Romano, Shapir, and Merchant, integrate that resource with the care of patients in the Divisions of Neonatal-Perinatal Medicine, Hematology-Oncology, Medical Genetics, and other disciplines. The efforts of these physicians honor the memory of our colleague, Robert Boxer, MD, whose untimely death cut short a pediatric cardiology career characterized by clinical excellence, perseverance, and humanity.

With the creation of the North Shore-Long Island Jewish Health System in 1997, the Division of Cardiology was established as a regional pediatric cardiac center. Unification of the pediatric cardiology and cardiothoracic surgical faculty, concentration of interventional cardiac care at SCH, and the extension of consultation services to the SCH consultation centers by Michael LaCorte,

MD, have amplified the resources available for cardiac care for children in the region. The thread tying the history of the Division of Cardiology of the Department of Pediatrics of the Long Island Jewish Medical Center to the future of the division is a steadfast commitment to clinical excellence. The dedication of the Division of Cardiology to the highest standard of pediatric medical care, which Dr. Norman Gootman established in 1965 and was sustained by the full-time and voluntary physicians, nurses, and technologists of the division, will go forward into the twenty-first century under the guidance and leadership of Dr. Bierman and the administration of the Schneider Children's Hospital.

CRITICAL CARE MEDICINE

In the late 1960s, Norman Gootman, MD, chief of the Division of Pediatric Cardiology, developed a monitored pediatric intensive care unit (PICU) consisting of a four-bed room on Four South, the pediatric floor at LIJ. There were no trained intensivist attendings working in the unit in those years, and the daily clinical work in the PICU was done by the pediatric chief residents supervised by pediatric attendings with considerable input from the pediatric cardiologists, under Dr. Gootman's direction. This four-bed unit existed until 1983.

In 1983, when the Schneider Children's Hospital (SCH) opened, the pediatric intensive care unit (PICU) consisted of twelve beds. In 1984 Emile Scarpelli, MD, PhD, was appointed chief of both the Division of Pulmonary Medicine and the Division of Critical Care Medicine. Two pediatric pulmonologists worked side by side with Dr. Scarpelli in the combined Division of Critical Care Medicine and Pulmonary Medicine: Bella Clutario, MD, and Mary Catalano, MD.

During the second half of the 1980s, the Division of Critical Care Medicine separated from the Division of Pulmonary Medicine. Janis Schaeffer, MD, a graduate of the pediatric

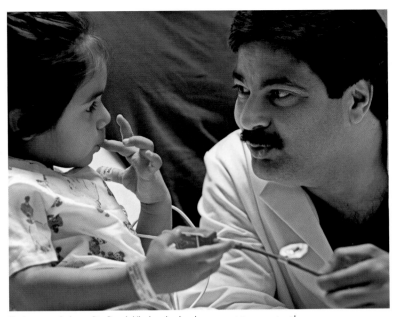

Pediatric cardiologist Dr. Dipak Kholwadwala, shares a quiet moment with three-year-old patient prior to an interventional cardiac procedure.

pulmonary medicine fellowship program at Columbia Presbyterian Hospital in New York, was appointed the chief of the Division of Critical Care Medicine. The PICU became much busier, and attendings from other divisions had to help with its clinical coverage. Among these attendings were Andrew Steele, MD, (currently medical director of SCH), Donald Leichter, MD, (a pediatric cardiologist), Angela Romano, MD, (currently a member of the pediatric cardiology faculty), Howard Trachtman, MD (currently chief of the Division of Nephrology), and Michael Nussbaum, MD, (Division of Adolescent Medicine). Toward the late 1980s, Karen Powers, MD, was appointed to the Division of Critical Care Medicine as the first trained intensivist following the completion of her pediatric critical-care fellowship at Montefiore Medical Center of Albert Einstein College of Medicine in the Bronx.

Early in the 1990s, the Division of Critical Care Medicine and the related Divisions of Cardiothoracic Surgery and Cardiology underwent significant reorganization. Following the resignation of Janis Schaeffer, MD, Mayer

Sagy, MD, was appointed chief of the Division of Critical Care Medicine. Dr. Sagy had completed pediatric critical-care training at the Children's Hospital of Philadelphia, worked at the Chaim Sheba Medical Center in Israel, and subsequently directed the Pediatric Critical Care Division at Morristown Memorial Hospital in Morristown, New Jersey. Joseph Amato, MD, and Fredrick Z. Bierman, MD, were appointed chiefs of the Division of Cardiothoracic Surgery and chief of the division of Cardiology in 1989 and 1991

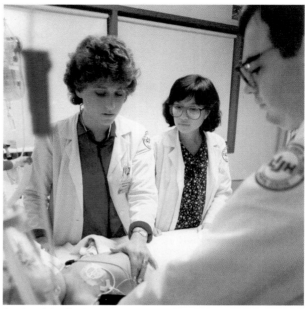

Dr. Janis Schaeffer, founding chief of the Division of Critical Care Medicine, 1985–1991, examining an infant in the PICU.

CRITICAL CARE MEDICINE FACULTY

Chiefs

1984–1985	Emile Scarpelli, MD*
1985–1991	Janis Schaeffer, MD
1991–present	Mayer Sagy, MD

*Initially chief of combined divisions of critical care medicine and pulmonary medicine.

Staff

1984–1989	Emile Scarpelli, MD
1984–1989	Bella Clutario, MD
1984–1988	Mary Cataletto, MD
1990–1992	Karen Powers, MD
1993–1997	Laura Nimkoff, MD
1993–present	Peter Silver, MD
1996–1998	Catherine Caronia, MD
1997–1998	Cynthia Rosenthal, MD
2000–2002	Mary Baldauf, MD
2000–present	Kevin Bock, MD
2000–present	Sharon Dial
2001–2008	Brenda Marcano, MD
2002–2005	Gregory Kraus, MD
2003–present	Maria Esperanza, MD
2004–present	Randi Trope, MD
2006–present	Michael Miller, MD
2008–present	James Schneider, MD

Inpatient Admissions

2007	580

respectively. In 1993 the pediatric critical fellowship program received its accreditation from the American Council for Graduate Medical Education (ACGME) and Dr. Sagy became the program director.

The Division of Critical Care Medicine at SCH has evolved over the past thirty years from a small four-bed unit at LIJ that provided basic measures of life support and electronic surveillance to critically ill pediatric patients to an advanced twenty-bed PICU at SCH as part of a nationally recognized division. It has grown from two attendings in the late 1980s to four attendings in the mid-1990s to the current staff of eight attendings, providing clinical services in the PICU. In September 1997 Dr. Sagy developed an extracorporeal membrane oxygenation (ECMO) center for neonatal and pediatric patients, one of only two ECMO programs in the New York metropolitan area.

The faculty members of the division have assumed specific responsibilities over the years to ensure the highest quality of care as well as excellent training of fellows and residents in pediatric critical-care medicine. Dr. Sagy oversees the

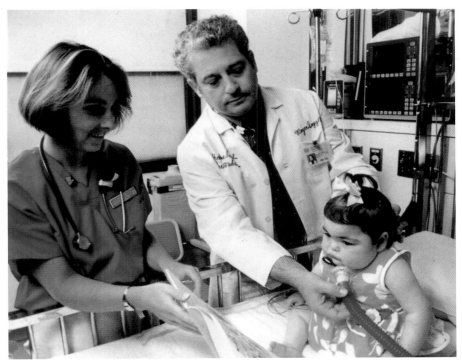

Dr. Mayer Sagy, chief of the Division of Critical Care Medicine, 1991–present, examining patient in PICU.

CYSTIC FIBROSIS CENTER

The first comprehensive description of the disease referred to as cystic fibrosis of the pancreas was reported in 1938 by the late Dorothy H. Anderson, MD, of Babies Hospital in New York City. Her publications on the condition in the pediatric literature alerted pediatricians to be more aware of this disease. In 1953, Paul di Sant'Agnese, MD, recognized that a symptom inherent in patients with cystic fibrosis was an excessive sweat salt loss. This observation was followed by the diagnostic "sweat test" procedure.

fellows' scholarly activities, ensures that they are qualified for the board examination in pediatric critical-care medicine, and is responsible for the hospital's pediatric emergency preparedness.

Dr. Silver was appointed clinical director of the Division of Critical Care Medicine in 2005 and is responsible for the clinical services in the PICU with particular focus on the cardiac intensive care and ECMO services. Kevin Bock, MD, is head of the renal replacement therapy program and the director of the Center for Pediatric Sleep Disorders. Maria Esperanza, MD, is director of the pediatric transport system of SCH. This program has increased its activities to close on 3,000 transports per year. Michael Miller, MD, is head of the Pediatric Medical Simulation Center of SCH. Under his supervision, pediatric residents, fellows, and nurses receive courses in measures of life support and CPR using medical simulators.

The number of patients treated in the PICU has increased considerably, as has the clinical severity over the years.

Drs. Dennis Davidson, and Mayer Sagy, with ECMO circuit, 1998.

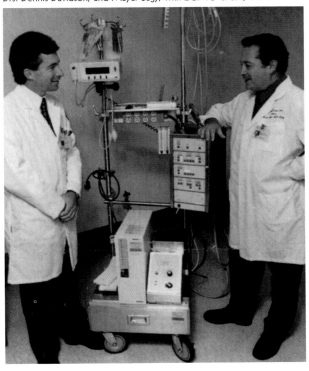

In the mid-1950s, during the early years in private practice of Jack Gorvoy, MD, he referred an eight-week-old infant with recurrent diarrhea and failure to thrive to Dr. Anderson for consultation. The diagnosis of cystic fibrosis of the pancreas was established by symptoms and stool chemistry.

Dr. Gorvoy's efforts on behalf of patients with cystic fibrosis, starting with the eight-week-old infant, led to the establishment of the Cystic Fibrosis Center at Long Island Jewish Medical Center (LIJ). Dr. Gorvoy was appointed director of the Cystic Fibrosis Center shortly after the founding of the Department of Pediatrics at LIJ. The goal of the center was to provide a diagnostic, treatment, and teaching program at LIJ, especially in response to the expanding needs of

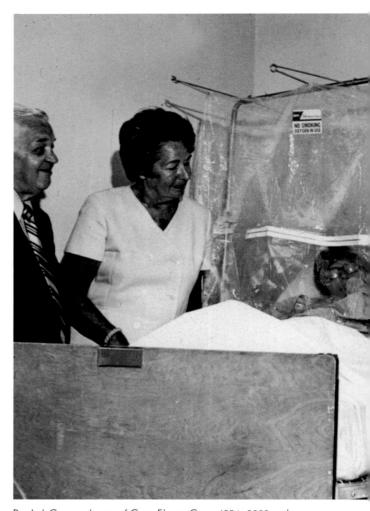

Dr. Jack Gorvoy, director of Cystic Fibrosis Center 1954–2002, with a cystic fibrosis patient circa 1960.

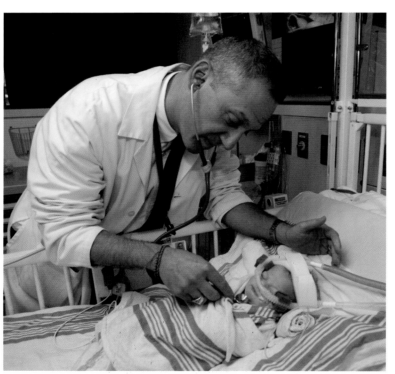

Dr. Peter Silver, on rounds in the pediatric intensive care unit, 2007.

the children of Queens and Nassau Counties.

The National Cystic Fibrosis Foundation, founded in 1955, designated LIJ as a Cystic Fibrosis Care Center. The program grew to be the largest in the New York metropolitan area, a

distinction it maintains to date. As the National Cystic Fibrosis Foundation grew, it began to differentiate between centers using specific criteria. The center at LIJ and subsequently at SCH has always held the highest distinction possible—the designation of care, teaching, resource, and research center.

Dr. Gorvoy acted as director of the Cystic Fibrosis Center from 1954 until 2002 and is currently director emeritus. In 1999 a co-director, Joan Germana, MD, was added to enhance the program. Dr. Germana has been director of the program since Dr. Gorvoy's retirement in 2002.

Essential to the care of the patient with cystic fibrosis is the Cystic Fibrosis Center care team.

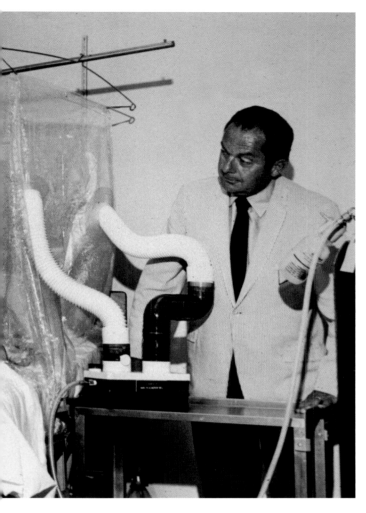

of the pathophysiology of cystic fibrosis, and ongoing clinical research have all contributed to an increase in the life expectancy. In 2005 the median life expectancy in the United States for a person with cystic fibrosis was 36 years of age. We have come a long way in improving both the quality of life and life expectancy of children with cystic fibrosis.

Critical staff members have been added throughout the history of the program to enhance the team, with comprehensive patient care as the goal. A clinical nurse specialist was the first to be added, and a designated social worker, nutritionist, physical therapist, respiratory therapist, research nurse, and psychologist are now essential components of the team.

When the Cystic Fibrosis Center at LIJ was established, the life expectancy for a child with cystic fibrosis was less than a year. Comprehensive specialized care, new pharmaceutical agents, improved antibiotics, development of enteric-coated pancreatic enzyme supplements, lung transplantation, better understanding

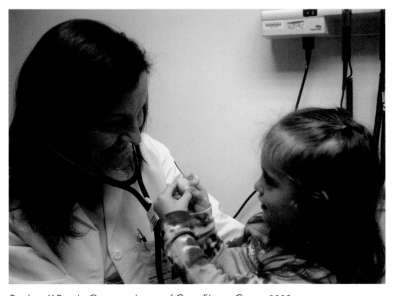

Dr. Joan K Decelie-Germana, director of Cystic Fibrosis Center, 2002–present.

DERMATOLOGY

Samuel Weinberg, MD, was appointed as physician-in-charge of pediatric dermatology in 1961. He conducted a weekly clinic at the hospital and was available for consultations on the inpatient units.

A gifted clinician, Dr. Weinberg taught pediatric dermatology to several generations of residents. In 1965, sponsored by LIJ, he lectured at the first international pediatric congress in Tokyo, Japan. In 1970 Dr. Weinberg, with three other like-minded colleagues, founded the Society for Pediatric Dermatology and served as one of its first presidents. In 2000 Dr. Weinberg was recognized for his teaching contributions by the American Academy of Dermatology with the Clark W. Finnerud Award. He co-authored the extremely popular *Color Atlas of Pediatric Dermatology* and completed the fourth edition of this atlas one week prior to his death on January 26, 2007.

In 1994 Dr. Weinberg resigned his position as chief of pediatric dermatology and Leonard Kristal, MD, was appointed. In 2000 Robert Hayman, MD, joined the pediatric dermatology staff. Both Dr. Kristal and Dr. Hayman conduct the dermatology clinic at SCH and are consultants on the inpatient units.

Dr. Samuel Weinberg, chief of Division of Dermatology, 1961–1994.

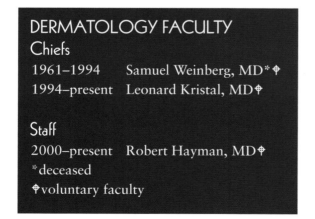

DERMATOLOGY FACULTY
Chiefs
1961–1994   Samuel Weinberg, MD*✢
1994–present Leonard Kristal, MD✢

Staff
2000–present Robert Hayman, MD✢
*deceased
✢voluntary faculty

DEVELOPMENTAL AND BEHAVIORAL PEDIATRICS

The programmatic foundation for this division was first laid in 1970 with the formation of the Learning Diagnostic Program (LDP) under the auspices of the Department of Pediatrics at Long Island Jewish Medical Center (LIJ) under Eugene Schwalb, MD. This was made possible by a 1969 grant of $40,000 from the Rosenstock Foundation.

The LDP was initially housed in the basement of the Hearing and Speech Center at LIJ. Psychologists and educational specialists performed diagnostic assessments of children with learning and emotional difficulties under the administrative directorship of Robert Bushell, PhD. The excellence of services provided by the LDP resulted in slow but substantial programmatic growth. The LDP subsequently relocated to another building on LIJ's campus (410 Lakeville Road) and came under the medical supervision of Marvin Klein, MD, who was appointed in 1971 as the founding physician-in-charge of the Division of Neurology in the Department of Pediatrics. Just a few years after its inception, the LDP came under the directorship of Irene

Dr. Andrew Adesman, chief of the Division of Developmental and Behavioral Pediatrics, 1994–present.

Hassett, PhD. Dr. Hassett joined the LDP in a full-time capacity, having worked previously part-time performing school liaison work in the Department of Psychiatry at LIJ.

Working with a growing staff of psychologists and educators, Dr. Hassett steadily expanded the size of the LDP patient base until she left LIJ in 1993. Throughout the 1970s and 1980s, the LDP performed psycho-educational testing and offered educational remediation, as well as psychotherapy and counseling.

The Division of Child Development, as it was originally named, was established shortly following the opening of Schneider Children's Hospital (SCH). In December 1985 Yeou-Cheng Ma, MD (sister of the renowned cellist, Yo-Yo

Ma), was hired as the Department of Pediatrics' first developmental pediatrician. Six months later, two additional physicians joined Dr. Ma in the division. Andrew Adesman, MD, came to SCH from a fellowship in child development and rehabilitation at Children's Hospital of Philadelphia, and Paul Lipkin, MD, had completed a similar fellowship at the Kennedy Institute, which is affiliated with Johns Hopkins University.

Dr. Adesman served as acting physician-in-charge of the division from 1986 until March 1989 when Esther Wender, MD, came to SCH from Montefiore to assume the position of chief of the division. Shortly following Dr. Wender's arrival, the name of the division was changed to the Division of Developmental and Behavioral

Pediatrics. This change reflected the greater medical focus of the division as well as the inclusion of behavioral problems. Under Dr. Wender's leadership the division attained considerable stature.

With the addition of more developmental pediatricians, the division was in an even better position to offer comprehensive diagnostic and treatment services for children with disorders of learning, attention, or behavior.

Although the LDP fell victim to financial constraints, all of the division's other programs and services have expanded over the years.

In the late 1970s Dr. Hassett established an early intervention program for young children with developmental problems. This program was funded by grants through the New York State Family Court system (for infants and toddlers)

and through the New York State Education Department (for preschool children). With Dr. Hassett's departure in the early 1990s, administrative directorship was taken over by Ellen Palermo, PhD. At its peak, the division's early intervention program had approximately 150 professional and support staff, and provided services to approximately 250 children, either at home or at its offices. Children enrolled in these programs received special education services as well as speech-language therapy, occupational therapy, and physical therapy. In 2005, this program left the administrative umbrella of the North Shore-LIJ Health System and affiliated with the Association for the Help of Retarded Children (AHRC) of Nassau County, an organization dedicated to servicing children and adults with developmental disabilities.

During the 1990s developmental pediatricians within the division provided clinical consultations for a myriad of developmental problems including speech-language delay, mental retardation, autism, motor delay, and attention deficit hyperactivity disorder (ADHD). In addition to performing diagnostic assessments, developmental pediatricians within the division have established a growing treatment program for the medical management of children with ADHD.

In 2000 the Division of Developmental and Behavioral Pediatrics at SCH merged with its divisional counterpart at NSUH. David Meryash, MD, then chief of developmental pediatrics at NSUH, joined the clinical staff of the SCH division, and the combined faculty assumed newly developed clinical space near the hospital at 1983 Marcus Avenue in Lake Success.

The merger of the division was an important step forward for many reasons. To begin with, since all pediatric residents are required to spend one month on a developmental pediatrics rotation, merging of the two developmental divisions facilitated clinical training with the unification

DEVELOPMENTAL AND BEHAVIORAL PEDIATRICS FACULTY

Chiefs

1985–1986	Yeou-Cheng Ma, MD (interim)
1986–1989	Andrew Adesman, MD (acting)
1989–1994	Esther Wender, MD
1994–present	Andrew Adesman, MD

Staff

1985–1986	Yeou-Cheng Ma, MD
1986–1995	Paul Lipkin, MD
1989–1994	Andrew Adesman, MD
1992–2005	Dorie Hankin, MD
1997–1997	Marcie Wexler-Silverman, MD
1997–present	Patricia Bigini-Quinn, MD
2000–present	David Meryash, MD
2000–present	Alyson Gutman, MD
2003–2003	Cecilia Amisola Rivera, MD
2005–present	Ruth Milanaik, DO
2006–present	Julie Jacob, MD

Ambulatory Visits

2000	4,569
2007	7,040

of the NSUH and SCH pediatric residencies. Integration of the two divisions also allowed for greater faculty collaboration, space consolidation, and programmatic integration. Since Dr. Meryash had a unique long-standing clinical relationship with the Association for Children with Down's Syndrome, this clinical alliance allowed SCH residents to visit a special education program dedicated to children with this disorder.

The other large clinical program is the Neonatal Developmental Follow-up Program. All high-risk neonates in SCH's neonatal intensive care unit (NICU) are evaluated prior to discharge. These patients are then followed as outpatients, so that each child's developmental profile and course can be monitored and recommendations can be made regarding the need for early intervention services. With the merger of pediatrics at NSUH and SCH, the Neonatal Developmental Follow-up Program was expanded to include evaluation and management of high-risk newborns discharged from the NICU at NSUH.

Apart from clinical endeavors, the division has played a significant role in medical house staff training as well as continuing medical education. In 1986 the division accepted its first fellow in child development. As of 2007 the division has trained a total of twenty-one fellows in developmental and behavioral pediatrics. In addition, the division has assumed primary responsibility for residency training in the area of normal and abnormal behavior and development, which has been given increased emphasis by the American Board of Pediatrics. In 2006 the division received formal accreditation for its fellowship program in developmental and behavioral pediatrics from the American Board of Medical Specialties.

Over the years the division has sponsored many continuing education programs. These programs, focused on ADHD, autism and related topics, have featured nationally prominent speakers and attracted audiences in excess of 500 registrants. Over the years several thousand professionals and parents have attended educational programs sponsored by the Division.

To the extent that developmental pediatrics interfaces with many other developmental disciplines and needs to work in a multidisciplinary model, the division's physicians have had various affiliations with other not-for-profit organizations that provide therapeutic services to children with developmental delays or disabilities. At different times the faculty provided clinical services to the Suffolk Child Development Center (now known as Developmental Disabilities Institute or DDI) and to Stepping Stones in Queens. The division continues to provide services to Building Blocks Pre-school in Commack, and the Association for Children with Down's Syndrome in Plainview.

In the mid-1990s a growing number of young children were being adopted from orphanages overseas. Because there were also increasing concerns about the health and development of some of these children, families needed guidance to assess their risks. To address this need, Dr. Adesman created the Adoption Evaluation Center. The primary focus of this program was to help prospective parents evaluate the risks associated with adopting a specific child referred by an adoption agency. Once children arrived in this country, they were evaluated by Dr. Adesman and then followed until the family felt comfortable with their development. Dr. Adesman was the first developmental pediatrician in the country to provide this service, which garnered considerable attention for SCH in this area. The first press coverage for this new program was a 1996 story in the *New York Times*. Eight years later Dr. Adesman co-authored a book for adoptive parents entitled *Parenting Your Adopted Child: A Positive Approach to Building a Strong Family*.

In addition to the article in the *New York Times*, the division has gained considerable media attention in recent years. Given frequent public concerns about the increased prevalence of some developmental disorders and the controversy surrounding some alternative therapies, experts from within the Division of Developmental and Behavioral Pediatrics are often sought for comment. Dr. Adesman has been repeatedly quoted in prominent newspapers and national magazines, and has also appeared on various network television programs. In 2000, *Newsweek* published a one-page article he'd written on medical treatment of ADHD. Dr. Adesman has been repeatedly quoted in the *New York Times* and *Newsday*, and has also been cited in the *Chicago Sun-Times*, the *Los Angeles Times*, *U.S. News & World Report*, and other prominent periodicals. Dr. Adesman has represented SCH on the *Today Show*, the *CBS Evening News*, CNN programming, and other national programs.

Apart from clinical training and service, the division has been active in clinical research. Original research relating to ADHD has been presented at various national meetings over the years. Results from two studies have been published in *Pediatrics*, and findings from other studies have appeared in prominent peer-reviewed journals. The division has also participated in several industry-sponsored multicenter clinical trials looking at new pharmacologic therapies for ADHD and autism.

The rapid evolution in the financing of healthcare services and medical education will undoubtedly pose future challenges, but the division will continue to provide excellent clinical service to families and to train its physician staff in developmental and behavioral disorders in children.

EMERGENCY MEDICINE

In the 1970s and early 1980s, pediatric emergency medicine did not exist as a separate entity from emergency medicine for adults. Children were seen by pediatric house officers in rooms scattered throughout the emergency department (ED) at Long Island Jewish Medical Center (LIJ) that were in no way distinct from those in which adults were cared for. The pediatric minor trauma cases were cared for by physician assistants supervised by the attendings who were also supervising the adult cases. Pediatric patients in the emergency department were triaged by nurses with no specific pediatric training.

When Michael Frogel, MD, was appointed in 1984 as chief of the Division of General Pediatrics at the Schneider Children's Hospital (SCH) he was also given responsibility for pediatric emergency medicine. Dr. Frogel established a distinct pediatric area (in the LIJ emergency department) consisting of three rooms staffed by pediatric nurses. He also instituted the supervision of the pediatric house staff by assigning Philip Case, MD, the ambulatory care fellow within the division, to oversee the pediatric area on a part-time basis. During the following academic year the supervised time was increased with the presence of two ambulatory care fellows, each of whom spent half his or her time in the emergency department.

In July 1986 Joy S. Nagelberg, MD, formerly an ambulatory care fellow, was appointed the first chief of the Division of Emergency Medicine at SCH. In July 1989 two additional full-time physicians, Philomena Thomas, MD, and Nancy Rosenblum, MD, were hired to work exclusively in the pediatric emergency department. This expanded the attending supervision of the pediatric house staff to sixteen hours a day. Finally, in July 1990, the pediatric emergency medicine faculty was expanded to a total of five attendings, including Robert Gochman, MD, and Robert Katz, MD. The pediatric emergency area was then covered twenty-four hours a day, seven days a week.

The success of the establishment of a separate area for pediatric patients staffed by pediatric nurses and pediatric emergency medicine physi-

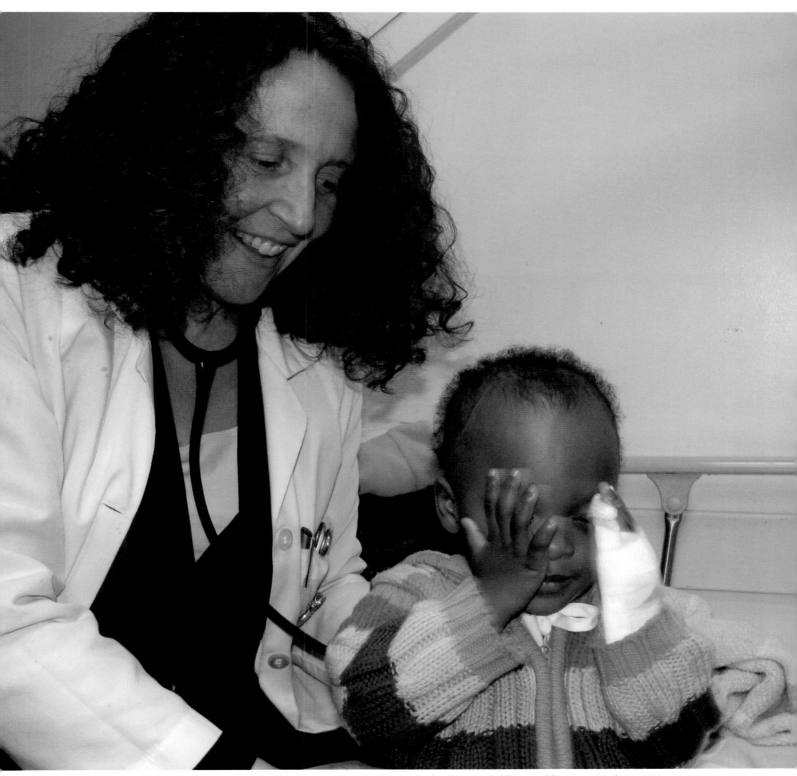

Dr. Joy S. Nagelberg, chief of Division of Emergency Medicine, 1986—present.

cians was evidenced by the dramatic increase in the number of visits. Between 1984 and 1992 the visits increased from 12,500 visits to 19,000 visits with an increasing level of acuity. In spite of the fact that the pediatric area had expanded to five spaces, there was marked overcrowding with prolonged waiting times. A pediatric urgicenter in SCH was established in October 1992.

In July 1993 a fellowship program in pediatric emergency medicine was established with Robert Gochman, MD, appointed as the fellowship director. The three-year fellowship program, which has a total of five fellows at a time, has successfully trained twenty-seven fellows to date. They are practicing throughout the country as board-certified physicians in pediatric emergency medicine.

As part of the goal of continued improvement of emergency care to pediatric patients, the division expanded its services in 1994 to include the care of pediatric patients with minor trauma. In 1996 SCH was the first facility in New York to be designated a dedicated Level I Pediatric Trauma Center. The trauma center is approved by the New York City 911 EMS system and receives critically injured patients from a large catchment area. Nelson G. Rosen, MD, director of the Pediatric Trauma Center, and the trauma coordinator, George Berry, PA, work together with the faculty and nurses in pediatric emergency medicine to provide the highest level of care to these patients. A multidisciplinary team consisting of the pediatric emergency medicine faculty, pediatric surgeons, pediatric critical-care faculty, anesthesiologists, pediatric emergency medicine and critical-care nurses, and respiratory therapists has been created to care for these critically injured children. Support is also provided to the team by pediatric social workers and child life workers. Two pediatric trauma resuscitation rooms are dedicated to the care of these children. More than 300 children who had suffered significant trauma were admitted to SCH in 2006.

The Division of Emergency Medicine is central to the development of emergency preparedness for the hospital. Susan Lee Chan, MD, is co-chair of the Emergency Preparedness Committee, which is responsible for establishing policies and procedures governing the hospital's response to external and internal disasters. This committee deals with initial response, surge capacity, and utilization of personnel and resources in emergency situations.

Nursing care in the Division of Emergency Medicine is provided exclusively by pediatric nurses under the supervision of a pediatric nurse manager. All pediatric emergency medicine nurses are certified in pediatric advanced life support, advanced cardiac life support, trauma nursing core curriculum, and basic life support, with a pediatric nurse educator responsible for ensuring their training. The nurses are responsible for quickly triaging the pediatric patients who arrive in the ED, identifying those who need immediate care. Additionally, they are responsible for all of the bedside care including the monitoring of all patients requiring critical care. They are also an integral part of the trauma team. In addition to providing medical care, as pediatric nurses they provide the emotional support necessary for the children and their families.

EMERGENCY MEDICINE FACULTY

Chiefs
1986–present	Joy S. Nagelberg, MD

Staff
1989–1999	Nancy Rosenblum, MD
1989–present	Philomena Thomas, MD
1990–present	Robert Gochman, MD
1990–1993	Robert Katz, MD
1997–2003	Roy Vega, MD
1998–present	Arlene Silverio, MD
2001–present	Susan Lee Chan, MD
2001–present	Diana Crevi, MD
2002–2006	Jean Klig, MD
2003–present	William Krief, MD
2005–present	Cara Bornstein, MD
2006–present	Nafis Khan, MD
2007–present	Joshua Rocker, MD

As visits and acuity have grown, so has the Division of Emergency Medicine. It presently consists of ten attending physicians providing twenty-four-hour coverage, with a second attending present during the afternoon and evening hours. All of the physicians are subspecialty board certified in pediatric emergency medicine.

As pediatric emergency medicine is a relatively young subspecialty (the first subspecialty boards were given in 1992), the faculty of the division is an integral part of the growing movement toward the recognition of the need for childhood emergencies to be managed by physicians with extensive training in pediatric emergency medicine. As part of this crusade, all of the physicians in the division attend national meetings and conferences on pediatric emergency medicine. Additionally, the faculty participates in the training of physicians and other healthcare professionals at other institutions. This takes the form of grand rounds on topics in pediatric emergency medicine at these institutions, as well as participation in the Pediatric Advances Life Support (PALS) course. The PALS course teaches the recognition and management of the critically ill child, and is under the medical direction of Dr. Nagelberg. It is conducted eight to ten times a year, with a full enrollment of physicians and nurses from throughout the metropolitan area.

House staff education is a high priority within the division. In addition to training fellows, the division is responsible for the education of the SCH pediatric house staff, as well as emergency medicine house staff from LIJ and North Shore University Hospital (NSUH). The education includes bedside supervision of all cases, as well as a formal lecture/case presentation/journal club series coordinated by Diana Crevi, MD, and Joshua Rocker, MD. Additionally, medical students, physician assistants, emergency medical technicians, and paramedics in training rotate through the emergency department.

The division is quite prolific in its research endeavors, under the leadership of its research coordinator, William Krief, MD. The division's research interests are varied and have included studies on bacteremia, clinical assessment of appendicitis, utilization of topical anesthetics, conscious sedation, international medicine, trauma, assessment of cerebrospinal fluid in the ED, parental compliance in filling prescriptions written in the ED, x-ray exposure of trauma patients, and childhood safety.

As one of the goals of the division is to ensure the complete care of patients, an extensive program of social workers and child life specialists has been developed. Two pediatric social workers are dedicated to the pediatric emergency department, providing sixteen hours of coverage per day. The pediatric social workers give emotional support to the children and their families, provide assistance in ensuring that the patients have adequate follow-up care, assist in the identification and management of "at-risk" families, provide crisis intervention, and aid in the care of victims of physical abuse, sexual abuse, and child neglect.

The Child Life Program in the emergency department began in 1995, and in 2006 expanded to two child life specialists. They play a crucial role in the hectic and often anxiety-provoking environment of the emergency department. In the youngest children—infants and toddlers who are often frightened by the entire experience—they provide distractions so that the physician may perform an adequate examination. For the somewhat older children, they prepare them in advance for what might be painful and/or scary experiences, such as x-rays, CT scans, and intravenous placements. In addition, during the painful procedures, they provide age-appropriate diversions and coping techniques. They ensure family-centered care throughout the hospital stay, which helps to alleviate the anxiety of all who are involved.

Over the twenty-four years since the estab-

View of inpatient tower showing new emergency department to be completed in 2011.

lishment of a separate pediatric area in the LIJ emergency department, SCH has grown as well as having developed a reputation for delivering the highest level of care for children in our area. Over this time the number of visits to the pediatric emergency department has doubled, with a dramatic increase in the percentage of patients admitted to the hospital. Presently, 20 percent of children who come to the pediatric emergency area are admitted, which is among the highest admission rates of children's hospitals throughout the country and triple the national average. The pediatric emergency department has expanded from three treatment rooms to ten treatment rooms and two trauma resuscitation rooms with dedicated pediatric triage and waiting areas. In 2008, a state-of-the-art pediatric emergency facility including a separate pediatric waiting room, pediatric triage and registration, and a total of sixteen pediatric treatment rooms, and two pediatric trauma rooms opened. It will be utilized until SCH has its own discrete emergency department at which time this facility will be used for adults. Construction of a thirty-five-bed pediatric emergency department exclusively for SCH, started in August 2008 and is due to be completed in January 2011. This will be a state-of-the-art freestanding pediatric emergency

department adjacent to SCH and will be a unique regional facility for emergency care for children.

The Division of Emergency Medicine is committed to providing the highest quality of care to the children in the emergency department and actively participating in injury prevention programs, while at the same time contributing to the larger goal of ensuring that all children have access to the high level of care provided by pediatric emergency medicine specialists.

ENDOCRINOLOGY

The Division of Endocrinology was first established within the Department of Pediatrics at Long Island Jewish Medical Center (LIJ) in 1970. The founding physician-in-charge was the late Leonard Sussman, MD. Dr. Sussman was also involved with resident education and conducted clinics both at LIJ and at the Queens Hospital Center.

Dr. Cyril Abrams, chief of Division of Endocrinology, 1976–1992.

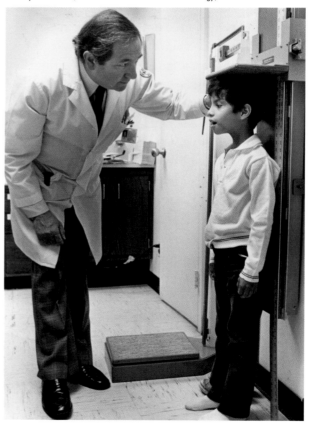

Cyril Abrams, MD, joined the division as chief in 1976 following the untimely death of Dr. Sussman. Formerly in private pediatric practice in South Africa, Dr. Abrams immigrated to the United States and completed a fellowship in pediatric endocrinology at the College of Physicians and Surgeons of Columbia University under the direction of Melvin Grumbach, MD. Before he came to LIJ, Dr. Abrams was chief of pediatric endocrinology and head of the Cytogenetics Research Laboratory at Roosevelt Hospital in New York City and was also assistant professor of clinical pediatrics at the College of Physicians and Surgeons of Columbia University.

Dr. Abrams developed a program for children with juvenile diabetes that was certified as an approved program by the New York City Department of Health, Bureau for Handicapped Children. In 1980 New York State approved LIJ as a neonatal hypothyroid treatment center for the County of Queens with Dr. Abrams as director. All newborn infants in Queens County with abnormal thyroid screening tests were referred to the center for evaluation and treatment. As a forerunner to the training program in pediatric endocrinology, Dr. Abrams provided a six-month elective in pediatric endocrinology for several pediatric residents including Robert Rappaport, MD, who went on to become chief of endocrinology at Mount Sinai Hospital in New York City.

With the opening of the Schneider Children's Hospital (SCH), the full-time professional staff was increased with the appointment of Sandra Blethen, MD, PhD, and Fred Chasalow, PhD, both of whom came from Washington University in St. Louis. Both had extensive research training and experience. Dr. Blethen assumed the role of clinical coordinator for the division while Dr. Chasalow developed and directed the pediatric endocrinology laboratory performing clinical assays as well as doing basic research focused on the investigation of growth hormone molecule variants and steroid biochemistry. Together

with Dr. Abrams as program director, Drs. Blethen and Chasalow developed the pediatric endocrinology fellowship program and were instrumental in fostering research as well as clinical skills in their trainees. Under the guidance of Drs. Blethen and Chasalow, the fellows' research led to presentations at international meetings and publications in peer review journals.

In 1988 Paula Kreitzer, MD, who had completed her fellowship in the division, joined the faculty as a full-time attending. During the next few years, Dr. Kreitzer was instrumental in the expansion of the division in other areas. The Bernard Worob Center for Gender Identity was created as a collaborative endeavor of the Divisions of Endocrinology, Child Psychiatry, and Human Genetics. In addition, Dr. Kreitzer opened a satellite center at Good Samaritan Hospital in West Islip, providing care for patients on the South Shore of Long Island. Dr. Kreitzer has continued her clinical research on the endocrinological aspects of anorexia nervosa.

In 1992 Dennis Carey, MD, succeeded Dr. Abrams as division chief. Dr. Carey completed his residency at LIJ where his elective with Dr.

ENDOCRINOLOGY FACULTY

Chiefs

1971–1976	Leonard Sussman, MD*
1976–1992	Cyril Abrams, MD
1992–1999	Dennis E. Carey, MD
1999–present	Phyllis W. Speiser, MD

Staff

1993–1995	Cyril Abrams, MD
1984–1990	Sandra Blethen, MD, PhD
1988–present	Paula Kreitzer, MD
1999–present	Dennis E. Carey, MD
1994–present	Graeme Frank, MD
1984–1991	Fred Chasalow, PhD
1993–1995	Maureen Lynch, PhD
1992–2003	Doug Yoon, PhD
1999–present	Pavel Fort, MD
*Deceased	

Ambulatory Visits

2000	6,508
2007	8,826

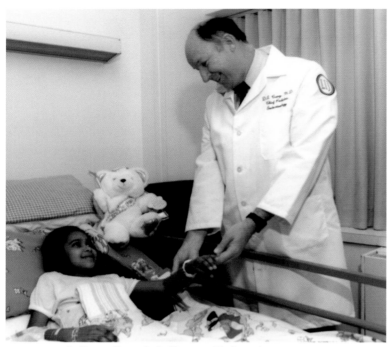
Dr. Dennis Carey, chief of Division of Endocrinology, 1992–1999.

Abrams led him to pursue a fellowship in pediatric endocrinology at the University of California in San Diego. Following his training he was appointed to the University of Connecticut Health Center, where he was associate professor as well as director of the Growth Disorders Clinic at Newington Children's Hospital. Dr. Carey has been involved in both clinical and basic research in the areas of bone growth and mineral metabolism. His work in calcium and phosphorus metabolism has led to the reformulating of infant formula for premature infants and the prevention of "rickets of prematurity." Under Dr. Carey's leadership, the Program for Childhood Diabetes was established as a full-service multidisciplinary-team center stressing education, nutrition, and behavioral medicine.

Dr. Carey expanded the division's basic research activities in the investigation of testicular development as well as growth plate maturation as Doug Yoon, PhD, and Maureen Lynch, PhD, joined the faculty. Dr. Yoon additionally took over as director of the clinical

laboratory. The training of young pediatric endocrinologists remained a high priority.

In 1994 Graeme Frank, MD, a former chief resident, returned to SCH from a fellowship at Cincinnati Children's Hospital. Dr. Frank's description of the first male patient with a genetic defect in the estrogen receptor led to the elucidation of the role of estrogen in men. Dr. Frank continues his research interest in the physiology of estrogen in growth and bone maturation.

Following the 1999 merger of LIJ with North Shore University Hospital (NSUH), Phyllis Speiser, MD, professor of pediatrics at New York University School of Medicine, assumed the role of chief of pediatric endocrinology and director of the fellowship training program for the newly merged Division of Endocrinology based at SCH. Dr. Speiser had previously served as chief of pediatric endocrinology at NSUH from 1993 to 1999 and associate program director of the Children's Clinical Research Center at Cornell Medical College from 1988 to 1993. An internationally recognized expert in adrenal disease, Dr. Speiser has helped plan international medical meetings, including the International Consensus Conference on congenital adrenal hyperplasia held under the sponsorships of North American and European pediatric endocrine societies to establish treatment guidelines for this condition. Her research interests have mainly centered on genetic and clinical correlations among patients with adrenal disorders with publications in the *New England Journal of Medicine,* the *Journal of Clinical Investigation,* and the *Journal of Clinical Endocrinology and Metabolism*, where she has served two terms on the editorial board. Dr. Speiser is a member of the Pediatric Endocrinology Sub-Board of the American Board of Pediatrics. She also serves as an advisory board member of several patient support groups, is a member of several prestigious national medical societies, and is a fellow of the American College of Endocrinology.

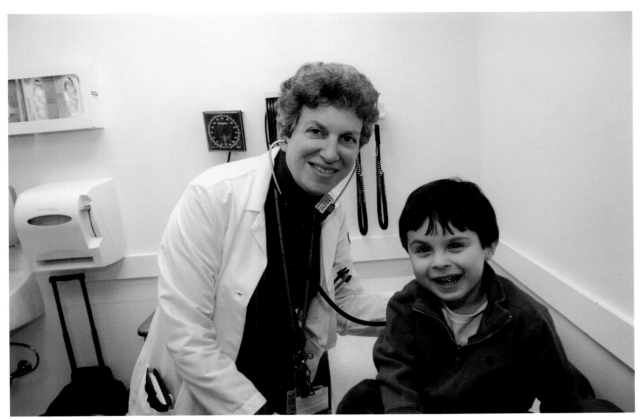

Dr. Phyllis Speiser, chief of Division of Endocrinology, 1999–present.

Joining Drs. Speiser, Carey, Frank, and Kreitzer in 1999 was Pavel Fort, MD, a native of the Czech Republic and graduate of Charles University School of Medicine in Prague. Dr. Fort did his residency and fellowship training at NSUH with Fima Lifshitz, MD, former chief of endocrinology at NSUH. He remained on the NSUH medical attending staff until joining the SCH staff. He is a well-respected clinician who has written several book chapters on the management of childhood diabetes and thyroid disease.

The division's support staff includes several nurses and nutritionists who are certified diabetes educators. Margaret Pellizzarri, RN, CDE, serves as head nurse for the division. She has organized patient education programs and support groups for families of children with diabetes and coordinated several clinical trials. She is assisted by Linda Bokor, pediatric nurse practitioner, Barbara Ryan, and Ellen Kagan.

The SCH diabetes program has been recognized as a Pediatric Diabetes Education Center by the American Diabetes Association. Nurse Katherine Brunner performs endocrine stimulation tests and coordinates clinical trials involving growth hormone studies.

GASTROENTEROLOGY AND NUTRITION
(Formerly Gastroenterology)

In the early 1960s and 1970s, pediatric gastroenterology coverage and consultation were provided by Arnold Schussheim, MD, a man who also maintained a large general pediatric practice, as well as Irwin Katzka, MD, the chief of adult gastroenterology at Long Island Jewish Medical Center (LIJ).

In 1979, the Division of Gastroenterology was established within the Department of

Pediatrics at LIJ with the arrival of Murray Davidson, MD. Dr. Davidson graduated from City College of New York and earned his medical degree from New York University. He did a research fellowship in gastroenterology in the Department of Medicine at Cornell University Medical College. Dr. Davidson was internationally recognized as a pioneer in the field of

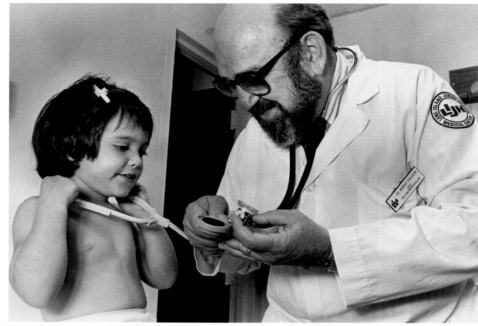

Dr. Murray Davidson, founding physician-in-charge of Gastroenterology and Nutrition, 1979–1989.

pediatric gastroenterology. Prior to his arrival at LIJ, he was the director of pediatrics at Bronx-Lebanon Hospital, and professor of pediatrics and assistant dean at the Albert Einstein College of Medicine.

Dr. Davidson's arrival coincided with the phase of intense planning for the children's hospital, and he established both the pediatric endoscopy suite and an active clinical gastroenterology laboratory. Babu Bangaru, MD, served with Dr. Davidson from 1979 to 1981, followed by Anastasios Angelides, MD, from 1981 to 1984. Michael Pettei, MD, PhD, joined the division in 1984 from Columbia Presbyterian Medical Center. Jeremiah Levine, MD, from Harvard, and Allan Olson, MD, from Oklahoma were recruited in 1985. In 1988 Dr. Olson resigned his position and relocated to Michigan and Bradley Kessler, MD, who trained at Baylor, was appointed to the full-time faculty. Toba Weinstein, MD, and David Gold, MD, both of whom received their fellowship training in the division, were recruited to join the faculty in 1991 and 1993 respectively.

Dr. Pettei was appointed director of the

nutrition support service in 1988 and with the incorporation of all nutritional responsibilities at the Schneider Children's Hospital (SCH), the division was officially renamed the Division of Gastroenterology and Nutrition. Dr. Davidson retired in 1989 and Drs. Levine and Pettei were appointed co-chiefs of the division. In 1991 both Drs. Levine and Pettei became associate professors of pediatrics at the Albert Einstein College of Medicine and in 1998 Dr. Levine became professor of pediatrics at Albert Einstein College of Medicine.

The members of the Division of Gastroenterology and Nutrition and the nutrition support service were instrumental in establishing home care at SCH. Working with Kathy Marshall, RN, the divisional nurse, the hospital established Schneider Children's Hospital at Home, an independent, full-service home-care company specifically for children. Drs. Pettei and Levine were named medical directors of this company until 1996 when it merged with LIJ to form LIJ at Home.

The division has had a long-standing interest in the impact of environmental factors on gastrointestinal disease. This interest led to the establishment of the Center for Pediatric Environmental Studies in 1996 with Dr. Levine named director.

Over the last ten years the divisional staff has grown significantly, culminating in the merger of the SCH and NSUH divisions into a unified Division of Gastroenterology and Nutrition in November 2002. Lisa Iofel, MD, a graduate of the NSUH fellowship training program, joined the faculty in November 2000 and initially spent half her time running the pediatric gastroenterology program at Jacobi Hospital in the Bronx in a cooperative arrangement with the SCH Division of Gastroenterology and Nutrition. Dr. Kessler resigned his position in September 2001 to assume the position of chief of pediatric gastroenterology at Good Samaritan Hospital in West Islip. He was joined at the same hospital by Dr. Gold in August 2003. Cindy Haller, MD, who had been an attending at SUNY Stony Brook, joined the faculty in November 2001 and Carlotta Hample, MD, formerly of Winthrop University Hospital, assumed a faculty position in January 2003.

With the North Shore-LIJ merger in November 2002, Fredric Daum, MD, and James Markowitz, MD, joined the SCH faculty along with pediatric nurse practitioner Joanne Rosa, RN. Harvey Aiges, MD, continued with his duties at NSUH while continuing to see patients in the combined division. In September 2003, Libia Moy, MD, along with physician's assistant Kerry Romeo, both formerly of Winthrop University Hospital, joined the SCH faculty. Melanie Greifer, MD, formerly on staff at New York Hospital-Cornell Medical Center, joined the staff in September 2005. In January 2006 Dr. Aiges resigned his faculty position to assume the chairmanship of the Department of Pediatrics at Nassau University Medical Center in East Meadow, New York.

GASTROENTEROLOGY AND NUTRITION FACULTY

Chiefs

1979–1989	Murray Davidson, MD*
1989–2002	Jeremiah Levine, MD, Co-Chief, Gastroenterology and Nutrition
	Michael Pettei, MD, PhD. Co-Chief, Gastroenterology and Nutrition
2002–2003	Fredric Daum, MD, Co-Chief, Gastroenterology and Nutrition
	Jeremiah Levine, MD, Co-Chief, Gastroenterology and Nutrition
2004–present	Jeremiah Levine, MD, Chief, Gastroenterology
2004–present	Michael Pettei, MD, PhD, Chief, Nutrition

Staff

1979–1981	Babu Bangaru, MD
1981–1984	Anastasios Angelides, MD
1984–present	Michael Pettei, MD, PhD
1985–present	Jeremiah Levine, MD
1985–1988	Allan Olson, MD
1988–2001	Bradley Kessler, MD
1991–present	Toba Weinstein, MD
1993–2003	David Gold, MD
2002–2005	Harvey Aiges, MD*
2000–2007	Lisa Iofel, MD
2001–present	Cindy Haller, MD
2002–2004	Fredric Daum, MD
2002–present	James Markowitz, MD
2003–present	Carlotta Hample, MD
2003–present	Libia Moy, MD
2005–present	Melanie Greifer, MD

*deceased

Ambulatory Visits

2000	8,877
2007	12,326

With the North Shore-LIJ merger, Drs. Levine and Daum were named co-chiefs of the combined Division of Gastroenterology and Nutrition. Dr. Pettei was appointed section head of pediatric nutrition for the North Shore-LIJ Health System. In August 2003 Dr. Daum resigned his faculty position and assumed a position at an affiliated hospital within the Yale System in Connecticut at which time Dr. Levine was named chief of the Division of Gastroenterology and Nutrition. In 2004 Dr. Pettei was appointed chief of the Division of Nutrition with Dr. Levine chief of the Division of Gastroenterology, both within a single administrative unit called the Division of Gastroenterology and Nutrition.

The division has grown significantly and remains technologically at the forefront of pediatric gastroenterology and nutrition. In the summer of 2002 a state-of-the-art pediatric endoscopy suite was opened at SCH adjacent to new divisional offices. This expansion created a new procedure room equipped for anesthesiology services, a separate post-procedure recovery area with three bays utilized also for infusion therapy, and additional rooms for separate indirect calorimetry measurement and breath testing for carbohydrate malabsorption. With its own pediatric nursing staff, patients in the endoscopy suite receive preparation, undergo procedures, and recover—all in the caring and friendly environment that is appropriate for children. The division employs the new technology encompassed in wireless capsule endoscopy. In this method a capsule with a video camera is swallowed. The images are sent to a telemetry-recording device that is carried by the patient. In this way, a video of the entire small bowel, an area not readily accessible to endoscopy, is obtained. This has revolutionized the ability to diagnose small bowel lesions found in such diverse problems as gastrointestinal bleeding, isolated polyps, and early Crohn's disease. Similarly, the division employs the newer capsule

Dr. Jeremiah Levine, co-chief, Division of Gastroenterology and Nutrition, 1989–present.

version of esophageal pH recording. A capsule is attached endoscopically to the interior of the lower esophagus and pH data is transmitted to a recording device carried by the patient for computer download after twenty-four to forty-eight hours. With the development of this procedure, the child must no longer endure a catheter inserted nasally for that length of time.

The nutritional responsibilities of the division have grown to include all children on intravenous or specialized feedings, as well as outpatients with specific nutritional difficulties. Several nurses have served as inpatient nurse clinicians on the nutrition support team; currently Elizabeth Weglarz, RN, CNS, oversees this aspect of the division. The divisional outpatient nutritionist staff reporting to Dr. Pettei has expanded from one to three, encompassing new responsibilities in pediatric metabolism and in-patient services at SCH and NSUH as well as the Cystic Fibrosis Center. In June 2001 the division welcomed its first nutritionist, Laurie Ann McMahon, MS, RD, to serve on the inpatient service nutritional support team, thus expanding the capabilities of the team, particularly with regard to the bone marrow transplantation, hematology-oncology, and pediatric intensive care units. The nutritional evaluation of children is enhanced by several new noninvasive procedures within the division that can precisely determine nutritional requirements.

Research activities within the division are extensive, with many papers being published and abstracts presented at national meetings. A particular research focus has been multiple aspects of pediatric inflammatory bowel diseases—ulcerative colitis and Crohn's disease—ranging from epidemiology to diagnosis to therapy. Other specific areas of interest include capsule endoscopy, pH monitoring, celiac disease, motility abnormalities, the influence of nitric oxide on motility and intestinal inflammation, fatty acid and prostaglandin metabolism, and neonatal liver disease.

Members of the division are also active on a national level. Dr. Levine has been the chairman of the Long Island Chapter Medical Advisory Committee of the Crohn's and Colitis Foundation as well as on the scientific advisory board of the American Liver Foundation. Dr. Pettei is long-standing chairman of the Nutrition Committee of the American Academy of Pediatrics (New York Chapter) and has been on the Long Island Chapter Medical Advisory Committee of the Crohn's and Colitis Foundation of America. Dr. Markowitz has held various positions on the national level within the North American Society for Pediatric Gastroenterology, Hepatology and Nutrition (NASPGHAN) and the American College of Gastroenterology (ACG), most recently serving on the NASPGHAN Executive Board. Drs. Weinstein, Moy, and Greifer also currently serve on

national committees of NASPGHAN. The faculty has served as reviewers for numerous publications including *Gastroenterology*, the *Journal of Pediatric Gastroenterology and Nutrition*, and the *American Journal of Gastroenterology*.

There is a strong emphasis on teaching within the division. The division has trained many fellows, all of whom are active in clinical and/or academic gastroenterology. At all times one to two pediatric residents rotate on a monthly basis within the division. In addition, second- and third-year residents interested in the field of pediatric gastroenterology are assigned to an individual attending in the outpatient area for one to two years. In 1996 Dr. Levine was named a visiting professor in the Department of Pediatrics, Hadassah Medical Center in Jerusalem, Israel. Dr. Levine was also visiting professor in the Department of Pediatrics, Shaare Zedek Medical Center in 2005 and 2006.

The division conducts multiple weekly teaching conferences and through the efforts of Dr. Weinstein as course director, an SCH pediatric gastroenterology grand rounds program with continuing medical education (CME), was sponsored by the North Shore-Long Island Jewish (NS-LIJ) Health System. In October 2003 Dr. Weinstein was named program director for the division's fellowship program.

Dr. Michael Pettei, co-chief, Division of Gastroenterology and Nutrition 1989–present.

Over the last twenty-nine years the Division of Gastroenterology and Nutrition has grown rapidly and acquired a national and international reputation for expert patient care and academic excellence.

GENERAL PEDIATRICS

In the beginning, circa 1970–1983 BCH (before the children's hospital), the Division of General Pediatrics at Long Island Jewish Medical Center (LIJ) was staffed by one physician, Bruce Bogard, MD, one secretary, Emily Solomon, and one nurse, Karen Halom. Dr. Bogard trained at the Children's Hospital of Philadelphia before joining the LIJ pediatric program as chief resident and he remained on as physician-in-charge of general pediatrics.

Dr. Bogard was an outstanding teacher, clinician, and advocate for children. Under his direction the pediatric clinic developed into an established faculty practice. Before it became national policy, he implemented weekly resident primary care sessions and he established and headed one of the first hospital child protection teams in the country. He worked closely with

Dr. Bruce Bogard, founding physician-in-charge of General Pediatrics, 1971–1989.

local schools and parents to help children with special needs and was a recognized expert on attention deficit disorders and developmental issues. During the Christmas holiday season, he would don his Santa outfit and bring joy to the pediatric patients waiting to be seen.

After a chronic illness, Dr. Bogard passed away in 2001. As the founder of general pediatrics he left a grand legacy. To this day, patients, parents, doctors, and nurses remember his dedication and benevolent demeanor. He truly mastered the art of pediatrics.

In those days there was a rudimentary pediatric clinic with occasional attendance by pediatric residents.

By 2008 the Division of General Pediatrics had developed into the largest division at the Schneider Children's Hospital (SCH) with over 50,000 outpatient visits, thousands of newborn and inpatient admissions, and a staff of eleven full-time physicians, five nurses, an office manager, and six secretaries. The division provides comprehensive primary care, anticipatory guidance, and preventive services to patients from birth to adolescence with the full gamut of pediatric illnesses. There is a strong emphasis on proper nutrition, exercise, reading, and education so that children reach their full potential.

Significant programs include a busy pediatric faculty practice (training eighty-nine pediatric residents per week), an urgicenter, a Section on Child Advocacy and Protection attending to the needs of abused children, the Queens Child Advocacy Center (QCAC), the Special Supplemental Nutrition Program for Women, Infants and Children (known as the WIC program), sports medicine and weight management, Reach Out and Read (sponsored by a national nonprofit group), the New York State Department of Health's Vaccines for Children program providing free immunizations, and a lead poisoning treatment center.

GENERAL PEDIATRICS FACULTY

Chiefs

1971–1989	Bruce Bogard, MD*
1989–present	Michael Frogel, MD

Staff

1984–1989	Michael Frogel, MD
1989–2001	Bruce Bogard, MD*
1986–1988	Irene Landau, MD
1989–1994	Patricia Elvir, MD
1989–1994	Harry Kipperman, MD
1989–1994	Jill Leavens-Maurer, MD
1990–present	Lynda Gerberg, MD
1990–present	Robert Katz, MD
1991–1998	Erica Waterman, MD
1991–1994	Scott Svitek, MD
1995–present	Clifford Nerwen, MD
1998–2001	Kathleen T. O'Connor, MD
1998–2001	Victor Turow, MD
1998–present	Deborah Esernio-Jenssen, MD
1998–present	Shoshanna Wind, MD
1999–present	Minu George, MD
2001–2003	Ethan Weiner, MD
2001–2003	Jason Kronberg, MD
2001–2003	Jeremy Adler, MD
2001–2003	Andrew Hart, MD
2001–2204	Inna Novak, MD
2001–2005	Jocelyn Kohn, MD
2001–present	Stephen Barone, MD
2002–2003	Lisa Thebner, MD
2002–2003	Gila Schiowitz, MD
2002–2004	Karen Raksis, MD
2002–2005	Lynn Cetin, MD
2002–2005	Leslie Aiuto, MD
2003–present	Mark Wells, MD
2004–present	Jamie Hoffman-Rosenfeld, MD
2005–present	Maryanne Wolert, MD
2006–present	Toni Clare, MD
2008–present	Nancy Palumbo, MD

*deceased

Ambulatory Visits

2000	47,884
2007	49,148

Dr. Michael Frogel, chief of Division of General Pediatrics, 1989–present.

Dr. Frogel joined the Division of General Pediatrics in 1984 while also serving as director of the house staff training program and physician-in-charge of the pediatric emergency room. Two nurses from the inpatient units, Christine Reilly and Yvonne Bailey, joined the division the same year and have continued in the division for over two decades.

Through the years, a number of pediatric attendings who appear on the faculty list have come and gone to other positions for various reasons. In 1989 Dr. Frogel was appointed chief of the Division of General Pediatrics at SCH.

In October 1992, the pediatric urgicenter was opened in order to decompress the high volume of patients in the pediatric emergency unit of LIJ's emergency department (See Chapter 14.)

In 2003 the Queens Child Advocacy Center (QCAC) was opened on Queens Boulevard in Forest Hills in the former Queens Medical Society Building. In 2005, Jamie Hoffman-Rosenfeld, MD, joined the division as director of the QCAC. It is a child-friendly, fully coordinated, multidisciplinary program dedicated to the evaluation, treatment, and follow-up of the victims of child abuse, neglect, and maltreatment. It is also a colocated center for the collection of forensic evidence. The New York City Police Department's Child Abuse Squad, the New York City Administration for Children's Services, the Queens County District Attorney's Office, Corporation Counsel, the Schneider Children's Hospital, and Safe Horizon are all at one site. Coordination of care and efficient expert collection of evidence are performed in a child-friendly manner. The cases are immediately discussed and reviewed on an ongoing basis to ensure appropriate outcomes. Dr. Hoffman-Rosenfeld, a recognized pediatric expert in child abuse, provides full medical services. An examination room with state-of-the-art equipment facilitates the comprehensive medical and forensic evaluation.

The Section on Child Advocacy and Protection is very involved in state- and city-wide initiatives to promote prevention as well as enhance services and provide ongoing education to health professionals. Dr. Hoffman-Rosenfeld frequently testifies at state and city legislative meetings on these issues.

In May 2004 the division launched the WIC (Women, Infants and Children) program, sponsored by an agency of the U.S. Department of Agriculture. Coordinated by Dawn Kempa, RN, SCH's WIC program provides supplemental food for pregnant women and high-risk children from birth to age five. The program emphasizes nutritional education, physical activity, breast-feeding, and the prevention of childhood obesity. The program includes a farmers' market, which has been sponsored through a Healthy Lifestyle Initiative State Grant since 2006. The WIC program treats some of the most complex patients in the state and has a breastfeeding initiation rate of 85 percent (the state average is 60 percent). The WIC program is presently at 2,000 encounters per month and experiencing explosive growth.

Prior to the merger that created the North Shore-Long Island Health System, North Shore University Hospital had a Division of General Pediatric located at 865 Northern Boulevard in Great Neck, directed by James Fagin, MD. In 2005 the two separate Divisions of General Pediatrics were combined in one location at 410 Lakeville Road under the direction of Michael Frogel, MD, in keeping with the merging of all divisions of pediatrics under unified leadership in a single location on the North Shore-LIJ campus.

HEMATOLOGY-ONCOLOGY AND STEM CELL TRANSPLANTATION
(Formerly Hematology-Oncology)

Prior to 1970, pediatric hematology-oncology at Long Island Jewish Medical Center (LIJ) was practiced predominantly by adult hematologists, led by Arthur Sawitsky, MD, chief of the Division of Hematology-Oncology, assisted by Bruce Bocklan, MD, and Robert Levy, MD. Frank Desposito, MD, a fully trained pediatric hematologist-oncologist, joined the pediatric department of the Queens Hospital Center and provided pediatric hematology-oncology services to LIJ from 1964 until 1970.

When Philip Lanzkowsky, MD, assumed the directorship of pediatrics at LIJ in 1970, he was also appointed the founding physician-in-charge of the Division of Pediatric Hematology-Oncology, and he started the training program in this discipline. The first two trainees, Tribhavans

Vats, MD, and Theresa Silberman-Procupez, MD, came with Dr. Lanzkowsky from New York Hospital-Cornell University Medical Center. Ashok Shende, MD, who had trained in pediatric hematology-oncology at the Queens Hospital Center, joined the division as a fellow and then as a member of the faculty.

Dr. Philip Lanzkowsky, founding divisional chief of Hematology-Oncology from 1970–1999.

In the early days, the secretary for the pediatrics department acted as the secretary for the Division of Pediatric Hematology-Oncology, as well as the technologist doing required blood tests for the division. In 1970, a laboratory for pediatric hematology-oncology was established for clinical applications as well as research. The laboratory studied DNA, RNA, and protein synthesis in iron-depleted and iron-replete rats, a topic of considerable interest to pediatric hematologists of that era. Subsequently, work was done on the gastrointestinal effects of iron deficiency, both in rats and in children, which demonstrated a decrease in disaccharidases in both iron-deficient animals and iron-deficient infants.

In 1972, Gungor Karayalcin,MD, joined the staff as a full-time attending within the Division of Pediatric Hematology-Oncology. The division grew rapidly from the late 1970s to the 1990s. Robert Festa, MD, who trained at Children's Hospital of Philadelphia, joined the division as a full-time attending in 1978, followed by Perry Nissen, MD, Joseph McNamara, MD, Mark

Cheah, MD, Carole Paley, MD, John Donahue, MD, and Arlene Redner, MD.

In the early 1970s, the division was located in a small space adjacent to the chairman's office, which served as the office for the attendings and the fellows, the microscope room, as well as a place for taking histories of patients and administering chemotherapy. The patients utilized the chairman's waiting room shared with Edward Meilman, MD, chairman of medicine. During this time, Jane Moore, CPNP, joined the division as a nurse practitioner to assist with the administration of chemotherapy to a growing number of ambulatory patients and she has remained on in the division until the present.

Ms. Moore, remembers, "Back then, our quarters were so tiny, we had to share a room with geriatric patients with lung disorders. We sat in swivel chairs at a counter and mixed each child's chemotherapy ourselves and then we would literally turn the chairs around and administer the chemotherapy. It was distressing for the adults to watch, of course, because back then, the nausea from the treatment was harder to control. And the kids had no other place to go during the stressful treatment. That's how strapped we were for space and resources."

Things improved with the opening of the Schneider Children's Hospital (SCH) in 1983. The division acquired a considerable amount of space in which to perform its functions—a separate chemotherapy room consisting of seven stations, faculty

Dr. Gungor Karayalcin on rounds with pediatric residents, 2008.

offices, outpatient facilities, a secretarial area, and a large clinical laboratory. SCH became known for its Division of Hematology-Oncology and patients came from far and wide.

In 1988, Raj Pahwa, MD, established the bone marrow transplantation program using a converted single-patient room fitted with a HEPA filter on the fourth floor of the children's hospital. In October 1991, the four-bed Gambino Medical and Science Foundation transplantation unit was opened at the Schneider Children's Hospital. The unit had a laminar airflow system, and was the only bone marrow transplantation unit approved by New York State specifically for children.

Throughout the years, the division trained a large number

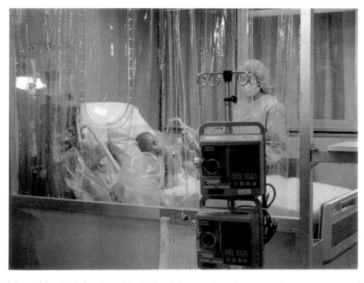

View of four-bed Gambino Medical and Science Foundation transplantation unit opened in 1991.

of pediatric hematologist-oncologists, most of whom became board certified. Many joined pediatric faculties throughout the country.

Significant research in hematology, particularly iron deficiency anemia, emanated from the division. Hundreds of scientific papers were published in national and international peer-reviewed journals, and Dr. Lanzkowsky and his staff (predominantly Dr. Shende and Dr. Karayalcin) presented their research at national and international meetings.

Dr. Lanzkowsky published six textbooks during his tenure in the Division of Hematology-Oncology. The first, *Pediatric Hematology-Oncology*, (1980) and the second, *Pediatric Oncology*, (1983) were published by McGraw-Hill, followed by the first and second editions of the *Manual of Pediatric Hematology-Oncology*, (1989 and 1995), which were published by Churchill Livingstone. The third edition was published by Academic Press (1999), and the fourth by Elsevier Academic Press (2005). These books have been translated into a number of languages and are used as standard texts by pediatric hematologists and oncologists worldwide.

HEMATOLOGY-ONCOLOGY AND STEM-CELL TRANSPLANTATION FACULTY

Chiefs

1970–1999	Philip Lanzkowsky, MD
1999–present	Jeffrey Lipton, MD, PhD

Staff

1970–2007	Ashok Shende, MD
1972–present	Gungor Karayalcin, MD
1978–1992	Robert Festa, MD
1986–1990	Perry Nissen, MD, PhD
1987–1989	Joseph McNamara, MD
1988–1995	Raj Pahwa, MD
1989–1992	Mark Cheah, MD*
1990–2004	Carole Paley, MD
1992–1993	John Donahue, MD
1992–present	Arlene Redner, MD
1999–present	Philip Lanzkowsky, MD
2000–present	Adrianna Vlachos, MD
2000–2005	Steven Arkin, MD
2001–present	Mark Atlas, MD
2001–2007	Banu Aygun, MD
2001–present	Indira Sahdev, MD
2004–present	Johnson Liu, MD
2006–2008	Deepa Manwani, MD
2006–2007	Muhammad Hasan, MD
2008–present	Carolyn Fein-Levy, MD
2008–present	Sharon Singh, MD
2008–present	Jonathan Fish, MD
*deceased	

Ambulatory Visits

2000	11,500
2007	12,080

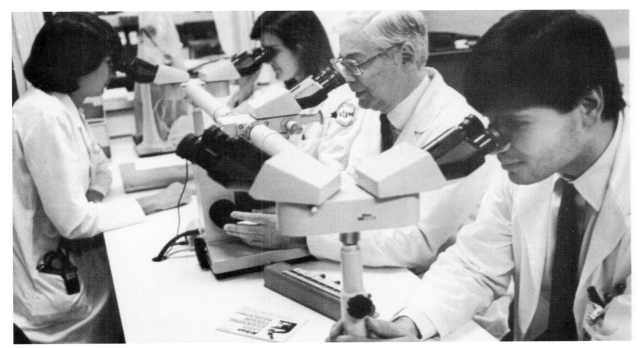

Dr. Philip Lanzkowsky with trainees at a teaching microscope, 1989.

In 1995 the division joined a national childhood cancer cooperative, the Pediatric Oncology Group (POG).

By 1999 the growth of the Division of Hematology-Oncology and the rest of the Department of Pediatrics was so great that Dr. Lanzkowsky could no longer fulfill the demands of serving as both chairman of the Department of Pediatrics and chief of the Division of Hematology-Oncology. In September 1999, Dr. Lanzkowsky, following a national search, appointed Jeffrey M. Lipton, MD, PhD, as chief of hematology-oncology and the name was changed to the Division of Hematology-Oncology and Stem Cell Transplantation.

Dr. Lipton had been trained at Children's Hospital Boston and the Dana-Farber Cancer Institute. After almost ten years in Boston, Dr. Lipton had been recruited to Babies Hospital (Columbia Presbyterian Medical Center) in New York City and then had spent twelve years as the chief of pediatric hematology-oncology at the Mount Sinai Medical Center. Dr. Lanzkowsky and Dr. Lipton set in motion a comprehensive

merger plan for the division of hematology-oncology at SCH and NSUH that resulted in the division as it stands today, a highly respected clinical, research, and teaching program.

When Dr. Lipton arrived, the faculty of the academic program at SCH consisted of Drs. Karayalcin, Shende, Redner, and Paley, and the clinical program at NSUH, led by Joseph Kochen, MD, PhD, was staffed by three clinical hematologist-oncologists and Indira Sahdev, MD, who headed up the pediatric bone marrow transplantation program within the combined adult/pediatric program there. Over the next two years the hematopoietic stem cell transplantation program moved to SCH under the leadership of Dr. Sahdev, who was trained at Memorial Sloan-Kettering Cancer Center.

In 2000, Adrianna Vlachos, MD, a former fellow of Dr. Lipton at Mount Sinai, was recruited to join the faculty as a stem cell transplanter and to join Dr. Lipton in establishing the Bone Marrow Failure Program and the Diamond Blackfan Anemia (DBA) Care Center. Today Dr. Vlachos heads the program, which is funded by grants from the National Heart, Lung, and Blood Institute (NHLBI) of the National Institutes of Health (NIH) and the U.S. Centers for Disease Control (CDC). With the retirement of Dr. Kochen in 2001, the attending hematologists at NSUH were replaced in 2001 by Mark Atlas, MD (trained at Children's Memorial Hospital, Chicago), Steven Arkin, MD (trained at Babies Hospital, New York), and Banu Aygun, MD, a graduate of Dr. Lanzkowsky's program at SCH. In 2004, with the closing of the program at NSUH, these physicians joined the faculty of SCH. The first phase of the merger was complete. In 2005 and 2006, respectively, Drs. Paley and Arkin left academic medicine to pursue opportunities in the pharmaceutical industry arena. Deepa Manwani, MD, a former fellow with Dr. Lipton at Mount Sinai, was recruited from Mount Sinai to replace Dr. Arkin as the pediatric head of the hemophilia treatment program. Under the leadership of Dr. Aygun, Dr. Manwani also joined the hemoglobinopathy program. At this time, Dr. Atlas established the brain and spinal tumor program within the division. The Division of Orthopaedic Surgery at SCH appointed an orthopaedic oncologist, Samuel Kanen, MD, permitting the creation of

Dr. Jeffrey Lipton, chief of Division of Hematology-Oncology from 1999–present.

the bone tumor program under the leadership of Dr. Aygun. Thus with the expanded faculty, these programs joined the clinical oncology program headed by Dr. Redner, the principal investigator at SCH for the National Cancer Institute-funded cooperative, the Children's Oncology Group (previously called the Pediatric Oncology Group, or POG.). Thus new faculty had been recruited to complement the existing faculty. The resulting array of programs established the paradigm for clinical care and research, providing broad expertise upon which to build and continue growth.

The next step was the establishment of a laboratory research program based at The Feinstein Institute for Medical Research, within the North Shore-Long Island Jewish Health System. Dr. Lipton's laboratory was established upon his arrival to study the cellular and molecular biology of erythroid failure. With a $5 million donation from the Nelkin family, Dr. Lipton was able to recruit Johnson Liu, MD, as the Les Nelkin Professor of Pediatric Oncology to head the laboratory and become head of experimental hematology in the division. Dr. Liu, formerly of the hematology branch of the NHLBI and more recently from Mount Sinai School of Medicine, joined Dr. Lipton and within two years established a robust research enterprise working in the area of hematopoietic failure. The laboratory at The Feinstein Institute is training a former fellow, Gulay Sezgin, MD, to receive a doctorate in molecular medicine from its graduate school. The Feinstein Institute also has numerous hematology-oncology and post-doctoral fellows. In addition, fellows from the program have joined with researchers at The Feinstein Institute to create a collaboration with the division in the area of neurooncology. An integrated approach from basic to translational to clinical research that serves as the paradigm for the division has been established to further our efforts to cure brain and spinal cord tumors.

Dr. Indira Sahdev, head of stem cell transplantation program (right), and Dr. Adrianna Vlachos with transplant patient (standing) who received a stem cell transplant from one of her young twin brothers, 2005.

Thus an excellent clinical program with a history of a small laboratory research program has expanded dramatically. Nurse practitioners and a physician's assistant, five social workers, and Margaret Tippy, PsyD, a dedicated doctoral-level psychologist, support the current clinical program. The division has over $3 million in federal funds (NIH, NCI, and CDC) as well as New York State and foundation grant support. At the time of this writing, the Division of Hematology-Oncology and Stem Cell Transplantation has established itself at SCH as a preeminent academic, clinical, teaching, and research program.

Dr. Lipton's interest in bone marrow failure patients, especially those with Diamond Black-fan anemia (DBA), has made SCH a nationally recognized center for these diseases and the location for a national DBA registry. On October 15, 2007, Schneider Children's Hospital received honorable mention on the floor of the United States House of Representatives for providing the first comprehensive clinical care center for patients across the United States and developing a national DBA patient registry during a motion to support House Resolution 524 by New York State Representative Carolyn McCarthy.

The division continues to expand its scientific and training efforts as it offers the best clinical care based upon the science and art of medicine, dedicated to moving advances from the laboratory to the patients in order to cure and prevent the cancers and blood disorders of childhood.

INFECTIOUS DISEASES

Even though in the early years the majority of children's hospital admissions were due to infections, infectious diseases was not an acknowledged subspecialty of pediatrics.

Samuel Karelitz, MD, who in 1955 became the founding chairman of the Department of Pediatrics at Long Island Jewish Medical Center (LIJ), had a particular interest in infectious diseases and should be considered the first infectious diseases specialist in the department. Dr. Karelitz was affiliated with the Willard Parker Hospital, an infectious diseases hospital in Manhattan, established in 1935, and served on the Committee of Immunizations and Therapeutic Procedures of the American Academy of Pediatrics. He worked with Bela Schick, MD, on diphtheria at Mount Sinai Hospital, and published articles on many topics in infectious diseases including diphtheria, hepatitis, scarlet fever, intravenous rehydration for treatment of gastroenteritis, and antibiotic therapy of infections. However, he is most well known for his work on measles immunity and prevention and was the author of the chapter on measles in several editions of Holt's *Diseases of Infancy and Children*.

In the 1960s and early 1970s, Max Stillerman, MD, a long-standing member of the department's voluntary staff who practiced in Great Neck, had an avid interest in infectious diseases. He performed many clinical studies and was the author of thirty-seven articles, particularly in the area of antibiotic therapy of streptococcal pharyngitis. He was a member of the Infectious Diseases Society of America and the American Pediatric Society. In his professional life he served as a role model for a pediatrician in private practice who also performed clinical research.

Several months prior to the November 1983 opening of the Schneider Children's Hospital

INFECTIOUS DISEASES FACULTY	
Chief	
1983–present	Lorry G. Rubin, MD
Staff	
1984–1990	Leonard Krilov, MD
1990–present	Sunil K. Sood, MD
2000–present	Sujatha Rajan, MD
Ambulatory Visits	
2000	1,110
2007	829

(SCH), Lorry G. Rubin, MD, joined the full-time faculty of the LIJ Department of Pediatrics as first physician-in-charge of the division of pediatric infectious diseases. Following his pediatrics training at Children's Hospital of Los Angeles, Dr. Rubin was an NIH fellow in infectious diseases at Johns Hopkins University School of Medicine under the direction of Walter Hughes and E. Richard Moxon. He then served on the faculty of Johns Hopkins University. After his arrival at LIJ, he developed an active consultation service and a teaching program in infectious diseases for pediatric residents and medical students, and he established a pediatric infectious diseases fellowship program. He shaped policy concerning the use of antimicrobials and vaccines in the department. In 1989, he was appointed chief of the division, and in 1995, he was promoted to professor of pediatrics at Albert Einstein College of Medicine. He serves as chair of the Schneider Children's Hospital Pharmacy and Therapeutics Committee and is a member of the Pharmacy and Therapeutics Committee at LIJ. He is also associate director of the Infection Control Committee, and a past member of the Human Subjects Review Committee. He developed and has maintained a research laboratory where his work focuses on the pathogenesis, diagnosis, and prevention of bacterial infections, particularly those due to *Haemophilus influenzae* and *Streptococcus pneumoniae*. In 2004 he was awarded a research grant RO1 from the National Institutes of Health to develop assays for study of pneumococcal infections. Since 2003 he has been an investigator at The Feinstein Institute for Medical Research of the North Shore-Long Island Jewish Health System, and since 2004, a member of the General Clinical Research Center Advisory Committee at The Feinstein Institute.

Dr. Rubin was elected to membership in the Society for Pediatric Research and to fellowship in the Infectious Diseases Society of America, and is a member and past president of the Long

Dr. Lorry Rubin, founding physician-in-charge, Division of Infectious Diseases 1983–present.

Island Infectious Diseases Society. He serves on the editorial board or as a reviewer for several journals. He has authored more than 150 scientific publications and is a member of the Committee on Infectious Diseases ("Redbook Committee") of the American Academy of Pediatrics.

Leonard Krilov, MD, joined the division in 1984 after completing a pediatric residency at Johns Hopkins Hospital and a fellowship in infectious diseases at Children's Hospital Boston under the direction of Kenneth McIntosh, MD. Dr. Krilov earned a reputation for excellence in both clinical medicine and teaching. He received the attending-of-the-year award from the SCH house staff in 1987. His research activities involved study of respiratory syncytial virus (RSV), specifically, antibody-mediated enhancement of infection. In 1990, he resigned to take a position as chief of pediatric infectious diseases at NSUH.

Sunil K. Sood, MD, joined the division in 1990 after serving as assistant professor of pediatrics at Tulane School of Medicine. Dr. Sood completed a pediatric residency at Georgetown University Medical Center and a fellowship in infectious diseases at Tulane School of Medicine under the direction of Robert Daurn, MD. Dr. Sood is highly respected as an astute clinician and excellent teacher and received the attending-of-the-year award from the pediatric house staff in 2001 and 2005. With the merger and the resulting creation of the North Shore-Long Island Jewish Health System in 1997, Dr. Sood was appointed head of pediatric infectious diseases at SCH at North Shore and director of education in the division. His laboratory research in the areas of *Haemophilus influenzae* type b immunization and laboratory testing and pathogenesis of Lyme disease has resulted in important publications.

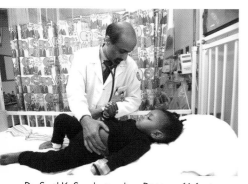

Dr. Sunil K. Sood, attending, Division of Infectious Diseases, 2008.

In addition, he has received several competitive research grants for his research on Lyme disease. He has given several invited lectures on pediatric Lyme disease nationally and internationally, was appointed as a member of the Society for Pediatric Research and as a fellow of the Infectious Diseases Society of America, and is a member and past president of the Long Island Infectious Diseases Society. He has been promoted to professor of clinical pediatrics at Albert Einstein College of Medicine. Dr. Sood has been a reviewer for several pediatric and infectious diseases journals, for selection of abstracts submitted for the Society for Pediatric Research annual meeting and for Center for Disease Control (CDC) grant applications. Dr. Sood has served on LIJ's Investigational Review Board and the Biomedical Research Alliance of New York.

Sujatha Rajan, MD, joined the division in 2001. She completed a fellowship in pediatric infectious diseases at Columbia University in 2000 and was on the faculty of Columbia University until 2001. She is an assistant professor of pediatrics at Albert Einstein College of Medicine, and is noted for her outstanding clinical acumen and dedication. She has a research interest in antimicrobial therapy of fungal and opportunistic infections in oncology patients. She is the site principal investigator for several clinical studies.

A fellowship training program was established in 1985, and fourteen fellows have completed training. The most accomplished former fellows are Vicki Peters (fellow, 1987–1990), who served as a full-time faculty member in the Department of Pediatrics at Mount Sinai School of Medicine; Marc Salzman (fellow, 1990–1992), who is a full-time pediatrician and pediatric infectious diseases consultant at Kaiser Permanente of Southern California, and has published several important studies on varicella; and Itzhak Levy (fellow, 1995–1997), who is a full-time faculty member in infectious diseases at the Schneider Children's Medical Center in Israel.

In 1993, in conjunction with Norman Ilowite, who was chief of the Division of Rheumatology, the Pediatric Lyme Disease Center was established for the care of children with tick bites or proven or suspected Lyme disease. The center provides both comprehensive clinical care and specific laboratory evaluation. In addition, Dr. Sood leads the clinical and basic research in Lyme disease conducted at the center.

The Pediatric Travel and Immunization Center was established in 2000 under the direction of Dr. Sood. The center provides travel advice and appropriate immunizations and preventive medications for children traveling outside the United States. It is a yellow fever vaccination center authorized by the State of New York.

MEDICAL GENETICS
(Formerly Human Genetics)

The Division of Human Genetics was established within the Department of Pediatrics at Long Island Jewish Medical Center (LIJ) in 1972 with the appointment of Eugene Pergament MD, PhD, from Chicago, as the first physician-in-charge of human genetics and the opening of the Cytogenetics Laboratory at LIJ with a grant of $200,000 from the Children's Medical Fund (CMF).

Audrey Heimler, MS, was appointed the first genetics counselor. In 1972 the Division of Human Genetics was designated a regional diagnostic center by the Birth Defects Institute of the New York State Department of Health. Dr. Pergament returned to Chicago in 1974, and Ernest Lieber, MD, joined the division in 1974 as physician-in-charge and remained in the division until 1985. He further developed the Cytogenetics Laboratory by increasing its staff by two technicians. Another genetics counselor, Jane Engelberg, MS, was hired in 1975 and remained with the division until 1988.

The Cytogenetics Laboratory was expanding, and Judith Stamberg, PhD, was appointed full-time director in 1984. Lewis Waber, MD, PhD, was recruited as division chief in 1985. He expanded the division by hiring Donna Blumenthal, MS, and Connie Cucinotta, MS, as genetics counselors in 1985. Joyce Fox MD, was then appointed as a second medical geneticist in 1986. In 1988, two more genetics counselors, Roberta Ebert, MS, and Suzanna Allan, MS, were added. Ms. Cucinotta relocated and was followed by Jane Schuette, MS, who subsequently moved to Michigan in 1992. Audrey Heimler retired as senior genetics counselor in 1990 after serving in this position for eighteen years, and Meredith Masiello, MS, joined the division in 1992. Roberta Ebert retired in 2000 and was replaced by Jenna Antonelli who left in 2006. Meredith Masiello left the division in 2005 and was

replaced by Peter Thom.

The Cytogenetics Laboratory flourished during Dr. Stamberg's four-year tenure as director. In 1988 Alan Shanske, MD, became interim director, and in 1991 Ann-Leslie Zaslav, PhD, was recruited as the new director. Under her guidance, the laboratory was expanded, and new procedures and techniques were instituted with funds from the Fan Fox Foundation. The laboratory was moved to the Department of Pathology at LIJ in 1998, and Dr. Zaslav remained director until 2006.

Dr. Waber left the division in 1989, and Dr. Fox became the chief. Shari Fallet, DO, joined the division in 1993 and relocated in 1998. With the merger that created the North Shore-LIJ Health System, Drs. Bialer and Mehta joined the SCH division. The name of the division was changed from the Division of Human Genetics to the Division of Medical Genetics. Dr. Mehta had worked as a clinical geneticist at NSUH since 1994, and she organized and ran the Lysosomal

---

MEDICAL GENETICS FACULTY

Chiefs

1972–1974	Eugene Pergament, MD
1974–1985	Ernest Lieber, MD
1985–1989	Lewis Waber, MD, PhD
1989–present	Joyce Fox, MD

Staff

1984–1988	Judith Stamberg, PhD
1986–1989	Joyce Fox, MD
1988–1991	Alan Shanske, MD
1991–2006	Ann-Leslie Zaslav, PhD
1993–1998	Shari Fallet, DO
2004–present	Martin Bialer, MD
2004–2007	Lakshmi Mehta, MD

Ambulatory Visits

2000	2,675
2007	2,800

Storage Disease Program at SCH. Dr. Bialer had been a resident at NSUH but left for a brief period to complete his fellowship in clinical, biochemical, and molecular genetics. He returned to NSUH in 1989. After the two divisions merged, he became section head of metabolism in 2005. Dr. Mehta resigned in 2007.

The Comprehensive Genetics Disease Program has been an integral part of the Division of Medical Genetics. The staff of this program has initiated and put forth considerable effort to ensure the availability of needed comprehensive genetics services in areas of Queens and Nassau Counties. The program was initially instituted in conjunction with the Queens Hospital Center, with which LIJ had an affiliation, and has been funded by the Department of Health of New York State. The Sickle Cell Outreach Program, also funded by New York State, has been providing community-based genetics education service since the fall of 1974. Educational presentations to the lay population include reasons to seek service, and expectations of the benefits of genetics counseling services. Genetics counseling services are available regardless of the ability to pay. Wanda Jones-Robinson, MPH, was coordinator of these programs from 1983 until 1996, and William Molette assumed these responsibilities in 1996. Barbara Davidoff-Feldman, MS, and Janice Rinsky, MS, provided genetics counseling services to this program along with Nina Sitron, MS, who has been with the division since 1983. Peter Thom, MS, works in this program.

The Division of Medical Genetics was involved with the Craniofacial-Cleft Clinic at LIJ.

Dr. Joyce Fox, chief of Division of Medical Genetics, 1989–present.

Alan Shanske, MD, the physician-in-charge of the Division of Human Genetics at the Queens Hospital Center, was the director of the Craniofacial-Cleft Clinic from 1980 to 1993. From 1993 to 2003 Dr. Fox was co-director, along with Lyle Leipziger, MD, chief of the Division of Plastic Surgery at LIJ. Dr. Fox became actively involved with the Hagedorn Cleft Palate and Craniofacial Center in 2006.

The staff of the Division of Medical Genetics provides genetics counseling, consultation, and evaluation to patients in the Departments of Pediatrics at SCH and Obstetrics and Gynecology at LIJ and NSUH. Residents from these departments and dental medicine are trained by the genetics staff. The members of the team are also actively involved in the Marfan clinic, the neurofibromatosis clinic, and the hemophilia clinic. Clinical and research interests include dysmorphology, metabolic disease, and the application of new cytogenetic techniques to diagnosis. Mrs. Heimler and Dr. Fox described a new syndrome characterized by sensorineural hearing loss, enamel hypoplasia, and nail abnormalities.

METABOLISM

Prior to the merger of Long Island Jewish Medical Center (LIJ) with the North Shore Health System (NSHS) to create the North Shore-Long Island Jewish Health System, treatment of metabolic disorders fell into the purview of the Division of Endocrinology and was the responsibility of the endocrinology faculty.

Following the merger, metabolic diseases were treated by Alfred Slonim, MD, who was the chief of metabolism at NSUH. Metabolism became a pediatric division separate from endocrinology for a few years until Dr. Slonim resigned his position in 2005. Dr. Slonim had an international

METABOLISM FACULTY
Chiefs
1997–2005   Alfred Slonim, MD
2005–present   Martin Bialer, MD

Dedication of premature nursery center, May 27, 1956. Left to right: Dr. Bela Schick, Dr. Ethel C. Dunham, Mr. and Mrs. David A. Travis, Sr., and Dr. Samuel Karelitz.

reputation, and patients were referred to him from many countries abroad. When Dr. Slonim resigned, Martin Bialer, MD, who was board certified in metabolic genetics, became section head of metabolism, and this section was placed in the Division of Medical Genetics.

NEONATAL-PERINATAL MEDICINE
(Formerly Premature Center and later Neonatology)

In 1956, Long Island Jewish Medical Center (LIJ) started admitting premature babies to a special dedicated nursery. This nursery, which was designated a "premature center" by the Bureau of Maternity and Family Planning of New York City, was built as an afterthought. It looked almost like a very large and long trailer, an appendage to the hospital in close proximity to the emergency department. Bela Schick, MD, who discovered the skin test for susceptibility to diphtheria, was the honored guest at the premature nursery center dedication on May 27, 1956.

Beatrice Holland, RN, was the first nursing supervisor of the unit. Premature babies from New York City and the metropolitan area were referred to the center and transported in ambulances originating from Bellevue Hospital. This was the beginning of a neonatal transport system. Infants were transported in metal boxes with oxygen piped in, without any temperature control. They often arrived at their destination hypoxic and hypothermic. Herbert Goldman, MD, a voluntary attending pediatrician on the staff of LIJ,

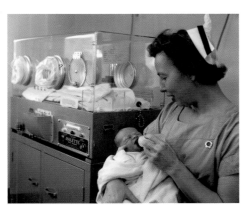

Beatrice Holland, RN, feeding a premature baby, early 1960s.

NEONATAL-PERINATAL MEDICINE FACULTY
Chiefs

1956–1972	Herbert Goldman, MD
1972–1974	Bruce Ackerman, MD
1974–1998	Philip Lipsitz, MD
1998–present	Dennis Davidson, MD

Staff

1965–present	Hedda Acs, MD
1977–1978	David Brown, MD
1978–1980	Marie Casalino, MD
1980–present	Andrew Steele, MD
1982–1989	Ellen Eisenberg, MD
1985–2000	Katherine King, MD
1986–1989	Josiah Wedgewood, MD
1987–present	Dennis Davidson, MD
1988–1989	Eitan Kilchevsky, MD
1993–2007	Alice Garner, MD
1993–present	Robert Koppel, MD
1998–present	Philip Lipsitz, MD
1998–present	Philip Lipsitz, MD
2000–2002	Rita Harper, MD
2000–2002	Concepcion Sia, MD
2000–2002	Sharon Buckwald, MD
2000–present	Susanna Castro-Alcarez, MD
2001–present	Jerrold Schlessel, MD
2002–2007	Sherry Courtney. MD
2002–present	Regina Spinazzola, MD
2002–present	Richard Schanler, MD
2003–present	Howard Heiman, MD
2008–present	Mohammad Ahmed, MD

was assigned by Samuel Karelitz, MD, director of pediatrics, to be the part-time physician-in-charge of the premature center, which was dedicated to the care of premature newborns, both "inborn" and "outborn." Dr. Goldman's salary in 1970 for this arduous task was $7,000 per year.

In 1970, a neonatology fellowship program was introduced and a committed pediatrician was now present in the premature nursery at all times.

Because of an increasing need for neonatal transport from community hospitals in Queens, Nassau, and Suffolk Counties, the pediatric department decided to start its own neonatal transport system. Before commercial vehicles specially designed and equipped for neonatal transport became available, a "mobile intensive care unit" was designed and built by LIJ. The cabin space was now adequate for the transport of more than one newborn at a time.

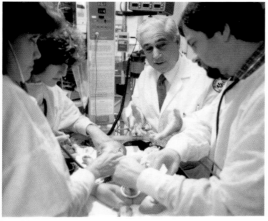

Dr. Philip Lipsitz, chief of Division of Neonatal-Perinatal Medicine 1974–1998, on rounds with pediatric house staff.

In 1972, Bruce Ackerman, MD, from the University of Southern California, was appointed as the first full-time physician-in-charge of neonatology and advanced respiratory care and monitoring of sick newborns. Dr. Ackerman resigned in 1974.

The neonatal special unit now had a thirty-bed capacity including a four-bed room dedicated to the care of very sick newborns. This was the forerunner of the newborn intensive care unit (NICU) within the special care unit. The NICU concept was now emerging and standards of care were being developed.

Philip J. Lipsitz, MD, who was previously on the staff at the Medical College of Georgia, chief of neonatology at Beth Israel in New York

City and director of pediatrics at LIJ-South Shore Division in the Rockaways, became physician-in-charge of the Division of Neonatology in 1974 and Dr. Goldman became the coordinator for community neonatology. Dr. Lipsitz trained in Cape Town, South Africa, and Sheffield, England, and did his neonatal fellowship at Cleveland and Boston in the United States. At this time, there was an increasing demand for neonatal beds in the New York metropolitan area and hospitals were requested by the New York Health Department to increase their number. Renovations took place and the bed capacity was increased to thirty-four beds—six ICU, six intermediate, and twenty-two convalescent beds. The National Institute for Child Health and Development (NICHD) collaborative phototherapy study started in 1974, and LIJ became one of the six U.S. centers awarded contracts. A six-year follow-up of participating neonates was completed, and all the study data contributed to the collaborative reports published in 1985 and 1990.

In 1977, the commissioner of health of the City of New York designated LIJ a neonatal intensive care center, and the New York State Department of Health approved this special-care unit as a tertiary-level care center. A neonatal follow-up clinic was implemented. More and more high-risk newborns and prematures were now being referred to LIJ because of the growth in programs and medical expertise available in the Department of Pediatrics. The management and care of the high-risk mother were continually improving, and more mothers with high-risk pregnancies were referred to LIJ for delivery and stabilization of their newborn. The fellowship program was well established and attracted numerous applicants. In 1978 the intensive care capacity in the nursery was expanded to ten beds.

The increasing complexity and severity of illness and the management of a larger number of sick newborns necessitated the appointment of additional board-certified neonatologists to the full-time staff in 1977 and 1978. David Brown, MD, a graduate of the LIJ pediatric and neonatal fellowship programs, and Marie Casalino, who trained at Beth Israel hospital in New York were appointed. Over the next couple of years, new opportunities and positions for neonatologists were rapidly developing nationally in 1980, Andrew M. Steele, MD, was appointed staff neonatologist.

With the opening of the Schneider Children's Hospital (SCH) in 1983, the neonatal unit, which had been adjacent to the emergency department at LIJ, was relocated to the new hospital's third floor adjacent to LIJ's labor and delivery suite. SCH had state approval for expanding the bed capacity to a forty-bed unit with eighteen intensive-care beds, eighteen intermediate, and four "growers." This new specially designed, state-of-the-art NICU became a showplace for SCH. In 1985, Katherine C. King, MD, joined the faculty, followed by Dennis Davidson, MD, in 1987. In 1989 a fifth neonatologist was added to the division; Robert Koppel, MD, has held that position since 1993. The number of fellows in training also increased gradually to six.

In 1987 SCH was designated a Regional Perinatal Center (RPC) by New York State. That year the NICU at SCH became the first hospital on Long Island to use a mammalian preparation

of surfactant for the *prevention* of respiratory distress syndrome in premature newborns.

In October 1987 the first set of quintuplets was delivered by cesarean section at LIJ. The neonatal team was well rehearsed for this event and easily managed the administration of endotracheal surfactant to each infant in the delivery room. The neonatal care of these infants had its ups and downs, but all five were discharged home. Soon other newborns were recruited for the Phase 3 trial of surfactant and its administration for the *treatment* of respiratory distress in premature newborns. In 1993 and in 1996, the second and third sets of quintuplets were delivered at LIJ and cared for in the NICU. All these newborns were discharged home to their parents.

The follow-up program for high-risk newborns was expanded in 1987 to incorporate developmental pediatrics in evaluation of the newborn at the time of discharge and at regular follow-up.

The census continued to be above maximum capacity, and the New York State Department of Health in 1991 approached SCH to expand the neonatal unit by four additional intermediate-care beds.

Upon the arrival of Dr. Davidson, work began in the laboratory regarding nitric oxide in the perinatal pulmonary circulation. The first two papers in the field came from this laboratory. In 1990, Dr. Davidson wrote an editorial in the *American Review of Respiratory Diseases* describing the urgent need and design for clinical trials to test the safety and efficacy of inhaled nitric oxide (I-NO) for persistent pulmonary hypertension (PPHN). Subsequently, Dr. Davidson was recruited to become the principal investigator for a national multicenter clinical trial. With the assistance of Dr. Steele, SCH became a lung rescue center for PPHN. Dr.

Cangiolosi quintuplets being discharged from neonatal unit, 1987.

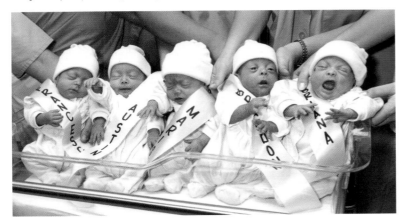

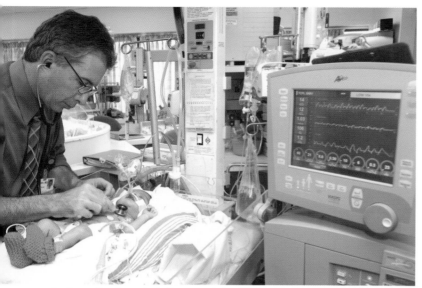

Dr. Dennis Davidson, chief of Division of Neonatal-Perinatal Medicine 1999–present, examining sick neonate.

Davidson's trial, as well as other major clinical trials, ultimately led to the approval of I-NO for PPHN by the U.S. Food and Drug Administration (FDA). However, it became apparent to members of the division that in order to become a lung rescue center we also needed to be able to transport babies on I-NO and have the backup of extracorporeal membrane oxygenation (ECMO) if necessary. SCH became the first center and remains one of the only centers with transport isolettes equipped with nitric oxide. In addition, in collaboration with Mayer Sagy, MD, and Peter Silver, MD, of the Division of Critical Care Medicine and the Department of Nursing, ECMO was established. As a result of the work on I-NO and ECMO the NICU became regionally recognized with multiple reports in print media and on television.

An important component of the NICU was the establishment in 1990 of a neonatal database and computerized high-quality discharge summaries by Dr. Davidson and Christine Grippi, RN, the regional perinatal coordinator. The database allows the faculty to benchmark outcomes and compare them to those of other centers. It has

become extremely helpful from the standpoint of internal administration and communication to referring or follow-up physicians.

In 1998 Dr. Davidson became chief of the Division of Neonatal-Perinatal Medicine when Dr. Lipsitz retired. The NICU now had twenty-four intensive-care beds and twenty semi-ICU beds. Owing to past research accomplishments and involvement in other clinical trials, the fellowship program became highly competitive with high-quality fellow applicants.

The division has been involved in a number of important clinical trials, on retinopathy of prematurity, hematopoietic growth factors (GCSF and GMCSF) in neonatal infections, and superoxide dismutase (SOD) to prevent bronchopulmonary dysplasia, and an important and successful clinical trial of selective brain cooling for hypoxic ischemic encephalopathy. This laborious and intense clinical trial required immediate cooling (less than six hours from birth) of the brain for infants who developed encephalopathy. Starting in 1999, the NICU was the only center other than one in Manhattan that offered this important experimental therapy. The results of the brain cooling study showed that there was a fifty percent reduction in severe disabilities for newborns with moderate encephalopathy at birth by examination and amplitude-integrated EEG. Again, the SCH NICU received media attention, this time being described as a "brain rescue center." Without the round-the-clock help from Barbara Wilkens, RN, Dr. Steele, and Dr. Castro, the brain cooling project could not have been as successful as it was.

Also of note with regard to research developments, Dr. Koppel's research demonstrated the usefulness of pulse oximetry screening to detect occult cardiac conditions in the newborn. As a result of his work, this screening tool is now considered standard practice in New York State and other areas of the country and the world.

With the merger of the North Shore Health

System and Long Island Jewish Medical Center to create the North Shore-Long Island Jewish Health System, the opportunity to have new academic faculty was an important milestone in the NICU. Dr. Davidson was appointed the first director of neonatal services for the North Shore-Long Island Jewish Health System and the first director of the combined fellowship program. Three new faculty members were hired who had impressive academic credentials, and subsequently contributed greatly to the quality of clinical care, teaching, and research. Richard Schanler, MD, professor of pediatrics, was recruited from Baylor College of Medicine and Texas Children's Hospital as the chief of neonatal-perinatal medicine at NSUH. He is internationally known for his work in neonatal nutrition and breastfeeding. Howard Heiman, MD, former director of the NICU at Wilford-Hall in Texas, was recruited next as a full-time attending neonatologist. He came with extensive experience in neonatal transport and an academic interest in gastrointestinal immunology. Dr. Heiman has become a leader in high-frequency ventilation transport, which has been a life-saving technique unique to the New York metropolitan area, bolstering the reputation of the neonatal lung rescue center. Sherry E. Courtney, MD, who was also hired, was previously well known to the division because of its involvement in her multicenter clinical trial of high-frequency oscillatory ventilation (HFOV) to prevent bronchopulmonary dysplasia (BPD). Dr. Courtney's trial was an important success and was published in the *New England Journal of Medicine* in 2002.

With the merger, the Division of Neonatal-Perinatal Medicine now had nine neonatologists, eleven neonatal fellows, and ninety-five beds between SCH and NSUH. As of 2002, there were greater than 1,200 discharges annually from the SCH NICU alone. Dr. Davidson organized and published guidelines for best neonatal practices, which are applied system-wide. Dr. Castro developed and organized a neonatal board-related curriculum with weekly seminars for the fellows and attendings. Regina Spinazzola, MD, plays an important role in centralizing and organizing neonatal follow-up, as well as scheduling neonatal services at affiliate hospitals. Jerrold Schlessel, MD, is responsible for setting up the monthly neonatal teleconference, which is viewed by affiliate neonatologists throughout the healthcare system, as well as Schneider Children's Hospital in Israel.

By 2006, the Division of Neonatal-Perinatal Medicine was in full swing, with new faculty and major clinical advances in hand. Dr. Davidson was awarded an independent NIH grant for basic research in neonatal lung inflammation. Dr. Schanler became the senior editor of a book entitled *Breastfeeding for Physicians* sponsored by the American Academy of Pediatrics (AAP).

In November 2008 a new state-of-the-art twenty-four-bed addition to the Schneider Children's Hospital NICU was opened, which will provide a greater degree of family-centered care. The delivery room and operative suites of the women's hospital (under construction) will be on the same floor as the new NICU at SCH, and there will be a four-bed neonatal stabilization unit (NSU) located between the two principal operating rooms of the new women's hospital. The NSU will be unique for the New York metropolitan region, providing cutting-edge resuscitation advances and immediate neonatal intensive care that will be able to be implemented with a baby's first breath.

NEPHROLOGY

During the early years of the Department of Pediatrics at Long Island Jewish Medical Center (LIJ), there was no staff member assigned exclusively to handling renal problems in children.

Dr. Bernard Gauthier, founding chief of Division of Nephrology 1975–1995, with a patient.

Leonard Ehrlich, MD, and Maurice Teitel, MD, members of the voluntary pediatric staff, had an interest in nephrology and though they handled some renal patients, they did not have any formal training in nephrology. Many of the cases were handled by internists. Bernard Gauthier, MD, was appointed as the founding physician-in-charge of the new Division of Nephrology in 1975 after completing his fellowship in pediatric nephrology at SUNY Downstate Medical Center under the supervision of Melinda McVicar, MD, who later became chief of nephrology at NSUH.

Over the next ten years, Dr. Gauthier *was* the division. He was assisted from the earliest days of his tenure by Barbara Ho, who worked as the divisional secretary for both the Division of Nephrology and the Division of Endocrinology.

During Dr. Gauthier's tenure, which lasted through 1995, he established a full array of pediatric nephrology services that included treatment of the entire gamut of kidney diseases, performance of renal biopsies, and the management of children requiring dialysis and transplantation. Dr. Gauthier participated in a number of the teaching exercises at the Albert Einstein College of Medicine. He participated in a broad array of clinical research studies and was a participant in the International Study of Kidney Diseases in Children. The only other staff members in the division during this period were Rachel Frank, RN, the divisional nurse, and Carol Cialeo, MSW, a social worker who also assisted in the Division of Pulmonary Medicine. Ms. Cialeo, an outstanding social worker, had cystic fibrosis and was treated even as an adult by Dr. Jack Gorvoy in the Cystic Fibrosis Center in the Department of Pediatrics. Sadly, she died in December 1994 following a lung transplant. Ms. Frank continues to work in the division and became a certified nephrology nurse (CNN) in 1995.

In December 1976, the first chronic hemodialysis was performed on a child at LIJ, and in April 1977, Dr. Gauthier successfully used the first hemoperfusion column for reversing coma due to a dilantin overdosage. In September 1980 the first pediatric patient received continuous ambulatory peritoneal dialysis (CAPD) at LIJ.

Howard Trachtman, MD, joined the division in 1985. Dr. Trachtman completed his residency in pediatric nephrology at Albert Einstein College of Medicine. When the division doubled in size from one to two doctors, Drs. Gauthier and Trachtman began to perform a much broader array of clinical and basic science research in addition to maintaining the high standard of clinical care that had been established under Dr. Gauthier's leadership.

NEPHROLOGY FACULTY

Chiefs

1975–1995	Bernard Gauthier, MD
1995–present	Howard Trachtman, MD

Staff

1985–1995	Howard Trachtman, MD
1995–2004	Bernard Gauthier, MD
1999–2007	Manju Chandra, MD
2000–2005	Marcella Vergara, MD
2007–present	Beatrice Goilav, MD
2008–present	Christine Sethna, MD

Ambulatory Visits

2000	2,669
2007	2,252

Over the next eleven years, Drs. Gauthier and Trachtman co-edited a monograph entitled *Pediatric Nephrology* that included contributions from colleagues in the New York area, as well as other national authorities.

Dr. Trachtman set up a registry for patients with renal disease treated in the New York-New Jersey area under the aegis of the Kidney Urological Foundation of America. The division also conducted numerous clinical trials and research studies in clinical nephrology as well as in basic sciences. The bench research focused on the role of taurine in osmoregulation, the use of antioxidants in the prevention of kidney disease, and the pathophysiology of diabetic nephropathy.

With the merger of LIJ and NSUH, Manju Chandra, MD, who was chief of nephrology at NSUH, joined the Division of Nephrology at SCH. She had established a urodynamics laboratory at NSUH in 1983 and developed recognized expertise in voiding dysfunction in pediatric patients. Dr. Chandra resigned her position at SCH in June 2007.

Dr. Trachtman was promoted to professor of pediatrics at the Albert Einstein College of Medicine in 1995 and assumed the position of chief of the Division of Nephrology at SCH. Marcella Vergara, MD, was hired as a third nephrologist in 2000 and was a part of the division until 2005, when she resigned her position. Dr. Gauthier retired from the division in 2004. In the summer of 2005 the Division of Nephrology at NSUH became fully integrated with the SCH division in a unified facility on the third floor of SCH, where the division continues to reside to this day. This involved closure of the outpatient services at NSUH and consolidation of all dialysis services at the Julia & Israel Waldbaum Dialysis Center on Community Drive.

Over the last ten years, the clinical research activity of the division has expanded exponentially. Dr. Trachtman has been the principal investigator for clinical trials in hemolytic uremic syndrome (HUS) and focal segmental glomerulosclerosis (FSGS). Several outstanding research coordinators have been part of the division over the last decade. These include Erica Christen, RN, who was the principal coordinator for the HUS-SYNSORB study; Suzanne Vento, RN, who joined the division in 2003 to serve as coordinator for the FSGS clinical trial; and Ann Way, RN, who was a member of the division briefly in 2004 as the coordinator for a trial in novel therapies in resistant FSGS. Cathy Hoffman, RN, joined the division in 2006 to assist in the creation of an international registry and biorepository for thrombotic microangiopathy, a project that was supported by the National Institutes of Health (NIH). Virginia Crosby, RN, a former dialysis nurse, was hired to oversee the clinical activities of the pediatric end-stage renal disease patients in 2005. She returned to the dialysis unit in 2006. Beatrice Goilav, MD, joined the division in July 2007 after she completed her fellowship in pediatric nephrology at Mount Sinai School of Medicine.

Dr. Howard Trachtman, chief of Division of Nephrology 1995–present, with Rachel Frank, RN, BS, entertaining a patient.

The division continues to be one of the premier nephrology services in the greater metropolitan area. The physicians have routinely been recognized as among the top doctors in this region, and Dr. Trachtman has been the principal investigator in a number of NIH-supported clinical trials, and a member of national review boards for clinical research. He also serves on the educational programs of the American Academy of Pediatrics and the American Board of Pediatrics.

NEUROLOGY

The Division of Neurology was founded within the Department of Pediatrics at Long Island Jewish Medical Center (LIJ) in June 1971 when Marvin Klein, MD, was appointed the founding physician-in-charge.

Prior to that time, the pediatric neurology service was covered by local voluntary adult neurologists. Upon his arrival at LIJ, Dr. Klein also started the first learning disability clinic. He served as chief of both the division and the clinic until 1985, when he resigned his position to go into private practice.

In July 1975, Barbara Stewart, MD, was recruited as a full-time attending and remained on the full-time staff until September 1981. Lydia Eviatar, MD, joined the staff in September 1979. She became acting chief in 1985 after Dr. Klein's resignation and in 1986 became the chief of the Division of Neurology at the Schneider Children's Hospital (SCH).

Dr. Marvin Klein, founding divisional chief of Neurology 1971–1985.

Over the years, Marcia Bergtraum, MD, Ram Kairam, MD, and Ingrid Taff , MD, joined the pediatric neurology staff. Joseph Maytal, MD, was recruited in 1987 and Gerald Novak, MD, in 1988. Both are certified in neurology with special competence in child neurology and clinical neurophysiology. Both graduated from the pediatric neurology training program at Albert Einstein College of Medicine.

In 1990, LIJ and SCH were selected as one of the four sites in New York State for a designated epilepsy center. The center provides specialized diagnostic facilities such as short- and long-term EEG monitoring for patients with intractable seizures for the purposes of treatment with new, experimental anticonvulsants or epilepsy surgery.

Video EEG monitoring of patients facilitates differentiation between true seizures, pseudo-seizures, and movement disorders. The division has been involved in multi-institutional collaborative studies for the use of investigational antiepileptic drugs. Video EEG monitoring with subdural electrodes and electrocorticography is also available in preparation for epilepsy surgery. Auditory evoked potentials and visual evoked potentials are also tested in the electrophysiology laboratory.

NEUROLOGY FACULTY

Chiefs

1971–1985	Marvin Klein, MD*
1986–2000	Lydia Eviatar, MD
2000–present	Joseph Maytal, MD

Staff

1975–1981	Barbara Stewart, MD
1982–1988	Marcia Bergtraum, MD
1985–1986	Ram Kairam, MD
1986–1988	Ingrid Taff, MD
1987–present	Joseph Maytal, MD
1988–2001	Gerald Novak, MD
1998–present	Li Kan, MD
1998–present	Rosemarrie Sy-Kho, MD
2000–present	Lydia Eviatar, MD
2002–2005	Leonid Topper, MD
2002–present	Robin Smith, MD
2002–present	Zipora Fefer, MD
2007–present	Patricia Krief, MD

*Deceased

Ambulatory Visits

2000	11,091
2007	12,902

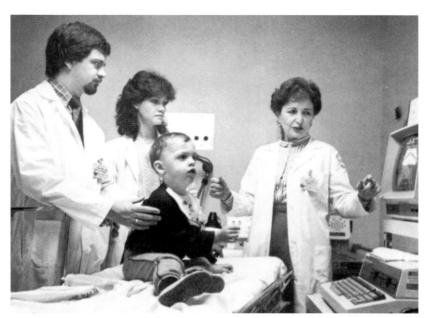

Dr. Lydia Eviatar, chief of Division of Neurology 1986–2000, with patient and house staff.

Specialized clinics for neuromuscular disorders are also available.

Since 1990, the Michaels Foundation has generously contributed to the growth and development of the division. With their help, a sophisticated neurovestibular laboratory that evaluated dizziness and balance difficulties in children, with the help of a special computerized rotational chair, was established. In 1995, their generous support provided funds to remodel the division in order to accommodate a much larger staff and a growing patient population.

In 1998 Rosemarrie Sy-Kho, MD, and Li Kan, MD, who completed her fellowship training at SCH, were appointed to the staff of the division. In 2000 Dr. Maytal was appointed chief of the division. In 2002 Dr. Maytal collaborated with neurooncologists, neurosurgeons, radiation oncologists, and neuroradiologists to form the Childhood Brain and Spinal Cord Tumor Center. Members of the center meet once a week to review each patient's case and progress to determine the best course of treatment.

The division has an active training program accredited by the American Council for Graduate Medical Education (ACGME). Two pediatric neurology trainees per year are recruited. The training program consists of hands-on experience in clinical pediatric neurology as well as didactic instruction with weekly conferences covering subspecialty areas such as electrophysiology, neuroradiology, neuropathology, neurochemistry, and psychiatry. The division is based at SCH but has strong ties to LIJ's neurology department, where the trainees spend a year of clinical training in adult neurology.

The population base serviced by the division has steadily increased over time, and the range of neurological problems seen includes developmental delay, neuromuscular disorders, seizure disorders and degenerative disorders, tumors of the central nervous system and spinal cord, as well as neurological complications of infections or collagen disorders. The approach to patients is multidisciplinary, involving related disciplines such as neuropsychology, psychiatry, rehabilitation medicine, genetics, and orthopaedics.

Dr. Joseph Maytal, chief of Division of Neurology 2000–present, reading EEG on monitor.

PULMONARY MEDICINE

In 1984, shortly after the Schneider Children's Hospital (SCH) opened, Emile M. Scarpelli, MD, PhD, was appointed founding chief of the Division of Pulmonary Medicine and director of the Pulmonary Function Diagnostic Laboratory. A distinguished graduate of Duke University Medical School and former fellow of Abraham Rudolph, MD, the renowned pediatric cardiologist, he was chief of pediatric pulmonology and professor of pediatrics at Albert Einstein College of Medicine before joining the SCH faculty.

Dr. Scarpelli is a scholar and an internationally recognized researcher in pulmonary mechanics and development. He has an extensive body of research on first breath mechanics and the biophysical and biochemical characteristics of the alveolar surface network.

He contributed to the development of pulmonary surfactant for the treatment of respiratory distress syndrome in premature infants, received several prestigious National Institutes of Health (NIH) grants, and published numerous scientific papers, books, and monographs on pulmonary development and surfactant. He mentored many clinical and research fellows in pediatric pulmonology. He brought a staff of clinicians, basic researchers, and fellows to the Schneider Children's Hospital and directed clinical care in pulmonary medicine and critical care, as well as serving as director of pediatric research.

Robert S. Bienkowski, PhD, assistant professor of pediatrics at Albert Einstein College of Medicine, came with Dr. Scarpelli as assistant director of pediatric research in 1984. He published extensively in the areas of pulmonary extracellular matrix biology and intracellular protein trafficking. Dr. Bienkowski organized postdoctoral training programs to guide and advise trainees in the conduct of clinical and basic research at SCH. He provided forums wherein various researchers at LIJ could share and collaborate in basic science research. Alan Mautone, PhD, studied the biophysical properties of pulmonary surfactant biofilms together with Dr. Scarpelli. Anthony Sica, PhD, collaborated with Phyllis Gootman, PhD, of SUNY Downstate and conducted research on autonomic control of breathing during postnatal development, focusing particularly on sympathetic and respiratory rhythm generators. Faculty members and postdoctoral fellows at SCH availed themselves of their colleagues' expertise and laboratory facilities for conducting basic science research.

Bella Clutario, MD, formerly associate professor of pediatrics at Albert Einstein College of Medicine, also came to SCH with Dr. Scarpelli in 1984. She collaborated with Dr. Scarpelli on many studies on first breath mechanics and the alveolar surface network, but was also an experienced clinician who evaluated and managed children with pulmonary disease. She assisted Jack Gorvoy, MD, in the treatment of

PULMONARY MEDICINE FACULTY

Chiefs

1984–1989	Emile Scarpelli, MD, PhD
1998–2002	Arthur DeLuca, MD
2002–2003	Maria Teresa Santiago, MD (interim)
2003–present	Anastassios Koumbourlis, MD

Staff

1984–1999	Robert Bienkowski, PhD
1984–1989	Bella Clutario, MD
1984–1988	Mary Cataletto, MD
1984–1985	Stuart Weinberg, MD
1989–1990	Alan Mautone, PhD
1989–1990	William Yee, MD
1998–present	Joan DeCelie-Germana, MD
2003–present	Marie Theresa Santiago, MD

Ambulatory Visits

2000	2,447
2007	3,590

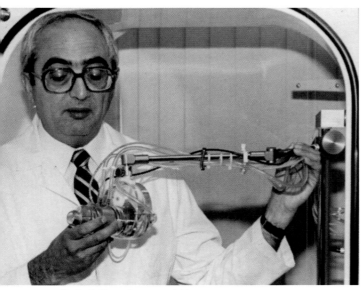
Dr. Emile Scarpelli in research laboratory.

patients at the Cystic Fibrosis Center. She helped supervise a state-of-the-art pediatric pulmonary function laboratory where a full-time technician undertook the challenges of testing young children with various respiratory disorders. Dr. Clutario spearheaded the formation of a chronic ventilator unit at Blythedale Children's Hospital in Westchester, a collaborative venture with New York Medical College and SCH. In this pediatric rehabilitation facility, primary caregivers of children with chronic respiratory failure who needed tracheostomies and ventilator support were taught to care for their children at home. The unit continues to provide transitional care for many of the pediatric patients discharged from the inpatient intensive care units at SCH.

In 1984, Mary Cataletto, MD, a pediatric anesthesiologist who had completed her pediatric pulmonary fellowship with Dr. Scarpelli, and Stuart Weinberg, MD, managed patients in the pediatric intensive care unit (PICU). With the help of the pediatric chief residents, including Joy Nagelberg, MD, who now heads the Division of Emergency Medicine at SCH, she supervised the care of critically ill children. Dr. Cataletto helped establish a chronic ventilator program so that children requiring various forms of ventilator support

and would otherwise remain hospitalized indefinitely were transitioned home and followed by the pulmonologists and intensive care specialists.

William F. Yee, MD, was with the faculty of the Division of Pulmonary Medicine briefly in 1989. He was also trained in pediatric pulmonology by Dr. Scarpelli at Albert Einstein College of Medicine and was assistant professor of pediatrics at the Floating Hospital for Children at Tufts-New England Medical Center. He is an outstanding teacher and clinician with experience both in pulmonary medicine and in critical care. He returned to Tufts in 1990 in the Division of Pediatric Pulmonology and Allergy.

Arthur DeLuca, MD, joined the faculty of SCH in 1998 as chief of the division (*pro tem*) after completing his pediatric pulmonary fellowship at the Children's Hospital of Pittsburgh, and brought his expertise in pediatric flexible bronchoscopy to the patients at SCH. Prior to his arrival, direct assessment of subglottic airways, particularly in critically ill children, was limited to rigid bronchoscopy, which pediatric surgeons or otolaryngologists could only perform in the operating room. He established a pediatric flexible bronchoscopy service where procedures are performed either at the bedside in critically ill patients in the intensive care units or in the endoscopy suite at SCH.

Maria Teresa Santiago, MD, was Dr. Scarpelli's first clinical fellow at SCH, and she returned to SCH as interim chief of the Division of Pulmonary Medicine in 2002. In 2004, she was named co-director of the CMF Center for Childhood Asthma, a collaborative venture with the SCH Division of Allergy and Immunology, where children with asthma can be fully evaluated and managed in a multidisciplinary setting.

Anastassios Koumbourlis, MD, assumed the role of chief of the Division of Pulmonary Medicine and Cystic Fibrosis Center in July 2003. He was associate professor of clinical pediatrics, attending physician in pediatric pulmonology

Drs. Koumbourlis and Santiago performing bronchoscopy.

and pediatric critical care, and director of the Pulmonary Function and Exercise Laboratories at the Morgan Stanley Children's Hospital of New York-Presbyterian Hospital prior to joining the SCH faculty. He completed fellowships in pediatric pulmonology and pediatric critical care at the Children's Hospital of Pittsburgh and is board certified in pediatrics and pediatric pulmonology. Dr. Koumbourlis is an experienced clinician and flexible bronchoscopist with expertise in the care of children with complex pulmonary problems. Since his arrival, the Cystic Fibrosis Center has been fully incorporated into the Division of Pulmonary Medicine. He is also a distinguished teacher and mentor who trained numerous pulmonary fellows and pediatric residents since joining the Columbia University faculty in 1991. He has published extensively on pulmonary mechanics in the critical-care setting, as well as on pulmonary function testing in both infants and children with various pulmonary disorders including sickle cell disease, congenital diaphrag-

matic hernia, pectus excavatum, and pulmonary hypertension. He is a member of several national and international scientific societies, was elected to the Society of Pediatric Research in 1998, and is a reviewer for several peer-reviewed journals including *Pediatric Research*, *Pediatric Pulmonology*, *Lung*, *Respiratory Medicine*, *Circulation*, the *European Journal of Pediatrics*, and *Intensive Care Medicine*. He is a member of the American Thoracic Society/European Respiratory Society Working Group on Infant Pulmonary Function Testing, and is currently a member of the expert panel of the International Spinal Muscular Atrophy (SMA) Standard of Care Committee.

The Division of Pulmonary Medicine has a staff that provides education and clinical support for pulmonary patients. Both Trudy Leicht, RN, BS, MS, a clinical nurse specialist, and Susan Kline, RN, BSN, a nurse clinician, have extensive clinical experience with the acute and chronic care of children. Edward Cranston, RPFT, is a respiratory therapist, pulmonary function technologist, and asthma educator with extensive experience in pulmonary function testing in children and asthma management.

RESEARCH

An account of research activities in the Department of Pediatrics at Long Island Jewish Medical Center (LIJ) divides naturally into three periods: the *early period* beginning in 1955 when Samuel Karelitz, MD, organized the department; the *middle period* beginning in 1970 when Philip Lanzkowsky, MD, became chairman; and the *recent period* beginning with the opening of the Schneider Children's Hospital (SCH) in 1983.

The Early Period

In the early days Dr. Karelitz was the only full-time staff pediatrician. The other attending physicians worked at the hospital approximately half-time usually *pro bono* and maintained private practices in the area. Research in the department was completely clinical, driven by problems the physicians encountered in treating their patients. Among the faculty who were active in research were Max Stillerman, MD, who is remembered for seeming always to bring culture plates from his office to the hospital, and Herbert Goldman, MD, who was an active member of the voluntary faculty in private practice, working in neonatology.

The 1950s and early 1960s were a time of tremendous development of new antibiotics. Dr. Karelitz and Henry Isenberg, PhD, who was the chief of microbiology at LIJ, were in the forefront of evaluating new antibiotics to treat various pediatric infectious diseases such as the bacterial complications of measles. Dr. Stillerman and Dr. Isenberg carried out several investigations on Group A hemolytic streptococcal infections, which became increasingly common after 1956. Particularly noteworthy was their large study comparing clindamycin and penicillin, which was carried out in collaboration with investigators at

the U.S. Centers for Disease Control (CDC). The faculty also participated in landmark trials of the killed measles vaccine and the Salk polio vaccine.

Dr. Karelitz had a long-standing interest in crying activity in neonates. Together with Dr. Isenberg, he demonstrated differences in the biochemical composition of tears from children with Down syndrome and that of tears from normal children. With Victor Fisichelli, PhD, a psychologist on the faculty of Lehman College of the City University of New York, he conducted extensive studies on the phonetic structure of babies' cries and the ways that different types of cries related to different emotional and disease states. Those early papers from the 1960s exhibit a rather different approach to clinical research from the present-day approach. For example, Dr. Karelitz recruited volunteers from the Women's Service Guild of the hospital to assist in making audiotapes and recording data.

Dr. Karelitz was well known for his personal and professional integrity. One small but very telling example of his intellectual honesty occurs in a footnote to a 1966 paper in the *Journal of Psychology* that reads: "The data which are summarized here are available for each of the 60 subjects studied. A copy may be secured by citing the Document number and remitting $1.25 to the Library of Congress." In a time when scientists' ethics are routinely questioned, Karelitz's footnote indicating where the data were stored and how a reader could access them shows that he set a very high standard for good research practices.

Herbert Goldman, MD, who worked in the premature nursery at LIJ, conducted important research on nutritional requirements of neonates. In a series of papers beginning in 1969, Dr. Goldman and colleagues demonstrated that "low" birth weight infants (less than 2,000 grams) fared much better on low-protein formula than on high-protein formula. Furthermore, the IQ deficit associated with high-protein diet was evident after seven years. This study was notable for its size and design (more than 300 infants were enrolled in a randomized, double-blind trial) and for the statistical rigor of the analysis.

Dr. Goldman was one of the first to recognize a connection between formula feeding and a high incidence of hemorraghic disease, and studies conducted by Dr. Goldman and colleagues were cited in a 1971 Statement of the American Academy of Pediatrics Committee on Nutrition recommending vitamin K supplementation of infant formulas.

During this early period, Dr. Karelitz involved the residents in research studies. He sent them to the laboratory to carry out assays, and he sent them to meetings to present their work. Karelitz and his colleagues were very successful in obtaining external funds from pharmaceutical companies and the National Institutes of Health (NIH) to support their work.

Norman Gootman, MD, joined the department in 1965, working half-time at LIJ and half-time at the Queens Hospital Center, which had recently affiliated with LIJ. In addition to establishing the Division of Cardiology within the Department of Pediatrics at LIJ, Dr. Gootman, who had trained with Abraham Rudolph at Albert Einstein College of Medicine, began an active program of basic research into neural control of cardiovascular function. In many ways, Dr. Gootman was a bridge between early and middle periods; he became the principal force driving research in the department.

The Middle Period

Several aspects of Dr. Gootman's work are noteworthy. It was based on a highly productive twenty-year collaboration with investigators at other institutions, namely, his wife Phyllis Gootman, PhD, in the Department of Physiology at SUNY Downstate and Nancy Buckley, PhD, in the Department of Physiology at Albert Einstein College of Medicine. Dr. Gootman's research

program was the first in the Department of Pediatrics to make extensive use of laboratory animals, and his group was one of the first to demonstrate that the piglet was an excellent model for studying the physiology of the human neonate. Many cardiology and neonatology fellows received their research training in Dr. Gootman's group. Among the neonatology fellows was Andrew Steele, MD, who learned the basics of research in Dr. Gootman's laboratory at LIJ and then as a junior attending spent a six-month sabbatical in Phyllis Gootman's laboratory learning the techniques of neural recording. Joy Nagelberg, MD, another trainee in the seventies, has remained at SCH and is now chief of the Division of Emergency Medicine.

Philip Lanzkowsky, MD, became chairman of the Department of Pediatrics in 1970. He established the Division of Hematology-Oncology, which included a research laboratory. Together with Gungor Karayalcin, MD, and Ashok Shende, MD, he carried out basic research into the effects of iron deficiency on DNA, RNA, and protein synthesis in various organs in iron-deficient rats and the effect of iron deficiency anemia on gut function in infants.

Within the Division of Neonatology, Philip Lipsitz, MD, was the local principal investigator for a large NIH-sponsored trial of phototherapy for neonatal jaundice. Dr. Steele, together with Allan Abramson, MD, in LIJ's Department of Otorhinolaryngology, demonstrated the value of using flow-volume loops in diagnosing laryngotracheal disease.

In the Division of Adolescent Medicine, I. Ronald Shenker, MD, and Michael Nussbaum, MD, were beginning important studies on eating disorders that remain a focus of research in the division to this day. Their 1980 paper demonstrating cerebral atrophy in anorexia nervosa is a landmark in the field.

The Recent Period

The opening of the Schneider Children's Hospital in 1983 fundamentally changed the character of the pediatric department. The influx of new faculty including many basic scientists, the expansion of existing divisions, and the founding of new ones created an explosion in research activity. Emile Scarpelli, MD, PhD, was recruited from the Albert Einstein College of Medicine in June 1984 to organize and direct the Pediatric Research Center. He brought with him Robert Bienkowski, PhD, as associate director. Several thousand square feet of laboratory space were renovated for the department, and core facilities for instrumentation and tissue culture were established. Dr. Scarpelli continued his work on pulmonary surfactant, and Anthony Sica, PhD, who came as a postdoctoral research fellow, organized a laboratory to study the development of neural control of breathing. He also collaborated extensively with Drs. Norman and Phyllis Gootman. Dr. Bienkowski was studying the effects of extracellular matrix on pneumocyte differentiation and collagen metabolism in lung cells. Most of the divisions established laboratories, and the newly recruited faculty brought new technologies with them.

Several divisions established clinical laboratories to perform special tests, and the wealth of patient-derived material stimulated many research projects. In addition to the increase in laboratory-based research, there was a rapid growth in clinical studies, with many faculty members initiating their own projects, as well as participating in multicenter trials. Collaborations within pediatrics and with faculty in other departments grew rapidly. Active research programs flourish in many divisions at SCH and those programs are fully discussed within the individual divisional histories in this section of the book.

With the NS-LIJ merger and the development of The Feinstein Institute for Medical Research of the NS-LIJ Health System, researchers at SCH conduct their research in the institute and no longer at SCH.

RHEUMATOLOGY

Clinical programs in rheumatology were established within the Department of Pediatrics at Long Island Jewish Medical Center (LIJ) in July 1976 by Lazar Fruchter, MD, an immunologist with an interest in juvenile rheumatoid arthritis and other rheumatic conditions.

After Dr. Fruchter immigrated to Israel, Bruce Bogard, MD, in the Division of General Pediatrics within LIJ's Department of Pediatrics, cared for many of the children with juvenile rheumatoid arthritis. Patients with systemic lupus erythematosus were cared for by Dr. Bernard Gauthier or Dr. Philip Lanzkowsky since many had significant kidney or hematologic involvement. Patients with dermatomyositis were seen by Dr. Marvin Klein in the Division of Neurology.

Care of patients with the rheumatic diseases of childhood was centralized when Norman Ilowite, MD, became section head of pediatric rheumatology in the Division of Allergy-Immunology and Rheumatology at the Schneider Children's Hospital (SCH)

RHEUMATOLOGY FACULTY

Chiefs

1991–2006	Norman Ilowite, MD
2006–present	Beth Gottlieb, MD

Staff

1984–1991	Norman Ilowite, MD
1992–2005	Peter LoGalbo, MD
1998–2006	Beth Gottlieb, MD
2001–present	Barbara Anne Eberhard, MD
2008–present	Lilliana Barillas-Arias, MD

Ambulatory Visits

2000	2,973
2007	3,737

in 1984. Dr. Ilowite and Naynesh Kamani, MD, of the bone marrow transplantation unit, constituted the immunology service of the newly constructed children's hospital and established the clinical laboratory in immunology and rheumatology.

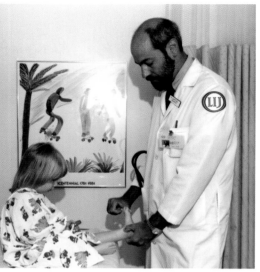

Dr. Norman Ilowite, founding chief of Division of Rheumatology, 1991–2006.

One year later, Vincent Bonagura, MD, became chief of SCH's Division of Allergy-Immunology and Rheumatology and established important research programs in autoimmunity relevant to the pathogenesis of rheumatic diseases. As part of this newly formed division, Dr. Ilowite developed and expanded clinical and research programs in pediatric rheumatology. In collaboration with Gary Walco, PhD, of the Division of Developmental and Behavioral Pediatrics at SCH, programs in pain assessment and treatment of the childhood rheumatic diseases were established with support from the Easter Seals Research Foundation. In collaboration with Marc Jacobson, MD, of the Division of Adolescent Medicine, programs in prevention of atherosclerosis in patients with childhood rheumatic disease were established with support from the Arthritis Foundation and the Lupus Foundation. In collaboration with Dr. Bonagura, research programs on the role of rheumatoid factors in juvenile rheumatoid arthritis were established, supported by the Arthritis Foundation, the Lupus Foundation, and the Easter Seals Research Foundation. The center became a member of the Pediatric Rheumatology Collaborative Study Group and participated in trials of nonsteroidal antiinflammatory drugs, intravenous immunoglobulin, methotrexate, and

newly emerging biologic agents for the treatment of juvenile rheumatoid arthritis.

By 1991, clinical programs in rheumatology had expanded at the Schneider Children's Hospital to the degree that it was deemed necessary to establish an independent Division of Rheumatology. Eileen Pagano, RN, was the division's first nurse clinician, helping to develop programs in patient education and advocacy. Establishment of an arthritis center with input from Angeles Badel, MD, from the Division of Physical Medicine and Rehabilitation and Jack Handelsman, MD, from the Division of Orthopaedics supported a multidisciplinary approach to patients with complex and severe musculoskeletal disease.

Peter LoGalbo, MD, became the division's second attending physician in 1992. Clinical programs in intraarticular injection therapy using conscious sedation were developed. Dr. Ilowite and Lorry Rubin, MD, chief of the Division of Infectious Diseases established the Lyme Disease Center, and along with Sunil Sood, MD, developed programs in tick identification, as well as immunodiagnostic and molecular testing.

In 1992, Dr. Ilowite was among the first group of eighty-three pediatric rheumatologists to be certified by the Sub-Board of Pediatric Rheumatology of the American Board of Pediatrics. In 1996 he was elected chairman of the Sub-Board of Pediatric Rheumatology.

In 1992 Kevin Schlessel, MD, the first pediatric rheumatology fellow, was recruited. Terry Kwong, MD, was recruited from Australia to be the second fellow in 1993. In 1996 the Residency Review Committee (RRC) of the American Council for Graduate Medical Education (ACGME) approved certification of SCH's pediatric rheumatology fellowship training program. SCH was among the first twenty programs nationally given this distinction. Beth Gottlieb, MD, became the first pediatric rheumatology fellow at SCH in 1995 to become board eligible because of the ACGME approval of the program.

Fellows Christine Hom, MD, and Diana Milojevic, MD, did their basic research training on the role of autoantibodies in rheumatic disease with Dr. Bonagura. Dr. Milojevic's abstract was named the best basic science abstract at the international pediatric rheumatology meeting in 2003. Patricia Irigoyen, MD, was mentored by Peter Gregersen, MD, at The Feinstein Institute for Medical Research of the North Shore-Long Island Jewish Health System in studies on immunogenetics of rheumatic disease and received a Physician Scientist Development Award for further studies from 2006 to 2009 from the Research and Education Foundation of the American College of Rheumatology.

From 1995 to 2006 the division remained active in clinical research, with studies of biologic therapies in juvenile rheumatoid arthritis as well as projects in atherosclerosis prevention in pediatric systemic lupus erythematosus and gene expression in juvenile rheumatoid arthritis, funded by grants from the National Institutes of Health (NIH) from 2003 to 2007. Nurses Trudy Leicht, RN (1991–2000), Eileen Pagano, RN (2000–2005), and Marilyn Orlando, RN (2002–present), coordinated this clinical research activity. These investigator-initiated studies were sponsored by an emerging clinical research network called the Childhood Arthritis and Rheumatology Research Alliance, which Dr. Ilowite was instrumental in establishing. Patricia Lee, RN, joined the division in 2000, taking over the nurse clinician duties from Eileen Pagano, RN. Dr. Gottlieb was appointed to the faculty of the division in 1998. She received a five-year clinical science grant from the Arthritis Foundation to study outcomes of two inception cohorts of patients with juvenile rheumatoid arthritis (JRA). This study continues to follow the largest collection of JRA patients in North America. Anne Eberhard, MD, trained in Australia and at Boston Children's Hospital, joined the division in 2001. She directed studies on intra-articular

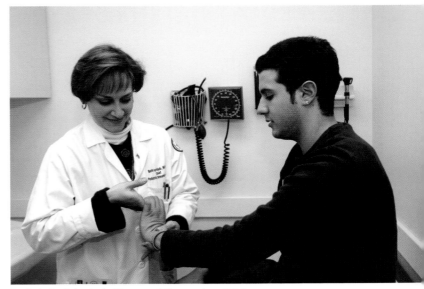

Dr. Beth Gottlieb, chief of Division of Rheumatology 2006–present, examining a patient.

steroid injection in JRA and characterization of flares in pediatric lupus. She mentored Jennifer Weiss, MD, in studies in this area. Her resulting abstract presentation at the American College of Rheumatology meeting in 2004 was awarded the Earl J. Brewer Research Award from the American Academy of Pediatrics Section on Rheumatology.

In 2006 Dr. Ilowite resigned his position at SCH to assume the directorship of a new division of rheumatology at the Albert Einstein College of Medicine and Dr. Beth Gottlieb succeeded him as chief of the Division of Rheumatology.

Beginning with the efforts of Dr. Lazar Fruchter, the division has evolved over the decades to be one of only a few centers of pediatric rheumatology in the country, and presently enjoys a national and international reputation for excellence.

PEDIATRIC SURGERY

CARDIOTHORACIC SURGERY

The Division of Cardiothoracic Surgery of the Department of Surgery at LIJ encompassed both adult and pediatric cardiac and general thoracic surgical patients. The program involved both a clinical service and an accredited residency teaching program in the specialty, one of about 100 in the country.

Walter Phillips, MD, came from South Africa to direct the program in the 1960s and organized the teaching service with the help of Dr. Philip Crastnopol, MD, and other members on the voluntary staff. (Note from Dr. Lanzkowsky: As a point of interest, I was Dr. Phillips's intern in 1955 in Cape Town at the Groote Schuur Hospital, the teaching hospital of the University of Cape Town, where he was chief of cardiothoracic surgery. This was before open heart surgery, when the only cardiac surgery performed was tight mitral valve surgery done blindly through a purse-string suture in the left atrial appendix and closure of patent ductus arteriosus [extra-cardiac]. In those days cardiothoracic surgery was performed once a week, and it was a harrowing experience for the entire surgical team. The duration was long, anesthesia was marginal, the blood consumption was enormous, and the mortality high. Successful

Drs. John Luber and Norman Gootman examining post-operative cardiac patient, 1982.

outcomes, which were few and far between, were dramatic and life saving and created memories that are still powerful fifty years later.)

George Wisoff, MD, was recruited to join the staff in 1967 from Mount Sinai Hospital, and with the retirement of Dr. Phillips, Dr. Wisoff took over as a full-time director in 1970. Other surgeons from other academic centers added talent and quality. Alan Wolpowitz, MD, trained by Christiaan Barnard, MD, in South Africa, was appointed and concentrated on pediatric cardiothoracic surgery. Julius Garvey, MD, came from Montefiore Hospital and directed the program at the Queens Hospital Center. (He was the son of Marcus Mosiah Garvey, Jr. [1887-1940], the national hero of Jamaica who advanced a Pan-African philosophy to inspire a mass movement focusing on Africa known as Garveyism.)

Pediatric cardiac surgery was a relatively young specialty in 1970. Norman Gootman, MD, chief of the Division of Pediatric Cardiology, ran an extremely active clinical and diagnostic service, and patients were attracted locally as well as from more distant areas. These activities helped to build the pediatric cardiothoracic program in the early days.

The requirement for at least fifty pediatric open heart surgical cases per year to maintain

CARDIOTHORACIC SURGERY FACULTY

Chiefs

Early 1960s	Walter Phillips, MD
1967–1977	George Wisoff, MD
1977–1982	Alan Wolpowitz, MD
1982–1989	John Luber, MD
1989–1995	Joseph Amato, MD
1995–1999	Hanni Hannein, MD
2000–present	Vincent Parnell, MD

Staff

2000–2008	Sheel K. Vatsia, MD
2008–present	David Meyer, MD

Ambulatory Visits

2007	547

state accreditation and a teaching program was easily exceeded. The variety and volume of general thoracic and cardiac problems presented

Dr. Joseph Amato with patient, 1990.

for evaluation and care strengthened the clinical and training program.

In 1982 John Luber, MD who came from Children's Hospital Boston, became the first fellowship-trained pediatric cardiac surgeon to be appointed as chief of pediatric cardiothoracic surgery. He and Dr. Gootman continued to expand the scope of cardiology and cardiac surgery services at the children's hospital. Dr. Luber left in 1989, and after a short hiatus, Joseph Amato, MD, a nationally recognized leader in pediatric cardiac surgery, replaced him as chief of the division. The program was further strengthened by the addition of Fredrick Z. Bierman, MD, as chief of the Division of Pediatric Cardiology, who succeeded Dr. Gootman at SCH when he resigned because of a serious illness. In 1994 Dr. Amato carried out the first surgical ligation of the ductus arteriosus in a premature infant at the bedside in the neonatal intensive care unit (NICU). When Dr. Amato left for Chicago in 1995, Hanni Hannein MD, who trained in Ann Arbor and San Francisco, was recruited to become chief of cardiothoracic surgery. By this time, surgical palliation of hypoplastic left heart syndrome and mechanical support of the heart and lungs with extracorporeal membrane oxygenation (ECMO) had been added to the repertoire of the surgical program.

Coincident with the merger that created the North Shore-Long Island Jewish (NS-LIJ) Health System and Dr. Hannein's departure to Cleveland, the existing pediatric cardiothoracic

surgical programs at North Shore University Hospital (NSUH) and at SCH were combined at SCH under the leadership of Vincent Parnell, MD, assisted by Sheel K. Vatsia, MD. Dr. Vatsia resigned in 2008 and David Meyer, MD, was appointed.

In March of 2001, all pediatric cardiac surgery within the health system was moved to SCH. Currently, the program handles over 300 patients per year and has become the second largest in New York State. The division provides surgical treatment of the entire spectrum of congenital heart disease and is an integral part of a large multidisciplinary approach to congenital heart disease at SCH, which includes diagnostic and interventional cardiac catheterization, electrophysiology for children and young adults, complete cardiac imaging, including MRI, CT, and echocardiography, critical care, and the highly specialized care of adults with congenital heart disease.

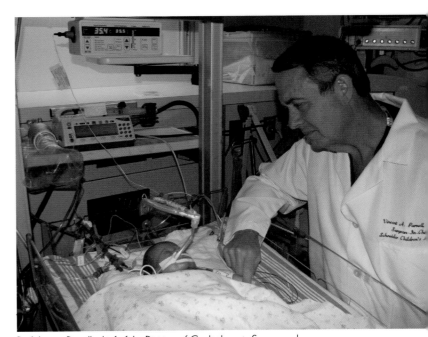

Dr. Vincent Parnell, chief of the Division of Cardiothoracic Surgery and Surgeon-In-Chief, 2000–Present.

GENERAL SURGERY

In 1956, Jerrold Becker, MD, was appointed to the surgical staff of Long Island Jewish Medical Center (LIJ) as the first pediatric surgeon.

Among the earliest group of surgeons in the United States specially trained in the care of

Dr. Jerrold Becker, founding chief of General Surgery from 1956–1985 with patient Ehud Baram and his mother from Israel.

children, he had received training from Robert Gross, MD, at Children's Hospital Boston and C. Everett Koop, MD, at Children's Hospital of Philadelphia. These were the two most prominent figures training the early group of leaders in pediatric surgery in the United States. Dr. Becker established the first pediatric surgical service on Long Island, which rapidly expanded due in part to the large number of obstetrical deliveries at LIJ, the many board-certified pediatricians on staff, as well as the presence of a pediatric residency program. The service became the premier referral center for major pediatric surgical problems. Dr Becker, the founding chief of pediatric surgery at LIJ, attracted a number of pediatric surgeons onto the voluntary staff during the 1960s to the early 1980s as listed in the accompanying faculty list.

In 1958, additions to the staff included Burton Bronsther, MD, who trained at Children's Memorial Hospital in Chicago, and Keith Schneider, MD, who trained at Children's Hospital Boston and in 1960, Martin W. Abrams, MD, who trained at Children's Hospital of Philadelphia.

As the hospital developed, surgical specialization blossomed with the addition of pediatric orthopaedists, urologists, neurosurgeons, anesthesiologists, pathologists, and radiologists. Pediatric surgical conferences were held weekly with attendance by the pediatric radiologists and pathologists. The staff published many pediatric surgical papers in major pediatric and pediatric surgical journals.

In 1975 the American Board of Surgery (ABS) held its first certifying examination in pediatric surgery. This certification was then added to the requirements for appointment to the pediatric surgical staff.

In 1985 Alberto Peña, MD, who specialized in the innovative operative correction of the imperforate anus and other anorectal malformations, was appointed from Mexico City as the new full-time chief of the Division of Surgery at SCH. He was world famous in his field, and his unique expertise added luster to the surgical service at SCH. He conducted regular courses in his operative approach that attracted pediatric surgeons from a total of sixty-four countries all over the world. In January 1997, after he had performed more than 1,000 surgical corrections of anorectal mal-

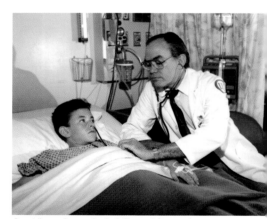

Dr. Alberto Peña, chief of General Surgery from 1985–2005.

formations, his patients honored him at a gala dinner at the Garden City Hotel on Long Island.

In 1996 SCH received official designation as a Regional Pediatric Trauma Center, one of only three in New York State. More than 300 pediatric admissions yearly result from traumatic injuries. The center is directed by Nelson G. Rosen, MD, a surgeon who trained in general surgery at LIJ before completing his pediatric surgery fellowship training at Sainte Justine Hospital for Children in Montreal and joined the faculty at SCH in 2003. He has helped maintain the division's excellence in the management of anorectal malformations and the care of children with these problems.

When Andrew R. Hong, MD, joined the full-time staff in 1997, he was already an established pediatric surgeon, having served on the faculty at the University of Vermont School of Medicine and having been in private practice on Long Island for several years. He earned a reputation at SCH for surgical excellence and led the innovative use of minimally invasive techniques for pediatric surgery. The division has become a regional leader in these modern approaches to children's surgery.

In 1997 SCH established its extracorporeal life support program. It is one of two such programs in the metropolitan area providing extracorporeal membrane oxygenation (ECMO) to desperately ill children who cannot be adequately oxygenated and ventilated by standard means. Between sixteen and twenty newborns and children are placed on ECMO at SCH each year. The pediatric surgical team plays an important role in the placement of lines in these critically ill patients.

The pediatric surgery fellowship program at SCH was approved in 2004 because of the hospital's large surgical volume, particularly for neonatal surgery, and because of its proven reputation for outstanding teaching and education. It is one of only three pediatric surgical training programs in the state and one of only thirty-two in North America. One resident graduates annually from the two-year program. These young surgeons are among the best in the American surgical arena and a distinct achievement and source of pride for SCH.

GENERAL SURGERY FACULTY

Chiefs

1956–1985	Jerrold Becker, MD✝
1985–2005	Alberto Peña, MD
2005–present	Stephen E. Dolgin, MD

Staff

1958–1990	Burton Bronsther, MD✝*
1958–1982	Keith Schneider, MD✝*
1960–2003	Martin W. Abrams, MD✝*
1964–1977	Irwin Krasna, MD✝
1960s–1970s	Kenneth Kenigsberg, MD✝
1960s–1970s	Elizabeth Corrylos, MD✝
1973–present	David Schwartz, MD✝
1976–1995	Henry So, MD✝*
1983–present	Neil Kutin, MD✝
1986–2007	Stuart Bohrer, MD✝
1988–present	Charles Coren, MD✝
1990–1993	Kenneth Kimura, MD
1992–1996	Peter Shrock, MD
1995–present	Andrew R. Hong, MD
1995–present	Edmund Kessler, MD✝
1999–2001	Richard Scriven, MD✝
2001–2002	Thomas Lee, MD✝
2002–2004	Marc Levitt, MD
2002–2004	Peter Midulla, MD
2003–present	Nelson G. Rosen, MD
2003–present	Richard D. Glick, MD
2005–present	Samuel Z. Soffer, MD

✝voluntary faculty, *deceased

Ambulatory Visits

2000	1,518
2007	4,422

Inpatient Admissions

2007	1,122

In 2003 Richard Glick, MD, joined the staff at SCH. His background includes general surgical training at Cornell University and pediatric surgery at Texas Children's Hospital. Dr. Glick spent two years during his general surgery residency at the Memorial Sloan-Kettering Cancer Center gaining expertise in pediatric surgical oncology.

In 2005 Samuel Z. Soffer, MD, joined the staff. He trained in general surgery at LIJ, spent four years at Columbia University in basic science research, and completed his pediatric surgery residency at the Morgan Stanley Children's Hospital of New York-Presbyterian Columbia University Medical Center. He is establishing a career as a clinician-scientist with an appointment to The Feinstein Institute for Medical Research, part of the North Shore-Long Island Jewish Health System, where he is working on pediatric solid tumor angiogenesis and creative ways to inhibit the growth of these tumors by blocking blood vessel formation.

In 2005 Dr. Peña resigned his position to assume the position of head of the newly established Colorectal Center at Cincinnati Children's Hospital Medical Center. Dr. Dolgin, recruited from the Mount Sinai Medical Center in New York City where he held the position of chief of pediatric surgery for many years, replaced Dr. Pena as the chief of general surgery at SCH. Dr. Dolgin had trained in general surgery at Harvard University's Peter Bent Brigham Hospital and in pediatric surgery at Children's Memorial Hospital in Chicago. With his established reputation as an outstanding clinician and educator, Dr. Dolgin brought to SCH his extensive experience with the surgical management of pediatric inflammatory bowel disease.

General surgeons at SCH, 2006. Left to right: Drs. Nelson G. Rosen, Richard D. Glick, Samuel Z. Soffer, Andrew R. Hong, and Stephen E. Dolgin, chief of General Surgery from 2005–present.

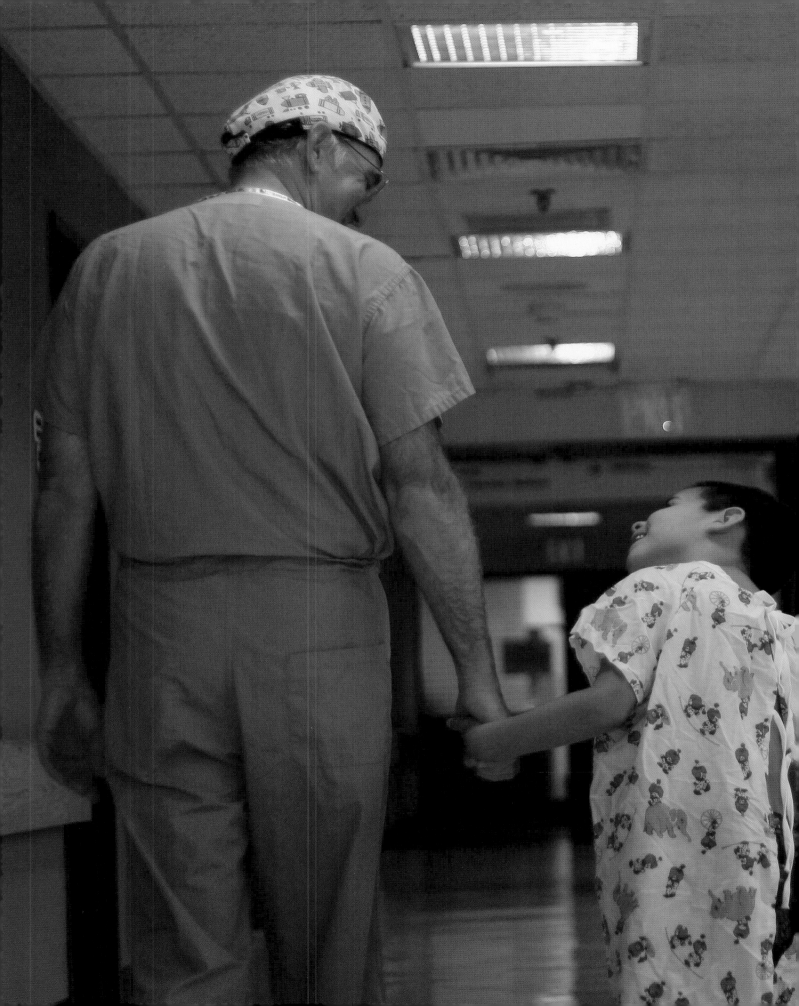

NEUROSURGERY

In 1969, Joseph Epstein, MD, chief of the division of neurosurgery at LIJ, recruited Alan Rosenthal, MD, from Children's Hospital Boston to join his neurosurgery practice in order to develop a regional pediatric neurosurgery division. Dr. Rosenthal trained under Donald Matson, MD, the most prominent leader in the early evolution of the subspecialty. At that time surgical subspecialization was a new concept not universally accepted and pediatric neurosurgery was not even fully recognized as a specialty.

LIJ was forward-thinking at that time, and many of the building blocks required for a sophisticated service were simultaneously being developed. The Division of Neuroradiology at LIJ was initially led by Bernard Epstein, MD, Joseph's brother, a pioneer in that field. Neonatal and pediatric intensive care units were thriving, and their leaders, Philip Lipsitz, MD, and Norman Gootman, MD, lent great support to building pediatric neursurgery. Pediatric neurology, initially led by Marvin Klein, MD, provided a complementary approach to neurologic diseases of childhood. Simultaneous development of the plastic surgery, otolaryngology, ophthalmology, general surgery, and orthopaedic divisions created a well-rounded and multidisciplinary surgical approach to pediatric patients.

Robert Decker, MD, joined the neurosurgery division in 1970 adding special expertise in skull

Drs. Steven Schneider and Mark Mittler, co-divisional chiefs, Neurosurgery (2003-present).

NEUROSURGERY FACULTY	
Chiefs	
1969-1986	Alan Rosenthal, MD✢
1987-2003	Steven Schneider, MD✢
Staff	
1999-2003	Mark Mittler, MD✢
Co-Chiefs	
2003-present	Steven Schneider, MD✢
2003-present	Mark Mittler, MD✢
✢ voluntary faculty	

base pituitary, microscopic, and seizure surgery. Over the next decade, Nancy Epstein, MD, and David Chalif, MD, both joined the group, adding respectively spinal and vascular experience. Each member of the group participated in the care of children during that time.

In 1986, the pediatric patient load was sufficient to recruit Steven Schneider, MD, who had completed a formal fellowship in pediatric neurosurgery with Fred Epstein, MD, at New York University Medical Center. Dr. Schneider became the first board-certified pediatric neurosurgeon on Long Island.

During this time period, the region's pediatric neurosurgical care was predominantly split between the newly created Schneider Children's Hospital and North Shore University Hospital. As the North Shore-Long Island Jewish Health System came to fruition, most neurosurgical cases were operated on at Schneider Children's Hospital.

In 1999 Mark Mittler, MD, was recruited from Children's Hospital of Los Angeles. With the retirement of Dr. Rosenthal, Drs. Schneider and Mittler focused their efforts at Schneider Children's Hospital, while still providing coverage to surrounding hospitals. It was felt that centralization and standardization would enhance the care of children with complex neurological conditions. (N.S. 1)

In 2002 a multidisciplinary brain and spinal cord tumor center with a full-time dedicated coordinator was established.

Advances have also been made in craniofacial surgery, microscopic techniques, endoscopic skull base and intraventricular surgery, epilepsy surgery, and surgery for spacticity.

With world-class research being undertaken at The Feinstein Institute for Medical Research of the North Shore-Long Island Jewish Health System, the Division of Neurosurgery initiated a translational program with Marc Symons, MD,

and Eric Shi, MD. The establishment of a brain tumor bank allowed for the preservation of clinical specimens for research purposes.

In 2007, a pediatric neurosurgical clinic was established to further advance the institution's mission and to provide care to the increasing number of uninsured patients. Schneider Children's Hospital has become the primary provider of neurosurgical care to Long Island's children.

OPHTHALMOLOGY

Prior to 1984, there were no specifically trained pediatric ophthalmologists at Long Island Jewish Medical Center (LIJ); ophthalmology in

Child being examined by ophthalmologist.

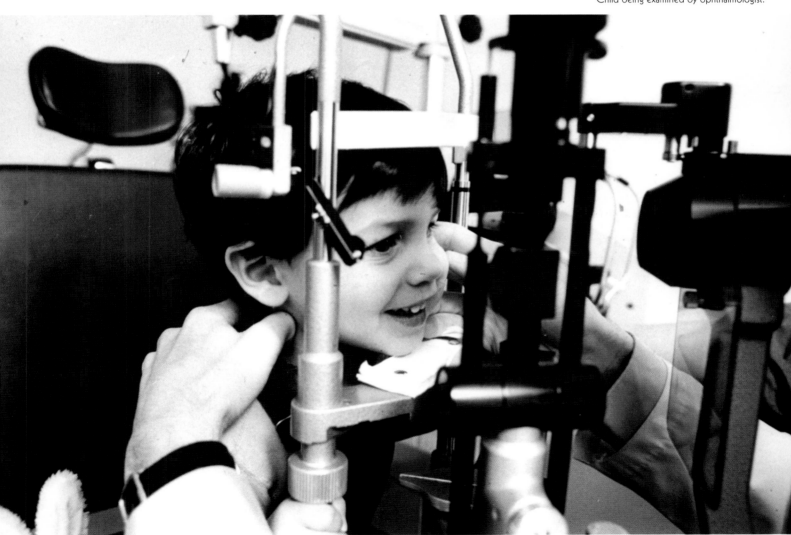

children was practiced by specialists in adult ophthalmology.

The Division of Ophthalmology was formed at the Schneider Children's Hospital (SCH) in 1984 with the appointment of Steven E. Rubin, MD, the first trained pediatric ophthalmologist in the region. Dr. Rubin started an outpatient service and provided inpatient consultations, including an active program in the neonatal intensive care unit (NICU) caring for premature infants with retinopathy of prematurity.

Dr. Rubin moved to the full-time staff of North Shore University Hospital (NSUH) in 1991 and was replaced in 1994 by Sylvia Kodsi, MD, who rebuilt the inpatient and outpatient services. As part of the general migration of outpatient-based specialties and subspecialties to nearby off-campus sites, LIJ and NSUH moved their ophthalmology departments to the same floor of a nearby office building on Northern Boulevard in Great Neck, effecting a partial "merger" prior to the official institutional merger in the late 1990s.

As the Children's Health Network of the Schneider Children's Hospital added satellite offices, Corina Gerontis, MD, joined the attending staff, based primarily at the SCH Satellite Center at Commack, Suffolk County. With advances in retinal surgery, Philip Ferrone, MD, and Eric Shakin, MD, both of whom trained specifically as retinal specialists, were appointed to identify and manage retinal disease with particular reference to retinopathy of prematurity.

OPHTHALMOLOGY FACULTY
Chiefs
1984–1991	Steven E. Rubin, MD
1994–present	Sylvia Kodsi, MD

ORTHOPAEDIC SURGERY AND REHABILITATION MEDICINE

The history and treatment of musculoskeletal injuries and disorders date back to antiquity;

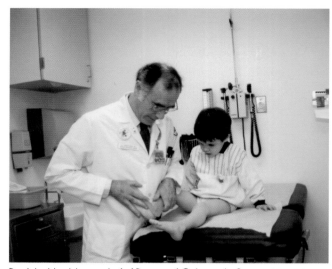

Dr. John Handelsman, chief of Division of Orthopaedic Surgery 1986–2003.

however, the specialty of orthopaedics, as a branch of medicine and surgery, is relatively young. In 1741, Nicholas Andry, then a professor of medicine in Paris, published a book entitled *The Art of Preventing and Correcting Deformities in Children*. In this book, he coined the term *orthopaedia* from the words *orthos* (straight) and *pais* (child).

Prior to 1975 all pediatric orthopaedics at LIJ was carried out by adult orthopaedic surgeons. In 1975 Hormozin Aprin, MD, was the first trained pediatric orthopaedic surgeon appointed as chief of the Division of Pediatric Orthopaedic Surgery at Long Island Jewish Medical Center (LIJ). John E. Handelsman, MD, succeeded him in 1986.

Dr. Handelsman has had a distinguished academic career, has performed seminal research in pediatric orthopaedic surgery, has presented many papers at national meetings, and has published numerous articles and abstracts in peer-reviewed surgical journals. In 2003, David H. Godfried, MD, was appointed chief to succeed Dr. Handelsman.

In 2004 the Division of Pediatric Orthopaedic Surgery and Rehabilitation was separated from the LIJ Department of Orthopaedic Surgery, becoming a formal division within the Schneider Children's Hospital (SCH), and since then it has grown exponentially. While the treatment of pediatric fractures and the management of various congenital and developmental deformities have always represented an important aspect of the care, the scope and volume of services have steadily evolved. The Schneider Children's Hospital has become a major regional referral center for children with a broad range of musculoskeletal injuries and deformities. The program attracts patients from the entire region.

The Division of Orthopaedic Surgery and Rehabilitation Medicine at the Schneider Children's Hospital has developed a local and regional reputation for excellence in the care of fractures, scoliosis, congenital deformities, bone and joint infections, musculoskeletal tumors, hand problems, and impairments related to childhood neurologic disorders such as cerebral palsy and spina bifida. Multidisciplinary programs have been developed to provide state-of-the-art care for children with complex orthopaedic problems. Close interactions between this division and the Divisions of Neurology, Infectious Diseases, and Rheumatology have provided patients a more comprehensive level of care. In recent years, there has been a dramatic increase in the volume of patients with orthopaedic fractures and injuries who have transferred to the hospital's Level I Pediatric Trauma Center.

Since 2003 various specialty programs have developed in orthopaedics in partnership with select, highly specialized surgeons within the region who share a commitment to the treatment of children. Section heads have been appointed in neuromuscular movement disorders, scoliosis and spinal deformity, musculoskeletal tumors, hand and upper extremity, orthopaedic trauma, and clinical and basic science research.

In 2003 the Divisions of Hematology-Oncology and Orthopaedic Surgery and Rehabilitation Medicine developed an interdisciplinary musculoskeletal tumor program that permitted the multidisciplinary management of malignant bone and extremity tumors. Samuel Kenan, MD, coordinated this program.

In 2004 a formal spine program was initiated, led by Dr. Godfried, Anthony Petrizzo, MD, and Jeffrey Silber, MD.

ORTHOPAEDIC SURGERY AND REHABILITATION MEDICINE FACULTY

Chiefs

1975–1986	Hormozin Aprin, MD
1986–2003	John E. Handelsman, MD
2003–present	David H. Godfried, MD

Staff

1987–1994	Kathleen Raggio, MD
1986–present	Hormozin Aprin, MD♦
1999–2006	Harold Von Bosse, MD
1999–2001	Ronald Lewis, MD
2003–present	John E. Handelsman, MD,♦ Research & Education
2004–present	Javier Laplaza, MD, Neuromuscular Movement Diseases
2005–present	Samuel Kenan, MD,♦ Orthopaedic Oncology
2008–present	Anthony Petrizzo, MD,♦ Scoliosis & Spinal Deformities
2004–present	Russell Crider, MD♦
2005–present	Neal L. Hochwald, MD,♦ Hand & Upper Extremities
2001–present	Jeffrey Silber, MD♦ Scoliosis & Spinal Deformities

♦voluntary faculty

Ambulatory Visits

2000	4,126
2007	7,103

Inpatient Admissions

2007	304

The division plays an important role in training orthopaedic and pediatric residents at the Schneider Children's Hospital. Medical students rotating from affiliated medical programs at the Albert Einstein School of Medicine and New York University School of Medicine also spend time in the division as part of their surgical specialty elective.

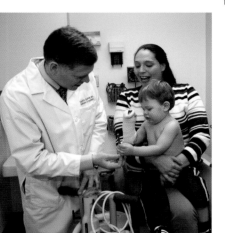

Dr. David Godfried, chief of Orthopaedic Surgery 2003–present, with patient.

Clinical and basic research plays a central part in the academic and teaching mission of the division. There are active clinical research projects underway to evaluate the role of small fragment external fixators for stabilization of the periarticular corrective osteotomies in young children, preoperative regional nerve blocks to improve management of post-surgical pain in children, and prospective data collection related to development of a pediatric spinal deformity program. Basic science studies in progress in collaboration with researchers at The Feinstein Institute for Medical Research of the North Shore-Long Island Jewish Health System are focused on describing the differential response of articular cartilage to injury based on skeletal maturity.

OTORHINOLARYNGOLOGY

Merrill Goodman, MD, was chief of the Division of Otolaryngology at Long Island Jewish Medical Center (LIJ) from 1965 to1973. He was assisted by a number of otolaryngology specialists, none of whom had any specific training in pediatric otolaryngology.

In those years, tonsillectomy and adenoidectomy were the treatments of choice for many childhood ailments. There was a special four-bed room on the pediatric unit on Four South called the "tonsil room," and every day four to six children would be admitted for tonsillectomy. This was before evidence-based medicine became the guiding principle for medical practice. When Philip Lanzkowsky, MD, arrived at LIJ as director of the Department of Pediatrics in 1970, he banned routine tonsillectomy and required specific indications for this surgery. That put a fairly abrupt end to the tonsillectomy business on patients in whom there were no clear-cut indications.

In 1973, Allan Abramson, MD, became the first full-time chief of otolaryngology at LIJ. For the past thirty-five years he has served as the chairman of what is now called the Department of Otorhinolaryngology and Communicative Disorders. He established the residency program in this specialty in 1977. Since its inception, three physicians have pursued a career in pediatric otolaryngology: Ari Goldsmith, MD (1993), trained at Children's Hospital Boston; Michael Mendelsohn, MD (1995), trained at the University of Virginia; and James Batti, MD (1999), trained at Children's Hospital of Pittsburgh.

Bettie Steinberg, PhD, joined Dr. Abramson

Dr. Gerald Zahtz examinimg a patient, 2008.

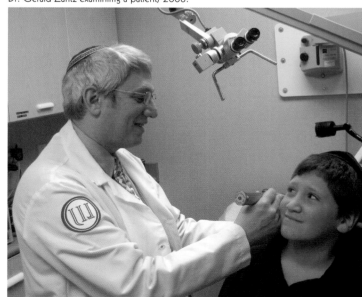

in 1980 as chief of the Division of Research within the Department of Otorhinolaryngology and Communicative Disorders. They have contributed extensive clinical, basic science, and translational research on pediatric laryngeal papillomatosis, carbon dioxide laryngeal surgery, and airway mechanics. The National Institutes of Health (NIH) has awarded this team over $13 million for research in human papillomavirus disease of the larynx. This has resulted in clinical trials using Interferon, photodynamic therapy, and now Celebrex, a COX-2 inhibitor (2007–2012). Drs. Steinberg and Abramson published their landmark work in the *New England Journal of Medicine* (1983) establishing the concept of latent HPV infection of the larynx.

Dr. Abramson handled all the pediatric otolaryngology cases in the 1970s and early 1980s. He was joined by Gerald Zahtz, MD, in 1982, who concentrated on ambulatory otolaryngology, and Mark Shikowitz, MD, in 1987, who concentrated on complex sinus and skull-based surgery in children. These physicians were not specifically trained in pediatric otorhinolaryngology and treat adults as well as children.

Under the direction of Lynn Spivak, PhD, the Hearing and Speech Center became one of the sites in New York State to investigate the efficacy of newborn hearing screening. This procedure has now become the standard throughout New

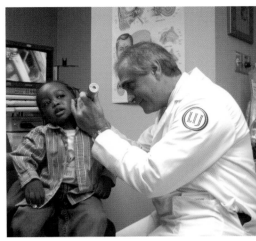

Dr. Mark Shikowitz examinimg a patient, 2008.

York State and the country. The North Shore-Long Island Jewish Health System now averages 23,000 newborn hearing screening studies each year and is the largest screening program in the country.

Andrea Vambutas, MD, developed the cochlear implant program in 2001, which has enabled many children to hear even though they were deaf at birth.

In June 2008, the Department of Otorhinolaryngology and Communicative Disorders moved out of its offices in LIJ into a new expanded facility in the Speech and Hearing Center on the grounds of LIJ.

UROLOGY

Until 1980, Long Island Jewish Medical Center (LIJ) had no specifically trained urologists within the Department of Pediatrics. Children were cared for by adult urologists, predominantly Henry Abrams, MD, and Alfred Sutton, MD.

In 1980 Moneer Hanna, MD, was the first pediatric urologist to be appointed chief with the formation of the Division of Pediatric Urology. In 1985 Dr. Hanna resigned and was succeeded by William A. Brock, MD, who became chief of the Division of Urology at the Schneider Children's Hospital (SCH).

Prior to joining SCH, Dr. Brock was chairman of the Department of Urology at San Diego Children's Health and Hospital Center and an associate professor of surgery (urology) and pediatrics at the University of California San Diego.

Dr. Brock was the author of numerous peer-reviewed articles in pediatric urology and several

OTORHINOLARYNGOLOGY FACULTY

1973–present	Alan Abramson, MD, Chairman
1982–present	Gerald Zahtz, MD
1987–present	Mark Shikowitz, MD
1993–present	Lynn Spivak, PhD
1998–present	Andrea Vambutas, MD

Ambulatory Visits

2000	2,803
2007	3,768

chapters in textbooks of pediatric urology. He lectured at educational meetings of pediatric urology and at pediatric surgical societies throughout the United States, in Europe and South America, and presented several clinical research papers at the annual meetings of the American Urological Association and the American Academy of Pediatrics (AAP) annual meetings.

In 1987 Dr. Brock was appointed a research scholar of the American Foundation for Urologic Diseases and began the first externally funded laboratory research in the Division of Urology at SCH. He studied the use of monoclonal antibodies directed against renal

Dr. Selwyn Levitt, chief of Division of Urology 1999–2005.

tubular antigens in the diagnosis of pyelonephritis. With Mark Rich, MD, a urology resident at LIJ, he began collaborative work on the use of oncogenes in the differentiation of Wilms' tumor and neuroblastoma. Dr. Rich joined the faculty and became the head of the new pediatric urology research laboratory, working with Leslie Kushner, PhD. After three years, Dr. Rich relocated to Orlando, Florida, to become the chief of urology at the Arnold Palmer Women's and Children's Hospital. In 1994 Dr. Brock established a fellowship training program in pediatric urology at SCH. This fellowship is approved by the American Council for Graduate Medical Education (ACGME), one of only fourteen train-

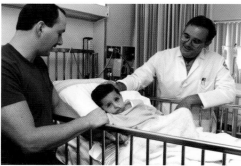

Dr. William A. Brock, chief of Division of Urology 1985–1993.

ing programs in the United States and the only active training program for pediatric urologists in the New York tri-state area and between Boston and Philadelphia as well.

Selwyn Levitt, MD, was appointed chief of the division in 1999. Under his leadership, the clinical volume of the division grew, as did its faculty. Dr. Levitt is a true pioneer in pediatric urology, being the first urologist in New York who committed himself exclusively to pediatric urology. He received the prestigious lifetime award from the National Kidney Foundation. Dr. Levitt received his fellowship training in pediatric urology at Babies Hospital, Columbia Presbyterian Medical Center in New York, and at Hospital for Sick Children at Great Ormond Street in London. He is the author of numerous peer-reviewed scientific papers and chapters in many textbooks on the subject of pediatric urol-

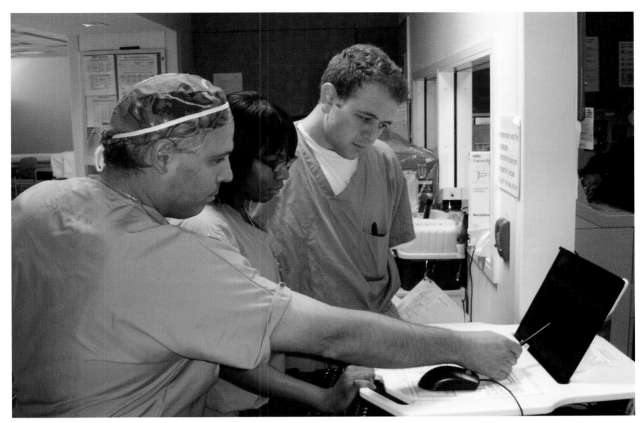

Dr. Lane Palmer, chief of Division of Urology 2005–present.

ogy. Dr. Levitt retired in 2006.

In 2005 Dr. Palmer was promoted to chief of the division and director of the fellowship program. Under Dr. Palmer's direction the faculty grew to ten urologists, the largest division of urology in this country, and developed a national reputation for laparoscopy, reconstructive urologic surgery, and voiding dysfunction.

Dr. Palmer trained in urology at the Montefiore Medical Center in the Bronx and completed research and clinical fellowships in pediatric urology at Children's Memorial Hospital in Chicago. He is associate clinical professor of urology and pediatrics at the Albert Einstein College of Medicine. Dr. Palmer has published 100 papers in the urologic and pediatric literature on different areas of pediatric urology. He has leadership positions in several organizations including the Society for Pediatric Urology, the Kidney and Urology Foundation of America, the National

Kidney Foundation, and the American College of Surgeons. He has directed several national courses and has presented papers at most major international and national urologic meetings. He is on the editorial boards of several journals and is a reviewer for most major urologic journals.

OTHER DEPARTMENTS

PEDIATRIC DENTAL MEDICINE

The Department of Dental Medicine was founded when Long Island Jewish Hospital opened in 1954. The department initially included a Division of Pediatric Dental Medicine. Leon Eisenbud, DDS, the founding chairman of the department, was extremely influential in the development of the children's dental facility within the Schneider Children's Hospital and was involved with its design and architectural nuances together with Saul Kamen, DDS, the first chief of pediatric dentistry.

Both doctors had the foresight to develop a clinical dental facility that was intended to provide comprehensive oral health care to a cadre of medically, physically, and emotionally impaired children and adolescents. Dr. Saul Kamen was considered to be one of the pioneers in the area of dentistry for children with special needs. When the children's hospital opened in 1983, the pediatric dental facility, with its expansive skylight and state-of-the-art dental equipment, provided an unmatched bright and cheerful environment for the provision of dental care to both inpatient and ambulatory children.

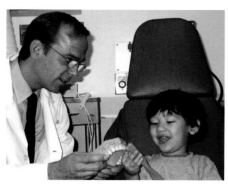

Dr. Ronald Kosinski examining a patient in a dental clinic, 2008.

Under the continued influence of Drs. Kamen and Eisenbud, the children's dental division rapidly developed a reputation for the management of the developmentally disabled and the dental surgical management of children requiring sedation and/or anesthesia for their oral surgical care.

In 1987 Paul V. Crespi, DDS, was appointed chief of the Division of Dental Medicine. He developed the pediatric dental medicine residency curriculum and became the first program director for the two-year pediatric dental residency training program. This post-doctoral training program became fully accredited by the American Dental Association in 1990 with the graduation of the first two pediatric dentists. The program maintained and expanded its involvement in the oral health care of pediatric dental patients, particularly those requiring sedative and anesthetic services to facilitate their dental care. The children's dental program continued to evolve with the assistance of the LIJ Section of Orthodontics and the LIJ Divisions of Oral Pathology and Oral and Maxillofacial Surgery, which specialized in the management of craniofacial and dentofacial anomalies like cleft lip and palate. Stephen Sachs, DDS, chief of oral and maxillofacial surgery, and Stewart Grauer, DDS,

PEDIATRIC DENTAL MEDICINE FACULTY

Chiefs

1954–1985	Saul Kamen, DDS
1987–1997	Paul V. Crespi, DDS
1997–present	Ronald Kosinski, DMD

Chiefs of Oral and Maxillofacial Surgery

1953–1978	Eugene Friedman, DDS, BSD
1973–1988	Stephen Sachs, DDS
1988–1990	Leon Assael, DMD
1990–1993	James Murphy, DMD
1994–2000	John Kelly, DMD
2000–2006	Salvatore Ruggiero, DMD, MD
2006–2007	Ronald Schneider, DDS

Chiefs of Orthodontics

1953–1983	Richard Pasternak, DDS✤
1988–1990	George D'Arienza, DDS✤
1990–1997	Stewart Grauer, DDS✤
1992–2003	Christopher Paladino, DDS✤
2004–present	Kera Kim-Berman, DDS✤

General Pediatric Dental Surgery

1978–present	Charles Pillar, DDS✤
1982–present	Mary George, DDS✤
1997–present	Paul Crespi, DDS
1988–present	Mary Ellen Nesnay, DMD✤
1989–present	Deborah Troy, DDS✤
1990–present	Sharon Essner, DDS✤
1993–present	John Melinski, DMD✤
1997–present	Ronald Kosinski, DMD
2003–present	Jason Glick, DDS✤
2003–present	Dawn Sosnick, DDS✤

✤voluntary faculty

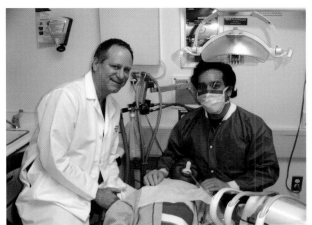

Dr. Paul V. Crespi in dental clinic, 2008.

head of the Section of Orthodontics, played a major role in developing a comprehensive program in the orthognathic management of the child with significant dental and facial anomalies.

Many committed voluntary faculty staff members contributed enormously to the maturation of the pediatric dental residency training program and the expanded dental surgical service the children's dental division provided to the community. Many of the voluntary faculty members have contributed over twenty-five years of didactic and clinical acumen to the residents and have provided an invaluable contribution to the care of the pediatric dental population.

In 1997 Paul V. Crespi, DDS, resigned as chief to enter private practice but he continued as program director until the present time. Ronald Kosinski, DMD, was appointed chief in 1997 and in 2002 he expanded the residency program to include six residents, three in each of the years, which was a testament to the American Dental Association's Commission on Dental Accreditation recognition of the quality of care and training provided at the institution. The Division of Pediatric Dental Medicine continues to provide dental surgical services to a large number of children with unusual concomitant medical and behavioral conditions that preclude their management in the routine dental setting.

CHILD AND ADOLESCENT PSYCHIATRY

In the 1960s the Division of Child and Adolescent Psychiatry consisted of the child psychotherapy unit at the Hillside Hospital, directed by Hershey Marcus, MD. When Dr. Marcus retired, Sol Nichtern, MD, became the first director of the newly named Division of Child Psychiatry and he developed the fellowship program in child psychiatry in the Department of Psychiatry of Long Island Jewish Medical Center (LIJ). The ambulatory clinic for pediatric psychiatry, which became known as the Children's Psychiatric Clinic, was directed first by Jesse Schumer, MD, and subsequently by Rita Reuben, MD. Child and adolescent psychiatry was the first and only recognized subspecialty in psychiatry for the next thirty years.

About 1970 Dr. Nichtern left LIJ and was replaced by Judith Roheim, MD, who was director of child psychiatry until 1977. In the early 1970s the Adolescent Day Hospital was developed at Hillside Hospital. Herbert Levowitz, MD was its first director and was succeeded in 1982 by Stanley Hertz, MD. From 1986 to 1990 Dr. Hertz was in charge of the consultation service in the Schneider Children's Hospital and in 1990 he joined Ronald Shenker, MD, and Michael Nussbaum, MD, in the Eating Disorders Program where he continued to work until 2008.

In 1975 Lawrence Sheff, MD, replaced Dr. Reuben as the director of the Children's Psychiatric Clinic, which was renamed the Child and

CHILD AND ADOLESCENT PSYCHAITRY FACULTY
Chiefs

1960's–1970	Sol Nichtern, MD
1970–1977	Judith Roheim, MD
1977–1985	Stuart Kaplan, MD
1985–1996	Harold Koplewicz, MD
1996–2006	Carmel Foley, MD
2006–Present	Victor Fornari, MD

Family Outpatient Clinic to reflect the growing emphasis on treating families as a whole.

In 1977 Stuart Kaplan, MD, became the chief of the division. He expanded mental health services for children by establishing the consultation service in the Department of Pediatrics at LIJ. He also established the Children's Day Hospital and

Dr. Harold Koplewicz, chief of Division of Child and Adolescent Psychiatry 1985–1996.

began a fledgling research program. At that time treatment still had a significant psychodynamic focus, but Dr. Kaplan, fresh from training with the renowned Salvador Minuchin, MD, in Philadelphia, brought a new skill set in family therapy. Behavior therapy was also starting to be recognized as an effective intervention and was being taught to trainees. Dr. Sheff assumed the role of director of training, as well as being in charge of the outpatient clinic.

When SCH opened in 1983 it had a fifteen-bed inpatient psychiatric unit for children under thirteen years of age, and the psychiatric ambulatory clinic was housed on the ground floor of the children's hospital. Dr. Kaplan played an integral part in the design and program planning for the inpatient service.

In 1983 Dr. Hertz, Dr. Nussbaum, and their group were the first to demonstrate that anorexic patients had significant shrinkage of brain tissue on CT scans.

Burt Weston, MD, was the first chief of the new inpatient psychiatric unit at SCH, succeeded by Victor Fornari, MD, who served in this position from 1984 to 1986, followed by Carmel Foley, MD, from 1986 to 1996. When Dr. Foley became divisional chief in 1996, Gina Padula, MD, became the unit chief, assisted by Stelios Zodiatis, MD. Both resigned their positions in July 2006 when Dr. Foley reassumed responsibil-

ity for both inpatient and consultation services, assisted by Sol Lee, MD. The child psychiatry inpatient unit has developed an excellent reputation in the local and regional community. Its unique location in a tertiary-care children's hospital has allowed for the management of children with complicated medical and psychiatric problems. Over the years, as outpatient services have improved and special education options have expanded, the inpatient unit treats more developmentally disabled children.

Following Dr. Kaplan's departure in 1985, Harold Koplewicz, MD, became divisional chief and served in this position for the next ten years. Since all of the institution-based levels of service were already in place (child inpatient, adolescent inpatient, child and adolescent day treatment, the consultation/liaison service, as well as the hospital-based outpatient clinic), Dr. Koplewicz focused on expanding services into the community with an emphasis on preventive psychiatry. He began an alternative high school program at Hewlett High School where local high school students with emotional problems could receive their education in an annex to the regular high school while being treated on site by a mental health team consisting of a psychiatrist, psychologist, and social worker. This was considered a significant innovation in managing this population of patients. Rather than bringing one child at a time to a hospital-based day program, it was more appropriate and efficient to provide mental health services at the child's school. Versions of this model now exist all over the region. Dr. Koplewicz also established what became known as the School Mental Health Alliance. This was staffed largely by talented psychologists who provided case-based consultation to a myriad of school districts throughout Queens, Nassau, and Suffolk Counties. These teams also provided research-based bully prevention programs as well as trauma treatment to children affected by the September 11, 2001, disaster. Dr. Koplewicz forged integration with the satellite clinic called Hillside Eastern Queens, located in Jamaica, Queens, and also with three elementary-school-based mental health programs in Far Rockaway, Queens.

Following the first World Trade Center attack in 1993, Dr. Koplewicz was able to garner

Dr. Carmel Foley, chief of Division of Child and Adolescent Psychiatry 1996–2006.

wide community- and school-based support to study the children who were trapped on top of the World Trade Center and evacuated by helicopter. Dr. Koplewicz received national recognition for his book entitled *Nobody's Fault*. This was a sorely needed explanation of the psychiatric diseases of children and adolescents with the overall goal of relieving parental guilt for so many things that were clearly not the parents' fault. Dr. Koplewicz also began the publication of a monthly newsletter, the *Youth Mental Health Update*, which was circulated to local professionals and hundreds of school personnel.

Dr. Koplewicz resigned in 1996 to become director of the Child Study Center at New York University School of Medicine and Dr. Foley was appointed divisional chief, a position she held until 2006. The theme of her leadership was ensuring that evidence-based psychotherapy and psychopharmacology be integrated into all services of the division. A particularly innovative program of dialectical behavior therapy for adolescents suffering from borderline personality disorder was instituted. This patient population is well known to overuse expensive institutional services, and the goal of treatment is to maintain such children successfully in the community.

Extensive in-service training took place to bring staff up to date in the provision of cognitive behavior therapy and cutting-edge training in trauma treatment.

The adolescent inpatient service first began at Hillside Hospital in the 1960s and was headed by a series of directors, including Muriel Stra, MD, in the sixties, followed by Mary Friedman, MD, in the late 1960s and early 1970s, Sheldon Novick, MD, in the late 1970s, Dr. Foley in 1980, Glenn Hirsch, MD, in 1986, and Keith Ditkowsky, MD, circa 2000. The current unit chief is Ema Saito, MD, who is assisted by N. Okereke, MD.

The Adolescent Pavilion continues to be a very strong training and clinical service for the local community. In 2003, the space requirements of the Department of Pediatrics had increased so greatly that the Child Psychiatry Outpatient Clinic moved out of SCH. It is currently located in the new Ambulatory Pavilion at Zucker-Hillside Hospital.

In 2006, the Divisions of Child and Adolescent Psychiatry at SCH and NSUH merged, and Dr. Fornari became the chief of the combined division created by the merger.

On the training front, Avi Kreichman succeeded Dr. Sheff until 1991, and was in turn succeeded by Dr. Foley until 1996, followed by Richard Pleak, MD. In 2008, with the merger of the LIJ and NSUH programs, Dr. Fornari became the training program director of both campuses with eighteen trainees in the combined program.

Research topics in the division include prodromal schizophrenia (with NIMH grant funding), bipolar disorder, genetic studies of major mental illnesses, and weight gain secondary to atypical neuroleptics.

Because of space needs at SCH for tertiary medical services, the inpatient psychiatric ward was moved from the children's hospital to Holliswood Hospital in Queens in 2008.

PEDIATRIC PATHOLOGY

Until 1974, all pediatric pathology at Long Island Jewish Medical Center (LIJ) was performed by general pathologists who did not focus on the requirements, subtleties, and nuances of pediatric pathology. However, as pediatric medicine evolved, so did the practice of pediatric pathology, and the understanding that clinico-pathologic relationships in children are different from those in the adult population and required special training and expertise.

In 1974, Elsa Valderrama, MD, was recruited from Mount Sinai School of Medicine in New York. She had completed her pathology residency at the University of Bogota, Colombia, in 1960 followed by a pediatric pathology fellowship. Although there was no formal division of pediatric pathology, Dr. Valderrama was responsible for all anatomic pathology in children.

The role played by pediatric pathology became critical with the opening of the Schneider Children's Hospital (SCH) in 1983. Prior to the 1980s, pathology relied on hematoxylin and eosin staining for morphology supplemented by ultra-structural morphology. The 1980s were characterized by major advances in the field of surgical pathology, one of which was immunohistochemistry. This allowed for antibody recognition and chromogenic localization of specific epitopes in tissue. In addition, flow cytometry has for several years been an integral part of the diagnostic armamentarium in the assessment of hematopathology specimens. More recently, fluorescent in situ hybridization (FISH) and molecular analysis requiring Southern blot or polymerase chain reaction (PCR) analysis have become critical in pediatric pathology diagnosis. All these studies are performed at SCH.

From 1991 until 2005 Dr. Valderrama was chief of the Division of Pathology at the Schneider Children's Hospital. In 2005 Morris Edelman, MD, was appointed chief of pediatric pathology. Dr. Edelman completed his pathology residency in 1996 at the Albert Einstein College of Medicine in the Bronx followed by a one-year

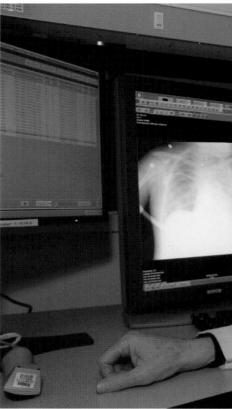

Dr. Edward S. Wind, the first radiologist at LIJ to concentrate on pediatric radiology, 1972 to present.

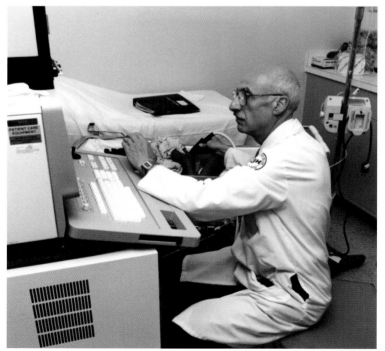

Dr. John C. Leonidas, chief Division of Pediatric Radiology 1984–2002.

cytopathology fellowship. Dr. Edelman had several years of pediatric pathology experience at Montefiore Medical Center and at Winthrop University Hospital. Dr. Edelman has enhanced the activities of the Division of Pathology. He interacts on a daily basis with the clinical divisions at SCH, providing not only routine surgical pathology diagnoses but also intraoperative consultations to the appropriate surgical specialties. The division also participates in subspecialty clinicopathology conferences and is responsible for teaching pathology to residents and fellows.

PEDIATRIC RADIOLOGY

In the mid-1970s, Bernard S. Epstein, MD, who was the first chairman of the Department of Radiology at Long Island Jewish Medical Center (LIJ), gathered his small attending staff together to discuss changing the inner workings of the department.

Up to that time, the radiologist was expected to interpret any film taken. That included patients of all ages, any organ studied, whether there was, for example, a suspected fracture, a duodenal ulcer, or lung cancer. But in the early years of that decade, subspecialization was a growing trend, and hospitals were beginning to implement that practice. The radiology department at LIJ had to adapt. In order to do that, radiologists were expected to become experts in subjects of their interest. Dr. Epstein went around the room and assigned the physicians their new specialties.

Since Edward S. Wind, MD, had been a pediatric resident prior to arriving at LIJ for training in radiology, he was given the title of pediatric radiologist, even though he had no special training in pediatric imaging. However, there were many resources available to help him gain the experience needed to handle an ever-increasing number of pediatric images, including attendance at monthly meetings of the local pediatric radiologists held at the Babies Hospital in New York, national conferences, and textbooks. Perhaps the most important resource was on-the-job training with some of the most dedicated and respected pediatric specialists at the hospital.

Jerrold Becker, MD, and the other members of his superb pediatric surgical group taught Dr. Wind the safest and most accurate way to perform an emergency barium enema on infants suffering from intussusception, a potentially deadly form of intestinal obstruction. Jack Gorvoy, MD, who devoted his pediatric practice

PEDIATRIC RADIOLOGY FACULTY	
Chiefs	
1972–1984	Edward S. Wind, MD
1984–2002	John C. Leonidas, MD*
2002–2008	Daniel Barlev, MD
Staff	
1972–present	Edward S. Wind, MD
2003–present	Jeanne Choi-Rosen, MD
*deceased	

to the care of patients with cystic fibrosis, became a role model for compassion in dealing with the gravely ill patients he served on a daily basis. In the neonatal unit, Philip Lipsitz, MD, provided a source of expertise in the care of the very ill premature infants whose management relied on the changes seen on daily x-rays.

Pediatric patients, with the exception of the neonates, were relegated to the fourth floor of the main building at LIJ. Imaging was performed on the second floor. At that early stage, no special services were provided to differentiate the frightened child from the aging adult in the austere fluoroscopic and conventional radiographic rooms.

As years went by and the Schneider Children's Hospital (SCH) evolved from a dream to a reality, plans were made to provide a full-time pediatric radiology service. John C. Leonidas, MD, who was recognized world wide as an expert in the field, was recruited to become the full-time chief of the Division of Radiology, arriving from the Mount Sinai Hospital the year after SCH opened in 1984. A fellowship program in pediatric radiology was approved by the American Council for Graduate Medical Education (ACGME) and became a training site for future pediatric radiologists. Meanwhile, a revolution was occurring in medical imaging as technologies such as ultrasound, CT scanning, and MRI emerged over the next two decades, providing incredibly crisp head-to-toe images of the body. No longer would films be misplaced as computer monitors now stored digital images which became accessible, not only to the radiologist, but to the clinicians at multiple sites including the emergency department.

After directing the Division of Radiology for nearly twenty years, Dr. Leonidas resigned his position in 2002. Although he continued to work in the department, he died in 2007 of complications of Parkinson's disease. Daniel Barlev, MD, was appointed in 2002 to serve as the new chief. Dr. Barlev came to the Schneider Children's Hospital from Jacobi Medical Center, a major teaching institute of the Albert Einstein College of Medicine in the Bronx, where he had been practicing pediatric radiology for six years. He continued to maintain the high standards demanded for optimum clinical care and brought a dedication, enthusiasm, and continuous presence to the division. Dr. Barlev resigned his position in 2008.

Medical breakthroughs are ongoing phenomena, and a tertiary institution must be in the forefront. The Division of Radiology continues to provide the imaging capability that will ensure that the simple and complex pediatric cases that arrive at the Schneider Children's Hospital are resolved in an expeditious and satisfactory way.

NURSING

The Department of Nursing at Schneider Children's Hospital (SCH) has a rich tradition

DIRECTORS OF NURSING	
1971–1974	Marie Monaco (Four South-LIJ)
1974–1985	Mary Lou Martin (Four South-LIJ & SCH)
1985–1987	Kathy Kane
1987–1991	Gloria Blatti
1991–1993	Lucille O'Leary
1993–1995	Rita Fogel
1995–1999	Elaine Rosenblum
1999–2002	Linda Vassallo
2002–present	Carolyn Quinn

Jane Moore, RNNP, Pediatric Hematology-Oncology Nurse Practitioner, circa early 70s

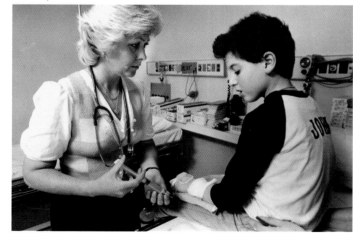

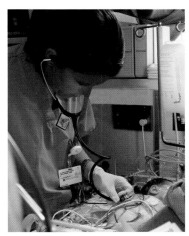

Lori McKee, RN,CCRN, Pediatric Critical Care Nurse, 2006

of dedicated, compassionate care. In its early years, the department consisted of registered nurses (RNs) and licensed practical nurses (LPNs). It grew into a robust department of more than 600 RNs, many of whom are practicing as nurse practitioners and clinical nurse specialists in various specialty areas. A large percentage of the nurses are credentialed by the American Association Credentialing for Nursing (AACN) in their specialty. SCH, as part of LIJ, was the first children's hospital in New York State to receive Magnet Award status in recognition of nursing excellence.

The development of a vibrant nursing education program has brought to the bedside a team of competent, knowledgeable, critical-thinking individuals who provide care of the highest quality. Under the leadership of a director of nursing education, nurse educators conduct orientation programs to meet the needs of new graduate nurses and offer continuing support to the staff. This division, together with the nursing leadership team, was able to produce the first evidence-based nursing journal (*Pediatric Nursing Journal-PNJ*) written for nurses by nurses.

SCH's nursing staff has collaborated with the patient care team in the development of nursing care standards (standards of care, standards of practice). These tools enable the nursing staff to provide patient care of consistently high quality. As technology advances, these tools will continue to support evidence-based nursing practice.

Under the leadership of a strong nursing administration consortium, the Department of Nursing is well recognized and respected in the wider nursing community and is a favorite destination for nursing students from many nursing schools.

SCH has been fortunate and privileged to have had a series of highly talented and committed nurse executives. Each of the leaders have brought their own talents and has contributed to the remarkable success of nursing at the children's hospital.

SOCIAL WORK

The Department of Social Work Services, as part of the Long Island Jewish Medical Center (LIJ), has had a distinguished forty-five-year history.

At its inception, the department provided social work staff in the inpatient and outpatient medical and surgical services and in the Division of Child and Adolescent Psychiatry as well as in the Division of Developmental and Behavioral Pediatrics, including the early intervention program. The department initially had twenty-five social workers; it has grown to thirty-five social workers as of 2008. Currently there is a greater emphasis on inpatient and outpatient medical and surgical services, as there are fewer community agencies to care for the multiple needs of children and adolescents with acute and chronic illnesses. In addition, we have an extensive continuum of care for eating disorders and well-established health centers in high-risk and/or alternative schools. SCH is located in one of the most culturally diverse populated areas in the United States and the Department of Social Work Services is sensitive to the needs of this multicultural hospital population. Services are tailored to

DIRECTORS OF SOCIAL WORK

1983–1989	Ruth Blustein, CSW
1989–1995	Diana Guida Brown, LCSW
1995–present	Kathleen Krieg, LCSW, MBA

various ethnic and cultural groups.

The mission of the Department of Social Work Services is to meet the psychosocial needs of children and families in order to maximize the physical and psychological health of all. It has also been a major contributor to assessing and advocating for the needs of the child and family for quality discharge planning while contributing to considerable reduction in length of stay of hospital patients. It has been in the forefront of aiding families by integrating new insurance legislation for access to care for children (Child Health Plus) as a component of all social work interaction with families. A hallmark of the department has been assisting the medical team in determining issues of neglect and abuse and working with liaison agencies to assist families in these situations. It was instrumental in the creation of the Queens Child Advocacy Center (QCAC), which provides comprehensive psychosocial investigation and medical management of sexually and physically abused children in that county.

Child who lost a parent sends a message from Camp Hope.

The department has always been viewed as having an innovative, high-quality graduate program, sought after by many candidates. It provides training in medical and psychiatric social work to social work interns from all metropolitan New York graduate schools of social work.

The department utilizes a continuity-of-care model of social work within the specialty medical services. Each patient and family is assigned a primary social worker upon diagnosis. Whether the patient is treated as an inpatient or an outpatient, the same social worker will meet with the patient and family to assess needs and determine a plan of care. This increases the support the family comes to rely on, as the social worker is aware of changes that the patient goes through during medical management. It also maximizes the social worker's contact with the child and family, increasing the ability to follow through on both concrete service referrals and psychological support. In addition, the social worker is much better equipped to manage his or her caseload of families since he or she can determine differing levels of psychosocial support required by families in different situations.

The Department of Social Work Services has also received grant support to explore a number of innovative programs and integrate best models of care. By implementing psychosocial support services early in the medical treatment of patients with failure to thrive, it was able to decrease the number of admissions in children with this diagnosis. In addition, a series of educational pamphlets for parents of infants and toddlers was developed to assist families with some of the issues that commonly lead to referrals to child protection agencies.

In February 2002 the department received a grant from Baptist Medical Center of Memphis, Tennessee, to assist children and adolescents who had been affected by the 9/11 tragedy as well as grieving families. The Center for HOPE (Healing, Opportunity, Perseverance and Enlightenment) was opened with the grant. The program provides free social work support to children and their families who have experienced the loss of a parent or sibling. The center has become a beacon of support for families from a wide geographic area who have experienced the unfortunate loss of a child from all types of situations and medical diagnoses. In addition, many community agencies and schools for education and training regarding children's grief services frequently consult the center for help in meeting the needs of grieving families.

The Society for Social Work Leadership in

A bird from the Bronx Zoo Outreach Program sits on a young patient's head.

"Lefty," a golden retriever, in the pet therapy program patiently allows a young patient to pet him.

Child using a computer in the Resource Center.

Health Care named Kathleen Krieg the National Health Care Social Work Leader of the Year in 2002.

The Department of Social Work Services has responded to the changing needs of children, adolescents, and their families as advances in medicine have occurred simultaneously with changes in the social, economic, and political environments.

CHILD LIFE

The Child Life Program was established in 1983 at the time SCH opened and has been generously supported throughout the years by the Children's Medical Fund of New York (CMF). Prior to 1983 the entire department of pediatrics had only one playroom attended by a volunteer play therapist. There were no professionals responsible for the supervision of the playroom. At the present time eleven child life specialists are available throughout the hospital six days a week in addition to a certified music therapist and an art therapist. Our Child Life Program provides many special activities for our patients to help ease the stress of hospitalization.

A visit to the hospital can be traumatic for any youngster, and hospitalized children require comfort and emotional support from trained professionals who recognize and understand their unique needs. Specialists from our Child Life Program help children continue normal development, as well as recuperate from the emotional and physical effects of illness.

The Child Life Program offers pediatric patients and their families a sense of normalcy and choice, thus helping them to respond to their hospital experience in a positive way, which includes providing age-appropriate play opportunities. Play helps develop a sense of mastery in this challenging setting and enables the child to exert control over some aspects of his or her environment. Appropriate developmental medical play is used as a way of making children aware of what is likely to happen next in their hospital experience and how they can best get through it.

In order to assist parents and children accessing information concerning their illness, a Resource Center has been developed consisting of an array of books providing medical information in lay terms and computers for searching

DIRECTORS OF CHILD LIFE	
1983–1990	Joan Chan
1991–2000	Susan Wjotasik
2000–2005	Joan Alpers
2005–2007	Michelle Neuhaus
2008–present	Ann Marie DeFrancesca

Music therapist with patients.

Clown blows bubbles for young patients.

Art therapist painting with patients.

First director of the Child Life Program of SCH, Joan Chan, in playroom with children, mid-1980s.

medical information. A medical librarian, ready to assist any patient searching for information, staffs the center.

In order to accomplish the objectives of child life, various programs have been developed.

Pet Therapy

This program offers emotional support and comfort to patients by providing therapeutic interactions with specially trained dogs and occasionally other animals, birds, and reptiles. This therapy is offered in an effort to normalize the environment and help reduce the stress of hospitalization. In addition, pet therapy may enhance positive physical, cognitive, emotional, and social interactions. Each volunteer handler of these pets must complete volunteer training through the Schneider Children's Hospital Volunteer Services, and all therapy dogs must pass a series of skill and aptitude tests to become certified.

Music Therapy

This program allows for the expression of complex thoughts, feelings, and emotions. Music therapy supports medical treatment and can reduce the intensity of pain, decrease the length of a hospital stay, and increase positive feelings. The music therapist at SCH is a board-certified professional who uses music to effect positive changes in the psychological, physical, cognitive, or social functioning of individuals with health or educational problems.

Clown Care Therapy

"Clown doctors" are specially selected professional performers who are trained to work in the sensitive hospital environment. The clown doctors make one-on-one bedside visits throughout the hospital. They spread their specialized humor therapy to help bring a smile to the faces of children and their family members.

Art Therapy

When children are in the hospital, they often find it easier to communicate through art rather than through verbal means. Through this program, children use pictures and metaphors to explore their emotions related to their illness. Patients are free to choose the type of art they are most comfortable with, whether it is drawing, painting, collage, or sculpture. Art therapy can take place at the bedside or in the playrooms, with patients of all ages participating. The making of art encourages children and adolescents to share their creativity and meaningful insights into their hospital experience.

Scenes from graduation ceremonies at SCH 1988–2008

THE ALUMNI AND MEDICAL STAFF

From its beginning in 1954 until June 30, 2008, a total of 1,294 pediatricians and pediatric sub-specialists graduated from the training program. During my tenure as chairman of pediatrics I personally trained and shepherded close to one thousand of these graduates through the three years of the program.

The fellowship programs commenced in the late 1960s, with neonatology and cardiology followed by hematology. By June 30, 2008, a total of 433 fellows had graduated from twenty training programs at Schneider Children's Hospital. I personally trained 38 hematologist-oncologists during my tenure as chief of that division from 1970 until 2000.

The graduates of the program have settled in many states in this country and in many countries abroad. They have made major contributions in providing pediatric care in their communities, and many occupy top academic and leadership positions.

What follows is a directory of the alumni of the programs from their inception.

GUIDE TO THE ALUMNI DIRECTORY

ALUMNI BIOGRAPHICAL INFORMATION

This directory includes updated biographical information for alumni who responded to our survey. In some cases, alumni information appears as obtained through our research. Information on some alumni is sketchy despite our efforts to obtain more complete data. We apologize in advance for any omissions or errors. This section lists each alumnus alphabetically with the following information (if available):

- Graduation year in pediatrics
- Graduation year in subspecialty
- Address
- Email address

Where pediatrics or the subspecialty is not followed by a date, training did not occur at LIJ or SCH. The asterisk indicates that the individual is deceased.

ALUMNI BY YEAR OF GRADUATION

This section lists alumni by the final year of their residency or fellowship training.

ALUMNI BY GEOGRAPHIC LOCATION

This section lists alumni by the state or country they reside in. The name is followed by the year of graduation.

ALUMNI BY SPECIALTY

This section lists alumni by their medical specialty of study. The name is followed by the year of graduation.

ALUMNI APPOINTED CHIEF RESIDENTS

This section lists the alumni who were appointed chief residents from 1954 to 2008. The asterisk before a name indicates the individual is deceased.

ALUMNI APPOINTED TO FULL-TIME FACULTY

This section lists alumni appointed to the full-time faculty, specialty and year of graduation from SCH. The asterisk before a name indicates the individual is deceased. The cross following a name indicates that he or she served as chief resident.

MEDICAL STAFF DIRECTORY

This section lists all the medical staff appointed from 1954 to 2008. All members of the medical staff hold an MD, DO, DDS, DMD, or PhD degree. Those in bold type at one time or another have been members of the full-time faculty. The asterisk before a name indicates the individual is deceased.

International map indicating locations of house staff origins.

ALUMNI BIOGRAPHICAL INFORMATION

ABDULRAHMAN, Eiman *Pediatrics 2008;* 260-33 Langston Avenue (Apt 1), Glen Oaks, NY 11004 *eiman144@yahoo.com*

ABELS, Jane *Pediatrics 1973;* 422 Linden Avenue, Westfield, NJ O7090

ACKERMAN-STEINBOCK, Gila *Pediatrics 2003;* 2790 Lafayette Drive, Boulder, CO 80305 *glaack@hotmail.com*

ACS, Hedda *Pediatrics 1959, Neonatal-Perinatal Medicine;* 78 Hilltop Drive, Manhasset, NY 11030

ADAMS, Lawrence *Pediatrics 1985, Gastroenterology 1987;* 5325 Greenwood Avenue (Suite 304), West Palm Beach, FL 33407

ADARAMOLA-OJO, Mojisola *Pediatrics 2006;* 465 Scarsdale Road, Tuckahoe, NY 10707

ADEYINKA, Adebayo *Pediatrics, Critical Care Medicine 2008;* 697 Crescent Street, Brooklyn, NY 11208

ADLER, Liora *Pediatrics 2004;* Coral Springs Medical Center, 201 Sample Road, Pompano Beach, FL 33065 *liora00@yahoo.com*

AEINITZ, Jennifer *Pediatrics 2001;* 1770 Motor Parkway, Hauppauge, NY 11749 *drjenn10@optonline.net*

AGGARWAL, Alpna *Pediatrics 2008;* Children's Hospital Boston, 300 Longwood Avenue, Boston, MA O2115 *agoyal@nyit.edu*

AHLUWALIA, Amardeep *Pediatrics, Neonatal-Perinatal Medicine 2006;* Phoenix Children's Hospital, 901 East Willetta Street (Suite 2503), Phoenix, AZ 85006

AHMAD, Saed *Pediatrics 2006, Rheumatology;* 300 South Wells Street, Sisterville, WV 26175 *saed_ahmed@yahoo.com*

AIDLEN, Jeremy Todd *Surgery 2008;* 330 Sunderland Road (Unit 78), Worcester, MA O1604 *jaidlen@charter.net*

ALENICK, D. Scott *Pediatrics 1987, Cardiology;* 200 Closter Dock Road, Closter, NJ O7624 *salenick@pvhospital.org*

ALEXANDER-MURUGIAH, Vanaja *Pediatrics 2007;* *vanaalexander@yahoo.com*

*ALI, Asad *Pediatrics, Neurology 1986*

ALKON, Jaime *Pediatrics 2003, Cardiology;* Dupont Children's Hospital, 15 Georgetown Plaza, Georgetown, DE 19947 *jalkon@hotmailcom*

ALLAWI, Diane *Pediatrics 1981;* 7 Park Street, Norwalk, CT O6851

ALSHANSKY, Anna *Pediatrics 1996, Neurology 1998;* 69 Sand Pit Road (Suite 300), Danbury, CT O6810 *aalshansky@hotmail.com*

ALTMAN, Stuart *Pediatrics 1977;* 50 Underhill Blvd, Syosset, NY 11791 *saltman@kidfixer.com*

ALVARADO, Doris *Pediatrics 1985, Cardiology;* 10 Swans Mill Lane, Scotch Plains, NJ O7076

ALVARADO, Nestor *Pediatrics 1996;* Mid-Atlantic Permanente Medical Group, 20407 Seneca Meadow Parkway, Germantown, MD 20876 *nestor.a.alvarado@kp.org*

ALVAREZ, Miguel *Pediatrics 1978, Child Psychiatry 1980;* 215 Sixth Avenue, Greenport, NY 11944 *malvarez@optonline.net*

AMANULLAH, Adoor *Pediatrics, Hematology-Oncology 1976;* Beaumont Hospital, 3577 West 13 Mile Road, Royal Oak, MI 48073 *adoor@umich.edu*

AMARO-GALVEZ, Rodolfo *Pediatrics 1999, Pulmonary Medicine;* University of Texas Health Center at Tyler, 11937 U.S. Highway 271, Tyler, TX 75708 *rodolfo.amaro@uthct.edu*

AMIGO, Therese *Pediatrics 1993;* 105 Ramona Drive, Muskogee, OK 74401 *tamigo@pol.net*

AMISOLA, Rogelio *Pediatrics, Adolescent Medicine 2003;* 2322 Lakeview Drive, Beavercreek, OH 45431

AMODIO, Stefano *Pediatrics 1996, Cardiology 1999;* St. John's Hospital, 90-02 Queens Blvd., Elmhurst, NY 11373 *dioamo@aol.com*

AMOONA, Raphael *Pediatrics 1970, Hematology-Oncology 1973;* 1573 Broadway, Hewlett, NY 11557

ANAND, Shikha *Pediatrics 2001;* 20 York Street, New Haven, CT O6504

ANDERSON, Nancy *Pediatrics 1985, Hematology-Oncology 1986;* 7837 East Walnut Ridge Road, Orange, CA 92869 *gsdoc@earthlink.net*

ANDREWS, Diana *Pediatrics 1988;* 5900 North Burdick Avenue, East Syracuse, NY 13057 *eastsidepeds@hotmail.com*

ANG, Renato *Pediatrics 1995;* 902 Lexington Circle (Apt F), Edinburg, TX 78539

ANTHONY, Thiele Umali *Pediatrics, Infectious Diseases 1998;* 121 South Front Street, Seaford, DE 19973

ANTOKOLETZ, Marilyn *Pediatrics 1967;* 32 Shelter Rock Road, Manhasset, NY 11030 *hoffmanmarilyn@aol.com*

APEATU, Samuel *Pediatrics, Neurology 1994;* 347 North Smith Avenue, St. Paul, MN 55102

APFEL, Howard *Pediatrics 1992;* 823 Winthrop Road, Teaneck, NJ O7666

APOLLONSKY, Nataly *Pediatrics, Hematology-Oncology 2007;* St. Barnabus Medical Center, 94 Old Short Hills Road, Livingston, NJ O7039

APPEL, Cheryl *Pediatrics 1984;* Andrus Children's Center, 1156 North Broadway, Yonkers, NY 10701 *cappel@jdam.org*

APPLEBAUM, Eric *Pediatrics, Allergy-Immunology 1992;* 50 Cherry Hill Road, Parsippany, NJ O7054

ARANDA, Diane *Pediatrics 2005;* Morris Heights Health Center, 85 West Burnside Avenue, Bronx, NY 10453 *daranda@mhhc.org*

ARBITMAN, Mikhail *Pediatrics 1985;* 102-10 66th Road (Suite 1G), Forest Hills, NY 11375

ARBITMAN, Raisa *Pediatrics 1985;* 102-10 66th Road (Suite 1G), Forest Hills, NY 11375 *ryeagermd@pol.net*

ARDEN, Martha *Pediatrics, Adolescent Medicine 1990;* 706 Esplanade, Pelham, NY 10803

ARENA, Marina *Pediatrics 2004;* 5 Pinnacle Drive, Newtown, CT 06470

ARNOLD, Lisa *Pediatrics 2008;* *lisagold@aol.com*

ARONOFF, David *Urology, 2003;* 3612 22nd Place, Lubbock, TX 79410

ARORA, Satish *Pediatrics 1980, Endocrinology;* 3 Regents Park, East Amherst, NY 14051

ARROYO, Alexander *Pediatrics 2005, Emergency Medicine 2008;* 1758 East 38th Street, Brooklyn, NY 11234 *aarroyomd@gmail.com*

ARYEL, Ron *Pediatrics 1996;* 3732 Jefferson Street, Kansas City, MO 64111 *raryel@att.net*

ASCHETTINO, Diana *Pediatrics, Adolescent Medicine 2008;* *dianalynnaschettino@hotmail.com*

ASHOURZADEH, Kourosh *Pediatrics 1993;* 37 Meridian Road, Levittown, NY 11756 *caringpeds@optonline.net*

ASRA, Irfan *Pediatrics 2002, Endocrinology 2004;* 4260 Main Street, Flushing, NY 11355

AUERBACH, Harvey *Pediatrics 1980;* 62 Pine Tree Drive, Centerville, MA 2632

AUNG, Lei *Pediatrics 1992;* 7 Barkley Court, Monmouth Junction, NJ O8855

AUYEUNG, Valerie *Pediatrics 2002;* 214 Rochambeau Avenue, Providence, RI O2906

AVARELLO, Jahn *Pediatrics 2005, Emergency Medicine;* 750 East Adams Street, Syracuse, NY 13210
avarellj@upstate.ed8u

AVARICIO, Elizabeth *Pediatrics 2002;* 95-11 101 Avenue, Ozone Park, NY 11416

AVSHALOMOV, Gad *Pediatrics 1999, Allergy-Immunology 2001;* 560 Northern Blvd., Great Neck, NY 11020

AVVOCATO, Gloria P. *Pediatrics 1994;* 222 Westchester Avenue (Suite 202), New Rochelle, NY 10604
pgpmd2003@optonline.net

AYDIN, Scott *Pediatrics 2006, Critical Care Medicine 2008;* 240 East 47th Street (Apt 18E), New York, NY 10017
saydin@nshs.edu

AYGUN, Banu *Pediatrics, Hematology-Oncology 2000;* St. Jude Children's Research Hospital, 332 North Lauderdale, Room S4039, Memphis, TN 38105
banu.aygun@stjude.org

AYYAGARI-SIEGEL, Subhadra *Pediatrics 2007, Allergy-Immunology 2010;* Schneider Children's Hospital, 269-01 76th Avenue, New Hyde Park, NY 11040
ssiegel@nshs.edu

AZAM, Shabana *Pediatrics, Neurology 1996;* Brookdale Hospital Medical Center, One Brookdale Plaza, Brooklyn, NY 11212

BABINSKI, Eleanor *Pediatrics 1996;* 380 Dogwood Avenue, Franklin Square, NY 11010

BACHMAN, Michael *Pediatrics 2001;* 3872 Porter Street Northwest (Apt D358), Washington, DC 20016

BAER, Aryeh *Pediatrics, Infectious Diseases 2005;* Hackensack University Medical Center, 30 Prospect Avenue, Hackensack, NJ O7601

BAILEY, Beth *Pediatrics, Developmental &Behavioral Pediatrics 2003;* 36 Guilroy Street, Glen Cove, NY 11542

BAILEY, Denyse *Pediatrics 2000;* 39978 Mary Helen Way, Leonardtown, MD 20650
drbailey69@hotmail.com

BAIN, Russell *Pediatrics 1990, Nephrology;* 5132 U.S. Highway 19, New Port Richey, FL 34652

BAKERYWALLA, Rubina *Pediatrics 2006, Neurology 2009;* 24 Darina Court, Hempstead, NY 11550
docrubina1@aol.com

BALASNY, Jennifer *Pediatrics 1997;* 458 First Street, Brooklyn, NY 11215

BALBUS, Michael *Pediatrics 1988, Neonatal-Perinatal Medicine;* 201 State Street, Erie, PA 16550

BALDAUF, Mary *Pediatrics 2000, Critical Care Medicine 2003;* Brookdale Hospital Medical Center, One Brookdale Plaza, Brooklyn, NY 11212

BALMAGIYA, Tovy *Pediatrics 1987;* 14-16 Heyward Street, Brooklyn, NY 11211

BALSON, Boris *Pediatrics 1994;* 1180 Beacon Street, Brookline, MA 2446

BANDEL, Jack *Pediatrics 1993;* Hospital de Clinicas Caracas Av., Panteon Cons. 429 San Bernardino, Caracas, Venezuela
jbandel@pol.net

BANGUG, Samuel *Pediatrics , Hematology-Oncology 2001;* 4250 Broadway, New York, NY 10033

BANKS, Mitchell *Pediatrics 1981, Child and Adolescent Psychiatry 1988;* 399 Conklin Street (Suite 305), Farmingdale, NY 11735
mbanksmd@msn.com

BARILARI, Rafael *Pediatrics 1997;* 201 Lyons Avenue, Newark, NJ O7112

BARKAN, Craig *Pediatrics 2003;* 111 Arrandale Blvd., Exton, PA 19341

BARLEV, Dan *Pediatrics 1991, Radiology ;* 114 Patton Blvd., New Hyde Park, NY 11040

BARLOW, Douglas *Pediatrics 1992;* Boca Raton Community Hospital, 8194 Glades Road, Boca Raton, FL 33434

BASSOUL, Albert *Pediatrics 1999;* 2149 East 5th Street, Brooklyn, NY 11223
albassoul@yahoo.com

BATAYKIN, Yelena *Pediatrics, Adolescent Medicine 2007;* 2530 Ocean Avenue (Apartment C6), Brooklyn, NY 11229

BATTISTA, Anthony *Pediatrics 1983;* 173 Mineola Blvd (Suite 100), Mineola, NY 11501
ajbattista@aol.com

BAYRAK, Beril *Pediatrics, Hematology-Oncology 2001;* 43 Columbia Place (Apt 11), Brooklyn, NY 11201

BEARD, Rachel *Pediatrics 2000;* 810 Geronimo Drive, Frederick, MD 21701

BEKKER, David *Pediatrics 1977;* 115 Commonwealth Avenue, Dedham, MA O2026

BELLIN, Anne *Pediatrics, Critical Care Medicine 2005;* New York Methodist Hospital, 506 Sixth Street, Brooklyn, NY 11215
aebellin@hotmail.com

BELLOTTI, Christopher *Pediatrics 2008;* Rainbow Babies & Children's Hospital, 11100 Euclid Avenue, Cleveland, OH 44106
cbelloti@hotmail.com

BELOSTOTSKY, Olga *Allergy-Immunology 2005;* 350 East 82 Street, New York, NY 10028

BENERI, Christy *Pediatrics 2005, Infectious Diseases 2008;* 32 Restful Lane, Levittown, NY 11756
christybny@aol.com

BENJAMIN-THORPE, Solange *Pediatrics, Critical Care Medicine 2005;* 260-23 Union Tpke, Glen Oaks, NY 11004

BENNETT, Douglas *Pediatrics 1996;* 485 Titus Avenue, Rochester, NY 14617

BEN-ZEEV, Uri *Pediatrics 1979;* 9 Schenck Avenue, Apt 1G, Great Neck, NY 11021

BERCHIN, Bernard *Pediatrics 1992;* 1807 Avenue P, Brooklyn, NY 11229

BERGER, Karl *Pediatrics, Hematology-Oncology 1974;* 1141 Franklin St, Johnstown, PA 15905
smart_doc@msn.com

BERGER, Jay *Pediatrics 2002;* 2 ProHealth Plaza, Lake Success, NY 11042
jberger@prohealthcare.com

BERGTRAUM, Marcia *Pediatrics 1977, Neurology 1982;* 3003 New Hyde Park Road, New Hyde Park, NY 11042
drmb@optonline.net

BERGWERK, Ari *Pediatrics 1992;* 4650 Sunset Blvd (MS78), Los Angeles, CA 90027

BERGWERK, Katherine *Pediatrics 1992;* 444 South San Vincente Blvd., Los Angeles, CA 90027

BERLIN, Hilary *Pediatrics 1990, Physical Medicine & Rehabilitation 2004;* 1800 Rockaway Avenue (Suite 100), Hewlett, NY 11557
pmr4kids@aol.com

BERLIN, Paul *Pediatrics 1988;* 188 Frier Mill Road (Suite A1), Turnersville, NJ O8012
pjberlin@pol.net

BERMAN, David *Pediatrics 1998, Infectious Diseases;* University of South Florida College of Medicine, 880 Sixth Street South (Suite 240), St Petersburg, FL 33701
bermand@allkids.org

BERMAN, Lori *Pediatrics 1995;* 99 South Central Avenue, Valley Stream, NY 11580
valleystreampeds@optonline.net

BERMAN, Robert *Pediatrics 1965*

BERNSTEIN, Frederic *Pediatrics 2006;* 344 First Street, Mineola, NY 11501
fbernste@iris.nyit.edu

BEUZEVILLE, Carlos *Pediatrics 1972;* 640 West Boston Post Road, Mamaroneck, NY 10543

BHASKAR, Mahesh *Pediatrics 2003;* Queens-Long Island Medical Group, 350 South Broadway, Hicksville, NY 11801
mbhask@hotmail.com

BHATIA, Narinder *Pediatrics, Critical Care Medicine 1997;* Texas Tech University Health Science Center, 3601 Fourth Street, Lubbock, TX 79430

BICHOTTE, Sophia Ligonde *Pediatrics 2005;* 112-18 Springfield Blvd., Queens Village, NY 11429

BIENSTOCK, Jeffrey *Pediatrics 1988;* 20-20 Fair Lawn Avenue, Fair Lawn, NJ O7410
jbienstock@verizon.net

BIGWOOD, Jonathan *Pediatrics 2003;* East Texas Medical Center, 18780 Three Lakes Road, Tyler, TX 75703
jmbigwood@yahoo.com

BILOG, Agnes *Pediatrics, Developmental & Behavioral Pediatrics 1998;* 5020 Shea Blvd, Scottsdale, AZ 85254

BINDRA, Tejwant *Pediatrics , Neurology 2006;* Department of Neurology, Stony Brook University Hospital, Stony Brook, NY 11794

> To study the phenomena of disease without books is to sail an unchartered sea, while to study books without patients is not to go to sea at all.
>
> —Sir William Osler
>
> (1849-1919)

BIRNBAUM, Lynette *Pediatrics 2003;* 124 Main Street, Huntington, NY 11743
lbirn01@hotmail.com

BISWAS, Saumitra *Pediatrics 1997, Cardiology; Critical Care Medicine;* 2149 South Cedar Hill Avenue, Springfield, MO 65809
sbiswas@pol.net

BLATT, Stanley *Pediatrics 1965;* 4098 Corie Bella Drive, Broomfield, CO 80021

BLAU, Hannah *Pediatrics, Pumlmonary Medicine 1987;* Schneider Children's Medical Center of Israel, 14 Kaplan Street, Petah Tikveh, Israel 49202
hannahblau@hotmail.com

BLAU, Irwin *Pediatrics 1976, Neurology;* 3003 New Hyde Park Road, New Hyde Park, NY 11042
nyneuro@hotmail.com

BLEIBERG, Alan *Pediatrics 1996;* Children's Medical Center, 1935 Medical District Drive, Dallas, TX 75235

BLICHARSKI, Danuta *Pediatrics, Hematology-Oncology 1977;* Memorial Hermann Family Medicine, 7737 Southwest Freewy, #420, Houston, TX 77074
danuta_blicharski@memorialhermann.com

BLUMENREICH, Robert *Pediatrics 1989;* 206-10 Lori Drive, Bayside, NY 11360

BLUMENTHAL, Steven *Pediatrics 1983;* Maine Medical Center, 22 Bramhall Street, Portland, ME O4102
blumes@mmc.org

BLUMER, Steven *Pediatrics 2005;* 2328 Halyard Drive, Merrick, NY 11566
Steven.blumer@unmc.sunysb.edu

BOCCHICCHIO, Jeffrey *Pediatrics 2001;* 4604 Shoalwood Ave, Austin, TX 78756
jeffboa65@yahoo.com

BOCK, Kevin *Pediatrics, Critical Care Medicine 2000;* Schneider Children's Hospital, 269-01 76th Avenue, New Hyde Park, NY 11040
kbock@lij.edu

BODI, Janice *Pediatrics 1979;* 1499 Laurel Hollow Road, Syosset, NY 11791
jbodi@optonline.net; janicebodi@yahoo.com

*BOGARD, Bruce *Pediatrics 1972*

BOLLAMPALLI, Vidyasagar Reddy *Pediatrics 1985;* 1720 South Queen Street, York, PA 17403

BOMBART, Felice *Pediatrics, Endocrinology 1991;* 46 Bacon Road, Old Westbury, NY 11568

BONTEMPO-BLAUSTEIN, Silvia *Pediatrics 1994, Adolescent Medicine 1996;* 361 Clinton Street (Apt 1D), Brooklyn, NY 11231

BORCZUK, Mrinalini *Pediatrics 1994, Allergy-Immunology 1996;* 216 Willis Avenue (Suite 002), Roslyn Heights, NY 11577

BORNSTEIN-MAYERSON, Cara *Pediatrics 2002, Emergency Medicine 2005;* Schneider Children's Hospital, 269-01 76th Avenue, New Hyde Park, NY 11040

BOROWSKA, Halina *Pediatrics 1997, Emergency Medicine 2001;* Good Samaritan Hospital Medical Center, 1000 Montauk Highway, West Islip, NY 11795
halina.borowski@chsli.org

BOXER, Harriet *Pediatrics , Neonatal-Perinatal Medicine 1977;* Nassau University Medical Center, 2201 Hempstead Turnpike, East Meadow, NY 11559
hboxer@numc.edu

BOYAR, Vitaliya *Pediatrics , Neonatal-Perinatal Medicine 2008;* Schneider Children's Hospital, 269-01 76th Avenue, New Hyde Park, NY 11040
vboyar@gmail.com

BOYER, Clark *Pediatrics , Cardiology 2004;* 1325 East 80th Street, Brooklyn, NY 11236
clarfedo135431@pol.net

BRADY, Jodi *Pediatrics, Adolescent Medicine 2005;* 733 Naamans Road (Apt 19-A), Claymont, DE 19703

BRAIER, Karin *Pediatrics 2002;* 531 Central Park Avenue, Scarsdale, NY 10583

BRANDT, Penny *Pediatrics 2004;* University of New Mexico, 2211 Lomas Blvd Northeast (ACC), Albuquerque, NM 87131

BRANT-DEITCH, Deborah *Pediatrics 2000;* 15 Seward Drive Woodbury, NY 11797
deitichpd@optonline.net

BRATT, James *Pediatrics 2006;* Medacs Doctors, Kirkdale House, Kirkdale Road, Geytonstone, London, UK E11 1HP

BRAUN, Rochelle *Pediatrics 1992;* 1555 East 7th Street, Brooklyn, NY 11230

BRAVERMAN, Isaac *Pediatrics 1998;* 164 Flintlock Drive, Lakewood, NJ O8701
pedidoc9@aol.com

BREGLIO, Keith *Pediatrics 2005;* 5 East 98 Street, New York, NY 10021
bregs0522@aol.com

BRENNER, Dennis *Pediatrics 2000, Endocrinology 2003;* Baystate Children's Hospital, 759 Chestnut Street (S3584), Springfield, MA 01107
db999@mail.com

BRODTMAN, Daniel *Pediatrics 2000, Allergy-Immunology 2002;* 840 U.S. Highway 1 (Suite 235), North Palm Beach, FL 33408

BROSGOL, Yuri *Pediatrics 1993, Neurology 1996;* 30 West End Avenue (Bldg #1), Brooklyn, NY 11235
gbrosg@msn.com

BROWN, David *Pediatrics 1975, Neonatal-Perinatal Medicine 1978;* 6 Northwestern Drive, Bloomfield, CT O6002
dbrown@prohealthmd.com

BROWN, Dennis *Pediatrics 1981;* Nationwide Health Plans, 5525 Park Center Drive, Dublin, OH 43017

BROWN, Erica *Pediatrics 2006;* 6876 Rolling Creek Way, Alexandria, VI 22315

BROWN, Robert *Pediatrics 1966;* 11211 Boca Woods Lane, Boca Ratton, FL 33428

BROWN-McDANIEL, Barbara *Pediatrics 2001;* Tanner Medical Center, 148 Clinic Avenue, Carrollton, GA 30117
totdoc71@yahoo.com

BROWNSTEIN, William *Pediatrics 1983;* 160 Wolcott Street, Bristol, CT O6010 *wbrownstein@prohealthmd.com*

BRUNO, Sandra *Pediatrics 2002;* 208-F East Baldwin Road, Panama City, FL 32405

BRUNSON, Sandra *Pediatrics 1976, Cardiology 1979;* 2035 Lakeville Road, New Hyde Park, NY 11040 *sognbird11247@aol.com*

BRYANT-RENNIE, Janet *Pediatrics 1993;* 113 South Delaware Street, Smyrna, DE 19977 *newrennie@verizon.net*

BUDOW, Lauren *Pediatrics , Adolescent Medicine 1990;* 14 East 90 Street, New York, NY 10128

BULINOUN, Paul *Pediatrics 1988;* 188 Irien Mill Road, Turnersville, NJ 08012 *pjbencin@pol.net*

BURKE, Christine Maroon *Pediatrics 2001;* 639 Main Street, Johnson City, NY 13790 *cmaroon_2000@yahoo.com*

BURKES, Lynn *Pediatrics 1971, Child Psychiatry;* 185 West End Avenue, New York, NY 10023 *lynnburkes@aol.com*

BUTENSKY, Arthur *Pediatrics 1983;* 1129 Bloomfield Avenue, West Caldwell, NJ 07006 *abuten@comcast.net*

CABALLERO, Felipe *Pediatrics, Neonatal-Perinatal Medicine 2002;* St Catherine of Sienna Medical Center, 50 Route 25A, Smithtown, NY 11787

CALLEJA, Gregorio *Pediatrics 1980;* 10710 Shore Front Parkway, Rockaway Park, NY 11694 *gregorio.callejo@gmail.com*

CAMACHO, Jose Angel *Pediatrics, Cardiology 1987;* Geisinger Medical Center, 100 North Academy Avenue, Danville, PA 17822

CAMPOS, Francisco *Pediatrics 1997;* 855 West Brambleton Avenue, Norfolk, VA 23510

CANLAS-SUCGANG, Maria *Pediatrics 1994;* 109 Lake Ridge Drive, Enterprise, AL 36330 *nolimarrapepe@yahoo.com*

CANTATORE-FRANCIS, Julie *Pediatrics 2004, Dermatology ;* SUNY Downstate Medical Center, 450 Clarkson Avenue (Box 46), Brooklyn, NY 11203 *julie.contatore@gmail.com*

CANTOS, Eric *Pediatrics 1984, Radiology;* Advanced Medical Imaging, 900 Northern Blvd., Great Neck, NY 11021 *elc900@aol.com*

CAPPELLI, Frank *Pediatrics 1968;* 380 Dogwood Avenue, Franklin Sq, NY 11010 *fcapp@mac.com*

CAREY, Dennis *Pediatrics 1976, Endocrinology;* Schneider Children's Hospital, 269-01 76th Avenue, New Hyde Park, NY 11040 *dcarey@lij.edu*

CARONIA, Catherine *Pediatrics 1992, Critical Care Medicine 1995;* Good Samaritan Hospital, 1000 Montauk Highway, West Islip, NY 11795 *catherine.caronia@chsli.org*

CARREIRO, Jennifer *Pediatrics 2006;* 3 Foxtail Lane, Brookfield, CT O6804

CARRO-SACKLER, Lorna *Pediatrics 1990;* 4C Medical Park Drive, Pamona, NY 10970

CASADONTE, Joseph *Pediatrics, Neurology 1989;* Pinellas County Medical Society, 860 6th Street South (Suite 430), St. Petersburg, FL 33701

CASE, Philip *Pediatrics 1984, Ambulatory Pediatrics 1985;* 4251 U.S. Highway 9 (Suite E), Freehold, NJ O7728 *plcasemd@pol.net*

CASSON, Ira *Pediatrics 1976, Neurology;* 112-03 Queens Blvd., Forest Hills, NY 11375 *iradocdad@aol.com*

CASTIGLIA, Luisa *Pediatrics 1985;* 156 First Street, Mineola, NY 11501 *luisacmd@aol.com*

CATALANO, Lorraine *Pediatrics 1996;* 164 Commack Road, Commack, NY 11725 *lcatal@optonline.net*

CAVANAUGH, Lisa *Pediatrics 1996;* 77 Glenwood Road, Glen Head, NY 11545 *dcavanau@optonline.net*

CAVUOTO, Marie *Pediatrics, Allergy-Immunology 2004;* Schneider Children's Hospital, 269-01 76th Avenue, New Hyde Park, NY 11040

CELIKER, Mahmut *Pediatrics, Hematology-Oncology 1999;* Stony Brook School of Medicine, Stony Brook, NY 11794

CHAKRABATI, Chandrama *Pediatrics, Infectious Diseases 2002;* 306 East Trailwood Drive, Terre Haute, IN 47802

CHAN, Raymond K. *Pediatrics, Emergency Medicine 1989;* Highland Hospital, 1000 South Avenue (Box 31), Rochester, NY 14620

CHANG, Barry *Urology 2001;* 4614 East Shea Blvd (Suite D-110), Phoenix, AZ 85028

CHANG, Philip *Pediatrics 2007;* 347 North New River Drive East (Suite 2211), Fort Lauderdale, FL 33301 *philipchang77@yahoo.com*

CHARYTAN, Morris *Pediatrics 1983;* 353 Elm Street, West Hempstead, NY 11552 *charytan@cpfh.net*

CHASE-WANDERMAN, Nancy *Pediatrics 1971, Cardiology 1974;* 805 Estate Place (Suite 1), Memphis, TN 38120 *pedcardiologypc@aol.com*

CHATTERGEE, Manjula *Pediatrics, Endocrinology 2008;* The Brooklyn Hospital Center, 121 DeKalb Ave, Brooklyn, NY 11201 *mchatts@gmail.com*

CHEMIATILLY, Wassim *Pediatrics 2008;* Children's Hospital of Pittsburgh, 3705 Fifth Avenue, Pittsburgh, PA 15213

CHEN, Ashton *Pediatrics 2007;* C.S. Mott Children's Hospital, 1500 East Medical Center Drive (SPC 5297), Ann Arbor, MI 48109

CHEN, Ellen *Pediatrics 2001;* 280 West Macarthur Blvd, Oakland, CA 94611

CHEONG, Keith *Pediatrics, Neurology 2000;* 374 Stockholm Street, Brooklyn, NY 11237

CHERRICK, Irene *Pediatrics 1989, Hematology-Oncology 1992;* Upstate Medical University, 750 East Adams Street, Syracuse, NY 13210 *cherrick@upstate.edu*

CHESNER, Rina *Pediatrics 2000;* 728 North Main Street, Spring Valley, NY 10977

CHEUNG, Helen *Pediatrics 2006;* 158-49 84 Street, Howard Beach, NY 11413

CHIANG, Angela *Pediatrics 1988;* 1425 South Main Street, Walnut Creek, CA 94596

CHIANG, Nancy *Pediatrics 1999;* 42 Stanwood Road, New Hyde Park, NY 11040

CHIKEZIE, Augustine *Pediatrics, Endocrinology 1996;* Atlanticare duPont Children's Hospital, 2500 English Creek Drive, Egg Harbor Twp., NJ O8234

CHINNAIRUSAN, Muthamilan *Pediatrics 2008;* Methodist Hospital, 4221 Cobble Stone Drive, Henderson, KY 42420 *muthamilanc@yahoo.co.in*

CHO, Eunsung *Pediatrics 2006;* 98-41 64th Road, Rego Park, NY 11374

CHO, Jason *Pediatrics 1999;* 2601 Louis Bauer Drive, Brooks City-Base, TX 78235

CHOI, Rosa *Pediatrics 1969, Neonatal-Perinatal Medicine;* 6853 North Avenue, Oak Park, IL 60302 *rchoi6853@aol.com*

CHOI, Sook *Pediatrics, Neonatal-Perinatal Medicine 1974;* 159 Executive Drive, New Hyde Park, NY 11040

CHOWDHARI, Antonina *Pediatrics, Neonatal-Perinatal Medicine 1992;* University of South Florida, 4202 East Fowler Avenue, Tampa, FL 33620

CHUNG, David *Pediatrics, Hematology-Oncology 1983;* 37-28 Parsons Blvd, Flushing, NY 11354 *davidigchung@hotmail.com*

CIANNELLA, John *Pediatrics 2008;* 333 Ovington Avenue (Apt 49), Brooklyn, NY 11209 *ciajoh@scu.edu*

CITARELLA, Brett *Pediatrics, Neonatal-Perinatal Medicine 2007;* Lawrence and Memorial Hospital, 365 Montauk Avenue, New London, CT O6320

CITERMAN, Stephanie *Pediatrics 1985;* 11 Clinton Lane, Jericho, NY 11753
sciterman@optonline.net

CLAUS, Mark *Pediatrics 1986;* 178 York Road, Mansfield, MA O2048

CLEMENTI, Jennifer *Pediatrics 2004;* 30 Hempstead Avenue, Rockville Centre, NY 11570
CO, Margaret *Pediatrics 1987, Allergy-Immunology;* 75 North Maple Avenue, Ridgewood, NJ O7450

COHEN, Cynthia *Pediatrics 1988;* 6 Iroquois Trail, Harrison, NY 10528

COHEN, Jack *Pediatrics 1976;* 11808 South Island Road, Cooper City, FL 33026
jecohen@bellsouth.net

COHEN, Joseph *Pediatrics 1999;* 37 Stauber Drive, Plainview, NY 11803

COHEN, Michele *Pediatrics 2008, Cardiology;* Saint Peter's University Hospital, 254 Easton Avenue, New Brunswick, NJ O8901
rofcohen@yahoo.com

COHEN, Pamela *Pediatrics 1981, Hematology-Oncology;* Novartis Oncology, One Health Plaza, East Hanover, NJ 07932
pamela.cohen@novartis.com

COHEN, Sheryl *Pediatrics 1999;* 61-34 188th Street (Suite 211), Fresh Meadows, NY 11365
fmpeds@msn.com

COHEN, Stanley *Pediatrics 1981;* 7 West 96 Street (Apt 3A), New York, NY 10025

COLEMAN, Cathy *Pediatrics 1985;* 37 Furwood Drive, East Northport, NY 11731

COLEY-PICCIRILLO, Karen *Pediatrics 1993;* 114 Broadway, Malverne, NY 11565

COLON-LEDEE, Athos *Pediatrics, Cardiology 1995;* 3702 20th Street, Lubbock, TX 79410

CONROY-RICHARDS, Rushika *Pediatrics 2008;* 68-38 Yellowstone Blvd (B 67), Forest Hills, NY 11375
rushikar@hotmail.com

CONSTANT, Mireille *Pediatrics, Endocrinology 1993;* 3250 Sunrise Highway, East Islip, NY 11730

COONEY, Maureen *Pediatrics 1993, Adolescent Medicine 1995;* 311 North Midland Avenue, Nyack, NY 10960
drmaureencooney@yahoo.com

COPE, Jennifer *Pediatrics 1997, Neurology 2000;* 1200 East Ridgewood Avenue, Ridgewood, NJ O7450

COPPER, Donna *Pediatrics 1986;* Queens Health Network, 134-64 Springfield Blvd, Flushing, NY 11413
CopperD@nychhc.org

COPPERMAN, Stuart *Pediatrics 1963;*
smcmd@aol.com

CORDICE-FORD, Candida *Pediatrics 1998;* 111-20 Merrick Blvd., St. Albans, NY 11423

COTLER, Donald *Pediatrics 1986;* 171 Millburn Avenue, Millburn, NJ O7041

COUROUCLI, Xanthi *Pediatrics 1995;* 6621 Fannin Street, Houston, TX 77030

COX, Amanda *Pediatrics 2005, Allergy-Immunology 2007;* Schneider Children's Hospital, 269-01 76th Avenue, New Hyde Park, NY 11040
acox@nshs.edu

CRAMER, Andrea *Pediatrics 1982;* 1600 Republic Parkway (Suite 140), Mesquite, TX 75150
pairadocs3@aol.com

CREVI, Diana *Pediatrics, Emergency Medicine 2002;* Schneider Children's Hospital, 269-01 76th Avenue, New Hyde Park, NY 11040
bulboc@worldnet.att.net

CRISS-SMITH, Cynthia *Pediatrics 2000;* 327 Beach 19 Street, Far Rockaway, NY 11691

CUTLER, Adam *Pediatrics 1992;* Pediatric Associates, 9331 Vedra Pointe Lane, Boca Raton, FL 33496
adam.cutler@alumni.duke.edu

DADA, Lesley *Pediatrics 2001;* 900 Caton Avenue, Baltimore, MD 21229

DAMOUR, Yvon *Pediatrics, Neonatal-Perinatal Medicine 1995;* 113 Wedgewood Drive, Hauppauge, NY 11788

DAVIS, Carol *Pediatrics 2007;* 107 Clarendon Drive, Valley Stream, NY 11580
cdavis@aol.com

DAVIS, Jennifer *Pediatrics 2007;* 320 East 94th Street, New York, NY 10128
Jennifer.Davis@mssm.edu

DAVIS, Jonathan *Pediatrics 2002;* 636 Wantagh Avenue, Levittown, NY 11566

DAYAN, Nimrod *Pediatrics, Infectious Diseases 2005;* 15 Corporate Drive, Trumbull, CT 06611

DE ALDAY, Marietta Yumana *Pediatrics 1993;* 44256 North 10 Street West, Lancaster, CA 91327

DE BLASIO, Eugene *Pediatrics 1976;* 14-14 Bonnie Lane, Bayside, NY 11360
medicalconsultants@NYC.rr.com

DECARMINE, Philip *Pediatrics, Critical Care Medicine 1988;* Jacobi Medical Center, 1400 Pelham Parkway South, Bronx, NY 10461

DECASTRO-GROUSSE, Denise *Pediatrics 1987;* Boston Medical Center, One Boston Medical Center Place, Boston, MA O2118

DEE, Sandra *Pediatrics 1996;* Florida Hospital, 1061 Medical Center Drive, Orlando, FL 32763
sandradeemd@yahoo.com

DEGENHARDT, Karl *Pediatrics 2004, Cardiology;* Children's Hospital of Philadelphia, 34th Street and Civic Center Blvd, Philidelphia, PA 19104
karldehenhardt@yahoo.com

DEGUZMAN, Jocelyn *Pediatrics, Endocrinology 2002;* 505 Copper Street, Elko, NV 89801

DE JESUS, Julisa *Pediatrics 2008;* 263-45 73rd Avenue, Glen Oaks, NY 11004
julisadj@hotmail.com

DE JESUS, Socorro *Pediatrics 1994;* 1029 Rosedale Road, North Woodmere, NY 11581

DEL CARMEN, Ruby *Pediatrics 1988, Anesthesiology;* 2117 Terraza Place, Fullerton, CA 92835

DEL CARMEN, Renato *Pediatrics 1988;* 2117 Terraza Place, Fullerton, CA 92835

DELANEY, Angela *Pediatrics 2008;* National Institutes of Health, 9000 Rockville Pike, Bethesda, MD 20892
angela.delaney@gmail.com

DELLORUSSO, Ana *Pediatrics 1991;* 271 Jericho Turnpike, Floral Park, NY 11001
joeana@aol.com

DELLORUSSO, Giuseppe *Pediatrics 1991;* 58 Main Street, East Rockaway, NY 11518
joeana@aol.com

DENIZ, Yamo *Pediatrics 1997;* 12 Richie Road, Attleboro, MA O2703

DESPOSITO, Franklin *Pediatrics 1961, Hematology-Oncology; Genetics;* 161 Mayhew Drive, South Orange, NJ O7079
desposfr@umdnj.edu

DESROSIERS, Florence *Pediatrics, Adolescent Medicine 2008;* 1243 East 49th Street, Brooklyn, NY 11234
foyde@yahoo.com

DEUTCH, Robert *Pediatrics 2006, Emergency Medicine;* University of Rochester Medical Center, 601 Elmwood Avenue (Box 655), Rochester, NY 14642
dr.robbie@gmail.com

DEVER, Lynn *Pediatrics 1987;* Lakeside, 20 North Main Street, Yardley, PA 19067
ldever@aol.com

DHANANTWARI, Preeta *Pediatrics, Cardiology 2007;* Schneider Children's Hospital, 269-01 76th Avenue, New Hyde Park, NY 11040

DIAL, Sharon *Pediatrics, Critical Care Medicine 2000;* 269-01 76th Avenue, New Hyde Park, NY 11040
sdial@nshs.edu

DIAMANT, Shmuel *Pediatrics, Cardiology 1986;* Dana Children's Hospital of Tel Aviv Sourasky Medical Center, 6 Weizmann Street, Tel Aviv, Israel 64239

DICK, Gilbert *Pediatrics 1979;* 173 East Shore Road, Great Neck, NY 11023

DICKSON, Pamela *Pediatrics 1984;* 1611 Northwest 12th Avenue, Miami, FL 33136

DIEJOMAH, Ejiro *Pediatrics, Neonatal-Perinatal Medicine 2004;* Nemours Pediatrics at Milford, 703 North DuPont Highway, Teal Creek Plaza, Milford, DE 19963

DI LELLO, Edmund *Pediatrics 1979, Cardiology 1981, Neonatal-Perinatal Medicine 1983;* St. John's Hospital, 9002 Queens Blvd, Elmhurst, NY 11373

DI TURI-HARTLEY, Suzanne *Pediatrics 1998;* 10 Broadway, Denville, NJ O7834

DIXON, Earl *Pediatrics 1994;* 36458 U.S. Highway 19-N, Palm Harbor, FL 34684

DIZON, Louis *Pediatrics 2001, Physical Medicine & Rehabilitation;* Carroll & Tate Streets, Lebanon, VA 24266
Lrodizon@aol.com

DOBKIN-FARIN, Michelle *Pediatrics 1991, Neonatal-Perinatal Medicine;* Exempla Lutheran Medical Center, 8300 West 38th Avenue, Wheat Ridge, CO 80033
mfarin@sbhcs.com

DOLMAIAN, Gigliola Copaescu *Pediatrics 2004, Neonatal-Perinatal Medicine;* Flushing Hospital Medical Center, 45th Avenue & Parsons Blvd., Flushing, NY 11355

DOS SANTOS, Christiane *Pediatrics , Neonatal-Perinatal Medicine 1992;* Germany

DOYLE, James *Pediatrics 1990, Ophthalmology;* 119 North Park Avenue (Suite 208), Rockville Center, NY 11570
jdoyle@jamesmdoylemd.com

DRAGOI, Elena *Pediatrics, Hematology-Oncology 2005;* 70 Mansfield Avenue, Willimantic, CT 06226
eddragoi@yahoo.com

DUROSEAU, Herold *Pediatrics, Hematology-Oncology 1993;* 1771 Utica Avenue, Brooklyn, NY 11234

DUVDEVANY, Neta *Pediatrics 1995;* 1610 Medical Drive, Cottstown, PA 19464

DVORIN, Donald *Pediatrics 1983, Allergy-Immunology;* Hahnemann University Hospital, 205 N Broad Street (Suite 300) Philadelphia, PA 19107
ddorin3@aol.com

DYER, Lori Landau *Urology 2006;* Pediatric Urology Associates, 159 White Plains Road, Tarrytown, NY 10591

EAPEN, Santhosh *Pediatrics 1996, Endocrinology 1999;* Jersey Shore University Medical Center, 1945 Route 33, Neptune, NJ O7753
seapen@meridianhealth.com

ECKSTEIN, Ira *Pediatrics, Emergency Medicine 1998;* Good Samaritan Hospital Medical Center, 1000 Montauk Highway, West Islip, NY 11795

EDWARDS, Bruce *Allergy-Immunology 1989;* 700 Old Country Road, Plainview, NY 11803

EISEN, Louis *Pediatrics 1993;* 279 Main Street (Suite 103), New Paltz, NY 12561

EISENBERG, Bruce *Pediatrics 1986;* Miami Beach Pediatrics, 524-41 Arthur Godfrey Road (Suite 201), Miami Beach, FL 33140
mbpeds@bellsouth.net

EISENSTAT, Jennifer *Pediatrics 2001;* 340 Dogwood Avenue, Franklin Square, NY 11010
jdeisenstat@optonline.net

ELBASH, Lina *Pediatrics 2005, Neonatal-Perinatal Medicine 2008;* SUNY Stony Brook University Hospital, Stony Brook, NY 11979
lina.elbash@gmail.com

ELBASTY, Azza *Pediatrics 1994;* Elbasty Pediatric Associates, 100 Commons Way (Suite 130), Holmdel, NJ O7733
moelbasty@aol.com

ELDEMERDASH, Alaa *Pediatrics, Neonatal-Perinatal Medicine 1990;* Section on Neonatology, Alwasl Hospital, Dubai, UAE
aaeldemerdash@dohms.gov.ae

ELIE, Marie-Theresa *Pediatrics, Neonatal-Perinatal Medicine 1984*

ELLIOTT, Michelle *Pediatrics, Adolescent Medicine 2005;* 913 East 48 Street, Brooklyn, NY 11203

No class of men needs to call to mind more often the wise comment of Plato that education is a life-long business.

—Sir William Osler
(1849-1919)

ELLIS, Jeffrey *Pediatrics 2003, Dermatology;* 79 Hillside Lane, New Hyde Park, NY 11040
doctorellis@Gmail.com

ELLWOOD, Joanmarie *Pediatrics 2008;* 306 Community Drive (Apartment 1F), Manhasset, NY 11030
jellwood@nyit.edu

ELVIR, Patricia *Pediatrics 1988;* 156 First Street, Mineola, NY 11501

EMRALINO, Feliciano *Pediatrics, Neonatal-Perinatal Medicine 1995;* St. Barnabus Medical Center, 4422 Third Avenue, Bronx, NY 10457

ENG, Christine *Pediatrics 1986, Medical Genetics;* Mt. Sinai School of Medicine, One Gustave Levy Place (Suite 1203), New York, NY 10029

ENG, Jennifer *Pediatrics 2007, Hematology-Oncology;* 220-07 Hempstead Avenue, Queens Village, NY 11429
engJ1628@hotmail.com

ERMITANO, Maria Luisa *Pediatrics 1997;* 204 Plantation Drive, Winchester, KY 40391
hlim66@yahoo.com

ESPERANZA, Maria *Pediatrics, Critical Care Medicine 2003;* Schneider Children's Hospital, 269-01 76th Avenue, New Hyde Park, NY 11040
mesperan@nshs,edu

ESPOSITO, Linda *Pediatrics 1986, Ophthalmology;* 3218 Fordham Road, Wilmington, DE 19807
espa24@gmail.com

ESSANDOH, Yvonne *Pediatrics 2007*
yessandoh@yahoo.co m

ESTRADA, Elizabeth *Pediatrics 1993;* 383-050 Fortieth Street East (Suite 100), Palmdale, CA 93550

ETESS, Melanie Stein *Pediatrics 2000, Emergency Medicine;* 260 Ellen Place, Jericho, NY 11753
etess@optonline.net

*EVERETT, Stanley *Pediatrics 1967*

ETWARU, Kumarie *Pediatrics 1999, Emergency Medicine;* Beth Israel Medical Center, First Avenue & 16th Street, New York, NY 10003

EYAL, Dalit *Pediatrics, Emergency Medicine 1998;* 3376 Manor Road, Huntington Valley, PA 19006

FALK, Theodore *Pediatrics 1980;* 63 Grand Avenue (Suite 100), River Edge, NJ O7607
teanecka@aol.com

FALKOVICH, Ruvim *Pediatrics 1996;* Joseph C. Wilson Health Center, 800 Carter Street, Rochester, NY 14621
zuni61@frontiernet.net

FANELLA, Frank *Pediatrics 1997;* 120 Park Lane Road (Suite A-101), New Milford, CT O6776
ffanella@charter.net

*FARIN, Mark *Pediatrics 1991, Cardiology*

FASANO, Andrew *Pediatrics 2000;* 2073 Newbridge Road, Bellmore, NY 11710

FATICA, Nunzia *Pediatrics 1982, Cardiology;* New York Hospital Cornell University Medical Center, 525 East 68 Street, New York, NY 10022
ratican@hss.edu

FEBER, Kevin *Urology 2007;* 2221 Livernois Road (Suite 103), Troy, NY 48083

FEFER, Zipora *Pediatrics 1999, Neurology 2002;* Schneider Children's Hospital, 269-01 76th Avenue, New Hyde Park, NY 11040

FEINSTEIN, Ronald *Pediatrics 1979, Adolescent Medicine;* Schneider Children's Hospital, 269-01 76th Avenue, New Hyde Park, NY 11040
ronfeinstein@hotmail.com

FEINSTEIN, Stuart *Pediatrics 1986;* 2266 Dutch Broadway, Elmont, NY 11003
info@kids-care.com

FELDMAN, Doron *Pediatrics 1993, Anesthesiology;* 219 Bryant Street, Buffalo, NY 14222
dfeldman@adelphia.net

FELDMAN, Robert *Pediatrics, Neurology 1985;* 806 14th Avenue, Albany, GA 31701

FELDT, Matthew *Pediatrics 2006;* Rainbow Babies and Children's Hospital, 11100 Euclid Avenue, Cleveland, OH 44106

FELL, Brad *Pediatrics 1995;* 1171 Old Country Road, Plainview, NY 11803
drbfell@aol.com

FERNANDEZ, Mariely *Pediatrics 2007;* Center for Comprehensive Health Practice, 1900 Second Avenue (9th Floor), New York, NY 10029
mariely1@aol.com

FERNANDO, Anusha *Pediatrics 2008;* 245 East 63rd Street, New York, NY 10021
anushaf@hotmail.com

FERREIRA, Carmen *Pediatrics, Neurology 2005;* 508 South Havana Avenue, Tampa, FL 33609

FERREIRA, Jose *Pediatrics, Neurology 1993;* 508 South Havana Avenue, Tampa, FL 33609

FIGLOZZI, Christina *Pediatrics 2001;* 1947 Winding Ridge Road, Winston Salem, NC 27127
cfiglozzi@yahoo.com

FIGUEROA, Nitza Lugo *Pediatrics, Critical Care Medicine 1997;* 252 Calle San Jorge, San Juan, PR 00926

FINK, Lawrence *Pediatrics 1986;* 125 Franklin Avenue, Franklin Square, NY 11010
drlfink@optonline.net

FIORENTINOS, Dionysia *Pediatrics 2008;* 69-15 Little Neck Parkway, Glen Oaks, NY 11004
dfiorent@nyit.edu

FISH, Jonathan *Pediatrics 2004 Hematology-Oncology;* Schneider Children's Hospital, 269-01 76th Avenue, New Hyde Park, NY 11040

FISHER, Karen *Pediatrics 1976;* Davis Avenue @ East Post Road, White Plains, NY 10601

FISHER, Martin *Pediatrics 1978, Adolescent Medicine 1980;* Schneider Children's Hospital, 269-01 76th Avenue, New Hyde Park, NY 11040
fisher@nshs.edu

FIUMANO, Margaret *Pediatrics 2002;* 720 Montauk Hwy, West Islip, NY 11795
mags11743@yahoo.com

FLAMENBAUM, Helen *Pediatrics 1979, Dermatology;* 3003 New Hyde Park Road, New Hyde Park, NY 11042
hflame@aol.com

FLICKER, Jason *Pediatrics 1998, Ophthalmology;* 2185 Wantagh Avenue, Wantagh, NY 11793
jf1206es@hotmail.com

FLIEGENSPAN, Jeffrey *Pediatrics 1986;* 1835 North Corporate Lakes Blvd, Weston, FL 33326
jfliegenspan@pediatricassociates.com

FLITMAN, Sheila *Pediatrics 1968;* 221 Jericho Turnpike, Syosset, NY 11791
sflitman@yahoo.com

FONG, Jane *Pediatrics 1988, Critical Care Medicine 1991;* 506 Sixth Street, Brooklyn, NY 11215

FONT, Luis *Pediatrics, Endocrinology 2008;* 212-30 16th Avenue, Bayside, NY 11360

FORGIONE, Lisa *Pediatrics 1997;* 165 North Village Avenue (Suite 215), Rockville Centre, NY 11570

FORREST, Emily *Pediatrics 2005;* Department of Pediatrics, NYU/Bellevue Medical Center, 462 First Avenue (3rd floor), New York, NY 10016
forree01@med.nyu.edu

FORTE, Louis *Pediatrics 1985;* 503 George McClaim Drive, Benton, KY 42025

FRANCES, Adriana *Pediatrics 1991;* Children's Mercy Hospitals and Clinics, 2401Gillham Road, Kansas City, MO 64108

FRANK, Graeme *Pediatrics 1991, Endocrinology;* Schneider Children's Hospital, 269-01 76th Avenue, New Hyde Park, NY 11042
gfrank@lij.edu

FREED, Jay *Pediatrics 1976;* 233 Union Avenue, Holbrook, NY 11741

FREEDMAN, Samuel *Pediatrics 1991, Endocrinology 1994;* Joe DiMaggio Children's Hospital, 601 North Flamingo Road (Suite 207), Pembroke Pines, FL 33028
s.freedman@BellSouth.net

FREYLE, Jamie *Urology 2004;* Pediatric Urology Associates, 909 49th Street, Brooklyn, NY 11029

FRIEDMAN, Benyamin *Pediatrics 2001;* 441 Route 306 (Suite 1), Monsey, NY 10952
benyamin@dymedpediatrics.com

FRIEDMAN, Daniel *Pediatrics 2000;* 271 Jericho Turnpike, Floral Park, NY 11001

FRIEDMAN-GOLDMAN, Sharon *Pediatrics 1995;* 4525 Henry Hudson Pkwy, Bronx, NY 10471

FRIEDMAN-OPPENHEIMER, Orit *Pediatrics 2001, Hematology-Oncology;* Memorial Sloan-Kettering Cancer Institute, 1275 York Avenue, New York, NY 10021

FRIED-SIEGEL, Judy *Urology 1996;* 623 Warburton Avenue, Hastings-on-Hudson, NY 10706

FRISS, Helena *Pediatrics 1983, Neonatal-Perinatal Medicine 1986;* Temple University School of Medicine, 3401 North Broad Street, Philadelphia, PA 19140
frissh@tuhs.temple.edu

FROGEL, Michael *Pediatrics 1978;* Schneider Children's Hospital, 269-01 76th Avenue, New Hyde Park, NY 11042
frogel@lij.edu

FRUCHTMAN, Deborah *Pediatrics 1981;* 11 Rappleye Court, West Orange, NJ O7052
eyedocmom3@aol.com

FRUMPKIN-KANTROVITZ, Farla *Pediatrics, Adolescent Medicine 1991*

FUCHS, Howard *Pediatrics 1981;* 3920 Bee Ridge Road, Sarasota, FL 34233
Tavas1@comcast.net

FURMAN, Gilbert *Pediatrics 1977, Neonatal-Perinatal Medicine;* Citrus Valley Medical Center, 1115 South Sunset Avenue, West Covina, CA 91790
g.furman@comcast.net

FURMAN, Melissa *Pediatrics 1994;* 91 Schoolhouse Lane, Roslyn Hts, NY 11577
melfur@optonline.net

FUSCO, Tara *Pediatrics 1999;* 160-23 80th Street, Howard Beach, NY 11414

GALANG, Luz *Pediatrics, Neonatal-Perinatal Medicine 1999*

GALOSO, Maria *Pediatrics 1998;* Unity Health System, Physician Clinic, 1518 Mulberry Avenue, Muscatine, IA 52761
mtrg@machlink.com

GAMENG, Mary Ann Flynn *Pediatrics 2007;* Kids First Pediatrics, 815 Hallock Avenue, Port Jefferson, NY 11776
maflynncat@aol.com

GAMUNDI JOAQUIN, Rosa *Pediatrics, Neonatal-Perinatal Medicine 1999;* 289 Monroe Street, Passaic, NJ O7055

GANAL-ESPERANZA, Pamelynn *Pediatrics 2005;* 1249 Park Avenue (Apartment 17B), New York, NY 10029
pamelynn_esperanca@rush.edu

GANGULY, Rekha *Pediatrics 1981*

GARA, Lori *Pediatrics 1993;* 258 Washington Street (Suite 201), Wellesly Hills, MA O2481

GARCIA, Maria *Pediatrics, Hematology-Oncology 1996;* Hospital Ramon y Cajal, Universidad de Alcala de Henares, Madrid, Spain

GAROFALO-MONACO, Melissa *Pediatrics 2008, Critical Care Medicine 2011;* Pediatric Specialists, 90 Prospect Avenue, Hackensack, NJ O7601

GATES, Robert *Surgery 2005;* University of California, Davis Medical Center, 5275 F Street (Suite 3), Sacramento, CA 95819 *robert.gates@ucdmc.ucdavis.edu*

GAYNOR, Michael *Pediatrics, Adolescent Medicine 1985;* 3638 Madaca Lane, Tampa, FL 33618 *mdgmd1@aol.com*

GEDACHIAN, Robert *Pediatrics 1969, Allergy-Immunology;* 6 Tsienneto Road, Derry, NH O3038 *rgedachian@snhima.com*

GELABERT-LEMUS, Carmen *Pediatrics 1955;* 18535 S. Santana Avenue, Cerritos, CA 90703

GELLIS, Richard *Pediatrics 1983;* 43 Kensico Road, Mt. Kisco, NY 10549

GENNARO, Margaret *Pediatrics 1990;* 3004 Robin Ridge Court, Fairfax, VA 22031 *drgennaro@webTC.net*

GENNINO, Christopher *Pediatrics 1990, Adolescent Medicine;* 7 Crozier Court, Oxford, CT O6478

GENSER, Alan *Pediatrics 1984;* 31 Burnham Court, Scotch Plains, NJ O7076

GENSLER, Zev *Pediatrics 1999;* 150 Sunrise Highway, Lindenhurst, NY 11757 *gensler@pol.net*

GEORGE, Matthew *Pediatrics, Critical Care Medicine 2005;* 102 Thomas Road (Suite 113), West Monroe, LA 71291

GEORGE, Minu *Pediatrics 1999;* Schneider Children's Hospital, 269-01 76th Avenue, New Hyde Park, NY 11004 *mgeorge@lij.edu*

GERBERG, Bruce *Pediatrics 1998;* 164 East Main Street, Huntington, NY 11743 *kiddoc4@optonline.net*

Medical education is not completed at the medical school: it is only begun.

—William H. Welch

(1850-1934)

GERBERG, Lynda *Pediatrics 1993, Sports Medicine;* Schneider Children's Hospital, 269-01 76th Avenue, New Hyde Park, NY 11040 *lgerberg@lij.edu*

GERO, Bernard *Pediatrics 1985;* 415 East Rolling Oaks Drive, Thousand Oaks, CA 91361

GERSHKOVICH, Irina *Pediatrics 2006;* 723 Mulberry Place, N. Woodmere, NY 11581 *zakarpote@aol.com*

GIAMPIETRO, Philip *Pediatrics 1989, Medical Genetics;* Marshfield Clinic Center, 1000 North Oak Avenue, Marshfield, WI 54449 *giampietro.philip@marshfieldclinic.org*

GIDWANEY, Rita *Pediatrics 2007;* Kaplan Test Preparation and Admissions, 1440 Broadway, New York, NY 10018 *rgidwaney@gmail.com*

GINEBRA, Fernando *Pediatrics, Neonatal-Perinatal Medicine 1997;* Coral Springs Medical Center, 3000 Coral Hills Drive, Coral Springs, FL 33065

GINSBURG, Mark *Pediatrics 1980;* 7001 Southwest 87th Avenue, Miami, FL 33173 *mginsburg@bellsouth.net*

GIORDANO, Ida *Pediatrics 1972;* 17 Prospect Street, Huntington, NY 11743 *idagiordano@aol.com*

GIORGI, Marilyn *Pediatrics, Neonatal-Perinatal Medicine 2005;* 225-03 114th Road, Cambria Heights, NY 11411

GLEIT-CADURI, Daphne *Pediatrics 1992;* 6268 Jericho Tpke. (Suite 11), Commack, NY 11725 *drcaduri@hotmail.com*

GLIKSMAN, Felicia *Pediatrics 2006;* 306 Community Drive (Apt 4J), Manhasset, NY 11030 *doctorfelicia@hotmail.com*

GLOBERMAN, Hadas *Pediatrics 1986;* Carmel Hospital, Haifa, Israel 34362

GO, Anita *Pediatrics 1995, Cardiology;* 5229 Lark Lane, Alexandria, LA 71303 *atacgo@yahoo.com*

GOCHOCO, Aurora *Pediatrics, Neurology 1984;* 460 North Main Street (Box 228), Warsaw, NY 14569

GOLD, David *Pediatrics 1990, Gastroenterology 1993;* Good Samaritan Hospital Medical Center, 1000 Montauk Highway, West Islip, NY 11795 *david.gold@chsli.org*

GOLD, Nina *Pediatrics 1990, Emergency Medicine 1996;* 34 Kershner Place, Fair Lawn, NJ O7410

GOLDBERG, Barry *Pediatrics 1992, Cardiology 1995;* Good Samaritan Hospital Medical Center, 1000 Montauk Highway, West Islip, NY 11795 *barry.goldberg@chsli.org*

GOLDBERG, Michael *Pediatrics, Neonatal-Perinatal Medicine 1975;* 8-A Herzog Street, Rechovot, Israel

GOLDBERG, Michael *Pediatrics 1992*

GOLDBERG, Tracie *Pediatrics, Hematology-Oncology 2007;* Schneider Children's Hospital, 269-01 76 Avenue, New Hyde Park, NY 11040 *tgoldberg@nshs.edu*

GOLDMAN, Arnold *Pediatrics 1977;* 332 Willis Avenue, Roslyn Hts, NY 11577 *drajgoldman@aol.com*

GOLDMAN, Robert *Pediatrics 1997, Allergy-Immunology 1999;* Hudson Valley Asthma and Allergy Association, 35 South Riverside Avenue, Croton-on-Hudson, NY 10520 *robertgoldman@optonline.net*

GOLDSTEIN, Alvin *Pediatrics 1963;* 109 Woodmere Blvd. South, Woodmere, NY 11598 *summerjoel@cs.com*

GOLDSTEIN, Ilene *Pediatrics 1991, Allergy-Immunology 1993;* 158 East Main Street, Huntington, NY 11743 *iad18@aol.com*

GOLDSTEIN, Stanley *Pediatrics 1978, Allergy-Immunology; Pulmonary Medicine;* 242 Merrick Road (Suite 401), Rockville Centre, NY 11570 *drsgoldstein@pol.net*

GOLDSTEIN, Steven *Pediatrics 1981;* Kew Garden Hills Pediatrics, 141-49 70 Road, Flushing, NY 11367 *SJG34@cornell.edu*

GOLOMBECK, Arel *Pediatrics 2007;* 24 Arleigh Road, Great Neck, NY 11021

GOMBOS, Michal *Pediatrics, Emergency Medicine 1995;* Montefiore Medical Center 1400 Pelham Parkway South, Bronx, NY 10467

GONZALEZ, Jeanette *Pediatrics 2007;* Children's Hospital at Montefiore, 3415 Bainbridge Avenue, Bronx, NY 10467 *junabug77@hotmail.com*

GONZALEZ, Maripaz *Pediatrics, Cardiology 1994;* 34 Graves Street, Staten Island, NY 10314

GONZALEZ, Rosa Ana *Pediatrics, Hematology-Oncology 2000;* Mexican Army, Mexico City, Mexico

GOODMAN, Karen Meier *Pediatrics 2005;* 1343 Trafalgar Street, Teaneck, NJ 07666

GORDON, Charles *Pediatrics 1980;* 261 Central Park West, New York, NY 10024

GORDON, Laurie *Pediatrics 1982;* New York Hospital at Queens, 56-45 Main Street, Flushing, NY 11355 *laurie.gordon@earthlink.net*

GORDON, Seth *Pediatrics 2004;* Pediatrics East of New York, 157 East 81st Street (Suite 1A), New York, NY 10028
setsdg@aol.com

GOROZA, Edmund *Pediatrics, Critical Care Medicine 2008;* The Children's Hospital at St. Peter's University Hospital, 254 Easton Avenue, New Brunswick, NJ O8901
edmund.goroza@gmail.com

GOTTESMAN, Avraham *Pediatrics 2007;* 85-21 124th Street, Kew Gardens, NY 11415
avrahamgottesman@yahoo.com

GOTTLIEB, Beth *Pediatrics 1995, Rheumatology 1998;* Schneider Children's Hospital, 269-01 76th Avenue, New Hyde Park, NY 11040
gottlieb@lij.edu

GOULD, Eric *Pediatrics 1971;* 15 Barstow Road, Great Neck, NY 11021

GRAF, Alisa *Pediatrics 1991;* Queens-Long Island Medical Group, 125-06 101 Avenue, Richmond Hill, NY 11419

GRAF, Jeannette *Pediatrics 1985, Dermatology;* 88 Bayview Avenue, Great Neck, NY 11021

GRAF, Lillian *Pediatrics 1980, Dermatology;* 214-18 24th Avenue, Bayside, NY 11360

GRANAT, Lloyd *Pediatrics 1973;* 3945 San Jose Park Drive, Jacksonville, FL 32217
llgranat@aol.com

GRAZIANO, Joan *Pediatrics 1993, Hematology-Oncology 1996;* 168 Jules Drive, Staten Island, NY 10314

GREENBAUM, Dorothy *Pediatrics 1981;* 158-49 84th Street, Howard Beach, NY 11414

GREEN-BILELLO, Rachel *Pediatrics 2008;* Beach Pediatrics, 312 Long Beach Road, Island Park, NY 11558
rgreen@nyit.edu

GREENBLATT, Daniel *Pediatrics 2006, Neurology;* SUNY Downastate Medical Center, 450 Clarkson Avenue, Brooklyn, NY
degreenblatt@gmail.com

GREENFIELD, Elizabeth *Pediatrics 1985;* Richmond Hill Center, Richmond Hill, NY 11419

GREENHILL, Philip *Pediatrics 1974, Cardiology 1976;* 151 Route 10 East (Suite 106), Succasunna, NJ O7876
pgmd12@optonline.net

GREIF, Jules *Pediatrics 1986, Ambulatory Pediatrics 1987;* 303 Overton Road, Dallas, TX 75216
jgreif@parknet.pmh.org

GREISING, Joanne *Pediatrics 1989;* 18 Menyas Court, Washingtonville, NY 10992
derm999@earthlink.net

GREISSMAN, Allan *Pediatrics 1991, Critical Care Medicine 1994;* Joe DiMaggio Children's Hospital, 3501 Johnson Street, Hollywood, FL 33021
joedpicu@au.com

GRELLO, Stephen *Pediatrics 2001;* 390 Montauk Highway, West Islip, NY 11795

GRIJNSZTEIN, Mark *Pediatrics 2001, Allergy-Immunology 2004;* 8170 Laguna Blvd (Suite 200), Elk Grove, CA 95758

GROENING, Portia *Pediatrics 2006;* 7 Martin Road, Ossining, NY 10562

GROSSMAN, Heather *Pediatrics, Hematology-Oncology 2003;* Lincoln Hospital, 234 East 149th Street, Bronx, NY 10032

GROSSMAN, Rami Raphael *Pediatrics 1990, Neurology 1993;* 6 Tuxedo Avenue, New Hyde Park, NY 11040
ramiavi@aol.com

GUBITOSI, Terry Ann *Pediatrics, Pulmonary Medicine 1988;* Five Dorchester Lane, Morristown, NJ O8057

GUINTO, Danilo *Pediatrics 1993;* 144 Chilton Street, Elizabeth, NJ O7202

GUPTA, Krishna *Pediatrics 1971;* 214-08 Hillside Avenue, Queens Village, NY 11427

GUTERMAN, Carl *Pediatrics 1987, Ophthalmology;* 385 Prospect Avenue, Hackensack, NJ O7601
NJKidsEyes@aol.com

*HABER, Alan *Pediatrics 1962*

HABERMAN, Elisa *Pediatrics 2002;* 14 Burning Hollow Road, Saddle River, NJ O7458

HADJIEV, Boyan *Allergy-Immunology 2005;* 2420 Overlook (Apt 1), Cleveland Heights, OH 44106

HAHN, Gary *Pediatrics 1980, Dermatology;* 283 Commack Road, Commack, NY 11725
gmh1@yahoo.com

HAIBY, William *Pediatrics 1979;* 411 Lakeview Avenue, Rockville Centre, NY 11570

HAIMI-COHEN, Yishai *Pediatrics, Infectious Diseases 2000;* Schneider Children's Medical Center of Israel, 14 Kaplan Street, Petah Tikvah, Israel 49100

HAIMOWITZ-REINITZ, Jennifer *Pediatrics 2001;* 1770 Motor Parkway, Hauppauge, NY 11795
drjenn10@optonline.net

HALEGOUA, Jason *Pediatrics 2004, Adolescent Medicine;* 270 Union Avenue, Holbrook, NY 11741
halegouaj@aol.com

HALLER, Jerome *Pediatrics 1965, Neurology;* 1415 Tulane Avenue, New Orleans, LA 70112

HAMETZ, Irwin *Pediatrics 1973;* 77-55 Schank Road, Freehold, NJ 07728

HAMMER-SANDOVAL, Ellen *Pediatrics 1990;* 299 Crane Road, Carmel, NY 10512

HAMMER, Michael *Pediatrics 1992;* 2254 Timothy Drive, Glenview, IL 60025

HANDELSMAN, Edward *Pediatrics 1991;* SUNY Downstate Medical Center, 451 Clarkson Avenue (Box 294), Brooklyn, NY 11203

HANDWERKER, Lisa *Pediatrics 1979;* 80 Saint Paul Street (4th Floor), Rochester, NY 14604

HANSROTE, Louis *Pediatrics, Cardiology 1991;* Children's Heart Center, 401 North 17th Street (Suite 309), Allentown, PA 18104

HARBERT, Mary Jo *Pediatrics 2007;* University of California at San Diego Medical Center, 402 West Dickinson Street, San Diego, CA 92103

HARDOFF, Daniel *Pediatrics, Adolescent Medicine, 1983;* Bnei Zion Medical Center, Haifa, Israel

HARNICK, Joel *Pediatrics, Cardiology 2007;* Children's Hospital Boston, 300 Longwood Avenue, Boston, MA O2116

HARRIS, Bradford *Pediatrics 1996;* 550 First Avenue, New York, NY 10016

HARVEY, Jay *Pediatrics 1991;* 5132 U.S. Highway 19, New Port Richey, FL 34652

HAUSDORFF, Mark *Pediatrics 1988, Anesthesiology ;* Children's Hospital of New Jersey, 201 Lyons Avenue, Newark, NJ 07112
madorf1@aol.com

HAWKINS, Lynn *Pediatrics 1987, Endocrinology 1990;* Select Physicians, 410 Lakeville Road, New Hyde Park, NY 11040
migdoc@optonline.net

HEAVENS-ALEXANDRE, Faith *Pediatrics, Neurology 2001;* 202-18 45 Drive, Bayside, NY 11361

HEITLER, Michael *Pediatrics 1962;* 41 East Mall Drive, Melville, NY 11747
drmheitler@aol.com

HEMPEL, Bridget *Pediatrics 2004;* 661 West End Avenue, New York, NY 10025

HENTSCHEL-FRANKS, Karen *Pediatrics 1996;* 5001 Shoal Creek Road, Suffolk, VA 23435

HERKO, Patricia *Pediatrics 1983;* Select Physicians, 410 Lakeville Road, New Hyde Park, NY 11040

HERMAN, Tali *Pediatrics 2008*
tali.herman@mssm.edu

HERZFELD, Sharon *Pediatrics 1996;* 530 First Avenue (Suite 3A), New York, NY 10016

HERZOG, Ronit *Pediatrics 1998, Allergy-Immunology;* 515 West 59th Street (Apt 19N), New York, NY 10019
rherzog@montefiore.org

HILAIRE, Chantal *Pediatrics 1995, Physical Medicine & Rehabilitation;* 15 Melton East Drive, Rockville Centre, NY 11570

HOGAN, Timothy *Pediatrics 1986;* 2611 Corporal Kennedy Street, Bayside, NY 11360

HOLLANDER-BOBO, Robin *Pediatrics 1994;* 2416 Ocean Avenue, Brooklyn, NY 11229

HOLZMAN, Bernard *Pediatrics 1974, Critical Care Medicine;* University of Miami School of Medicine, 7380 Southwest 114th Street, Miami, FL 33156

HOM, Christine *Pediatrics, Rheumatology 1999;* New York Medical College, Valhalla, NY 10595

HONIGMAN, Richard *Pediatrics 1979, Hematology-Oncology 1981;* 3601 Hempstead Tpke (Suite 416) Levittown, NY 11756

HORMAZDI, Bomi *Pediatrics 1977;* 1147 Rennie Drive, Katy, TX 77450

HOROWITZ, Jeffrey *Pediatrics 1984;* 10 Ronald Reagan Blvd, Warwick, NY 10990
jeffandannah@netscape.net

HORVATH, Lajos *Pediatrics, Neonatal-Perinatal Medicine 2005;* 1613 North Harrison Parkway, Sunrise, FL 33323

HORWITZ, Jonathan *Pediatrics 1974, Adolescent Medicine 1975;* 23-25 Bell Blvd, Bayside, NY 11360
lis49@yahoo.com

HOWARD, Renee *Pediatrics 1979;* 2914 Duncan Road, White Hall, MD 21161
reneeh947@yahoo.com

HSU, Penelope *Pediatrics 2004, Emergency Medicine;* Children's Hospital of Los Angeles, 4650 Sunset Blvd, MS-113, Los Angeles, CA 90027
penelopehsu@hotmail.com

HUANG, Andrew *Urology 1999;* 2025 Morse Avenue, Sacramento, CA 95825

HUBEL, Philip *Pediatrics 1982, Emergency Medicine;* 5 Shady Tree Lane, Port Jefferson, NY 11777

HUSAIN, Naghma *Pediatrics 1997, Hematology-Oncology 2000;* 3826 Freedom Drive, Eau Claire, WI 54703

HUSAN, Muhamad *Pediatrics, Hematology-Oncology 2006;* Peninsula Hospital, 5115 Beach Channel Drive, Far Rockaway, NY 11691

HUTNER, Aline *Pediatrics 1990;* East Boston Neighborhood Health Center, 10 Gove Street, East Boston, MA O2128
hutnera@ebnhc.org

HWANG, Juliet *Pediatrics 2006;* 444 East 88 Street (Apt 2E), New York, NY 10128
juliet.hwang@mssm.edu

IGARTUA, Jon *Pediatrics, Critical Care Medicine 1999;* Avda.Los Chopos 55, 3E, Getxo Bizkaia, Spain 48990

IMUNDO, Jason *Pediatrics 2008;* 15 Ron Court, Commack, NY 11725
jason.imundo

IRAKAM, Anitha *Pediatrics, Neonatal-Perinatal Medicine 2002;* 25 North Road, Warren, NJ 07059

IRIGOYEN, Patricia *Pediatrics, Rheumatology 2006;* Children's Hospital at Montefiore, 3415 Bainbridge Avenue, Bronx, NY 10467
pirigoe@montefiore.org

ISAKSON, Loren *Pediatrics 2006, Allergy-Immunology;* University of South Florida, 4202 East Fowler Avenue, Tampa, FL 33620
loren_I@hotmail.com

ISRAEL, David Moshe *Pediatrics 1987, Gastroenterology 1989;* British Columbia Children's Hospital, 4480 Oak Street (Rm K4-200), Vancouver, British Columbia, Canada V6H3V4
disrael@cw.bc.ca

IVINS, Rhea *Pediatrics 1986, Adolescent Medicine 1988;* 10 Narla Lane, Utica, NY 13501
nasalcpap@yahoo.com

IVKER-GOLDSTEIN, Cindee *Pediatrics 1995;* 244 Westchester Avenue (Suite 210), White Plains, NY 10604
medcing@aol.com

IYPE, Jay *Pediatrics 2004;* 270 Union Avenue, Holbrook, NY 11741

IZENBERG, Neil *Pediatrics 1978, Adolescent Medicine;* Alfred duPont Hospital for Children, 1600 Rockland Road, Wilmington, DE 19803
izenberg@kidshealth.org

JACOB, Julie *Pediatrics 2003, Developmental & Behavioral Pediatrics 2006;* Schneider Children's Hospital, 269-01 76th Avenue, New Hyde Park, NY 11040

JACOBY-LOW, Gail *Pediatrics 1991;* 2410 Nnortheast 48th Avenue, Portland, OR 97213

JACQUE, Celeste *Pediatrics 1979, Child & Adolescent Psychiatry;* 201 South Livingston Avenue, Livingston, NJ O7039
cajacque@aol.com

JAIN, Varsha *Pediatrics 1992, Infectious Diseases 1995;* 82 Lords Way, New Hyde Park, NY 11040

JAISWAL, Paresh *Pediatrics 2003;* 433 Sykes Circle, Rio Rico, AZ 85648
pjaiswal@hotmail.com

JAMAL, Yousaf *Pediatrics, Hematology-Oncology 1998*

JANDER, Isabel Granja *Pediatrics 2005;* 2655 Prosperity Avenue (Suite 313), Fairfax, VA 22631
granja_isabel@hotmail.com

JANKELOVITS, Eric *Pediatrics 1988;* 760 Summer Street, Stamford, CT 06901

JARENWATTANANON, Marisa *Pediatrics, Cardiology 1985;* 4031 North Lake Drive, Shorewood, WI 53211

JEAN-BAPTISTE, Stefanie *Pediatrics 2007;* 144-32 78th Avenue (Apt 2E), Flushing, NY 11367

JENNINGS, Gloria *Pediatrics 1987;* 317 Cleveland Avenue, Highland Park, NJ 08816

JEROME, Robert *Pediatrics 1983;* 5721 S. Crescent Park (Suite 208), Playa Vista, CA 90094
robertsjeromemd@aol.com

JESSANI, Shabana *Pediatrics, Developmental & Behavioral Pediatrics 2004;* Melmed Center, 5020 East Shea Blvd, Scottsdale, AZ 85254

JIWANI, Amyn Ali *Pediatrics 1996, Cardiology 1999;* 9410 59th Avenue (Apt 4J), Elmhurst, NY 11373

JOHNSTON-MADINGER, Jean *Pediatrics 1986, Hematology-Oncology 1989;* 164 Commack Road, Commack, NY 11725

JORDAN, Jo-Ann *Pediatrics 2002;* 272 Broad Street, Red Bank, NJ O7701

JOSE, Bessey *Pediatrics 2008;* 212 Hales Avenue, Staten Island, NY 10312
bess_jose@yahoo.com

JOSEPH, Keanna *Pediatrics 2003;* 2675 Henry Hudson Pkwy (Suite 4F), Bronx, NY 10463
josephke@aol.com

JOSEPH, Natalie Pierre *Pediatrics 1995;* 850 Harrison Avenue (ACC), Boston, MA 02118

JOVINO, Louise *Pediatrics 1993;* 311 North Midland Avenue, Nyack, NY 10960
loujo3@juno.com

JOY, Rosemary *Pediatrics 2006;* 233 West Joe Orr Road, Chicago Heights, IL 60911

JUDMAN-LEDER, Eva *Pediatrics 2007, Pulmonary Medicine;* Children's Hospital Boston, 300 Longwood Avenue, Boston, MA O2108
eva.leder@ztaxreturn.com

JUSTER, Fern R. *Pediatrics, Ambulatory Pediatrics 1986;* 19 Bradhurst Avenue (Suite 800), Hawthorne, NY 10532

KABARITI, Jack *Pediatrics 2000;* Brooklyn Community Medical PC, 2935 Avenue S, Brooklyn, NY 11229
jkabariti@aol.com

KABAT, Loren Gail *Pediatrics 1987;* 1400 Pelham Parkway South, Bronx, NY 10461

KACPERSKI, Joanne *Pediatrics 2008, Neurology 2011;* Schneider Children's Hospital, 269-01 76th Avenue, New Hyde Park, NY 11040

KADEN, Gail Goodman *Pediatrics 1988;* Pediatrics Associates of Plainview, 400 South Oyster Bay Road (Suite 207), Hicksville, NY 11801

KAGANOWICZ-GORELICK, Eliza *Pediatrics 1975;* 48 Highland Blvd, Dix Hills, NY 11746

KAHAN, Joel *Pediatrics 1982;* 2611 Corporal Kennedy Street, Bayside, NY 11360
Drjlk@aol.com

KAHN, Doron *Pediatrics 2004, Neonatal-Perinatal Medicine 2007;* Joe DiMaggio Children's Hospital, 1000 Joe DiMaggio Drive, Hollywood, FL 33021
dorankahn@yahoo.com

KAIN, Zeev *Pediatrics 1989, Anesthesiology;* 333 Cedar Street, New Haven, CT 06520
zeev.kain@yale.edu

KAINE, Richard *Pediatrics 1971;* 6615 West Boynton Beach Blvd, Boynton Beach, FL 33437
rkaine@eqma.com

KAN, Li *Pediatrics, Neurology 1998;* Schneider Children's Hospital, 269-01 76th Avenue, New Hyde Park, NY 11040
lkan@lij.edu

KANG, Richard *Pediatrics 2003;* Children's Hospital of Los Angeles, 4650 Sunset Blvd., Los Angeles, CA 90027
richard_kang@nymc.edu

KANIA, Patricia *Pediatrics 1994*

KANTOR, Paul *Pediatrics 1990;* PO Box 338, Middle Saskachuan, Canada SOC1SO

KAPADIA, Shailee *Pediatrics, Allergy-Immunology 2002;* 2995 Fort Henry Drive (Suite 100), Kingsport, TN 37614
shaileedoc@hotmail.com

KAPLAN, Eric *Pediatrics 1976, Adolescent Medicine 1977;* 33 Bartlett Street, Lowell, MA O1852
epkpedi@massmed.org

KAPOOR, Vishwa *Pediatrics, Hematology-Oncology 1985;* 1560 South Imperial Avenue, El Centro, CA 92243

KARAKAS, Sabiha Pinar *Pediatrics 2003;* 9500 Euclid Avenue (HB-6), Cleveland, OH 44195

KARIDIS, Argyro *Pediatrics 2008;* 5 Hill Court, Glen Head, NY 11545
rorokar@yahoo.com

KAROLL, Doreen *Pediatrics, Developmental & Behavioral Pediatrics 1988;* Franciscan Hospital for Children, 30 Warren Street, Brighton, MA O2135
dkaroll@fharc.org

KARPF, Laurie *Pediatrics 1987;* 22047 State Road 7, Boca Raton, FL 33428

KASLOFF, Ilene *Pediatrics 1985;* 11294 Stones Throw Drive, Reston, VA 20194

KASNICKI, Laurie *Pediatrics 1981;* 515 Abbott Road, Buffalo, NY 14220
kasnicki@aol.com

KATSEVA, Ida L. *Pediatrics 1978;* 105-15 66 Road (Apt 1E), Forest Hills, NY 11375

KATZ, David *Pediatrics 1980;* 3333 Bardstown Road, Louisville, KY 40218
dkatz@ka.net

KATZ, Elizabeth *Pediatrics 1994;* 380 Dogwood Avenue, Franklin Square, NY 11010

KATZ, Laura *Pediatrics 2007;* Hasbro Children's Hospital, 593 Eddy Street, Providence, RI 2908

KATZ, Lisa *Pediatrics 2008;* 1780 Route 106, Syosset, NY 11791
klisa802@yahoo.com

KATZ, Uriel *Cardiology 2000;* Sheba Medical Center, Tel Hashomer, Israel 49100

KAUSHAL-JOHAL, Sandeep *Pediatrics 2005, Emergency Medicine;* 130 Dartmouth Street (Suite 1101), Boston, MA 02116
sandyjohal@aol.com

KAVIT, Gary *Pediatrics 1986;* 139 Beechwood Hills, Newport News, VA 23608

KAW, Saroj *Pediatrics, Neonatal-Perinatal Medicine 1986;* 47 White House, Panchuati, Ambawadi Ahmedabad, Gujarat, India 38006

KAYE, Arthur *Pediatrics 1975;* 271 Jericho Turnpike, Floral Park, NY 11002
suffydoc@aol.com

KEATES-BALEEIRO, Jennifer *Pediatrics 2000;* 2220 Pierce Avenue, Nashville, TN 37232

KELMINSON, Leslie *Pediatrics 1964;* 1010 East 19th Avenue (Suite 617), Denver, CO 80208

KEMPIAK, Stephan *Pediatrics 2007;* University of California at San Diego Medical Center, 402 West Dickinson Street, San Diego, CA 92103

KENDALL, Roxanne *Pediatrics 1982;* 25 Hageman Lane, Princeton, NJ O8540
drroxi@hotmail.com

KENNEDY, Joanne M. *Pediatrics 1989;* 2401 Gillham Road, Kansas City, MO 64108

KESSLER, Oded *Urology 1995;* Schneider Children's Medical Center of Israel, 14 Kaplan Street, Petah Tiqva, Israel 49100

KHABBAZE, Youssef *Pediatrics, Hematology-Oncology 2001;* 509 6th Street (Apt 3-D), Brooklyn, NY 11215

KHADAVI, Alan *Pediatrics 2003, Allergy-Immunology;* 199-A West Shore Road, Great Neck, NY 11024
akhadavi@yahoo.com

KHAN, Abu *Pediatrics 1995, Emergency Medicine;* Morgan Stanley Children's Hospital, 622 West 168 Street (PH 137), New York, NY 10032
ank14@columbia.edu

KHAN, Aliya *Allergy-Immunology 1997;* Dayton Arthritis and Allergy, 3075 Governors Place Blvd (Suite 110), Dayton, OH 45409
draliyakhan@aol.com

KHAN, Ambreen *Pediatrics, Emergency Medicine 2003;* 73-12 Yellowstone Blvd., Forest Hills, NY 11375

KHAN, Kishwar *Pediatrics 1995;* 5 Pischke Road, Campbell Hall, NY 10916

KHAN, Nafis *Pediatrics , Emergency Medicine 1995;* Schneider Children's Hospital, 269-01 76th Avenue, New Hyde Park, NY 11040

KHAN, Zahida *Pediatrics 1980;* 115 Irving Avenue, Brooklyn, NY 11237

KHANNA, Happy Neera *Pediatrics 1998;* 544 North Glendale Avenue, Glendale, CA 91206

KIBLAWI, Fuad *Pediatrics 1998, Cardiology 2001;* 123 Bobolink Court, Wayne, NJ O7470
fkiblawi@optonline.net

KILCHEVSKY, Eitan *Pediatrics 1983, Neonatal-Perinatal Medicine;* Danbury Hospital, 24 Hospital Avenue, Danbury, CT O6810
amikefy@yahoo.com

KILIMNICK, Joseph *Pediatrics 1998;* 39 North Goodman Street, Rochester, NY 14607
dryosef@yahoo.com

KIM, Theresa *Pediatrics 1970;* 150 North Finley Avenue, Basking Ridge, NJ O7920

KIM, Urian *Pediatrics 2003;* 201 East Franklin Turnpike, HoHoKus, NJ 07423

KIMPO, Joycelyn *Pediatrics 1995, Endocrinology;* National Health Service, 3409 Calloway Drive, Bakersvield, CA 93312

KIMPO, Miriam *Pediatrics, Hematology-Oncology 2002;* 79-06 68 Road (Apt 2B), Middle Village, NY 11379

KIRSCHNER, Jessica *Pediatrics 2008;* 571 Chestnut Street, Cedarhurst, NY 11516
jessica@adelsberg.com

KLEIGER, Richard *Pediatrics 1985;* 108 Main Street, New Paltz, NY 12561

KLEIMAN, Michele *Pediatrics 1988;* 147 Saybrook Road, Middletown, CT O6457
mdkmd@cnskids.com

KLEIN, Susan *Pediatrics 1984;* 41 East Post Road, White Plains, NY 10601
sklein3240@optonline.net

KLEIN, Thomas *Pediatrics 1983, Allergy-Immunology;* 400 West Township Line Road, Havertown, PA 19083
tkleinmd@hotmail.com

KLEINBERG, Mitchell *Pediatrics 1983;* 270 Union Avenue, Holbrook, NY 11741
mitdeb@aol.com

KNOBLER, Stacey *Pediatrics 1991, Neurology 1994;* 3732 Jefferson Street, Kansas City, MO 64111

*KNOLLWELL-ROTH, Sharon *Pediatrics 2006*

KOHN, Michael *Pediatrics, Adolescent Medicine 1996;* Locked Bag 4001, Westmead, NSW 2145, Australia
michaek2@chw.edu.au

KOHN, Gary *Pediatrics, Critical Care Medicine 2002;* 16 Helene Drive, Randolph, NJ 07869

KOKAN, Farhat *Pediatrics 1996, Allergy-Immunology;* 2116 Craig Road, Eau Claire, WI 54701
kokanfarhat@marshfieldclinic.org

KOMITAS, Mahi *Pediatrics 2000;* 22-21 72nd Stree (3rd Floor), Jackson Heights, NY 11370
gkmk99@yahoo.com

KORN, Sheila *Pediatrics 1992;* 2073 Newbridge Road, Bellmore, NY 11710
seal498@aol.com

KOROPECKY, Christine *Allergy-Immunology 1996;* 285 Sills Road, East Patchogue, NY 11772

KOSLOWE, Oren *Pediatrics 2006;* 525 East 68 Street, New York, NY 10021
koslowe@aecom.edu

KOSTER, Divya *Pediatrics 2006;* 50 Amaral Street, Riverside, RI O2915
divyakoster@hotmail.com

KOSTER, Michael *Pediatrics 2007, Infectious Diseases;* 593 Eddy Street, Providence, RI O2915
michael_koster@brown.edu

KOVACS, George *Pediatrics 1997;* 23 Bond Street, Great Neck, NY 11021
gkdoc1@aol.com

KRAUS, Gregory *Pediatrics 1999, Critical Care Medicine 2002;* SUNY Downstate Medical Center, 450 Clarkson Avenue (Box 49), Brooklyn, NY 11203
gregory.kraus@downstate.edu

KRAUSS, Joel *Pediatrics 1997;* 1111 Amsterdam Avenue, New York, NY 10025

KRAUSS, Richard *Pediatrics 1990, Anesthesiology;* Long Island Jewish Medical Center, 269-01 76th Avenue, New Hyde Park, NY 11040
pkrk38@aol.com

KRECO, Edvins *Pediatrics 2000;* 28 Spruce Mountain Rd, Danbury, CT O6810
latmed7@aol.com

KREITZER, Paula *Pediatrics 1985, Endocrinology 1988;* Schneider Children's Hospital, 269-01 76th Avenue, New Hyde Park, NY 11040
pcritzer@lij.edu

KRIEF, Patricia *Pediatrics 2004, Neurology 2007;* Schneider Children's Hospital, 269-01 76th Avenue, New Hyde Park, NY 11040
pkrief@nshs.edu

KRIEF, William *Pediatrics 1999, Emergency Medicine;* Schneider Children's Hospital, 269-01 76th Avenue, New Hyde Park, NY 11040
willeve@pol.net

KRISHNAN, Venkatesan *Pediatrics, Neonatal-Perinatal Medicine 1974;* 2142 North Cove, Toledo, OH 43606

KRONBERG, Jason *Pediatrics 2001;* 270 Union Avenue, Holbrook, NY 11741
jdkronberg@optonline.net

KRONFELD, Gary *Pediatrics 1983;* 2 Cobblefield Road, Mendham, NJ O7945

KUMAR, Cathie *Pediatrics 2005;* 398 Neponset Avenue, Dorchester, MA 02062
cathiekumar@hotmail.com

KUMAR, Gogi *Pediatrics, Neurology 2005;* One Children's Plaza, Dayton, Ohio 45404
kumarg@childrensdayton,org

KUMAR, Munish *Pediatrics 2008, Neonatal-Perinatal Medicine;* St John's Children's Hospital of Southern Illinois, 800 East Carpenter Street, Springfield, IL 62769

KUMAR, Pankaj *Pediatrics, Neonatal-Perinatal Medicine 2003;* 4380 Brentwood Drive, South Boston, MA 24592

KUMAR, Vasanth *Pediatrics, Hematology-Oncology 1978;* 111 (C) Brittany Farms Road, New Britain, CT O6053

KUNCEWITCH, William *Pediatrics, 1981;* 380 Dogwood Avenue, Franklin Square, NY 11010

KUSHNER-CUSHMAN, Susan *Pediatrics, 1989;* Hackensack University Hospital, 90 Prospect Avenue, Hackensack, NJ 07601
evsu@aol.com

KWOK, Maria *Pediatrics 2001;* Morgan Stanley Children's Hospital, 622 West 168 Street, New York, NY 10032

KWONG, Terry *Pediatrics, Rheumatology 1995;* Australia

KYRIAKAKOS, Anastassios *Pediatrics 1981;* 699 West 239 (Suite 3M), Riverdale, NY 10463

LACANILAO, Ramon *Pediatrics, Endocrinology 1997;* 250 Stanaford Road, Beckley, WV 25801

LaCORTE, Justin *Pediatrics 2006, Emergency Medicine 2009;* 105 East Mauser Street, Valley Stream, NY 11580

LACY-KING, Roxanne *Pediatrics 2002;* 687 Northern Pkwy, Uniondale, NY 11553

LAKSHMINARAYANAN, Sonali *Pediatrics, Hematology-Oncology 2005;* 2726 Croasdaile Drive, Durham, NC 27705

LALLY, Michelle *Pediatrics, Developmental & Behavioral Pediatrics 1992;* 135 Rutledge Avenue, Charleston, SC 29425

LANDA, Dahlia *Allergy-Immunology 2008;* ENT Associates of NY, 875 Old Country Road, Plainview, NY 11803

LANTZOUNI, Eleni *Pediatrics 1996, Adolescent Medicine 1999;* 113 Hunt Club Drive (Apt 3D), Copley, OH 44321

LANZONE, Theresa *Pediatrics 1983;* 350 National Blvd (Suite 2C), Long Beach, NY 11561
redbeachrosie@aol.com

LAO, Jimmy *Pediatrics, Neonatal-Perinatal Medicine 1991;* 1978 Industrial Blvd., Housa, LA 70363

LAPIDUS, Sivia *Pediatrics 2006;* 3131 Connecticut Avenue Northwest, Washington, DC 20008
siviakerry@yahoo.com

LAPTOOK, Abbot *Pediatrics 1979, Neonatal-Perinatal Medicine;* 101 Dudley Street (Suite 1100), Providence, RI 2905

LARKIN, Anne Marie *Pediatrics 1998*

LASHANSKY, Gayle *Pediatrics 1989;* Queens Hospital Center, 82-68 164th Street, Jamaica, NY 11432
lashansg@nychhc.org

LASKARI, Cleo Vassilios *Cardiology 1995;* 15 Xenokratous, Athens, Greece 10675

LAU, Alice *Pediatrics 1983;* 4265 Kissena Blvd (Suite L-4), Flushing, NY 11365

LAU, Bernard *Pediatrics 1999;* 1344 Middle Country Road, Centereach, NY 11720

LAU, Joshua Hung Tin *Pediatrics 2005;* 8 Franklin Road, Great Neck, NY 11024
joshuahtlau@aol.com

LAWRENCE, Donald *Pediatrics 1969;* 37 Stewart Street, Hewlett, NY 11557
drs.4kids@aol.com

LAWRENCE, Emily *Pediatrics 2008;* Mt. Sinai Hospital, One Gustave Levy Place, New York, NY 10029
emilyjlawrence@hotmail.com

LAWRENCE, Philip *Pediatrics 1985;* Pocono Medical Bldg, 206 East Brown Street, East Stroudsburg, PA 18301

LAZAR, Linda *Pediatrics 1980, Gastroenterology;* Le Bonheur Children's Medical Center, 50 North Dunlap Street, Memphis, TN 38103 *llazar@utmem.edu*

LEARSY, Dawn *Pediatrics 2003;* PO Box 208064, New Haven, CT O6520

LEAVENS-MAURER, Jill *Pediatrics 1989;* Winthrop University Hospital, 259 First Street, Mineola, NY 11501

LEBO, Debra *Allergy-Immunology 1993;* 74-11 37 Avenue, Jackson Heights, NY 11372

LEBOVIC, Daniel *Pediatrics 1985;* 326 Main Street, Metuchen, NJ O8840

LEE, Chi *Urology 1997;* 2999 Regent Street(Suite 612), Berkley, CA 94705

LEE, Jeong *Pediatrics 1994;* ODA Primary Care Health Clinic, 14-16 Heyward Street, Brooklyn, NY 11211

LEEDS, Andrea *Pediatrics 1993;* 3178 Lee Place, Bellmore, NY 11710 *mom5doc30@hotmail.com*

LEIB, Martin *Pediatrics 1975, Ophthalmology;* The Edward S. Harkness Eye Institute, 635 West 165th Street (Suite 230), New York, NY 10032

LEMON-MULE, Heather *Pediatrics 2006;* 704 166 Street, Whitestone, NY 11357

LENARSKY, Carl *Pediatrics 1980, Hematology-Oncology;* Medical City Children's Hospital, 7777 Forest Lane (D400), Dallas, TX 75230 *clenar3526@aol.com*

LEONOR-GILRANE, Marixie Q. *Pediatrics, Neonatal-Perinatal Medicine 1985;* 7454 Hannover Parkway, Stockbridge, GA 30281

LEONOV, Andrey *Pediatrics 2006;* 1020 Laurel Oak Road, Voorhees, NJ O8043

LERIAS, Edgar *Pediatrics 1987;* 2017 Deer Park Avenue, Deer Park, NY 11729 *efleriasmd@aol.com*

LESSER, Eric *Pediatrics 1991;* 703 Main Street, Paterson, NJ O7503

LEUPOLD, Kerry *Pediatrics 2000, Emergency Medicine 2003;* Robert Wood Johnson University Hospital, One Robert Wood Johnson Place, New Brunswick, NJ 08903

LEVENE, Eric *Pediatrics 1993;* 15 North Broadway (Suite F), White Plains, NY 10601 *elevene@chesterpediatrics.com*

LEVI, Michelle *Pediatrics 2004;* Wishard Health Services, 1001 West Tenth Street, Indianapolis, ID 46202

LEVIN, Marina *Pediatrics, Hematology-Oncology 1997;* Nassau University Medical Center, 2201 Hempstead Turnpike, East Meadow, NY 11554

LEVINE, Alan *Pediatrics, Hematology-Oncology 1982;* 3601 Hempstead Turnpike (Suite 416), Levittown, NY 11756

LEVINE, Daniel *Pediatrics 1991, Endocrinology 1994;* 90 Prospect Avenue, Hackensack, NJ O7452 *dbl1@optonline.net*

LEVINE, Jack *Pediatrics 1981;* 5 Aspen Place, Great Neck, NY 11021 *jmlevine@optonline.net*

LEVINE, Marc *Pediatrics 1975, Cardiology 1981;* 3 Cooper Plaza, Camden, NJ 08103 *levinemm@umdnj.edu*

LEVINE-BOSIN, Stephanie *Pediatrics 1992, Adolescent Medicine 1994;* 2345 Lamington Road, Bedminster, NJ O7921

LEVIT, Orly *Pediatrics 2006;* Yale-New Haven Children's Hospital, 20 York Street (Room 493 WP), New Haven, CT O6504 *levits@hotmail.com*

LEVY, Itzhak *Pediatrics, Infectious Diseases 1997;* Schneider Children's Medical Center of Israel, 14 Kaplan Street, Petah Tikva, Israel 49202

LEVY, Moshe *Pediatrics 1999;* 831 Tennent Road, Manalapan, NJ O8701

LEW, Lai-Ping *Pediatrics 1999;* 163 East 97th Street, New York, NY 10029

LIBERT, Melissa *Pediatrics 2007;* Northshore Children's Healthcare, 3 School Street (Suite 302), Glen Cove, NY 11542 *mms428@yahoo.com*

*LIBRIK, Leon *Pediatrics 1960, Endocrinology*

LIEBER, Marvin *Pediatrics 1976;* 233 Union Avenue, Holbrook, NY 11741

LIGHTMAN, Hylton *Pediatrics 1985, Allergy-Immunology 1987;* 601 Jarvis Avenue, Far Rockaway, NY 11691 *thebestdoc4kids@yahoo.com*

LIM, Wilma *Pediatrics 1986*

LIMAYE, Deepa *Pediatrics 1995, Developmental & Behavioral Pediatrics 1997;* 8 Robin Road, Farmington, CT O6032 *plimaye@pol.net*

LINDER, Alice *Pediatrics 1982, Child & Adolescent Psychiatry 1984;* The Astor Home for Children (PO Box 5005), Rhinebeck, NY 12572 *alinder@astorservices.org*

LINDGREN, Bruce *Urology 1998;* 2300 Children's Plaza, Chicago, IL 60614

LINDT, Josephine *Pediatrics 1992, Developmental & Behavioral Pediatrics;* 1402 Solano Avenue, Albany, CA 94706 *jojolindt@yahoo.com*

LIPTSEN, Ellina *Pediatrics, Neonatal-Perinatal Medicine 2005;* 1835 Franklin Street, Denver, CO 80218 *ellinamd@yahoo.com*

LIQUORNIK, Karen *Pediatrics 1992;* Thornhill Pediatrics, Thornhill, Ontario, Canada

LIU, Yingxue *Pediatrics 1998;* 557 Cranbury Road (Suite 18), East Brunswick, NJ O8816 *shelleyleemd@hotmail.com*

LIWAG, Celerina *Pediatrics 1995;* 159 North Reading Road, Ephrata, PA 17522 *slimperial@hotmail.com*

LOBEL, Danielle *Pediatrics, Neurology 1995;* Schneider Children's Medical Center of Israel, 14 Kaplan Street, Petah Tikva, Israel 49100

LONG, Jennifer *Pediatrics, Neonatal-Perinatal Medicine 2005;* Pediatric Health Center, 1951 Southwest 172nd Avenue (Suite 304), Miramar, FL 33029

LOPEZ, Carmen *Pediatrics 2002;* 435 East 79 Street, New York, NY 10021

LOYOLA, Rosa *Pediatrics, Developmental & Behavioral Pediatrics 1997;* 40690 (A) California Oaks Road, Murrieta, CA 92562

LUA, Jorge *Pediatrics, Neonatal-Perinatal Medicine 2000;* 3901 Beaubien Blvd., Detroit, MI 48201

LUCK, Raemma Paredes *Pediatrics 1993;* Temple University Children's Medical Center, 3401 North Broad Street (6th Floor) Philadelphia, PA 19140

LUFTIG-WEISS, Jennifer *Pediatrics 2001, Rheumatology 2004;* 130 Dean Street, Marrington Park, NJ 7040 *jweiss@humed.com*

LUGO, Nitza *Pediatrics, Critical Care Medicine 1997;* 252 Calle San Jorge, San Juan, PR

LUJAN-ZILBERMANN, Jorge *Pediatrics 1998, Infectious Diseases;* 17 Davis Boulevard (Suite 313), Tampa, FL 33606 *jlujanzi@hsc.usf.edu*

LUNA, Betty *Pediatrics 1998;* 731 White Plains Road, Bronx, NY 10473

LYNCH, Patricia Kania *Pediatrics 1994;* 60 Prospect Avenue, Middletown, NY 10940

MACHEN, Heather *Pediatrics, Emergency Medicine 2006;* Texas Children's Hospital, 6621 Fannin Street, Houston, TX 77030

MACHUCA, Hildred *Pediatrics 2004;* 112-15 72 Road, Forest Hills, NY 11375

MADAD, Saiyeda *Pediatrics 1978;* 226 Clinton Street, Hempstead, NY 11550 *s.madad@olmig.com*

MADDUR, Shantha Devi *Pediatrics 1985;* 1105 Essex Drive, Sierra Vista, AZ 85635

MADHOK, Ashish *Pediatrics, Cardiology 2003;* 2312 Knob Creek Road (Suite 208), Johnson City, TN 37604
ashisshailee@hotmail.com

MAGALETTI, Francine *Pediatrics 1987;* 2825 North Service Road No. 7, Margate, FL 33063

MAHADEO, Robby *Pediatrics 1993, Emergency Medicine;* 197-27 Hillside Avenue, Hollis, NY 11423

MAHMOOD, Khawaja *Allergy-Immunology 1996*

MAISEL, Mercedes *Pediatrics 1993;* 19669 Estuary Drive, Boca Raton, FL 33498

MAITINSKY, Steven *Pediatrics 1968, Developmental & Behavioral Pediatrics;* 16 Bailey Avenue, East Meadow, NY 11554

MAJEED, Salamat *Pediatrics 1995, Emergency Medicine;* 263-18 Hillside Avenue, Floral Park, NY 11004
doctormajeed@gmail.com

MAKATAN, Marjan *Pediatrics 2001;* 609 Mercer Street, Albany, NY 12208
marjan@comuserve.com

MAKORNWATTANA, Porawat *Allergy-Immunology 2004;* 321 East 13 Street (Apt 3-A), New York, NY 10003
porawat@hotmail.com

MALKIN, Elfrida *Pediatrics, Neurology 1991;* 90 North Broadway, Nyack, NY 10960
drmalkin@optonline.net

MALLARE, Johanna *Pediatrics 1997, Endocrinology 2000;* 50 North Dunlap, Memphis, TN 38103
jmallare@utmem.edu

MAMANI, Sylvia *Pediatrics 2007;* 114 Lee Road, Garden City, NY 11530

MAMONLUK, Maribel *Pediatrics, Allergy-Immunology 2000;* 156 Island Creek Road, Pikeville, KY 41501

MANALO, Erlinda *Pediatrics 1993, Neonatal-Perinatal Medicine;* 6501 Coyle Avenue, Carmichael, CA 95608
edmanalo@aol.com

MANDEL, Corey *Pediatrics, Cardiology 2003;* 901 7th Avenue (Suite 310), Fort Worth, TX 76104
cmandel@cookchildrens.org

MANDELKER, Lisa *Pediatrics 2008*
lisagold@aol.com

MANICONE, Paul *Pediatrics 2002;* 111 Michigan Avenue N.W., Washington, DC 20010
pmanicon@cnmc.org

MANOHAR, Priti *Pediatrics, Neurology 2004;* 3125 Center Pointe Drive, Edinburg, TX 78539

MANTZOURANIS, Jessica *Pediatrics 2006;* 229 South Street, Oyster Bay, NY 11771

MARCANO, Brenda *Pediatrics 1998, Critical Care Medicine 2001;* Good Samaritan Hospital Medical Center, 1000 Montauk Highway, West Islip, NY 11795
bmarcano@lij.edu

MARCHITELLI, Roberto *Pediatrics 1988, Pulmonary Medicine 1989;* 6 Old Homestead Way, Albertson, NY 11507
piccolomd@aol.com

MARCHLEWSKI, Robert *Pediatrics 2005, Allergy-Immunology 2007;* 25 Canterbury Road (2T), Great Neck, NY 11021
rmarchlewski@hotmail.com

MARCU, Mariana *Allergy-Immunology 2000;* 30 East 40 Street, New York, NY 10016

MARCUS, Carole *Pediatrics 1984;* Children's Hospital of Philadelphia, 34 Street & Civic Center Blvd., Philadelphia, PA 19104

MARDY, Gisele *Pediatrics, Infectious Diseases 1994;* 9299 Southwest 152 Street, Miami, FL 33157

MARILAO, Hilario *Cardiology 1989;* 4000 Fourteenth Street (211), Riverside, CA 92501

MAROON, Christine *Pediatrics 2001;* 639 Main Street, Johnson City, NY 13790

MARRIA, Pooja *Pediatrics 2007, Gastroenterology;* Kennedy Krieger Institute, Johns Hopkins University, 707 North Broadway, Baltimore, MD 21205
pbmarria@alum.mit.edu

MARSHALL, Ian *Pediatrics 1999;* Robert Wood Johnson University Hospital, One Robert Wood Johnson Place, New Brunswick, NJ 08901

MARTINEZ, Alfred *Pediatrics 2003;* 20 Edwards Road, Foxboro, MA 02035
amartine@aecom.hu.edu

MARTINEZ, Maritza *Pediatrics 2008;* 19 Firewood Road, Manorhaven, NY 11050
mariposa00@gmail.com

MARTON, Freddie *Pediatrics 1988, Neurology;* 123 Grove Avenue (100), Cedarhurst, NY 11516

MARTYNEC, Lydia *Pediatrics 1987;* Food & Drug Administration, Center for Drug Evaluation & Research, 10903 New Hampshire Avenue (Bldg 22, Rm 2344), Silver Spring, MD 20903
Lydia.Martynec@fda.hhs.gov

MASAKAYAN, Adelaide *Pediatrics 1994;* 32 Setakott Place, Setauket, NY 11733
bency@optonline.net

MASER, Dennis *Pediatrics 1982;* 417 Henry Street, Herkimer, NY 13350
timeoff296@aol.com

MASSEY, Laurie O'Brien *Pediatrics 1999;* 35 Sproul Road, Hanover, MA 02339

MATHEW, Kolathu A. *Pediatrics 1972;* 720 Montauk Highway, West Islip, NY 11795

MATHEW, Rajamma *Pediatrics, Critical Care/Pulmonary Medicine 1986;* Blythedale Children's Hospital, Bradhurst Avenue, Valhalla, NY 10595

MATHIAS, Liesl *Pediatrics 1996, Hematology-Oncology;* Loma Linda University Medical Center, 11234 Anderson Street, Loma Linda, CA 92354

MATTHEWS, Benjamin *Pediatrics 1994, Critical Care Medicine;* 42 Adella Avenue, West Newton, MA 02465

MATTHEWS, Lori Gara *Pediatrics 1993, Developmental & Behavioral Pediatrics;* 42 Adella Avenue, West Newton, MA 02465

MATTHEWS, Zacharias *Pediatrics 1954*

MAYBANK, Karen *Pediatrics 2003;* 225 Rabro Drive East, Hauppauge, NY 11788
aletha.maybank@suffolkcountyny.gov

MAYTAL, Joseph *Pediatrics 1982, Neurology;* Schneider Children's Hospital, 269-01 76th Avenue, New Hyde Park, NY 11040

MAZE, Aubrey *Pediatrics 1974, Anesthesiology;* 21901 North Central Avenue (Suite 500), Phoenix, AZ 85012
mazevalley@aol.com

MAZIN, Howard *Pediatrics 2006;* 987 Allen Court, Teaneck, NJ 07666

MC CARTHY, Patricia *Pediatrics 1977;* 300 Bay Shore Road, North Babylon, NY 11703
pkmdr@qlimg.com

MC COLLUM, Alexandra *Pediatrics 2008;* Rady Children's Hospital, 8010 Frost Street (Suite 602), San Diego, CA 92123
dr.alexandramccollum@yahoo.com

MC DADE, Jenny *Pediatrics 2006;* 332 North Lauderdale (MS 260), Memphis, TN 38105

McDERMOTT-ADAMS, Nancy *Pediatrics 1987;* 777 Bannock Street, Denver, CO 80204
njmcdermott@comcast.net

MC DONOUGH, Christian *Pediatrics 2006, Anesthesiology;* Robert Wood Johnson University Hospital, One Robert Wood Johnson Place, New Brunswick, NJ 08903

MC GOVERN, Margaret *Pediatrics 1987, Medical Genetics;* Mt. Sinai Hospital, One Gustave Levy Place, New York, NY 10029
margaret.mcgovern@mssm.edu

MC INERNEY-LOPEZ, Regina *Pediatrics 2005;* 3137 Elmmede Road, Ellicot City, MD 21042 *rmcine7771@aol.com*

MC LAUGHLIN, Reginald *Pediatrics 1975;* Queens-Long Island Medical Group, 125-06 101st Avenue, Richmond Hill, NY 11419

McNAMARA, Joseph *Pediatrics, Hematology-Oncology 1987;* Connecticut Hospice, 100 Double Beach Road, Homeport Cove, Branford, CT 06405

MC SHERRY, Kevin *Pediatrics 1987, Hematology-Oncology 1990;* 355 Grand Street, Jersey City, NJ O7302

MEHROTRA, Deepti *Pediatrics 1999;* 61-34 188 Street (Suite 211), Fresh Meadows, NY 11365 *tistibhommi@yahoo.com*

MEISLER, Susan *Pediatrics 1987;* 145 Huguenot Street, New Rochelle, NY 10801 *babydocshm@aol.com*

MELA, Suzanne *Pediatrics 2007* *suzanne0023@aol.com*

MELTZER-KRIEF, Eve *Pediatrics 1998;* 129 Hayes Place, Centerport, NY 11721 *wlleve@aol.com*

MENSCH, Deborah *Pediatrics, Cardiology 2008;* Schneider Children's Hospital, 269-01 76th Avenue, New Hyde Park, NY 11040 *deborahmensch@hotmail.coom*

MERCHANT-SOOMAR, Sanah *Pediatrics , Cardiology 2006;* 213 Katemeya Heights (Zone 11), Cairo, Egypt *sanah_m@hotmail.com*

MEYAPPAN, Thiyagaraja *Pediatrics 2002;* 2320 Taylor Street, Dallas, TX 75201

MEYERSON, Lisa Linzer *Pediatrics 1993;* 3156 Shore Road, Bellmore, NY 11710

MIJARES-ZIMMERMAN, Jennifer *Pediatrics 1996;* 5962 Berryhill Road, Milton, FL 32570

MILANAIK, Ruth *Pediatrics, Developmental & Behavioral Pediatrics 2004;* Schneider Children's Hospital, 269-01 76th Avenue, New Hyde Park, NY 11040

MILGRAUM, Sandy *Pediatrics 1981;* 81 Brunswick Woods Drive, East Brunswick, NJ O8816

MILLER, Harvey *Pediatrics 1980;* 2330 Union Blvd, Islip, NY 11751

MILLER, Karen *Pediatrics, Developmental & Behavioral Pediatrics 1996;* 1731 Beacon Street (Suite 1513), Brookline, MA O2445

MILLER, Margarita *Pediatrics 1998;* 2801 North I-35 East (Suite 110), Carrollton, TX 75007 *mmiller@medscape.com*

MILLER, Michael *Pediatrics 2003, Critical Care Medicine 2006;* Schneider Children's Hospital, 269-01 76th Avenue, New Hyde Park, NY 11040 *mmiller1002@yahoo.com*

MILMAN, Marina *Pediatrics 1997;* 21 Hunting Hill Road, Woodbury, NY 11797 *mmilman@optonline.net*

MILOJEVIC, Diana *Pediatrics 2003, Rheumatology 2002;* 533 Parnassus Avenue, San Francisco, CA 94143 *milojevic@ped.ucsf.edu*

MINIKES, Neil *Allergy-Immunology 1989;* 570 Piermont Road (Suite 17), Closter, NJ O7624 *doctorneil@aol.com*

MINTZ, Jesse *Pediatrics 1979;* 885 Main Street, Hackensack, NJ O7601

MINUSKIN, Tal *Pediatrics 2000;* Edmond and Lily Safra Children's Hospital, Chaim Sheba Medical Center, Tel HaShomer, Ramat-Gan, Israel 52621

> The bedside is always the true center of medical teaching.
>
> —Oliver Wendell Holmes
> (1809-1894)

MIRER, Mikhail *Pediatrics, Neurology 1999;* Good Samaritan Hospital Medical Center, 1000 Montauk Highway, West Islip, NY 11795

MITSOTAKIS-HOWARD, Demetra *Pediatrics 2004;* 243 87th Street, Brooklyn, NY 11209 *demimd@hotmail.com*

MODI, Sangita Kumari *Pediatrics 1999;* 984 North Broadway, Yonkers, NY 10701

MOERCK, Linda *Pediatrics 2000;* 1014 Fort Salonga Road, Northport, NY 11768

MOERCK-JOHNSON, Deborah *Pediatrics 2000;* 312 Long Beach Road, Island Park, NY 11558

MOHAMED, Yasser *Pediatrics, Hematology-Oncology 1998*

MOISSIDIS, Ioannis *Pediatrics 1997, Allergy-Immunology;* Mezonos 304, Patra, Greece 26222 *moissidis@gmail.com*

MOKIDES, Valerie *Pediatrics 1991;* 1575 Hillside Avenue, New Hyde Park, NY 11040

MOLLICK, Lawrence *Pediatrics 1975, Otolaryngology;* 560 Northern Blvd, Great Neck, NY 11021 *lmollick@optonline.net*

MONES, Karen *Pediatrics 1996, Developmental & Behavioral Pediatrics;* 10 Grosvenor Place, Great Neck, NY 11021

MORALES, Yesenia *Pediatrics, Neonatal-Perinatal Medicine 2008;* 9408 Avenue K, Brooklyn, NY 11236 *morales_y@yahoo.com*

MORAN, Oscar *Pediatrics 1956;* Shis-QL10 Conj. 10, Casa 15, Brasilia 71600

MORENO, Lisa *Pediatrics 2003, Allergy-Immunology 2005;* 102-31 46th Avenue, Corona, NY 11368

MORGANSTERN, Jeffrey *Pediatrics 2003, Gastroenterology & Nutrition;* 120 Deer Valley Drive, Nesconset, NY 11767 *jmorganstern@notes.cc.sunysb.edu*

MORGENSTERN, Bruce *Pediatrics 1981, Nephrology;* 1919 East Thomas Road, Phoenix, AZ 85016 *bmorgenstern@mayo.edu*

MORGENSTERN, Joel *Pediatrics 1982;* 45 Route 25A (Suite E2), Shoreham, NY 11786

MORGENSTERN, Solomon S. *Pediatrics 2004, Emergency Medicine;* 935 Northfield Road, Woodmere, NY 11598 *ssmorgenstern@hotmail.com*

MORRIS, Elliot *Pediatrics 1983;* 271 Jericho Turnpike, Floral Park, NY 11001 *m61376@optonline.net*

MOUSTAFA, Usama *Pediatrics 2006;* 1814 78 Street [Apt 1E], Brooklyn, NY 11214

MUKHERJEE, Sarmistha *Pediatrics 2005;* 256-08 86th Avenue, Floral Park, NY 11001 *docsarmi@hotmail.com*

MULALE, Unami *Pediatrics 2008, Critical Care Medicine 2011;* Schneider Children's Hospital, 269-01 76th Avenue, New Hyde Park, NY 11040 *umulale@yahoo.com*

MURPHY, Susan *Pediatrics 1988, Hematology-Oncology 1991;* 94 Old Short Hills Road (1-F), Livingston, NJ O7039

MURZA, Gina *Pediatrics 1995, Neonatal-Perinatal Medicine 1998;* Good Samaritan Hospital, 1000 Montauk Highway, West Islip, NY 11795

MUSIKER-NEMIROV, Jamie *Pediatrics 1990, Emergency Medicine;* Good Samaritan Hospital, 1000 Montauk Highway, West Islip, NY 11795 *nemi@optonline.net*

MYERS, Christine *Pediatrics 2006;* 181 Franklin Ave., Malverne, NY 11565

NACHMAN, Sharon *Pediatrics 1986, Infectious Diseases;* SUNY Stony Brook University Hospital, Stony Brook, NY 11794 *sharon.nachman@stonybrook.edu*

NADARAJ, Sumekala *Pediatrics, Cardiology 2005;* 254 Easton Avenue, New Brunswick, NJ 08901 *snadaraj@email.chop.edu*

NAFICY-PAKRAVAN, Parvin *Pediatrics 1969;* 665 Broadway, Paterson, NJ O7514

NAGEL, Michael *Pediatrics 1986, Neurology 1989;* 4235 Secor Road, Toledo, OH 43623

NAGELBERG, Joy *Pediatrics 1985, Ambulatory Pediatrics 1986, Emergency Medicine;* Schneider Children's Hospital, 269-01 76th Avenue, New Hyde Park, NY 11040
jnagelbe@lij.edu

NAGPAL, Rajeev *Pediatrics 1989, Gastroenterology & Nutrition;* 4440 West 95th Street, Oak Lawn, IL 60453

NAIK, Vibhuti *Pediatrics 2004,*
vnaik@yahoo.com

NAKAR, Charles *Pediatrics 2007, Hematology-Oncology;* Memorial Sloan-Kettering Cancer Center, 1275 York Avenue, New York, NY 10065
charlesnakar@hotmail.com

NALABOFF, Kenneth *Pediatrics 1997;* 3000-12 Stevens Street, Oceanside, NY 11572

NANADIEGO, Maria *Pediatrics 1981;* 5225 Canyon Crest Drive, Riverside, CA 92507

NANGIA, Srishti *Pediatrics 2002;* 780 Davis Avenue, Staten Island, NY 10310

NAPOLITANO, Jeanmarie *Pediatrics 1976;* 150 Sunrise Highway (Suite 200), Lindenhurst, NY 11757
docjeanmarie@yahoo.com

NARAIN-CHAWLA, Bindoo *Pediatrics 1990;* 1070 Flagler Avenue, Leesburg, FL 34748
bnarain21@hotmail.com

NARAN, Navyn *Pediatrics 1997, Critical Care Medicine 2011;* 403 Unquowa Road, Fairfield, CT 06824
navynn@rocketmail.com

NARUCKI, Wayne *Pediatrics 2004;* 23-00 Rte. 208 South, Fairlawn, NJ O7410

NASS, Howard *Pediatrics 1989;* 76-01 113th Street, Forest Hills, NY 11375
hwrdnss@aol.com

NAYOR, Ilyse *Pediatrics 1993;* 400 South Oyster Bay Road (Suite 207), Hicksville, NY 11801
cgreen567@yahoo.com

NAZNIN, Dixit *Pediatrics 1999, Endocrinology;* 615 Princeton Street, Orlando, FL 32803

NERWEN, Clifford *Pediatrics 1995;* Schneider Children's Hospital, 269-01 76th Avenue, New Hyde Park, NY 11040

NEUMANN, David *Pediatrics 1986, Radiology;* 164 Summit Street, Providence, RI 02906
dneumann@lifespan.org

NEUSTEIN, Sherrie *Pediatrics 2008;* 3001 Arlington Avenue, Riverdale, NY 10463
shergoldie@aol.com

NEWBRUN, Daniel *Pediatrics 1989, Anesthesiology;* 280 West MacArthur Blvd., Oakland, CA 94611
Daniel.Newbrun@kp.org

NEWFIELD, Liora *Pediatrics 1993;* 3332 Venture Drive, Huntington Beach, CA 92649

NEWFIELD, Ron *Pediatrics 1993, Endocrinology;* Rady Children's Hospital of San Diego, 3020 Childrens Way (MC 5103), San Diego, CA 92123
rnewfield@ucsd.edu

NG, Elizabeth *Pediatrics 2002;* 11 Fair Street, Carmel, NY 10512

NGHI, Phuong *Pediatrics 2004;* 1111 Amsterdam Avenue, New York, NY 10025
Phuong_Nghi@yahoo.com

NICHOLS, Christiana *Pediatrics 2008;* 104-21 68th Drive (Apt A40), Forest Hills, NY 11375
nichols_christy@yahoo.com

NICOLOPOULOS, Efthemia *Pediatrics 2004;* 210-01 43rd Avenue (Apt 3G), Bayside, NY 11360
nicolopoulose@aol.com

NIEVES, Jorge *Pediatrics 1996;* 108-48 70th Road, Forest Hills, NY 11375

NIMKOFF, Laura *Pediatrics 1990, Critical Care Medicine 1993;* Good Samaritan Hospital, 1000 Montauk Highway, West Islip, NY 11795
Laura.Nimkoff@chsli.org

NITZBERG, Benjamin *Pediatrics 1960;* 7330 Pyramid Drive, Los Angeles, CA 90046
benwn1@adelphia.net

NOLAN, Lizabeth *Pediatrics 2008;* 4001 Little Neck Pkwy (Apt 19B), Little Neck, NY 11363
lknolan78@yahoo.com

NORMAN, Shannon *Pediatrics 2008;* 19 Hope Lane, Hicksville, NY 11801
normanshannon@yahoo.com

NOVAK, Inna *Pediatrics 2005;* 12 Claremont Lane, Suffern, NY 10901

NUNEZ, Ann *Pediatrics 1979, Pathology&Laboratory Medicine;* 600 Westage Business Court, Fishkill, NY 12524
anunez@mhmgpc.com

NUSSBAUM, Michael *Pediatrics 1976, Adolescent Medicine 1978;* 233 Union Avenue, Holbrook, NY 11741

OCAMPO, Stella *Pediatrics, Developmental & Behavioral Pediatrics 2000;* 1100 Carson Avenue (Suite 201), La Junta, CO 81050

OCHOTORENA, Josiree *Pediatrics, Hematology-Oncology 1995;* 513 Washington Street, Watertown, NY 13601

O'CONNELL, Karen *Pediatrics 2002, Emergency Medicine;* Children's National Medical Center, 111 Michigan Avenue N.W., Washington, DC 20010
koconnel@cnmc.org

O'DONNELL, Lisa-Mary *Pediatrics 2005;* Hackensack University Medical Center, 55 Summit Avenue, Hackensack, NJ 07601
drlisamary@yahoo.com

O'GRADY-IANDOLI, Mary Lou *Pediatrics 2001;* Breeze Pediatrics, 204 Center Road, Gulf Breeze, FL 32561
mlogrady@hotmail.com

OHRING, Marshall *Pediatrics 1987;* 4500 Sheridan Street, Hollywood, FL 33021
ohringm@bellsouth.net

OHSON, Gunwant *Pediatrics 1980;* 230 Cold Spring Road, Syosset, NY 11791

OLIN, Jeffrey *Pediatrics, Cardiology 1988;* 1575 Broadway, Hewlett, NY 11557
win95netmd@aol.com

OLSHANSKY, Cheryl *Pediatrics 1984, Neonatal-Perinatal Medicine*

OMLAND, Omar *Pediatrics 1973, Psychiatry;* 14620 Quince Orchard Road, North Potomac, MD 20878

ONG-DEE, Elizabeth *Pediatrics, Hematology-Oncology 1998;* 1200 West State Street, Rockford, IL 61102

ONG, Manuel *Pediatrics, Neonatal-Perinatal Medicine 1988;* 7105 Wareham Drive, Tampa, FL 33647

OPITZ, Lynne *Pediatrics 1987, Pathology & Laboratory Medicine;* 29th Street and Avenue E, Bayonne, NJ O7022
lopitz@bayonnemedicalcenter.org

ORNSTEIN, Rollyn *Pediatrics, Adolescent Medicine 2002;* 905 West Governor Avenue (Suite 250), Hershey, PA 17033
rornstei@nshs.ede

ORT, Howard *Pediatrics 1979, Allergy-Immunology;* Magan Medical Clinic, 420 West Rowland Street, Covina, CA 91723
h.ort@verizon.net

OVED, Kfir *Pediatrics 2007*
kifi48@yahoo.com

OXMAN, David *Pediatrics 1977;* 1050 Galloping Hill Road, Union, NJ O7090
djrb58500@aol.com

PADMANABHAN, Pradeep *Pediatrics 1997, Emergency Medicine;* 7406 Steeplecrest Circle (Apt 211), Louisville, KY 40222
pradeeppmd@yahoo.com

PALACIO, Liliana *Pediatrics 1997;* Riverside Pediatrics, 300 Riverside Drive East (Suite 1300), Bradenton, FL 34208

PALATHRA, Mary Lou *Pediatrics 2007*
mpalathra@yahoo.com

PALAZZO, Marie *Pediatrics 2007,*
mpalazzo13@yahoo.com

PALUMBO, Nancy *Pediatrics 2008;* 1320 81st
Street, Brooklyn, NY 11228

PANES, Susan *Pediatrics 1992, Allergy-
Immunology;* North Shore Allergy and Asthma
Institute, 32 Village Square, Glen Cove, NY 11542

PAPAIOANNOU, Helen *Pediatrics 2006,
Developmental & Behavioral Pediatrics 2009;* 263-
38 74th Avenuue (Apt H6), Glen Oaks, NY 11004
elenipappas22@hotmail.com

PAREDES-LUCK, Raemma *Pediatrics 1994,
Emergency Medicine;* Temple University Children's
Medical Center, 3401 North Broad Street, 6th Floor,
Philadelphia, PA 19140

PARK, KunTae *Pediatrics 2008;* Lucille Packard
Children's Hospital, 725 Welch Road, Palo Alto,
CA 94304
ktpark@alumni.duke.edu

PARK, Seung-Dae *Pediatrics, Gastroenterology &
Nutrition 2004;* National Center for Child Health
and Development, 2-10-1, Okura, Setagaya-ku,
Tokyo, Japan 157-8535

PARK, Yohan *Pediatrics 2005;* 263-34 74th
Avenue, Flushing, NY 11355

PARRA, Angelica *Pediatrics 2006;* 12145 Sheridan
Street, Cooper City, FL 33328

PARRISH, Samuel K. *Pediatrics, Adolescent
Medicine 1984;* 2900 Queen Lane, Philadelphia, PA
19129

PARRISH, Daniel *Pediatrics 1997;* 29-30 150
Street, Flushing, NY 11354

PARSONS, Scott *Pediatrics 2000;* 2 Martha Ann
Way, Beaufort, SC 29907

PATANKAR, Srikanth *Pediatrics 1989, Pediatric
Cardiac Anesthesia 1991;* 124 Lincoln Road,
Westfield, NJ O7090
sspatankar@aol.com

PATEL, Kalpana *Pediatrics, Allergy-Immunology
1998;* 4 Blackwell Court, Stonyboook, NY 11790

PATEL, Shipra *Pediatrics 2005, Endocrinology;*
University of North Carolina Children's Hospital,
110E North Medical Drive, Chapel Hill, NC 27599
shaipra26@hotmail.com

PEARLMAN, Stephen *Pediatrics 1984, Neonatal-
Perinatal Medicine;* Christiana Hospital, 4755
Ogletown Stanton Road (Suite 217), Newark, DE
19718
spearlman@christianacare.org

PEDROSO, Manuel *Pediatrics 1997;* 115 South
17th Avenue, Hollywood, FL 33020
mpedrosomd@hotmail.com

PEK, Monika *Pediatrics 2005;* 1837 Fair Avenue,
Honesdale, PA 18431

PELOSO, Marie Azzu *Pediatrics 1992;* 1414 Rhode
Avenue, Merrick, NY 11566

PEREIRA-ARGENZIANO, Lucy *Pediatrics 2006;* 9
Laurel Street, Garden City, NY 11530

PEREZ, Lucille *Pediatrics 1982, Adolescent
Medicine;* The Cave Institute, 6419 Dahlonega
Road, Suite 300, Bethesda, MD 20816

PERLMAN, Varisa *Pediatrics 2002;* 3850 Pelham
Road, Dearborn, MI 48124
lperlman1@excite.com

PERNICE, Mercedes Tiongo *Pediatrics 1990,
Allergy-Immunology;* Southeastern Allergy &
Asthma Specialists, 4343 West Newberry Road
(Suite 1), Gainesville, FL 32607

PETERS, Vicki *Pediatrics 1987, Infectious Diseases
1990;* 444 E 84th Street (Apt 4G), New York, NY
10028

PETROZZINO, Jeffrey *Pediatrics , Neonatal-
Perinatal Medicine 2005;* University of California
at San Diego Medical Center, 402 West Dickinson
Street (MPF 1-140), San Diego, CA 92103
jpetrozzino@acm.com

PHILIP, Smitha *Pediatrics 2008*
sphilip79@yahoo.com

PHILIP, Soman *Pediatrics 1996;* 4045 West
Chandler Blvd., Chandler, AZ 85226

PHILIPS, Jeffrey *Pediatrics, Adolescent Medicine
1979;* 1044 Hazel Place, Woodmere, NY 11598

PICKERING, Olufunke *Pediatrics 2008*
olufun@sgu.edu

PIELA, Christina *Pediatrics 1996;* ABC Pediatrics,
Brick, NJ O8724
krysia1058@aol.com

PIERRE, Louisdon *Pediatrics, Critical Care
Medicine 1998;* 121 DeKalb Avenue, Brooklyn, NY
11201

PINTO, Matthew *Pediatrics 2004, Critical Care
Medicine 2007;* 1755 York Avenue (Apt 37-E), New
York, NY 10128

PIRRAGLIA, Don *Pediatrics 1994, Child &
Adolescent Psychiatry;* Wyckoff Heights Hospital,
374 Stockholm Street, Bklyn, NY 11237
dop9015@nyp.org

PLANER, Benjamin *Pediatrics 1992, Neonatal-
Perinatal Medicine;* Hackensack University Medical
Center, 30 Prospect Avenue, Hackensack, NJ 7601
dplaner@humed.com

PLATT, Anne *Pediatrics 1983, Pathology &
Laboratory Medicine;* 9 Oxford Court, Wyandanch,
NY 11798

PLAUT, Allan *Pediatrics 1982;* 372 Kingston
Avenue, Brooklyn, NY 11213
aplaut@att.biz

POLSINELLI, Rosanna *Pediatrics 1988;* 156 First
Street, Mineola, NY 11501

PONDA, Punita *Pediatrics 2003, Allergy-
Immunology 2006;* 180 Manetta Hill Road,
Plainview, NY 11803
punitaponda@hotmail.com

POOLE, Claudette *Pediatrics 2005;* 180 East
Pulaski Road, Huntington Station, NY 11746
claudette@poole.com

POSNER, Mark , *Allergy-Immunology 1990;*
Allergy and Asthma Specialists, 470 Sentry Parkway
East (Suite 200), Blue Bell, PA 19422
marckhway@comcast.net

POTDAR, Meenu *Pediatrics, Adolescent Medicine
2005;* 511 Cross Anchor Road, Woodruff, SC 29388

PREMINGER, Nizza *Pediatrics 1974;* 31 Lincoln
Place, Brooklyn, NY 11217

PRUSHIK, Kenneth *Pediatrics 2003;* 241 East Main
Street, Huntington, NY 11743

PUGLIESE, Madeline *Pediatrics 1994;* 211 Main
Street, Port Washington, NY 11050
pugliesem@prodigy.net

PUGLISI, Gregory , *Allergy-Immunology 2007;*
Mid Island Allergy Group, 1171 Old Country Road,
Plainview, NY 11803

PUGLISI, Vincent *Pediatrics , Hematology-
Oncology 1988;* Sheridan Children's Healthcare
Services, 1613 N. Harrison Parkway (Bldg C, Suite
200), Sunrise, FL 33323
vpuglisi@aol.com

PUNSALAN, Imelda *Pediatrics 1990;* 8900 Van
Wyck Expressway, Jamaica, NY 11418

QADIR, Maqbool *Pediatrics 1995, Neonatal-
Perinatal Medicine 1998;* 1315 St. Joseph Parkway,
Houston, TX 77002

QUERSHI, Masarrat *Pediatrics , Neurology 2002;*
802 Ash Court Street, Sessner, FL 33584

QUIJANO, Claudia *Pediatrics 1991;* 700 Parnassus
Avenue (Apt 17), San Francisco, CA 94122
medcq@yahoo.com

QUITTELL, Lynne *Pediatrics 1984, Pulmonary
Medicine;* Columbia University Medical Center, 630
West 168th Street, New York, NY 10032
lmq1@columbia.edu

RABINOWICZ, Morris *Pediatrics 1978;* 995 Old
Country Road, Plainview, NY 11803
doctormoe@aol.com

RABINOWITZ, Brian *Pediatrics 1998;* 400 South
Oyster Bay Road (Suite 207), Hicksville, NY 11801

RABINOWITZ, Deborah *Pediatrics 2005;* 2701
Calvert Street (404 Northwest), Washington, DC
20008

RADINSKY, Stacey *Pediatrics 2001, Allergy-Immunology 2003;* 1699 Merrick Avenue, Merrick, NY 11566

RAFFALLI, Peter *Pediatrics 1989, Neurology 1992;* Children's Hospital Boston, 300 Longwood Avenue, Boston, MA O2115
perter.raffalli@childrens.harvard.edu

RAHEJA, Ravi *Pediatrics 2000;* 310 25th Avenue, Nashville, TN 37203
RajejaRavi@hotmail.com

RAHSHID, Iqbal *Pediatrics 2007;* Copper Queen Community Hospital, 101 Cole Avenue, Bisbee, AZ 85603
iqbalrashidmd@yahoo.com

RAIFMAN, Mark *Pediatrics 1977;* 431 Beach 129th Street, Belle Harbor, NY 11694
brminwood@aol.com

RAISSI-FARD, Ehteram *Pediatrics 1993;* 758 North Sun Drive (108), Lake Mary, FL 32746

RAKOWSKA, Urszula *Pediatrics 1996;* 150 Sunrise Highway (Suite 200), Lindenhurst, NY 11757
urszula@ix.netcom.com

RAKSIS, Karen R., *Pediatrics 2002;* 1825 Madison Avenue (Apt 5H), New York, NY 10035
kraksis@aol.com

RAMAKRISHNAN, T.R. *Allergy-Immunology 1989;* 1728 Jonathan Street (Suite 100), Allentown, PA 18104

RAMANAN, Aruna *Pediatrics, Hematology-Oncology 1997;* 65 Kane Street, West Hartford, CT 06119

RANDEL, Sidney *Pediatrics 1984;* 6275 Northwest 76th Terrace, Parkland, FL 33076
ran4444@aol.com

RANGWALA, Nikita *Pediatrics, Emergency Medicine 2004;* Children's Healthcare of Atlanta, 1001 Johnson Ferry, North Atlanta, GA 30342

RAPPAPORT, Mark *Pediatrics 1991, Endocrinology;* Pediatric Endocrine Associates, 1100 Lake Hearn Drive (Suite 350), Atlanta, GA 30342

RAPPAPORT, Robert *Pediatrics 1977, Endocrinology;* Mt. Sinai Hospital, One Gustave Levy Place, New York, NY 10029

RAVAL, Nikhilkumar *Pediatrics 1991, Neonatal-Perinatal Medicine;* 2307 Montaigne Avenue, Nederland, TX 77627

RAVID, Sarit *Pediatrics, Neurology 2001;* Rambam Medical Center, Aalia Street 6. P.O. Box 9602, Bat Galim, Haifa, Israel 31096
s_ravid@rambam.health.gov.il

RAVISHANKAR, Chitra *Pediatrics 1997, Cardiology;* Children's Hospital of Philadelphia, 34th & Civic Center Blvd., Philadelphia, PA 19104

READ, Rosemarie *Pediatrics 2006;* 100 Manetto Hill Road, Plainview, NY 11803

REDDY, Damodar *Cardiology 2001;* 43-43 Kissena Blvd, Flushing, NY 11355

REDDY, Uday *Allergy-Immunology 2003;* Allergy and Asthma Clinic of South Texas, 6600 South Mo Pac Expressway, Austin, TX 78749

REGAN, Brian *Pediatrics, Gastroenterology & Nutrition 2007;* The Floating Hospital for Children at Tufts New England, 800 Washington Street, Boston, MA O2111
bregan@tuftsmedicalcenter.org

REICH, Harvey *Pediatrics 1974, Developmental & Behavioral Pediatrics;* Children's Primary Care Medical Group, 6699 Alvarado Road (Suite 2200), San Diego, CA 92120

RELVAS, Monica de Stefani *Pediatrics 1999, Critical Care Medicine 2002;* Virginia Commonwealth University, Main Hospital, 401 North 12th Street (Box 980530), Richmond, VA 23298
mrelvas@aol.com

RESMOVITS, Marvin *Pediatrics 1982;* 107 Northern Blvd., Great Neck, NY 11021
mresmo@gmail.com

REYES, Miraflor *Pediatrics, Physical Medicine & Rehabilitation 1993;* 4229 Locust Lane, Jackson, MI 49201

REZNIKOV, Alexandra *Pediatrics 2001;* SUNY Downstate Medical Center, 450 Clarkson Avenue (Box 49), Brooklyn, NY 11203

RICHARDS, Andrea Telak *Pediatrics 2005, Neurology;* 254 Easton Avenue, New Brunswick, NJ 08903

RIFKIN-ZENENBERG, Stacey *Pediatrics , Hematology-Oncology 2001;* 300 Second Avenue, Long Branch, NJ O7740

RINGHEANU, Mihaela *Pediatrics, Gastroenterology & Nutrition 2003;* Valley Baptist Medical Center, 2121 Pease Street (Suite 600), Harlingen, TX 78551

RIVERA, Loyda *Pediatrics, Cardiology 1990;* 3204 Allaire Road, Wall, NJ O7719
lirmd@aol.com

RIVERA-AMISOLA, Cecilia *Pediatrics , Developmental & Behavioral Pediatrics 2002;* Dayton Children's Medical Center, One Children's Plaza, Dayton, Ohio 45404
rivera-amisola@childrensdayton.org

ROBBINS, Michael *Pediatrics 1975, Neurology;* 220 Sutton Street, North Andover, MA O1845

ROBERTS, Marc *Pediatrics 1975;* 559 Broad Street, Newark, NJ O7102
mrobe90551@aol.com

ROCKER, Joshua *Pediatrics, Emergency Medicine 2007;* Schneider Children's Hospital, 269-01 76th Avenue, New Hyde Park, NY 11040
yehoshuabendavid@yahoo.com

RODRIGUEZ, Rhina *Pediatrics, Hematology-Oncology 1985;* 3 South Bay Avenue, Amityville, NY 11701
rodiqu@optonline.net

RODRIGUEZ, Ruth *Pediatrics 1993;* 1109 Seminole Drive, Rockledge, FL 32955

ROMANO, Alicia *Pediatrics 1988, Endocrinology 1991;* New York Medical College, 19 Bradhurst Avenue, Hawthorne, NY 10532
aromano@olmhs.org

RONCA, Lorraine *Pediatrics 1993;* 24 Windmill Place, Armook, NY 10504

ROONEY, Elizabeth *Pediatrics 1996;* 2714 Elm Drive, North Bellmore, NY 11710

ROONEY, John , *Allergy-Immunology 1995;* 1165 Wantagh Avenue, Wanatagh, NY 11793

RORER, Eva Maria *Pediatrics 1993, Ophthalmology;* 600 North WolfeAvenue, Baltimore, MD 21287

ROSE, Marion *Pediatrics 1994, Cardiology 1997;* Good Samaritan Hospital Medical Center, 1000 Montauk Highway, West Islip, NY 11795

ROSEN, Dov *Pediatrics 1998;* Nachal Luz 8/7, Bet Shemash, Israel 99640
rosendov@netvision.net.il

ROSENBERG, Steven *Pediatrics 1976, Allergy-Immunology;* Allergy & Asthma Associates of Central Florida, 1890 State Road 436 (215), Winter Park, FL 32792
stevenr597@aol.com

ROSENBERG, Zehava Sadka *Pediatrics 1981, Radiology;* Hospital for Joint Diseases, 301 East 17th Street, New York, NY 10003
zehava@ramtogo.com

ROSENBLUM, Howard *Pediatrics 1979, Nephrology;* 45 Gloucester Court, E Brunswick, NJ 8816
mulenesore@aol.com

ROSENCRANTZ, Richard *Pediatrics 1997, Gastroenterology & Nutrition;* Weill Cornell Medical College, 525 E 68th Street (Box 214), New York, NY 10021
rar2016@med.cornell.edu

ROSENN, Greg *Pediatrics 1989, Neurology 1992;* 522 Old Country Road, Plainview, NY 11803

ROSENSTEIN, Jonathan *Pediatrics, Adolescent Medicine 1979;* P.O. Box 777087, Henderson, NV 89077

ROSENTHAL, Cynthia *Pediatrics 1994, Critical Care Medicine 1997;* Good Samaritan Hospital Medical Center, 1000 Montauk Highway, West Islip, NY 11795
cynthia.rosenthal@chsli.org

ROSENTHAL, David *Pediatrics , Allergy-Immunology 2006;* 865 Northern Blvd (Suite 102), Great Neck, NY 11021
drrosenthal@lij.edu

ROSSI, Wilma *Pediatrics 1982, Endocrinology;* 22 Periwinkle Drive, Mount Laurel, NJ 08054
rossin@email.chop.edu

ROTELLA, Alessandra *Pediatrics 2003;* 877 Stewart Avenue, Garden City, NY 11530
alessandrarotella@hotmail.com

ROTHSTEIN, David Hershel *Surgery 2007;* Children's Memorial Hospital, 2300 Children's Plaza (Box 63), Chicago, IL 60614
drothstein@childrensmemorial.org

ROUVALIS, Fotis *Pediatrics 2002, Cardiology;* Greece

ROY, Kevin *Pediatrics 2006, Critical Care Medicine 2009;* Schneider Children's Hospital, 269-01 76th Avenue, New Hyde Park, NY 11040

ROZENBAUM, Joseph *Pediatrics 1988;* 571 Chestnut Street, Cedarhurst, NY 11516

RUBIN, Andrew *Pediatrics 1991;* 700 Old Bethpage Road, Old Bethpage, NY 11804

RUBIN, Irina *Pediatrics 1983;* Friendly Medical Group, 207 Hallock Road (Suite 106), Stony Brook, NY 11790

RUBIN, Jamie *Pediatrics 2007;* 505 LaGuardia Place, New York, NY 10003
jamiebloomberg@hotmail.com

RUBIN, Michael *Pediatrics 1982, Cardiology*

RUSSELL, Barbara *Pediatrics 1983*

*SAAD, Sam *Pediatrics 1986*

SACKLER, Lorna Carro *Pediatrics 1990;* Pomona Pediatrics, 4C Medical Park Drive, Pomona, NY 10970

SAFIER, Brian *Pediatrics 2008;* Children's Hospital of Buffalo, 1260 Delaware Avenue, Buffalo, NY 14209
bsafier@nshs.edu

SALEK, Allyson *Pediatrics 2008;* Bedford Hills Pediatric Associates, 701 Bedford Road, Bedford Hills, NY 10507
aabo77@hotmail.com

SALES, Serafin *Developmental & Behavioral Pediatrics 1996;* 6 Crossfield Court, Shoreham, NY 11786

SALUJA, Gurbir *Pediatrics 1973, Hematology-Oncology 1975;* 47 Graphic Blvd., Sparta, NJ 07871
gssalujamd@aol.com

SALZMAN, Mark *Pediatrics, Infectious Diseases 1992;* 6041 Cadillac Avenue, Los Angeles, CA 90034

SAMONTE, Frank *Pediatrics 2007;* Floating Hospital, 750 Washington Street, Boston, MA 02111

SAMUEL, Maritza *Pediatrics 1987;* 141 South Main Street (Rm 131), Belle Glade, FL 33430

SAMUELS, Roya *Pediatrics 2008;* 144-05 69th Avenue, Flushing, NY 11367
royasamuels@yahoo.com

SANBORN, Chad *Pediatrics 2006;* 2775 North East 187 Street, Aventura, FL 33180

SAND, Harold *Pediatrics 1978;* 25 Kilmer Drive, Morganville, NJ 07751
hsand23@comcast.net

SANDOVAL, Claudio *Pediatrics 1990, Hematology-Oncology;* New York Medical College, Munger Pavilion (Room 110), Valhalla, NY 10595
claudio_sandoval@nymc.edu

SANTANGELO, Christina *Pediatrics 2003;* Queens-Long Island Medical Group, 300 Bayshore Road, Babylon, NY 11703
csanta1219@yahoo.com

SANTIAGO, Maria Teresa *Pediatrics, Pulmonary Medicine 1988;* Schneider Children's Hospital, 269-01 76th Avenue, New Hyde Park, NY 11040

SANTIAGO, Myla *Pediatrics 2007;* Pikeville Medical Center, 911 Bypass Road, Pikeville, KY 41501
doktormyles@yahoo.com

SANTOS-NANADIEGO, Maria Catalina *Pediatrics 1981, Child&Adolescent Psychiatry;* Kaiser Permanente, 5225 Canyon Crest Drive (Suite 103), Riverside, CA 92507

SAPIRE, Kenneth *Pediatrics 1988, Anesthesiology;* MD Anderson Cancer Center, 1515 Holcombe Blvd (Box 42), Houston, TX 77030
ksapire@mdanderson.org

SARUMI, Oludayo *Pediatrics 2006;* Marshfield Clinic of Eau Claire Center, 2116 Craig Road, Eau Claire, WI 54701

SAUNDERS, Jay *Pediatrics 1985, Adolescent Medicine;* 5177 Route 9W, Newburgh, NY 12550

SAVARESE, David *Pediatrics 1994;* 5525 Broadway, Bronx, NY 10463

SAVARGAONKAR, Rajesh *Pediatrics 1997;* Martin Luther King Jr. Community Health Center, 1556 Straight Path Road, Wyandanch, NY 11793

SAXENA, Harshita *Pediatrics 2005, Adolescent Medicine;* Children's National Medical Center, 111 Michigan Ave., NW, Washington, DC 20010
hjsaxena@hotmail.com

SCERBO, Jessica *Pediatrics 2008, Hematology-Oncology 2011;* Schneider Children's Hospital, 269-01 76th Avenue, New Hyde Park, NY 11040
jesscerbo@aol.com

SCHAEFFER, Janis *Pediatrics 1982, Pulmonary Medicine;* 3003 New Hyde Park Road (Suite 204), New Hyde Park, NY 11042
lungmd1@aol.com

SCHARE, Rachel *Pediatrics 2000;* Beaches Family Health Center, 1522 Penman Road, Jacksonville Beach, FL 32250

SCHECHTMAN-FREEDMAN, Merryl *Pediatrics 1988, Developmental & Behavioral Pediatrics 1990;* Rose F. Kennedy Center, 1410 Pelham Parkway South, Bronx, NY 10461
dottoresa@aol.com

SCHER, Herschel *Pediatrics 1998;* 9980 Central Park Blvd (Suite 318), Boca Raton, FL 33428

SCHIFF, Russell *Pediatrics 1984, Cardiology 1986;* Winthrop University Hospital, 259 First Street, Mineola, NY 11501

SCHIFF, Stuart *Pediatrics 1995;* 571 Chestnut Street, Cedarhurst, NY 11516
stuschiff@hotmail.com

SCHIOWITZ, Gila *Pediatrics 2003;* 682 Washington Avenue, West Hempstead, NY 11552

SCHLESSEL, Kevin *Pediatrics, Rheumatology 1992;* Columbus Arthritis Center, 1211 Dublin Road, Columbus, OH 43215

SCHLOSSBERGER, Norman *Pediatrics 1988;* 300 Pasteur Drive, Stanford, CA 94305

SCHMERLER, Alan *Pediatrics 1975, Child & Adolescent Psychiatry;* Manchester Memorial Hospital, 71 Haynes Street, Manchester, CT 06040

SCHNEIDER, David *Pediatrics 1993;* Pediatric Associates, One General Wing Road, Rutland, VT 05701

SCHROEDER, Marie *Pediatrics 1995;* 109 Garden Street, Garden City, NY 11530

SCHULKIND, Martin *Pediatrics 1963*

SCHULMAN, Jason *Pediatrics 1998;* 4104 North 48 Avenue, Hollywood, FL 33021

SCHUVAL, Susan *Pediatrics , Allergy-Immunology 1991;* Schneider Children's Hospital, 269-01 76th Avenue, New Hyde Park, NY 11040

SCHWARTZ, Fred *Pediatrics, Emergency Medicine 1999*; 1 Moran Road, West Orange, NJ O7050

SCHWARTZ, Gerald *Pediatrics 1972*; 351 Merline Road (Suite 103), Vernon, CT O6066

SCHWARTZ, Lisa *Pediatrics 1987*; 64 Ottawa Road South, Marlboro, NJ O7746

SCHWARTZ, Robert *Pediatrics 2007*; Children's Hospital of Pittsburgh, 3705 Fifth Avenue, Pittsburgh, PA 15213

SCHWARTZ, Saara *Allergy-Immunology 2003*; Florida International University, 11200 Southwest 8th Street, Miami, FL 33174

SCHWARTZ, Susan *Pediatrics 1991*

SCHWARZ, Gavin *Pediatrics 2007, Allergy-Immunology 2011*; Schneider Children's Hospital, 269-01 76th Avenue, New Hyde Park, NY 11040

SCHWOB, Netanel *Pediatrics 1993*; 4000 Old Court Road, Baltimore, MD 21208

SCIMEME, Jason *Pediatrics 2008*; Nationwide Children's Hospital, 700 Children's Drive, Columbus, OH 43205
jasonscimeme@yahoo.com

SEIDLER-LISS, Alice F. *Pediatrics, Emergency Medicine 1988*; North Central Bronx Hospital, 3424 Kossuth Avenue, Bronx, NY 10467

SEITZ, Michele L. *Pediatrics, Adolescent Medicine 1986*; 90 Blossom Heath Avenue, Lynbrook, NY 11563

SEKHON, Aman *Pediatrics 2007*; St. John's Episcopal Hospital, 327 Beach 19th Street, Far Rockaway, NY 11691
amansekhon111@hotmail.com

SELIGSOHN, Jacob *Pediatrics 2006*; 4500 Sheridan Street, Hollywood, FL 33021

SELTZER, Alexandra *Pediatrics 2004*; NYU Medical Center, 550 First Avenue, New York, NY 10016
shadowboxer3@hotmail.com

SERRUYA, Jose *Pediatrics, Neurology 1998*; Pediatric Neurology and Neurophysiology, 95-25 Queens Blvd (Suite 520), Rego Park, NY 11374

SEZGIN, Gulay *Pediatrics, Hematology-Oncology 2005*; 264-40 Langston Avenue, Glen Oaks, NY 11004

SHABBIR, Azfar *Pediatrics, Neonatal-Perinatal Medicine 1994*; Elmhurst Hospital, 7901 Broadway, Elmhurst, NY 11373

SHAFINOORI, Shideh *Pediatrics, Infectious Diseases 2003*; 104 Legacy Drive, Bereau, KY 40403

SHAH, Atul Navnitlal *Pediatrics, Allergy-Immunology 1998*; 2 Coraci Blvd (Suite 14), Shirley, NY 11967

SHAH, Binod *Pediatrics 1998, Physical Medicine & Rehabilitation 2002*; Montefiore Medical Center, 111 East 210th Street, Bronx, NY 10467
binodshah@yahoo.com

SHAH, Jesika *Pediatrics 2006*

SHAH, Nikhil *Pediatrics 2003, Emergency Medicine 2006*; Weill-Cornell Medical Center, 525 East 68 Street (Emergency Medicine), New York, NY 10021

SHAHDADPURI, Jean *Pediatrics 2000*; 45066 Cougar Circle, Freemong, CA 94539

SHAINHOUSE, Tsippora *Pediatrics 2004, Neurology*; 40 Kristin Lane, Hauppauge, NY 11788

SHAMIM, Tabassum *Pediatrics, Adolescent Medicine 1999*; 1800 Silas Deane Highway, Rocky Hill, CT O6067

SHAPIRO, Warren *Pediatrics 1988*; 4405 Vandever Avenue, San Diego, CA 92120
warren.1.shapiro@kp.org

SHARAF, Mohamed *Pediatrics, Neonatal-Perinatal Medicine 1996*; 2131 South 17 Street, Wilmington, NC 28401

SHARMA, Anjali *Pediatrics, Hematology-Oncology 2002*; 7807 Laguna Blvd (Suite440), Elk Grove, CA 95758

SHAW-BRACHFELD, Jennifer *Pediatrics 1992, Developmental & Behavioral Pediatrics 1994*; Touchpoint Pediatrics, 17 Watchung Avenue, Chatham, NJ 7928
touchpointpeds@aol.com

SHEFFER-BABILA, Sharone *Pediatrics 2006*; Nassau University Medical Center, 2201 Hempstead Turnpike, East Meadow, NY 11554

SHEFLIN, Marla *Pediatrics 1997, Emergency Medicine 2000*; Jamaica Hospital Medical Center, 8900 Van Wyck Expressway, Jamaica, NY 11418

SHEINBAUM, Karen (Blum) *Pediatrics 1989*

SHENKER, I. Ronald *Pediatrics 1961, Adolescent Medicine*; Schneider Children's Hospital, 269-01 76th Avenue, New Hyde Park, NY 11040
rshenker@lij.edu

SHERMAN, Martin *Pediatrics 1978, Dermatology*; 193 Broadway (Box 568), Amityville, NY 11701
drmpsherman@aol.com

SHERNOCK, Marsha *Pediatrics 1977*; 9704 Rolling Ridge, Fairfax Station, VA 22039
msirdofsky@aol.com

SHERTZ, Mitchell *Pediatrics, Developmental & Behavioral Pediatrics 1994*; 20 Ha'shahafim Street, Ra'anana, Israel

SHETH, Shashank *Pediatrics 2002*; 10 Dennis Street (Apt 321), New Brunswick, NJ O8901

SHETREAT-KLEIN, Maya *Pediatrics 2004, Neurology*; 110 South Bedford Road, Mount Kisco, NY 10549

SHIH, Chie-Youn *Pediatrics 2002, Critical Care Medicine*; Children's Specialty Group, 601 Children's Lane, Norfolk, VI 23507
heatherandchie@sbcglobal.net

SHIH, San *Pediatrics, Hematology-Oncology 1994*; 133-29 41 Road (Suite 2D), Flushing, NY 11355

SHIRSAT, Pratibha *Pediatrics 1978*; Texas Tech University, 4800 Alberta Avenue, El Paso, TX 79905
pratibha.shirsat@ttuhsc.edu

SHORSER, James *Pediatrics 1986, Anesthesiology*; Northeastern Anesthesia Services, 43 Kensico Drive (2nd floor), Mount Kisco, NY 10549

SHROFF, Amita *Pediatrics 2001, Emergency Medicine 2007*; Emory University, 1440 Clifton Road, Atlanta, GA 30322

SHULMAN, Peter *Pediatrics 1975*; Pediatric Associates, 9611 West Broward Blvd, Ft Lauderdale, FL 33324
pshulman@pediatricassociates.com

SIAREZI, Shaghayegh (Sherry) *Pediatrics 2002*; 601 East 15th Street, Austin, TX 78701

SIDDIQI, Shaz *Pediatrics 2000, Allergy-Immunology 2005*; 150 Chevy Chase Street (Suite 303), Gaithersburg, MD 20878
shazsiddiqi7@hotmail.com

SIDDIQUE, Razia *Pediatrics 1993*; Queens Hospital Center, 82-68 164 Street, Jamaica, NY 11432

SIEGEL, David *Pediatrics 1977*; 9803 Glynshire Way, Potomac, MD 20854

SIEGEL, Janet *Adolescent Medicine 1992*; 35 Fairview Avenue, Great Neck, NY 11023

SIEGEL, Mark *Pediatrics 1996, Critical Care Medicine*; Hackensack University Medical Center, 30 Prospect Ave, Hackensack, NJ O7601
msiegel@humed.com

SIEGEL, Melissa *Pediatrics 2001, Hematology-Oncology 2004*; 201 East 28th Street (Apt 21-F), New York, NY 10016

SIEGEL, Scott *Pediatrics 1989*; 18 Melanie Manor, East Brunswick, NJ O8816

SILBER, Gail *Pediatrics 1984*; 8915 Datapoint Drive (Suite 51-C), San Antonio, TX 78229

SILBERMAN-PROCUPEZ, Theresa *Pediatrics, Hematology-Oncology 1971*; 1000 North Oak Avenue, Marshfield, WI 54449

SILBERMINTZ, Ari *Pediatrics, Gastroenterology & Nutrition 2006*; Shaare Zedek Medical Center, Box 3235, Jerusalem, Israel 91031
arisilb1@yahoo.com

SILTON, Akiva *Pediatrics 2003*; 3 Hayshar Street, Hashmonaim, Israel

SILVER, Peter *Pediatrics 1990, Critical Care Medicine 1993;* Schneider Children's Hospital, 269-01 76th Avenue, New Hyde Park, NY 11040
psilver@lij.edu

SILVERIO, Arlene *Pediatrics 1994, Emergency Medicine 1996;* Schneider Children's Hospital, 269-01 76th Avenue, New Hyde Park, NY 11040
arlene@silverio.md

SILVERIO-REYES, Soledad *Pediatrics 1965;* County of Riverside Public Health Medical Clinic, 4065 County Circle Drive, Riverside, CA 92513

SILVERMAN, Lawrence *Pediatrics 1990, Endocrinology;* Goryeb Children's Hospital at Morristown Memorial Hospital, 100 Madison Avenue, Morristown, NJ O7962
lawrence.silverman@ahsys.org

SILVERMAN, Sarah *Pediatrics 2008;* Park Avenue Medical Professionals, 120 East 86th Street (2nd Street), New York, NY 10028

SILVERSTEIN, Michael *Pediatrics 1973, Emergency Medicine;* Plantation General Hospital, 401 North West 42nd Avenue, Plantation, FL 33317
topdoc25@aol.com-home

SIM, Alfonso *Pediatrics 1979;* 9620 Church Avenue, Brooklyn, NY 11212

SIM, Geoffrey *Pediatrics 2000;* 39 Lloyd Street, New Hyde Park, NY 11040

SIMAI, David *Pediatrics 2003;* 660 Central Avenue (Suite 3), Cedarhurst, NY 11516
davidsimai@yahoo.com

SIMHI, Eliahu *Pediatrics 1992;* 3705 Fifth Avenue, Pittsburgh, PA 15213

SIMON-GOLDMAN, Phyllis *Pediatrics 2007;* 230 Middleneck Road (Suite 3), Great Neck, NY 11021
DrPSimon201@yahoo.com

SINGALA, Ravinder *Pediatrics 2006;* 2281 Nandi Hills, Smartz Creek, MI 48473

SINGH, Jayati *Pediatrics 1996;* 3807 East Millers Bridge Road, Tallahassee, FL 32312
drsingh@tpcadocs.com

SINGH, Rachana *Pediatrics, Neonatal-Perinatal Medicine 2006;* Tufts New England Medical Center, 800 Washington Street, Boston, MA O2111

SINGH, Sharon *Pediatrics, Hematology-Oncology 2008;* Schneider Children's Hospital, 269-01 76th Avenue, New Hyde Park, NY 11040
ssingh1@nshs.edu

SINGLA, Manav *Pediatrics 2001, Allergy-Immunology;* Asthma, Allergy & Sinus Center, 9478 Latchkey Row, Columbia, MD 21045
msingla@singla.net

SIRNA, Paul *Pediatrics 1999;* 39 Park Avenue, Verona, NJ 07044

SIVAKUMAR, Preethi *Pediatrics 1995;* 10200 North 92nd Street (Suite 102), Scottsdale, AZ 85258

SIVITZ, Adam *Pediatrics 2005;* 84 Walpole Street (7-H), Canton, MA 02021

SIVITZ, Jennifer *Pediatrics 2005, Endocrinology 2008;* 84 Walpole Street (7-H), Canton, MA 02021
jensivitz@yahoo.com

SIYAHREZAEI, Shaghayegh *Pediatrics 2002;* 811 New York Avenue (Suite 703), Brooklyn, NY 11203

SKOLNICK, Eric *Pediatrics 1984, Anesthesiology;* Ambulatory Surgery Center of Westchester, 34 South Bedford Road, Mt. Kisco, NY 10549
eskolnick@westchesterrsurgery.com

SKOOG-LAUFER, Dagna *Pediatrics 1987;* 2050 Pine Street, Philadelphia, PA 19107

SLUTZAH, Meredith *Pediatrics 2006, Neonatal-Perinatal Medicine 2009;* 261-83 Langston Avenue, Glen Oaks, NY 11004
merri0928@aol.com

SMITH, Carol *Pediatrics 1983, Psychiatry;* 8600 West 110th Street (Suite 214), Overland Park, KS 66210

SMITH, Michael *Pediatrics 2008;* North Shore Children's Healthcare, 3 School Street, Suite 301, Glen Cove, NY 11542
mas132@yahoo.com

SMITH, Robin *Pediatrics 1998, Neurology 1997;* Schneider Children's Hospital 269-01 76th Avenue, New Hyde Park, NY 11040
rsmith@lij.edu

SMITH, Steven *Pediatrics 1992, Allergy-Immunology 1994;* 9150 Marshall Street (Suite 2), Philadelphia, PA 19114
allergy.doc@verizon.net

SNOW, Ayelet *Pediatrics 2006;* 6629 Westwood Drive, Charlestown, IN 47111
ayeletsnow@gmail.com

SOFOCLEOUS, Constantinos *Pediatrics 1994, Radiology;* Memorial Sloan-Kettering Cancer Center, 1275 York Avenue (H-201), New York, NY 10021
constant@pol.net

SOGAWA, Yoshimi *Pediatrics 2005, Neurology 2003;* Montefiore Medical Center, 111 East 210th Street, Bronx, NY 110467
ysogawa@aol.com

SOKOL, Scott *Pediatrics 1976;* Queens-Long Island Medical Group, 350 South Broadway, Hicksville, NY 11801
mdkids47@hotmail.com

SOMMERS, Ross *Pediatrics 2007;* One Taft Avenue, Providence, RI O2906
ross_sommers@yahoo.com

SONDIKE, Stephen *Pediatrics 1997, Adolescent Medicine 2000;* Charleston Area Medical Center, 830 Pennsylvania Avenue (Suite 103), Charleston, WV 25302
ssondike@hsc.wrv.edu

SONENBLUM, Michael *Pediatrics 1990;* 4269 North West 88th Avenue, Sunrise, FL 33351
msonenblum@pediatricassociates.com

SORIANO-AGUILLAR, Edita *Pediatrics 1993;* 203-88 Northwest Colonade Drive, Hillsboro, OR 97124

SOSULSKI, Richard *Pediatrics 1980, Neonatal-Perinatal Medicine;* 30 Riverview Terrace, Smithtown, NY 11787
sosmd77@aol.com

SPATOLIATORE, Rosa Linda *Pediatrics 1996;* 731 Saw Mill River Road, Ardsley, NY 10502

SPERLING, Randi *Pediatrics 1995;* University of Miami School of Medicine, 4104 North 48th Avenue, Hollywood, FL 33021

SPINNER, Milton *Pediatrics 1960;* 14750 Caminito Punta Arenas Street, Delmar, CA 92014

SPIOTTA, Roseann *Pediatrics 1981;* 133-03 Jamaica Avenue, Richmond Hill, NY 11418

SREEDHARA, Malathi *Pediatrics, Neonatal-Perinatal Medicine 1999;* 7259 Sylvan Glade Court, Weeki Wachee, FL 34607

ST. VICTOR, Rosemarie *Pediatrics, Adolescent Medicine 1993;* Brookdale Hospital Medical Center, One Brookdale Plaza, Brooklyn, NY 11212

STEEG, Carl *Pediatrics 1967, Cariology;* 315 West 70th Street (Apt 2K), New York, NY 10023
cnsteeg@gmail.com

STEELE, Andrew *Pediatrics 1978, Neonatal-Perinatal Medicine 1980;* Schneider Children's Hospital, 269-01 76th Avenue, New Hyde Park, NY 11040
steele@lij.edu

STEIN, Lawrence *Pediatrics 1976;* 18350 Roscoe Blvd (Suite 200), Northridge, CA 91325

STEIN, Michael *Pediatrics 1977;* Mid Suffolk Pediatrics, 1770 Motor Parkway, Hauppauge, NY 11749
jetmike@mac.com

STEIN, Rodd *Pediatrics 1999;* 1880 Commerce Street, Yorktown, NY 10598
docrodd@optonline.net

STEIN-ALBERT, Marcie *Pediatrics 1987, Ambulatory Pediatrics 1989;* Queens Hospital Center. 82-68 164 Street, Jamaica, NY 11432
steinm@nychhc.org

STEINBOCK, Roy *Pediatrics 2002;* 2790 Lafayette Drive, Boulder, CO 80305
bockny@hotmail.com

STEIN-ETESS, Melanie *Pediatrics 2000;* 260 Ellen Place, Jericho, NY 11753
estess@optonline.net

STEINER, Deborah *Pediatrics 1992;* 30 Hempstead Avenue, Rockville Centre, NY 11570

STERLING, Karen Mathurin *Pediatrics 1998;* Hoboken University Medical Center for Family Health, 122 Clinton Street, Hoboken, NJ O7030

STEVENS-MORRISON, Cynthia *Pediatrics, Emergency Medicine 1989;* Carrol Hospital Center, 96 Harry S. Truman Drive (Suite 220), Largo, MD 20774
pediatricwellnesscenter@verizon.net

STEVENSON, Amanda *Pediatrics 2007;* New Britain General Hospital, 100 Grand Street, New Britain, CT O6050
amalandas@hotmail.com

STEWART, Constance *Pediatrics 1980, Endocrinology;* 515 Hempstead Avenue, Rockville Centre, NY 11570
medoffices@yahoo.com

STOLL, Matthew *Pediatrics 2004, Immunology-Rheumatology;* Childrens Hospital Boston, 300 Longwood Avenue, Boston, MA 02115
Matthew.Stoll@Childrens.Harvard.Edu

STONE, Hilary *Pediatrics 2006;* 2050 Route 22, Brewster, NY 10509

STONE, Josie *Pediatrics 1996;* 5458 Towncenter Road, Boca Raton, FL 33486

*STORM, Jack *Pediatrics 1962*

STORM, Richard *Pediatrics 1978, Ophthalmology;* 303 East Park Avenue, Long Beach, NY 11561

STRAUSS, Raphael *Pediatrics 1989, Allergy-Immunology 1991;* 242 Merrick Road, Rockville Centre, NY 11570
rrsmd@optonline.net

STROBER, Jonathan *Pediatrics 1995, Neurology;* University of California, San Francisco, 350 Parnassu Avenue (Suite 609), San Francisco, CA 94143
stroberj@neuropeds.ucsf.edu

STROTHER, Christopher *Pediatrics 2005, Emergency Medicine;* 353 East 72nd Street (Apt 31-B), New York, NY 10021
christopher.strother@mssm.edu

STROZUK, Stephanie *Pediatrics, Adolescent Medicine 2004;* Child Health Institute of New Jersey, 89 French Street (Room 2300), New Brunswick, NJ O8901

STULBACH, Harry *Pediatrics 1984;* St. Barnabus Medical Center, 94 Old Short Hills Road, Livingston, NJ O7039

SUAREZ, Elizabeth *Pediatrics 1995, Endocrinology 1997;* 1600 162nd Avenue (Apt 16), San Leandro, CA 94578

SUCHOFF, Monica *Pediatrics, Developmental & Behavioral Pediatrics 1990;* Discovery Developmental Center, 840 East Redd Road (Suite 3), El Paso, TX 79912
monicasuchoff@juno.com

SUH, Michael *Pediatrics , Neurology 2008;* 35-26 190th Street, Flushing, NY 11358

SUKHOV, Renat *Pediatrics/ Physical Medicine & Rehabilitation 2000;* 29-01 216 Street, Bayside, NY 11360

SULITZER, Karen *Pediatrics, Hematology-Oncology 1994;* 208 Sylvan Drive, Wading River, NY 11792

SUN, Lena *Pediatrics 1982, Anesthesiology;* Morgan Stanley Children's Hospital of New York, 630 West 168 Street (CH4-440 North), New York, NY 10032
LSS4@Columbia.edu

SUN, Shyan-Chu *Pediatrics, Neonatal-Perinatal Medicine 1972;* St. Barnabus Medical Center, 94 Old Short Hills Road, Livingston, NJ O7039
ssun@sbhcs.com

SUN, Sirisak *Pediatrics 1972;* Alton Health Center, 550 Landmarks Blvd, Alton, IL 62002
sirisak@netscape.com

SUPASWUD, Tingnong *Pediatrics, Neonatal-Perinatal Medicine 2008;* 100 Market Street (Apartment 405), des Moines, IA 50309
ting_supaswud@hotmail.com

SURGAN, Victoria Zolot *Pediatrics 2003, Neurology 2006;* 97 Paterson Street, New Brunswick, NJ 08901

*SUSER, Fredric *Pediatrics 1976*

SUSSMAN, Joel *Pediatrics 1972, Developmental & Behavioral Pediatrics;* 2 Tiftgreen Circle, Columbia, SC 29223
addsuss@aol.com

SVITEK, Scott *Pediatrics 1994;* 164 Commack Road, Commack, NY 11725

SY-KHO, Rose Marrie *Pediatrics, Neurology 1991;* Schneider Children's Hospital, 269-01 76th Avenue, New Hyde Park, NY 11040
rsykho@lij.edu

SYLVESTER, Julie *Pediatrics 2008*
julie12@hotmail.com

TAFRESHI-ORAEE, Parisa *Pediatrics 1995;* 275 Sprain Road, Scarsdale, NY 10583

TAHZIB-KHADEM, Munirih *Pediatrics 1999, Allergy-Immunology 2001;* 79 Hudson Street, Hoboken, NJ O7030

*TALLAL, Lisa *Pediatrics 1957, Hematology-Oncology*

TALWAR, Rohit *Pediatrics, Cardiology 1998;* Good Samaritan Hospital Medical Center, 1000 Montauk Highway, West Islip, NY 11795

TAMIR, Akiva *Pediatrics, Cardiology 1993;* Save a Child's Heart at Wolfson Medical Center, One Borochov Street Azir, Azur, Israel 58008

TAN, Bernardo *Pediatrics 1995;* 2645 Washington Street (Suite 430), Waukegan, IL 60085

TAN, Noel *Pediatrics 1992, Neonatal-Perinatal Medicine 1999;* 5006 Ashington Landing Drive, Tampa, FL 33647

TAN, Patricia *Pediatrics, Physical Medicine & Rehabilitation 1992;* 1158 Atlantic Avenue, Baldwin, NY 11510
ptanmd@aol.com

TANG-HUANG, Lin-Lan *Pediatrics 1987, Developmental & Behavioral Pediatrics 1989;* 27 Mountain Blvd (Suite 2), Warren, NJ O7059
faaplin@yahoo.com

TATZ, Gary *Critical Care Medicine 2005;* Woods Road, Valhalla, NY 10595

TAURASSI, Cheryl *Pediatrics 2003, Critical Care Medicine 2006;* 160 East 32nd Street (2nd Floor), New York, NY 10016
ctaurassi@hotmail.com

TAWAKOL, Heshem *Pediatrics, Neonatal-Perinatal Medicine 2001;* New Hanover Regional Medical Center, 2131 South 17th Street, Wilmington, NC 28401

TAYLOR-DURDAN, Danielle *Pediatrics 2004;* 3959 Broadway (CHC1-115), New York, NY 10032

TEICHMAN, Faye *Pediatrics 1987, Neonatal-Perinatal Medicine 1989;* 280 North Central Avenue, Hardsdale, NY 10530

TELEGA, Dorota *Pediatrics 1997, Neurology;* 4495 Compton Lane, Brookfield, WI 53045
gtelega@wi.rr.com

TELEGA, Gregory *Pediatrics 1997;* 4495 Compton Lane, Brookfield, WI 53045
telega@mcw.edu

TELLECHEA, Natasha *Pediatrics 1998;* 380 North Broadway (Suite L-2), Jericho, NY 11753

TELLER, Filip *Pediatrics 2007;* St. Luke's-Roosevelt Hospital Center, 1111 Amsterdam Avenue, New York, NY 10025
filipteller@hotmail.com

TELSEY, Aimee *Pediatrics 1985, Neonatal-Perinatal Medicine;* Beth Israel Medical Center, 16 First Avenue (7 Baird), New York, NY 10003
atelsey@bethisraelny.org

TENG, David *Pediatrics 2000, Emergency Medicine;* Columbia University Medical Center, 622 West 168 Street, New York, NY 10032

TEYAN, Frederick *Pediatrics 1971;* 36 Lincoln Avenue, Rockville Centre, NY 11570
fgjteyan@ix.netcom.com

THECKEDATH, Jose *Allergy-Immunology 1998;* 1911 Palmyra Road, Albany, GA 31701

THOMAS, Philomena *Pediatrics, Ambulatory Pediatrics 1987, Emergency Medicine;* Schneider Children's Hospital, 269-01 76th Avenue, New Hyde Park, NY 11040
unipedpc@hotmail.com

THOMASEN, Tanya-Marie *Pediatrics, Neurology 2008;* 224 Riverside Drive (1A), New York, NY 10025
tbag21@yahoo.com
TIONGO, Mercedes *Pediatrics 1990*

TIYYAGURA, Sripriya *Pediatrics 2006;* NYU Medical Center, 550 First Avenue, New York, NY 10012

TIZER, Karen *Pediatrics 1993;* SUNY Downstate Medical Center, 450 Clarkson Avenue (Box 49), Brooklyn, NY 11203

TOBIN-SIMON, Cecily *Pediatrics 1992;* 429 Summit Street, Ridgewood, NJ 07450

TOPPER, Leonid *Pediatrics, Neurology 2000;* Chilton Memorial Hospital, 97 West Parkway, Pompton Plains, NJ 07444

TOPSIS, Julie *Pediatrics 1984, Neonatal-Perinatal Medicine;* Beth Israel Medical Center, 16 First Avenue (Baird Hall), New York, NY 10003
jtopsis@chpnet.org; Jjpran@comcast.net

TRAN, Loanne *Pediatrics, Neonatal-Perinatal Medicine 2007;* Schneider Children's Hospital, 269-01 76th Avenue, New Hyde Park, NY 11040

TRECARTIN, Susan *Pediatrics 1975, Adolescent Medicine 1976;* Queens-Long Island Medical Group, 350 South Broadway, Hicksville, NY 11801
strecartin@qlimg.com

TREPEL, Robert *Pediatrics, Neurology 1987;* 66 Commack Road, (Suite 200), Commack, NY 11725
childbrain@aol.com

TROPE, Juliette *Pediatrics 2006;* 347 Twin Lane South, Wantagh, NY 11793

TROPE, Randi *Pediatrics 2000, Critical Care Medicine 2004;* Schneider Children's Hospital, 269-01 76th Avenue, New Hyde Park, NY 11040
Rtrope@lij.edu

TRUCCO, Jamie *Pediatrics 1965;* Bogota, Columbia

TRUXAL, Brian Andrew *Pediatrics, Adolescent Medicine 1982;* Monmouth Medical Center, 223 Monmouth Road, West Long Branch, NJ 07764
m.pediatric@comcast.net

TRYZMEL, John *Pediatrics, Neonatal-Perinatal Medicine 2003;* 3765 Northeast 209th Terrace, Aventura, FL 33180

TSIMOYIANIS, George *Pediatrics, Adolescent Medicine 1987;* 106 North Avenue, Darien, CT 06820
gvtmd@aol.com

TU, Lan Chau Hang *Pediatrics 1989, Pulmonary Medicine*

TUCKER, Stephanie *Pediatrics 2003;* 333 Oakgrove Street (Apt 304), Minneapolis, MN 55403
Tuckerwoo@aol.com

TUER, William *Pediatrics 1972;* 1117 North Olive Avenue, West Palm Beach, FL 33401

TURNER, Peter *Pediatrics 1980;* 1304 Laurel Oak Road, Voorhees, NJ 08043
pturner@forkidcare.com

TUROW, Victor *Pediatrics 1981;* 833 Northern Blvd, Great Neck, NY 11021

TYAGI, Swayamprabha (Pat) *Pediatrics, Developmental & Behavioral Pediatrics 1992;* 555 Old Norcross Road, Lawrenceville, GA 30045

UCKAN, Duygu *Pediatrics, Hematology-Oncology 1994;* 1529 Eden Isle Blvd Northeast, St Petersburg, FL 33704
uduckan@hacettepe.edu.tr

UDDIN, Zia *Pediatrics, Neonatal-Perinatal Medicine 2002;* 251 East Antietam Street, Hagerstown, MD 21740

UEBLER-YOKOIS, Nancy *Pediatrics 1988, Gastroenterology & Nutrition ;* Arizona Children's Gastroenterology, 9-155 North 90 Street (Suite C200), Scottsdale, AZ 85258

UKRAINCIK, Miro *Pediatrics 1999;* 9 Manor Court, Edison, NJ 08817
mimeyo1@juno.com

UNAL, Elif *Pediatrics 2001, Hematology-Oncology 2004;* Ridvanpasa SOK 26/19, Istanbul, Turkey

UNCYK, Avraham *Pediatrics 1985;* 3251 Westchester Avenue, Bronx, NY 10461

VALCOURT, Lucienne Deltor *Pediatrics 1995;* 15205 Collier Blvd (Suite 102), Naples, FL 34119

VALENTINE-RICHARDSON, Keena *Pediatrics 2007;* Mt Sinai Medical Center, One Gustave Levy Place, New York, NY 10029
kenavalentine@yahoo.com

VALOIS, Katherine *Pediatrics 2002;* Kaiser Permanente Medical Group, 39400 Paseo Padre Parkway, Freemont, CA 94538
Katherine.k.valois@kp.org

VALSAMIS, Christina *Pediatrics 2007;* Westchester Medical Center, 95 Grasslands Road, Valhalla, NY 10595
christinoula17@aol.com

VAN OORDT-CESPEDES, Karen *Pediatrics 1992*

VANSTONE, Michelle *Pediatrics 2006;* Johns Hopkins Medical Center, 600 North Wolfe Street, Baltimore, NY 21287

VARMA, Rupa *Pediatrics, Developmental & Behavioral Pediatrics 2001;* Family Health Care Network, 1107 West Popular Avenue, Porterville, CA 932557

VASILESCU, Alexandra *Pediatrics 2008;* Johns Hopkins Medical Center, 600 North Wolfe Street, Baltimore, MD 21287
abianca2000@yahoo.com

VASISHTHA, Sanjeev *Pediatrics 1996;* 1256 Culver Avenue, Utica, NY 13501
superjeeva101@yahoo.com

VATS, Tribhavans *Pediatrics, Hematology-Oncology 1971;* 4700 Waters Avenue, Savannah, GA 31404
vatstrl@memorialhealth.com

VEGA, Roy *Pediatrics 1991, Emergency Medicine;* North Shore University Hospital, 300 Community Drive, Manhasset, NY 11030

VENIT, Bethany *Pediatrics 1977;* 881 North Church Street, Hazleton, PA 18201

VIJAYAN, Radhika *Pediatrics, Hematology-Oncology 1982;* 30 Prospect Place, Hackensack, NJ 07601
taraarts@hotmail.com

VILLASECA, Miriam *Pediatrics 1993;* 1665 Castlefield Road, Virginia Beach, VA 23456

VINOGRAD, Alexander *Pediatrics 1980;* 3065 Brighton 13th Street, Brooklyn, NY 11235

VIRAY, Jose *Pediatrics, Neonatal-Perinatal Medicine 1990;* Mount Sinai Medical Center, One Gustave Levy Place, New York, NY 10029
jose.viray@mssm.edu

VITALE, Leonard *Pediatrics 1967;* 269 Everett Place, Englewood, NJ 07631

VOGT-LOWELL, Robert *Pediatrics, Cardiology 1992;* 7765 Southwest 87 Avenue, Miami, FL 33196

VOLK, Barbie *Pediatrics 1988;* 667 Stoneleigh Avenue (Suite 116), Carmel, NY 10512
shorser@optonline.net

VUKSANAJ, Dila *Pediatrics 1985;* 103 Wildwood Circle, Columbia, TN 38401

WAJNRAJCH, Michael *Pediatrics 1992, Endocrinology;* Pfizer Inc., 235 East 42nd Street, NY, NY 10017
michael.wajnrajch@pfizer.com

WALD, Barton *Pediatrics 1978;* 199 East Los Robles Avenue, Pasadena, CA 91101
bwald@pahealth.com

WALD, Pamela *Pediatrics 1978;* Southern California Permanente Medical Group, 1011 Baldwin Park Blvd, Baldwin Park, CA 91706
pambwald@kp.org

WALSH, Rowan *Pediatrics, Cardiology 2007;* Children's Hospital of New Jersey, 201 Lyons Avenue, Newark, NJ O7112

WANDERMAN, Richard *Pediatrics 1972, Adolescent Medicine;* 6077 Apple Tree Drive (Suite 5), Memphis, TN 38115
drrich@bellsouth.net/richwander@medscape.com

WASEEM, Amira *Pediatrics 2001;* Mitchel Field Complex Family Health Center, Bldg 19 West Road, Garden City, NY 11530
awaseem@svcmcny.org

WASTI, Azra *Pediatrics 1992;* 2417 Ocean Parkway, Brooklyn, NY 11235
drawasti@aol.com

WATCHI, Ralph *Pediatrics, Infectious Diseases 1990;* 1300 North Vermont Avenue (Suite 901), Los Angeles, CA 90027

WEILER, Mitchell *Pediatrics 1983;* 86 Carman Avenue, Cedarhurst, NY 11516

WEINBERGER, Sylvain *Pediatrics 1978, Neonatal-Perinatal Medicine 1982;* NYU Medical Center, 550 First Avenue, New York, NY 10010

WEINER, Monica *Pediatrics 2004;* University of Medicine & Dentistry of New Jersey, 42 East Laurel Road (Suite 1100), Stratford, NJ O8084
mbweiner@hotmail.com

WEINER, Stacy *Pediatrics 2007;* NYU Medical Center, 550 First Avenue (NBV 7W 11), New York, NY 10016

WEINHOUSE, Elliott *Pediatrics, Cardiology 1977;* William Beaumont Hospital, 3601 West 13 Mile Road, Royal Oak, MI 48067
eweinhouse@beaumont,edu

WEINREB, Mark *Pediatrics 1991;* 110 Decker Drive, Gloversville, NY 12078

WEINSTEIN, Gloria *Pediatrics 1977;* 2823 42nd Street Northwest, Gig Harbor, WA 98335
drglo2@aol.com

WEINSTEIN, Toba *Pediatrics, Gastroenterology & Nutrition 1991;* Schneider Children's Hospital, 269-01 76th Avenue, New Hyde Park, NY 11040

WEINSTOCK, Michael *Pediatrics 1970, Emergency Medicine;* 1200 S. Cedar Crest Boulevard, Allentown, PA 18105
michael.weinstock@lvh.com

WEISELBERG, Eric *Pediatrics, Adolescent Medicine 1989;* Schneider Children's Hospital, 269-01 76th Avenue, New Hyde Park, NY 11040
eweiselb@lij.edu

WEISER, Adam *Urology 2003;* 750 Mount Carmel Mall (Suite 3), Columbus, OH 43222

WEISS, Christopher *Pediatrics 2001;* Washington Avenue Pediatrics, 263 Washington Avenue, Dumont, NJ O6079
drchristopherweiss@gmail.com

WEISS, Jeffrey *Allergy-Immunology 2002;* 44 Route 23 North (Suite 6), Riverdale, NJ O7457
jweiss@yahoo.com

WEISS, Mark *Pediatrics, Gastroenterology & Nutrition 1983;* 1224 Summit Avenue (Suite 304), Oakbrook Terrace, IL 60181

WEISS, Michael *Pediatrics 1969;* 382 Between the Lakes Road (Box 48), Taconic, CT 06079
gmweisss10@comcast.net

WEISS, Steven *Pediatrics 1994, Allergy-Immunology 1996;* 175 Jericho Tpke (Suite 121), Syosset, NY 11791
drsjweiss@aol.com

WEISSMAN, Avraham *Pediatrics 1991;* 6208 Sale Avenue, Haifa, Israel 34355
aweisman@yahoo.com

WEITZ, Theodore *Pediatrics 1991;* 11041 West 134th Street (Apt 12), Overland Park, KS 66213
ofanoa@gmail.com

WELLS, John *Pediatrics 1991, Neurology;* 109 East 67th Street, New York, NY 10021
johwtwellsmd@aol.com

WENICK, Gary *Pediatrics 1985, Endocrinology 1987;* 2050 Route 22 (Suite 101), Brewster, NY 10509
gwenick@aol.com

WERTHEIM, David *Pediatrics 1992, Allergy-Immunology 1994;* 310 East Shore Road (Suite 207), Great Neck, NY 11023
davidw1621@aol.com

WERTHER, Joseph *Pediatrics 1986;* 455 East 6th Street, Mesa, AZ 85203
jwerther@behcon.com

WHITE, Stacey *Pediatrics 1993;* 112 Chicken Valley Road, Old Brookville, NY 11545

WHITMAN, Bradley *Pediatrics 1990;* PO Box 6873, Delray Beach, FL 33482

WILLIAMS, Lisa *Pediatrics 2007, Hematology-Oncology;* Johns Hopkins Medical Center, 600 North Wolfe Street, Baltimore, MD 21287
bioteach23@yahoo.com

WILLIAMS, Sophia *Pediatrics 2007;* 579 East 34 Street, Brooklyn, NY 11203

WILNER, Jennifer *Pediatrics 2008;* 1356 First Avenue (Apt 4G), New York, NY 10021
jwilner7@gmail.com

WINGERIN, Ruth *Pediatrics 1989, Developmental & Behavioral Pediatrics;* British Columbia Self Tower Oakridge Mall, 650 West 41st Avenue (Suite 203), Vancouver, BC V5Z2M9
rwingerin@cw.bc.ca

WINTER-ANNUNZIATO, Paula *Pediatrics 1991;* 1130 Cleaver Road, Ambler, PA 19002
paula_annunziato@merck.com

WITTEK, Alec *Pediatrics 1981;* 300 Pasteur Dr (Suite S-322), Palo Alto, CA 94304

WOLF, Todd *Pediatrics, Emergency Medicine 2004;* 114 Killdeer Court, Southlake, TX 76092

WOLFF, Richard *Pediatrics 1978;* 10521 Martinque Isle Drive, Tampa, FL 33647

WOLFSON, Scott *Pediatrics, Hematology-Oncology 2003;* 700 Old Bethpage Road, Old Bethpage, NY 11804

WOLKOFF, Leslie *Pediatrics 1992, Neonatal-Perinatal Medicine;* Connecticut Children's Medical Center, 282 Washington Street, Hartford, CT 06106
lwolkof@ccmck305.org

WOLLOCH, Norbert *Pediatrics 1984;* 1010 Central Park Avenue, Yonkers, NY 10704
nwolloch@montefiore.org

WOODBURN-HOURIE, Karen *Pediatrics 1989;* 29-15 Far Rockaway Blvd., Far Rockaway, NY 11691
karenh356@aol.com

WOU, Margaret *Pediatrics 2002;* 217 Grand Street, New York, NY 10013

WREN-GLUPE, Margaret *Pediatrics 2000;* 2245 Jackson Avenue, Seaford, NY 11783
megwren@yahoo.com

WRIGHT, Lucinda Thurman *Pediatrics 2001, Cardiology 2004;* 571 South Floyd Street (Suite 334), Louisville, KY 40202
LTWRIG01@louisville.edu

WURZEL, Carol *Pediatrics 1985, Infectious Diseases 1987;* Blythedale Children's Hospital, 95 Bradhurst Avenue, Valhalla, NY 10595
carolw@blythedale.org/clwmd59@optonline.net

XAVIER, Frederico *Pediatrics 2007;* St. Jude Children's Research Hospital, 332 North Lauderdale, Memphis, TN 38105
frederico.xavier@stjude.org

YADOO, Moshe *Pediatrics , Neonatal-Perinatal Medicine 1988;* 29-01 216th Street, Bayside, NY 11360
myadoo@stmarykids.org

YAGUDAYEV, Yakov *Pediatrics 1998;* 85-15 Main Street, Briarwood, NY 11435

YAN, Karen *Pediatrics 2001;* 2 ProHealth Plaza, Lake Success, NY 11042
kyan@prohealthcare.com

YANG, LiMin *Pediatrics 2006;* 41 Mott Street, New York, NY 10013

YARIS-NEWMAN, Andrea *Pediatrics 1990;* Human Services Center at Sunnybrook, 10 Sunnybrook Road, Raleigh, NC 27610
anewman@co.wake.nc.us

YELLIN, Loren Kabat *Pediatrics 1987;* 1400 Pelham Parkway South (Room 512), Bronx, NY 10641
loren.yellin@nbhn.net

YOUNG, Guy *Pediatrics 1995, Hematology-Oncology;* 455 South Main Street, Orange, CA 92868
gyoung@choc.org

YOUNG, Ju Kim *Pediatrics 1978, Hematology-Oncology*

YOUSSEF-AHMED, Maged *Pediatrics, Critical Care Medicine 1996;* 384 DeMott Avenue, Rockville Centre, NY 11570

YOZAWITZ, Elissa *Pediatrics 2007;* Children's Hospital at Montefiore, 3415 Bainbridge Avenue, Bronx, NY 10467

YUDKOWITZ, Francine *Pediatrics 1984, Anesthesiology;* Mt. Sinai Medical Center, One Gustave Levy Place (Box 1010), New York, NY 10029
francine.yudkowitz@msnyouhealth.org

YUSUF, Fazlul *Pediatrics, Hematology-Oncology 1993;* 57-07 146th Street, Flushing, NY 11355

YUSUPOV, Roman *Pediatrics 2006;* Partners Healthcare Center, Children's Hospital Boston, 300 Longwood Avenue (Fegan 10), Boston, MA O2115
romanyu1@yahoo.com

ZACH, Tamara *Pediatrics 2006, Neurology;* Children's Hospital at Montefiore, 3415 Bainbridge Avenue, Bronx, NY 10467

ZALEWITZ, Jodi *Pediatrics 2004;* Saint Peter's Hospital, 317 Cleveland Avenue (2nd floor), Highland Park, NJ 08904

ZAR, Heather *Pediatrics 1991;* Red Cross War Memorial Children's Hospital, Rondebosch, Cape Town, SA

ZAVOLKOVSKAYA, Sabina *Pediatrics 2006;* 1111 Amsterdam Avenue, New York, NY 10025

ZAYTSEVA, Alla *Pediatrics 2008;* 66-15 Wetherole Street (Apartment B7), Rego Park, NY 11374
allochka5@yahoo.com

ZECHOWY, Racine *Pediatrics 1996;* 105 Renaissance Drive, Cherry Hill, NJ 8003
russandracine@aol.com

ZEIRA, Shelly *Pediatrics 1998;* 12 Medical Drive, Port Jefferson Station, NY 11776

ZELKOVIC, Paul *Urology 2005;* 159 White Plains Road, Tarrytown, NY 10591

ZENTAY, Zoltan *Pediatrics, Neonatal-Perinatal Medicine 1999;* 399 East Highland Avenue (Suite 527), San Bernardino, CA 92404

ZEROLNICK, Lawrence *Pediatrics 1975;* 11 Oak Hill Court, Owings Mills, MD 21117
docz4u@aol.com

ZIA, Ahmad *Pediatrics 2005, Medical Genetics;* Columbia University Medical Center, 630 West 168 Street, New York, NY 10032

ZILKHA, Naomi *Pediatrics 1996, Allergy-Immunology 1997;* 636 Wantagh Avenue, Levittown, NY 11756
nzilkha@optonline.net

ZWICK, Deborah *Pediatrics 1985;* 1120 South Jackson Highway (Suite 304), Sheffield, AL 35660
deborah1@hiwaay.net

ZYSKIND, Israel *Pediatrics 2007;* Borough Park Pediatric Associates, 4406 12th Avenue, Brooklyn, NY 11219
israelzyskind@yahoo.com

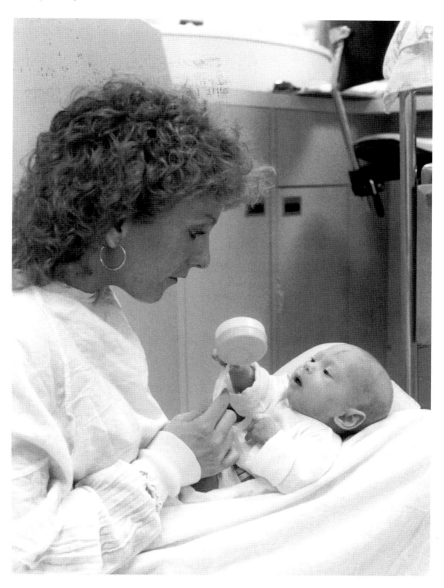

ALUMNI BY YEAR OF GRADUATION

The list of names for the years between 1954 and 1970 may be incomplete because the records for those years were not available for verification.

1954
MATHEWS, Zacharias

1955
GELABERT-LEMUS, Carmen

1956
MORAN, Oscar

1957
*TALLAL, Lisa

1959
ACS, Hedda

1960
*LIBRIK, Leon
NITZBERG, Benjamin
SPINNER, Milton

1961
DESPOSITO, Franklin
SHENKER, I. Ronald

1962
*HABER, Alan
HEITLER, Michael
*STORM, Jack

1963
COPPERMAN, Stuart
GOLDSTEIN, Alvin
SCHULKIND, Martin

1964
KELMINSON, Leslie

1965
*BERMAN, Robert
BLATT, Stanley
HALLER, Jerome
SILVERIO-REYES, Soledad
TRUCCO, Jaime

1966
BROWN, Robert

1967
ANTOKOLETZ, Marilyn
*EVERETT, Stanley
STEEG, Carl
VITALE, Leonard

1968
CAPPELLI, Frank
FLITMAN, Sheila
MAITINSKY, Steven

1969
CHOI, Rosa
GEDACHIAN, Robert
LAWRENCE, Donald
NAFICY-PAKRAVAN, Parvin
WEISS, Michael

1970
KIM, Theresa
WEINSTOCK, Michael

1971
BURKES, Lynn
GOULD, Eric
GUPTA, Krishna
KAINE, Richard
SILBERMAN-PROCUPEZ, Theresa
TEYAN, Frederick
VATS, Tribhavans

1972
BEUZEVILLE, Carlos
*BOGARD, Bruce
GIORDANO, Ida
MATHEW, Kolathu A.
SCHWARTZ, Gerald
SUN, Shyan-Chu
SUN, Sirisak
SUSSMAN, Joel
TUER, William
WANDERMAN, Richard

1973
ABELS, Jane
AMOONA, Raphael
GRANAT, Lloyd
HAMETZ, Irwin
OMLAND, Omar
SILVERSTEIN, Michael

1974
BERGER, Karl
CHASE-WANDERMAN, Nancy
CHOI, Sook
HOLZMAN, Bernard
KRISHNAN, Venkatesan
MAZE, Aubrey
PREMINGER, Nizza
REICH, Harvey

1975
GOLDBERG, Michael
HORWITZ, Jonathan
KAGANOWICZ-GORELICK, Eliza
KAYE, Arthur
LEIB, Martin
MC LAUGHLIN, Reginald
MOLLICK, Lawrence
ROBBINS, Michael
ROBERTS, Marc
SALUJA, Gurbir
SCHMERLER, Alan
SHULMAN, Peter
ZEROLNICK, Lawrence

1976
AMANULLAH, Adoor
BLAU, Irwin
CAREY, Dennis
CASSON, Ira
COHEN, Jack
DE BLASIO, Eugene
FISHER, Karen
FREED, Jay
GREENHILL, Philip
LIEBER, Marvin
NAPOLITANO, Jeanmarie
ROSENBERG, Steven
SOKOL, Scott
STEIN, Lawrence
*SUSER, Fredric

TRECARTIN, Susan

1977
ALTMAN, Stuart
BEKKER, David
BLICHARSKI, Danuta
BOXER, Harriet
FURMAN, Gilbert
GOLDMAN, Arnold
HORMAZDI, Bomi
KAPLAN, Eric
MC CARTHY, Patricia
OXMAN, David
RAIFMAN, Mark
RAPPAPORT, Robert
SHERNOCK, Marsha
SIEGEL, David
STEIN, Michael
VENIT, Bethany
WEINHOUSE, Elliott
WEINSTEIN, Gloria

1978
ALVAREZ, Miguel
BROWN, David
FROGEL, Michael
GOLDSTEIN, Stanley
IZENBERG, Neil
KATSEVA, Ida L.
KUMAR, Vasanth
MADAD, Saiyeda
NUSSBAUM, Michael
RABINOWICZ, Morris
SAND, Harold
SHERMAN, Martin
SHIRSAT, Pratibha
STORM, Richard
WALD, Barton
WALD, Pamela
WOLFF, Richard
YOUNG, Ju Kim

1979
BEN-ZEEV, Uri
BODI, Janice
BRUNSON, Sandra
DICK, Gilbert
FEINSTEIN, Ronald
FLAMENBAUM, Helen
HAIBY, William
HANDWERKER, Lisa
HOWARD, Renee
JACQUE, Celeste
LAPTOOK, Abbot
MINTZ, Jesse
NUNEZ, Ann
ORT, Howard
PHILIPS, Jeffrey
ROSENBLUM, Howard
ROSENSTEIN, Jonathan
SIM, Alfonso

1980
ALVAREZ, Miguel
ARORA, Satish
AUERBACH, Harvey
CALLEJA, Gregorio
FALK, Theodore
FISHER, Martin
GINSBURG, Mark

GORDON, Charles
GRAF, Lillian
HAHN, Gary
KATZ, David
KHAN, Zahida
LAZAR, Linda
LENARSKY, Carl
MILLER, Harvey
OHSON, Gunwant
SOSULSKI, Richard
STEELE, Andrew
STEWART, Constance
TURNER, Peter
VINOGRAD, Alexander

1981
ALLAWI, Diane
BROWN, Dennis
COHEN, Pamela
COHEN, Stanley
FRUCHTMAN, Deborah
FUCHS, Howard
GANGULY, Rekha
GOLDSTEIN, Steven
GREENBAUM, Dorothy
HONIGMAN, Richard
KASNICKI, Laurie
KUNCEWITCH, William
KYRIAKAKOS, Anastassios
LEVINE, Jack
LEVINE, Marc
MILGRAUM, Sandy
MORGENSTERN, Bruce
NANADIEGO, Maria
ROSENBERG, Zehava Sadka
SANTOS-NANADIEGO, Maria
    Catalina
SPIOTTA, Roseann
TUROW, Victor
WITTEK, Alec

1982
BERGTRAUM, Marcia
CRAMER, Andrea
FATICA, Nunzia
GORDON, Laurie
HUBEL, Philip
KAHAN, Joel
KENDALL, Roxanne
LEVINE, Alan
LINDER, Alice
MASER, Dennis
MAYTAL, Joseph
MORGENSTERN, Joel
PEREZ, Lucille
PLAUT, Allan
RESMOVITS, Marvin
ROSSI, Wilma
RUBIN, Michael
SCHAEFFER, Janis
SUN, Lena
TRUXAL, Brian
VIJAYAN, Radhika
WEINBERGER, Sylvain

1983
BATTISTA, Anthony
BLUMENTHAL, Steven
BROWNSTEIN, William
BUTENSKY, Arthur

CHARYTAN, Morris
CHUNG, David
DI LELLO, Edmund
DVORIN, Donald
GELLIS, Richard
HARDOFF, Daniel
HERKO, Patricia
JEROME, Robert
KILCHEVSKY, Eitan
KLEIN, Thomas
KLEINBERG, Mitchell
KRONFELD, Gary
LANZONE, Theresa
LAU, Alice
MORRIS, Elliot
NUSSBAUM, Michael
PLATT, Anne
RUBIN, Irina
RUSSELL, Barbara
SMITH, Carol
WEILER, Mitchell
WEISS, Mark

1984
APPEL, Cheryl
CANTOS, Eric
DICKSON, Pamela
ELIE, Marie-Theresa
GENSER, Alan
GOCHOCO, Aurora
HOROWITZ, Jeffrey
KLEIN, Susan
MARCUS, Carole
OLSHANSKY, Cheryl
PARRISH, Samuel K.
PEARLMAN, Stephen
QUITTELL, Lynne
RANDEL, Sidney
SILBER, Gail
SKOLNICK, Eric
STULBACH, Harry
TOPSIS, Julie
WOLLOCH, Norbert
YUDKOWITZ, Francine

1985
ALVARADO, Doris
ARBITMAN, Mikhail
ARBITMAN, Raisa
BOLLAMPALLI, Vidyasagar Reddy
CASE, Philip
CASTIGLIA, Luisa
CITERMAN, Stephanie
COLEMAN, Cathy
FELDMAN, Robert
FORTE, Louis
GAYNOR, Michael
GERO, Bernard
GRAF, Jeannette
GREENFIELD, Elizabeth
JARENWATTANANON, Marisa
KAPOOR, Vishwa
KASLOFF, Ilene
KLEIGER, Richard
LAWRENCE, Philip
LEBOVIC, Daniel
LEONOR-GILRANE, Marixie Q.
MADDUR, Shantha Devi
RODRIGUEZ, Rhina
SAUNDERS, Jay
TELSEY, Aimee

UNCYK, Avraham
VUKSANAJ, Dila
ZWICK, Deborah

1986
*ALI, Asad
ANDERSON, Nancy
CLAUS, Mark
COPPER, Donna
COTLER, Donald
DIAMANT, Shmuel
EISENBERG, Bruce
ENG, Christine
ESPOSITO, Linda
FEINSTEIN, Stuart
FINK, Lawrence
FLIEGENSPAN, Jeffrey
FRISS, Helena
GLOBERMAN, Hadas
GREIF, Jules
HOGAN, Timothy
JUSTER, Fern R.
KAVIT, Gary
KAW, Saroj
LIM, Wilma
MATHEW, Rajamma
NACHMAN, Sharon
NAGELBERG, Joy
NEUMANN, David
*SAAD, Sam
SCHIFF, Russell
SEITZ, Michele L.
SHORSER, James
WERTHER, Joseph

1987
ADAMS, Lawrence
ALENICK, D. Scott
BALMAGIYA, Tovy
BLAU, Hannah
CAMACHO, Jose Angel
CO, Margaret
DECASTRO-GROUSSE, Denise
DEVER, Lynn
GREIF, Jules
GUTERMAN, Carl
HALLER, Jerome
JENNINGS, Gloria
KABAT, Loren Gail
KARPF, Laurie
LERIAS, Edgar
LIGHTMAN, Hylton
MAGALETTI, Francine
MARTYNEC, Lydia
McDERMOTT-ADAMS, Nancy
McGOVERN, Margaret
McNAMARA, Joseph
MEISLER, Susan
OHRING, Marshall
OPITZ, Lynne
SAMUEL, Maritza
SCHWARTZ, Lisa
SKOOG-LAUFER, Dagna
TEICHMAN, Faye
THOMAS, Philomena
TREPEL, Robert
TSIMOYIANIS, George
WENICK, Gary
WURZEL, Carol
YELLIN, Loren Kabat

1988
ANDREWS, Diana
BALBUS, Michael
BANKS, Mitchell
BERLIN, Paul
BIENSTOCK, Jeffrey
BULINOUN, Paul
CHIANG, Angela
COHEN, Cynthia
DECARMINE, Philip
DEL CARMEN, Renato
DEL CARMEN, Ruby
ELVIR, Patricia
GUBITOSI, Terry Ann
HAUSDORFF, Mark
IVINS, Rhea
JANKELOVITS, Eric
KADEN, Gail Goodman
KAROLL, Doreen
KLEIMAN, Michele
KREITZER, Paula
MARTON, Freddie
OLIN, Jeffrey
ONG, Manuel
POLSINELLI, Rosanna
PUGLISI, Vincent
ROZENBAUM, Joseph
SANTIAGO, Maria Teresa
SAPIRE, Kenneth
SCHLOSSBERGER, Norman
SEIDLER-LISS, Alice F.
SHAPIRO, Warren
UEBLER-YOKOIS, Nancy
VOLK, Barbie
YADOO, Moshe

1989
BLUMENREICH, Robert
CASADONTE, Joseph
CHAN, Raymond
EDWARDS, Bruce
GIAMPIETRO, Philip
GREISING, Joanne
ISRAEL, David Moshe
JOHNSTON, Jean Madinger
KAIN, Zeev
KENNEDY, Joanne M.
KUSHNER-CUSHMAN, Susan
LASHANSKY, Gayle
LEAVENS-MAURER, Jill
MARCHITELLI, Roberto
MARILAO, Hilario
MINIKES, Neil
NAGEL, Michael
NAGPAL, Rajeev
NASS, Howard
NEWBRUN, Daniel
RAMAKRISHNAN, T.R.
SHEINBAUM, Karen (Blum)
SIEGEL, Scott
STEIN-ALBERT, Marcy
STEVENS-MORRISON, Cynthia
TANG-HUANG, Lin-Lan
TU, Lan Chau Hang
WEISELBERG, Eric
WINGERIN, Ruth
WOODBURN-HOURIE, Karen

1990
ARDEN, Martha
BAIN, Russell

BUDOW, Lauren
CARRO-SACKLER, Lorna
DOYLE, James
ELDEMERDASH, Alaa
GENNARO, Margaret
GENNINO, Christopher
HAMMER-SANDOVAL, Ellen
HAWKINS, Lynn
HUTNER, Aline
KANTOR, Paul
KRAUSS, Richard
MC SHERRY, Kevin
MUSIKER-NEMIROV, Jamie
NARAIN-CHAWLA, Bindoo
PERNICE, Mercedes Tiongo
PETERS, Vicki
POSNER, Mark
PUNSALAN, Imelda
RIVERA, Loyda
SACKLER, Lorna Carro
SANDOVAL, Claudio
SCHECHTMAN-FREEDMAN,
   Merryl
SILVERMAN, Lawrence
SONENBLUM, Michael
SUCHOFF, Monica
TIONGO, Mercedes
VIRAY, Jose
WATCHI, Ralph
WHITMAN, Bradley
YARIS-NEWMAN, Andrea

1991
BARLEV, Dan
BOMBART, Felice
BRUNSON, Sandra
DELLORUSSO, Ana
DELLORUSSO, Giuseppe
DOBIN-FARIN, Michelle
*FARIN, Mark
FONG, Jane
FRANCES, Adriana
FRANK, Graeme
FRUMPKIN-KANTROVITZ, Farla
GRAF, Alisa
HANDELSMAN, Edward
HANSROTE, Louis
HARVEY, Jay
JACOBY-LOW, Gail
LAO, Jimmy
LESSER, Eric
MALKIN, Elfrida
MOKIDES, Valerie
MURPHY, Susan
PATANKAR, Srikanth
QUIJANO, Claudia
RAPPAPORT, Mark
RAVAL, Nikhilkumar
ROMANO, Alicia
RUBIN, Andrew
SCHUVAL, Susan
SCHWARTZ, Susan
STRAUSS, Raphael
SY-KHO, Rose Marrie
VEGA, Roy
WEINREB, Mark
WEINSTEIN, Toba
WEISSMAN, Avraham
WEITZ, Theodore
WELLS, John
WINTER-ANNUNZIATO, Paula

ZAR, Heather

1992
APFEL, Howard
APPLEBAUM, Eric
AUNG, Lei
BARLOW, Douglas
BERCHIN, Bernard
BERGWERK, Ari
BERGWERK, Katherine
BRAUN, Rochelle
CHERRICK, Irene
CHOWDHARI, Antonina
CUTLER, Adam
DOS SANTOS, Christiane
GLEIT-CADURI, Daphne
GOLDBERG, Michael
HAMMER, Michael
KORN, Sheila
LALLY, Michelle
LINDT, Josephine
LIQUORNIK, Karen
MAISEL, Mercedes
PANES, Susan
PELOSO, Marie Azzu
PLANER, Benjamin
RAFFALLI, Peter
ROSENN, Greg
SALZMAN, Mark
SCHLESSEL, Kevin
SIEGEL, Janet
SIMHI, Eliahu
STEINER, Deborah
TAN, Patricia
TOBIN-SIMON, Cecily
TYAGI, Swayamprabha (Pat)
VAN OORDT-CESPEDES, Karen
VOGT-LOWELL, Robert
WAJNRAJCH, Michael
WASTI, Azra
WERTHEIM, David
WOLKOFF, Leslie

1993
AMIGO, Therese
ASHOURZADEH, Kourosh
BANDEL, Jack
BRYANT-RENNIE, Janet
COLEY-PICCIRILLO, Karen
CONSTANT, Mireille
DE ALDAY, Marietta Yumana
DUROSEAU, Herold
EISEN, Louis
ESTRADA, Elizabeth
FELDMAN, Doron
FERREIRA, Jose
GARA, Lori
GERBERG, Lynda
GOLD, David
GOLDSTEIN, Ilene
GROSSMAN, Rami Raphael
GUINTO, Danilo
JOVINO, Louise
LEBO, Debra
LEEDS, Andrea
LEVENE, Eric
LUCK, Raemma Paredes
MAHADEO, Robby
MANALO, Erlinda
MATTHEWS, Lori Gara
MEYERSON, Lisa Linzer

NAYOR, Ilyse
NEWFIELD, Liora
NEWFIELD, Ron
NIMKOFF, Laura
RAISSI-FARD, Ehteram
REYES, Miraflor
RODRIGUEZ, Ruth
RONCA, Lorraine
RORER, Eva Maria
SCHNEIDER, David
SCHWOB, Netanel
SIDDIQUE, Razia
SILVER, Peter
SORIANO-AGUILLAR, Edita
ST. VICTOR, Rosemarie
TAMIR, Akiva
TIZER, Karen
VILLASECA, Miriam
WHITE, Stacey
YUSUF, Fazlul

1994
APEATU, Samuel
AVVOCATO, Gloria P.
BALSON, Boris
CANLAS-SUCGANG, Maria
DE JESUS, Socorro
DIXON, Earl
ELBASTY, Azza
FREEDMAN, Samuel
FURMAN, Melissa
GONZALEZ, Maripaz
GREISSMAN, Allan
HOLLANDER-BOBO, Robin
KANIA, Patricia
KATZ, Elizabeth
KNOBLER, Stacey
LEE, Jeong
LEVINE, Daniel
LEVINE-BOSIN, Stephanie
LYNCH, Patricia Kania
MARDY, Gisele
MASAKAYAN, Adelaide
MATTHEWS, Benjamin
PAREDES-LUCK, Raemma
PIRRAGLIA, Don
PUGLIESE, Madeline
SAVARESE, David
SHABBIR, Azfar
SHAW-BRACHFELD, Jennifer
SHERTZ, Mitchell
SHIH, San
SMITH, Steven
SOFOCLEOUS, Constantinos
SULITZER, Karen
SVITEK, Scott
UCKAN, Duygu
WERTHEIM, David

1995
ANG, Renato
BERMAN, Lori
CARONIA, Catherine
COLON-LEDEE, Athos
COONEY, Maureen
COUROUCLI, Xanthi
DAMOUR, Yvon
DUVDEVANY, Neta
EMRALINO, Feliciano
FELL, Brad
FRIEDMAN-GOLDMAN, Sharon

GO, Anita
GOLDBERG, Barry
GOMBOS, Michal
HILAIRE Chantal
IVKER-GOLDSTEIN, Cindee
JAIN, Varsha
JOSEPH, Natalie Pierre
KESSLER, Oded
KHAN, Abu
KHAN, Kishwar
KHAN, Nafis
KIMPO, Joycelyn
KWONG, Terry
LASKARI, Cleo Vassilios
LIWAG, Celerina
LOBEL, Danielle
MAJEED, Salamat
NERWEN, Clifford
OCHOTORENA, Josiree
ROONEY, John
SCHIFF, Stuart
SCHROEDER, Marie
SIVAKUMAR, Preethi
SPERLING, Randi
STROBER, Jonathan
TAFRESHI-ORAEE, Parisa
TAN, Bernardo
VALCOURT, Lucienne Deltor
YOUNG, Guy

1996
ALVARADO, Nestor
ARYEL, Ron
AZAM, Shabana
BABINSKI, Eleanor
BENNETT, Douglas
BLEIBERG, Alan
BONTEMPO-BLAUSTEIN, Silvia
BORCZUK, Mrinalini
BROSGOL, Yuri
CATALANO, Lorraine
CAVANAUGH, Lisa
CHIKEZIE, Augustine
DEE, Sandra
FALKOVICH, Ruvim
FRIED-SIEGEL, Judy
GARCIA, Maria
GOLD, Nina
GRAZIANO, Joan
HARRIS, Bradford
HENTSCHEL-FRANKS, Karen
HERZFELD, Sharon
KOHN, Michael
KOKAN, Farhat
KOROPECKY, Christine
MAHMOOD, Khawaja
MATHIAS, Liesl
MIJARES-ZIMMERMAN, Jennifer
MILLER, Karen
MONES, Karen
NIEVES, Jorge
PHILIP, Soman
PIELA, Christina
RAKOWSKA, Urszula
ROONEY, Elizabeth
SALES, Serafin
SHARAF, Mohamed
SIEGEL, Mark
SILVERIO, Arlene
SINGH, Jayati
SPATOLIATORE, Rosa Linda

STONE, Josie
VASISHTHA, Sanjeev
WEISS, Steven
YOUSSEF-AHMED, Maged
ZECHOWY, Racine

1997
BALASNY, Jennifer
BARILARI, Rafael
BHATIA, Narinder
BISWAS, Saumitra
CAMPOS, Francisco
DENIZ, Yamo
ERMITANO, Maria Luisa
FANELLA, Frank
FIGUEROA, Nitza Lugo
FORGIONE, Lisa
GINEBRA, Fernando
KHAN, Aliya
KOVACS, George
KRAUSS, Joel
LACANILAO, Ramon
LEE, Chi
LEVIN, Marina
LEVY, Itzhak
LIMAYE, Deepa
LOYOLA, Rosa
LUGO, Nitza
MILMAN, Marina
MOISSIDIS, Ioannis
NALABOFF, Kenneth
NARAN, Navyn
NIMKOFF, Laura
PADMANABHAN, Pradeep
PALACIO, Liliana
PARRISH, Daniel
PEDROSO, Manuel
RAMANAN, Aruna
RAVISHANKAR, Chitra
ROSE, Marion
ROSENCRANTZ, Richard
ROSENTHAL, Cynthia
SAVARGAONKAR, Rajesh
SUAREZ, Elizabeth
TELEGA, Dorota
TELEGA, Gregory
ZILKHA, Naomi

1998
ALSHANSKY, Anna
ANTHONY, Thiele Umali
BERMAN, David
BILOG, Agnes
BRAVERMAN, Isaac
CORDICE-FORD, Candida
DI TURI-HARTLEY, Suzanne
ECKSTEIN, Ira
EYAL, Dalit
FLICKER, Jason
GALOSO, Maria
GERBERG, Bruce
GOTTLIEB, Beth
HERZOG, Ronit
JAMAL, Yousaf
KAN, Li
KHANNA, Happy Neera
KILIMNICK, Joseph
LARKIN, Anne Marie
LINDGREN, Bruce
LIU, Yingxue
LUJAN-ZILBERMANN, Jorge

LUNA, Betty
MELTZER-KRIEF, Eve
MILLER, Margarita
MOHAMED, Yasser
MURZA, Gina
ONG-DEE, Elizabeth
PATEL, Kalpana
PIERRE, Louisdon
QADIR, Maqbool
RABINOWITZ, Brian
ROSEN, Dov
SCHER, Herschel
SCHULMAN, Jason
SERRUYA, Jose
SHAH, Atul Navnitlal
SHAH, Binod
SMITH, Robin
STERLING, Karen Mathurin
TALWAR, Rohit
TELLECHEA, Natasha
THECKEDATH, Jose
YAGUDAYEV, Yakov
ZEIRA, Shelly

1999
AMARO-GALVEZ, Rodolfo
AMODIO, Stefano
BASSOUL, Albert
CELIKER, Mahmut
CHIANG, Nancy
CHO, Jason
COHEN, Joseph
COHEN, Sheryl
EAPEN, Santhosh
ETWARU, Kumarie
FUSCO, Tara
GALANG, Luz
GAMUNDI JOAQUIN, Rosa
GENSLER, Zev
GEORGE, Minu
GOLDMAN, Robert
HOM, Christine
HUANG, Andrew
IGARTUA, Jon
JIWANI, Amyn Ali
KRIEF, William
LANTZOUNI, Eleni
LAU, Bernard
LEVY, Moshe
LEW, Lai-Ping
MARSHALL, Ian
MASSEY, Laurie O'Brien
MEHROTRA, Deepti
MIRER, Mikhail
MODI, Sangita Kumari
NAZNIN, Dixit
SCHWARTZ, Fred
SHAMIM, Tabassum
SIRNA, Paul
SREEDHARA, Malathi
STEIN, Rodd
TAN, Noel
UKRAINCIK, Miro
ZENTAY, Zoltan

2000
ANTOKOLETZ, Marilyn
AYGUN, Banu
BAILEY, Denyse
BEARD, Rachel
BOCK, Kevin

BRANT-DEITCH, Deborah
CHEONG, Keith
CHESNER, Rina
COPE, Jennifer
CRISS-SMITH, Cynthia
DIAL, Sharon
ETESS, Melanie Stein
FASANO, Andrew
FRIEDMAN, Daniel
GONZALEZ, Rosa Ana
HAIMI-COHEN, Yishai
HUSAIN, Naghma
KABARITI, Jack
KATZ, Uriel
KEATES-BALEEIRO, Jennifer
KOMITAS, Mahi
KRECO, Edvins
LUA, Jorge
MALLARE, Johanna
MAMONLUK, Maribel
MARCU, Mariana
MINUSKIN, Tal
MOERCK, Linda
MOERCK-JOHNSON, Deborah
OCAMPO, Stella
PARSONS, Scott
RAHEJA, Ravi
SCHARE, Rachel
SHAHDADPURI, Jean
SHEFLIN, Marla
SIM, Geoffrey
SONDIKE, Stephen
STEIN ETESS, Melanie
SUKHOV, Renat
TENG, David
TOPPER, Leonid
WREN-GLUPE, Margaret

2001
AEINITZ, Jennifer
ANAND, Shikha
AVSHALOMOV, Gad
BACHMAN, Michael
BANGUG, Samuel
BAYRAK, Beril
BOCCHICCHIO, Jeffrey
BOROWSKA, Halina
BROWN-McDANIEL, Barbara
BURKE, Christine Maroon
CHANG, Barry
CHEN, Ellen
DADA, Lesley
DIZON, Louis
EISENSTAT, Jennifer
FIGLOZZI, Christina
FRIEDMAN, Benyamin
FRIEDMAN-OPPENHEIMER, Orit
GRELLO, Stephen
HAIMOWITZ-REINITZ, Jennifer
HEAVENS-ALEXANDRE, Faith
KHABBAZE, Youssef
KIBLAWI, Fuad
KRONBERG, Jason
KWOK, Maria
MAKATAN, Marjan
MARCANO, Brenda
MAROON, Christine
O'GRADY-IANDOLI, Mary Lou
RAVID, Sarit
REDDY, Damodar
REZNIKOV, Alexandra

RIFKIN-ZENENBERG, Stacey
SINGLA, Manav
TAHZIB-KHADEM, Munirih
TAWAKOL, Heshem
VARMA, Rupa
WASEEM, Amira
WEISS, Christopher
YAN, Karen

2002
AUYEUNG, Valerie
AVARICIO, Elizabeth
BERGER, Jay
BRAIER, Karin
BRODTMAN, Daniel
BRUNO, Sandra
CABALLERO, Felipe
CHAKRABATI, Chandrama
CREVI, Diana
DAVIS, Jonathan
DEGUZMAN, Jocelyn
FEFER, Zipora
FIUMANO, Margaret
HABERMAN, Elisa
IRAKAM, Anitha
JORDAN, Jo-Ann
KAPADIA, Shailee
KIMPO, Miriam
KOHN, Gary
KRAUS, Gregory
LACY-KING, Roxanne
LOPEZ, Carmen
MANICONE, Paul
MEYAPPAN, Thiyagaraja
NANGIA, Srishti
NG, Elizabeth
O'CONNELL, Karen
ORNSTEIN, Rollyn
PERLMAN, Varisa
QUERSHI, Masarrat
RAKSIS, Karen R.
RELVAS, Monica de Stefani
RIVERA-AMISOLA, Cecilia
ROUVALIS, Fotis
SHARMA, Anjali
SHETH, Shashank
SHIH, Chie-Youn
SIAREZI, Shaghayegh (Sherry)
SIYAHREZAEI, Shaghayegh
STEINBOCK, Roy
UDDIN, Zia
VALOIS, Katherine
WEISS, Jeffrey
WOU, Margaret

2003
ACKERMAN-STEINBOCK, Gila
ALKON, Jaime
AMISOLA, Rogelio
ARONOFF, David
BAILEY, Beth
BALDAUF, Mary
BARKAN, Craig
BHASKAR, Mahesh
BIGWOOD, Jonathan
BIRNBAUM, Lynette
BRENNER, Dennis
ELLIS, Jeffrey
ESPERANZA, Maria
GROSSMAN, Heather
JAISWAL, Paresh

JOSEPH, Keanna
KANG, Richard
KARAKAS, Sabiha Pinar
KHADAVI, Alan
KHAN, Ambreen
KIM, Urian
KUMAR, Pankaj
LEARSY, Dawn
LEUPOLD, Kerry
LUFTIG-WEISS, Jennifer
MADHOK, Ashish
MANDEL, Corey
MARTINEZ, Alfred
MAYBANK, Karen
MILOJEVIC, Diana
MORGANSTERN, Jeffrey
PRUSHIK, Kenneth
RADINSKY, Stacey
REDDY, Uday
RINGHEANU, Mihaela
ROTELLA, Alessandra
SANTANGELO, Christina
SCHIOWITZ, Gila
SCHWARTZ, Saara
SHAFINOORI, Shideh
SILTON, Akiva
SIMAI, David
TRYZMEL, John
TUCKER, Stephanie
WEISER, Adam
WOLFSON, Scott

2004
ADLER, Liora
ARENA, Marina
ASRA, Irfan
BERLIN, Hilary
BOYER, Clark
BRANDT, Penny
CANTATORE-FRANCIS, Julie
CAVUOTO, Marie
CLEMENTI, Jennifer
DEGENHARDT, Karl
DIEJOMAH, Ejiro
DOLMAIAN, Gigliola Copaescu
FISH, Jonathan
FREYLE, Jamie
GORDON, Seth
GRIJNSZTEIN, Mark
HALEGOUA, Jason
HEMPEL, Bridget
HSU, Penelope
IYPE, Jay
JESSANI, Shabana
LEVI, Michelle
LUFTIG-WEISS, Jennifer
MACHUCA, Hildred
MAKORNWATTANA, Porawat
MANOHAR, Priti
MILANAIK, Ruth
MITSOTAKIS-HOWARD, Demetra
MORGENSTERN, Solomon S.
NAIK, Vibhuti
NARUCKI, Wayne
NGHI, Phuong
NICOLOPOULOS, Efthemia
PARK, Seung-Dae
RANGWALA, Nikita
SELTZER, Alexandra
SHAINHOUSE, Tsippora
SHETREAT-KLEIN, Maya

SIEGEL, Melissa
STOLL, Matthew
STROZUK, Stephanie
TAYLOR-DURDAN, Danielle
TROPE, Randi
UNAL, Elif
WEINER, Monica
WOLF, Todd
WRIGHT, Lucinda Thurman
ZALEWITZ, Jodi

2005

ARANDA, Diane
AVARELLO, Jahn
BAER, Aryeh
BELLIN, Anne
BELOSTOTSKY, Olga
BENJAMIN-THORPE, Solange
BICHOTTE, Sophia Ligonde
BLUMER, Steven
BORNSTEIN-MAYERSON, Cara
BRADY, Jodi
BREGLIO, Keith
DAYAN, Nimrod
DRAGOI, Elena
ELLIOTT, Michelle
FERREIRA, Carmen
FORREST, Emily
GANAL-ESPERANZA, Pamelynn
GATES, Robert
GEORGE, Matthew
GIORGI, Marilyn
GOODMAN, Karen Meier
HADJIEV, Boyan
HORVATH, Lajos
JANDER, Isabel Granja
KAUSHAL-JOHAL, Sandeep
KUMAR, Cathie
KUMAR, Gogi
LAKSHMINARAYANAN, Sonali
LAU, Joshua Hung Tin
LIPTSEN, Ellina
LONG, Jennifer
MC INERNEY-LOPEZ, Regina
MORENO, Lisa
MUKHERJEE, Sarmistha
NADARAJ, Sumekala
NOVAK, Inna
O'DONNELL, Lisa-Mary
PARK, Yohan
PATEL, Shipra
PEK, Monika
PETROZZINO, Jeffrey
POOLE, Claudette
POTDAR, Meenu
RABINOWITZ, Deborah
RICHARDS, Andrea Telak
SAXENA, Harshita
SEZGIN, Gulay
SIDDIQI, Shaz
SIVITZ, Adam
SIVITZ, Jennifer
SOGAWA, Yoshimi
STROTHER, Christopher
TATZ, Gary
ZELKOVIC, Paul
ZIA, Ahmad

2006

ADARAMOLA-OJO, Mojisola
AHLUWALIA, Amardeep
AHMAD, Saed
BAKERYWALLA, Rubina
BERNSTEIN, Frederic
BINDRA, Tejwant
BRATT, James
BROWN, Erica
CARREIRO, Jennifer
CHEUNG, Helen
CHO, Eunsung
DEUTCH, Robert
DYER, Lori Landau
FELDT, Matthew
GERSHKOVICH, Irina
GLIKSMAN, Felicia
GREENBLATT, Daniel
GROENING, Portia
HASAN, Muhamad
HWANG, Juliet
IRIGOYEN, Patricia
ISAKSON, Loren
JACOB, Julie
JOY, Rosemary
*KNOLLWELL-ROTH, Sharon
KOSLOWE, Oren
KOSTER, Divya
LaCORTE, Justin
LAPIDUS, Sivia
LEMON-MULE, Heather
LEONOV, Andrey
LEVIT, Orly
MACHEN, Heather
MANTZOURANIS, Jessica
MAZIN, Howard
MC DADE, Jenny
MC DONOUGH, Christian
MERCHANT-SOOMAR, Sanah
MILLER, Michael
MOUSTAFA, Usama
MYERS, Christine
PAPAIOANNOU, Helen
PARRA, Angelica
PEREIRA-ARGENZIANO, Lucy
PONDA, Punita
READ, Rosemarie
ROSENTHAL, David
ROY, Kevin
SANBORN, Chad
SARUMI, Oludayo
SELIGSOHN, Jacob
SHAH, Jesika
SHAH, Nikhil
SHEFFER-BABILA, Sharone
SILBERMINTZ, Ari
SINGALA, Ravinder
SINGH, Rachana
SLUTZAH, Meredith
SNOW, Ayelet
STONE, Hilary
SURGAN, Victoria Zolot
TAURASSI, Cheryl
TIYYAGURA, Sripriya
TROPE, Juliette
VANSTONE, Michelle
YANG, LiMin
YUSUPOV, Roman
ZACH, Tamara
ZAVOLKOVSKAYA, Sabina

2007

ALEXANDER-MURUGIAH, Vanaja
APOLLONSKY, Nataly
AYYAGARI-SIEGEL, Subhadra
BATAYKIN, Yelena
CHANG, Philip
CHEN, Ashton
CITARELLA, Brett
COX, Amanda
DAVIS, Carol
DAVIS, Jennifer
DHANANTWARI, Preeta
ENG, Jennifer
ESSANDOH, Yvonne
FEBER, Kevin
FERNANDEZ, Mariely
GAMENG, Mary Ann Flynn
GIDWANEY, Rita
GOLDBERG, Tracie
GOLOMBECK, Arel
GONZALEZ, Jeanette
GOTTESMAN, Avraham
HARBERT, Mary Jo
HARNICK, Joel
JEAN-BAPTISTE, Stefanie
JUDMAN-LEDER, Eva
KAHN, Doron
KATZ, Laura
KEMPIAK, Stephan
KOSTER, Michael
KRIEF, Patricia
LIBERT, Melissa
MAMANI, Sylvia
MARCHLEWSKI, Robert
MARRIA, Pooja
MELA, Suzanne
NAKAR, Charles
NICHOLS, Christiana
OVED, Kfir
PALATHRA, Mary Lou
PALAZZO, Marie
PINTO, Matthew
PUGLISI, Gregory
RAHSHID, Iqbal
REGAN, Brian
ROCKER, Joshua
ROTHSTEIN, David Hershel
RUBIN, Jamie
SAMONTE, Frank
SANTIAGO, Myla
SCHWARTZ, Robert
SCHWARZ, Gavin
SCIMEME, Jason
SEKHON, Aman
SHROFF, Amita
SIMON-GOLDMAN, Phyllis
SOMMERS, Ross
STEVENSON, Amanda
TELLER, Filip
TRAN, Loanne
VALENTINE-RICHARDSON, Keena
VALSAMIS, Christina
WALSH, Rowan
WEINER, Stacy
WILLIAMS, Lisa
WILLIAMS, Sophia
XAVIER, Frederico
YOZAWITZ, Elissa
ZYSKIND, Israel

2008

ABDULRAHMAN, Eiman
ADEYINKA, Adebayo
AGGARWAL, Alpna
AIDLEN, Jeremy Todd
ARNOLD, Lisa
ARROYO, Alexander
ASCHETTINO, Diana
AYDIN, Scott
BELLOTTI, Christopher
BENERI, Christy
BOYAR, Vitaliya
CHATTERGEE, Manjula
CHEMIATILLY, Wassim
CHINNAIRUSAN, Muthamilan
CIANNELLA, John
COHEN, Michele
CONROY-RICHARDS, Rushika
DE JESUS, Julisa
DELANEY, Angela
DESROSIERS, Florence
ELBASH, Lina
ELLWOOD, Joanmarie
FERNANDO, Anusha
FIORENTINOS, Dionysia
FONT, Luis
GAROFALO-MONACO, Melissa
GOROZA, Edmund
GREEN-BILELLO, Rachel
HERMAN, Tali
IMUNDO, Jason
JOSE, Bessey
KACPERSKI, Joanne
KARIDIS, Argyro
KATZ, Lisa
KIRSCHNER, Jessica
KUMAR, Munish
LANDA, Dahlia
LAWRENCE, Emily
MANDELKER, Lisa
MARTINEZ, Maritza
MC COLLUM, Alexandra
MENSCH, Deborah
MORALES, Yesenia
MULALE, Unami
NEUSTEIN, Sherrie
NOLAN, Lizabeth
NORMAN, Shannon
PAPAIOANNOU, Helen
PALUMBO, Nancy
PARK, KunTae
PHILIP, Smitha
PICKERING, Olufunke
SAFIER, Brian
SALEK, Allyson
SAMUELS, Roya
SCERBO, Jessica
SCIMEME, Jason
SILVERMAN, Sarah
SINGH, Sharon
SMITH, Michael
SUH, Michael
SUPASWUD, Tingnong
SYLVESTER, Julie
THOMASEN, Tanya-Marie
VASILESCU, Alexandra
WILNER, Jennifer
ZAYTSEVA, Alla

ALUMNI BY GEOGRAPHIC LOCATION

UNITED STATES

ALABAMA
CANLAS-SUCGANG, Maria *1994*
ZWICK, Deborah *1985*

ARIZONA
AHLUWALIA, Amardeep *2006*
BILOG, Agnes *1998*
CHANG, Barry *2001*
JAISWAL, Paresh *2003*
JESSANI, Shabana *2004*
MADDUR, Shantha Devi *1985*
MAZE, Aubrey *1974*
MORGENSTERN, Bruce *1981*
PHILIP, Soman *1996*
RAHSHID, Iqbal *2007*
SIVAKUMAR, Preethi *1995*
UEBLER-YOKOIS, Nancy *1988*
WERTHER, Joseph *1986*

CALIFORNIA
ANDERSON, Nancy *1986*
BERGWERK, Ari *1992*
BERGWERK, Katherine *1992*
CHEN, Ellen *2001*
CHIANG, Angela *1988*
DE ALDAY, Marietta Yumana *1993*
DEL CARMEN, Renato *1988*
DEL CARMEN, Ruby *1988*
ESTRADA, Elizabeth *1993*
FURMAN, Gilbert *1977*
GATES, Robert *2005*
GELABERT-LEMUS, Carmen *1955*
GERO, Bernard *1985*
GRIJNSZTEIN, Mark *2004*
HARBERT, Mary Jo *2007*
HSU, Penelope *2004*
HUANG, Andrew *1999*
JEROME, Robert *1983*
KANG, Richard *2003*
KAPOOR, Vishwa *1985*
KEMPIAK, Stephan *2007*
KHANNA, Happy Neera *1998*
KIMPO, Joycelyn *1995*
LEE, Chi *1997*
LINDT, Josephine *1992*
LOYOLA, Rosa *1997*
MANALO, Erlinda *1993*
MARILAO, Hilario *1989*
MATHIAS, Liesl *1996*
MC COLLUM, Alexandra *2008*
MILOJEVIC, Diana *2003*
NANADIEGO, Maria *1981*
NEWBRUN, Daniel *1989*
NEWFIELD, Liora *1993*
NEWFIELD, Ron *1993*
NITZBERG, Benjamin *1960*
ORT, Howard *1979*
PARK, KunTae *2008*
PETROZZINO, Jeffrey *2005*
QUIJANO, Claudia *1991*
REICH, Harvey *1974*
SALZMAN, Mark *1992*
SANTOS-NANADIEGO, Maria Catalina *1981*
SCHLOSSBERGER, Norman *1988*

SHAHDADPURI, Jean *2000*
SHAPIRO, Warren *1988*
SHARMA, Anjali *2002*
SILVERIO-REYES, Soledad *1965*
SPINNER, Milton *1960*
STEIN, Lawrence *1976*
STROBER, Jonathan *1995*
SUAREZ, Elizabeth *1997*
VALOIS, Katherine *2002*
VARMA, Rupa *2001*
WALD, Barton *1978*
WALD, Pamela *1978*
WATCHI, Ralph *1990*
WITTEK, Alec *1981*
YOUNG, Guy *1995*
ZENTAY, Zoltan *1999*

COLORADO
ACKERMAN-STEINBOCK, Gila *2003*
BLATT, Stanley *1965*
DOBKIN-FARIN, Michelle *1991*
KELMINSON, Leslie *1964*
LIPTSEN, Ellina *2005*
McDERMOTT-ADAMS, Nancy *1987*
OCAMPO, Stella *2000*
STEINBOCK, Roy *2002*

CONNECTICUT
ALLAWI, Diane *1981*
ALSHANSKY, Anna *1998*
ANAND, Shikha *2001*
ARENA, Marina *2004*
BROWN, David *1978*
BROWNSTEIN, William *1983*
CARREIRO, Jennifer *2006*
CITARELLA, Brett *2007*
DAYAN, Nimrod *2005*
DRAGOI, Elena *2005*
FANELLA, Frank *1997*
GENNINO, Christopher *1990*
JANKELOVITS, Eric *1988*
KAIN, Zeev *1989*
KILCHEVSKY, Eitan *1983*
KLEIMAN, Michele *1988*
KRECO, Edvins *2000*
KUMAR, Vasanth *1978*
LEARSY, Dawn *2003*
LEVIT, Orly *2006*
LIMAYE, Deepa *1997*
NARAN, Navyn *1997*
RAMANAN, Aruna *1997*
SCHMERLER, Alan *1975*
SCHWARTZ, Gerald *1972*
SHAMIM, Tabassum *1999*
STEVENSON, Amanda *2007*
TSIMOYIANIS, George *1987*
WEISS, Michael *1969*
WOLKOFF, Leslie *1992*

DELAWARE
ALKON, Jaime *2003*
ANTHONY, Thiele Umali *1998*
BRADY, Jodi *2005*
BRYANT-RENNIE, Janet *1993*
DIEJOMAH, Ejiro *2004*

ESPOSITO, Linda *1986*
IZENBERG, Neil *1978*
PEARLMAN, Stephen *1984*

DISTRICT OF COLUMBIA
BACHMAN, Michael *2001*
LAPIDUS, Sivia *2006*
MANICONE, Paul *2002*
O'CONNELL, Karen *2002*
RABINOWITZ, Deborah *2005*
SAXENA, Harshita *2005*

FLORIDA
ADAMS, Lawrence *1987*
ADLER, Liora *2004*
BAIN, Russell *1990*
BARLOW, Douglas *1992*
BERMAN, David *1998*
BRODTMAN, Daniel *2002*
BROWN, Robert *1966*
BRUNO, Sandra *2002*
CASADONTE, Joseph *1989*
CHANG, Philip *2007*
CHOWDHARI, Antonina *1992*
COPPERMAN, Stuart *1963*
COHEN, Jack *1976*
CUTLER, Adam *1992*
DEE, Sandra *1996*
DICKSON, Pamela *1984*
DIXON, Earl *1990*
EISENBERG, Bruce *1986*
FERREIRA, Carmen *2005*
FERREIRA, Jose *1993*
FLIEGENSPAN, Jeffrey *1986*
FREEDMAN, Samuel *1994*
FUCHS, Howard *1981*
GAYNOR, Michael *1985*
GINEBRA, Fernando *1997*
GINSBURG, Mark *1980*
GRANAT, Lloyd *1973*
GREISSMAN, Allan *1994*
HARVEY, Jay *1991*
HOLZMAN, Bernard *1974*
HORVATH, Lajos *2005*
ISAKSON, Loren *2006*
KAHN, Doron *2007*
KAINE, Richard *1971*
KARPF, Laurie *1987*
LONG, Jennifer *2005*
LUJAN-ZILBERMANN, Jorge *1998*
MAGALETTI, Francine *1987*
MAISEL, Mercedes *1993*
MARDY, Gisele *1994*
MIJARES-ZIMMERMAN, Jennifer *1996*
NARAIN-CHAWLA, Bindoo *1990*
NAZNIN, Dixit *1999*
O'GRADY-IANDOLI, Mary Lou *2001*
OHRING, Marshall *1987*
ONG, Manuel *1988*
PALACIO, Liliana *1997*
PARRA, Angelica *2006*
PEDROSO, Manuel *1997*
PERNICE, Mercedes Tiongo *1990*
PUGLISI, Vincent *1988*
QUERSHI, Masarrat *2002*

RAISSI-FARD, Ehteram *1993*
RANDEL, Sidney *1984*
RODRIGUEZ, Ruth *1993*
ROSENBERG, Steven *1976*
SAMUEL, Maritza *1987*
SANBORN, Chad *2006*
SCHARE, Rachel *2000*
SCHER, Herschel *1998*
SCHULMAN, Jason *1998*
SCHWARTZ, Saara *2003*
SELIGSOHN, Jacob *2006*
SHULMAN, Peter *1975*
SILVERSTEIN, Michael *1973*
SINGH, Jayati *1996*
SONENBLUM, Michael *1990*
SPERLING, Randi *1995*
SREEDHARA, Malathi *1999*
STONE, Josie *1996*
TAN, Noel *1999*
TRYZMEL, John *2003*
TUER, William *1972*
UCKAN, Duygu *1994*
VALCOURT, Lucienne Deltor *1995*
VOGT-LOWELL, Robert *1992*
WHITMAN, Bradley *1990*
WOLFF, Richard *1978*
ZENTAY, Zoltan *1999*

GEORGIA
BROWN-McDANIEL, Barbara *2001*
FELDMAN, Robert *1985*
LEONOR-GILRANE, Marixie Q. *1985*
RANGWALA, Nikita *2004*
RAPPAPORT, Mark *1991*
SHROFF, Amita *2007*
THECKEDATH, Jose *1998*
TYAGI, Swayamprabha (Pat) *1992*
VATS, Tribhavans *1971*

IDAHO
LEVI, Michelle *2004*

ILLINOIS
CHOI, Rosa *1969*
HAMMER, Michael *1992*
JOY, Rosemary *2006*
KUMAR, Munish *2008*
LINDGREN, Bruce *1998*
NAGPAL, Rajeev *1989*
ONG-DEE, Elizabeth *1998*
ROTHSTEIN, David Hershel *2007*
SUN, Sirisak *1972*
TAN, Bernardo *1995*
WEISS, Mark *1983*

INDIANA
CHAKRABATI, Chandrama *2002*
SNOW, Ayelet *2006*

IOWA
GALOSO, Maria *1998*
SUPASWUD, Tingnong *2008*

KANSAS
SMITH, Carol *1983*
WEITZ, Theodore *1991*

KENTUCKY
CHINNAIRUSAN, Muthamilan 2008
ERMITANO, Maria Luisa 1997
FORTE, Louis 1985
KATZ, David 1980
MAMONLUK, Maribel 2000
PADMANABHAN, Pradeep 1997
SANTIAGO, Myla 2007
SHAFINOORI, Shideh 2003
WRIGHT, Lucinda Thurman 2004

LOUISIANA
GEORGE, Matthew 2005
GO, Anita 1995
HALLER, Jerome 1965
LAO, Jimmy 1991

MAINE
BLUMENTHAL, Steven 1983

MARYLAND
ALVARADO, Nestor 1996
BAILEY, Denyse 2000
BEARD, Rachel 2000
DADA, Lesley 2001
DELANEY, Angela 2008
HOWARD, Renee 1979
MARRIA, Pooja 2007
MARTYNEC, Lydia 1987
MC INERNEY-LOPEZ, Regina 2005
OMLAND, Omar 1973
PEREZ, Lucille 1982
RORER, Eva Maria 1993
SCHWOB, Netanel 1993
SIDDIQI, Shaz 2005
SIEGEL, David 1977
SINGLA, Manav 2001
STEVENS-MORRISON, Cynthia 1989
UDDIN, Zia 2002
VASILESCU, Alexandra 2008
WILLIAMS, Lisa 2007
ZEROLNICK, Lawrence 1975

MASSACHUSETTS
AGGARWAL, Alpna 2008
AIDLEN, Jeremy Todd 2008
AUERBACH, Harvey 1980
BALSON, Boris 1994
BEKKER, David 1977
BRENNER, Dennis 2003
CLAUS, Mark 1986
DECASTRO-GROUSSE, Denise 1987
DENIZ, Yamo 1997
GARA, Lori 1993
HARNICK, Joel 2007
HUTNER, Aline 1990
JOSEPH, Natalie Pierre 1995
JUDMAN-LEDER, Eva 2007
KAPLAN, Eric 1977
KAROLL, Doreen 1988
KAUSHAL-JOHAL, Sandeep Johal 2005
KUMAR, Cathie 2005
KUMAR, Pankaj 2003
MARTINEZ, Alfred 2003
MASSEY, Laurie O'Brien 1999
MATTHEWS, Benjamin 1994
MATTHEWS, Lori Gara 1993

MILLER, Karen 1996
RAFFALLI, Peter 1992
REGAN, Brian 2007
ROBBINS, Michael 1975
SAMONTE, Frank 2007
SINGH, Rachana 2006
SIVITZ, Adam 2005
SIVITZ, Jennifer 2005
STOLL, Matthew 2004
YUSUPOV, Roman 2006

MICHIGAN
AMANULLAH, Adoor 1976
CHEN, Ashton 2007
LUA, Jorge 2000
PERLMAN, Varisa 2002
REYES, Miraflor 1993
SINGALA, Ravinder 2006
WEINHOUSE, Elliott 1977

MINNESOTA
APEATU, Samuel 1994
TUCKER, Stephanie 2003

MISSOURI
ARYEL, Ron 1996
BISWAS, Saumitra 1997
FRANCES, Adriana 1991
KENNEDY, Joanne M. 1989
KNOBLER, Stacey 1994

NEW HAMPSHIRE
GEDACHIAN, Robert 1969

NEVADA
DEGUZMAN, Jocelyn 2002
ROSENSTEIN, Jonathan 1979

NEW JERSEY
ABELS, Jane 1973
ALENICK, D. Scott 1987
ALVARADO, Doris 1985
APFEL, Howard 1992
APOLLONSKY, Nataly 2007
APPLEBAUM, Eric 1992
AUNG, Lei 1992
BAER, Aryeh 2005
BARILARI, Rafael 1997
BERLIN, Paul 1988
BIENSTOCK, Jeffrey 1988
BRAVERMAN, Isaac 1998
BULINOUN, Paul 1988
BUTENSKY, Arthur 1983
CASE, Philip 1985
CHIKEZIE, Augustine 1996
CO, Margaret 1987
COHEN, Michele 2008
COHEN, Pamela 1981
COPE, Jennifer 2000
COTLER, Donald 1986
DESPOSITO, Franklin 1961
DI TURI-HARTLEY, Suzanne 1998
EAPEN, Santhosh 1999
ELBASTY, Azza 1994
FALK, Theodore 1980
FRUCHTMAN, Deborah 1981
GAMUNDI JOAQUIN, Rosa 1999
GAROFALO-MONACO, Melissa 2008
GENSER, Alan 1984
GOLD, Nina 1996

GOODMAN, Karen Meier 2005
GOROZA, Edmund 2008
GREENHILL, Philip 1976
GUBITOSI, Terry Ann 1988
GUINTO, Danilo 1993
GUTERMAN, Carl 1987
HABERMAN, Elisa 2002
HAMETZ, Irwin 1973
HAUSDORFF, Mark 1988
IRAKAM, Anitha 2002
JACQUE, Celeste 1979
JENNINGS, Gloria 1987
JORDAN, Jo-Ann 2002
KENDALL, Roxanne 1982
KIBLAWI, Fuad 2001
KIM, Theresa 1970
KIM, Urian 2003
KOHN, Gary 2002
KRONFELD, Gary 1983
KUSHNER-CUSHMAN, Susan 1989
LEBOVIC, Daniel 1985
LEONOV, Andrey 2006
LESSER, Eric 1991
LEUPOLD, Kerry 2003
LEVINE, Daniel 1994
LEVINE, Marc 1981
LEVINE-BOSIN, Stephanie 1994
LEVY, Moshe 1999
LIU, Yingxue 1998
LUFTIG-WEISS, Jennifer 2003
MARSHALL, Ian 1999
MAZIN, Howard 2006
MC DONOUGH, Christian 2006
MC SHERRY, Kevin 1990
MILGRAUM, Sandy 1981
MINIKES, Neil 1989
MINTZ, Jesse 1979
MURPHY, Susan 1991
NADARAJ, Sumekala 2005
NAFICY-PAKRAVAN, Parvin 1969
NARUCKI, Wayne 2004
O'DONNELL, Lisa-Mary 2005
OPITZ, Lynne 1987
OXMAN, David 1977
PATANKAR, Srikanth 1991
PIELA, Christina 1996
PLANER, Benjamin 1992
RICHARDS, Andrea Telak 2005
RIFKIN-ZENENBERG, Stacey 2001
RIVERA, Loyda 1990
ROBERTS, Marc 1975
ROSENBLUM, Howard 1979
ROSSI, Wilma 1982
SALUJA, Gurbir 1975
SAND, Harold 1978
SCHWARTZ, Fred 1999
SCHWARTZ, Lisa 1987
SHAW-BRACHFELD, Jennifer 1994
SHETH, Shashank 2002
SIEGEL, Mark 1996
SIEGEL, Scott 1989
SILVERMAN, Lawrence 1990
SIRNA, Paul 1999
STERLING, Karen Mathurin 1998
STROZUK, Stephanie 2004
STULBACH, Harry 1984
SUN, Shyan-Chu 1972
SURGAN, Victoria Zolot 2006
TAHZIB-KHADEM, Munirih 2001
TANG-HUANG, Lin-Lan 1989
TOBIN-SIMON, Cecily 1992

TOPPER, Leonid 2000
TRUXAL, Brian Andrew 1982
TURNER, Peter 1980
UKRAINCIK, Miro 1999
VIJAYAN, Radhika 1982
VITALE, Leonard 1967
WALSH, Rowan 2007
WEINER, Monica 2004
WEISS, Christopher 2001
WEISS, Jeffrey 2002
ZALEWITZ, Jodi 2004
ZECHOWY, Racine 1996

NEW MEXICO
BRANDT, Penny 2004

NEW YORK
ABDULRAHMAN, Eiman 2008
ACS, Hedda 1959
ADARAMOLA-OJO, Mojisola 2006
ADEYINKA, Adebayo 2008
AEINITZ, Jennifer 2001
ALTMAN, Stuart 1977
ALVAREZ, Miguel 1980
AMODIO, Stefano 1999
AMOONA, Raphael 1973
ANDREWS, Diana 1988
ANTOKOLETZ, Marilyn 1967
APPEL, Cheryl 1984
ARANDA, Diane 2005
ARBITMAN, Mikhail 1985
ARBITMAN, Raisa 1985
ARDEN, Martha 1990
ARORA, Satish 1980
ARROYO, Alexander 2008
ASHOURZADEH, Kourosh 1993
ASRA, Irfan 2004
AVARELLO, Jahn 2005
AVARICIO, Elizabeth 2002
AVSHALOMOV, Gad 2001
AVVOCATO, Gloria P. 1994
AYDIN, Scott 2008
AYYAGARI-SIEGEL, Subhadra 2007
AZAM, Shabana 1996
BABINSKI, Eleanor 1996
BAILEY, Beth 2003
BAKERYWALLA, Rubina 2006
BALASNY, Jennifer 1997
BALDAUF, Mary 2003
BALMAGIYA, Tovy 1987
BANGUG, Samuel 2001
BANKS, Mitchell 1981
BARLEV, Dan 1991
BASSOUL, Albert 1999
BATAYKIN, Yelena 2007
BATTISTA, Anthony 1983
BAYRAK, Beril 2001
BELLIN, Anne 2005
BELOSTOTSKY, Olga 2005
BENERI, Christy 2008
BENJAMIN-THORPE, Solange 2005
BENNETT, Douglas 1996
BEN-ZEEV, Uri 1979
BERCHIN, Bernard 1992
BERGER, Jay 2002
BERGTRAUM, Marcia 1982
BERLIN, Hilary 2004
BERMAN, Lori 1995
BERNSTEIN, Frederic 2006
BEUZEVILLE, Carlos 1972
BHASKAR, Mahesh 2003

BICHOTTE, Sophia Ligonde 2005
BINDRA, Tejwant 2006
BIRNBAUM, Lynette 2003
BLAU, Irwin 1976
BLUMENREICH, Robert 1989
BLUMER, Steven 2005
BOCK, Kevin 2000
BODI, Janice 1979
BOMBART, Felice 1991
BONTEMPO-BLAUSTEIN, Silvia 1996
BORCZUK, Mrinalini 1996
BORNSTEIN-MAYERSON, Cara 2005
BOROWSKA, Halina 2001
BOXER, Harriet 1977
BOYAR, Vitaliya 2008
BOYER, Clark 2004
BRAIER, Karin 2002
BRANT-DEITCH, Deborah 2000
BRAUN, Rochelle 1992
BREGLIO, Keith 2005
BROSGOL, Yuri 1996
BRUNSON, Sandra 1979
BUDOW, Lauren 1990
BURKE, Christine Maroon 2001
BURKES, Lynn 1971
CABALLERO, Felipe 2002
CALLEJA, Gregorio 1980
CANTATORE-FRANCIS, Julie 2004
CANTOS, Eric 1984
CAPPELLI, Frank 1968
CAREY, Dennis 1976
CARONIA, Catherine 1995
CARRO-SACKLER, Lorna 1990
CASSON, Ira 1976
CASTIGLIA, Luisa 1985
CATALANO, Lorraine 1996
CAVANAUGH, Lisa 1996
CAVUOTO, Marie 2004
CELIKER, Mahmut 1999
CHAN, Raymond K. 1989
CHARYTAN, Morris 1983
CHATTERGEE, Manjula 2008
CHEONG, Keith 2000
CHERRICK, Irene 1992
CHESNER, Rina 2000
CHEUNG, Helen 2006
CHIANG, Nancy 1999
CHO, Eunsung 2006
CHOI, Sook 1974
CHUNG, David 1983
CIANNELLA, John 2008
CITERMAN, Stephanie 1985
CLEMENTI, Jennifer 2004
COHEN, Cynthia 1988
COHEN, Joseph 1999
COHEN, Sheryl 1999
COHEN, Stanley 1981
COLEMAN, Cathy 1985
COLEY-PICCIRILLO, Karen 1993
CONROY-RICHARDS, Rushika 2008
CONSTANT, Mireille 1993
COONEY, Maureen 1995
COPPER, Donna 1986
CORDICE-FORD, Candida 1998
COX, Amanda 2007
CREVI, Diana 2002
CRISS-SMITH, Cynthia 2000
DAMOUR, Yvon 1995

DAVIS, Carol 2007
DAVIS, Jennifer 2007
DAVIS, Jonathan 2002
DE BLASIO, Eugene 1976
DE JESUS, Julisa 2008
DE JESUS, Socorro 1994
DECARMINE, Philip 1988
DELLORUSSO, Ana 1991
DELLORUSSO, Giuseppe 1991
DESROSIERS, Florence 2008
DEUTCH, Robert 2006
DHANANTWARI, Preeta 2007
DIAL, Sharon 2000
DICK, Gilbert 1979
DI LELLO, Edmund 1983
DOLMAIAN, Gigliola Copaescu 2004
DOYLE, James 1990
DUROSEAU, Herold 1993
DYER, Lori Landau 2006
ECKSTEIN, Ira 1998
EDWARDS, Bruce 1989
EISEN, Louis 1993
EISENSTAT, Jennifer 2001
ELBASH, Lina 2008
ELLIOTT, Michelle 2005
ELLIS, Jeffrey 2003
ELLWOOD, Joanmarie 2008
ELVIR, Patricia 1988
EMRALINO, Feliciano 1995
ENG, Christine 1986
ENG, Jennifer 2007
ESPERANZA, Maria 2003
ETESS, Melanie Stein 2000
ETWARU, Kumarie 1999
FALKOVICH, Ruvim 1996
FASANO, Andrew 2000
FATICA, Nunzia 1982
FEBER, Kevin 2007
FEFER, Zipora 2002
FEINSTEIN, Ronald 1979
FEINSTEIN, Stuart 1986
FELDMAN, Doron 1993
FELL, Brad 1995
FERNANDEZ, Mariely 2007
FERNANDO, Anusha 2008
FINK, Lawrence 1986
FIORENTINOS, Dionysia 2008
FISH, Jonathan 2008
FISHER, Karen 1976
FISHER, Martin 1980
FIUMANO, Margaret 2002
FLAMENBAUM, Helen 1979
FLICKER, Jason 1998
FLITMAN, Sheila 1968
FONG, Jane 1991
FONT, Luis 2008
FORGIONE, Lisa 1997
FORREST, Emily 2005
FRANK, Graeme 1991
FREED, Jay 1976
FREYLE, Jamie 2004
FRIEDMAN, Benyamin 2001
FRIEDMAN, Daniel 2000
FRIEDMAN-GOLDMAN, Sharon 1995
FRIEDMAN-OPPENHEIMER, Orit 2001
FRIED-SIEGEL, Judy 1996
FROGEL, Michael 1978
FURMAN, Melissa 1994

FUSCO, Tara 1999
GAMENG, Mary Ann Flynn 2007
GANAL-ESPERANZA, Pamelynn 2005
GELLIS, Richard 1983
GENSLER, Zev 1999
GEORGE, Minu 1999
GERBERG, Bruce 1998
GERBERG, Lynda 1993
GERSHKOVICH, Irina 2006
GIDWANEY, Rita 2007
GIORDANO, Ida 1972
GIORGI, Marilyn 2005
GLEIT-CADURI, Daphne 1992
GLIKSMAN, Felicia 2006
GOCHOCO, Aurora 1984
GOLD, David 1993
GOLDBERG, Barry 1995
GOLDBERG, Tracie 2007
GOLDMAN, Arnold 1977
GOLDMAN, Robert 1999
GOLDSTEIN, Alvin 1963
GOLDSTEIN, Ilene 1993
GOLDSTEIN, Stanley 1978
GOLDSTEIN, Steven 1981
GOLOMBECK, Arel 2007
GOMBOS, Michal 1995
GONZALEZ, Jeanette 2007
GONZALEZ, Maripaz 1994
GORDON, Charles 1980
GORDON, Laurie 1982
GORDON, Seth 2004
GOTTESMAN, Avraham 2007
GOTTLIEB, Beth 1998
GOULD, Eric 1971
GRAF, Alisa 1991
GRAF, Jeannette 1985
GRAF, Lillian 1980
GRAZIANO, Joan 1996
GREENBAUM, Dorothy 1981
GREEN-BILELLO, Rachel 2008
GREENBLATT, Daniel 2006
GREENFIELD, Elizabeth 1985
GREISING, Joanne 1989
GRELLO, Stephen 2001
GROENING, Portia 2006
GROSSMAN, Heather 2003
GROSSMAN, Rami Raphael 1993
GUPTA, Krishna 1971
HAHN, Gary 1980
HAIBY, William 1979
HAIMOWITZ-REINITZ, Jennifer 2001
HALEGOUA, Jason 2004
HAMMER-SANDOVAL, Ellen 1990
HANDELSMAN, Edward 1991
HANDWERKER, Lisa 1979
HARRIS, Bradford 1996
HAWKINS, Lynn 1990
HEAVENS-ALEXANDRE, Faith 2001
HEITLER, Michael 1962
HEMPEL, Bridget 2004
HERKO, Patricia 1983
HERZFELD, Sharon 1996
HERZOG, Ronit 1998
HILAIRE, Chantal 1995
HOGAN, Timothy 1986
HOLLANDER-BOBO, Robin 1994
HOM, Christine 1999
HONIGMAN, Richard 1981

HOROWITZ, Jeffrey 1984
HORWITZ, Jonathan 1975
HUBEL, Philip 1982
HUSAN, Muhamad 2006
HWANG, Juliet 2006
IMUNDO, Jason 2008
IRIGOYEN, Patricia 2006
IVINS, Rhea 1988
IVKER-GOLDSTEIN, Cindee 1995
IYPE, Jay 2004
JACOB, Julie 2006
JAIN, Varsha 1995
JEAN-BAPTISTE, Stefanie 2007
JIWANI, Amyn Ali 1999
JOHNSTON, Jean Madinger 1989
JOSE, Bessey 2008
JOSEPH, Keanna 2003
JOVINO, Louise 1993
JUSTER, Fern R. 1986
KABARITI, Jack 2000
KABAT, Loren Gail 1987
KACPERSKI, Joanne 2008
KADEN, Gail Goodman 1988
KAGANOWICZ-GORELICK, Eliza 1975
KAHAN, Joel 1982
KAN, Li 1998
KARIDIS, Argyro 2008
KASNICKI, Laurie 1981
KATSEVA, Ida L. 1978
KATZ, Elizabeth 1994
KATZ, Lisa 2008
KAYE, Arthur 1975
KHABBAZE, Youssef 2001
KHADAVI, Alan 2003
KHAN, Abu 1995
KHAN, Ambreen 2003
KHAN, Kishwar 1995
KHAN, Nafis 1995
KHAN, Zahida 1980
KILIMNICK, Joseph 1998
KIMPO, Miriam 2002
KIRSCHNER, Jessica 2008
KLEIGER, Richard 1985
KLEIN, Susan 1984
KLEINBERG, Mitchell 1983
KOMITAS, Mahi 2000
KORN, Sheila 1992
KOROPECKY, Christine 1996
KOSLOWE, Oren 2006
KOVACS, George 1997
KRAUS, Gregory 2002
KRAUSS, Joel 1997
KRAUSS, Richard 1990
KREITZER, Paula 1988
KRIEF, Patricia 2007
KRIEF, William 1999
KRONBERG, Jason 2001
KUNCEWITCH, William 1981
KWOK, Maria 2001
KYRIAKAKOS, Anastassios 1981
LACORTE, Justin 2006
LACY-KING, Roxanne 2002
LANDA, Dahlia 2008
LANZONE, Theresa 1983
LASHANSKY, Gayle 1989
LAU, Alice 1983
LAU, Bernard 1999
LAU, Joshua Hung Tin 2005
LAWRENCE, Donald 1969
LAWRENCE, Emily 2008

LEAVENS-MAURER, Jill *1989*
LEBO, Debra *1993*
LEE, Jeong *1994*
LEEDS, Andrea *1993*
LEIB, Martin *1975*
LEMON-MULE, Heather *2006*
LERIAS, Edgar *1987*
LEVENE, Eric *1993*
LEVIN, Marina *1997*
LEVINE, Alan *1982*
LEVINE, Jack *1981*
LEW, Lai-Ping *1999*
LIBERT, Melissa *2007*
LIEBER, Marvin *1976*
LIGHTMAN, Hylton *1987*
LINDER, Alice *1982*
LOPEZ, Carmen *2002*
LUNA, Betty *1998*
LYNCH, Patricia Kania *1994*
MACHUCA, Hildred *2004*
MADAD, Saiyeda *1978*
MAHADEO, Robby *1993*
MAITINSKY, Steven *1968*
MAJEED, Salamat *1995*
MAKATAN, Marjan *2001*
MAKORNWATTANA, Porawat *2004*
MALKIN, Elfrida *1991*
MAMANI, Sylvia *2007*
MANTZOURANIS, Jessica *2006*
MARCANO, Brenda *2001*
MARCHITELLI, Roberto *1989*
MARCHLEWSKI, Robert *2007*
MARCU, Mariana *2000*
MAROON, Christine *2001*
MARTINEZ, Maritza *2008*
MARTON, Freddie *1988*
MASAKAYAN, Adelaide *1994*
MASER, Dennis *1982*
MATHEW, Kolathu A. *1972*
MATHEW, Rajamma *1986*
MAYBANK, Karen *2003*
MAYTAL, Joseph *1982*
MC CARTHY, Patricia *1977*
MC GOVERN, Margaret *1987*
MC LAUGHLIN, Reginald *1975*
MEHROTRA, Deepti *1999*
MEISLER, Susan *1987*
MELTZER-KRIEF, Eve *1998*
MENSCH, Deborah *2008*
MEYERSON, Lisa Linzer *1993*
MILANAIK, Ruth *2004*
MILLER, Harvey *1980*
MILLER, Michael *2006*
MILMAN, Marina *1997*
MIRER, Mikhail *1999*
MITSOTAKIS-HOWARD, Demetra *2004*
MODI, Sangita Kumari *1999*
MOERCK, Linda *2000*
MOERCK-JOHNSON, Deborah *2000*
MOKIDES, Valerie *1991*
MOLLICK, Lawrence *1975*
MONES, Karen *1996*
MORALES, Yesenia *2008*
MORENO, Lisa *2005*
MORGANSTERN, Jeffrey *2003*
MORGENSTERN, Joel *1982*
MORGENSTERN, Solomon S. *2004*
MORRIS, Elliot *1983*

MOUSTAFA, Usama *2006*
MUKHERJEE, Sarmistha *2005*
MULALE, Unami *2008*
MURZA, Gina *1998*
MUSIKER-NEMIROV, Jamie *1990*
MYERS, Christine *2006*
NACHMAN, Sharon *1986*
NAGELBERG, Joy *1986*
NAKAR, Charles *2007*
NALABOFF, Kenneth *1997*
NANGIA, Srishti *2002*
NAPOLITANO, Jeanmarie *1976*
NASS, Howard *1989*
NAYOR, Ilyse *1993*
NERWEN, Clifford *1995*
NEUSTEIN, Sherrie *2008*
NG, Elizabeth *2002*
NGHI, Phuong *2004*
NICHOLS, Christiana *2008*
NICOLOPOULOS, Efthemia *2004*
NIEVES, Jorge *1996*
NIMKOFF, Laura *1993*
NOLAN, Lizabeth *2008*
NORMAN, Shannon *2008*
NOVAK, Inna *2005*
NUNEZ, Ann *1979*
NUSSBAUM, Michael *1978*
OCHOTORENA, Josiree *1995*
OHSON, Gunwant *1980*
OLIN, Jeffrey *1988*
PALUMBO, Nancy *2008*
PANES, Susan *1992*
PAPAIOANNOU, Helen *2006*
PARK, Yohan *2005*
PARRISH, Daniel *1997*
PATEL, Kalpana *1998*
PELOSO, Marie Azzu *1992*
PEREIRA-ARGENZIANO, Lucy *2006*
PETERS, Vicki *1990*
PHILIPS, Jeffrey *1979*
PIERRE, Louisdon *1998*
PINTO, Matthew *2007*
PIRRAGLIA, Don *1994*
PLATT, Anne *1983*
PLAUT, Allan *1982*
POLSINELLI, Rosanna *1988*
PONDA, Punita *2006*
POOLE, Claudette *2005*
PREMINGER, Nizza *1974*
PRUSHIK, Kenneth *2003*
PUGLIESE, Madeline *1994*
PUGLISI, Gregory *2007*
PUNSALAN, Imelda *1990*
QUITTELL, Lynne *1984*
RABINOWICZ, Morris *1978*
RABINOWITZ, Brian *1998*
RADINSKY, Stacey *2003*
RAIFMAN, Mark *1977*
RAKOWSKA, Urszula *1996*
RAKSIS, Karen *2002*
RAPPAPORT, Robert *1977*
READ, Rosemarie *2006*
REDDY, Damodar *2001*
RESMOVITS, Marvin *1982*
REZNIKOV, Alexandra *2001*
ROCKER, Joshua *2007*
RODRIGUEZ, Rhina *1985*
ROMANO, Alicia *1991*
RONCA, Lorraine *1993*
ROONEY, Elizabeth *1996*

ROONEY, John *1995*
ROSE, Marion *1997*
ROSENBERG, Zehava Sadka *1981*
ROSENCRANTZ, Richard *1997*
ROSENN, Greg *1992*
ROSENTHAL, Cynthia *1997*
ROSENTHAL, David *2006*
ROTELLA, Alessandra *2003*
ROY, Kevin *2006*
ROZENBAUM, Joseph *1988*
RUBIN, Andrew *1991*
RUBIN, Irina *1983*
RUBIN, Jamie *2007*
SACKLER, Lorna Carro *1990*
SAFIER, Brian *2008*
SALEK, Allyson *2008*
SALES, Serafin *1996*
SAMUELS, Roya *2008*
SANDOVAL, Claudio *1990*
SANTANGELO, Christina *2003*
SANTIAGO, Maria Teresa *1988*
SAUNDERS, Jay *1985*
SAVARESE, David *1994*
SAVARGAONKAR, Rajesh *1997*
SCERBO, Jessica *2008*
SCHAEFFER, Janis *1982*
SCHECHTMAN-FREEDMAN, Merryl *1990*
SCHIFF, Russell *1986*
SCHIFF, Stuart *1995*
SCHIOWITZ, Gila *2003*
SCHROEDER, Marie *1995*
SCHUVAL, Susan *1991*
SCHWARZ, Gavin *2007*
SEIDLER-LISS, Alice F. *1988*
SEITZ, Michele L. *1986*
SEKHON, Aman *2007*
SELTZER, Alexandra *2004*
SERRUYA, Jose *1998*
SEZGIN, Gulay *2005*
SHABBIR, Azfar *1994*
SHAH, Atul Navnitlal *1998*
SHAH, Binod *2002*
SHAH, Nikhil *2006*
SHAINHOUSE, Tsippora *2004*
SHEFFER-BABILA, Sharone *2006*
SHEFLIN, Marla *2000*
SHENKER, I. Ronald *1961*
SHERMAN, Martin *1978*
SHETREAT-KLEIN, Maya *2004*
SHIH, San *1994*
SHORSER, James *1986*
SIDDIQUE, Razia *1993*
SIEGEL, Janet *1992*
SIEGEL, Melissa *2004*
SILVER, Peter *1993*
SILVERIO, Arlene *1996*
SILVERMAN, Sarah *2008*
SIM, Alfonso *1979*
SIM, Geoffrey *2000*
SIMAI, David *2003*
SIMON-GOLDMAN, Phyllis *2007*
SINGH, Sharon *2008*
SIYAHREZAEI, Shaghayegh *2002*
SKOLNICK, Eric *1984*
SLUTZAH, Meredith *2006*
SMITH, Michael *2008*
SMITH, Robin *1998*
SOFOCLEOUS, Constantinos *1994*
SOGAWA, Yoshimi *2005*
SOKOL, Scott *1976*

SOSULSKI, Richard *1980*
SPATOLIATORE, Rosa Linda *1996*
SPIOTTA, Roseann *1981*
ST. VICTOR, Rosemarie *1993*
STEEG, Carl *1967*
STEELE, Andrew *1980*
STEIN, Michael *1977*
STEIN, Rodd *1999*
STEIN ETESS, Melanie *2000*
STEIN-ALBERT, Marcy *1989*
STEINER, Deborah *1992*
STEWART, Constance *1980*
STONE, Hilary *2006*
STORM, Richard *1978*
STRAUSS, Raphael *1991*
STROTHER, Christopher *2005*
SUH, Michael *2008*
SUKHOV, Renat *2000*
SULITZER, Karen *1994*
SUN, Lena *1982*
SVITEK, Scott *1994*
SY-KHO, Rose Marrie *1991*
TAFRESHI-ORAEE, Parisa *1995*
TALWAR, Rohit *1998*
TAN, Patricia *1992*
TATZ, Gary *2005*
TAURASSI, Cheryl *2006*
TAYLOR-DURDAN, Danielle *2004*
TEICHMAN, Faye *1989*
TELLECHEA, Natasha *1998*
TELLER, Filip *2007*
TELSEY, Aimee *1985*
TENG, David *2000*
TEYAN, Frederick *1971*
THOMAS, Philomena *1987*
THOMASEN, Tanya-Marie *2008*
TIYYAGURA, Sripriya *2006*
TIZER, Karen *1993*
TOPSIS, Julie *1984*
TRAN, Loanne *2007*
TRECARTIN, Susan *1976*
TREPEL, Robert *1987*
TROPE, Juliette *2006*
TROPE, Randi *2004*
TUROW, Victor *1981*
UNCYK, Avraham *1985*
VALENTINE-RICHARDSON, Keena *2007*
VALSAMIS, Christina *2007*
VANSTONE, Michelle *2006*
VASISHTHA, Sanjeev *1996*
VEGA, Roy *1991*
VINOGRAD, Alexander *1980*
VIRAY, Jose *1990*
VOLK, Barbie *1988*
WAJNRAJCH, Michael *1992*
WASEEM, Amira *2001*
WASTI, Azra *1992*
WEILER, Mitchell *1983*
WEINBERGER, Sylvain *1982*
WEINER, Stacy *2007*
WEINREB, Mark *1991*
WEINSTEIN, Toba *1991*
WEISELBERG, Eric *1989*
WEISS, Steven *1996*
WELLS, John *1991*
WENICK, Gary *1987*
WERTHEIM, David *1994*
WHITE, Stacey *1993*
WILLIAMS, Sophia *2007*
WILNER, Jennifer *2008*

WOLFSON, Scott *2003*
WOLLOCH, Norbert *1984*
WOODBURN-HOURIE, Karen *1989*
WOU, Margaret *2002*
WREN-GLUPE, Margaret *2000*
WURZEL, Carol *1987*
YADOO, Moshe *1988*
YAGUDAYEV, Yakov *1998*
YAN, Karen *2001*
YANG, LiMin *2006*
YELLIN, Loren Kabat *1987*
YOUSSEF-AHMED, Maged *1996*
YOZAWITZ, Elissa *2007*
YUDKOWITZ, Francine *1984*
YUSUF, Fazlul *1993*
ZACH, Tamara *2006*
ZAVOLKOVSKAYA, Sabina *2006*
ZAYTSEVA, Alla *2008*
ZEIRA, Shelly *1998*
ZELKOVIC, Paul *2005*
ZIA, Ahmad *2005*
ZILKHA, Naomi *1997*
ZYSKIND, Israel *2007*

NORTH CAROLINA
FIGLOZZI, Christina *2001*
LAKSHMINARAYANAN, Sonali *2005*
PATEL, Shipra *2005*
SHARAF, Mohamed *1996*
TAWAKOL, Heshem *2001*
YARIS-NEWMAN, Andrea *1990*

OHIO
AMISOLA, Rogelio *2003*
BELLOTTI, Christopher *2008*
BROWN, Dennis *1981*
FELDT, Matthew *2006*
HADJIEV, Boyan *2005*
KARAKAS, Sabiha Pinar *2003*
KHAN, Aliya *1997*
KRISHNAN, Venkatesan *1974*
KUMAR, Gogi *2005*
LANTZOUNI, Eleni *1999*
NAGEL, Michael *1989*
RIVERA-AMISOLA, Cecilia *2002*
SCHLESSEL, Kevin *1992*
SCIMEME, Jason *2008*
WEISER, Adam *2003*

OKLAHOMA
AMIGO, Therese *1993*

OREGON
JACOBY-LOW, Gail *1991*
SORIANO-AGUILLAR, Edita *1993*

PENNSYLVANIA
BALBUS, Michael *1988*
BARKAN, Craig *2003*
BERGER, Karl *1974*
BOLLAMPALLI, Vidyasagar Reddy *1985*
CAMACHO, Jose Angel *1987*
CHEMIATILLY, Wassim *2008*
DEGENHARDT, Karl *2004*
DEVER, Lynn *1987*
DUVDEVANY, Neta *1995*
DVORIN, Donald *1983*
EYAL, Dalit *1998*

FRISS, Helena *1986*
HANSROTE, Louis *1991*
KLEIN, Thomas *1983*
LAWRENCE, Philip *1985*
LIWAG, Celerina *1995*
LUCK, Raemma Paredes *1993*
MARCUS, Carole *1984*
ORNSTEIN, Rollyn *2002*
PAREDES-LUCK, Raemma *1994*
PARRISH, Samuel K. *1984*
PEK, Monika *2005*
POSNER, Mark *1990*
RAMAKRISHNAN, T.R. *1989*
RAVISHANKAR, Chitra *1997*
SCHWARTZ, Robert *2007*
SIMHI, Eliahu *1992*
SKOOG-LAUFER, Dagna *1987*
SMITH, Steven *1994*
VENIT, Bethany *1977*
WEINSTOCK, Michael *1970*
WINTER-ANNUNZIATO, Paula *1991*

RHODE ISLAND
AUYEUNG, Valerie *2002*
KATZ, Laura *2007*
KOSTER, Divya *2006*
KOSTER, Michael *2007*
LAPTOOK, Abbot *1979*
NEUMANN, David *1986*
SOMMERS, Ross *2007*

SOUTH CAROLINA
LALLY, Michelle *1992*
PARSONS, Scott *2000*
POTDAR, Meenu *2005*
SUSSMAN, Joel *1972*

TENNESSEE
AYGUN, Banu *2000*
CHASE-WANDERMAN, Nancy *1971*
KAPADIA, Shailee *2002*
KEATES-BALEEIRO, Jennifer *2000*
LAZAR, Linda *1980*
MADHOK, Ashish *2003*
MALLARE, Johanna *2000*
MC DADE, Jenny *2006*
RAHEJA, Ravi *2000*
VUKSANAJ, Dila *1985*
WANDERMAN, Richard *1972*
XAVIER, Frederico *2007*

TEXAS
AMARO-GALVEZ, Rodolfo *1999*
ANG, Renato *1995*
ARONOFF, David *2003*
BHATIA, Narinder *1997*
BIGWOOD, Jonathan *2003*
BLEIBERG, Alan *1996*
BLICHARSKI, Danuta *1977*
BOCCHICCHIO, Jeffrey *2001*
CHO, Jason *1999*
COLON-LEDEE, Athos *1995*
COUROUCLI, Xanthi *1995*
CRAMER, Andrea *1982*
GREIF, Jules *1987*
HORMAZDI, Bomi *1977*
LENARSKY, Carl *1980*
MACHEN, Heather *2006*
MANDEL, Corey *2003*

MANOHAR, Priti *2004*
MEYAPPAN, Thiyagaraja *2002*
MILLER, Margarita *1998*
QADIR, Maqbool *1998*
RAVAL, Nikhilkumar *1991*
REDDY, Uday *2003*
RINGHEANU, Mihaela *2003*
SAPIRE, Kenneth *1988*
SHIRSAT, Pratibha *1978*
SIAREZI, Shaghayegh (Sherry) *2002*
SILBER, Gail *1984*
SUCHOFF, Monica *1990*
WOLF, Todd *2004*

VERMONT
SCHNEIDER, David *1993*

VIRGINIA
CAMPOS, Francisco *1997*
DIZON, Louis *2001*
GENNARO, Margaret *1990*
HENTSCHEL-FRANKS, Karen *1996*
JANDER, Isabel Granja *2005*
KASLOFF, Ilene *1985*
KAVIT, Gary *1986*
RELVAS, Monica de Stefani *2002*
SHERNOCK, Marsha *1977*
VILLASECA, Miriam *1993*

WASHINGTON
WEINSTEIN, Gloria *1977*

WEST VIRGINIA
AHMAD, Saed *2006*
LACANILAO, Ramon *1997*
SONDIKE, Stephen *2000*

WISCONSIN
GIAMPIETRO, Philip *1989*
HUSAIN, Naghma *2000*
JARENWATTANANON, Marisa *1983*
KOKAN, Farhat *1996*
SARUMI, Oludayo *2006*
SILBERMAN-PROCUPEZ, Theresa *1971*
TELEGA, Dorota *1997*
TELEGA, Gregory *1997*

INTERNATIONAL

AUSTRALIA
KOHN, Michael *1996*
KWONG, Terry *1995*

BRITISH COLUMBIA
WINGERIN, Ruth *1989*

BRAZIL
MORAN, Oscar *1956*

CANADA
ISRAEL, David Moshe *1989*
KANTOR, Paul *1990*
LIQUORNIK, Karen *1992*

COLOMBIA
TRUCCO, Jamie *1965*

EGYPT
MERCHANT-SOOMAR, Sanah *2006*

GERMANY
DOS SANTOS, Christiane *1992*

GREECE
LASKARI, Cleo Vassilios *1995*
MOISSIDIS, Ioannis *1997*
ROUVALIS, Fotis *2002*

INDIA
KAW, Saroj *1980*

ISRAEL
BLAU, Hannah *1987*
DIAMANT, Shmuel *1986*
GLOBERMAN, Hadas *1986*
GOLDBERG, Michael *1975*
HAIMI-COHEN, Yishai *2000*
HARDOFF, Daniel *1992*
KATZ, Uriel *2000*
KESSLER, Oded *1995*
LEVY, Itzhak *1997*
LOBEL, Danielle *1995*
MINUSKIN, Tal *2000*
RAVID, Sarit *2001*
ROSEN, Dov *1998*
SHERTZ, Mitchell *1994*
SILBERMINTZ, Ari *2006*
SILTON, Akiva *2003*
TAMIR, Akiva *1993*
WEISSMAN, Avraham *1991*

JAPAN
PARK, Seung-Dae *2004*

MEXICO
GONZALEZ, Rosa Ana *2000*

PUERTO RICO
FIGUEROA, Nitza Lugo *1997*
LUGO, Nitza *1997*

SOUTH AFRICA
ZAR, Heather *1991*

SPAIN
GARCIA, Maria *1996*
IGARTUA, Jon *1999*

TURKEY
UNAL, Elif *2004*

UNITED ARAB EMIRATES
ELDEMERDASH, Alaa *1990*

UNITED KINGDOM
BRATT, James *2006*

VENEZUELA
BANDEL, Jack *1993*

VIRGIN ISLANDS
SHIH, Chie-Youn *2002*

LOCATION UNKNOWN
ALEXANDER-MURUGIAH, Vanaja *2007*
ARNOLD, Lisa *2008*

ASCHETTINO, Diana *2008*
COPPERMAN, Stuart *1963*
ELIE, Marie-Theresa *1984*
ESSANDOH, Yvonne *2007*
FRUMPKIN-KANTROVITZ, Farla *1991*
GALANG, Luz *1999*
GANGULY, Rekha *1981*
GOLDBERG, Michael *1992*
HERMAN, Tali *2008*
JAMAL, Yousaf *1998*
KANIA, Patricia *1994*
LARKIN, Anne Marie *1998*
LIM, Wilma *1986*

MAHMOOD, Khawaja *1996*
MANDELKER, Lisa *2008*
MATHEWS, Zacharias *1954*
MELA, Suzanne *2007*
MOHAMED, Yasser *1998*
NAIK, Vibhuti *2004*
OLSHANSKY, Cheryl *1984*
ONG, Elizabeth *1998*
OVED, Kfir *2007*
PALATHRA, Mary Lou *2007*
PALAZZO, Marie *2007*
PHILIP, Smitha *2008*
PICKERING, Olufunke *2008*
RUBIN, Michael *1982*

RUSSELL, Barbara *1983*
SCHULKIND, Martin *1963*
SCHWARTZ, Susan *1991*
SHAH, Jesika *2006*
SHEINBAUM, Karen (Blum) *1989*
SYLVESTER, Julie *2008*
TIONGO, Mercedes *1990*
TU, Lan Chau Hang *1989*
VAN OORDT-CESPEDES, Karen *1992*
YOUNG, Ju Kim *1978*

DECEASED
ALI, Asad *1986*
BERMAN, Robert *1965*
BOGARD, Bruce *1972*
EVERETT, Stanley *1967*
FARIN, Mark *1991*
HABER, Alan *1962*
KNOLLWELL-ROTH, Sharon *2006*
LIBRIK, Leon *1960*
SAAD, Sam *1986*
STORM, Jack *1962*
SUSER, Fredric *1976*
TALLAL, Lisa *1957*

House Staff Graduation 2006

ALUMNI BY SPECIALTY

GENERAL PEDIATRICS

ABDULRAHMAN, Eiman *2008*
ABELS, Jane *1973*
ACKERMAN-STEINBOCK, Gila *2003*
ACS, Hedda *1959*
ADAMS, Lawrence *1985*
ADARAMOLA-OJO, Mojisola *2006*
ADLER, Liora *2004*
AEINITZ, Jennifer *2001*
AGGARWAL, Alpna *2008*
AHMAD, Saed *2006*
ALENICK, D. Scott *1987*
ALEXANDER-MURUGIAH, Vanaja *2007*
ALKON, Jaime *2003*
ALLAWI, Diane *1981*
ALSHANSKY, Anna *1996*
ALTMAN, Stuart *1977*
ALVARADO, Doris *1985*
ALVARADO, Nestor *1996*
ALVAREZ, Miguel *1978*
AMARO-GALVEZ, Rodolfo *1999*
AMIGO, Therese *1993*
AMODIO, Stefano *1996*
AMOONA, Raphael *1970*
ANAND, Shikha *2001*
ANDERSON, Nancy *1985*
ANDREWS, Diana *1988*
ANG, Renato *1995*
ANTOKOLETZ, Marilyn *1967*
APFEL, Howard *1992*
APPEL, Cheryl *1984*
ARANDA, Diane *2005*
ARBITMAN, Mikhail *1985*
ARBITMAN, Raisa *1985*
ARENA, Marina *2004*
ARNOLD, Lisa *2008*
ARORA, Satish *1980*
ARROYO, Alexander *2005*
ARYEL, Ron *1996*
ASHOURZADEH, Kourosh *1993*
ASRA, Irfan *2002*
AUERBACH, Harvey *1980*
AUNG, Lei *1992*
AUYEUNG, Valerie *2002*
AVARELLO, Jahn *2005*
AVARICIO, Elizabeth *2002*
AVSHALOMOV, Gad *1999*
AVVOCATO, Gloria P. *1994*
AYDIN, Scott *2006*
AYYAGARI-SIEGEL, Subhadra *2007*
BABINSKI, Eleanor *1996*
BACHMAN, Michael *2001*
BAILEY, Denyse *2000*
BAIN, Russell *1990*
BAKERYWALLA, Rubina *2006*
BALASNY, Jennifer *1997*
BALBUS, Michael *1988*
BALDAUF, Mary *2000*
BALMAGIYA, Tovy *1987*
BALSON, Boris *1994*
BANDEL, Jack *1993*
BANKS, Mitchell *1981*
BARILARI, Rafael *1997*
BARKAN, Craig *2003*

BARLEV, Dan *1991*
BARLOW, Douglas *1992*
BASSOUL, Albert *1999*
BATTISTA, Anthony *1983*
BEARD, Rachel *2000*
BEKKER, David *1977*
BELLOTTI, Christopher *2008*
BENERI, Christy *2005*
BENNETT, Douglas *1996*
BEN-ZEEV, Uri *1979*
BERCHIN, Bernard *1992*
BERGER, Jay *2002*
BERGTRAUM, Marcia *1977*
BERGWERK, Ari *1992*
BERGWERK, Katherine *1992*
BERLIN, Hilary *1990*
BERLIN, Paul *1988*
BERMAN, David *1998*
BERMAN, Lori *1995*
*BERMAN, Robert *1965*
BERNSTEIN, Frederic *2006*
BEUZEVILLE, Carlos *1972*
BHASKAR, Mahesh *2003*
BICHOTTE, Sophia Ligonde *2005*
BIENSTOCK, Jeffrey *1988*
BIGWOOD, Jonathan *2003*
BIRNBAUM, Lynette *2003*
BISWAS, Saumitra *1997*
BLATT, Stanley *1965*
BLAU, Irwin *1976*
BLEIBERG, Alan *1996*
BLUMENREICH, Robert *1989*
BLUMENTHAL, Steven *1983*
BLUMER, Steven *2005*
BOCCHICCHIO, Jeffrey *2001*
BODI, Janice *1979*
*BOGARD, Bruce *1972*
BOLLAMPALLI, Vidyasagar Reddy *1985*
BONTEMPO-BLAUSTEIN, Silvia *1994*
BORCZUK, Mrinalini *1994*
BORNSTEIN-MAYERSON, Cara *2002*
BOROWSKA, Halina *1997*
BRAIER, Karin *2002*
BRANDT, Penny *2004*
BRANT-DEITCH, Deborah *2000*
BRATT, James *2006*
BRAUN, Rochelle *1992*
BRAVERMAN, Isaac *1998*
BREGLIO, Keith *2005*
BRENNER, Dennis *2000*
BRODTMAN, Daniel *2000*
BROSGOL, Yuri *1993*
BROWN, David *1975*
BROWN, Dennis *1981*
BROWN, Erica *2006*
BROWN, Robert *1966*
BROWN-McDANIEL, Barbara *2001*
BROWNSTEIN, William *1983*
BRUNO, Sandra *2002*
BRUNSON, Sandra *1976*
BRYANT-RENNIE, Janet *1993*
BULINOUN, Paul *1988*
BURKE, Christine Maroon *2001*
BURKES, Lynn *1971*

BUTENSKY, Arthur *1983*
CALLEJA, Gregorio *1980*
CAMPOS, Francisco *1997*
CANLAS-SUCGANG, Maria *1994*
CANTATORE-FRANCIS, Julie *2004*
CANTOS, Eric *1984*
CAPPELLI, Frank *1968*
CAREY, Dennis *1976*
CARONIA, Catherine *1992*
CARREIRO, Jennifer *2006*
CARRO-SACKLER, Lorna *1990*
CASE, Philip *1984*
CASSON, Ira *1976*
CASTIGLIA, Luisa *1985*
CATALANO, Lorraine *1996*
CAVANAUGH, Lisa *1996*
CHANG, Philip *2007*
CHARYTAN, Morris *1983*
CHASE-WANDERMAN, Nancy *1971*
CHEMIATILLY, Wassim *2008*
CHEN, Ashton *2007*
CHEN, Ellen *2001*
CHERRICK, Irene *1989*
CHESNER, Rina *2000*
CHEUNG, Helen *2006*
CHIANG, Angela *1988*
CHIANG, Nancy *1999*
CHINNAIRUSAN, Muthamilan *2008*
CHO, Eunsung *2006*
CHO, Jason *1999*
CHOI, Rosa *1969*
CIANNELLA, John *2008*
CITERMAN, Stephanie *1985*
CLAUS, Mark *1986*
CLEMENTI, Jennifer *2004*
CO, Margaret *1987*
COHEN, Cynthia *1988*
COHEN, Jack *1976*
COHEN, Joseph *1999*
COHEN, Michele *2008*
COHEN, Pamela *1981*
COHEN, Sheryl *1999*
COHEN, Stanley *1981*
COLEMAN, Cathy *1985*
COLEY-PICCIRILLO, Karen *1993*
CONROY-RICHARDS, Rushika *2008*
COONEY, Maureen *1993*
COPE, Jennifer *1997*
COPPER, Donna *1986*
COPPERMAN, Stuart *1963*
CORDICE-FORD, Candida *1998*
COTLER, Donald *1986*
COUROUCLI, Xanthi *1995*
COX, Amanda *2005*
CRAMER, Andrea *1982*
CRISS-SMITH, Cynthia *2000*
CUTLER, Adam *1992*
DADA, Lesley *2001*
DAVIS, Carol *2007*
DAVIS, Jennifer *2007*
DAVIS, Jonathan *2002*
DE ALDAY, Marietta Yumana *1993*
DE BLASIO, Eugene *1976*
DE JESUS, Socorro *1994*

DECASTRO-GROUSSE, Denise *1987*
DEE, Sandra *1996*
DEGENHARDT, Karl *2004*
DE JESUS, Julisa *2008*
DEL CARMEN, Renato *1988*
DEL CARMEN, Ruby *1988*
DELANEY, Angela *2008*
DELLORUSSO, Ana *1991*
DELLORUSSO, Giuseppe *1991*
DENIZ, Yamo *1997*
DESPOSITO, Franklin *1961*
DEUTCH, Robert *2006*
DEVER, Lynn *1987*
DICK, Gilbert *1979*
DICKSON, Pamela *1984*
DI LELLO, Edmund *1979*
DI TURI-HARTLEY, Suzanne *1998*
DIXON, Earl *1994*
DIZON, Louis *2001*
DOBKIN-FARIN, Michelle *1991*
DOLMAIAN, Gigliola Copaescu *2004*
DOYLE, James *1990*
DUVDEVANY, Neta *1995*
DVORIN, Donald *1983*
EAPEN, Santhosh *1996*
EISEN, Louis *1993*
EISENBERG, Bruce *1986*
EISENSTAT, Jennifer *2001*
ELBASH, Lina *2005*
ELBASTY, Azza *1994*
ELLIS, Jeffrey *2003*
ELVIR, Patricia *1988*
ENG, Christine *1986*
ENG, Jennifer *2007*
ERMITANO, Maria Luisa *1997*
ESPOSITO, Linda *1986*
ESSANDOH, Yvonne *2007*
ESTRADA, Elizabeth *1993*
ETESS, Melanie Stein *2000*
ETWARU, Kumarie *1999*
EVERETT, Stanley *1967*
FALK, Theodore *1980*
FALKOVICH, Ruvim *1996*
FANELLA, Frank *1997*
*FARIN, Mark *1991*
FASANO, Andrew *2000*
FATICA, Nunzia *1982*
FEFER, Zipora *1999*
FEINSTEIN, Ronald *1979*
FEINSTEIN, Stuart *1986*
FELDMAN, Doron *1993*
FELDT, Matthew *2006*
FELL, Brad *1995*
FERNANDEZ, Mariely *2007*
FERNANDO, Anusha *2008*
FIGLOZZI, Christina *2001*
FINK, Lawrence *1986*
FIORENTINOS, Dionysia *2008*
FISH, Jonathan *2004*
FISHER, Karen *1976*
FISHER, Martin *1978*
FIUMANO, Margaret *2002*
FLAMENBAUM, Helen *1979*
FLICKER, Jason *1998*

FLIEGENSPAN, Jeffrey 1986
FLITMAN, Sheila 1968
FONG, Jane 1988
FORGIONE, Lisa 1997
FORREST, Emily 2005
FORTE, Louis 1985
FRANCES, Adriana 1991
FRANK, Graeme 1991
FREED, Jay 1976
FREEDMAN, Samuel 1991
FRIEDMAN, Benyamin 2001
FRIEDMAN, Daniel 2000
FRIEDMAN-GOLDMAN, Sharon 1995
FRIEDMAN-OPPENHEIMER, Orit 2001
FRISS, Helena 1983
FROGEL, Michael 1978
FRUCHTMAN, Deborah 1981
FUCHS, Howard 1981
FURMAN, Gilbert 1977
FURMAN, Melissa 1994
FUSCO, Tara 1999
GALOSO, Maria 1998
GAMENG, Mary Ann Flynn 2007
GANAL-ESPERANZA, Pamelynn 2005
GANGULY, Rekha 1981
GARA, Lori 1993
GAROFALO-MONACO, Melissa 2008
GEDACHIAN, Robert 1969
GELABERT-LEMUS, Carmen 1955
GELLIS, Richard 1983
GENNARO, Margaret 1990
GENNINO, Christopher 1990
GENSER, Alan 1984
GENSLER, Zev 1999
GEORGE, Minu 1999
GERBERG, Bruce 1998
GERBERG, Lynda 1993
GERO, Bernard 1985
GERSHKOVICH, Irina 2006
GIAMPIETRO, Philip 1989
GIDWANEY, Rita 2007
GINSBURG, Mark 1980
GIORDANO, Ida 1972
GLEIT-CADURI, Daphne 1992
GLIKSMAN, Felicia 2006
GLOBERMAN, Hadas 1986
GO, Anita 1995
GOLD, David 1990
GOLD, Nina 1993
GOLDBERG, Barry 1992
GOLDBERG, Michael 1992
GOLDMAN, Arnold 1977
GOLDMAN, Robert 1997
GOLDSTEIN, Alvin 1963
GOLDSTEIN, Ilene 1991
GOLDSTEIN, Stanley 1978
GOLDSTEIN, Steven 1981
GOLOMBECK, Arel 2007
GONZALEZ, Jeanette 2007
GOODMAN, Karen Meier 2005
GORDON, Charles 1980
GORDON, Laurie 1982
GORDON, Seth 2004
GOTTESMAN, Avraham 2007
GOTTLIEB, Beth 1995
GOULD, Eric 1971
GRAF, Alisa 1991

GRAF, Jeannette 1985
GRAF, Lillian 1980
GRANAT, Lloyd 1973
GRAZIANO, Joan 1993
GREEN-BILELLO, Rachel 2008
GREENBAUM, Dorothy 1981
GREENBLATT, Daniel 2006
GREENFIELD, Elizabeth 1985
GREENHILL, Philip 1974
GREIF, Jules 1986
GREISING, Joanne 1989
GREISSMAN, Allan 1991
GRELLO, Stephen 2001
GRIJNSZTEIN, Mark 2001
GROENING, Portia 2006
GROSSMAN, Rami Raphael 1990
GUINTO, Danilo 1993
GUPTA, Krishna 1970
GUTERMAN, Carl 1987
*HABER, Alan 1962
HABERMAN, Elisa 2002
HAHN, Gary 1980
HAIBY, William 1979
HAIMOWITZ-REINITZ, Jennifer 2001
HALEGOUA, Jason 2004
HALLER, Jerome 1965
HAMETZ, Irwin 1973
HAMMER, Michael 1992
HAMMER-SANDOVAL, Ellen 1990
HANDELSMAN, Edward 1991
HANDWERKER, Lisa 1979
HARBERT, Mary Jo 2007
HARRIS, Bradford 1996
HARVEY, Jay 1991
HAUSDORFF, Mark 1988
HAWKINS, Lynn 1987
HEITLER, Michael 1962
HEMPEL, Bridget 2004
HENTSCHEL-FRANKS, Karen 1996
HERKO, Patricia 1983
HERMAN, Tali 2008
HERZFELD, Sharon 1996
HERZOG, Ronit 1998
HILAIRE, Chantal 1995
HOGAN, Timothy 1986
HOLLANDER-BOBO, Robin 1994
HOLZMAN, Bernard 1974
HONIGMAN, Richard 1979
HORMAZDI, Bomi 1977
HOROWITZ, Jeffrey 1984
HORWITZ, Jonathan 1974
HOWARD, Renee 1979
HSU, Penelope 2004
HUBEL, Philip 1982
HUSAIN, Naghma 1997
HUTNER, Aline 1990
HWANG, Juliet 2006
IMUNDO, Jason 2008
ISAKSON, Loren 2006
ISRAEL, David Moshe 1987
IVINS, Rhea 1986
IVKER-GOLDSTEIN, Cindee 1995
IYPE, Jay 2004
IZENBERG, Neil 1978
JACOB, Julie 2003
JACOBY-LOW, Gail 1991
JACQUE, Celeste 1979
JAIN, Varsha 1992
JAISWAL, Paresh 2003
JANDER, Isabel Granja 2005

JANKELOVITS, Eric 1988
JARENWATTANANON, Marisa 1981
JEAN-BAPTISTE, Stefanie 2007
JENNINGS, Gloria 1987
JEROME, Robert 1983
JIWANI, Amyn Ali 1996
JOHNSTON-MADINGER, Jean 1986
JORDAN, Jo-Ann 2002
JOSE, Bessey 2008
JOSEPH, Keanna 2003
JOSEPH, Natalie Pierre 1995
JOVINO, Louise 1993
JOY, Rosemary 2006
JUDMAN-LEDER, Eva 2007
KABARITI, Jack 2000
KABAT, Loren Gail 1987
KACPERSKI, Joanne 2008
KADEN, Gail Goodman 1988
KAGANOWICZ-GORELICK, Eliza 1975
KAHAN, Joel 1982
KAHN, Doron 2004
KAIN, Zeev 1989
KAINE, Richard 1971
KANG, Richard 2003
KANIA, Patricia 1994
KANTOR, Paul 1990
KAPLAN, Eric 1976
KARAKAS, Sabiha Pinar 2003
KARIDIS, Argyro 2008
KARPF, Laurie 1987
KASLOFF, Ilene 1985
KASNICKI, Laurie 1981
KATSEVA, Ida L. 1978
KATZ, David 1980
KATZ, Elizabeth 1994
KATZ, Laura 2007
KATZ, Lisa 2008
KAUSHAL-JOHAL, Sandeep 2005
KAVIT, Gary 1986
KAW, Saroj 1980
KAYE, Arthur 1975
KEATES-BALEEIRO, Jennifer 2000
KELMINSON, Leslie 1964
KEMPIAK, Stephan 2007
KENDALL, Roxanne 1982
KENNEDY, Joanne M. 1989
KHADAVI, Alan 2003
KHAN, Abu 1995
KHAN, Kishwar 1995
KHAN, Zahida 1980
KHANNA, Happy Neera 1998
KIBLAWI, Fuad 1998
KILCHEVSKY, Eitan 1983
KILIMNICK, Joseph 1998
KIM, Theresa 1970
KIM, Urian 2003
KIMPO, Joycelyn 1995
KIRSCHNER, Jessica 2008
KLEIGER, Richard 1985
KLEIMAN, Michele 1988
KLEIN, Susan 1984
KLEIN, Thomas 1983
KLEINBERG, Mitchell 1983
KNOBLER, Stacey 1991
*KNOLLWELL-ROTH, Sharon 2006
KOKAN, Farhat 1996
KOMITAS, Mahi 2000
KORN, Sheila 1992

KOSLOWE, Oren 2006
KOSTER, Divya 2006
KOSTER, Michael 2007
KOVACS, George 1997
KRAUS, Gregory 1999
KRAUSS, Joel 1997
KRAUSS, Richard 1990
KRECO, Edvins 2000
KREITZER, Paula 1985
KRIEF, Patricia 2004
KRIEF, William 1999
KRONBERG, Jason 2001
KRONFELD, Gary 1983
KUMAR, Cathie 2005
KUMAR, Munish 2008
KUNCEWITCH, William 1981
KUSHNER-CUSHMAN, Susan 1989
KWOK, Maria 2001
KYRIAKAKOS, Anastassios 1981
LaCORTE, Justin 2006
LACY-KING, Roxanne 2002
LANTZOUNI, Eleni 1996
LANZONE, Theresa 1983
LAPIDUS, Sivia 2006
LAPTOOK, Abbot 1979
LARKIN, Anne Marie 1998
LASHANSKY, Gayle 1989
LAU, Alice 1983
LAU, Bernard 1999
LAU, Joshua Hung Tin 2005
LAWRENCE, Donald 1969
LAWRENCE, Emily 2008
LAWRENCE, Philip 1985
LAZAR, Linda 1980
LEARSY, Dawn 2003
LEAVENS-MAURER, Jill 1989
LEBOVIC, Daniel 1985
LEE, Jeong 1994
LEEDS, Andrea 1993
LEIB, Martin 1975
LEMON-MULE, Heather 2006
LENARSKY, Carl 1980
LEONOV, Andrey 2006
LERIAS, Edgar 1987
LESSER, Eric 1991
LEUPOLD, Kerry 2000
LEVENE, Eric 1993
LEVI, Michelle 2004
LEVINE, Daniel 1991
LEVINE, Jack 1981
LEVINE, Marc 1975
LEVINE-BOSIN, Stephanie 1992
LEVIT, Orly 2006
LEVY, Moshe 1999
LEW, Lai-Ping 1999
LIBERT, Melissa 2007
*LIBRIK, Leon 1960
LIEBER, Marvin 1976
LIGHTMAN, Hylton 1985
LIM, Wilma 1986
LIMAYE, Deepa 1995
LINDER, Alice 1982
LINDT, Josephine 1992
LIQUORNIK, Karen 1992
LIU, Yingxue 1999
LIWAG, Celerina 1995
LOPEZ, Carmen 2002
LUCK, Raemma Paredes 1993
LUFTIG-WEISS, Jennifer 2001
LUJAN-ZILBERMANN, Jorge 1998
LUNA, Betty 1998

LYNCH, Patricia Kania *1994*
MACHUCA, Hildred *2004*
MADAD, Saiyeda *1978*
MADDUR, Shantha Devi *1985*
MAGALETTI, Francine *1987*
MAHADEO, Robby *1993*
MAISEL, Mercedes *1993*
MAITINSKY, Steven *1968*
MAJEED, Salamat *1995*
MAKATAN, Marjan *2001*
MALLARE, Johanna *1997*
MAMANI, Sylvia *2007*
MANALO, Erlinda *1993*
MANDELKER, Lisa *2008*
MANICONE, Paul *2002*
MANTZOURANIS, Jessica *2006*
MARCANO, Brenda *1998*
MARCHITELLI, Roberto *1988*
MARCHLEWSKI, Robert *2005*
MARCUS, Carole *1984*
MAROON, Christine *2001*
MARRIA, Pooja *2007*
MARSHALL, Ian *1999*
MARTINEZ, Alfred *2003*
MARTINEZ, Maritza *2008*
MARTON, Freddie *1988*
MARTYNEC, Lydia *1987*
MASAKAYAN, Adelaide *1994*
MASER, Dennis *1982*
MASSEY, Laurie O'Brien *1999*
MATHEW, Kolathu A. *1972*
MATHIAS, Liesl *1996*
MATTHEWS, Benjamin *1994*
MATTHEWS, Lori Gara *1993*
MATTHEWS, Zacharias *1954*
MAYBANK, Karen *2003*
MAYTAL, Joseph *1982*
MAZE, Aubrey *1974*
MAZIN, Howard *2006*
MC CARTHY, Patricia *1977*
MC COLLUM, Alexandra *2008*
MC DADE, Jenny *2006*
McDERMOTT-ADAMS, Nancy *1987*
MC DONOUGH, Christian *2006*
MC GOVERN, Margaret *1987*
MC INERNEY-LOPEZ, Regina *2005*
MC LAUGHLIN, Reginald *1975*
MC SHERRY, Kevin *1987*
MEHROTRA, Deepti *1999*
MEISLER, Susan *1987*
MELA, Suzanne *2007*
MELTZER-KRIEF, Eve *1998*
MEYAPPAN, Thiyagaraja *2002*
MEYERSON, Lisa Linzer *1993*
MIJARES-ZIMMERMAN, Jennifer *1996*
MILGRAUM, Sandy *1981*
MILLER, Harvey *1980*
MILLER, Margarita *1998*
MILLER, Michael *2003*
MILMAN, Marina *1997*
MILOJEVIC, Diana *2003*
MINTZ, Jesse *1979*
MINUSKIN, Tal *2000*
MITSOTAKIS-HOWARD, Demetra *2004*
MODI, Sangita Kumari *1999*
MOERCK, Linda *2000*
MOERCK-JOHNSON, Deborah *2000*

MOISSIDIS, Ioannis *1997*
MOKIDES, Valerie *1991*
MOLLICK, Lawrence *1975*
MONES, Karen *1996*
MORAN, Oscar *1956*
MORENO, Lisa *2003*
MORGANSTERN, Jeffrey *2003*
MORGENSTERN, Bruce *1981*
MORGENSTERN, Joel *1982*
MORGENSTERN, Solomon S. *2004*
MORRIS, Elliot *1983*
MOUSTAFA, Usama *2006*
MUKHERJEE, Sarmistha *2005*
MULALE, Unami *2008*
MURPHY, Susan *1988*
MURZA, Gina *1995*
MUSIKER-NEMIROV, Jamie *1990*
MYERS, Christine *2006*
NACHMAN, Sharon *1986*
NAFICY-PAKRAVAN, Parvin *1969*
NAGEL, Michael *1986*
NAGELBERG, Joy *1985*
NAGPAL, Rajeev *1989*
NAIK, Vibhuti *2004*
NAKAR, Charles *2007*
NALABOFF, Kenneth *1997*
NANADIEGO, Maria *1981*
NANGIA, Srishti *2002*
NAPOLITANO, Jeanmarie *1976*
NARAIN-CHAWLA, Bindoo *1990*
NARAN, Navyn *1997*
NARUCKI, Wayne *2004*
NASS, Howard *1989*
NAYOR, Ilyse *1993*
NAZNIN, Dixit *1999*
NERWEN, Clifford *1995*
NEUMANN, David *1986*
NEUSTEIN, Sherrie *2008*
NEWBRUN, Daniel *1989*
NEWFIELD, Liora *1993*
NEWFIELD, Ron *1993*
NG, Elizabeth *2002*
NGHI, Phuong *2004*
NICHOLS, Christiana *2008*
NICOLOPOULOS, Efthemia *2004*
NIEVES, Jorge *1996*
NIMKOFF, Laura *1990*
NITZBERG, Benjamin *1960*
NOLAN, Lizabeth *2008*
NORMAN, Shannon *2008*
NOVAK, Inna *2005*
NUNEZ, Ann *1979*
NUSSBAUM, Michael *1976*
O'CONNELL, Karen *2002*
O'DONNELL, Lisa-Mary *2005*
O'GRADY, Mary Lou Iandoli *2001*
OHRING, Marshall *1987*
OHSON, Gunwant *1980*
OLSHANSKY, Cheryl *1984*
OMLAND, Omar *1973*
OPITZ, Lynne *1987*
ORT, Howard *1979*
OVED, Kfir *2007*
OXMAN, David *1977*
PADMANABHAN, Pradeep *1997*
PALACIO, Liliana *1997*
PALATHRA, Mary Lou *2007*
PALAZZO, Marie *2007*
PALUMBO, Nancy *2008*
PANES, Susan *1992*
PAPAIOANNOU, Helen *2006*

PAREDES-LUCK, Raemma *1994*
PARK, KunTae *2008*
PARK, Yohan *2005*
PARRA, Angelica *2006*
PARRISH, Daniel *1997*
PARSONS, Scott *2000*
PATANKAR, Srikanth *1989*
PATEL, Shipra *2005*
PEARLMAN, Stephen *1984*
PEDROSO, Manuel *1997*
PEK, Monika *2005*
PELOSO, Marie Azzu *1992*
PEREIRA-ARGENZIANO, Lucy *2006*
PEREZ, Lucille *1982*
PERLMAN, Varisa *2002*
PERNICE, Mercedes Tiongo *1990*
PETERS, Vicki *1987*
PHILIP, Smitha *2008*
PHILIP, Soman *1996*
PHILIPS, Jeffrey *1979*
PICKERING, Olufunke *2008*
PIELA, Christina *1996*
PINTO, Matthew *2004*
PIRRAGLIA, Don *1994*
PLANER, Benjamin *1992*
PLATT, Anne *1983*
PLAUT, Allan *1982*
POLSINELLI, Rosanna *1988*
PONDA, Punita *2003*
POOLE, Claudette *2005*
PREMINGER, Nizza *1974*
PRUSHIK, Kenneth *2003*
PUGLIESE, Madeline *1994*
PUNSALAN, Imelda *1990*
QADIR, Maqbool *1995*
QUIJANO, Claudia *1991*
QUITTELL, Lynne *1984*
RABINOWICZ, Morris *1978*
RABINOWITZ, Brian *1998*
RABINOWITZ, Deborah *2005*
RADINSKY, Stacey *2001*
RAFFALLI, Peter *1989*
RAHEJA, Ravi *2000*
RAHSHID, Iqbal *2007*
RAIFMAN, Mark *1977*
RAISSI-FARD, Ehteram *1993*
RAKOWSKA, Urszula *1996*
RAKSIS, Karen *2002*
RANDEL, Sidney *1984*
RAPPAPORT, Mark *1991*
RAPPAPORT, Robert *1977*
RAVAL, Nikhilkumar *1991*
RAVISHANKAR, Chitra *1997*
READ, Rosemarie *2006*
REICH, Harvey *1974*
RELVAS, Monica de Stefani *1999*
RESMOVITS, Marvin *1982*
REZNIKOV, Alexandra *2001*
RICHARDS, Andrea Telak *2005*
ROBBINS, Michael *1975*
ROBERTS, Marc *1975*
RODRIGUEZ, Ruth *1993*
ROMANO, Alicia *1988*
RONCA, Lorraine *1993*
ROONEY, Elizabeth *1996*
RORER, Eva Maria *1993*
ROSE, Marion *1994*
ROSEN, Dov *1998*
ROSENBERG, Steven *1976*
ROSENBERG, Zehava Sadka *1981*

ROSENBLUM, Howard *1979*
ROSENCRANTZ, Richard *1997*
ROSENN, Greg *1989*
ROSENTHAL, Cynthia *1994*
ROSSI, Wilma *1982*
ROTELLA, Alessandra *2003*
ROUVALIS, Fotis *2002*
ROY, Kevin *2006*
ROZENBAUM, Joseph *1988*
RUBIN, Andrew *1991*
RUBIN, Irina *1983*
RUBIN, Jamie *2007*
RUBIN, Michael *1982*
RUSSELL, Barbara *1983*
*SAAD, Sam *1986*
SACKLER, Lorna Carro *1990*
SAFIER, Brian *2008*
SALEK, Allyson *2008*
SALUJA, Gurbir *1973*
SAMONTE, Frank *2007*
SAMUEL, Maritza *1987*
SAMUELS, Roya *2008*
SANBORN, Chad *2006*
SAND, Harold *1978*
SANDOVAL, Claudio *1990*
SANTANGELO, Christina *2003*
SANTIAGO, Myla *2007*
SANTOS-NANADIEGO, Maria Catalina *2004*
SAPIRE, Kenneth *1988*
SARUMI, Oludayo *2006*
SAUNDERS, Jay *1985*
SAVARESE, David *1994*
SAVARGAONKAR, Rajesh *1997*
SAXENA, Harshita *2005*
SCERBO, Jessica *2008*
SCHAEFFER, Janis *1982*
SCHARE, Rachel *2000*
SCHECHTMAN-FREEDMAN, Merryl *1988*
SCHER, Herschel *1998*
SCHIFF, Russell *1984*
SCHIFF, Stuart *1995*
SCHIOWITZ, Gila *2003*
SCHLOSSBERGER, Norman *1988*
SCHMERLER, Alan *1975*
SCHNEIDER, David *1993*
SCHROEDER, Marie *1995*
SCHULKIND, Martin *1963*
SCHULMAN, Jason *1998*
SCHWARTZ, Gerald *1972*
SCHWARTZ, Lisa *1987*
SCHWARTZ, Robert *2007*
SCHWARTZ, Susan *1991*
SCHWARZ, Gavin *2007*
SCHWOB, Netanel *1993*
SCIMEME, Jason *2008*
SEKHON, Aman *1997*
SELIGSOHN, Jacob *2006*
SELTZER, Alexandra *2004*
SHAH, Binod *1998*
SHAH, Jesika *2006*
SHAH, Nikhil *2003*
SHAHDADPURI, Jean *2000*
SHAINHOUSE, Tsippora *2004*
SHAPIRO, Warren *1988*
SHAW-BRACHFELD, Jennifer *1992*
SHEFFER-BABILA, Sharone *2006*
SHEFLIN, Marla *1997*
SHEINBAUM, Karen (Blum) *1989*
SHENKER, I. Ronald *1961*

SHERMAN, Martin *1978*
SHERNOCK, Marsha *1977*
SHETH, Shashank *2002*
SHETREAT-KLEIN, Maya *2004*
SHIH, Chie-Youn *2002*
SHIRSAT, Pratibha *1978*
SHORSER, James *1986*
SHROFF, Amita *2001*
SHULMAN, Peter *1975*
SIAREZI, Shaghayegh (Sherry) *2002*
SIDDIQI, Shaz *2000*
SIDDIQUE, Razia *1993*
SIEGEL, David *1977*
SIEGEL, Mark *1996*
SIEGEL, Melissa *2001*
SIEGEL, Scott *1989*
SILBER, Gail *1984*
SILTON, Akiva *2003*
SILVER, Peter *1990*
SILVERIO, Arlene *1994*
SILVERIO-REYES, Soledad *1965*
SILVERMAN, Lawrence *1990*
SILVERMAN, Sarah *2008*
SILVERSTEIN, Michael *1973*
SIM, Alfonso *1979*
SIM, Geoffrey *2000*
SIMAI, David *2003*
SIMHI, Eliahu *1992*
SIMON-GOLDMAN, Phyllis *2007*
SINGALA, Ravinder *2006*
SINGH, Jayati *1996*
SINGLA, Manav *2001*
SIRNA, Paul *1999*
SIVAKUMAR, Preethi *1995*
SIVITZ, Adam *2005*
SIVITZ, Jennifer *2005*
SIYAHREZAEI, Shaghayegh *2002*
SKOLNICK, Eric *1984*
SKOOG-LAUFER, Dagna *1987*
SLUTZAH, Meredith *2006*
SMITH, Carol *1983*
SMITH, Michael *2008*
SMITH, Robin *1998*
SMITH, Steven *1992*
SNOW, Ayelet *2006*
SOFOCLEOUS, Constantinos *1994*
SOGAWA, Yoshimi *2005*
SOKOL, Scott *1976*
SOMMERS, Ross *2007*
SONDIKE, Stephen *1997*
SONENBLUM, Michael *1990*
SORIANO-AGUILLAR, Edita *1993*
SOSULSKI, Richard *1980*
SPATOLIATORE, Rosa Linda *1996*
SPERLING, Randi *1995*
SPINNER, Milton *1960*
SPIOTTA, Roseann *1981*
STEEG, Carl *1967*
STEELE, Andrew *1978*
STEIN, Lawrence *1976*
STEIN, Michael *1977*
STEIN, Rodd *1999*
STEIN-ALBERT, Marcie *1987*
STEIN-ETESS, Melanie *2000*
STEINBOCK, Roy *2002*
STEINER, Deborah *1992*
STERLING, Karen Mathurin *1998*
STEVENSON, Amanda *2007*
STEWART, Constance *1980*
STOLL, Matthew *2004*
STONE, Hilary *2006*

STONE, Josie *1996*
*STORM, Jack *1962*
STORM, Richard *1978*
STRAUSS, Raphael *1989*
STROBER, Jonathan *1995*
STROTHER, Christopher *2005*
STULBACH, Harry *1984*
SUAREZ, Elizabeth *1995*
SUKHOV, Renat *2000*
SUN, Lena *1982*
SUN, Sirisak *1972*
SURGAN, Victoria Zolot *2003*
*SUSER, Fredric *1976*
SUSSMAN, Joel *1972*
SVITEK, Scott *1994*
SYLVESTER, Julie *2008*
TAFRESHI-ORAEE, Parisa *1995*
TAHZIB-KHADEM, Munirih *1999*
*TALLAL, Lisa *1957*
TAN, Bernardo *1995*
TAN, Noel *1992*
TAN, Patricia *1992*
TANG-HUANG, Lin-Lan *1987*
TAURASSI, Cheryl *2003*
TAYLOR-DURDAN, Danielle *2004*
TEICHMAN, Faye *1987*
TELEGA, Dorota *1997*
TELEGA, Gregory *1997*
TELLECHEA, Natasha *1998*
TELLER, Filip *2007*
TELSEY, Aimee *1985*
TENG, David *2000*
TEYAN, Frederick *1971*
TIONGO, Mercedes *1990*
TIYYAGURA, Sripriya *2006*
TIZER, Karen *1993*
TOBIN-SIMON, Cecily *1992*
TOPSIS, Julie *1984*
TRECARTIN, Susan *1975*
TROPE, Juliette *2006*
TROPE, Randi *2000*
TRUCCO, Jamie *1965*
TU, Lan Chau Hang *1989*
TUCKER, Stephanie *2003*
TUER, William *1972*
TURNER, Peter *1980*
TUROW, Victor *1981*
UEBLER-YOKOIS, Nancy *1988*
UKRAINCIK, Miro *1999*
UNAL, Elif *2001*
UNCYK, Avraham *1985*
VALCOURT, Lucienne Deltor *1995*
VALENTINE-RICHARDSON, Keena *2007*
VALOIS, Katherine *2002*
VALSAMIS, Christina *2007*
VAN OORDT-CESPEDES, Karen *1992*
VANSTONE, Michelle *2006*
VASILESCU, Alexandra *2008*
VASISHTHA, Sanjeev *1996*
VEGA, Roy *1991*
VENIT, Bethany *1977*
VILLASECA, Miriam *1993*
VITALE, Leonard *1967*
VOLK, Barbie *1988*
VUKSANAJ, Dila *1985*
WAJNRAJCH, Michael *1992*
WALD, Barton *1978*
WALD, Pamela *1978*
WANDERMAN, Richard *1972*

WASEEM, Amira *2001*
WASTI, Azra *1992*
WEILER, Mitchell *1983*
WEINBERGER, Sylvain *1978*
WEINER, Monica *2004*
WEINER, Stacy *2007*
WEINREB, Mark *1991*
WEINSTEIN, Gloria *1977*
WEINSTOCK, Michael *1970*
WEISS, Christopher *2001*
WEISS, Michael *1969*
WEISS, Steven *1994*
WEISSMAN, Avraham *1991*
WEITZ, Theodore *1991*
WELLS, John *1991*
WENICK, Gary *1985*
WERTHEIM, David *1992*
WERTHER, Joseph *1986*
WHITE, Stacey *1993*
WHITMAN, Bradley *1990*
WILLIAMS, Lisa *2007*
WILLIAMS, Sophia *2007*
WILNER, Jennifer *2008*
WINGERIN, Ruth *1989*
WINTER-ANNUNZIATO, Paula *1991*
WITTEK, Alec *1981*
WOLFF, Richard *1978*
WOLKOFF, Leslie *1992*
WOLLOCH, Norbert *1984*
WOODBURN-HOURIE, Karen *1989*
WOU, Margaret *2002*
WREN-GLUPE, Margaret *2000*
WRIGHT, Lucinda Thurman *2001*
WURZEL, Carol *1985*
XAVIER, Frederico *2007*
YAGUDAYEV, Yakov *1998*
YAN, Karen *2001*
YANG, LiMin *2006*
YARIS-NEWMAN, Andrea *1990*
YELLIN, Loren Kabat *1987*
YOUNG, Guy *1995*
YOUNG, Ju Kim *1978*
YOZAWITZ, Elissa *2007*
YUDKOWITZ, Francine *1984*
YUSUPOV, Roman *2006*
ZACH, Tamara *2006*
ZALEWITZ, Jodi *2004*
ZAR, Heather *1991*
ZAVOLKOVSKAYA, Sabina *2006*
ZAYTSEVA, Alla *2008*
ZECHOWY, Racine *1996*
ZEIRA, Shelly *1998*
ZEROLNICK, Lawrence *1975*
ZIA, Ahmad *2005*
ZILKHA, Naomi *1996*
ZWICK, Deborah *1985*
ZYSKIND, Israel *2007*

PEDIATRIC SUB-SPECIALTIES

ADOLESCENT MEDICINE
AMISOLA, Rogelio *2003*
ARDEN, Martha *1990*
ASCHETTINO, Diana *2008*
BATAYKIN, Yelena *2007*
BONTEMPO, Silvia Blaustein *1996*
BRADY, Jodi *2005*
BUDOW, Lauren *1990*

COONEY, Maureen *1995*
DESROSIERS, Florence *2008*
ELLIOTT, Michelle *2005*
FISHER, Martin *1980*
FRUMPKIN-KANTROVITZ, Farla *1991*
GAYNOR, Michael *1985*
HARDOFF, Daniel *1983*
HORWITZ, Jonathan *1975*
IVINS, Rhea *1988*
KAPLAN, Eric *1977*
KOHN, Michael *1996*
LANTZOUNI, Eleni *1999*
LEVINE-BOSIN, Stephanie *1994*
NUSSBAUM, Michael *1978*
ORNSTEIN, Rollyn *2002*
PARRISH, Samuel K. *1984*
PHILIPS, Jeffrey *1979*
POTDAR, Meenu *2005*
ROSENSTEIN, Jonathan *1979*
SEITZ, Michele L. *1986*
SHAMIM, Tabassum *1999*
SIEGEL, Janet *1992*
SONDIKE, Stephen *2000*
ST. VICTOR, Rosemarie *1993*
STROZUK, Stephanie *2004*
TRECARTIN, Susan *1976*
TRUXAL, Brian Andrew *1982*
TSIMOYIANIS, George *1987*
WEISELBERG, Eric *1989*

ALLERGY-IMMUNOLOGY
APPLEBAUM, Eric *1992*
AVSHALOMOV, Gad *2001*
AYYAGARI-SIEGEL, Subhadra *2010*
BELOSTOTSKY, Olga *2005*
BORCZUK, Mrinalini *1996*
BRODTMAN, Daniel *2002*
CAVUOTO, Marie *2004*
COX, Amanda *2007*
EDWARDS, Bruce *1989*
GOLDMAN, Robert *1999*
GOLDSTEIN, Ilene *1993*
GRIJNSZTEIN, Mark *2004*
HADJIEV, Boyan *2005*
KAPADIA, Shailee *2002*
KHAN, Aliya *1997*
KOROPECKY, Christine *1996*
LANDA, Dahlia *2008*
LEBO, Debra *1993*
LIGHTMAN, Hylton *1987*
MAHMOOD, Khawaja *1996*
MAKORNWATTANA, Porawat *2004*
MAMONLUK, Maribel *2000*
MARCHLEWSKI, Robert *2007*
MARCU, Mariana *2000*
MINIKES, Neil *1989*
MORENO, Lisa *2005*
PATEL, Kalpana *1998*
PONDA, Punita *2006*
POSNER, Mark *1990*
PUGLISI, Gregory *2007*
RADINSKY, Stacey *2003*
RAMAKRISHNAN, T.R. *1989*
REDDY, Uday *2003*
ROONEY, John *1995*
ROSENTHAL, David *2006*
SCHUVAL, Susan *1991*
SCHWARTZ, Saara *2003*
SCHWARZ, Gavin *2011*

SHAH, Atul Navnitlal *1998*
SIDDIQI, Shaz *2005*
SMITH, Steven *1994*
STRAUSS, Raphael *1991*
TAHZIB-KHADEM, Munirih *2001*
THECKEDATH, Jose *1998*
WEISS, Jeffrey *2002*
WEISS, Steven *1996*
WERTHEIM, David *1994*
ZILKHA, Naomi *1997*

AMBULATORY PEDIATRICS
CASE, Philip *1985*
GREIF, Jules *1987*
JUSTER, Fern R. *1986*
NAGELBERG, Joy *1986*
STEIN-ALBERT, Marcy *1989*
THOMAS, Philomena *1987*

ANESTHESIOLOGY (Pediatric Cardiac)
PATANKAR, Srikanth *1991*

CARDIOLOGY
AMODIO, Stefano *1999*
BOYER, Clark *2004*
BRUNSON, Sandra *1979*
CAMACHO, Jose Angel *1987*
CHASE-WANDERMAN, Nancy *1974*
COLON-LEDEE, Athos *1995*
DHANANTWARI, Preeta *2007*
DIAMANT, Shmuel *1986*
DiLELLO, Edmund *1981*
GOLDBERG, Barry *1995*
GONZALEZ, Maripaz *1994*
GREENHILL, Philip *1976*
HANSROTE, Louis *1991*
HARNICK, Joel *2007*
JARENWATTANANON, Marisa *1985*
JIWANI, Amyn Ali *1999*
KATZ, Uriel *2000*
KIBLAWI, Fuad *2001*
LASKARI, Cleo Vassilios *1995*
LEVINE, Marc *1981*
MADHOK, Ashish *2003*
MANDEL, Corey *2003*
MARILAO, Hilario *1989*
MENSCH, Deborah *2008*
MERCHANT-SOOMAR, Sanah *2006*
NADARAJ, Sumekala *2005*
OLIN, Jeffrey *1988*
REDDY, Damodar *2001*
RIVERA, Loyda *1990*
ROSE, Marion *1997*
SCHIFF, Russell *1986*
TALWAR, Rohit *1998*
TAMIR, Akiva *1993*
VOGT-LOWELL, Robert *1992*
WALSH, Rowan *2007*
WEINHOUSE, Elliott *1977*
WRIGHT, Lucinda Thurman *2004*

CHILD & ADOLESCENT PSYCHIATRY
ALVAREZ, Miguel *1980*
LINDER, Alice *1984*
BANKS, Mitchell *1988*

CRITICAL CARE MEDICINE
ADEYINKA, Adebayo *2008*
AYDIN, Scott *2008*
BALDAUF, Mary *2003*
BELLIN, Anne *2005*
BENJAMIN-THORPE, Solange *2005*
BHATIA, Narinder *1997*
BOCK, Kevin *2000*
CARONIA, Catherine *1995*
DECARMINE, Philip *1988*
DIAL, Sharon *2000*
ESPERANZA, Maria *2003*
FIGUEROA, Nitza Lugo *1997*
FONG, Jane *1991*
GAROFALO-MONACO, Melissa *2011*
GEORGE, Matthew *2005*
GOROZA, Edmund *2008*
GREISSMAN, Allan *1994*
IGARTUA, Jon *1999*
KOHN, Gary *2002*
KRAUS, Gregory *2002*
LUGO, Nitza *1997*
MARCANO, Brenda *2001*
MATHEW, Rajamma *1986*
MILLER, Michael *2006*
MULALE, Unami *2011*
NIMKOFF, Laura *1993*
PIERRE, Louisdon *1998*
PINTO, Matthew *2007*
RELVAS, Monica de Stefani *2002*
ROSENTHAL, Cynthia *1997*
ROY, Kevin *2009*
SILVER, Peter *1993*
TATZ, Gary *2005*
TAURASSI, Cheryl *2006*
TROPE, Randi *2004*
YOUSSEF-AHMED, Maged *1996*

DEVELOPMENTAL &BEHAVIORAL PEDIATRICS
BAILEY, Beth *2003*
BILOG, Agnes *1998*
JACOB, Julie *2006*
JESSANI, Shabana *2004*
KAROLL, Doreen *1988*
LALLY, Michelle *1992*
LIMAYE, Deepa *1998*
LOYOLA, Rosa *1997*
MILANAIK, Ruth *2004*
MILLER, Karen *1996*
OCAMPO, Stella *2000*
PAPAIOANNOU, Helen *2009*
RIVERA-AMISOLA, Cecilia *2002*
SALES, Serafin *1996*
SCHECHTMAN-FREEDMAN, Merryl *1990*
SHAW-BRACHFELD, Jennifer *1994*
SHERTZ, Mitchell *1994*
SUCHOFF, Monica *1990*
TANG-HUANG, Lin-Lan *1989*
TYAGI, Swayamprabha (Pat) *1992*
VARMA, Rupa *2001*

EMERGENCY MEDICINE
ARROYO, Alexander *2008*
BORNSTEIN-MAYERSON, Cara *2005*
BOROWSKA, Halina *2001*
CHAN, Raymond K. *1989*
CREVI, Diana *2002*

ECKSTEIN, Ira *1998*
EYAL, Dalit *1998*
GOLD, Nina *1996*
GOMBOS, Michal *1995*
KHAN, Ambreen *2003*
KHAN, Nafis *1995*
LaCORTE, Justin *2009*
LEUPOLD, Kerry *2003*
MACHEN, Heather *2006*
RANGWALA, Nikita *2004*
ROCKER, Joshua *2007*
SCHWARTZ, Fred *1999*
SEIDLER-LISS, Alice F. *1988*
SHAH, Nikhil *2006*
SHEFLIN, Marla *2000*
SHROFF, Amita *2007*
SILVERIO, Arlene *1996*
STEVENS-MORRISON, Cynthia *1989*
WOLF, Todd *2004*

ENDOCRINOLOGY
ASRA, Irfan *2004*
BOMBART, Felice *1991*
BRENNER, Dennis *2003*
CHATTERGEE, Manjula *2008*
CHIKEZIE, Augustine *1996*
CONSTANT, Mireille *1993*
DEGUZMAN, Jocelyn *2002*
EAPEN, Santhosh *1999*
FONT, Luis *2008*
FREEDMAN, Samuel *1994*
HAWKINS, Lynn *1990*
KREITZER, Paula *1988*
LACANILAO, Ramon *1997*
LEVINE, Daniel *1994*
MALLARE, Johanna *2000*
ROMANO, Alicia *1991*
SIVITZ, Jennifer *2008*
SUAREZ, Elizabeth *1997*
WENICK, Gary *1987*

GASTROENTEROLOGY & NUTRITION
ADAMS, Lawrence *1987*
GOLD, David *1993*
ISRAEL, David Moshe *1989*
PARK, Seung-Dae *2004*
REGAN, Brian *2007*
RINGHEANU, Mihaela *2003*
SILBERMINTZ, Ari *2006*
WEINSTEIN, Toba *1991*
WEISS, Mark *1983*

HEMATOLOGY-ONCOLOGY
AMANULLAH, Adoor *1976*
AMOONA, Raphael *1973*
ANDERSON, Nancy *1986*
APOLLONSKY, Nataly *2007*
AYGUN, Banu *2000*
BANGUG, Samuel *2001*
BAYRAK, Beril *2001*
BERGER, Karl *1974*
BLICHARSKI, Danuta *1977*
CELIKER, Mahmut *1999*
CHERRICK, Irene *1992*
CHUNG, David *1983*
DRAGOI, Elena *2005*
DUROSEAU, Herold *1993*
GARCIA, Maria *1996*
GOLDBERG, Tracie *2007*

GONZALEZ, Rosa Ana *2000*
GRAZIANO, Joan *1996*
GROSSMAN, Heather *2003*
HONIGMAN, Richard *1981*
HUSAIN, Naghma *2000*
HUSAN, Muhamad *2006*
JAMAL, Yousaf *1998*
JOHNSTON, Jean Madinger *1989*
KAPOOR, Vishwa *1985*
KHABBAZE, Youssef *2001*
KIMPO, Miriam *2002*
KUMAR, Vasanth *1978*
LAKSHMINARAYANAN, Sonali *2005*
LEVIN, Marina *1997*
LEVINE, Alan *1982*
Mc NAMARA, Joseph *1987*
MC SHERRY, Kevin *1990*
MOHAMED, Yasser *1998*
MURPHY, Susan *1991*
OCHOTORENA, Josiree *1998*
ONG-DEE, Elizabeth *1998*
PUGLISI, Vincent *1988*
RAMANAN, Aruna *1997*
RIFKIN-ZENENBERG, Stacey *2001*
RODRIGUEZ, Rhina *1985*
SALUJA, Gurbir *1975*
SCERBO, Jessica *2011*
SEZGIN, Gulay *2005*
SHARMA, Anjali *2002*
SHIH, San *1994*
SIEGEL, Melissa *2004*
SILBERMAN-PROCUPEZ, Theresa *1971*
SINGH, Sharon *2008*
SULITZER, Karen *1994*
UCKAN, Duygu *1994*
UNAL, Elif *2004*
VATS, Tribhavans *1971*
VIJAYAN, Radhika *1982*
WOLFSON, Scott *2003*
YUSUF, Fazlul *1993*

INFECTIOUS DISEASES
ANTHONY, Thiele Umali *1998*
BAER, Aryeh *2005*
BENERI, Christy *2008*
CHAKRABATI, Chandrama *2002*
DAYAN, Nimrod *2005*
HAIMI-COHEN, Yishai *2000*
JAIN, Varsha *1995*
LEVY, Itzhak *1997*
MARDY, Gisele *1994*
PETERS, Vicki *1990*
SALZMAN, Mark *1992*
SHAFINOORI, Shideh *2003*
WATCHI, Ralph *1990*
WURZEL, Carol *1987*

NEONATAL-PERINATAL MEDICINE
AHLUWALIA, Amardeep *2006*
BOXER, Harriet *1977*
BOYAR, Vitaliya *2008*
BROWN, David *1978*
CABALLERO, Felipe *2002*
CHOI, Sook *1974*
CHOWDHARI, Antonina *1992*
CITARELLA, Brett *2007*
DAMOUR, Yvon *1995*
DIEJOMAH, Ejiro *2004*

DiLELLO, Edmund 1983
DOS SANTOS, Christiane 1989
ELBASH, Lina 2008
ELDEMERDASH, Alaa 1990
ELIE, Marie-Theresa 1984
EMRALINO, Feliciano 1995
FRISS, Helena 1986
GALANG, Luz 1999
GAMUNDI JOAQUIN, Rosa 1999
GINEBRA, Fernando 1997
GIORGI, Marilyn 2005
GOLDBERG, Michael 1975
HORVATH, Lajos 2005
IRAKAM, Anitha 2002
KAHN, Doron 2007
KAW, Saroj 1986
KRISHNAN, Venkatesan 1974
KUMAR, Pankaj 2003
LAO, Jimmy 1991
LEONOR-GILRANE, Marixie Q.
   1985
LIPTSEN, Ellina 2005
LONG, Jennifer 2005
LUA, Jorge 2000
MORALES, Yesenia 2008
MURZA, Gina 1998
ONG, Manuel 1988
PETROZZINO, Jeffrey 2005
QADIR, Maqbool 1998
SHABBIR, Azfar 1994
SHARAF, Mohamed 1996
SINGH, Rachana 2006
SLUTZAH, Meredith 2009
SREEDHARA, Malathi 1999
STEELE, Andrew 1980
SUN, Shyan-Chu 1972
SUPASWUD, Tingnong 2008
TAN, Noel 1999
TAWAKOL, Heshem 2001
TEICHMAN, Faye 1989
TRAN, Loanne 2007
TRYZMEL, Johny 2003
UDDIN, Zia 2002
VIRAY, Jose 1990
WEINBERGER, Sylvain 1982
YADOO, Moshe 1988
ZENTAY, Zoltan 1999

NEUROLOGY
*ALI, Asad 1986
ALSHANSKY, Anna 1998
APEATU, Samuel 1994
AZAM, Shabana 1996
BAKERYWALLA, Rubina 2009
BERGTRAUM, Marcia 1982
BINDRA, Tejwant 2006
BROSGOL, Yuri 1996
CASADONTE, Joseph 1989
CHEONG, Keith 2000
COPE, Jennifer 2000
FEFER, Zipora 2002
FELDMAN, Robert 1985
FERREIRA, Carmen 2005
FERREIRA, Jose 1993
GOCHOCO, Aurora 1984
GROSSMAN, Rami Raphael 1993
HEAVENS-ALEXANDRE, Faith
   2001
KACPERSKI, Joanne 2011
KAN, Li 1998

KNOBLER, Stacey 1994
KRIEF, Patricia 2007
KUMAR, Gogi 2005
LOBEL, Danielle 1995
MALKIN, Elfrida 1991
MANOHAR, Priti 2004
MIRER, Mikhail 1999
NAGEL, Michael 1989
QUERSHI, Masarrat 2002
RAFFALLI, Peter 1992
RAVID, Sarit 2001
ROSENN, Greg 1992
SERRUYA, Jose 1998
SMITH, Robin 1997
SOGAWA, Yoshimi 2003
SUH, Michael 2008
SURGAN, Victoria Zolot 2006
SY-KHO, Rose Marrie 1991
THOMASEN, Tanya-Marie 2008
TOPPER, Leonid 2000
TREPEL, Robert 1987

PHYSICAL MEDICINE & REHABILITATION
BERLIN, Hilary 2004
REYES, Miraflor 1993
SHAH, Binod 2002
SUKHOV, Renat 2000

PULMONARY MEDICINE
BLAU, Hannah 1987
GUBITOSI, Terry Ann 1988
MARCHITELLI, Roberto 1989
SANTIAGO, Maria Teresa 1988

RHEUMATOLOGY
GOTTLIEB, Beth 1998
HOM, Christine 1999
IRIGOYEN, Patricia 2006
KWONG, Terry 1995
LUFTIG-WEISS, Jennifer 2004
MILOJEVIC, Diana 2002
SCHLESSEL, Kevin 1992

SURGERY - GENERAL
AIDLEN, Jeremy Todd 2008
GATES, Robert 2005
ROTHSTEIN, David Hershel 2007

UROLOGY
ARONOFF, David 2003
CHANG, Barry 2001
DYER, Lori Landau 2006
FEBER, Kevin 2007
FREYLE, Jamie 2004
FRIED-SIEGEL, Judy 1996
HUANG, Andrew 1999
KESSLER, Oded 1995
LEE, Chi 1997
LINDGREN, Bruce 1998
WEISER, Adam 2003
ZELKOVIC, Paul 2005

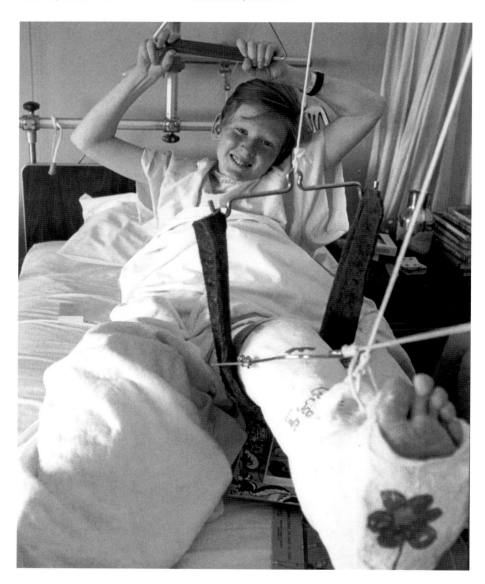

ALUMNI APPOINTED CHIEF RESIDENTS

The list of names for the years between 1954 and 1970 may be incomplete because the records for those years were not available for verification.

1954-1955
Matthews, Zacharias, MD

1955-1956
not available

1956-1957
*Tallal, Lisa, MD

1957-1958
not available

1958-1959
Acs, Hedda, MD

1959-1960
Desposito, Franklin, MD
*Librik, Leon, MD

1960-1961
Desposito, Franklin, MD

1961-1962
Heitler, Michael, MD
*Storm, Jack, MD

1962-1963
Acs, Hedda, MD

1963-1964
not available

1964-1965
Trucco, Jaime. MD

1965-1966
Brown, Robert, MD

1966-1967
*Everett, Stanley, MD

1967-1968
Cappelli, Frank, MD
Flitman, Sheila, MD
Maitinsky, Steven, MD

1968-1969
Weiss, Michael, MD
Lawrence, Donald MD

1969-1970
Gupta, K.K., MD
Weinstock, Michael, MD

1970-1971
Teyan, Fred, MD

1971-1972
*Bogard, Bruce, MD

1972-1973
Silverstein, Michael, MD

1973-1974
Holzman, Bernard, MD

1974-1975
McLaughlin, Reginald, MD

1975-1976
Goldman, Arnold, MD

1976-1977
Raifman, Mark, MD

1977-1978
Storm, Richard, MD

1978-1979
Dick, Gilbert, MD

1979-1980
Sosulski, Richard, MD

1980-1981
Morgenstern, Bruce, MD

1981-1982
Schaeffer, Janis, MD

1982-1983
Klein, Thomas, MD

1983-1984
Randel, Sidney, MD
Skolnick, Eric, MD

1984-1985
Nagelberg, Joy S., MD
Wurzel, Carol Lynn, MD

1985-1986
Fliegenspan, Jeffrey, MD
*Saad, Sam, MD
Werther, Joseph, MD

1986-1987
McDermott-Adams, Nancy, MD
Meisler, Susan, MD
Ohring, Marshall, MD

1987-1988
Cohen, Cynthia, MD
Elvir, Patricia, MD
Shapiro, Warren, MD

1988-1989
Kennedy, Joanne, MD
Lashansky, Gayle, MD
Nagpal, Rajeev, MD

1989-1990
Nimkoff, Laura, MD
Silver, Peter, MD
Sonenblum, Michael, MD

1990-1991
Frank, Graeme, MD
Harvey, Jay, MD
Zar, Heather, MD

1991-1992
Caronia, Catherine, MD
Goldberg, Barry, MD
Wertheim, David, MD

1992-1993
Graziano, Joan, MD
Jovino, Louise, DO
Levene, Eric, DO

1993-1994
Borczuk, Mrinalini, MD
Katz, Elizabeth, DO
Svitek, Scott, DO

1994-1995
Nerwen, Clifford, MD
Schroeder, Marie, MD
Sperling, Randi, MD

1995-1996
Bennett, Douglas, MD
Fell, Brad, MD
Stone, Josie, MD

1996-1997
Fanella, Frank, MD
Forgione, Lisa
Savargaonkar, Rajesh, MD

1997-1998
Gerberg, Bruce, MD
Lujan-Zilbermann, Jorge, MD
Smith, Robin MD

1998-1999
George, Minu, MD
Krief, William, MD
Mehrotra, Deepti, MD

1999-2000
Moerck, Linda, DO
Teng, David, MD
Wren-Glupe, Margaret, DO

2000-2001
Brown-McDaniel, Barbara, MD
O'Grady-Iandoli, Mary Lou, MD
Weiss, Christopher, DO

2001-2002
Berger, Jay S., MD
Grijnsztein, Mark, MD
Raksis, Karen R., MD

2002-2003
Kim, Urian, MD
Miller, Michael, MD
Moreno, Lisa, MD

2003-2004
Fish, Jonathan, MD
Machuca, Hildred, DO
Pinto, Matthew, MD

2004-2004
Beneri, Christy, DO
Marchlewski, Robert, MD
Sivitz, Adam, MD

2005-2006
Brown, Erica, MD
Koslowe, Oren, MD
LaCorte, Justin, DO
Lemon-Mule, Heather, MD
Roy, Kevin, MD

2006-2007
Ayyagari-Siegel, Subhadra A., MD
Fernandez, Mariely, MD
Koster, Michael, MD
Schwarz, Gavin, MD
Valentine-Richardson, Kena, MD

2007-2008
Conroy-Richards, Rushika. MD
Garofalo-Monaco, Melissa, MD
Nichols, Christiana, MD
Palumbo, Nancy, MD
Scimeme, Jason, MD

ALUMNI APPOINTED TO FULL-TIME FACULTY

ACS, Hedda+, *General Pediatrics,* 1963

AVSHALOMOV, Gadi, *Allergy-Immunology,* 2001

AYGUN, Banu, *Hematology-Oncology & Stem Cell Transplantation,* 2000

BALDAUF, Mary, *Critical Care Medicine,* 2000

BERGTRAUM, Marcia, *Neurology,* 1982

BOCK, Kevin, *Critical Care Medicine,* 2000

*BOGARD, Bruce+, *General Pediatrics,* 1972

BORNSTEIN, Cara, *Emergency Medicine,* 2005

CAREY, Dennis, *Endocrinology,* 1976

CARONIA, Catherine, *Critical Care Medicine,* 1995

CAVUOTO, Marie, *Allergy-Immunology,* 2004

DHANANTWARI, Preeti, *Cardiology,* 2008

DIAL, Sharon, *Critical Care Medicine,* 2000

ELVIR, Patricia+, *General Pediatrics,* 1988

ESPERANZA, Maria, *Critical Care Medicine,* 2003

FEFER, Zipora, *Neurology,* 2002

FEINSTEIN, Ronald, *Adolescent Medicine,* 1979

FISH, Jonathan+, *Hematology-Oncology & Stem Cell Transplantation,* 2004

FRANK, Graeme+, *Endocrinology,* 1991

FROGEL, Michael+, *General Pediatrics,* 1978

GEORGE, Minu+, *General Pediatrics,* 1999

GERBERG, Lynda, *General Pediatrics,* 1993

GOLD, David, *Gastroenterology,* 1993

GOLDBERG, Barry+, *Critical Care Medicine,* 1995

GOTTLIEB, Beth, *Rheumatology,* 1998

JACOB, Julie, *Developmental & Behavioral Pediatrics,* 2006

KHAN, Nafis, *Emergency Medicine,* 1995

KRAUS, Gregory, *Critical Care Medicine,* 2002

KREITZER, Paula, *Endocrinology,* 1988

KRIEF, Patricia, *Neurology,* 2007

KRIEF, William+, *Emergency Medicine,* 2003

KRONBERG, Jason, *General Pediatrics,* 2001

MARCANO, Brenda, *Critical Care Medicine,* 2001

MARCHLEWSKI, Robert, *Allergy-Immunology,* 2007

McNAMARA, Joseph, *Hematology-Oncology & Stem Cell Transplantation,* 1987

MENSCH, Deborah, *Cardiology,* 2008

MILANIAK, Ruth, *Developmental & Behavioral Pediatrics,* 2004

MILLER, Michael+, *Critical Care Medicine,* 2006

NAGELBERG, Joy+, *Emergency Medicine,* 1986

NERWEN, Clifford+, *General Pediatrics,* 1995

NIMKOFF, Laura+, *Critical Care Medicine,* 1993

NUSSBAUM, Michael, *Adolescent Medicine,* 1978

ORNSTEIN, Rollyn, *Adolescent Medicine,* 2002

PALUMBO, Nancy+, *General Pediatrics,* 2008

RAKSIS, Karen R.+, *General Pediatrics,* 2002

ROSENTHAL, Cynthia, *Critical Care Medicine,* 1997

SCHAEFFER, Janis+, *Critical Care Medicine,* 1982

SCHUVAL, Susan, *Allergy-Immunology,* 1991

SHENKER, I. Ronald, *Adolescent Medicine,* 1961

SHROFF, Amita, *Emergency Medicine,* 2007

SILVER, Peter+, *Critical Care Medicine,* 1993

SMITH, Robin+, *Neurology,* 1998

STEELE, Andrew, *Neonatal-Perinatal Medicine,* 1980

SVITEK, Scott+, *General Pediatrics,* 1994

TOPPER, Leonid, *Neurology,* 2000

TRAN, Louanne, *Neonatal-Perinatal Medicine,* 2007

TROPE, Randi, *Critical Care Medicine,* 2004

VEGA, Roy, *Emergency Medicine,* 1993

WEINSTEIN, Toba, *Gastroenterology,* 1991

WEISS, Steven, *Allergy-Immunology,* 1996

+Former Chief Residents

Abdelmoniem, Talaat A. - *Pediatrics*
Abraham, Alfred - *Pediatrics*
Abraham, Jamil - *Pediatrics*
*Aballi, Arturo J. – *Neonatology & Hematology*
Abramov-Pilosov, Esfira - *Pediatrics*
Abrams, Cyril - *Endocrinology*
*Abrams, Martin – *General Surgery*
Abrons, Mitchell Lloyd - *Pediatrics*
Accetta, Joseph Robert - *Pediatrics*
Acker, Diane – *Pediatrics*
Ackerman, Bruce – *Neonatal-Perinatal Medicine*
Acosta, Eloisa P. - *Pediatrics*
Acs, Hedda - *Neonatology*
Adesman, Andrew – *Developmental & Behavioral Pediatrics*
Adler, Albert - *Pediatrics*
Adler, Donald - *Pediatrics*
Adler, Jeremy - *Pediatrics*
Adler, Liora - *Pediatrics*
Adler, Robert George - *Pediatrics*
Agulneck, Milton - *Pediatrics*
Aharon, Albert - *Pediatrics*
Aiello, Angela M. - *Pediatrics*
*Aiges, Harvey - *Gastroenterology*
Aisenson, Milton - *Pediatrics*
Airen, Anju - *Pediatrics*
Aiuto, Leslie T. - *Pediatrics*
Alexander, James - *Pediatrics*
Aliprandis, Tjoyia - *Pediatrics*
Allen, Leslie A. – *Neonatal-Perinatal Medicine*
Altman, Stuart J. - *Pediatrics*
Alzoobaee, Faiz O. - *Pediatrics*
Amaravadi, Kameswari – *Pediatrics*
Amato, Joseph – *Cardiothoracic Surgery*
Amer, Jeffrey A. – *Pediatrics*
Amigo, Nancy - *Pediatrics*
Amodio, Stefano – *Pediatrics*
Amoona, Raphael - *Pediatrics*
Andrews, Diana - *Pediatrics*
Angelides, Anastasios - *Gastroenterology*
Anhalt, Herbert S. - *Pediatrics*
Antokoletz, Marilyn - *Pediatrics*
Aprin, Hormozan - *Pediatric Urology*
Arain, Sofia Yaseen - *Pediatrics*
Arbisser, Sherry L. - *Pediatrics*
Arden, Martha R. - *Adolescent Medicine*
Arkin, Steven - *Hematology-Oncology*
Aronow, Paul – *Pediatrics*
Aschenbrand, Leonard - *Pediatrics*
Ash, Zev - *Pediatrics*
Ashourzadeh, Kourosh - *Pediatrics*
Aspinall-Daley, Toni - *Pediatrics*
Atlas, Mark Peter - *Hematology-Oncology*
Auerbach, Marc - *Pediatrics*
Avaricio, Elizabeth - *Pediatrics*
Avigdor, Naftali - *Pediatrics*
Avshalomov, Gad – *Allergy-Immunology*
Axel, Peter J. - *Pediatrics*

Aygun, Banu - *Hematology-Oncology*
Babinski, Eleanor - *Pediatrics*
Bailey, Beth P. – *Pediatrics*
Bakhchi, Mozaffar - *Pediatrics*
Balachandar, Viswanathan - *Pediatrics*
Baldauf, Mary - *Critical Care Medicine*
Bangaru, Babu - *Gastroenterology*
Barash, Fred S. - *Pediatrics*
Barberis, Carl Louis - *Pediatrics*
Baricar, Febin Orlando F. – *Pediatrics*
Barillas-Arias, Lilliana - *Rheumatology*
Barlev, Dan M. - *Pediatric Radiology*
Barone, Stephen R. - *Pediatrics*
Barzideh, Shahla - *Pediatrics*
Basaca, Belinda C. – *Pediatrics*
Bass, Richard - *Pediatrics*
Battista, Anthony J.-*Pediatrics*
Bauer, Irving L. - *Pediatrics*
Baun, Carolina C. - *Pediatrics*
Becker, Jerrold – *General Surgery*
Beer, Myron - *Pediatrics*
Behr, Raymond - *Pediatrics*
Bell, Ralph - *Pediatrics*
Benilevi, Daniel - *Pediatrics*
Berger, Jay Seth. - *Pediatrics*
Berger, Lynn Claudine - *Pediatrics*
Bergtraum, Marcia - *Neurology*
Berlin, Hilary - *Physical Medicine/Rehabilitation*
*Berliner, Benjamin - *Pediatrics*
Berman, David - *Pediatrics*
Berman, Lori S. - *Pediatrics*
Berman, Robert - *Pediatrics*
Bernstein, Frederic Jacob - *Pediatrics*
Bharti, Des R. - *Pediatrics*
Bhaskar, Mahesh - *Pediatrics*
Bhatty, Samina B. - *Pediatrics*
Biancaniello, Thomas - *Cardiology*
Bialer, Martin G. - *Medical Genetics*
Bichotte-Ligonde, Sophia - *Pediatrics*
Bienkowski, Robert - *Research*
Bierman, Fredrick Z. - *Cardiology*
Bigini-Quinn, Patricia Emily – *Developmental & Behavioral Pediatrics*
Bikoff, William H. - *Pediatrics*
Birch, Ann. - *Pediatrics*
Bisacco, John - *Pediatrics*
*Blatman, Saul – *Pediatrics*
Blatt, Stanley - *Pediatrics*
Blau, Irwin H. - *Pediatrics*
Blaufox, Andrew David - *Cardiology*
Bleiweiss, Irwin - *Pediatrics*
Blethen, Sandra - *Endocrinology*
Blinderman, Brian - *Pediatrics*
Bloom, Allison - *Pediatrics*
Bloom, Thomas - *Pediatrics*
*Blumberg, Marvin – *Pediatrics*
Blumenfeld, Steven - *Pediatrics*
Bock, Kevin - *Critical Care Medicine*
*Bogard, Bruce - *Pediatrics*
Bohrer, Stuart L. – *General Surgery*
Bombart, Felice - *Pediatrics*
Bonagura, Vincent R. - *Allergy-Immunology*

Borczuk, Mrinalini - *Pediatrics*
Boris, Marvin - *Pediatrics*
Borne, Stanford - *Pediatrics*
Bornstein, Cara S. - *Emergency Medicine*
Borowski, Halina - *Pediatrics*
Bournias, Maria - *Pediatrics*
*Boxer, Robert - *Cardiology/Critical Care Medicine*
Boyar, Vita – *Neonatal-Perinatal Medicine*
Brant-Deitch, Deborah – *Pediatrics*
Braun, Rochelle - *Pediatrics*
Brignol, Marie Jose - *Pediatrics*
Brock, William A. – *Urologic Surgery*
*Bronsther, Burton – *General Surgery*
Brown, David – *Neonatal-Perinatal Medicine*
Brown, Erica - *Pediatrics*
Brown, Kimberly - *Pediatrics*
Brunell, Philip A. - *Pediatrics*
Brunn, Lauren Joy - *Pediatrics*
Brunson, Sandra C. - *Cardiology*
Bruzzone, Charles L. - *Pediatrics*
Bryer, Clifford J. - *Pediatrics*
Buckley, Nancy – *Research*
Buckwald, Sharon – *Neonatal-Perinatal Medicine*
Bungarz, William - *Pediatrics*
Cadet, Robyn A. - *Pediatrics*
Camillery, Daniel C. - *Pediatrics*
Canales, Marta Dinora – *Pediatrics*
Capilupi, Thomas - *Pediatrics*
Capozzi, Patrick Francis - *Pediatrics*
Cappelli, Frank - *Pediatrics*
Caramihai, Elena - *Hematology-Oncology*
Caravella, Salvatore J. - *Pediatrics*
Cardo-Hunter, Alice - *Pediatrics*
Carey, Dennis E. - *Endocrinology*
Carlsen, Andrea R. – *Child & Adolescent Psychiatry*
Carmine, Linda *Pediatrics*
Carnes, Moses - *Pediatrics*
Caronia, Catherine - *Critical Care Medicine*
Cascio-Leva, Melissa – *Pediatrics*
Casalino, Marie – *Neonatal-Perinatal Medicine*
Casden, Daniel D. – *Pediatrics*
Cassidy, Robert – *Bioethics and Social Policy*
Castiglia, Luisa - *Pediatrics*
Castro-Alcaraz, Susana - *Neonatal-Perinatal Medicine*
Catalano, Lorraine E. - *Pediatrics*
Cateletto, Mary - *Critical Care Medicine*
Cavanagh, James Patrick - *Pediatrics*
Cavanaugh, Lisa A. – *Pediatrics*
Cavuto, Marie – *Allergy-Immunology*
Celiker, Mahmut - *Hematology-Oncology*
Cerna-Helfer, Ana L. - *Pediatrics*
Cerniglia, Rose - *Pediatrics*
Cervantes, Cecilia D. - *Pediatrics*
Cetin, Lynn Talin. - *Pediatrics*

Chacko, Lissiamma - *Pediatrics*
*Chea, Marc - *Hematology-Oncology*
Chakrabarti, Chhaya - *Endocrinology*
Chalson, Margaret Kate. - *Pediatrics*
Champaneri, Charu - *Pediatrics*
Chan Amigo, Nancy - *Pediatrics*
Chandra, Manju M. - *Nephrology*
Charash, Leon I. - *Neurology*
Charytan, Morris - *Pediatrics*
Chasalow, Fred - *Endocrinology*
Chauhan, Alia - *Pediatrics*
Chawla, Anupama - *Gastroenterology*
Chen, Kenneth - *Pediatrics*
Cheruvanky, Thulasi - *Pediatrics*
Cheung, Helen – *Pediatrics*
Chianese, Maurice J. - *Pediatrics*
Chiang, Nancy L. – *Pediatrics*
Chiarmonte, Joseph - *Pediatrics*
Ching, Kevin Yuan Song. - *Pediatrics*
Chio, Jane L. - *Pediatrics*
Chiu, Mickey Yue K. - *Pediatrics*
Choi Rosen, Jeanne Susan – *Pediatric Radiology*
Chollop, Roger - *Pediatrics*
Choset, Karen Lindner - *Pediatrics*
Chowdhury, Devyani - *Cardiology*
Chung, David - *Pediatrics*
Chung, Wendy W. - *Pediatrics*
Chusid, Arnold - *Pediatrics*
Citerman, Stephanie H. - *Pediatrics*
Citron, Charles Ira - *Pediatrics*
Clare, Toni Ann - *Pediatrics*
Clutario, Bella - *Pulmonary Medicine*
Cogan, Steven F. - *Pediatrics*
Cohen, Alan J. - *Pediatrics*
Cohen, Claire O. - *Pediatrics*
Cohen, Herrick J. - *Pediatrics*
Cohen, Joseph B. - *Pediatrics*
Cohen, Lourdes Margarita - *Pediatrics*
Cohen, Martin B. - *Pediatrics*
Cohen, Matthew Scott - *Pediatrics*
*Cohen, Seymour - *Pediatrics*
Cohen, Sheryl S. – *Pediatrics*
Cohen, Stanley - *Pediatrics*
Coley-Piccirillo, Karen - *Pediatrics*
Constantatos, Constantinos - *Pediatrics*
Cooper, Rubin - *Cardiology*
Cooper, Seymour - *Pediatrics*
Copperman, Stuart M. - *Pediatrics*
Coren, Charles V. - *Pediatric Surgery*
Correll, Christoph - *Pediatrics*
Corriel, Robert N. - *Pediatrics*
Coryllos, Elizabeth – *General Surgery*
Costin, Valerie L. - *Pediatrics*
Courtney, Sherry E. - *Neonatal-Perinatal Medicine*
Crespi, Paul - *Dental Medicine*
Crevi, Diana – *Emergency Medicine*
Crider, Russell – *Orthopaedic Surgery*
Cruvant, David A. - *Pediatrics*
*Curtis, Bernard Marvin- *Pediatrics*
Danzi, Christine Marie – *Pediatrics*
D'Arienzo, Nicholas - *Pediatrics*
Dash, Barbara Ann - *Pediatrics*
Daum, Fredric – *Gastroenterology*
Davidson, Dennis - *Neonatal-*

Perinatal Medicine
*Davidson, Murray - *Gastroenterology*
Davis, Jason - *Pediatrics*
Davis, Jonathan - *Pediatrics*
Dayani, Farsima - *Pediatrics*
DeBlasio, Eugene - *Pediatrics*
Deegan-Haff, Mary - *Pediatrics*
de Jesus, Socorro M. - *Pediatrics*
DeCelie-Germana, Joan K. – *Cystic Fibrosis/Pulmonary*
Deegan-Haff, Mary B. - *Pediatrics*
Dellorusso, Ana M. - *Pediatrics*
Dellorusso, Giuseppe - *Pediatrics*
DeLuca, Arthur - *Pulmonary Medicine*
DeNise, Vivian - *Pediatrics*
Desposito, Franklin T. - *Hematology-Oncology*
Deutsch, Barbara G. - *Pediatrics*
Dial, Sharon P. - *Critical Care Medicine*
Diamond, William - *Pediatrics*
Diaz-Sy, Carmencita - *Pediatrics*
Dick, Gilbert A. - *Pediatrics*
Dicker, Robert – *Child and Adolescent Psychiatry*
DiLello, Edmund Sr. – *Pediatrics*
DiLello, Edmund Jr – *Neonatal-Perinatal Medicine*
DiLello, Pamela Louise - *Pediatrics*
Dillon, David C. - *Pediatrics*
Dixon, Jeremy J. - *Pediatrics*
Dolgin, Stephen Elliot - *General Surgery*
Dolgoff, Joanna - *Pediatrics*
Donahue, John - *Hematology-Oncology*
Dowel, Duane - *Pediatrics*
*Dreifuss, Richard L. - *Pediatrics*
Drucker, Susan - *Pediatrics*
Dube, Shiv Kumar – *Pediatrics*
Dubin, Philip - *Pediatrics*
Dupiton, Marie-Paule J. - *Pediatrics*
Duvivier, Tanya Eleanor - *Pediatrics*
Dyer, Lori - *Pediatrics*
Easton, Joan G. - *Pediatrics*
Eberhard, Barbara Anne – *Rheumatology*
Ebin, Eva – *Child and Adolescent Psychiatry*
Edelman, Morris - *Pathology*
Eden, Alvin N. - *Pediatrics*
Edwards, Bruce L. - *Allergy-Immunology*
*Ehrlich, Leonard I. - *Pediatrics*
Eichenfeld, Stuart - *Pediatrics*
Eisenberg, Ellen - *Neonatal-Perinatal Medicine*
Eisenberg, Melvin - *Pediatrics*
Eisenstat, Jennifer Dina - *Pediatrics*
Ejaz, Mariam Feroza - *Pediatrics*
El-Baba, Mohamad Fouad - *Pediatrics*
Eldemerdash, Alaa - *Neonatal-Perinatal Medicine*
Elice, Michael W. - *Pediatrics*
Elkin, Paul M. - *Pediatrics*
Elvir, Patricia - *Pediatrics*
Emmet, Marja Leena - *Pediatrics*
Engler, Danielle - *Pediatrics*
Ente, Gerald - *Pediatrics*

Epner, Michael - *Pediatrics*
Epstein, Shilpi - *Pediatrics*
Escobar, Celia C. - *Pediatrics*
Esernio-Jenssen, Debra D. - *Pediatrics*
Eskes, Philip W. - *Pediatrics*
Esperanza, Maria Cristina - *Critical Care Medicine*
Essner, Sharon A. - *Dental Medicine*
Evans, Martin J. - *Pediatrics*
*Everett, Stanley - *Pediatrics*
Everoski, Michael J. - *Pediatrics*
Eviatar, Lydia - *Neurology*
Ezer, Gay Elana - *Pediatrics*
Faber, Richard - *Dental Medicine*
Faber, Zackary Troy - *Dental Medicine*
Fagin, James C. – *Pediatrics/Allergy-Immunology*
Fallet, Shari - *Medical Genetics*
Fasano, Andrew J. - *Pediatrics*
Fefer, Zipora - *Neurology*
Feingold, Ellen – *Pediatrics*
Fein-Levy, Carolyn - *Hematology-Oncology*
Feinstein, Ronald – *Adolescent Medicine*
Feinstein, Stuart – *Pediatrics*
Feirstein, Kerri - *Pediatrics*
Fell, Brad E. - *Pediatrics*
Fernandez, Mariely - *Pediatrics*
Ferone, Carmine - *Pediatrics*
Festa, Robert - *Hematology-Oncology*
Fierstein, Kerry F. - *Pediatrics*
Fink, Lawrence S. - *Pediatrics*
Fischelli, Vincent - *Research*
Fish, Gladys A. – *Pediatrics*
Fish, Jonathan – *Hematology-Oncology*
Fishberger, Steven – *Cardiology*
Fisher, Beverly - *Pediatrics*
Fisher, Martin M. - *Adolescent Medicine*
Fitzgerald, Michael Patrick - *Pediatrics*
Flitman, Sheila - *Pediatrics*
Foley, Carmel A. - *Child and Adolescent Psychiatry*
Forgione, Lisa A. - *Pediatrics*
Fornari, Victor - *Child and Adolescent Psychiatry*
*Forray, Stanley - *Pediatrics*
Fort, Pavel F. - *Endocrinology*
Fox, Joyce - *Medical Genetics*
Franco, Israel – *Urologic Surgery*
Frank, Graeme R. - *Endocrinology*
Frank, Joshua Eric - *Pediatrics*
Frankel, Jack - *Pediatrics*
Freed, Jay A. - *Pediatrics*
Freyle, Jaime - *Pediatrics*
Fried, Steven M. - *Pediatrics*
Friedenthal, Esther - *Pediatrics*
Friedfeld, Douglas F. - *Pediatrics*
Friedman, Benyamin - *Pediatrics*
Friedman, Daniel Lawrence - *Pediatrics*
Friedman, Eugene B. – *Pediatrics*
Friedman, Marie – *Child and Adolescent Psychiatry*
Friedman, Steven Craig – *Urologic Surgery*
Frieri, Marianne - *Pediatrics*

Fries, Joseph - *Pediatrics*
Frogel, Michael P. - *Pediatrics*
Fruchter, Lazar - *Allergy-Immunology*
Fuchs, Sophie S. - *Pediatrics*
Fullerton, Katherine Tsao - *Pediatrics*
Galinkin, Lawrence J. - *Pediatrics*
Gallagher, Pamela - *Plastic Surgery*
Ganea, Gheorghe Romeo - *Pediatrics*
Ganesh, Lalitha - *Pediatrics*
Garabedian, Laura - *Pediatrics*
Garner, Alice M. - *Neonatal-Perinatal Medicine*
Gari, Lorraine - *Pediatrics*
Gauthier, Bernard - *Nephrology*
Gedarovich, Albin - *Pediatrics*
*Geller, Morton J. - *Pediatrics*
*Gemson, Bennett L. - *Pediatrics*
Geng, Yiping – *Pediatrics*
Gennaro, Margaret - *Pediatrics*
Gensler, Zev M. - *Pediatrics*
George, Mary L. - *Pediatrics*
George, Minu Daniel - *Pediatrics*
Gerba, William M. - *Pediatrics*
Gerberg, Bruce Edward - *Pediatrics*
Gerberg, Lynda - *Pediatrics*
Gerontis, Catherine Corina - *Ophthalmology*
Giglia, Therese M. - *Cardiology*
Gilbert, Michael L. - *Pediatrics*
Gitlin, Jordan - *Pediatric Urology*
*Gittleson, Stanley B. - *Pediatrics*
Gleit-Caduri, Daphne - *Pediatrics*
Glick, Jason Scott - *Dental Medicine*
Glick, Richard David - *Pediatric Surgery*
Gochman, Robert Francis - *Emergency Medicine*
Gocs, Diane Marie - *Pediatrics*
Godfried, David Harris - *Orthopaedic Surgery*
Godoy, Enriqueta Aurelia - *Pediatrics*
Goilav, Beatrice - *Gastroenterology*
Gold, David - *Gastroenterology*
Goldberg, Barry - *Cardiology*
Goldblum, Louis - Pediatrics
Golden, Neville - *Adolescent Medicine*
Goldman, Arnold J. - *Pediatrics*
Goldman, Herbert - *Neonatal-Perinatal Medicine*
Goldstein, Alvin P. - *Pediatrics*
Goldstein, Brian S. - *Pediatrics*
Goldstein (Ivker), Cindee - *Pediatrics*
Goldstein, Eric - *Pediatrics*
Goldstein, Heidi J. - *Pediatrics*
Goldstein, Jennie - *Pediatrics*
*Goldstein, Moe - *Pediatrics*
Goldstein, Stanley - *Pediatrics*
Goldstein, Steven - *Pediatrics*
Goldzier, Sanford E. - *Pediatrics*
Gombos, Michal M. - *Emergency Medicine*
Good, Leonard J. - *Pediatrics*
*Gootman, Norman - *Cardiology***
*Gootman, Phyllis - *Research*
Gordon, Hyman H. - *Pediatrics*
*Gordon, Milton - *Pediatrics*
Gorrin, Harvey - *Pediatrics*
Gorvoy, Jack D. - *Cystic Fibrosis*
Goslee, Leonard Thomas – *Pediatrics*
Gotsis, Constantinte - *Pediatrics*

Gottesman, Avraham MD - *Pediatrics*
Gottlieb, Beth Susan - *Rheumatology*
Gould, Eric F. - *Pediatrics*
Gould, Robert J. - *Neurology*
Graf, Alisa Joy - *Pediatrics*
Grant-Guimaraes, Jamilah - *Pediatrics*
Green, Abraham I. - *Pediatrics*
*Green, Marvin - *Pediatrics*
Green, Stephanie - *Pediatrics*
Greenbaum, Dorothy - *Pediatrics*
Greenberg, Judith J. - *Pediatrics*
Green-Mayer, Kimberly Jill - *Pediatrics*
Greensher, Joseph - *Pediatrics*
Greenwald, Richard M. - *Pediatrics*
Greifer, Ira - *Nephrology*
Greifer, Melanie - *Gastroenterology*
Grijnsztein, Jacob M. – *Pediatrics*
Grilli, Domenico - *Pediatrics*
Grillo, Anthony J. - *Pediatrics*
Gromisch, Donald S. - *Infectious Disease*
Gros, Shana - *Pediatrics*
Gross, Cathie C. - *Pediatrics*
Grossmann, Rami – *Neurology*
Grosso, Michael – *Pediatrics*
Guida, Louis - *Pediatrics*
Guidera, Blair Jessup - *Pediatrics*
Gulbransen, Greg - *Pediatrics*
Gunsberger, Maurice - *Pediatrics*
Gupta, Anil - *Pediatrics*
Gupta, Krishna K. - *Pediatrics*
Guram, Mohinder K. - *Pediatrics*
Gutkovich, Zinoviy - *Pediatrics*
Gutman, Alyson H. – *Developmental & Behavioral Pediatrics*
Guzowski, Dorothy - *Research*
Gyasi, Isaac Y. - *Pediatrics*
Gyves, William - *Pediatrics*
*Haber, Alan – *Pediatrics*
Haber, Calvin – *Child and Adolescent Psychiatry*
Hacker, Edith - *Pediatrics*
Hahami, Zivi - *Pediatrics*
Haimi, Joseph S. - *Pediatrics*
Hain, David - *Pediatrics*
Hajduk-Bennett, Ann M.- *Pediatrics*
Halegoua, Jason - *Pediatrics*
Haller, Cindy - *Gastroenterology*
Hammerman, Jeffrey - *Pediatrics*
Hample, Carlotta B. - *Gastroenterology*
Hampton, Phyllis A. - *Pediatrics*
Handelsman, John E. – *Orthopaedic Surgery*
Handler, Seymour - *Pediatrics*
Hankin, Dorie E. - *Developmental & Behavioral Pediatrics*
Hanna, Moneer - *Pediatric Urology*
Hannein, Hani – *Cardiothoracic Surgery*
Hanono, Monique - *Pediatrics*
Harnett-Robinson, Roy Edward - *Pediatrics*
Harper, Rita - *Neonatal-Perinatal Medicines*
Harris, Irwin L. - *Pediatrics*
Harris, Keith - *Pediatrics*
Hart, Andrew - *Pediatrics*
Harwin, Martin - *Pediatrics*

Hasan, Muhammad Akhtar - *Pediatrics*
Haskoor, Antwan - *Pediatrics*
Hass, Ada - *Pediatrics*
Hassett, Irene - *Developmental & Behavioral Pediatrics*
Hawkins, Lynn Ann. - *Endocrinology*
Hayman, Robert T. - *Dermatology*
Hebroni, Shohre - *Pediatrics*
Heiman, Howard S. - *Neonatal-Perinatal Medicine*
Heitler, Michael S. - *Pediatrics*
Heller, Gerald A. - *Pediatrics*
Herko, Patricia - *Pediatrics*
Hershey, Joel E. - *Pediatrics*
Hertz, Stanley M. – *Child and Adolescent Psychiatry*
Higgins, Kenneth J. - *Pediatrics*
Hirsch, Glenn S. – *Child and Adolescent Psychiatry*
Hirsch, Judith I. - *Pediatrics*
Hitner, Jason B. - *Pediatrics*
Hoch, Lori – *Pediatrics*
Hochwald, Neal – *Orthopaedic Surgery*
Hoffman, A. Charles - *Pediatrics*
Hoffman-Rosenfeld, Jamie Lyn – *Child Advocacy & Protection*
Hogan, Timothy - *Pediatrics*
Hollander, Melvin - *Pediatrics*
Hong, Andrew Richard – *General Surgery*
Honigman, Richard E. - *Pediatrics*
Horlick, Liat Jarkon – *Pediatrics*
Howoritz, Paul - *Pediatrics*
Horowitz, Roy - *Pediatrics*
Horwitz, Jonathan - *Pediatrics*
Hurwitz, David - *Pediatrics*
Husainy, Munira - *Pediatrics*
Hussain, Afia Akhtar - *Pediatrics*
Hyman, Susan S. - *Pediatrics*
Ibrahim, Iman William - *Pediatrics*
Ibrahim, Mahmoud Ahmed - *Neonatal-Perinatal Medicine*
Iglesias, Elba - *Adolescent Medicine*
Ilowite, Norman - *Rheumatology*
Imran, Sobia - *Pediatrics*
Ing, Frank - *Cardiology*
Inguagiato, Peter J. - *Pediatrics*
Iofel, Elizaveta - *Gastroenterology*
Iordanou, Christodoulos - *Pediatrics*
Iordanou, Michael - *Pediatrics*
Isenberg, Howard W. - *Pediatrics*
Issa-Basch, Elizabeth - *Pediatrics*
Itzkevitch, Mziya - *Pediatrics*
Iurato, Lori A. - *Pediatrics*
Jablonowski-Parada, Helen - *Pediatrics*
Jackman, Naomi Josephine - *Pediatrics*
Jacob, Josepheena J. - *Pediatrics*
Jacob, Julie – *Developmental & Behavioral Pediatrics*
Jacob, Stanley – *Pediatrics*
Jacobs, Katherine - *Pediatrics*
Jacobs, Linda H. - *Pediatrics*
*Jacobs, Martin H. - *Pediatrics*
Jacobs, Shari L. - *Pediatrics*
Jacobson, Marc - *Adolescent Medicine*
Jaffe, Rina - *Pediatrics*

Jassey, Lewis K. - *Pediatrics*
Jerome, Robert - *Pediatrics*
Jetter, Vicki E. - *Pediatrics*
Jhaveri, Meenaskshi - *Pediatrics*
Jiwani, Amyn - *Cardiology*
Jodorkovsky, Roberto - *Pediatrics*
Johnston, Jean Madinger - *Pediatrics*
Jongbloed, Audrey J. - *Pediatrics*
Jonisch, Elise L. - *Pediatrics*
Jose, Bessy - *Pediatrics*
Kabrawala, Pratibha B. - *Pediatrics*
Kadar, Robert Scott. - *Pediatrics*
Kaden, Gail - *Pediatrics*
Kafantaris, Vivian - *Child and Adolescent Psychiatry*
Kahan, Joel L. - *Pediatrics*
Kahn, Ronald Allan - *Pediatrics*
Kairam, Ram – *Neurology*
Kalenscher, Frederic - *Pediatrics*
Kamani, Naynesh - *Allergy-Immunology*
Kamen, Saul – *Dental Medicine*
Kaminsky, David M. - *Pediatrics*
Kan, Li - *Neurology*
Kantor, Howard L. - *Pediatrics*
Kantrow, Abraham H. - *Pediatrics*
Kaplan, A. Michael - *Pediatrics*
Kaplan, Blanka - *Allergy-Immunology*
Kaplan, Carl Philip – *Pediatrics*
Kaplan, Eugene - *Pediatrics*
Kaplan, Sandra J. - *Pediatrics*
Kaplan, Seymour – *Pediatrics/Allergy*
Kaplan, Stuart – *Child and Adolescent Psychiatry*
Kaplan, William - *Pediatrics*
Karakas, Sabiha Pinar - *Pediatrics*
Karayalcin, Gungor - *Hematology-Oncology*
*Karelitz, Samuel - *Pediatrics***
Karim, Rukshana O. – *Pediarics*
Kasat, Kavita - *Pediatrics*
Kasnicki, Laurie - *Pediatrics*
Katz, Elizabeth Young - *Pediatrics*
Katz, Lisa - *Pediatrics*
Katz, Robert K. - *Pediatrics*
Katz, Selig H. - *Pediatrics*
Kaufman, Arthur - *Pediatrics*
Kaye, Arthur - *Pediatrics*
Kaye, Shana Malka – *Pediatrics*
Kellner, Steven M. – *Pediatrics*
Kenan, Samuel – *Orthopaedic Surgery*
Kenigsberg, Kenneth - *Surgery*
Kent, Jeffrey D. - *Pediatrics*
Keschner, Alissa Sharon - *Pediatrics*
Keschner, Lori A. – *Pediatrics*
Kessler, David – *Pediatrics*
Kessler, Bradley - *Gastroenterology*
Kessler, Edmund - *Surgery*
Khadavi, Michael - *Pediatrics*
Khan, Ambreen – *Pediatrics*
Khan, Nafis Ahmad - *Emergency Medicine*
Khan, Shahana - *Pediatrics*
Khanna, Suresh - *Neonatal-Perinatal Medicine*
Kholwadwala, Dipak H. - *Cardiology*
Khoriaty, Florence - *Pediatrics*
Kilchevsky, Eitan - *Neonatal-Perinatal Medicine*
Kim, Yoojin - *Pediatrics*
Kim, Young - *Pediatrics*

Kim-Berman, Hera - *Pediatrics*
Kimura, Kenneth – *General Surgery*
King, Harry - *Pediatrics*
King, Katherine - *Neonatal-Perinatal Medicine*
Kipperman, Harry - *Pediatrics*
Kleiman, Jerrold I. - *Child and Adolescent Psychiatry*
Klein, Andrew J. - *Pediatrics*
*Klein, Marvin - *Neurology**
Kleinberg, Mitchell – *Pediatrics*
Klig, Jean – *Emergency Medicine*
Ko, Jesse - *Pediatrics*
Kodsi, Sylvia Rose - *Pediatric Ophthalmology*
Kohn, Jacelyn – *Pediatrics*
Koota, Ivan - *Pediatrics*
Koplewicz, Harold - *Child and Adolescent Psychiatry*
Koppel, Robert I. - *Neonatal-Perinatal Medicine*
Korn, Sheila S. - *Pediatrics*
Korn, Wallace - *Pediatrics*
Korsen, Glen Robert - *Pediatrics*
Kosinski, Ronald W. - *Pediatrics*
Koslowe, Oren Lewis - *Pediatrics*
Koster, Michael Philip - *Pediatrics*
Koumbourlis, Anastassios - *Pulmonary Medicine*
Koutras, Andreas K. - *Pediatrics*
Koutsoyiannis, Michael - *Pediatrics*
Kovacs, George - *Pediatrics*
Kove, Simon - *Pediatrics*
Kowal-Connelly, Suanne – *Pediatrics*
Krasna, Irwin – *General Surgery*
Kraus, Gregory - *Critical Care Medicine*
Krauss, Joel M. - *Pediatrics*
Kreitzer, Paula Michelle - *Endocrinology*
Kresic, Eva - *Pediatrics*
Kresic, Stoyanka - *Pediatrics*
*Kresky, Philip J. - *Pediatrics**
Krief, Patricia - *Neurology*
Krief, William Isaac - *Emergency Medicine*
Krigsman, Arthur Charles - *Pediatrics*
Krilov, Leonard - *Infectious Disease*
Kristal, Leonard - *Dermatology*
Kritchman, Benjamin - *Pediatrics*
Kronberg, Jason - *Pediatrics*
Kula, Roger W. - *Pediatrics*
Kuncewitch, William - *Pediatrics*
Kunjukunju, Grace - *Pediatrics*
Kunken, Frederic R. - *Pediatrics*
Kurer, Cheryl - *Cardiology*
Kuritzkes, Fedor - *Pediatrics*
Kutch, Joseph H. - *Pediatrics*
Kutin, Neil David – *General Surgery*
Kuttichira, Rachel J. - *Pediatrics*
Laboard, Barbara A. - *Pediatrics*
LaCorte, Jared C. - *Cardiology*
LaCorte, Michael A. - *Cardiology*
Landau, Irene - *Pediatrics*
Lalia, Madeline R. - *Pediatrics*
Lange, Joan Lisanne - *Pediatrics*
Lanzkowsky, Philip - *Hematology-Oncology*
Lanzone, Theresa C. - *Pediatrics*
Laplaza, Francisco - *Orthopaedic Surgery*

LaSala, Stephen R. - *Pediatrics*
Lashley, Marc S. - *Pediatrics*
Laskin, Emma J. - *Pediatrics*
Lau, Alice - *Pediatrics*
Lau, Nina Louie - *Pediatrics*
Lavy, Uri - *Pediatrics*
Lawrence, Donald P. - *Pediatrics*
Leavens-Maurer, Jill - *Pediatrics*
Lee, Jong-Won - *Pediatrics*
Lee, Siu Anthony - *Pediatrics*
Lee, Thomas – *General Surgery*
Lee, Wan Soo - *Pediatrics*
Lee Chan, Susan Meekyung. - *Pediatrics*
Leeds, Andrea J. - *Pediatrics*
Leichter, Donald - *Cardiology*
Lemon-Mule, Heather Frances - *Pediatrics*
Leonard, Henry - *Pediatrics*
Leonidas, John C. - *Radiology*
Levchuck, Sean Gerard - *Cardiology*
Levenbrown, Jack – *Radiology*
Levin-Carmine, Linda – *Adolescent Medicine*
Levine, Alan J. - *Pediatrics*
Levine, Howard Jay - *Pediatrics*
Levine, Jack - *Pediatrics*
Levine, Jeremiah J. – *Gastroenterology*
Levine, Marc - *Cardiology*
Levine, Mitchell Edward. - *Pediatrics*
*Levine, Stanley - *Immunology**
Levine, Stewart A. – *Pediatrics*
Levitt, Marc – *General Surgery*
Levitt, Selwyn – *Urologic Surgery*
Leviyeva, Natalya – *Pediatrics*
Levowitz, Herbert – *Child and Adolescent Psychiatry*
Levy, Harold - *Pediatrics*
Levy, Morton - *Pediatrics*
Lewis, Ronald - *Pediatrics*
Libert, Melissa M. - *Pediatrics*
*Librik, Leon - *Pediatrics**
Lidd, David - *Pediatrics*
Lieber, Ernest - *Medical Genetics*
Lief-Dienstag, Deborah - *Pediatrics*
Lightman, Hylton Ivan - *Pediatrics*
Lim, Henry Howard - *Pediatrics*
Linzer, Lisa - *Pediatrics*
Lipkin, Paul - *Developmental & Behavioral Pediatrics*
Lippman, Nancy Jo - *Pediatrics*
Lippmann, Richard Douglas - *Pediatrics*
Lipsitz, Philip - *Neonatal-Perinatal Medicine*
Lipskar, Aaron M. – *Plastic Surgery*
Lipton, Jeffrey M. - *Hematology-Oncology*
Liu, Johnson – *Hematology-Oncology*
Liu, Teddy - *Pediatrics*
Livoti, Angela - *Pediatrics*
LoGalbo, Peter - *Allergy-Immunology*
Love, Karen A. - *Pediatrics*
Lubov, Gary J. - *Pediatrics*
Lurie, Brian M. - *Pediatrics*
Luxenberg, Douglas Michael – *Pediatrics*
Lynch, Maureen - *Endocrinology*
Lynfield, Joshua - *Pediatrics*
Ma, Yeou-Chang - *Developmental & Behavioral Pediatrics*

Macaluso, Lauren Gale - *Pediatrics*
Machen, Heather Elizabeth - *Pediatrics*
Machuca, Hildred - *Pediatrics*
Madad, Saiyeda S. – *Pediatrics*
Magaletti, Francine - *Pediatrics*
Magnas, Tamar Elana - *Pediatrics*
Mahadeo, Robby - *Pediatrics*
Maisel, Jerome E. – *Pediatrics*
Maitinsky, Vera - *Pediatrics*
Majeed, Salamat – *Pediatrics*
Mandal, Paul - *Pediatrics*
Mandel, Clemens A. - *Pediatrics*
Manwani, Deepa G. - *Hematology-Oncology*
Maralit, Avelina - *Pediatrics*
Marcano, Brenda - *Critical Care Medicine*
Marchitelli, Roberto N. - *Pediatrics*
Marcus, Douglas - *Pediatrics*
Marder, Sidney S. - *Pediatrics*
Markouizos, Demetrios - *Pediatrics*
Markovics, Sharon B. - *Pediatrics*
Markowitz, James F. - *Gastroenterology*
*Marshall, Florence - *Pediatrics*
Martocci, Greg A. - *Pediatrics*
Marton, Freddie M. - *Pediatrics*
Massih, Raga A. - *Pediatrics*
Master, Kalpana R. - *Pediatrics*
Mathai-Jose, Beena - *Pediatrics*
Mathew, George - *Pediatrics*
Matos-Rivera, Irma M. – *Pediatrics*
Matthew, Kolathu - *Pediatrics*
Mauss, Irving H. - *Pediatrics*
Mauton, Alan - *Research*
Maybody, Shideh - *Pediatrics*
Maytal, Joseph - *Neurology*
McCarthy, Caro E. - *Pediatrics*
McCarthy, Patricia K. - *Pediatrics*
McGovern, Robert G. - *Pediatrics*
McInerney-Lopez, Regina - *Pediatrics*
McLaughlin, Reginald David - *Pediatrics*
McMahon, Donna-Marie - *Pediatrics*
McNamara, Joseph - *Hematology-Oncology*
Mehlman, Julia - *Pediatrics*
Mehrgut, Fabio M. - *Pediatrics*
Mehrotra, Deepti Ahuja. - *Pediatrics*
Mehta, Lakshmi - *Medical Genetics*
Mela, Suzanne - *Pediatrics*
Melamedoff, Monica - *Pediatrics*
Melinski, John Paul. – *Dental Medicine*
Meltzer Krief, Eve Ann. - *Pediatrics*
Mensch, Deborah - *Cardiology*
Merchant, Sanah R. - *Cardiology*
Merker, Robin - *Pediatrics*
Meryash, David L. – *Developmental & Behavioral Pediatrics*
Mesibov, William J. - *Pediatrics*
Messina Tsotsos, Deborah - *Pediatrics*
Meth, Rachelle H. – *Pediatrics*
Mickenberg, Norman - *Pediatrics*
Midulla, Peter - *Surgery*
Mienko, Iwona K. - *Pediatrics*
Mikhaylov, Arthur - *Pediatrics*
Milanaik, Ruth Lynn – *Developmental and Behavioral Pediatrics*

Miller, Bertram W. - *Pediatrics*
Miller, Laurence H. - *Pediatrics*
Miller, Michael Paul - *Critical Care Medicine*
Miller, Ruth - *Pediatrics*
Miller, Sheldon - *Pediatrics*
Millington-Capilupi, Deborah J. - *Pediatrics*
Milman, Marina - *Pediatrics*
Milton, Gayle P. - *Pediatrics*
Miner, Daniel W. - *Pediatrics*
Minikes, Neil - *Pediatrics*
Miranda, Louella Maria. - *Pediatrics*
Mirkin, Gary S. – *Pediatrics*
Mitchell, William - *Pediatrics*
Mitek-Gorecki, Aldona - *Pediatrics*
Mittler, Mark - *Neurosurgery*
Moerck, Linda Dawn. - *Pediatrics*
Moerck-Johnson, Deborah A. - *Pediatrics*
Moises, Marie-Jacq Leonor. - *Pediatrics*
Mokides, Valeria S. – *Pediatrics*
Mooalem, Frederick – *Pediatrics*
Morelli, Peter J. - *Pediatrics*
Moreno, Lisa - *Pediatrics*
Morris, Elliot - *Pediatrics*
Moxness, Margaret - *Child & Adolescent Psychiatry*
Moy, Libia C. - *Gastroenterology*
Mukherjee, Sarmistha - *Pediatrics*
Muscarello, Paul - *Pediatrics*
Nagelberg, Joy - *Emergency Medicine*
Napolitano, Jeanmarie Ann - *Pediatrics*
Narendra, Sudhanshu - *Pediatrics*
Nass, Howard - *Pediatrics*
Nathan, Janine - *Pediatrics*
Nayor, Ilyse Robin - *Pediatrics*
Naysan, Parviz - *Pediatrics*
Nazarian, Habib - *Pediatrics*
Needles, Carl - *Pediatrics*
Nehama, Jacqueline - *Critical Care Medicine*
Neman-Kuighadush, Mojgan - *Pediatrics*
Nerwen, Clifford B. - *Pediatrics*
Nesnay, Mary Ellen - *Dental Medicine*
Neumann, Karl - *Pediatrics*
Neuschotz, Frieda - *Pediatrics*
Nichols, Christiana – *Pediatrics*
Nichtern, Sol – *Child and Adolescent Psychiatry*
Nicolopoulos, Efthemia - *Pediatrics*
Niederer, Bettina S. - *Pediatrics*
Nieves, Jorge David - *Pediatrics*
Nimkoff, Laura - *Critical Care Medicine*
Nissen, Perry - *Hematology-Oncology*
Nitzberg, Benjamin W. – *Pediatrics*
Noble, Lawrence – *Neonatal-Perinatal Medicine*
Noghrey, Bobby - *Pediatrics*
Nolan, Lizabeth - *Pediatrics*
Novak, Gerald - *Neurology*
Novak, Inna - *Pediatrics*
Nudel, Dov - *Cardiology*
Nudelman, Jesse - *Pediatrics*
Nunez-Russotto, Grace - *Pediatrics*
Nussbaum, Michael - *Adolescent Medicine*

Ohebshalom, Robert - *Pediatrics*
*Oliker, Stanley - *Pediatrics*
Olin, Jeffrey Neal - *Pediatrics*
Olson, Allan - *Gastroenterology*
Olson, Madelyn E. - *Neurology*
Olstein, Dayna Lee – *Pediatric Dental Medicine*
Oppenheimer, Peter D. - *Pediatrics*
*Orange, Michael - *Pediatrics*
Ordonez, Julia I. – *Pediatrics*
Orens, Iris S. – *Child and Adolescent Psychiatry*
Orlando, Julia - *Pediatrics*
Orner, Hersch L. - *Pediatrics*
Orner, Shahnaz D. - *Pediatrics*
Ornstein, Rollyn Michelle - *Adolescent Medicine*
O'Rourke, Innis - *Pediatrics*
Ortiz, Carlos Adolfo. - *Pediatrics*
Oster, Julia - *Pediatrics*
Pagnotta, Laura Ann. - *Pediatrics*
Pahuja, Jagan N. - *Pediatrics*
Pahwa, Raj - *Stem Cell Transplantation*
Pahwa, Savita - *Allergy-Immunology*
Palathra, Mary - *Pediatrics*
Palazzo, Marie - *Pediatrics*
Paley, Carole - *Hematology-Oncology*
Palmer, Lane S. - *Pediatric Urology*
Palumbo, Nancy - *Pediatrics*
Palusci, Vincent - *Pediatrics*
Panes, Susan Ellen – *Pediatrics*
Panissidi, Nino - *Pediatrics*
Parisi, Mary S. – *Pediatrics*
Park, Yohan - *Pediatrics*
Parnell, Vincent A. - *Cardiothoracic Surgery*
Parris, O'Neall E. - *Pediatrics*
Patel, Mayank C. - *Pediatrics*
Patashny, Karen - *Pediatrics*
Peloso, Marie - *Pediatrics*
Peña, Alberto - *General Surgery*
Penefsky, Zia - *Pediatrics*
Penzer, Paul H - *Pediatrics*
Peress, Isaac - *Pediatrics*
Perez, Sania Rebecca - *Pediatrics*
Pergament, Eugene - *Medical Genetics*
Perlman, Sharon Michele - *Pediatrics*
Perrick, Steven L. - *Pediatrics*
Petinos, Konstantinos – *Pediatrics*
Petrizzo, Anthony – *Orthopaedic Surgery*
Petrovic, Michael - *Pediatrics*
Pettei, Michael Joseph – *Gastroenterology& Nutrition*
Philips, Smitha - *Pediatrics*
Piaser, Frederick J. - *Pediatrics*
Pilarte, Juan - *Pediatrics*
Pillar, Charles Jay – *Dental Medicine*
Pirraglia, Peter Dominic - *Pediatrics*
Platt, Louis - *Pediatrics*
Plaut, Allan - *Pediatrics*
Pleak, Richard R. - *Pediatrics*
Pockriss, Evan B. - *Pediatrics*
Polsinelli, Rosanna - *Pediatrics*
Pomerance, Herbert H. – *Pediatrics*
Ponda, Punita – *Allergy-Immunology*
Porges, Deborah Yourish - *Pediatrics*
Powers, Karen - *Critical Care Medicine*
Prendergast, Laura - *Pediatrics*

Prosper, Magally - *Pediatrics*
Pugliese, Madeline Melissa - *Pediatrics*
Putterman, Sheldon H. - *Pediatrics*
Quijano, Emelyn C. - *Pediatrics*
Quinn, Carrie Ann - *Pediatrics*
Rabinowicz, Morris - *Pediatrics*
Rabinowitz, Brian F. - *Pediatrics*
Rabinowitz, Leah - *Adolescent Medicine*
Radford, Richard - *Pediatrics*
Radinsky, Stacey - *Pediatrics*
Raggio, Kathleen - *Orthopaedic Surgery*
Raifman, Mark - *Pediatrics*
Rajan, Sujatha - *Infectious Disease*
Rakowska, Urszula K. - *Pediatrics*
Raksis, Karen - *Pediatrics*
Read, Rosemarie - *Pediatrics*
Recientes, Paz Tan. - *Pediatrics*
Reda, Edward - *Pediatrics*
Reddy, Gaddam - *Pediatrics*
Redner, Arlene Sara - *Hematology-Oncology*
Reejsinghani, Rosie - *Pediatrics*
Rehman, Khalil Ur. – *Pediatrics*
Reiman, Reuben - *Pediatrics*
Reischer, Izak - *Pediatrics*
Reiss, Joseph S. - *Pediatrics*
Reitman, Marc - *Pediatrics*
Reitman, Milton J. - *Cardiology*
Renna, Mary Ellen - *Pediatrics*
Resmovits, Marvin - *Pediatrics*
*Reuben, Richard N. - *Neurology*
Reuben, Rita S. - *Child and Adolescent Psychiatry*
Rhee, Jae C. - *Pediatrics*
Rhein, David Aron - *Pediatrics*
Rhein, Henry C. - *Pediatrics*
*Rie, Mary Louise - *Pediatrics*
Rivera-Amasola, Cecelia – *Developmental & Behavioral Pediatrics*
Rivkin, Nonna - *Pediatrics*
Roberto, Frank - *Pediatrics*
Robson, Yael Tabitha – *Pediatrics*
Rocker, Joshua – *Emergency Medicine*
Rodrigues, Maria Louella - *Pediatrics*
Rodrigues, Roy John - *Pediatrics*
Roe, Elsa – *Allergy-Immunology*
Roheim, Judith – *Child and Adolescent Psychiatry*
Romano, Angela - *Cardiology*
*Rook, George D. - *Cardiology*
Rooney, John – *Allergy-Immunology*
Rosemarin, Eve -*Pediatrics*
Rosen, Alexander S. - *Pediatrics*
Rosen, Nelson Garrett - *Pediatric Surgery*
Rosen, Stephanie Lynn - *Pediatrics*
Rosenberg, David - *Pediatrics*
Rosenberg, Jacob Judah - *Pediatrics*
Rosenbloom, Alan Jeffrey - *Pediatrics*
Rosenbloom, Andrew S. - *Pediatrics*
Rosenblum, Nancy - *Emergency Medicine*
Rosenn, Greg - *Pediatrics*
Rosenthal, Allan - *Neurosurgery*
Rosenthal, Cynthia - *Critical Care Medicine*
Rosenthal, David Walter – *Allergy-Immunology*

Rosman, Howard - *Pediatrics*
Ross, Avron - *Pediatrics*
Rotella, Alessandra M. - *Pediatrics*
Rothbort, Halana - *Pediatrics*
Rothenberg, Allan M. - *Pediatrics*
Rozenbaum, Joseph - *Pediatrics*
Rubel, Karen A. - *Pediatrics*
Rubin, Andrew P. - *Pediatrics*
Rubin, Elissa Hope - *Pediatrics*
Rubin, Jamie - *Pediatrics*
Rubin, Lorry Glen - *Infectious Disease*
Rubin, Steven E. - *Opthalmology*
Rubinos, Marcia - *Pediatrics*
Rubenstein, Allen A. - *Pediatrics*
Rubenstein, Ira S. - *Pediatrics*
Russ, Heidi R. - *Pediatrics*
Ruotolo, Rachel – *Surgery*
Rydzinski, Joyce – *Child and Adolescent Psychiatry*
*Saad, Sam - *Pediatrics*
Sachs, Hersch - *Pediatrics*
Sachse, Desiree K. - *Pediatrics*
Sadr, Iran - *Cardiology*
Sagy, Mayer - *Critical Care Medicine*
Sahdev, Indira - *Hematology-Oncology*
Saito, Ema - *Pediatrics*
Sajnani, Gina – *Pediatric Dental Medicine*
Salemi, Mozafer - *Pediatrics*
Salzman, Mark - *Pediatrics*
Samuel, Stewart - *Pediatrics*
Sanchez, Verisimo F. - *Pediatrics*
Santangelo, Christina - *Pediatrics*
Santangelo, Luzviminda S. - *Pediatrics*
Santiago, Maria Teresa Antonio – *Pulmonary Medicine*
Sarkar, Maya - *Pediatrics*
Sartori, Richard - *Pediatrics*
Saunders, Deborah S. - *Pediatrics*
Scalettar, Howard - *Pediatrics*
Scarpelli, Emile - *Pulmonary Medicine*
Schaeffer, Janis I. - *Critical Care Medicine*
Schanler, Richard - *Neonatal-Perinatal Medicine*
Scheidt, Joni D. - *Pediatrics*
Schell, Norman B. - *Pediatrics*
Scherz, Arnold - *Pediatrics*
Schertz, Mitchell - *Pediatrics*
Schiff, Russell - *Cardiology*
Schiff, Stuart - *Pediatrics*
Schildkrout, Mollie - *Child and Adolescent Psychiatry*
Schiowitz, Gila - *Pediatrics*
Schlessel, Jerrold S. - *Neonatal-Perinatal Medicine*
Schlusselberg, Moshe – *Pediatrics*
*Schneider, Keith – *General Surgery*
Schneider, James – *Critical Care Medicine*
Schneider, Philip – *Pediatrics*
Schneider, Steven - *Neurosurgery*
Schroeder, Marie B. - *Pediatrics*
Schroff, Amita - *Pediatrics*
*Schulkind, Martin L. - *Pediatrics*
Schultheis, Eric H. - *Pediatrics*
Schussheim, Arnold – *Pediatrics*
Schuval, Susan - *Allergy-Immunology*

Schwager, Arthur - *Pediatrics*
Schwalb, Eugene - *Pediatrics*
Schwarzer, Sigmund - *Pediatrics*
Schwartz, Bertram S. - *Pediatrics*
Schwartz, David Lipman - *General Surgery*
Schwartz, Ira M. - *Pediatrics*
Schwartz, Samuel E. - *Pediatrics*
Schwarz, Gavin - *Pediatrics*
Screnci, Catherine R. – *Pediatrics*
Scriven, Richard – *General Surgery*
Seiden, Howard Scott - *Cardiology*
Sekhon, Amon - *Pediatrics*
Sena, Vincent - *Pediatrics*
Shah, Manoj R. - *Pediatrics*
Shanske, Alan - *Genetics*
Shapir, Yehuda – *Cardiology*
Shapiro, Stacey D. - *Pediatrics*
Shear, Stephen E. - *Pediatrics*
Sheehy, John P. - *Pediatrics*
Sheff, Lawrence – *Child and Adolescent Psychiatry*
Sheflin, Marla Sue – *Pediatrics*
Shen, Edith - *Pediatrics*
Shende, Ashok Chintaman – *Hematology-Oncology*
Shenker, Ira Ronald - *Adolescent Medicine*
Sheppard, Beverly Anita - *Pediatrics*
Sherman, H. Peter - *Pediatrics*
Sherman, Steven – *Pediatrics*
Sherwyn, Albert - *Pediatrics*
Shibli, Syed Ahmed T. - *Pediatrics*
Shih, San Cheng - *Hematology-Oncology*
Shikowitz, Mark - *Otorhinolaryngology*
Shim, Thomas M. - *Pediatrics*
Shin, William Woosik - *Pediatrics*
Shoob, M. Philip – *Pediatrics*
Shrock, Peter – *General Surgery*
Shroff, Amita - *Emergency Medicine*
Shukla, Hari Krishna - *Pediatrics*
Sia, Concepcion G. - *Neonatal-Perinatal Medicine*
Sicklick, Marc J. – *Pediatrics*
Siddharth, Saroja - *Pediatrics*
Siedman, Howard - *Pediatrics*
Siegel, Subhadra – *Pediatrics*
Silber, Jeffrey – *Orthopaedic Surgery*
Silbermintz, Ari - *Pediatrics*
Silberstein, Warren – *Pediatrics*
Silbert, Daniel - *Cardiology*
Silver, Hilton - *Pediatrics*
Silver, Peter - *Critical Care Medicine*
Silverio, Arlene B. - *Emergency Medicine*
Simai, David Elazar - *Pediatrics*
Simela, Ernest – *Pediatrics*
Simon, Harvey - *Pediatrics*
Simon, Nina Jill – *Pediatrics*
Simon-Goldman, Phyllis - *Pediatrics*
Simpser, Edwin F. - *Nutrition*
Sinesi, Andrew P. – *Pediatrics*
Singer, Andrew - *Pediatrics*
Singh, A. Sharon – *Hematology-Oncology*
Slepowitz, Gary A. - *Pediatrics*
Slonim, Alfred E. - *Metabolism*
Small, Marvin - *Pediatrics*
Smith, Martha L. - *Pediatrics*

Smith, Robin Errol - *Neurology*
Smoller, Saul - *Pediatrics*
Snow, Amorita M. - *Pediatrics*
Snowe, Robert J. - *Pediatrics*
*So, Henry - *Pediatrics*
Soffer, Samuel Z. – *General Surgery*
Sokol, Scott K. - *Pediatrics*
*Solomon, Nathaniel - *Pediatrics*
Soloway, Josef - *Pediatrics*
Somma, Laura - *Pediatrics*
Sommer, Robert Jay – *Pediatrics*
Sonnenblick, Marcia - *Psychology*
Sood, Sunil Kumar - *Infectious Diseases*
Sparto, Robert - *Pediatrics*
Speiser, Phyllis W. – *Endocrinology*
Sperber, Mark - *Pediatrics*
Spina, Louis A. – *Pediatrics*
Spinner, Milton L. - *Pediatrics*
Spinazzola, Regina M. - *Neonatal-Perinatal Medicine*
Spiotta, Roseanne – *Pediatrics*
Spivak, Lynn - *Otorhinolaryngology*
Staiman, Keith - *Pediatrics*
Stamatos, Cathryn Gaye - *Pediatrics*
Stamberg, Judith - *Medical Genetics*
Steele, Andrew M. - *Neonatal-Perinatal Medicine*
Stein, Howard S. - *Pediatrics*
Stein, Joseph - *Pediatrics*
Stein, Martin L. - *Pediatrics*
Stein, Michael - *Pediatrics*
Stein-Albert, Marcy - *Pediatrics*
Steinberg, Allan - *Pediatrics*
Steinfeld, Philip S. - *Pediatrics*
Stern, Howard S. - *Pediatrics*
Stern, Michael Shlomo - *Pediatrics*
*Sternberg, S David - *Pediatrics*
Stewart, Barbara J. - *Neurology*
Stewart, Constance F. – *Endocrinology*
Stiefel, Fred H. - *Pediatrics*
*Stillerman, Maxwell - *Pediatrics*
Stillman, Susan C..- *Pediatrics*
Stiuso, Loriann M. - *Pediatrics*
*Storm, Jack - *Pediatrics*
Strassberg, Howard J. - *Pediatrics*
Strauss, Raphael E. - *Pediatrics*
*Suser, Fred - *Pediatrics*
Sussman, Leonard - *Endocrinology*
Sussman, Marvin – *Pediatrics*
*Sutin, Gerald - *Pediatrics*
Svitek, Scott - *Pediatrics*
Swersky, Charles - *Pediatrics*
Swezey, Susan H. - *Pediatrics*
Switzer, Richard - *Pediatrics*
Syalee, Jogesh - *Pediatrics*
Sy-Kho, Rose Marrie Yu - *Neurology*
Synowiedzka-Sawicki, Elzbieta - *Pediatrics*
Tabizadeh, Marjan Y. - *Pediatrics*
Taff, Ingrid P. - *Neurology*
Takhalov, Arkadiy - *Pediatrics*
Talebian, Behzad - *Pediatrics*
Talwar, Rohit - *Cardiology*
Tamaroff, Michael - *Research*
Tao, Wenjing – *Pediatrics*
Taubes, Harvey - *Pediatrics*
Taylor, Danielle - *Pediatrics*
Teitel, Maurice - *Pediatrics*
Telfeian, Arlin G. - *Pediatrics*
Tellechea, Natasha A. - *Pediatrics*

Tepper, Bradford - *Pediatrics*
Teyan, Frederick - *Pediatrics*
Thallur, Seetha D. - *Pediatrics*
Thambireddy, Damodar Reddy – *Pediatrics*
Thebner, Lisa - *Pediatrics*
Thomas, Philomena - *Emergency Medicine*
Thundercloud, Alex - *Pediatrics*
Tierney-O'Connor, Kathleen - *Pediatrics*
Tingir, Raffi N. - *Pediatrics*
Toback, Ira B. - *Pediatrics*
Tomei, Nina A. - *Pediatrics*
Tong, Man Yee Linda - *Pediatrics*
Topper, Leonid - *Neurology*
Toufexis, Christina - *Pediatrics*
Torrado-Jule, Carmen - *Pediatrics*
Trachtman, Howard - *Nephrology*
Trager, Jonathan - *Emergency Medicine*
Tran, Louanne - *Neonatal-Perinatal Medicine*
Trecartin, Susan E. - *Pediatrics*
Trepel, Robert - *Neurology*
Trepeta, Michael F. - *Pediatrics*
Trivilino, Alfred - *Pediatrics*
Trope, Randi - *Critical Care Medicine*
Troy, Deborah A. – *Pediatric Dental Medicine*
Tsoumpariotis, Apostolis N. - *Pediatrics*
Tsoutsouras, Steven - *Pediatrics*
Turow, Victor - *Pediatrics*
Vaccaro, Peter - *Pediatrics*
Valacer, David - *Allergy-Immunology*
Valderrama, Elsa - *Pathology*
Valentine, Kena - *Pediatrics*
Valins, Martin J. - *Pediatrics*
Vallone, Ambrose Martin – *Cardiology*
Vambutus, Andrea - *Otorhinolaryngology*
Van Bosse, Harold - *Orthopaedic Surgery*
Vatsia, Sheel - *Cardiothoracic Surgery*
Vega, Roy - *Emergency Medicine*
Vergara, Marcela Martha - *Nephrology*
Verrier, Tara - *Pediatrics*
Vianest, Jayne - *Pediatrics*
Vilela, Mary Gidget T. - *Pediatrics*
Vinograd, Alexander – *Pediatrics/Gastroenterology*
Vinograd, Annamma - *Pediatrics*
Viswanathan, Kusum - *Pediatrics*
Vlachos, Adrianna - *Hematology-Oncology*
Voght-Lowell, Robert - *Cardiology*
Vohra, Kiran - *Neonatal-Perinatal Medicine*
Vomvolakis, Maria A. - Pediatrics
Waber, Lewis – *Medical Genetics*
Wagner, Harold - *Pediatrics*
Walco, Gary - *Psychology*
Waldbaum, Ruth - *Child and Adolescent Psychiatry*
Wang, Linda - *Pediatrics*
Warren, Anat B. - *Pediatrics*
Wasser, Sidi B. - *Pediatrics*

Wassem, Amira - *Pediatrics*
Watman, Naomi Chaim - *Pediatrics*
Wasser, Sidi B. - *Pediatrics*
Waterman, Erica - *Pediatrics*
Wedgewood, Josiah - *Neonatal-
Perinatal Medicine*
Weeks, Mitchell - *Pediatrics*
Wehlou, Kicki Sara - *Pediatrics*
*Weichsel, Manfred - *Pediatrics*
Weiler, Mitchell I. - *Pediatrics*
*Weinberg, Samuel - *Dermatology*
Weinberg, Stuart - *Critical Care*
Medicine*
Weindorf, Stanley - *Pediatrics*
Weiner, Ethan - *Pediatrics*
Weinstein, Toba A. - *Gastroenterology*
Weinstock, Michael - *Pediatrics*
Weiselberg, Eric Charles –
Adolescent Medicine*
Weiser-Shlefstein, Julie - *Pediatrics*
Weiss, Michael - *Pediatrics*
Weiss, Steven Jay - *Allergy-*
Immunology*
Welles, Mark B. - *Pediatrics*
Wender, Esther - *Developmental &*
Behavioral Pediatrics*
Wertheim, David L. - *Allergy-*
Immunology
Werther, Joseph – *Pediatrics*
Weston, Bert – *Child and Adolescent*
Psychiatry*
Wexler-Silverman, Marcie
– *Developmental*
and Behavioral Pediatrics*
White, John – General Surgery
Whitelaw, Philip - *Pediatrics*
Wildes, Jerome - *Pediatrics*
Wilkie, Ormond L. - *Pediatrics*
Wilkins, Sania D. - *Pediatrics*
Wilks-Gallo, Lisa Sara - *Pediatrics*
Wind, Edward S. - *Radiology*
Wind, Shoshana M. - *Pediatrics*
Wininger, Michael – *Dental*
Medicine
Winkler, Ian - *Pediatrics*
Winston, John S. - *Pediatrics*
Wixsom, George Jory - *Pediatrics*
Wolert-Zaromatidis, Mary Ann
- *Pediatrics*
Wolfe, Harvey I. - *Pediatrics*
Wolfson, Scott J. - *Pediatrics*
Wong, Maicie - *Pediatrics*
Woroniecka, Monika Izabela
- *Pediatrics*
Woroniecki, Robert - *Pediatrics*
Wou, Margaret L. - *Pediatrics*
Xu, Rong - *Pediatrics*
Yadoo, Moshe - *Pediatrics*
Yagudayev, Yakov D. - *Pediatrics*
Yan, Karen Joan. - *Pediatrics*
Yee, Benetta - *Pediatrics*
Yee, William - *Critical Care Medicine*
Yeger-Arbitman, Raisa – *Pediatrics*
Yoon, Douglas - *Endocrinology*
Young, Rose Marie - *Pediatrics*
Yu, Ann Marie - *Pediatrics*
Yu, Robert M. - *Pediatrics*
Yusuf, Fazlul H. - *Hematology-*
Oncology
Zahtz, Gerald - *Otorhinolaryngology*
*Zahtz, Hyman - *Pediatrics*

Zaslav, Ann-Leslie - *Medical Genetics*
Zaso, John R. - *Pediatrics*
Zavolkovskaya, Sabina - *Pediatrics*
Zelkovic, Paul F. - *Pediatrics*
Zeng, Katherine - *Pediatrics*
Zeng, Lingling - *Pediatrics*
Zibners, Lara Marie - *Pediatrics*
Zilkha, Naomi Levine. - *Pediatrics*
Ziprkowski, Micha N. - *Pediatrics*
Zirin, Heddy J. - *Pediatrics*
Zitrin, Charlotte M. - *Psychiatry*
Zyskind, Israel - *Pediatrics*

AUTHOR'S BIOGRAPHY

Philip Lanzkowsky, MD, is executive director and chief-of-staff of the Schneider Children's Hospital, vice-president of the Children's Health Network of the North Shore–Long Island Jewish Health System, and professor of pediatrics at the Albert Einstein College of Medicine.

Born in Cape Town, South Africa, Dr. Lanzkowsky graduated as a physician from the University of Cape Town School of Medicine in 1954. He obtained his doctorate of medicine at the University of Cape Town in 1959. In 1960 he received a diploma in child health from the Royal College of Physicians of London and the Royal College of Surgeons of England, and in 1961 became a member of the prestigious Royal College of Physicians of Edinburgh. The Royal College of Physicians of Edinburgh honored Dr. Lanzkowsky in 1973 by appointing him a fellow of the college. In 1994 he received an honorary doctorate of science honoris causa from St. John's University in New York in recognition of his notable contributions to children of the world in the field of pediatric medicine.

Dr. Lanzkowsky did postgraduate research and clinical work in Edinburgh, Scotland; London, England; Duke University Medical School, Durham, North Carolina; and the University of Utah Medical School, Salt Lake City, Utah from 1960 to 1963 before returning to South Africa to take up a position as the first trained pediatric hematologist-oncologist in South Africa at the Red Cross War Memorial Children's Hospital in Cape Town, South Africa.

Dr. Lanzkowsky was recruited by the New York Hospital-Cornell University Medical Center and returned to the United States in 1965 to become the director of pediatric hematology at the New York Hospital and associate professor of pediatrics at the medical school. In 1970 he was appointed director of the Department of Pediatrics and chief of pediatric hematology-oncology at the Long Island Jewish Medical Center. Dr. Lanzkowsky was responsible for the planning and programmatic development of Schneider Children's Hospital starting in the early 1970s and has been its driving force and chief of staff since the hospital opened in 1983.

During his career, Dr. Lanzkowsky has received numerous honors and awards in South Africa, Edinburgh, and the United States. He sits on the boards of many organizations concerned with the health and welfare of children and has been a consultant to many institutions in this country as well as one of the consultants for the establishment and programmatic development of the first and only children's hospital in Israel—the Schneider Children's Medical Center of Israel.

Dr. Lanzkowsky is a member of numerous professional societies and has had many special appointments both in the United States and abroad. He has been an invited lecturer and visiting professor at numerous institutions and medical schools in this country, South Africa, Japan, England, Chile, Mexico, Brazil, Israel, India, Poland, Hungary, Spain, and China.

He is the author of six textbooks on pediatric hematology-oncology, many of which have been translated into other languages and are in use worldwide. He is the author of chapters in hematology and oncology in many standard textbooks and has 286 scientific publications to his name.

Dr. Lanzkowsky is married to Rhona Lanzkowsky, a psychotherapist in practice in Great Neck and Manhattan. They have five children—Shelley Lanzkowsky-Bienstock, MD, a pediatrician in Morristown, New Jersey; David Roy Lanzkowsky, MD, an anesthesiologist in Las Vegas, Nevada; Leora Lanzkowsky-Diamond, MD, a radiologist in Las Vegas, Nevada; Marc Lanzkowsky, an attorney in New York; and Jonathan Lanzkowsky, MD, an obstetrician-gynecologist in New York City, New York.

OTHER BOOKS BY PHILIP LANZKOWSKY, MD

Pediatric Hematology-Oncology, 1980, McGraw-Hill

Pediatric Oncology, 1983, McGraw-Hill

Manual of Pediatric Hematology and Oncology, First Edition, 1989, Churchill Livingstone

Manual of Pediatric Hematology and Oncology, Second Edition, 1995, Churchill Livingstone

Manual of Pediatric Hematology and Oncology, Third Edition, 1999, Academic Press

Manual of Pediatric Hematology and Oncology, Fourth Edition, 2005, Elsevier Academic Press

Rationale for a Children's Medical Center
By Philip Lanzkowsky, M.D.

This document is a preliminary working hypothesis for purposes of discussion.
May 30, 1972

PREAMBLE:

The essence of the medical center for children is the gathering under one roof for a combined attack on the manifold problems of health and disease of the infant, the child and the adolescent, doctors and medical workers whose major interests concern these age groups, with the aid of all the techniques and specialized knowledge available in the medical world today.

Editorial in the *New England Journal of Medicine* (234; 769-770, 1946)

Children are not adults in miniature; their entire medical and emotional makeup is wholly different from that of the adult and hence should be managed in a separate environment. That environment should be designed to appeal to the child and make him feel comfortable and "at home."

The social and medical advances of the past twenty-five years have changed the disability pattern of disease in children and thus the type of healthcare required for children. Coincidentally, an interesting amount of attention has been paid to the emotional effects of hospitalizing the child. It has been shown by numerous investigators that children under 5 years of age are emotionally disturbed by hospitalization, that improved hospital conditions can lessen trauma for children, and that arrangements that will permit the mother to stay with the child in the hospital are effective measures in preventing emotional disturbances. Changes in the care of children in hospitals must occur to avoid these emotional effects. These can

be brought about by modification of the traditional hospital routine to include recreational and educational activities, liberal parental visiting, family participation in ward care, and sleeping facilities for parents.

In addition, alternatives for healthcare for children in hospitals must be developed for those who require evaluation, those with chronic and not urgent diseases, and those requiring brief hospital-based procedures, e.g., minor surgery, etc.

Spiraling costs of medical care dictate the need for high bed utilization, and regionalization of services is required in order to accomplish this. Scrutinizing the large number of pediatric units in Nassau, Suffolk, and Queens indicates extremely low occupancy rates, which make these operations extremely expensive. Small units do not have available the necessary expertise for the optimal care of children because of the expense involved in the development of these types of services and the inability to attract well-trained specialists.

The recommendation for the building of the children's medical center is based on the following premises:

PREMISE I: The need for regionalization of pediatric care.

A survey of hospitals providing child care in Queens, Nassau, and Suffolk Counties indicated that there are too many facilities attempting to provide child care with extremely low occupancy, inadequate physical facilities, and incomplete medical coverage. This leads to spiraling costs and mediocre, often inadequate, care. The following data substantiate these statements:

	CHILDREN 14 YEARS AND UNDER	NUMBER OF HOSPITALS	NUMBER OF HOSPITAL BEDS	UTILIZATION PERCENTAGE	PATIENT DAYS	DISCHARGES
QUEENS COUNTY		20	660	57%		
NASSAU COUNTY	420,000	16	431	53%	73,600	16,000
SUFFOLK COUNTY	381,000	13	255	73%	67,700	17,857
LIJ-HMC			97	Peds/Adol 88.4% Neonatal 102.7%	22,105	3,807

Of the forty-nine hospitals only two have intensive care units for children or neonates and none have special adolescent facilities. Only LIJ-HMC has some full-time trained subspecialists.

The above table shows that the utilization and percentage occupancy rates of beds in the pediatric unit at Long Island Jewish-Hillside Medical Center are higher than that of all other hospitals providing childcare. This indicates that children are already gravitating to Long Island Jewish-Hillside Medical Center because of the medical staff, breadth of programs, and facilities available. A children's hospital with more adequate and optimal facilities will exaggerate this trend.

A large regional center can accomplish the following:

A. Reduce costs of medical care by increased utilization and decreased stay per disease process. To some extent we have demonstrated this already for medical and surgical admissions in the Department of Pediatrics.

B. Provide more optimum care for children through programs that smaller units cannot provide because of cost restrictions and the lack of medical expertise, e.g., cardiac surgery, hemophilia program, leukemia program, cystic fibrosis program, child development program, learning disability program, etc.

C. Increase safety for patients in large units where medical staff is available on a twenty-four-hour basis and can immediately respond to emergencies, e.g., bleeding, attention to cardiorespiratory arrest, etc.

D. Provide units with special equipment and facilities, e.g., neonatology, adolescent medicine, and intensive care units for the optimum care of children with special needs as well as individuals in particular age groups.

E. Make available distinguished academicians in the various specialty areas of pediatrics for consultation on a full-time basis, e.g., hematologists, neurologists, endocrinologists, cardiologists, geneticists, neonatologists, radiologists, surgeons, urologists, orthopaedic surgeons, etc.

F. Advance basic knowledge in pediatric medicine and surgery through research.

G. Better disseminate health education concerning children.

H. Provide special facilities (e.g., recreational, education, etc.) and sleeping accommodations for parents to reduce emotional trauma of children.

I. Provide special laboratory (ultra-microspecimens) and radiological facilities for children.

J. Provide emergency services and surgical operating facilities exclusively for children.

It is apparent that financial restrictions imposed on underutilized smaller pediatric units as well as the public's search for optimal medical care for children will force smaller pediatric units in Queens, Nassau, and Suffolk to close their doors. This trend is already apparent (e.g., LaGuardia Hospital). A number of other small institutions (e.g., Hillcrest General, Interboro, Peninsula General) have informal arrangements to send their more sophisticated and complicated cases to the Long Island Jewish-Hillside Medical Center, Department of Pediatrics. Special programs that have been developed have drawn patients from all over the Island and beyond. It is far better to plan for this regionalization of care in a rational way than to have it imposed on us by governmental funding agencies.

PREMISE II: The strain on and the limitations of the existing Department of Pediatrics at LIJ-HMC.

The trend to regionalization, which has already commenced, has pushed the Department of Pediatrics to the limits of its ability to provide care. Its physical facility is inadequate to carry out the job it is required to do for the following reasons:

•The high occupancy rate often requires that patients be nursed in the corridors.

•Isolation areas are inadequate for a constantly increasing number of patients who are immunocompromised, (e.g.,leukemics, children on cytotoxic agents), the critically ill, and psychiatric patients.

•Outpatient facilities for expanding pediatric programs are hopelessly inadequate (*vide infra*).

•Intensive care unit facilities are inadequate.

•Pediatric pre-anesthesia room, recovery room, and operating rooms exclusively for children are badly needed.

•There are no school facilities.

•Playroom facilities are inadequate.

•There are no parent facilities.

•Laboratory research space is hopelessly inadequate.

•Lecture rooms for pediatric students (paraprofessional, medical and nursing) are totally inadequate.

•Office and secretarial space is inadequate.

•There are no distinct pediatric radiology facilities (*vide infra*).

Because of the inherent inadequacies of a department of pediatrics within a general hospital, it is thought appropriate at this time to establish a physical plant specifically designed for the needs of children. There will be certain specific requirements, including parent sleeping accommodations in each room, sinks and toilets specifically designed for children, a school, adequate recreational facilities, an x-ray facility specifically for pediatric radiology work, and an outpatient department especially designed for the numerous pediatric clinics and special units to provide alternate types of healthcare for children in hospitals, e.g., day-care medical unit, day-care surgical unit, psychiatric unit (detoxification unit), chronic care unit, isolation unit, etc.

PREMISE III: The need for an enlarged ambulatory service in keeping with changing patterns in medical care in pediatrics.

This has come about for the following reasons:

•There is a recognition that many children now being hospitalized could be cared for totally or partially on an ambulatory basis.

•Advances in diagnostic and therapeutic techniques have decreased the need for inpatient hospitalization.

•Care of acute illnesses is taking place in ambulatory services and hospital emergency departments.

•Children with chronic diseases and handicapping disorders constitute a growing segment of the pediatric patient population.

•There is a growing emphasis on ambulatory medicine in the education of physicians, nurses, and allied health workers.

•Medical care is gradually becoming more concerned with preventive measures.

All of these aspects are accentuated in children.

PREMISE IV: The need for a distinct pediatric emergency department.

PREMISE V: The need for a distinct pediatric operating suite.

PREMISE VI: The need for distinct pediatric radiology.

The basic differences between pediatric radiology and adult radiology are:

•Infants and children are undergoing continuous growth and development.

•Emotional and physical reactions of infants and children to stress differ from those of adults.

•Diseases inherent in infants and children are different from those encountered in adults.

The following are some considerations for pediatric radiology:

A. Adequate supervision is necessary at all times—in the waiting room and radiographic room and during transportation from inpatient ward to the radiology suite.

B. Adequate immobilization during examination is necessary.

C. Appropriate exposure times are of utmost importance.

D. Adequate shielding of gonads is important.

E. Small errors of alignment of x-ray tube or in positioning of patient are magnified in infants.

F. Psychological effects must be taken into account.

G. Pediatric radiologists have special expertise in radiologic procedures in newborns and young children. "Ideally all radiologic procedures should be supervised and interpreted by a physician trained in pediatric radiology." (*American*

Academy of Pediatrics: Care of Children in Hospital, 1971).

PREMISE VII: The need for alternative types of healthcare for children.

In the past twenty-five years numerous changes have occurred in the disability pattern of disease in children and as a result the type of healthcare required for children. In addition to conventional pediatric hospital care the following facilities should be provided in a modern children's medical center:

A. Day-care medical unit

This is a hospital facility in which comprehensive professional and diagnostic laboratory and radiological facilities are provided to children on an ambulatory basis. It provides for the assessment and care of children by appointment, under the direction of hospital staff or a family physician. Children selected for the day-care medical units include those admitted for certain investigations or simple treatment, e.g., blood transfusion for Cooley's anemia, lumbar puncture, intravenous medication for leukemia, etc.

B. Day-care surgical unit

A day-care surgical unit would be devoted to the performance of elective surgical procedures or operations on patients who are admitted and discharged from the unit on the day of surgery. It is an extension of the surgical outpatient department and includes preanesthesia, operating, and recovery areas and an observation ward where parents may assist in routine post-operative care prior to discharge.

C. Extended-care custodial unit (in affiliation with a Children's Medical Center)

An extended-care custodial unit is a community facility for children in whom improvement is not anticipated, but who require continuing custodial nursing and medical care as inpatients.

D. Longer stay and rehabilitation unit (in affiliation with a Children's Medical Center)

This is a community facility for children

amenable to activation and rehabilitation:

• Children with medical, surgical, and orthopaedic problems who are not sufficiently recovered to return home but do not require acute hospital care;

• Children with chronic diseases thought likely to improve with a limited period of medical management in a hospital setting when such could not be achieved at home; and

• Children with physical disabilities requiring physiotherapy for specific rehabilitative goals, when such could not be achieved in a home setting.

E. A series of diagnostic clinics

These would assist the doctors of the area in dealing with children requiring specific investigations in the most economical and efficient manner.

F. Psychiatric unit

This unit would be devoted to the care of children with acute psychiatric disturbances.

G. Isolation unit

It is anticipated that a children's hospital will become a regional center for isolation of contagious disorders. It would also house children with impaired immunity, e.g., those with malignancies or leukemia and those on immunosuppressive drugs.

It appears that with rising costs of medical care, increasing demands for expertise, greater awareness of the psychiatric trauma of children who are hospitalized, and the need to attract subspecialists of pediatric medicine and pediatric surgery under one roof for the provision of optimum care for children, a large regional Children's Medical Center should be established. Because of the changing patterns of disease among children, imaginative alternative methods in the delivery of care should be sought. Some of these are outlined above.

PHYSICAL STRUCTURE

The following was prepared after a visit to Cleveland Children's Hospital (Case Western University Medical School), Toronto Children's Hospital (University of Toronto), and Montreal Children's Hospital (McGill University Medical School) May 1-3, 1972, by Drs. Philip Lanzkowsky, I. Ronald Shenker, Jerrold Becker, and Martin Abrams.

Preamble

The children's medical center should be a referral center for medical, surgical, dental, and psychiatric care for the neonate, child, and adolescent. It should provide primary care when called upon to do so for a defined area surrounding the hospital. In addition, it should become a center for undergraduate and postgraduate training for pediatricians, surgeons, psychiatrists, and dentists as well as other professionals such as nurses, physiotherapists, etc., and paraprofessionals such as physician associates and technicians. It should play a leading role in the development of basic and applied research with reference to children. To this end it should attract physicians of high academic caliber with a full-time commitment to these aims.

Bed Allocation

A total of 150 beds is proposed with the planned ability to increase to 200 beds. This number was arrived at after consideration of the following factors:

• Reasonable projection of the requirement for pediatric beds and the importance of maintaining a high occupancy rate with reference to reimbursement.

• Need to reduce the potential resistance that might arise from the regulatory agencies with reference to an application for the need for more pediatric hospital beds. (In this regard it should be noted that the mean occupancy rate for pediatrics is on the order of 60 percent in thirty-six pediatric units in the New York area.)

• The ability to staff the hospital with competent nursing and ancillary personnel.

• The size of other children's hospitals in this country (See list at the end of this document.)

The following breakdown of the beds is suggested:

Neonatal unit—40 beds. This should be a combined medical-surgical unit; thirty of the beds should be medical and ten surgical.

Pediatric unit—60 beds. Forty of the beds should be medical and twenty surgical. This would include an intensive care unit of ten beds, five medical and five surgical, and an isolation unit of ten beds. It is anticipated that this would become a regional center for the isolation of contagious disorders. It should house certain infectious diseases, e.g., diarrhea, infected wounds, and impaired immunologic disorders, e.g., leukemia, aplastic anemia.

Adolescent unit—20 beds. Twelve of the beds should be medical and eight surgical.

Psychiatric unit—15 beds.

Chronic care unit—15 beds. This will contain medical, orthopaedic, neurosurgical, and urologic patients. This unit will require low-care nursing and rehabilitative surgery, physiotherapy, and occupational therapy.

The breakdown into medical or surgical beds must be flexible, dictated by bed requirements and utilization.

The twenty-bed units should be arranged in two clusters of ten beds each. The clusters should be within sight and sound of the nurses' station to protect the child who cannot summon help and to enable children to observe activities. The child's world is oriented outward, and his interest can be held by watching staff carrying out their duties. Because of this and because of the lack of need of privacy for children, maximum use should be made of glass. A minimum of 25 percent of beds should be one-bed rooms for critically ill and psychiatric patients and those who require isolation. (*American Academy of Pediatrics*, 1971)

"Hospi-tel" Live-in Facility

This will be a unit designed for ambulatory, repetitive, non-nursing treatment or investigation. It will house both the patient and his parents. It is recommended that twenty such units be developed, each one consisting of a bedroom, little sitting room, toilet, and bathroom.

Emergency Department Beds

It is recommended that ten observation beds be available in the emergency department. (These will be used for such conditions as asthma, epilepsy, poisoning observation, head trauma observation.) It is not anticipated that anybody will remain under observation for a period longer than twelve hours. (If further observation is required, the child would be admitted to an inpatient ward.)

Physical Plant

Units: The following are the major features to be included in every unit:

Glass along corridors (except adolescent unit)

Modules of two beds (can be converted to one-bed rooms)

Parent's sleeping accommodations for each room

Sinks in every room

Service panels—suction, oxygen, clearly marked outlets for emergency power, and regular outlets

Doctor's room—to accommodate six doctors with desks, toilet, lockers

Sleeping facility/on-call room

Treatment room—view box, storage, bright lighting, crash cart

Conference room

Utility area

Laundry room

Storeroom—must be large enough to hold beds and cribs of different sizes, equipment

Nurse's station—including drug room, head nurse's office, nurse's lounge

Two offices for interviewing, history-taking,

social worker interviews, etc.

Parents' room—stove, table, shower, refrigerator

Lockers

Playroom

Note: This is not meant to be a comprehensive list.

General Facilities

Décor and furnishings, plumbing fittings (toilets, wash basins, water fountains), door handles, and closets in lobby and throughout building should be designed for children.

Pharmacy—central and outpatient department

Coat-check room for clothing of parents, doctors, and students on the first floor

Main x-ray facility—rooms for cystoscopy, angiography, and reading rooms

Regional x-ray facilities in the neonatal unit, intensive care unit, emergency department and outpatient department

Physiotherapy department

Social services department

Fog room (steam therapy)

Auditorium, lecture rooms

Central computer for laboratory data, x-ray reports

Library

Medical records room

Animal facility

Medical illustration facility (photography)

Surgical Suite:

    Holding (preanesthesia) room

    Induction room

    Five operating rooms (cystoscopy room)

    Recovery room

Intensive care units

House staff sleeping quarters

Heliport

Interdenominational chapel

School facilities

Play facilities

Parent education center (pre-surgery, immunization education)

Note: This is not meant to be a comprehensive list.

It is anticipated that the specialists in each of these areas would develop the specifications for their own areas. Ideally, the operating rooms would be separate and individually staffed.

Recommended Floor Plan

Basement: main x-ray department, record room, library

Ground floor: outpatient department, emergency department, main auditorium, administration

First floor: preanesthesia, operating room, post-anesthesia, intensive care unit

Rest of hospital: breakdown by age

Clinical Programs

It is anticipated that the following divisions will be developed at the outset:

Pediatric medicine

Adolescent medicine

Allergy-immunology

Cardiology

Endocrinology-metabolism

Gastroenterology

General pediatrics (division of private practice, part of HMO)

Hematology-oncology

Human genetics

Infectious diseases

Learning disability (requiring special facilities: one-way mirror classrooms, consultation rooms, rooms for psychologists, psychiatrists, pediatricians, neurologists, educators.)

Nephrology

Newborn medicine (in proximity to delivery suite—bridge, corridor)

Neurology
Pulmonology/cystic fibrosis

Pediatric surgery
    Cardiovascular Surgery
    General Surgery
    Neurosurgery
    Plastic Surgery
    Ophthalmology
    Orthopaedics
    Otolaryngology
    Urology
Pediatric anesthesiology
Pediatric dentistry
Pediatric psychiatry
    Mental health
    Crisis intervention (death of parent, sibling)
Pediatric physical medicine and rehabilitation
Pediatric radiology
Pediatric pathology (some may be shared with main hospital)
    Surgical Pathology—autopsy room
    Microbiology
    Biochemistry
    Hematology/blood bank substation
    Nuclear medicine
Pediatric emergency department

Each division should have its own suite of rooms. The outpatient department should be set up in modules, each module consisting of three medical or surgical divisions, a shared examining facility of twelve rooms, shared waiting room, and shared conference room. The x-ray facility and outpatient laboratory should be in a central location between these divisions.

The suite of rooms for each division should consist of:

- Division offices: secretaries, physician-in-charge, and fellows

- Laboratory: routine laboratory, e.g., neurology (EEG, EMG); cardiology (EKG, cardiac catheterization); and research laboratories

General medical outpatient department
    This should consist of:
    Twelve examining rooms
    Routine laboratory
    X-ray facility
    Social workers' office
    Small conference rooms (patients, parents, nurses, social workers, doctors)
    Large conference rooms for teaching
    Waiting areas
    Play areas

General surgical outpatient department
    This should consist of:
    Induction room
    Two operating rooms
    Recovery room
    Plaster room
    Twelve examining rooms

The laboratory, x-ray facility, social workers' office, conference rooms, and play areas can be shared with medicine.

Organizational Structure

From observations at Cleveland Babies' and Children's Hospital, Toronto Children's Hospital, and Montreal's Children's Hospital, as well as my knowledge of other children's hospitals in other countries, it is clear that they are separate structures, distinct hospitals in terms of public perception for fundraising purposes, but in terms of their working arrangements they are not truly independent. The reasons are as follows:

A. They are generally not isolated but part and parcel of a university system of hospitals consisting of general hospitals, geriatric hospitals, psychiatric hospitals, obstetrical hospitals—all under the aegis of a university, i.e., Case Western Reserve, University of Toronto, McGill University. In general, they are physically surrounded by these medical facilities and frequently share to a greater or lesser degree certain medical and other resources, e.g., radiotherapy units. Many use common kitchens, common purchasing arrangements, etc.

B. The surgeon in charge in the children's hospitals, the radiologist in charge, the pathologist in charge, etc., are all responsible to their counterparts in the corresponding departments of the general hospital who are chairmen of the university departments. There are slight variations in arrangements but in all cases the pediatric surgeon is responsible to the chairman of the department of surgery.

C. The relationship with the main hospital becomes essential with regard to residency rotation, for the training of general surgeons in pediatric surgery as well as the training of pediatric surgeons who are required to do a specific period of time in general surgery. A close link with the general department of surgery is a necessity.

Comparison with Existing Pediatric Facilities at Long Island Jewish-Hillside Medical Center

It was of considerable interest to note that throughout our travels we saw no program or procedure that we presently are not able to carry out within our Department of Pediatrics at Long Island Jewish-Hillside Medical Center. The following, however, are the differences:

A. Size: Children's hospitals vary in size; the largest has 820 beds. It should be noted here that size can become a major problem. We heard many complaints about the inefficiencies and communication problems in extremely large hospitals. There appears to be a critical level beyond which these problems start to arise.

B. Quality of treatment provided: Children's hospitals have special laboratories doing hematology, x-ray, micromethods, etc. These special laboratories have technicians and specialists highly trained and exclusively trained in the diseases of children and consequently the quality is better.

C. Regional laboratories and x-ray facilities for the outpatient department, the emergency room, neonatal unit, and intensive care unit: These permit more rapid and efficient processing of patients.

D. The number of specialists and the depth of specialties: These are greater than usually available to children in a general hospital.

E. The pre- and post-surgical techniques (holding room, induction room, recovery room): These are superior in hospitals designed exclusively for children.

F. Specially trained nursing staff and nursing-patient ratio in intensive care units and neonatal intensive care units: These are optimal in a children's hospital.

The following table lists the number of beds in various children's hospitals:

Children's Hospital	Number of Beds
Los Angeles	310
Washington, D.C.	220
Miami—Variety Children's	155
Children's Memorial, Chicago	240
Louisville	139
Baltimore	135
Boston	343
Detroit	215
St. Louis	188
Newark	84
Buffalo	315
Akron	253
Cincinnati	215
Columbus	301
Philadelphia	160-265
Philadelphia, St Christopher	146
Pittsburgh	------
Dallas	122
Salt Lake City	135
Seattle	223

Master Plan for Development of A *Children's Health Network* for the North Shore-Long Island Jewish Health System

By Philip Lanzkowsky, MD, ScD, FRCP, DCH, FAAP
Professor of Pediatrics, Albert Einstein College of Medicine
Chief of Staff, Schneider Children's Hospital
Executive VP and Medical Director, LIJMC

November 15, 1997
(Revised January 15, 1998)

Introduction

The merger of the North Shore Health System and Long Island Jewish Medical Center offers a unique opportunity to create a fully integrated regional healthcare network that will ensure that children from Staten Island to Montauk receive the right care, in the right environment, in the most cost-effective manner. To this end, this document proposes a plan of action for the integration of pediatric services throughout the new NS-LIJ Health System by creating a *Children's Health Network*, as well as laying out the principles that should guide the creation of this new network.

While recognizing and appreciating the sensitivity of the changes proposed herein, it is critical to the financial, clinical, and operational stability of pediatric services throughout the NS-LIJ Health System that the creation of the *Children's Health Network* be high on the agenda. The new network will serve as a model for providing children's healthcare for other health systems nationally, while identifying the NS-LIJ Health System as a leader in this endeavor.

As you will see, the action plan calls for the Schneider Children's Hospital (SCH) to become the hub for most of the pediatric tertiary and quaternary care, with the remaining hospitals in the NS-LIJ Health System providing primary, secondary, and some tertiary care where deemed strategically and clinically appropriate. In order to effectively implement this, clinical services will have to be fully integrated. Concurrently, faculty must also be integrated, with roles determined on a principles-based meritocracy. The only method for successfully accomplishing these tasks is to consolidate the competing pediatric departments into one common bottom line as soon as possible.

The following was developed using a practical, common sense approach and should serve as a basis for discussion on how to achieve the common vision of a unified *Children's Health Network* for the NS-LIJ Health System.

General Principles for Merging Clinical Departments

The basic business of the hospital is the clinical (intra- and extramural) programs directed by department chairs—the work product of physicians and the source of the hospital revenue. While a significant amount of care will be provided outside the hospital, the hospital component will always be significant (programmatically and economically) in our health system. From historic, experiential, and investment viewpoints the hospital will remain very important in the new entity.

The new entity is a unique opportunity, if set up correctly, to provide an example to be emulated nationally. The clinical component of the health system cannot be based on parochial considerations, expedience, or compromise, but should be a **principles-based meritocracy**. Departments should be fused with a singular vision and leadership in order to get a rapid economy of scale and reduce the expense side of the ledger to improve our competitive position. You cannot have two departments within one system vying for the same market share.

To this end, excellence in clinical leadership should be placed in position rapidly to lead the departments. In the short run this will be more difficult, but in the long run it will lay the foundation for success both financially and programmatically. Each clinical department is a multimillion-dollar corporation. Ambiguity at the top will be very costly and lead to failure.

With the fundamental goal of a **principles-based meritocracy,** chairs of departments of the new entity should be appointed as soon as possible, based, *inter alia*, on the following criteria:

- Academic and clinical track record (curriculum vitae)
- Proven leadership ability
- Entrepreneurial skills
- Management skills (both people and finance)
- Proven record of program development

They may come from the LIJ or the NSUH faculty or from the outside after a national search. Where a national search is required, interim chairs should be appointed. Some mistakes may be made and some people may be unhappy, but that is better than a lack of unified leadership of the clinical departments.

The new entity should be set up along department and product lines: mental health, cancer care, cardiac care, women's health, children's health, etc. (some product lines may be interdepartmental, in which cases the most suitable chair in a product line becomes medical director, e.g., women's center). This will add luster and value to the healthcare delivery system and provide the integration, added value, and excellence that will attract and maintain market share and managed care contracts. These product lines require:

- Single medical leadership
- Excellence
- Cost-effectiveness
- Wide geographic distribution
- Integration (ambulatory, inpatients, home care, satellites, urgicenters, etc.)

The product line will be network-wide and may not necessarily require a single site but rather may have a hub (tertiary and quaternary care) and spokes (ambulatory, home care, satellites, etc.) creating a tapestry of medical care.

Time is of the essence; the way we start out is the way we will be for a long time. I understand the reality and practical considerations and that occasional trade-offs may be necessary. That should be the exception, not the rule. If the reverse prevails, mediocrity will thrive, we will lose the competitive edge that we need, and we will miss a unique opportunity to reassess our existing staff and develop a world-class institution. To adopt a strategy of this type will take courage and commitment of the administration and the NS-LIJ Health System Board of Trustees.

Programmatic Scope, Inventory, and Principles of the Children's Health Network Within the NS-LIJ Health System

The health system created by the merger of the North Shore Health System and Long Island Jewish Medical Center will have approximately 1,000 pediatricians and subspecialists, 13,000 inpatient admissions, and 300,000 ambulatory care visits and serve a population of several million people. *This new "system" will represent one of the largest providers of pediatric care in the United States.*

The merger thus offers a unique opportunity to develop an innovative, integrated system that provides quality-driven, cost-effective care that meets the needs of children whether they are healthy or require specialized medicine and that trains pediatricians and pediatric and surgical subspecialists to do quality research. It should adhere to the fundamental concept of a **principles-based meritocracy.**

The mission could be accomplished through the development of a comprehensive continuum of children's health services (an integrated regional pediatric network) that will ensure that children are treated in the "right setting, at the right time, by the right provider." The new pediatric network would be academically based and would provide broad geographic access to high-quality care to children from Staten Island to Montauk through the vast array of hospitals, pediatricians, pediatric subspecialists, and satellite centers. It would be a center for medical education reflecting the broad clinical and research (basic and applied) resources of the NS-LIJ Health System.

Specifically, the new integrated delivery network for children, *inter alia*, would include close on 1,000 community-based pediatricians integrated into an interactive pediatric network, expanding on the existing SCH pediatric network and services to pediatricians and hospitals.

The following practice-management and other services would be included:

- Resident in situ
- On-call telephone coverage—"SCH On-Call"
- Inpatient coverage (hospitalists)
- Teleconferencing—"Gemini System"
- Partner recruitment
- Urgicenter
- Satellite availability
- Patient transportation
- Buying consortium
- Contract evaluation
- Practice broker
- Admission privileges
- Practice assessment by SCH consulting group
- Research participation
- Joint marketing venture
- LIJ-DOCS referral service
- Over 150 pediatric subspecialists at Sch-

neider Children's Hospital and the North Shore Health System representing the full range of pediatric clinical disciplines (seventeen subspecialties in pediatric medicine; nine pediatric surgical subspecialties; child and adolescent psychiatry; pediatric radiology; pediatric anesthesiology; and pediatric pathology)

- State-of-the-art tertiary- and quaternary-care programs including bone marrow transplantation, sophisticated cardiac surgery, and a pulmonary rescue program offering high-frequency ventilatory care, nitric oxide, and extracorporeal membrane oxygenation (ECMO)
- Pediatric tertiary-care ambulatory satellites and pediatric urgicenters located in neighborhoods throughout Long Island; expansion of existing satellites (Hauppauge and Hewlett) to other strategic locations in Queens, Brooklyn, Staten Island, Westchester, and northern New Jersey
- Emergency pediatric and neonatal transport services for coordination of the SCH/North Shore satellite hospitals
- Development of secondary inpatient pediatric services geographically and strategically placed to serve our tertiary-care satellites and urgicenters (e.g., Huntington and Southside Hospitals for Suffolk County and Staten Island Hospital for Staten Island and Brooklyn)
- Development of strategically located inpatient chronic care and chronic ventilatory units staffed by network pediatricians aimed at reducing length of stay in acute hospitals and providing a continuum of care
- Disease-specific centers of excellence, e.g., hemophilia, cystic fibrosis, bone marrow transplantation, cardio-thoracic surgery
- Specific facilities and programs for special children, e.g., infant stimulation program and preschool program

- Regional pediatric trauma care
- Regional teleconferencing of pediatric multidisciplinary conferences with affiliated hospitals and pediatricians and participation with other academic pediatric centers of excellence around the country and the world
- A pediatric medicine teaching program for physicians, surgeons, psychiatrists, dentists, nurses, child life, and other ancillary personnel
- A research program for basic and applied research in general pediatrics and pediatric specialties
- An extensive psychiatric service including the only locked in-patient unit for children
- The only Ronald McDonald House in the region to accommodate parents of hospitalized children
- A proactive network for setting clinical and healthcare delivery standards for children with advocacy of federal and state public policy legislative initiatives affecting the health and well-being of children
- A comprehensive philanthropic drive to raise funds for child health on Long Island

The product line will be network-wide and may not necessarily require a single site but rather require a hub (tertiary and quaternary care) and spokes (ambulatory, home care, satellites, urgicenters, etc.) creating a tapestry of integrated medical services for children.

The development of a unified, mission-driven, regional healthcare network for children will add luster and value to the overall healthcare delivery system and provide the integration, added value, and excellence that will attract and maintain market share and managed care contracts.

An integrated network of this type requires the fusion of departments into a system with a singular vision and leadership in order to accomplish an economy of scale, reduce the expense side of the ledger, and improve our competitive position. You cannot have two departments within one system vying for the same market share.

In order for the *Children's Health Network* to be effective, medical and administrative leadership would be required in the development and ongoing management of the resources allocated to the pediatric integrated delivery system. The *Children's Health Network* (the pediatric integrated delivery system) would serve as a national model to be emulated by other healthcare systems.

Implementation Plan For The Children's Health Network*
Core Values:
- All children should receive the best possible care from the most qualified people and in the most appropriate settings at the best value (quality/cost).
- Children should be treated in facilities exclusively designed for children and staffed by personnel specifically trained in pediatrics.
- The programs should be principles-based and developed according to objective criteria.

Objectives:
- To create a regional, academically based corporate division of Children's Health Services

The North Shore-LIJ Health System should identify the Children's Health Network as a priority for planning. The Children's Health Network should be a top priority of the system because an organized, cost-effective, high-quality delivery system for children will be a major strategy to attract managed-care contracts. According to a recent front-page article in Crain's New York Business (regarding the push by four major healthcare organizations in downstate New York to build children's hospitals), children's health services "will serve as the centerpieces of new healthcare networks" and "will be compelling, marketing showcases that networks will use to attract patients, insurers, and employees." We should take advantage of what we already have in place.

and develop an integrated pediatric network providing excellent primary, secondary, tertiary, and quaternary medical care under central administrative and clinical leadership.

- To establish universally applied standards of excellence, to be maintained and monitored irrespective of point of entry into the system, from Staten Island to Montauk, by a wide array of integrated services provided by pediatricians, pediatric subspecialties, and primary and tertiary ambulatory centers and hospitals.
- To ensure value, cost-effectiveness, and satisfaction of stakeholders (patients, payers, and providers).
- To develop a streamlined "process of care" designed to increase the likelihood of positive outcomes, based upon the effective/efficient use of resources throughout the system.
- To establish a single center for medical education and broad clinical and basic research.
- To integrate clinical programs, administrative responsibility, data management, and patient access with the ultimate goal of a common bottom line for the system.

Phase I (Three to Four Months)

- Appoint a medical director/executive vice president to direct all aspects of the new *Children's Health Network*.
- Name a corporate vice president for the *Children's Health Network* to work with the medical director to coordinate corporate objectives and carry out the mission of the network.
- Access physician performance within the network with reference to revenue, expenses, operating efficiency indices, and physician productivity standards.
- Apply to the Residency Review Committee (RRC) of the American Council for Graduate Medical Education (ACGME) to integrate residency effective July 1, 1999.

- Combine research efforts under one director of research so that economies of scale can be achieved.

Phase II (To Be Completed End of First Year)

- Set economic objectives for physician performance that are uniform for all pediatric departments and divisions within the network and develop a common bottom line for the Department of Pediatrics of the NS-LIJ Health System.
- Merge the departments (once individual department faculties are performing economically in a similar manner) based on core values. Appointment of divisional chiefs should be based, *inter alia*, on the following criteria:
  -- Professional rank: as a general rule; no chief should be below the rank of associate professor
  -- Academic and clinical track records (curriculum vitae)
  -- Proven leadership ability
  -- Proven entrepreneurial skills
  -- Proven management skills (both people and finance)
  -- Proven record of program development
     The divisional chiefs may come from North Shore's or LIJ's existing faculty or from the outside following a national search. Where a national search is required, an interim chief should be appointed.
- Establish marketable product lines, e.g., eating disorders, learning disorders, respiratory rescue, cancer care, etc. (Some product lines may be interdivisional, in which case the dominant chief in a product line becomes medical director.) This will add luster and value to the healthcare delivery system and provide the integration, added value, and excellence that will attract and maintain market share and managed-care contracts. These product lines require:

- Single medical leadership
- Excellence
- Cost-effectiveness
- Wide geographic distribution
- Integration (ambulatory, inpatients, home care, satellites, urgicenters, etc.)

The product lines will be network-wide and may not necessarily require a single site but rather may require a hub (tertiary and quaternary care) and spokes (ambulatory, homecare, satellites, etc.) creating a tapestry of medical care.

- Configure pediatric programs and hospital services based on clinical and economic criteria designed to locate the right services in the appropriate facilities with an economy of scale that maximizes quality of care and cost-effectiveness (what goes where and why?).

Phase III (Within First Two Years)

- Broaden the existing *Children's Health Network* to include the following:
  - Secondary inpatient pediatric units (e.g., Southside, Huntington) strategically located and staffed by existing faculty and house staff
  - Primary-care network including Medicaid managed care and new primary-care markets not currently served by community-based staff pediatricians
  - Inpatient chronic-and ventilatory-care units strategically located to reduce length of stay in acute-care hospitals
  - Tertiary-care satellites in southwestern Suffolk, Queens, Brooklyn, Staten Island,
  - Urgicenters linked to tertiary-care satellites
  - New and expanded school-based programs
  - Pediatric home care to provide a continuum of care from the existing home-care services in the network.
- Secure managed-care contracts for the *Children's Health Network*.
- Promote centrally administered clinical and

basic research in the *Children's Health Network*.
- Promote patient education and post-graduate and continuing medical education in the *Children's Health Network*.

Phase IV—Ongoing Management Systems/Issues

- Develop and monitor operating and capital budgets for the *Children's Health Network* (product line based, not institution based).
- Continue to conduct productivity analyses to ensure cost-efficient delivery of healthcare services to children within the network.
- Develop and maintain uniform standards for clinical care and delivery of services to children at all locations within the network (performance improvement).
- Develop and maintain a comprehensive database for the *Children's Health Network* that can be accessed at any location and may include data concerning demographics, utilization of services, finances, clinical care, performance improvement, etc.
- Develop a major fundraising arm of the *Children's Health Network* to raise money for capital priority projects and support of existing projects and the development of an endowment.
- Develop an aggressive marketing and public relations strategy to promote all aspects and all locations of the *Children's Health Network*.
- Identify opportunities for expansion and growth into new markets or new programs.
- Maintain emergency pediatric and neonatal transport services for coordination of care throughout the *Children's Health Network*.
- Continue to develop and expand the existing practice management services for all physicians within the *Children's Health Network*.

Executive Summary

Schneider Children's Hospital is one of

only two children's hospitals in New York State and the only children's hospital in the NS-LIJ Health System. SCH has an existing national and international reputation as an excellent academic center for pediatrics and its various disciplines, which should be promoted by the NS-LIJ Health System through the development of the *Children's Health Network*.

A guiding principle in the development of this network should be that **treatment of tertiary- and quaternary-care pediatric patients through the NS-LIJ Health System should be predominantly based at SCH, with primary and secondary care based at the other hospitals in the system.** NSUH should retain strategically appropriate tertiary care, especially neonatology and certain ambulatory and emergency services in pediatrics. The new *Children's Health Network* will provide broad geographic access to high-quality care to children from Staten Island to Montauk through a vast array of hospital, pediatricians, pediatric subspecialists, and urgi- and satellite centers.

This principle is supported by a review of recent mergers and the emergence of health systems around the country where existing children's hospitals within the system become the hub for the delivery of tertiary- and quaternary-care pediatrics for the entire system, for example, St. Louis Children's/Barnes Jewish Christian Health System; Children's Memorial/Evanston Health Systems Network; Michigan Children's/Detroit Medical Center Health System; LeBonheur Children's/Methodist Health System of Tennessee.

SOURCE MATERIAL
HOW IT ALL BEGAN: THE HISTORY OF A CHILDREN'S HOSPITAL

DOCUMENTS

Children's Medical Center of New York document, circa 1965

Children's Medical Center of New York Fund —Planning Committee Hearings
May 21, 1972
June 1, 6, 1972
June 14, 17, 1972
October 5, 16, 25, 1972

Application for Approval of Construction of Hospital and Amendments Parts I–V
Feb. 26, 1973 (Original submission date)
Supplementary data requested by State— June 20, 1977

Perkins & Will Master Plan and supplements— 1974

Minutes of Board of Trustees, Joint Conference Committee and Medical Board of LIJHMC—1970-1983

Inventing Great Neck, Judith S. Goldstein: Rutgers University Press, 2006

INTERVIEWS & DATES

Members of the Long Island Jewish Medical Center Board of Trustees

Rosalie (Mickey) Greenberg—June 21, 2006

Judge Bertram Harnett—Various times from 2006-2008.

Martin Lifton—June 6, 2006

Marcie Rosenberg—June, 2006

Michael Stein—September 18, 2006

Judge Sol Wachtler—June 7, 2006, and October 4, 2007

LIJ Legal Counsel in 1970s

Melvyn Ruskin, Esq.—August 25, 2006

Members of LIJ Planning Department and Consultants

Robert Boyer, Director of LIJ Planning Department 1978-1985—June 5, 2006

David Ginsberg, Architect for Perkins & Will —April, 2006

The Katz Consulting Group (KCG)—April 2006

Staff of North Shore University Hospital

Harvey Aiges, MD, Department of Pediatrics— February 3, 2006

Carol Hauptman, Director of Public Relations 1970s–1980s—January 12, 2006

Michael LaCorte, MD, Department of Pediatrics—June 29, 2006

Gary Wadler, MD, Director of Ambulatory Services 1970s—July 5, 2006

Medical Staff of Schneider Children's Hospital

Martin Abrams, MD, Pediatric Surgeon— May 2, 1996

Hedda Acs, MD, Attending Physician, Cystic Fibrosis, Neonatology—May 1, 1996, July 23, 2006

Jerry Becker, MD, Chief of Pediatric Surgery 1956-1985—September 20, 2006

Benjamin Berliner, MD, Pediatrician, Interim Director of Pediatrics 1969-1970—May 5, 1996

Burton Bronsther, MD, Pediatric Surgeon—May 10, 1996

Frank Cappelli, MD, Staff Pediatrician—May 3, 1996

Bernard Gauthier, MD, Pediatric Nephrologist—May 1, 1996

Herbert Goldman, MD, Neonatologist—May 1, 1996

Philip Lipsitz, MD, Chief, Neonatal-Perinatal Medicine—April 23, 1996

Jane Moore, RN, Clinical Nurse Specialist, Hematology-Oncology—May 3, 1996

I. Ronald Shenker, MD, Chief, Adolescent Medicine—May 1, 1996

David Sternberg, MD, Staff Pediatrician—May 8, 1996

Medical Staff of LIJ

Allan Abramson, MD, Chairman, Department of Otorhinolaryngology—June 4, 2006

Henry Isenberg, PhD, Director of Microbiology—May 10, 1996

Edward Meilman, MD, Chairman, Department of Medicine—September 22, 2006

Alumni

Jay Freed, MD—July 13, 2006

Eric Gould, MD—July 11, 2006

Jonathan Horowitz, MD—July 14, 2006

Mark Raifman, MD—May 3, 1996, July 11, 2006

Andrew Steele, MD—December 4, 2006

Fred Teyan, MD—June 20, 2006

Children's Medical Fund of New York

Gladys Cole—June 22, 2006

Marcia Goodman—July, 2006

Judge Bertram Harnett—Various times from 2006-2008

Rita Kay—June 29, 2006

Martin Lifton—June 6, 2006

Bernice Mager—June 6, 2006

Muriel Martin Springfield—June 5, 2006

Marcie Rosenberg—January 2006

Carol Zorfas—June 21, 2006

NEWSPAPER ARTICLES

Daily News

Far Rockaway Record

Glen Oaks News

Great Neck News

Great Neck Record

Herald Courier

Long Island Daily News

Long Island Herald

Long Island Press

Nassau Herald

New York Post

New York Times

Newsday

Pediatric World News

Queens Ledger

Rockaway Journal

South Shore Reporter

CMF Publications

In Touch

LIJ Publications

LIJ Reporter

New Horizons

Memories and Milestones

Aballi, Arturo, MD, 16, 20, 59, 242, 251

ABC-TV, 220

Abrams, Cyril A. MD, 19, 61, 358

Abrams, Martin W., MD, 8, 17, 44, 47, 71, 72, 74, 75, 77, 85, 99, 119, 126, 214

Abrams, Marie, 99

Abramson, Allan, MD, 30, 197, 198, 406

Abramson, Louis Allen, 31

Ackerman, Bruce, MD, 18

Acs, Hedda, MD, 9, 16, 44, 45, 47, 52, 59, 61, 241

Adelphi University, 39

Adesman, Andrew, MD, 227, 351

Adolescent Medicine Faculty, 334

AIDS, 21

Aiges, Harvey, MD, 242, 247, 301

Albert Einstein College of Medicine, 21, 39, 40, 104, 240, 242

Allergy-Immunolgy Faculty, 339

Alpert, Joel J., MD, 253, 254

Amato, Joseph, MD, 397

ambulatory chemotherapy unit, 322

Ambulatory visits, 237

American Council for Graduate Medical Education, The, 21, 416

American Pediatric Society, 57

Antokoletz, Marilyn, MD, 43

"Aqua Circus," 282, 283

Arbeli-Almozlino, Mrs. Shoshana, 252

Architects' Collaborative (TAC), 20, 145, 159, 185, 215

Arden, Martha, MD, 336

Art of the Children's Hospital, 259-293

Art Therapy, 421

Association for the Help of Retarded Children (AHRC), 18, 19, 60, 137, 352

Asthma Center, 21, 341

Astoria General Hospital, 134, 136

"Astronomy Lesson," 264, 267

Atlas, Mark, MD, 179

Atlas, Sol, 28

Bakst, Sylvia, 72

Baptist Memorial Health Care System of Tennessee, 22

Barell, Martin C., 40, 103, 105, 107, 113, 173, 190, 208, 209, 214, 219

Barnard, Christiaan Neethling, MD, 227, 396

Barnett, Henry, MD, 251

Baron, Murray, MD, 53

Barone, Stephen, MD, 247

Battaglia, Frederick, MD, 243

Beame, Abe, 207

Beardmore, Harvey E., MD, 75

Becker, Jerrold, MD, 126, 129, 398

Beckman, Albert, MD, 125

Beldock, Saul J., 107

Bell, Bertrand, MD, 246

Bell Commission, 240, 246

Bennett, Tony, 301

Bensonhurst, Brooklyn, multidisciplinary satellite center, 23, 233

Berger Commission, 144

Berkman, James, MD, 33, 34, 46, 53

Berliner, Benjamin, MD, 16, 45, 46, 334

Berman, Richard A., 157

Bernard Worob Center for Gender Identity, 359

Berne, Gustave (Gus), 10, 27, 40, 103, 104, 106, 107, 109, 112, 121, 127, 159

Bernstein, Abraham, 335

Bernstein, Fieda, 335

Bernstein, Harvey, 110, 187

"Bicycling In The Sun," 275

Bienkowski, Robert, PhD, 20, 393

Bierman, Frederick Z., MD, 22, 23, 59, 228, 303, 306, 314, 315, 321, 344

Bigel, Jack, 208

Bikur Cholim Room, 23

Kleinberg, Frederic A., 210

Koch, Mayor, 207

Kokol, Harold, 11

Kokol, Vivian, 11, 86, 90, 129, 209

Kollek, Teddy, 207

Koop, C. Everett, MD, 72, 75, 257

Koplewicz, Harold, MD, 412

Kosinski, Ronald, DMD, 410

Koumbourlis, Anastassios, MD, 23, 227

Kozma, William, 36

Krasnoff, Abraham, 296

Krauss, Herbert, 110

Kremer, Arthur, 207

Kumar, Sanjay and Sylvia Foundation, 234

LaCorte, Michael, MD, 23, 344

LaGuardia Hospital, 19, 58, 120, 135, 136

Lanzkowsky, Carly Beatrice, 292

Lanzkowsky, David, 10

Lanzkowsky, Jacob Tyler, 15

Lanzkowsky, Jonathan, 10

Lanzkowsky, Marc, 10

Lanzkowsky, Rhona, 10, 15, 50, 209, 314, 475

Lanzkowsky-Bienstock, Shelley, 10

Lanzkowsky-Diamond, Leora, 10

Lapidus, Morris, 74, 75, 181, 182

Larkin, Vincent DePaul, 75

Lazar, Fruchter, MD, 19

Lear, Philip, MD, 33, 34, 38, 46

Learning Diagnostic Center, 17

Learning Diagnostic Program (LDP), 350

Lehman, Dominik, 285

Leigh, Jean, 38

Leigh, Joe, 38

length of stay (LOS), 152, 153, 237

Leonidas, John C., MD, 414

Les Nelkin Professor fo Pediatric Oncology, 372

Level I Pediatric Trauma Center, 356, 405 *(see Trauma Center)*

Levin, Professor Stanley, MD, 21, 242, 252

Levine, Jeremiah, MD, 59, 243, 364

Levine, Larry, 303

Levitt, Selwyn, MD, 408

Levitt, William, 28

Levy, Alexander, 110

Levy, Bernard, 11, 81

Lexington School for the Deaf, 22

Lieber, Ernest, MD, 61

Liebowitz, Jack, 40, 103

Lifton, Martin, 11, 74, 81, 82, 93, 94, 96, 98, 109, 165, 218, 219

Lifton, Stephen, 81

Light, Harold, 118

Lightman, Hylton, MD, 338

LIJ Publications, 492

LIJ Reporter, 31

Lindsay, Mayor, John, 18, 84, 85

Lindsay, Mrs. John, 84, 85

Lipsitz, Philip, MD, 18, 52, 197, 289, 380, 392

Lipton, Jeffrey, MD, 59, 371, 372

Locastro, Laurie, 15, 51, 85, 105, 244, 296

Loeb and Trope, 113

LoGalbo, Peter, MD, 338

Logo, 98, 300

Lollipop Campaign, 90, 91

Long Beach Memorial Hospital, 175

Long Island Daily News, 158, 165, 167-170

Long Island Ducks, 290, 292

Long Island Hearing and Speech Society, 38

Long Island Herald, 78

Long Island Press, 61, 78, 183, 184

Long, Loretta, 87, 88

Luber, John, MD, 396

Lucey, Jerrold F., MD, 257

Lynn, Clyde, 202, 224, 266

Lyons, Jack, 210

Ma, Yeou-Cheng, MD, 227, 351

Mack, William, 10, 40, 41, 103, 127, 159, 190, 210

Nagelberg, Joy S., MD, 21, 227, 355, 392

Nanotechnology, 327

Nassau County Medical Center, 168, 170, 171 (see Meadowbrook Hospital)

Nassau County Medical Society, 165

Nassau Herald, 66

Nassau Hospital, 168

Nassau-Suffolk Health System Agency, 144, 153, 173, 174, 175

Nassau-Suffolk Hospital Council (NSHC), 165, 166, 169, 172

National Cystic Fibrosis Foundation, 348

National Institute of Child Health and Development, 21

National Institutes of Health (NIH), 16, 56, 340, 375, 395, 407

National Residency Matching Program (NIRMP), The, 55

Nauen, Richard, MD, 145, 146

NBC-TV, 220

neonatal intensive care, 323

Neonatal Transports, 230 (see Transport System)

Neonatal-Perinatal Medicine Faculty, 379

Nephrology Faculty, 384

Nester, Martin F., Jr., 175

Neurology Faculty, 386

Neurosurgery Faculty, 402

New Horizons, 149, 150

New York City Health System Agency (HSA), 19, 144, 157, 161, 228

New York City Police Department, 23

New York Hospital, 17, 227

New York Hospital-Cornell University Medical School, 49

New York Magazine, 313

New York Mets, 290

New York Post, 221

New York Presbyterian Hospital, 121

New York State Department of Health (NYSDH), 18, 23, 131, 144, 145, 149-157, 162, 174, 175, 187, 240, 246, 247, 305, 381

New York State Education Department, 352

New York State Hospital Review and Planning Council, 19, 95, 143, 152

New York State Journal of Medicine, 62-64

New York Telephone Company, 66

New York Times, 74-76, 160, 162-164, 167, 176-178, 220, 221, 354

New York University School of Medicine, 240

Newberger, May W., 114

Newsday, 78, 82, 158, 160, 162, 164, 167, 168, 170-176, 221

Newsweek, 354

NICU beds, 322

Non-Neonatal Transports, 230 (see Transport System)

Novak, Gerald, MD, 21

Nudel, Dov, MD, 61

Nursing Directors, 416

Nussbaum, Michael, MD, 61, 392

occupancy, 236

Oliver, Thomas K., Jr., MD, 253, 257

Olverd, Ms. Leah, 254

Ophthalmology Faculty, 404

Orthopaedic Surgery and Rehabilitation Medicine Faculty, 405

Oski, Frank A., MD, 253

Osmand, Marie, 288, 291

Otothinolaryngology Faculty, 407

Padavan, Frank, 114, 207

Pahwa, Raj, MD, 21, 22, 227, 370

Palermo, Ellen, PhD, 352

Paley, William, 28

Palmer, Lane, MD, 409

Rheumatology Faculty, 393

Rijn, Leo, 275

Rimmer, Murray, 36

Rivera, Geraldo, 87, 88

Robots, 327

Rockaway Journal, 164

Rogatz, Peter, MD, 30, 37, 38

"Roller Ball," 278

Romano, Ray, 99

Ronald McDonald House, 20, 23, 194, 195, 202, 203, 205, 235

Roosevelt, Eleanor, 28

Rosen, David, MD, 53

Rosen, Nelson G., MD, 400

Rosenberg, Marcie, 11, 81, 93, 97, 110, 209

Rosenfeld, Eugene, MD, 27, 29, 33, 34, 39

Rosenstock Foundation, 17

Rosenthal, Alexander, MD, 33, 34, 46

Rossetti Associates, 19, 20, 145, 182-185

Rothkopf, Gene, 11

Rotkovich, Rachel, RN, 54, 55

Rovinsky, Joseph, MD, 53

Rowe, Marc, MD, 123, 125

Roy, Kevin, MD, 245

Rubenstein, Barry, 110

Rubin, Lorry G., MD, 20, 227, 375

Rudin Foundation, 21, 342

Ruskin, Melvin, 108-109

Sabloff, Warren, 110

Safe Horizons, 23

Sagy, Mayer, MD, 227, 347, 382

Sahdev, Indira, MD, 227, 373

Sakaguchi, S., MD, 124

Salemi, M., MD, 64

Salk, Jonas, MD, 86, 87, 88, 89

Sandcastle Mural, 286

Sanders, Joe M., Jr., MD, 253

Santiago, Marie Theresa, MD, 390

Satellite Centers, 233

Sawitsky, Arthur, MD, 53

Scarpelli, Emile, MD, PhD, 20, 21, 227, 345, 393

SCH On-Call Program, 232

Schaeffer, Janis, MD, 227, 346

Schecter, Joel, 118

Schick, Bela, MD, 43, 374, 379

Schildkraut, Mollie, MD, 334

Schneider Children's Hospital at Home, 362

Schneider Children's Hospital at North Shore University Hospital, 204, 300

Schneider Children's Medical Center of Israel (SCMCI), 199, 201

Schneider, Helen, 172, 190, 197, 198, 201, 202, 203, 208, 209, 210, 211, 213, 217, 224, 252, 260, 264, 290

Schneider, Howard, 111, 118

Schneider, Irving, 40, 103, 105, 107, 111, 172, 190, 197, 198, 201, 202, 203, 204, 208, 210, 211, 217, 260, 290, 296, 313

Schneider, Lynn, 15, 203, 204, 208, 260, 261

Schneider Lesser, Mindy, 15, 203, 204, 208, 260, 261

school-based health programs, 336

Schulman, Jerome L., 75

Schumacher potato farm, 29, 31

Schumer, Charles, 207

Schwalb, Eugene, MD, 17

Schwartz, Elias, MD, 253

Schwartz, Harold Jr., 210

Science Museum of Long Island, 22

Seid, Gerry, 11

Seid, Walter, 11, 210

Seiden, Howard, MD, 178

Self-Portrait Tile Hallway, 285

Shanske, Alan, MD, 61

Shaw, Anthony, MD, 124

Shende, Ashok, MD, 61, 369, 392

Shenker, I. Ronald, MD, 16, 45, 55, 56, 59, 61, 126, 129, 242, 252, 257, 333, 336, 392

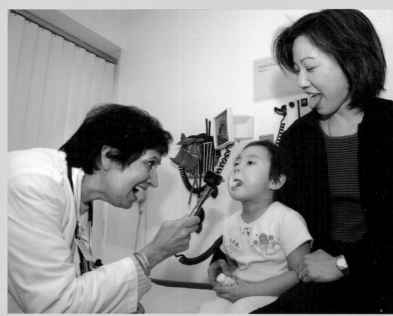

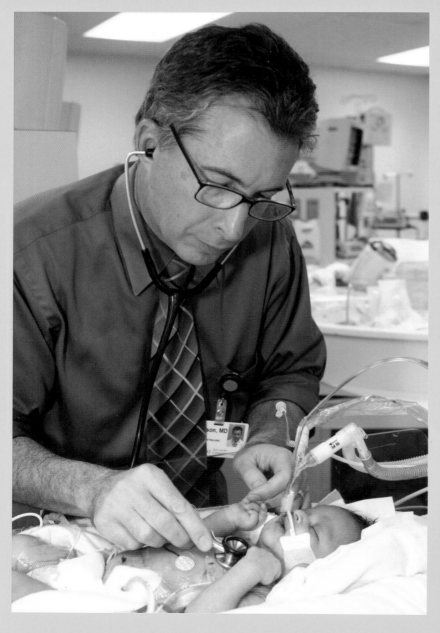

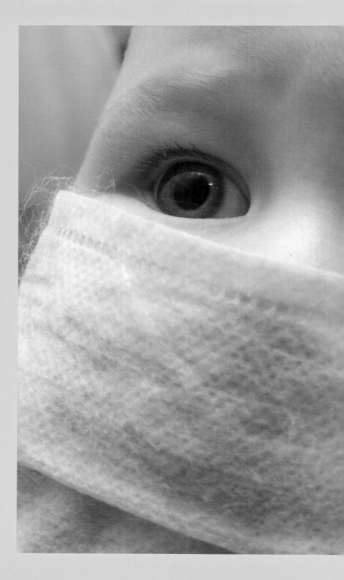